studies in jazz

Institute of Jazz Studies
Rutgers—The State University of New Jersey
General Editors: *Dan Morgenstern & Edward Berger*

1. BENNY CARTER: A Life in American Music, *by Morroe Berger, Edward Berger, and James Patrick*
2. ART TATUM: A Guide to His Recorded Music, *by Arnold Laubich and Ray Spencer*
3. ERROLL GARNER: The Most Happy Piano, *by James M. Doran*
4. JAMES P. JOHNSON: A Case of Mistaken Identity, *by Scott E. Brown;* Discography *by Robert Hilbert*
5. PEE WEE ERWIN: This Horn for Hire, *by Warren W. VacheÅ, Sr.*
6. BENNY GOODMAN: Listen to His Legacy, *by D. Russell Connor*
7. ELLINGTONIA: The Recorded Music of Duke Ellington and His Sidemen, *by W. E. Timner*
8. THE GLENN MILLER ARMY AIR FORCE BAND: Sustineo Alas / I Sustain the Wings, *by Edward F. Polic*
9. SWING LEGACY, *by Chip Deffaa*
10. REMINISCING IN TEMPO: The Life and Times of a Jazz Hustler, *by Teddy Reig, with Edward Berger*
11. IN THE MAINSTREAM, *by Chip Deffaa*
12. BUDDY DeFRANCO: A Biographical Portrait and Discography, *by John Kuehn and Arne Astrup*
13. PEE WEE SPEAKS: A Discography of Pee Wee Russell, *by Robert Hilbert, with David Niven*
14. SYLVESTER AHOLA: The Gloucester Gabriel, *by Dick Hill*
15. THE POLICE CARD DISCORD, *by Maxwell T. Cohen*
16. TRADITIONALISTS AND REVIVALISTS IN JAZZ, *by Chip Deffaa*
17. BASSICALLY SPEAKING: An Oral History of George Duvivier, *by Edward Berger;* Musical Analysis *by David Chevan*
18. TRAM: The Frank Trumbauer Story, *by Philip R. Evans and Larry F. Kiner, with William Trumbauer*
19. TOMMY DORSEY: On the Side, *by Robert L. Stockdale*

TRAM
The Frank Trumbauer Story

by
Philip R. Evans
and
Larry F. Kiner
with
William Trumbauer

Studies in Jazz, No. 18

Institute of Jazz Studies,
Rutgers—The State University
of New Jersey
and
The Scarecrow Press, Inc.
Metuchen, N.J., & London
1994

British Library Cataloguing-in-Publication data available

Library of Congress Cataloging-in-Publication Data

Evans, Philip R., 1935-
Tram : the Frank Trumbauer story / by Philip R. Evans and Larry F. Kiner with William Trumbauer.
p. cm. — (Studies in jazz ; no. 18)
Discography: p.
Includes bibliographical references (p.) and index.
ISBN 0-8108-2851-0 (acid-free paper)
1. Trumbauer, Frank. 2. Jazz musicians—United States—Biography. 3. Saxophonists—United States—Biography. I. Kiner, Larry F. II. Trumbauer, William, 1958- . III. Title. IV. Series.
ML419.T7E9 1994
788.7′165′092—dc20
[B] 94-706

Manufactured in the United States of America.

Printed on acid-free paper

DEDICATION

TO LINDA

For her continuous loving support
and encouragement during the
preparation of this book.

CONTENTS

A REMEMBRANCE

ALTHOUGH I DIDN'T KNOW IT at the time, my first awareness of Frank Trumbauer occurred when I heard the famous "chase chorus" on Paul Whiteman's "You Took Advantage of Me" shortly after the record was issued in June 1928. Compared to what I had been hearing on contemporary records, this whole approach to a tune was a new experience; the arrangement, the Bing Crosby vocal, and of course the Frank Trumbauer-Bix Beiderbecke "chase chorus."

I was only 15, still in high school, never dreaming that one day early in 1934 I would be meeting Frank personally to do an article about him for England's *The Melody Maker.* He had recently rejoined Paul Whiteman's organization, and he was enthusiastic about his new creations "Bouncing Ball," "Sun Spots," and "G Blues," which were frequently being played by the band.

From then on our paths crossed from time to time and we became good friends. I have always regretted that a severe snow storm prevented me from attending his Victor Records session in November 1934 when he recorded four tunes using Bunny Berigan and other all-stars. He had invited me, and it would have been my first experience of a recording session first-hand.

However, in 1940 I was privileged to supervise his later sessions for Varsity Records, and it was here that I had my last personal contact with Frank. These were busy times for all of us, and I didn't make the notes that I now wish I had.

Frank's style of playing was not one that could be easily copied, and his contribution to the American Music Scene, in my opinion, has yet to be appreciated fully. It is fitting that finally someone has seen fit to try to correct the situation, and this new book should do much to do just that!

Warren Scholl
Cincinnati, Ohio

FRANK'S INFLUENCE

AS A YOUTH GROWING UP around the formulative years of our American Jazz, I can recall the early saxophonist, Frank Trumbauer.

Rudy Wiedoeft was one of the first to play saxophone. He was a legitimate clarinet player that sort of introduced the instrument. He was a good technician, a good showman, and a good entertainer. But, he was not a jazz player!

Benny Krueger was probably the best known because he had bands and he made recordings. Perhaps the earliest "hot" saxophonist was Jack Pettis of the New Orleans Rhythm Kings. He had sort of a "swing" style to his playing.

Then came Frank Trumbauer!

I first heard Frank when he was a member of the Joe Kayser Band that played my hometown of Danville, Illinois. We usually had nightly dances. I heard this big, beautiful tone that he got on the C-melody saxophone and I became an instant and lifelong fan.

One of his first recordings was with the Mound City Blue Blowers of "San." I'm told this recording sold a million copies which were probably all purchased by musicians. He followed this up with a recording by the Benson Orchestra entitled "I Never Miss The Sunshine." Benny Carter said when he first heard this recording, it made him take up the saxophone.

I lost track of Tram until the Royal Peacock Orchestra of Indianapolis came to town and their trumpet player/vocalist, Dick Powell, later of the movies, started telling us about Bix and Miff. I was anxious to hear their recordings and Dick said that Miff was then with Ray Miller. I picked up a couple of their latest recordings and was delighted to hear Tram on the sides. I had "Doodle-Doo-Doo," "Mama's Gone Good-bye," and a tune that I am certain that some of today's sax men can't play, Tram's solo on "Lots O' Mama." As fast as Ray Miller made the recordings, we purchased them!

Everyone knows of Tram's recordings with Bix and well they should, as they are some of the finest solos put on wax.

I got to know Frank pretty well when I worked with Jack Tobin, a banjo player from New Orleans, in a chop suey joint in Chicago. Frank came in a lot and we got to be friends. In fact, we did a couple of recordings together in 1931.

During those years, all sax men copied Tram. They knew all of his choruses from his recordings and when he appeared in person, they'd flock to hear him play. Funny thing, I couldn't recall Frank sitting in with bands. I asked him about it. Frank said it was usually a disappointment for him, so he avoided it.

Frank had a great sense of humor. My wife, Blanche, really liked him. I remember one time when he was all excited about this new arrangement that he had. He sat there and told my wife how great it was and raved on and on about it. ''Who did the arrangement?'', Blanche finally asked. ''I did, of course,'' he said. They had a great laugh over that. Frank's humor even shows in his playing.

The most popular sax solo of all time had to be his ''Singin' The Blues.'' Everyone copied that solo. I remember Benny Goodman playing it on clarinet. It was such a direct change to anything being played at the time. I think it even topped Bix's solo on the recording, it has better composition. That one chorus assured Tram's place in Music History.

James ''Rosy'' McHargue
Santa Monica, California

AN APPRECIATION

I NEVER MET MY GRANDFATHER. Frank passed away in 1956. I was born two years later. I recall, as I was growing up, Frank's name was mentioned now and then around the house. Seems there was always a sense of reverence. Mitzi, my grandma, used to tell me stories of those days on the road with Frank.

We had in our house a great charcoal portrait of Frank. It was a great work, which I think was done in the thirties. As a boy, I remember that Frank's eyes seemed to follow you, no matter where you went in the room. I knew this was my grandpa, but yet it seemed somewhat haunting to me, and I have many times just stared at him, wondering and imagining. This picture is at my home now, and I sometimes catch my two young boys doing the same thing. Once in a while one will ask, "Is that Frank?" and I'll just smile and say, "Yes, it is!"

This book was not developed in a year or two. In fact, it was a goal of our families for over twenty years. Mitzi and my dad had started the process in the mid sixties. They were doing some research and solicited the help of Phil Evans in 1967. Things went along for a while, but by 1970 it all fell through. Looking back now, I think that there were certain things which they wanted to overlook. Perhaps it was that Mitzi and dad wanted to keep the story a bit too antiseptic. I can see why they felt that way. Time rolled along and, in 1978, dad died. Mitzi followed four years later. And that was that! Would their dream ever be realized? In 1989, while I was home one night, I decided to break out some of the many reel to reel tapes that were in my father's collection. I found one which was not marked, so I decided to listen. It was a tape that dad and Phil had been using to correspond back in 1967. I decided then and there to see what I could do to get things rolling again! I found Phil in the telephone book and called him the next day. "Yes" was Phil's reply. And here we are five years later! I can't describe how good I feel. I know that dad would be proud of me, and that's all that counts! Although I know that he's gone and I get very emotional thinking that this book is an everlasting memorial to not only Frank, but the last thing I ever did for my father. I can never repay him for all that he did for me. Perhaps this will, at least, show him how much I care—and remember!

I wanted this to be a true and honest account of Frank's life, so that meant having to make available all of the family information. This would include obvious things, such as scrapbooks and photographs, even information contained in family bibles. Frank's daughter, my aunt Lynne, opened her home to me on days when I'm sure she had many other things to take care of, and we spent hours going through those items of Frank's which she loaned to me. All of what she supplied was very valuable to this book.

During the development of this book, I became more and more familiar with Frank and his life. Many people out of the past called to talk with me about "Tram," and every last one of them would end by saying what a fine man he was. I soon became very proud to be his grandson.

The book is now finished and it is something that I'm proud of, and I hope my father and grandfather are too. To my lovely wife, Joan, I thank you for putting up with me as only you can.

I hope that Frank is happy with his story. I never met him, but I have come to know him. Perhaps now he is looking down with a smile, and I can look back and say "it's nice to finally meet you Frank! Until we meet again . . . "

William Trumbauer
Kansas City, Kansas

ACKNOWLEDGMENTS

THE AUTHORS WOULD LIKE TO TAKE this opportunity to thank the many folks who offered considerable assistance in the preparation of this work:

Academy Of Motion Picture Arts & Sciences, Danny Alguire, Herman "Trigger" Alpert, American Federation of Musicians (Chicago Local #10, Ed Ward; Detroit Local #5, Fred Nettling; Los Angeles Local #47, Serena Kay Williams; New York Local #802, Carl Janelli; St. Louis Local #2, Fred Laufketter), T. W. Anderson (N.F.F.A.), Bob Arnold, Ray Avery, Roy Bargy, Virginia Bargy, Bruce Bastin (England), George Baxter, Arlene Beiderbecke, Elizabeth Beiderbecke-Hart, Scott Black, Bob Boucher, Lawrence Brown, Nathanial Brewster (Columbia Records), Ralph Brewster, Alberta B. Brinkman, LeRoy Buck, Paul Burgess.

Also, Doug Caldwell, Mark Cantor, Hoagy Carmichael, Gregory Catsos, William Challis, Alan Cohn, Derek Coller (England), Ned Comstock, Max Connett, D. Russ Connor, Tom Corrigan (Lt. Col. USAF, Ret.), Ken Crawford, Jr., Herman Crone, Harry "Bing" Crosby, Mike Cuscuna, Modie Da Costa, William Dean-Myatt, Robert DeFlores, Tom DeLong, Kurt Dieterle, Marilyn Dunlap, J. A. W. Eekhoff (Netherlands), Alfie Evans, Federal Aviation Administration, Robert Fitzner, Chris Fletcher, Irving Friedman, Suzy Enns Frechette, John Fulton, General Services Administration, Saul Gilbert, Vincent Giordano, Jean Goldkette, Jim Gordon, Loretta Gragg (99ers).

Also, Friedrich Hachenberg (Germany), Phil Harris, Matt Hendrickson, Stan Hester, Steve Hester, Jay Hickerson, Robert Hilbert, Harold Hossle, Royal Howell, Don Ingle, Lillian Janssen, Carl Johnson, Richard J. Johnson (England), Harold Jones, Pershing Jung, Joe Kayser, Sylvia Kennick, Alice King, Vonnie King, Roger Kinkle, Kristine Krueger, Len Kunstadt, Stan Kuwik,

Steven Lasker, Joe Lauro, Stephen LaVere, Helen Leighow, Floyd Levin, Tor Magnuson (Sweden), Matty Matlock, Edwin Matthias (Library of Congress), Robert Mayhew, Brad McCuen, James "Rosy" McHargue, Charles McHenry, Tom McIntosh, John McNicholas (England), *The Melody Maker,* Homer Menge, Florence Mertz, Paul Mertz, Richard R. Miller, John Miner, John Molyneux, Nuncio "Toots" Mondello, Bernadette Moore (RCA Records), B. Joseph Moore (England), R. W. Murray.

Also, National Archives Of Canada, National Defence Headquarters (Canada), National Personnel Records, Ailiff Neal, A. Arthur Newman, Ralph Norton, "Red" Norvo, Herman Openner (Netherlands), Norm Orloff, Colleen Parkinson, Lou Paulsen, Maggie Pickett, Michael Pitts, Tom Pletcher, Ed Polic, Don Rayno, Record Research, Paul J. Ricci, Irving Riskin, Rockwell International Corp., Bonnie Ross, Johnnie Ross, Joseph Rushton, Priscilla Rushton, Brian A. L. Rust (England), Norma Ryker, Dave Saxon, Warren Scholl, Andy Secrest, Charles Senstock, Jr., Maggie Shedwill, Joe Showler (Canada), Andy Sindelar, John P. Smith, Warren Smith, Merv Sorenson, Russell Soule, William Soule, Cedric Spring, Esten Spurrier, John Steiner, Jean Steward, Gale Stout, Charles Strickfaden, Ruth Shaffner Sweeney.

Also, Harry Troxell, Tom Tsoti, Mary Trumbauer, Joseph Urso, University of Southern California Cinema-Television Library, Jane Vance, Joe Venuti, Tina Vinces (Columbia Records), Warren Vaché, Sr., Ate Van Delden (Netherlands), Peter Welding (Capitol Records), C. K. "Bozy" White, Paul Whiteman Collection (Williams College), Newell "Spiegle" Willcox, Laurie Wright (England), John Zentner, and Paulette Ziegfeld.

FOREWORD

FRANK TRUMBAUER'S WIFE, MITZI, and son, Bill, first approached Phil Evans about preparing a book on Frank in 1967. Following a series of telephone calls and correspondence, the project was agreed upon. Two years were spent in gathering information and interviewing former friends and associates, when Mitzi abruptly asked that the venture be discontinued. Her devotion to Frank was so great that the research was serving as a continual reminder that he was gone from her life, and the memories were too painful to relive. Her request was honored.

Frank's grandson, Bill Junior, contacted Phil again in 1989 and asked if he would resume the project. In the meantime, both Mitzi and her son, Bill, had passed away, and the grandson wanted to have their dream of a book on Frank Trumbauer fulfilled.

Larry F. Kiner and Phil had just completed a collaboration on *Al Jolson: A Bio-Discography,* and Bill's telephone call was timed right. Phil discussed the matter with Larry, and they agreed on another collaboration.

The same request was made of Bill Junior that had been made of his father and grandmother, and that was the promise of full cooperation and commitment. All of the available family information would be made available. Bill had access to his father's memorabilia, and he promised to consult with Frank's daughter, Lynne, about contributing what she could. He further was able to provide several names and addresses of former co-workers and associates of his late grandfather. Above all, he brought a refreshing enthusiasm to the project.

Bill turned up memos that Frank had written in 1953, which Frank had planned to use when he ''finally'' wrote his autobiography. All of those memos are contained within these pages, appropriately placed in the text so that the reader can have a feeling of Frank commenting on the events described during his life.

Lynne provided a wealth of material on Frank, locating his 1928 diary and a few scattered pages from three other diaries. She provided the family scrapbook and a host of papers vital to build a firm foundation for this book. All of Frank's comments taken from the diaries are found in the Chronology Section. The major "find" in the 1928 diary was that Frank noted the personnel on each of his Okeh recording dates and exactly how much he paid each musician. Lynne was able to provide additional ledgers that listed payments to Frank and his various bands, as well as receipts on some recording dates aside from the Okeh Record sessions.

The most difficult obstacle to overcome was that Frank was born in 1901 and all too many of his former associates are deceased. So many voices that could have offered memories are silent. Those former friends that remained were very gracious in assisting where they could, and words can never thank them enough. Frank had two professional worlds, music and aviation, and we attempted to offer as complete a story as possible.

In past years, various public libraries were all too helpful in checking dates and places from publications and newspaper, but now due to understaffing and budget cuts help is very limited. We are thankful for the help of John Molyneux, Arlene and Elizabeth Beiderbecke, Bob Fitzner, Len Kunstadt, Vince Giordano, Ralph Norton, John Miner, Steve LaVere, and Scott Black for their continual search of microfilms. Also the Reference Departments of the *Los Angeles Examiner* (now defunct) and the *Los Angeles Times.* Sylvia Kinnick provided valuable material from The Paul Whiteman Collection. Kristine Krueger opened the files of The Academy Of Motion Picture Arts And Sciences to us.

We are also indebted to *The Melody Maker* for their kind permission to quote from their past publications and for the exclusive photographs they offered to us.

A special appreciation is given to Bernadette Moore of RCA Victor Records, Peter Welding of Capitol Records, Tina Vinces and Nat Brewster of Columbia Records, Brian Rust, and devoted collectors Paul Burgess, John McNicholas, Friedrich Hachenberg, Joseph Moore, Ken Crawford Jr., William Dean-Myatt, Tor Magnuson, Steven Lasker, Tom DeLong, Joe Showler, Don Rayno, and the largest possible hooray to Richard Johnson, who can never be thanked enough times! Thanks to Stan Hester for "everything."

Date books were provided by Homer Menger, Matt Hendrickson, and Max Connett.

Tom Corrigan (Lt. Col., USAF, retired) provided not only information but suggestions and addresses that led to a wealth of material on Frank's aviation days. T. W. Anderson provided all of the journals of The Flying Farmers Association during the years 1946–1956. Many former pilots offered recollections included within the text, but one single man offered more than his recollections, John Zenter. John offered support and continual encouragement that is so vital to such an undertaking. None offered more light when things seemed darkest than Modie Da Costa and Bob Boucher. Their proofreading and suggestions were invaluable.

Finally, the task of researching and preparing the material was a difficult one. Anyone that has undertaken such a project knows that it has to be "a labor of love" because of the endless hours spent on the endeavor. Luckily the collaboration on this manuscript was a solid one. Phil fed a steady stream of writings to Larry, and Larry placed it within his computer. The main task was trying to keep the presentation in the same style as Frank's remarks, so that the reader would have an even flow of reading.

Phil has to offer a great deal of appreciation to his wife, Linda, who shared the "ups" and "downs" of these past five years. She can attest to the frustrations endured, the delight in locating new information, and the expenses needed to put such a book together. She could write a separate book on just the preparing of *The Frank Trumbauer Story*.

Considerable effort has been spent in compiling as complete an accurate discography as possible. It was considered of paramount importance to document the première issues and as many of subsequent reissues on other labels, including singles, long playing records, compact discs, and even the video recordings available for the historic film, *The King of Jazz*. Many of Tram's recordings are available today and most likely many will continue to be reissued in the future.

Some quotations, reviews, and/or comments have been edited for brevity and clarity, but some archaic spellings, phrases and punctuation (or lack thereof) are retained for period authenticity.

The final results are now before the reader, and it is our hope that we have presented a book worthy of Frank Trumbauer's memory. This was our goal, and now we await the public's decision.

Philip R. Evans
P. O. Box 10507
Stockdale Station
Bakersfield, CA. 93389–0507

Larry F.Kiner
P. O. Box 724
Redmond, WA. 98073–0724

SERIES EDITOR'S FOREWORD

There can be no question that Frank Trumbauer merits the meticulously detailed documentation of every aspect of his life and work contained in this imposing volume. Not only was he one of the most influential of the early jazz saxophonists and one of the first great improvisers in the music (as Lester Young put it, Tram "always told a little story when he played"), but he also was an important band leader and a complete professional.

As the co-authors point out in their foreword, this work could not have come into being without the collaboration of the Trumbauer family—and in a very real sense, the subject himself. Tram's diaries and autobiographical sketches provide insights both personal and discographical that flesh out the portrait of the man and the details about the music as no second-hand sources could have done. And it is touching indeed that William Trumbauer, who never knew his grandfather, feels that he has come to know him through this work, to which he himself contributed so much.

And it is touching as well to have the testimonials and collaborations from two octogenarians who knew Tram, the splendid clarinetist-saxophonist Rosy McHargue (still playing at this writing) and the pioneering writer-discographer Warren Scholl (whose annotated Whiteman discography, published serially in *Down Beat* in 1940, set standards still seldom met).

The editors of *Studies in Jazz* are pleased and proud to add this truly monumental work of dedicated research to the series. It will enhance appreciation and understanding of a significant chapter in 20th-century American music.

DAN MORGENSTERN
Director
Institute of Jazz Studies
Rutgers—The State University of New Jersey

CHAPTER ONE

THE EARLY YEARS 1901–1916

HENRY AND PAROLEE CROWELL HEARD the cries of their newly born grandchild, nine-pound Orie Frank Trumbauer, on Thursday, May 30, 1901, at 1:50 a.m. Frank was born in Carbondale, Illinois, in the living room of the Crowell home to their only daughter, Hannah Gertrude, and her husband since 1899, Fred Trumbauer, an employee of the Illinois Central Railroad.

As was often the case with newlyweds, they shared accommodations at 331 North West Street (later Illinois Avenue) in her parents' rambling wood-frame home, built by her father in 1892. The bedrooms were located on a second story that covered only the left half of the home. By the time that Orie Frank was nine months old, the Trumbauers managed to purchase a single-story home directly across the street.

Trumbauer's heritage could be traced back to being the great grandnephew of English author Charles Dickens. Charles's younger sister, Hannah Adeline Dickens, incurred the wrath of her parents when she fell in love with Wade Hampton Winchester, while both were studying in London. She became estranged from her family and elected to accompany her future husband to America in 1851. They were married and settled near Carbondale, Illinois, which was then but a village.

In December 1867, Charles Dickens began a tour of America that featured his reading *A Christmas Carol,* and the trial scene from *Pickwick Papers.* Before he returned to England in April 1868, he arranged a meeting with his sister and her husband in Nashville, Tennessee, to which Charles brought a gift, a green glass vase, scarcely nine inches high, flared and frilled at the top, and decorated with some simple little flowers. He knew Adeline had admired it in the family home, and he hoped that it would serve as a link to her family in England. He also gave her an unpublished manuscript, *The Life Of Our Lord.*[1] It was believed that the family now gave their blessings to Adeline's marriage and new life.

There is a direct relationship between Adeline's husband and the Winchesters who founded the Winchester Firearms And Ammunition Manufacturing Company. Oliver Winchester adapted and improved upon the repeating rifle; his Model 1873, a superior rifle with a steel mechanism and heavier center fire cartridge, came to be known as "the gun that won the West."

Sarah L. Winchester, widow of Oliver's son, is known today for the famed California Registered Historical Landmark #868, *The Winchester Mystery House,* in San Jose. She began constructing this home in 1884 and believed that as long as she continued to build, so would her life continue. The obsession reached 24-hour-a-day construction for thirty-eight years, resulting in an estate with 160 rooms and six acres of gardens. Today daily tours are conducted to display doors that open to a blank wall; stairs so tiny that no one could climb them; and various other mysterious building features.

Adeline and Wade's daughter, Parolee Gertrude, was born in 1855 and married Henry Bert Crowell, a member of the carpenter crew with the Illinois Central Railroad, in 1873. This marriage produced two children: Henry Lawrence Crowell, born in 1874, and Frank Trumbauer's mother, Hannah Gertrude Crowell, born in 1882.

Henry Lawrence entered the service of the Illinois Central Railroad as a fireman, where he served for three years before being promoted to engineer, a job that he held for four years, before moving to Waterloo, Iowa, in 1906. During the next several years, he was an apprentice instructor in various departments with the Illinois Central. He met his wife, Ethel, a school teacher from Salem, Illinois, and they decided to make Waterloo their lifelong residence.

Young Henry's placid life received a loud awakening when on March 6, 1916, Pancho Villa and 400 of his troops crossed the

[1]The previously unpublished Dickens manuscript was sold by the family in 1934 for $210,000. It was serialized in the Waterloo (Iowa) Daily Courier newspaper, starting on March 5, 1934. Dickens' tours reportedly netted him $140,000.

border into the United States and attacked the town of Columbus, New Mexico. A battle between Villa's men and 250 cavalry troops raged for a short time and resulted in the death of eight American soldiers, eighteen invaders, eight townspeople, and the loss of several buildings that were set afire by Villa's retreating forces. The surprise attack was concluded to have been that of a desperate man, who finding himself low on supplies, believed that he could capture the needed provisions with a quick raid.

This invasion by a foreign army met with national outrage, and cries for vengeance filled every newspaper across the United States. President Woodrow Wilson contacted Mexico's President Venustiano Carranza and sought permission to renew the "reciprocal privileges" that existed between 1880 to 1886 when both governments regularly crossed the border in pursuit of Geronimo and Victorio. President Carranza eagerly granted the request to pursue and capture Villa.

Immediate action was taken, and by March 15, Brigadier General John J. Pershing crossed the Mexican border at the head of seven columns, numbering 15,000 men from units of the cavalry, artillery, and infantry. One of the three mounted columns was made up of the famed Seventh Cavalry, historically associated with the late General George Custer.

Henry served with Pershing's Expedition Force.

While the American troops chased Pancho Villa throughout Mexico, they were never able to capture him. The army did succeed in breaking up Villa's forces and might have eventually captured Villa had not World War I threatened American shores, and President Wilson recalled the troops for service in Europe.

Upon his discharge from the army, with the ending of World War I, young Henry returned to Waterloo with what Gertrude proclaimed as "a chest full of medals."

Henry became head of the education department of the Illinois Central in his home town and held this job for many years. He distinguished himself at picnics and special events by offering exhibitions of his sharpshooting, both as an individual, and a member of the Illinois Central team.[2] One July Fourth picnic, he

[2]The ten-man team had only their last names entered in the files, and were as follows: Witry, Shepherd, Fairweather, Sutcliffe, Chapman, Shores, Hummel, Ingersoll, Webber, and (Henry) Crowell.

entered and won four shooting contests in Waverly, Iowa, with trapshooting scores of 81 breaks out of 87 tries, 49 out of 51, 47 out of 50, and 69 out of 75.

Meanwhile Gertrude, a gifted pianist, realized that the small town of Carbondale hindered her chances to advance her music career. She convinced Fred to request a transfer to St. Louis, and when it was accepted, they moved in 1907. Gertrude spent the first year playing piano for silent films in the smaller theatres known as "nickelodeons" (admission one nickel), but by 1908 she had gained a reputation as an outstanding pianist and was hired by the Lyric Theatre, one of St. Louis's finer theatres. The following year, she became owner and operator (for 18 months) of the Elite Amusement Company, a theatre where she employed a projectionist (name now forgotten) and a cashier (Maryann Walker), and charged the regular five cents admission on weekdays but raised it to a dime on Sundays.

> **Eventually music lessons came to me. Trying to find a suitable instrument was a task. I started with the violin, but the only thing that I really found of interest was the violin case which I used to carry my school books.**
>
> **Then I persuaded my parents to allow me to have a trombone and this lasted just long enough for me to add "Asleep In The Deep" to my repertoire. Then the neighbors persuaded my mother to select another instrument for me.**
>
> **I studied piano and concluded it abruptly while in a "moving picture" theatre. Mother was playing the piano for the silent film that was being shown, and one night she had to leave for the ladies room in a hurry, I decided to fill in for her. It seemed that I had mastered one certain polka and chose the middle of a very dramatic scene during the picture to slide under the rail of the pit and go into the tune. Mother returned to a very bewildered audience.**

Bill Trumbauer, Jr., has offered the following:

> I guess that it was 1911 when tragedy struck. The story the family heard was that a split in the marriage occurred and Fred brought young Frank to Carbondale to live with Gertrude's parents until such time as Fred could reconcile

> with Gertrude. Unfortunately, this was not to be, and Fred left Frank's life, never to see his son again.

Gertrude found work in 1912 at the Royal Theatre and sent for Frank. She often pushed folding chairs together in the theatre, so Frank could sleep, as she wanted him with her as much as possible, but her efforts to try and be both a father and mother were doomed.

Trumbauer's introduction to the saxophone occurred when Gertrude took him to the Arcadia Ballroom and he heard the band, and in particular saxophonist Ray Reynolds. When he discovered that Ray was making $125 a week, he persuaded his mother to purchase a sax for him.

A former Paul Whiteman musician, Charles Strickfaden, remembered Trumbauer's first saxophone during a 1966 interview:

> Frank told me about that first day. When he got that shiny instrument home, he held it in his hands, admiring it. He decided to play it, and blew through the three holes in the mouthpiece cap for almost an hour. He felt frustrated and betrayed by a horn that couldn't make a sound. In disgust, he tossed it on the couch, the cap flew off, and Frank discovered the reed.

> **I hadn't any books of any kind when I began to play the saxophone. My mother would sustain a chord on the piano while I sought out the corresponding arpeggio on the sax, she would strike chords related to the original, in addition to resolutions from one key to another, while I would continue with arpeggios and broken chords in each. This form continued until I had quite a command of the instrument.**
>
> **The saxophone was a C-melody and it made it possible for me to read violin parts, but these parts contained melody only and I wanted to try out my abilities. So, little by little, I began to improvise, using the violin part as a guide where my ear and chord training supplied the ideas.**
>
> **Up to this time, I had not read notes. All my ability was in the form of memorized key actions and chord response to my ear. I realized that the saxophone had a tremendous future and that if I could read as fast as I could improvise, it would be a real achievement. All of which**

brought on a spree of practice which consumed about eight hours a day and lasted approximately nine months.

In the fall of 1912, Gertrude decided to send Frank to live with her parents in Carbondale. She had signed a contract with the Palace Theatre for 1913 to share piano duties with Winnifred Green, and the hours were from 11 a.m. to midnight. She knew that it would be impossible to spend the proper time with Frank, so she packed his belongings and escorted him to Carbondale, 100 miles southeast of St. Louis.

At the turn of the century, Carbondale was recognized as an up and coming city with a population of about 5,000. It was located in the very center of the coal-mining district, hence its name. The city, centered on the Southern Illinois Fruit Belt, was considered the cultural center of Southern Illinois, broadly advertised as the ''Athens Of Illinois.'' The school system offered four public schools by 1905 with an enrollment of 900, and Southern Illinois Normal University (now known as Southern Illinois University), founded in 1874.

The city had two main streets, Illinois Avenue running north and south, and Main Street stretching east and west. The two streets intersected in the middle of the business district. It was then a popular saying that if someone had an umbrella that could cover a 40-mile radius, they could stand at the intersection and keep the rain off some 30 nearby towns, each of which had a population of about 1,000 people. All were located around coal mines. When the mines were being worked, everyone had money, but when the mines closed, everyone was broke.

Mayor Tom Hord, in his inaugural address of 1895, boasted that ''we now have the best lighted town in this part of the state,'' but the initial lighting company that placed the electricity in the homes and in the street lights, met with bankruptcy shortly thereafter, and it wasn't until 1902 that a permanent electric company was formed, later to be under the ownership of the Koppers Company.

In all of Trumbauer's applications where he was required to list his schooling, he listed his elementary school years as between September 1906 and June 1914, his high school years from September 1914 through June 1916, and followed with a notation of one year of ''normal school'' and one year of Mechanical Trade

School (apprentice) in St. Louis. (The St. Louis Public Schools were unable to offer any records from their files.)

Alan Cohn conducted research on the authors' behalf at the Carbondale schools:

> There have been several fires over the years, thus accounting for their lack of certification on Frank's schooling. There were not any elementary school records on Frank, although he did attend Lincoln School. The only information found was that he attended University High School, which was a teacher's training high school attached to what was then Southern Illinois Normal University.

Trumbauer was not pictured in any of the remaining school yearbooks. The lone enrollment card showed the first quarter (January–March) of 1916 at University High School, where Frank was given a grade of "88" in English I, and "85" in Medical Hygiene, a "credit" in Gym, and a "B-" in penmanship. One additional class where he averaged "80" is blurred on the card.

Alan found a registration dating from 1917 for S.I.N.U. but "Tram apparently never actually attended college as there are not any records of courses and grades, etc. I understand that then some University High School courses could be applied for credit with the college, so maybe Frank intended to go to S.I.N.U., enrolled, but never attended?"

Trumbauer, now living with his grandparents, offered these recollections:

> **I always remembered my grandmother, Parolee, with her jet black hair, copper skin, and beady black eyes. Her temper was just as you would imagine-fast and furious. Yet a more gentler woman did not exist.**
>
> **My grandfather, Henry, had a stoic understanding so characteristic of his nationality-Cherokee, The American Indian.**
>
> **He used to take me into the woods and show the wild flowers to me. "My boy, here is the best example of God that you will ever see-the basis for all religions. Man will never be able to duplicate this simple, little flower for it comes from a power greater than all of us."**
>
> **He gave me a bag of water-washed pebbles and took me to the bridge of a creek. "Son, I want you to drop two**

> **pebbles into the water every day for thirty days. You can not miss a single day. Then drop in four pebbles the next month-you must do this every day." It was his way of teaching me routine and discipline so necessary in our life.**
>
> **Another teaching I've remembered throughout my life, and one I've always tried to practice, is doing something good for someone every day of my life.**
>
> **"It is the most contagious thing in the world," grandfather told me. "It will always come back to you in some way."**
>
> **"Many people smoke the peace pipe, but very few inhale."**
>
> **"Never criticize your brother until you've walked in his moccasins for two weeks."**
>
> **How wonderful it would be if everyone practiced these Indian sayings.**

Royal Howell has recalled:

> Frank came to Lincoln School in 1912 and we were in the same grade together, with Nellie Weller as our teacher. I remember Frank as being a slender, tallish kid with very brown eyes and that straight, silky, brown hair that you could comb any way and it would stay put without using any kind of 'guke.' He was very mild mannered, not at all backward, but reserved.

Royal was one of five children that lived in a big ten-room house on South Illinois, and most importantly, he had a piano! Tram and Royal became inseparable, and it was not unusual to find Tram at the Howell home at all hours of the day, starting with breakfast and staying for dinner.

The new shiny saxophone that Tram received in St. Louis was now becoming a bit beat-up, with more dents and skinned places than an overly ripe cucumber, but, placed inside his carrying case, no one noticed.

The piano and sax duets that Royal and Tram enjoyed was soon joined by fellow student Bill Ashley, who brought along his guitar. Every Saturday the trio would practice. Then Sundays became "open house." Every kid in the neighborhood who could play an instrument showed up. Glenn Banuum brought his woodblocks, and various other instruments started to appear: violins, ukuleles, banjos, even a jew's-harp, and Royal's mother would just accept the crowd and bake cookies or a cake for refreshments. The neighbors put up with the "music" because it allowed them to know where their children were at those hours, but after five o'clock the telephone would start to ring and various parents would summon their children home for dinner. By 1915, the group added Claire Carr on trumpet and Omar Parker on drums.

None of this newly formed band could read much music except for Tram, so the job of teaching fell on him. Luckily everyone had a good ear, and he started out teaching everyone to harmonize, how to modulate from key to key, how to diminish, and how to memorize. Soon the band was able to play in seven keys: C, D, E-flat, F, G, A-flat, and B-flat.

They played at every party they could find: the Rotarians, the Lions, the PTA, and various church groups; All for free! Then one of the groups made a mistake. They paid the band for their performance; that ended their days of playing gratis. Word of mouth was their best advertisement. It became known that they were a good dance band and they played for little money. They called themselves "The Egyptian Jazzadores."

Frank Trumbauer was the leader. Royal's house seemed to be the headquarters, and, since he had a telephone, he became the booker. Royal took his role seriously and purchased a second-hand Maxwell touring car. This solved the transportation problems; with fairly good gravel roads to nearby towns, they were set. They'd book a job for a flat fee, no extra expenses, then, after deducting car expenses, they'd evenly divide the remainder. Sometimes they would have three or four jobs a week, and they'd end up with $20 to $25 apiece; quite a sum for that time.

Royal recalled those days vividly during an October 1968 interview:

> Frank had some pretty good ideas. He would take the choruses of four standard tunes and arrange them so they would fit with a little modulation. We would play two choruses of each song—that would give us eight choruses and add up to a reasonable dance. He thought up the idea of the soloist leaving the bandstand and going out onto the

> dance floor to mingle with the couples—serenading them individually. Boy, did that gag go over! Old Frank had it all down pat.

But 1916 proved to be Tram's downfall. He was devoting all of his time to the band. The school work started to suffer, and then he started to miss school. He missed a total of 22 days in April. The Crowells sadly informed Gertrude of the situation, and she asked them to send Tram to St. Louis immediately, so she could keep a close eye, and a firm hand, on him.

Tram had hoped to return to Carbondale for enrollment in September 1917, but the decision was made by his mother to enroll him in a trade school. Tram also obtained a part-time job with the Mobile and Ohio Railroad, shoveling coal into the boiler of the engine, and of course, the saxophone went with him, playing into the night air as the train traveled through the countryside.

CHAPTER TWO

WORLD WAR I
1917–1922

THE GERMAN SUBMARINE SINKING of the **Lusitania** on May 5, 1915, accounted for the total loss of 1152 lives, 102 of them Americans. Many newspapers printed editorials protesting this action, calling it an open act of war. President Woodrow Wilson maintained his pledge not to become involved in the European war that had started the previous year, and only offered written protests to Germany. Wilson made this his campaign promise in 1916 and easily won reelection. John Q. Public believed that "it was Europe's war," that it was "on the other side of the ocean," and besides, "I didn't raise my son to be a soldier."

President Wilson did everything possible to remain neutral but on January 31, 1917, Germany declared unrestricted submarine warfare, prompting the President to cut all diplomatic relations on February 3. America was later to learn that the German submarines promptly sank 134 vessels during that month.

On April 6, 1917, war was declared: Recruiting posters of Uncle Sam pointing an index finger and announcing "I Want You" sprang up across the land, as enlistment centers opened.

Bernice Tongate read about the Navy accepting women enlistments in Washington, D.C., and entered a Los Angeles Naval Recruiting Office that fateful day in 1917 when well-known poster artist, Howard Chandler Christy, happened to be there attempting to come up with an idea for the Navy's recruiting poster. Christy persuaded one of the men to give her a navy cap, a jumper, and a neckerchief, and he sketched a poster that appeared throughout the nation, showing Bernice with the slogan, "Gee, I

Wish I Were A Man, I'd Join The Navy.'' Join she did, and was a chief yeoman when she was discharged in 1920.

Perhaps it was this poster that appealed to Trumbauer's patriotism in 1918. One day short of his seventeenth birthday, he needed his mother's signature on his enlistment papers.

''After all,'' Tram assured her, ''the newspapers say that we are winning the war!''

The war seemed to take a turn on April 21 when German flying ace, ''The Red Baron,'' Baron Manfred von Richthofer was shot down and killed by artillery fire. He had been credited with destroying between 75 and 80 Allied aircraft. Then, as if to confirm the change of the direction of the war, Eddie Rickenbacker shot down his first German airplane eight days later, on his way to becoming the United States ''ace'' with 26 kills.

Gertrude gave in and signed the papers on May 29, 1918.

I reported to the Navy Recruiting Office in St. Louis where a big, tough petty officer barked, ''Take off your clothes!''

I swallowed hard, ''Right here?''

''Yeah, right here! Now whada'ya want, son, Regular D.O.W. Landsman Musician?''

I just stood there. I didn't have the vaguest idea of what he was saying.

''Speak up, son, speak up,'' he yelled.

I finally managed to say, ''I just want to join the navy, Captain.''

Well, that fixed me, but good! He signed me as ''Landsman Musician,'' the lowest rating the navy had to offer. I wasn't even eligible to go to sea.

Trumbauer was assigned to the Great Lakes Naval Training Center, near Chicago, on June 3.

I ate my first breakfast in pouring rain. I filled a mattress cover with wet straw and slept in a tent with about four inches of water on the ground. No wonder there was so much flu going around.

Two days of this and I was looking for someone to take my resignation. ''I quit!'' Well, it didn't take the Navy long to set me straight on that score.

We were soon assigned to quarters, but that was after

my three days in the brig. I neglected to salute an officer and then turned right around and saluted the same officer with a cigarette in my mouth!

One day the Master Of Arms lined us up and gave us the works, Navy style. Sopranio was his name and he was a big, husky Italian boy. He let us know that he was the boss. Did anyone doubt it? Did anyone think they could lick him? No one moved!

"Well, how about any two of you?" he finally asked.

Well now, my new friend, Bradley, didn't like the Navy either.

We had read somewhere in the rules that if anyone got into a fight he was thrown out of the Navy.

Bradley gave me the sign and we both stepped forward. Sopranio told us to follow him.

"Oh boy, here's where we get beat up and sent home."

Sopranio took us to the Company Commander. "Sir," he said, "here are the only two guys in the outfit with any guts!"

Do you know that we were put in charge of the work detail for our outfit!

Oh yes, we found out later that Sopranio was the middleweight boxing champion of the training station.

The Navy lost my number so I didn't receive any money for six months. I met an "old salt" who knew how to tie the square knots in the regulation black ties that we wore. I found an iron in the barracks and we went into business together. He'd tie 'em—I pressed 'em! Twenty-five cents.

Business was great, so with some of our profits we bought a chain stitch sewing machine and began altering and repairing uniforms. One turned the wheel and the other guided the cloth. We cleaned up for awhile but our luck didn't hold. Some of our alterations pulled out and sailors were observed marching on the field with just a front and back and plenty of ventilation on the side.

The company commander found out about our little racket, confiscated our equipment and assigned us to quarters for two weeks.

When Johnny went marching off to the sounds of distant cannons in 1917, the streets were filled with patriotic crowds, wildly cheering, assured that the Yanks would, quickly and decisively, end the campaign. Now a year later, having faced the reality of war's death and destruction, America was a nation united in prayer for the safe return of their loved ones and a quick end to the conflict. One million troops were stationed in Europe by June 30, 1918, and the reports of the dead and wounded were no longer numbers and statistics. Now names familiar to the families back home made the newspapers. Former President Teddy Roosevelt, lost his youngest son, Quentin, on July 17 in an aerial battle. Then poet Joyce Kilmer was killed on August 1.

The August 29, Great Lakes bulletin stated: ''For the last time for several weeks, the big band, which had always been one of the chief attractions at the weekly reviews, played en masse yesterday.'' This band battalion numbering 300 men was led by Lieutenant John Phillip Sousa. The plans now called for the band to be split into sections and sent all over the country in an effort to raise money in bond drives.

Trumbauer's unit, the second regiment, was slated to tour throughout Wisconsin, aided by an accompanying exhibit of war relics, and to present concerts to raise money for the war effort. They started their tour on September 17, but by the 24th they ran into serious trouble. They were struck hard by Spanish influenza. Three members were hospitalized in Chippewa Falls, two of them dying, and four more were hospitalized in Green Bay. The tour was immediately cancelled and the unit returned to Great Lakes.

Finally a higher rating came along, and Trumbauer was assigned to the troopship, **America,** originally **Amerika.** The steel-hulled, steam passenger liner, was launched on April 20, 1905, at Belfast, Ireland, for transatlantic service between Germany and the United States. When the war broke out, she was assigned to Boston harbor, and remained inactive until July 25, 1917, when John David, Commissioner of the United States Shipping Board, earmarked her for service. On August 6, she was placed in commission.

Her eighth return voyage, which sailed from France on August 30, returned with wounded. Among her passengers was the distinguished conductor and critic, Dr. Walter Damrosch (1862–1950), who, at the request of General John Pershing, commander of the American Expeditionary Force (AEF), was entrusted the mission of reorganizing the bands of the U. S. Army. He had founded a school for bandmasters at the general headquarters of the AEF at Chaumont, France.

Dr. Damrosch often offered inconsistent critical standards. In 1926, after he conducted the "Concerto In F" with George Gershwin at the piano with the New York Symphony Orchestra, he referred to "Lady Jazz" finding her white knight in Gershwin. But speaking before the Music Supervisors' National Conference in 1928 in New York, he stated according to the *New York Times:* "Jazz is a monotony of rhythm. It is rhythm without music and without soul. Personally, it annoys me. Jazz is quite unsatisfactory to any intelligent person."

On September 20, 1918, the **America** embarked on another trip from Boston to France at the start of an influenza epidemic. As a result, 997 cases of the flu and pneumonia occurred among the soldiers, and 56 cases broke out among the 940 crew members. When they completed the round trip to Hoboken, New Jersey, 53 soldiers and two sailors had died.

Trumbauer arrived, a proud sailor, in Philadelphia to accept his new assignment to the **America.** He arrived on October 15th—the very day the ship sank at the Hoboken dock. While anchored in Hoboken, the ship was completely fumigated to rid her of the influenza germ. To clear the air of the ship's hull, all portholes were left open. An "unofficial opinion" maintained that the ship had listed due to mud suction, that the ship had been resting on the bottom, and, when the tide rose, that the mud shifted and water rushed into the open portholes. She was raised and refloated on November 21, 1918, but due to needed repairs, not put back into active duty until February 1919.[3]

Trumbauer returned to the Great Lakes Naval Training Station:

> **J. Walter Guetter, our bandmaster, once asked me how I began playing and why I could improvise so well?**
>
> **Guetter's reason was obvious. He had conservatory graduates and fine musicians in the band who couldn't "fake note one." I wasn't a good musician but the officers always requested me to play for their dances.**
>
> **I told him of my desire to become a musician and all the help that my mother had given to me, teaching me**

[3]The **America** was laid up at Port Patience, Maryland in 1932, but recalled to service in 1940, and given a new name, *Edmünd B. Alexander.* After gallant service, she was placed in reserve on May 26, 1949 at Hawkin's Point, Maryland. On January 16, 1957, the Bethlehem Steel Company put the scrapper's torch to her.

how to modulate around any chord and I could practically play anything just by the sound of a chord.

Years later, I saw Mr. Guetter again. It was on July 29, 1935 at the Robin Hood Dell in Philadelphia. He was bassoon soloist with the Philadelphia Symphony Orchestra. I played a solo that night as the Paul Whiteman Orchestra combined with the Philadelphia Symphony Orchestra. I must say it was a big thrill, too.

The Armistice was announced on November 11, 1918. Now all of the armed services would be returning home, and sailors were being discharged from Great Lakes, but Trumbauer discovered that his enlistment officer in St. Louis had signed him not for the duration of the war but for a regular four-year hitch. When Gertrude learned of Tram's plight, she immediately contacted a congressman from Missouri and received a sympathetic listening. It took a few weeks, but Tram was finally discharged from the Navy on January 14, 1919.

On January 30, he applied for membership into the St. Louis Musicians Local #2. A game that Tram was to enjoy throughout his life now started. He would always list his correct birth date month and day, but not the year. It was always reported differently, and at this time he listed it as 1898. He listed his address as living with his mother at 2303 "A" Russell Avenue. He was accepted as a full member on February 28.

Max Goldman was a popular leader around town, so I went to see him. He told me to report that night for a tryout.

Goldman passed out some music and asked me what part I wanted.

"Any part you have left will be all right," I told him. That really startled him. To be perfectly honest, I didn't know what part to ask for.

Goldman handed me a cello part. I had to think fast. Now, let's see, the first four notes are whole notes. Count from the bottom. First line is "g," then "b," and the third line is "d." My first note is "d."

I had read the first four notes just fine and then I got lost so I had to fake the rest. After all, I was so excited that I couldn't even read the title.

The other men remarked about the fine cello part.

Max said, "This is a swell tune. Let's play it again."

Again I played the first four notes and faked the rest, but not the same as the first time. I explained that I had just added a little here and there.

I got the job and a fifty cent raise the second night. After the excitement wore off, I was able to read a little better.

From there I went to Cicardi's Cafe for $85 a week. This was more like it. I was slowly catching up with Ray Reynolds.

There is much to be said about the famous Cicardi's Cafe at Euclid and Delmar. Cicardi's was one of the most beautiful cafes in the middle west. It had a main dining room with a huge ballroom over it. The ceiling—a dome—was designed to give the illusion of the sky on a moonlit night, with tiny lights for stars. It was really a romantic setting. Around the dome was a balcony with exquisite oriental rugs draped over the banisters. Outside the dining room was a lovely terrace for the summer months.

The elite, the celebrities and artists stopping in St. Louis, the wealthy oil men from Oklahoma—they all gathered there. Whenever Fritz Kreisler, the great violinist, played in St. Louis, he always dined at Cicardi's.

One of the waiters, Robert Lang, told me that he usually made around four hundred dollars a week. It made me wonder if Ray Reynolds was so smart after all.

My first night at Cicardi's is so clear in my memory. I was the first one there and Al Sarli, the leader of the orchestra, came on the bandstand. He passed out the books and handed me three: flute, cello, and trumpet.

Oh, no! A concert session for the first three hours! Six to nine, every night! Then dance music. No one had told me about this.

Sarli picked a number and told me to play the cello part. What a mess I made of this! How different from having someone stomp off two beats and then every man for himself. I was miserable and wanted to go home.

Sarli took me in the back room and said, "Why, son, you can't read music!"

I remembered those words as long as I lived! He didn't think that I was much of a musician, but as long as I was there, I might as well finish the night, and he would replace me the next day.

I was sick and embarrassed. Besides, I had already given up my other job.

As we left the back room, Sarli gave me a pat on the shoulder and said, "Don't let it get you down, kid."

Well, they were the longest three hours in my whole life.

Nine o'clock and intermission. I took a long walk and made up my mind to go back to railroading.

Ten o'clock and back on the bandstand. Sarli gave me a big smile and said, "Now let's see what happens."

God must have been with me because Sarli picked a tune that I knew. I thought to myself, "Since this is my last night in the music business, I might as well blow my brains out."

After the number, Sarli grabbed me by the arm, rushed me to the bar and bought me a drink. "Great, kid, great! Forget what I said! You're in! We'll work out the concert session some way."

In just a few short hours, I had been to hell and back again!

I took home all of the parts of the concert numbers we were to play the next evening and stayed up all night learning them.

I did so much better the next night that I received a word of praise from Sarli. But that wasn't good enough! I was still very unhappy because I realized how little I knew about music, and I kept hearing those words, "Why, son, you can't read music!"

I made up my mind that I was going to study. I worked at the cafe every night and spent at least eight hours on my instruments. Study! Study! Study! I lost weight, I had very little sleep, but in nine months I could read and transpose any part. Flute parts—trumpet parts—trombone parts—clarinet parts—cello parts—anything at all. My technique had improved by leaps and bounds and I was beginning to get a little reputation with it. But, above all, Sarli was proud of me!

It was here that I first learned about unions. Earlier in the year, I had joined the Musicians Union but immediately forgot about it. I was working—making over scale—so why bother to read all of that fine print?

Joe Gonnalli opened a roof garden cafe across the street and offered me more money to work for him, so I left Cicardi's without telling anyone.

Poor August Cicardi called everyone in town that night, trying to locate me, and it wasn't until late that night that he learned that I was playing across the street.

The next day, I received my first call from the Musicians Union. The president wanted to see me in his office immediately.

I arrived at the union hall and found Mr. Cicardi there, too. I must say that he didn't look very happy. The president asked me what I was trying to do.

"Make more money," I replied. "Besides, it is very nice up there on the roof."

Mr. Cicardi stood up. "Frank, why didn't you ask me for a raise? I'll give you ten dollars more than Joe is paying you. Let's forget the union charges and quit this horseplay. What do you say?"

So I went back to Cicardi's that night, after some fatherly advice from the president of the Musicians Union.

Shortly after that, Jesse Holleweg took over the leadership of the orchestra. He brought in Alvin Steindel, violinist with the famous Steindel Trio, as featured artist with the concert group. I continued on because Cicardi liked me and by now I had quite a following.

Harry Grapengeter, saxophone player, was also a member of the famous Cicardi Orchestra. He later became Director of Music in the Los Angeles Public Schools. Harry was the practical joker in the band and drove us crazy.

One of Harry's favorite tricks was to put tabasco sauce on my mouthpiece just before my solo. By the time I finished playing my mouth would be burned to a crisp! Then he would hand me a glass of water with tabasco rubbed on the rim. Another of his tricks was putting a horse hair between the reed and mouthpiece.

I finally became so fed up with his tricks that I told Holleweg that I was going to fix Harry, once and for all! Jesse gave me his blessings.

I purchased a small drill and one night, during intermission, I took Harry's horn into a back room, removed a screw at the top of his horn, quickly drilled a

tiny hole and replaced the screw. That small hole served as an octave key and any low notes he played jumped up an octave. He tried and tried to find the trouble then finally asked me to look it over.

I went into the back room and put a small piece of a toothpick in the hole. I took it back and played it for Harry. "Nothing wrong. Here, you try it." Well, Harry was so happy that he bought me a drink.

The next day, I removed the toothpick and the same old trouble returned for Harry. I kept that up for thirty days—removing and replacing the toothpick! By now, Harry was almost out of his mind. He was about to go out and buy a new saxophone when I made a permanent repair for him, and advised Harry not to play any more tricks on us. That cured old Harry!

Harry once told me about taking his saxophone and climbing up among the pipes of a huge pipe organ. There are some notes on a pipe organ similar in tone quality to that of a saxophone. The organist played a melody and Harry continued it with his own phrase. The organist repeated the phrase, and Harry repeated his phrase. It wasn't long before the poor organist ran out of the building, screaming.

"But," as Harry said, "after that horn episode, I'm through with practical jokes!"

November 8, 1919 was selected as the date to hold a dance in Carbondale, it was midway between October 31 (Halloween) and November 11 (Armistice Day), and Tram was hired for the dance job. He asked Jesse Holleweg for the day off, and then telephoned Royal Howell and told him to "round up the old gang" for the dance date.

Royal's recollections in October 1968 were quite clear on the event:

> There was this man in Carbondale, John Brown, that had arranged for the dance, advertised Trumbauer's presence throughout southern Illinois and then became ill. When Tram called and asked about the "old gang," he was stunned to hear that Omar Parker had died suddenly from acute pneumonia, shortly after Tram left town. There was a long silence on his end of the telephone, as if reflecting on his memories of Omar.

"Well," Tram said, "I'll bring a few boys with me, and you see what you can do on your end. Okay?"

Frank felt that just because John Brown became ill, that was not any reason to cancel the dance. He suggested that we hire the hall ourselves, play the job, charge $3 per couple, and if we lost our fannies, we were just out our labor. Whooo-eee, we really jammed the hall. My younger brother sold tickets at the door. I don't know really how much he knocked down that night, but we paid Frank $300 plus his expenses, and still had money left over for the rest of us to be paid handsomely.

I do recall that Frank spent some time with his grandparents when he was in town. He would never have given a thought to have come to Carbondale and not take the opportunity to spend as much time with them as possible. He was very attached to the Crowell family.

Gertrude was remarried on January 6, 1920 to William Stevenson, employed by the St. Louis Fire Department as a fire fighter.

I stayed at Cicardi's until Prohibition closed it. Prohibition started at 12:01 on January 17, 1920. What a night—that last night before Prohibition. All the drinks we wanted—just anything—and champagne: the best in the house!

I drank some, saved some, and by the time we closed the doors I had loaded my old Model T coupe so full of champagne and instruments that I could barely see out! One of the singers in the show, a very luscious blonde, asked me for a lift to her hotel. I told her that I'd be waiting in my car, parked in the alley. The next thing I knew, a cop was shaking me. He saw all of the wine in my car and thought that I had stolen it. I kept telling him that I worked here, and I guess the sign of my instruments saved me. Just to be certain that I was telling the truth, he made me carry all of the champagne back into the cafe. I'll never forgive the girl for not showing up, nor losing all of that good wine.

Joe Kayser has recalled, in a letter dated March 12, 1968:

I left St. Louis in April 1917 for New York City and returned to St. Louis in May 1918 to join the Navy. After my discharge, I stayed in St. Louis until about June and then

> returned to New York where I played with bands headed by Meyer Davis and Earl Fuller. I decided to return to St. Louis and I went to see Gene Rodemich. When we were kids, we had a piano and drum duo known as ''Gene And Joe'' and we played many society affairs years prior to all of this. I didn't know Frank, but I knew that he was a standout musician and I asked Gene about borrowing Frank for a date that I had on December 20 in Danville, Illinois. Gene told Frank that it was 'just to help him out' and he went along with the arrangements.

At this point, James ''Rosy'' McHargue picked up the story during an interview with Richard Miller on October 30, 1989:

> In those days, we didn't have access to jazz except by phonograph records. Chicago was 135 miles to the north of us, and it might as well have been on another planet, as we didn't have any way to get there at our young age. The dance they played that night was an affair that was closed to us, so the best that we could do was gather outside a window and listen.
>
> During one of the intermissions, Frank stepped out to smoke a cigarette. I was the tallest of the group, so that sort of made me the spokesman when we approached him to tell Frank how much we enjoyed his playing. I guess we were one of the first fan clubs! Frank was so pleased to learn of our interest in him, and he vowed that once back inside, he would prop open the window a bit further, and direct all of his solos to the opening, so we could hear him clearer. What a tone he got! What a night!

It wasn't until the band returned to St. Louis that Tram learned that he was on ''permanent loan'' to Kayser. Joe made the sales pitch by saying that he needed someone who was well known throughout the area as a draw. Joe planned to make St. Louis the home base and do a series of one-nighters over the next few months to nearby towns. Kayser was aware of the traffic conditions. The winter months were upon them, and the towns had few paved roads; most were dirt roads that would prove nearly impassable when the snow and rains came. Joe decided that they'd take the trains to their engagements. The more he talked, the more Tram listened, and he finally agreed to join the band.

The band consisted of five pieces: Harry Sales on piano; Leo Lambertz on trumpet; Bob Chaudet on violin; Joe Kayser on drums; and Trumbauer on c-melody saxophone. Their uniforms were tuxedos. They were appropriately called "Joe Kayser's Band."

The tour continued into 1921 with a series of one-nighters throughout Illinois, Iowa, Wisconsin, and Indiana. The more stops they played, the more Leo grumbled, and soon Joe replaced him with banjoist Bob Marvin.

The band had a few novelty numbers worked up. When the band was introduced to the crowd, at the start of the performance, Joe would come up front, carrying a bass drum. The guys would give a sudden shout, it would scare Joe, and he'd fall onto his collapsible drum, and this always got a big laugh.

Each dance number was announced. A huge card was placed on an easel that proclaimed the next dance as a fox trot, turkey trot, waltz, or whatever. A dance known as "The Frisco" was becoming the rage, and this was included every night in the series. As the number neared its finish, Tram would start doing a little bit of dancing on the bandstand. This was designed to catch the eye of the dancers, and they would stop to watch Tram. He wore a derby, which he'd push forward on his head, and really offered some smart steps. This always resulted in a huge crowd gathering around the bandstand, urging on Tram's dancing ability, and ended with a mixing of laughter and great applause.

> **One night as we were riding the train to our next stop, Bob Chaudet and I hit upon an idea. It seemed that wherever we played, musicians would gather after the dance, and ask about my saxophone, as to the tone, etc. Bob and I purchased as many reeds as we could locate, and then sandpapered the manufacturer's name off of them, and rubber stamped "Trumbauer" on each one. We told the musicians that the reason for my tone was the secret in these reeds, and we promptly sold them for a dollar each! It was a good thing we were only doing one-nighters.**

Joe had promised a lengthy steady engagement, and on May 4, 1921, the band opened in Rockford, Illinois.

INGLATERRA
The Ballroom Beautiful
Dancing 8–12 Admission 15 cents

The *Rockford Republic* newspaper stated that this was the Joe Kayser's Novelty Orchestra's fourth engagement here. The ballroom had a balcony that extended across the width of the hall, then a long open space, across this was a long wooden railing with three gate entrances to the dance floor. The bandstand was round, open, and roofed with four supporting pillars.

Tom Totsi's correspondence with the late Merv Sorenson, has preserved Merv's memories:

> Frank and I became well acquainted during this time, and I often invited him to share a couch in my family's home, and he welcomed the change from the old dingy hotel rooms that he had shared for months. When you are on the road, every room looks the same! Many a night, after the dance, we'd walk over to my parents' home, whistling the latest tune or harmonizing on an old familiar one. The couch was located on a screened-in porch, and it was most pleasant sleeping with the night air breezing in and out. Besides, every morning mother prepared breakfast, usually pancakes, and Frank said that this was the closest to home that he could imagine!

Even with the steady work, Kayser managed to find jobs nearby on their nights off! This continued after they closed the Inglaterra Ballroom on May 27 and opened at the Harlem Park on May 30. This was advertised as ''Rockford's Coney Island,'' and they played the summer dances in a carnival-like atmosphere, sharing dancing honors with Herb Bailey's band from New York. The bandstand was located about midway through the dance floor and decorated with strings of lights and lanterns. Open air, all the way!

Bill Trumbauer, Jr., has recalled:

> It was June, Mitzi was known to all of the family by the nickname 'Honey.' We never called her grandma, or Mitzi, it was always 'Honey.' Anyway, Honey liked to tell the story of how she and Frank met. She was visiting a girlfriend in Rockford, as she was from Janesville, Wisconsin. The

> girlfriend told her of the band and wanting to listen to them, and maybe dance a bit, and she persuaded Mitzi to go along with her.
>
> At the time, Mitzi was engaged to a fellow back home. On the way to the dance site, they passed through several booths set up like a carnival, and Mitzi's girlfriend spotted a fortune teller's booth and suggested that they have their fortunes told. Mitzi sort of shied away from the idea, but the girlfriend persisted, and she finally agreed. The fortune teller predicted an early marriage for Honey, and she made a remark about the fortune teller saying that due to the ring that she was wearing. "No," she was assured by the fortune teller, "the man that she would marry was not the one she was engaged to at that time." Of course, Honey just laughed about it.
>
> She and the girlfriend attended the dance, and Honey was really taken with Frank, and during an intermission, persuaded her girlfriend to introduce them. Her real name was Myrtle Alice Hill, but after a few dates with Frank, he started to call the petite, red-haired girl "Mitzi" and the name stuck!

Many of the pilots from the war were barnstorming at fairs and festivals across the land, performing air shows and offering rides to the thrilled crowd at a price, from fifty cents to five dollars for a short ride over the nearest town and back. The vintage World War I aircraft seemed to be held together with chewing gum and wire, but Trumbauer was excited to see an airplane up close and actually have the chance for a ride!

Merv Sorenson told an almost identical story to Tom Tsotsi, but when Mitzi told the story, in subsequent years, it varied just a bit, but here are her recollections as Bill Trumbauer, Jr. recalled them:

> Frank and Mitzi were double dating with another couple *[Ed. note: Merv and his date]* and after a bit of coaxing, got the girls to agree to a flight. Merv and his date watched as Frank and Mitzi climbed into the cockpit of the World War I airplane, and were strapped in their seat. The pilot yelled "contact" as he switched on the engine, and an associate gave the propeller a spin. They were quickly airborne, and after a trip above the town, returned to land. Frank was hooked on flying and raved about it. On the other hand, Mitzi felt that there were better things to do.

> Merv and his date took the next trip. As they bounced and tumbled over the pasture, gaining speed for a liftoff into the air, a sense of danger arose, but once they were airborne, Frank and Mitzi dismissed their fears. Almost instantly they heard the sputtering and missing of the airplane engine, as the giant machine quickly turned to return to the field. The landing attempt was awkward and the plane tried to straighten itself before touching ground but was unable to make it a smooth landing, instead touched down and immediately flipped over, nose first, and tore off a wing. The spectators ran to the crash site and were relieved to see that Merv and his date had crawled out unharmed. Frank and Mitzi were trying to console the frightened girl when they started to look around for Merv. They spotted him, down on all fours, continually kissing the ground and murmuring, "Oh, thank you, thank you!"

Ted Jansen telephoned Trumbauer and told him of the opportunity to book a band into the Forest Park Highlands on August 21. Trumbauer decided to join the group, and gave immediate notice to Joe Kayser.

Tram's only regret was that he would be leaving Mitzi behind, but he kept telling himself that it might only be a summertime romance, and once he left, she'd forget him. Mitzi went to the station with Tram, and kissed him goodbye, as the train pulled out and headed for St. Louis.

Ted Jansen was a St. Louis drummer and booker of various bands, and he now extended an offer to Trumbauer that resulted in a partnership, to be billed as the Jansen-Trumbauer Orchestra. The idea was that sometimes Ted booked a double date, and by naming the band this way, should the case arise again, Tram could cover one date and Ted the other. Tram accepted.

The Forest Park Highlands was initially opened in 1896 and served as a beer garden and restaurant, but, when sold in 1897, it was transformed into an open air attraction that offered a family restaurant and "10 new and novel features including a scenic railway." Following Prohibition, the main restaurant became a penny arcade, and the center was planned for the family, to amuse the children, but at 6 P.M., the middle of the park lit up and they offered dance music and entertainment to complete the day.

The Jansen-Trumbauer Orchestra consisted of Frank Papila (accordion); Charles McHenry (xylophone); August Michener (piano); Norman Rathbert (banjo); Ted Jansen (drums); and Trumbauer.

The outdoor ''season'' lasted only 120 days, which proved to be a disaster in 1915, when rain closed down the dancing for 90 days. This engagement lasted until September 4, and ended with Ted completing the job, as Tram booked another unit of the Jansen-Trumbauer Orchestra into the Westminster Hall on September 1, 1921.

Mitzi and Tram started corresponding, but in the late summer, there were almost daily telephone conversations. Finally Tram was able to gather up the nerve to ask Mitzi to marry him. ''Sure, Frank, I'll marry you! Not in St. Louis, but in Rockford where we met.'' On September 14, 1921 they were married.

Eugene ''Gene'' F. Rodemich was born in St. Louis in 1890, the son of a southside dentist, Dr. Henry Rodemich, who in his younger days, studied violin. At the age of ten, Gene was studying piano with Louis Hammerstein, organist at Temple Israel, and was being schooled in the classics. The turning point in young Gene's life came in 1904 when St. Louis played host to the World's Fair, and as an attraction offered the music of ragtime piano players assembled from around the nation. Gene was thrilled with his ''syncopation music'' as he called it, and blessed with an ear of absolute pitch, began to offer his own interpretations of the popular music of his day.

He first obtained prominence as a pianist on the Governor's boat in President William Howard Taft's flotilla down the Mississippi River in 1909. Gene offered some of his ''jazzy'' selections and was well received by the accompanying smart set, who later arranged for him to play at private parties, social events, the Glenn Echo Club, and various country clubs.

In 1913, Gene decided to try the bright lights of New York, but he found limited opportunities, and, although a bit discouraged, he continued to find work in New York and other eastern cities. By 1917 he had become accompanyist for the outstanding vaudevillian, Elsie Janis. Janis's specialty was comic songs and impersonations of Eddie Foy, Eddie Cantor, and George M. Cohan. Gene was in her tour of the front lines of France when she entertained the troops and was called the ''Sweetheart Of The AEF.''

Following the association with Elsie Janis, Gene returned to St. Louis, where he put together smaller groups, at first, but by 1918 had fronted a 22-piece orchestra at the Liberty Theatre. He was now recognized as one of St. Louis' finest band leaders.

> **It was 1921. I had never made any recordings so when Gene Rodemich asked me to go to New York with his band to record for Brunswick Records I was plenty excited.**
>
> **My first trip to New York! I saw my first World Series game, and David Mendoza, conductor at the Capitol Theatre. In those days, the orchestra played the score for the silent pictures and it was quite a thrill to watch Mendoza follow the cues to the picture.**
>
> **Gus Haenschen, head of Brunswick Records, wanted to hear this sax man Gene had been raving about. We played some tunes for him and Gus and Gene went into the next room but neglected to close the door.**
>
> **I could hear Haenschen's voice. "My God, Gene, why bring a guy like him all the way from St. Louis on company expenses? Why, I could whistle out the window and get plenty of guys to blow him out of town."**
>
> **Now whether it took guts or ignorance to play that date, I don't know. But I do know that I was hurt beyond words and I guess a lot of these hurts can make you or break you.**
>
> **The records were released and sold like mad. "By The Pyramids," on which Benny Krueger and I played the first two-part, harmonized sax break ever recorded, turned out to be a big, big record. So, I was forgiven for intruding upon New York City and the Brunswick Record Company.**

Tram continued to work with Gene Rodemich after the band returned to St. Louis.

> **Gene said "sure" when I asked for a day off. I had booked a small band into Herrin, Illinois, for a one-nighter.**
>
> **On the way, we stopped in my home town, Carbondale, to see my old friend, Tom Entsminger. Tom owned**

a candy store and I wanted to pick up something for my grandparents, so I would not arrive at their home without something special for them.

When Tom and his pals found out where we were going to play, they begged us to forget the whole thing. Why that was "Bloody" Williamson County, just about the toughest place in the whole United States. We were determined to keep the date and left, but promised to stop to see Tom on our way back to St. Louis.

We arrived at the dance hall in Herrin—quite different from New York City, so fresh in my mind. We were setting up our music when a character out of a gangster picture came up to the bandstand.

"Who's da leader?"

The boys pointed to me. He came over to the piano, pulled a big pistol, gently tapped the keys and said, "This music better be good, Jack!" I thought this cat was kidding, so I pulled out a .45 automatic (which I used as protection for the money that we were paid after one-nighter jobs), tapped the keys and said, "This music will be good, Jack!"

"Okay! Okay!" he muttered as he walked away.

Good thing that I didn't know that he was serious.

"The boys" served us supper during intermission, paid us for the date, and even escorted us out of town that night. I wasn't so sure then that we were out of trouble. Finally, the lead car stopped and pulled across the road in front of us. Someone got out and was walking towards us. Yes, it was my friend with the gun.

"Youse guys is in the clear now! Drive like hell! Don't stop for nobody! We'll call you for a return date. We sure enjoyed your music."

I swallowed my heart as we drove away!

Tom was surprised when we returned to Carbondale, completely intact and nothing but kind words for "the boys." We found out later that our band was the first ever to be paid in full and finish an evening without at least one fight. Nevertheless, we turned down all future offers. "Let well enough alone" was our motto.

In Herrin, people went around with guns strapped on them, just like the old west pictures. Any old-timers can tell you about Williamson County.

On May 24, 1922, the following appeared in Rockford, Illinois, newspaper:

TOMORROW
IS THE BIG DAY
CENTRAL PARK GARDENS
(Rockford's Big City Amusement Resort)
FRANK TRUMBAUER'S ORCHESTRA
(8 musicians)

Opening night produced heavy rain that closed the rides and all other ground attractions, but the dance palace featured record crowds that came to hear the music and watch the accompanying "Wonder Girl Revue." Due to the weather, the crowd was disappointed when only a few of the girls could make it through the rain, but those that did tried their best, offering a few numbers, and were applauded by an appreciative audience.

Central Park Garden's second annual Mardi-Gras Ball was held on September 7. Pretty costumed girls, with fancy baskets on their arms, featuring confetti and serpentine rolls, as well as noise makers, sold confections to the attending patrons. Colored lights had replaced the normal ones that adorned the dance floor, and masked dancers weaved in and out, with serpentine streamers, all over the dance floor to provide an atmosphere of a real Mardi Gras celebration. The gala affair was noted in the next day's newspaper with "one of the best dance programs the capable Trumbauer musical aggregation has presented this summer."

Three nights later, the engagement folded. Tram informed the band that he was not returning to St. Louis. He had phoned Ted, who had promised to find new jobs for them all.

A decision was made to send Mitzi back to her parent's home. Trumbauer felt that he needed to become established, and he wanted to try his luck in Chicago. Once he was settled with a good job, he would send for Mitzi.

Mitzi agreed.

CHAPTER THREE

CHICAGO
1922–1923

ON SEPTEMBER 11, FRANK TRUMBAUER joined the Musicians Local #10 in Chicago, Illinois. He was issued card number 4884.

> **I spent most of my money just listening to all the good bands around town. I even forgot that I played an instrument. After a week, the Friars' Inn on South Wabash became my hangout. I went there every night and always heard something new.**
>
> **Paul Biese was the rage in Chicago. They said that he was the loudest sax man in town. Charlie Straight was there, too. Charlie once wrote a story about how he fired Bix. Bix loved to play with the band late at night, after Straight had gone home, but the arrangements were difficult. There were so many good men in that band that I guess they just didn't have time to fool around with a lad that didn't read too well.**
>
> **The number one band of the day was Isham Jones. He was playing at the College Inn in the Sherman Hotel. One night I had dinner there, and met Isham. I was surprised that he had heard about me! Imagine. It made me feel a little bit better because all of the good music that I had been hearing was making me a little unhappy about myself.**
>
> **Isham apologized for his band and explained that Artie Vanasec, his sax man, was ill. He then asked if I had my horns with me.**
>
> **"Me?" I asked surprisingly. "Oh, no, they're back at the hotel."**
>
> **"Well, why don't you rush over and get them, and sit-in with us on the late session."**

In fifteen minutes, I was back there, sitting on the bandstand, looking over the arrangements. I was so busy that I couldn't tell how I was doing, but after a few solos, I happen to catch a big smile from John Kuhn, the bass player, and just about the greatest, too.

In a quiet unassuming way, Isham simply said, "Nice work, kid, keep it up."

I had sense enough to watch the colored waiters and if they smiled at what I was playing then I was happy. Those boys know the score. During intermission, I went out through the kitchen with the band, and one, big lanky waiter stopped me.

"Pardon me, son, where you from?"

"St. Louis," I told him.

"You is? Well, you sure is makin' it tough on that boy that's sick. Mr. Isham better keep an eye on you."

I played with Isham for three days, during which time I played a lot of radio broadcasts. At the end of three days, Isham started to pay me but I was so thrilled that I said, "Never mind. Just give it to Van. He's been sick."

What was I saying? I was almost broke by then.

Now, fortified with three days of playing with the best band in town, I went to the Benson Office, on the second floor, of West Randolph Street, right in the heart of Chicago's Loop. Edgar A. Benson, retired cellist, was the biggest booker in town. He had Chicago in the palm of his hands.

Benson had heard that I had sat-in with Isham Jones and wanted to know how much salary I wanted. My success with Isham floated before my eyes and I said that I wouldn't consider anything less than one hundred and fifty dollars a week.

"You must be very good," Benson replied. "We'll look around, and give you a call in a few days."

Those "few days" stretched into a few weeks. I moved out of the hotel and took a small room near Kenmore and Wilson Avenue. The details of this adventure are too numerous to mention but I shall never forget them.

Every day, I would walk from Wilson Avenue to the Benson Office in the Loop, and back again. No work. Not even a Saturday night job!

To those who know Chicago, they will realize that

Wilson Avenue to 64 West Randolph Street, and home again, is quite a jaunt.

By now, I was down to my last fifteen cents. I went to a market, bought a bag of apples and put them in a dresser drawer in my room. Breakfast was one apple and a glass of water. Then walk downtown—with an apple in my pocket for lunch. Then walk home, stopping at the Wilson Avenue El Station to pick up discarded newspapers. Back to my room and dinner—two apples and a glass of water. Then to bed.

On the fourth day, I ran into Sam Wishnoff from St. Louis. I practically begged him to loan me some money, but he was broke, too. He did take me to a restaurant where his wife was working. What a wonderful girl, and what a delicious dinner she gave me. But, you know something? That food made me as sick as I have ever been in my life. My stomach just wasn't used to good food, and pushed it right back up.

That settled it. One more try and then a freight train back to St. Louis. At least I could eat there.

I barged right into the Benson Office. It might have been December, but I was boiling.

"Look, Mr. Benson, I don't care how much I make or where I work. I'm hungry, broke, and my rent is two weeks past due. Do I work or do I leave town?"

I'm certain Benson wasn't aware of my predicament because things started happening right away. He booked me for the afternoon sessions with Maurie Sherman at the old Bismarck Hotel. He handed me a ten dollar bill and sent me home for my horns. Just like that!

The personnel consists of: Wallace Bradley (piano); Andrew Padula (trumpet); Norman Lillis (sax); Ralph Smith (drums); Maurie Sherman (violin/leader); and myself.

I turned the calendar to January 1923, and the telephone rang with an offer from Tom Thatcher of the Benson Office. Don Bestor was going to organize the Benson Orchestra and there was a spot for me, if I wanted it. A few weeks ago, I was sitting in a small room, broke and hungry, reading discarded newspapers, and lying awake half the night trying to figure out what life was all about. Now I was with the famed Benson Orches-

> **tra of Chicago. To top it off, I was getting telephone calls from other men in Chicago who wanted to get in with the Benson Orchestra. They asked if I would put in a good word for them. How about that!**

The promotional advertisement on the band, issued by the Benson Orchestra, read as follows:

WALTER ZURAWSKI plays first trumpet and fluegelhorn. He is an incomparable interpreter of eccentric syncopation, with a grasp of every musical value, so alluring, and so necessary on the trumpet. The musical critic's estimate of Mr. Zurawski's work is highly flattering.

MYLES VANDERAUER plays second trumpet and reveals gift of melodies tonality. His cooperation forms an important factor where two-trumpet effects are desired.

ARTHUR WEISNER shows unusual skill in his performance on the trombone, euphonium, and baritone. He has an unusually fascinating tone, a quality rarely heard on the trombone. He has unique interpretational talent and he commands the attention and admiration of his listeners.

STUART WILLIAMS is a master of saxophones—soprano, tenor, baritone and bass—also of the clarinet, oboe, bassoon and English horn. On these related instruments he is exceptionally proficient, bringing out the peculiar tone qualities and the weird effects so popular in modern dance music.

FRANK TRUMBAUER is another renowned saxophone specialist, who has enjoyed the esteem of his numerous admirers with his unequaled syncopated "blues" and other novel effects. Besides he is a master of the sarusphone[4] and the soprano saxophone.

MARVIN T. THATCHER is a popular saxophonist whose accomplishment and experience has been looked upon with most signal success, and whose tonal qualities have sweetness appealing to the temperament of the dancers irresistibly.

GEORGE BASS is called by critics the peerless violinist. He is a pupil of Jacobsen and a former member of the Chicago Symphony Orchestra. His fine technique and beautiful tone quality has won for him musical fame, which he has enjoyed for several years now.

[4]A sarusphone is an E-flat contrabasslike bassoon but made of metal, four feet long in chainlink mode, and with three octave keys.

JOSEPH MUELLER is a banjo player of distinctive merit and his versatility on string instruments is quite exceptional, as he plays equally well the violin, mandolin, and guitar. His banjo playing is unusually brilliant and is the quintessence of rhythm, so necessary as an adjunct to piano playing in modern dancing.

PIERRE OLKER plays the sousaphone and string bass. His prominent accomplishments with the sousaphone are remarkable smoothness, richness, and unexcelled purity of tone. Those combined qualities are rarely produced on the sousaphone, which is a musical instrument very little known to the public at large.

GEORGE W. BROMMERBERG manipulates drums, xylophone, tympani, and accessories. The drum is one of the dominant factors in dance music. Mr. Brommerberg's "drum beats" have a style of their own, and are synonymous of "pep," so necessary in dance orchestra.

DON BESTOR, pianist, is the director.

The band went on the road, and their first engagement was the LeClaire Hotel and Theatre in Moline, Illinois, starting February 25, 1923.

Benson had contracted for and supplied the whole show—a large company, plus a line of chorus girls, and the band. Don Bestor had worked hard putting the show together and the results were good. Not only was Don to play piano, but conduct as well.

Just two days before we were to open, Don became seriously ill. Now what? No conductor! No pianist! The theatre manager was frantic and wanted to cancel the show. Benson was frantic because all of the contracts had been signed!

I finally got up enough nerve to tell the manager that I thought that we could get away with working around Don. He kept saying that he wouldn't pay us a cent.

I telephoned Benson. "Sure, okay," he said, "anything to save the show."

We had a tenor man (Stuart Williams) who could chord a bit, so I set out to find him. The poor boy had gotten a hold of some bad ice the night before, and was sick as a dog. He was pale green! He was sick three times during rehearsal, so, as a precaution, we put a bucket beside the piano and draped flowers, plants, and scenery around him. Good thing, too, because he was sick during the show.

I did so many things wrong that the audience thought it was all part of the show and laughed, long and loud. How I ever got through that day, I'll never know, but after the first show, the manager, hysterically happy, said, "Don't change nothin', boy. Just keep it up. I'll call Benson."

Then it dawned on me that in all of the excitement, I had completely forgotten about Don Bestor. I rushed to his hotel room to explain everything, but he was too sick to care. He rallied, later that evening, and played the final set with us.

Do you know that I never even got a "thank you" from Benson or Bestor? I even heard later that Don thought I was trying to take over the band. We had a saying in St. Louis that seemed to fit my feelings: "Now wouldn't that just cure your drawers?"

Don Bestor did go to bat for me later at our Victor recording date, so I guess he either liked me or thought that I had something to offer. I prefer to think that it was the former.

The theatre was part of the hotel, and it offered vaudeville from 1 P.M. to 11 P.M. The Benson Orchestra was one of seven attractions on the bill, and they did three shows a day. On opening night, they closed the bill with "Nola" (with a recovered Don Bestor featured on piano), "Runnin' Wild," "Down In Maryland," "Farewell Blues," and "Wonderful One."

Then the band switched to another part of the hotel, "The Winter Gardens," which was a combination ballroom and dining room, and provided continuous listening and dancing music until four in the morning. The engagement ended on March 3.

The band returned to Chicago in March and found that Rudolph Valentino was appearing at the Trianon Ballroom to fantastic crowds. Valentino was appearing while his divorce proceedings were taking place in Los Angeles, and due to his refusal to report to Paramount Pictures because of a dispute over both salary and script control. Valentino simply "had to get away from Hollywood," and Mineralava Beauty Clay Company was able to sign him to promote their products in connection with a tour that they had arranged. Rudy offered a dancing exhibition, under their sponsorship, at various cities across the nation, and left on March 15 for a six-week tour at $7,000 per week.

But, before Rudy left on his tour . . .

> **Remember the stories of when Benny Goodman played the Paramount Theatre in New York and the kids became so excited that they danced in the aisles? Or the girlish screams that were made when Frank Sinatra sang for the bobby soxers? Then, as ever, it was the same old story, "what is happening to our younger generation?"**
>
> **Well, let me tell you what I saw that night at the Trianon makes those generations tame to 1923. The women didn't just sigh, swoon, scream or applaud as they watched their idol dance. No sir! I watched them take off diamond rings from their fingers, bracelets from their arms, all kinds of jewelry, and wrap them in notes (containing their telephone numbers and addresses, no doubt!) and throw them at the dancing feet of Valentino. Never have I witnessed such an exhibition.**
>
> **The management returned such articles to their rightful owners with an apology that Mr. Valentino's limited engagement did not permit him time for such personal contacts.**

April 9 became the second most important day in Mitzi's and Tram's life. On this date, all eight-and-one-half pounds of him, William Francis Trumbauer, was born into their life.

During a July 1974 discussion, Esten Spurrier, recalled meeting Trumbauer for the first time:

> It was April 1923, Frank was in Davenport in March 1953 and I asked him if he remembered the incident, but he did not, and that is understandable. Bands, travelling from city to city, meet so many people that it is hard for the musicians to remember everyone they meet.
>
> Bix and I, went to the Coliseum to hear the Benson Orchestra of Chicago. We were both taken by Frank's tone and styling. We decided that we had to meet him, so we went up to the bandstand between sets. One thing that we had to ask him about was the band-aids that all of the sax and brass men wore across the bridge of their noses. Frank explained that this was a gimmick they used and told the dancers, when asked about the band-aids, that they played so "hot" that it would break the blood vessels in their nose, and this was put

on as a precaution. We had a good laugh about that and found Frank to be a very friendly person.

Larry Andrews, one of our local musicians, was playing banjo with a band at the Terrace Gardens at that time, and he said that the Benson gang came out to hear them after their dance was over. Larry said the band simply 'froze' when they realized who they were. Intermission came and the local musicians were very stiff in their playing. Frank Trumbauer motioned to a couple of his companions and they climbed up on the bandstand, after having gone out to the bus to pick up their instruments, and did two numbers, and this seemed to break the ice. The local musicians returned, smiling, as if to say "now we'll play for you."

The midwest tour headed towards Atlantic City, New Jersey, and an engagement at Young's Million Dollar Pier set for June 15. But three days before this opening, the band showed up in Camden on the 12th anticipating some recording work.

Don Bestor and I had sat up all night to make two arrangements for the Victor recording date. How well I remember those tunes: "My Pillow And Me" and "I Never Miss The Sunshine." We were convinced that we had something unusual when we turned in that morning.

I was plenty excited when we arrived at the Camden Studios. It was to be my first Victor date where we were doing two tunes that I helped arrange. I was putting my old trusty C-melody horn together when Eddie King, the recording director, passed by.

"What the hell have you got there?" King gasped. "No, no, it can't be! Don. Don Bestor. Where are you? We'll have to cancel the date."

While Don and King were in his office, I asked one of the recording engineers, "What's eating old laughing boy?" He smiled and said, "Don't let the old seahorse disturb you too much."

How was I to know that they had never been able to record the C-melody horn successfully? I later found out that Bestor read the riot act to King. We came here to record! I was the featured member in the band, and I deserved a chance! After a while, King cooled down, but he still wasn't sold on the idea.

We finally made a deal. If the recording was unsuc-

cessful, I was never to return to the studio again! That was my own idea. Fine way to start a recording date, wasn't it? Don and I decided to put our new arrangements on hold for now. We came back the next day, and we made a test and it sounded pretty good, so we made a master. Well, the chorus I played on "I Never Miss The Sunshine" was one of the most copied sax choruses in the world. The record outsold all current releases and from that day on, Eddie King and I were the best of friends.

Many musicians didn't like to record for Victor Records because King was so tough. He insisted on all drummers using his own personal cymbals because he thought that they recorded better.

Jimmy Dorsey and the Scranton Sirens were in Atlantic City during our stay, which lasted into September. Jimmy used to come over to hear our afternoon sessions, and when we finished at night, we would dash over to hear him.

Now back in Chicago, I decided to ask Edgar Benson for a raise. I was turned down! Tommy Thatcher, the daddy of the band, told me that loyalty to a band is great, but only if you were paid enough for it. After our talk, and at his suggestion, I quit!

CHAPTER FOUR

MIFF MOLE
1924–1925

BACK TO ST. LOUIS WITH MY SAVINGS, and home with Mitzi and Bill.

Ted Jansen and I had worked together before, and we both had a pretty good idea of how Gene Rodemich had made a lot of money in the booking business, so we decided to open our own office. We signed most of the good men in town and soon had a corner on all the business. We averaged about twenty engagements a week—everything from debutante parties to tough dance halls. Everyone loved our band, and why not? We had the best musicians in town under contract!

We packed the Westminster Dance Hall every night. Then the owner of the Arcadia Ballroom offered me a new car if I would sign a contract to play at his ballroom. This meant breaking up our enterprises so I refused! Upon hearing of this, the owner of the Westminster gave us a raise to stay.

Jack Ford was at the Arcadia for awhile, and then Danny Russo and his Oriole Terrace Band. Although Russo had a much bigger and better band, we still drew larger crowds.

Just a few years before, I played my first dance job with Max Goldman at the Westminster for two dollars and seventy-five cents a night!

Our booking business was flourishing when we booked ourselves into the Coronado Hotel for a New Year's Eve Dance. Everything was going great! Then I collapsed from overwork.

The first several weeks of 1924, I spent trying to

recover, and by the time that I did, both the money and business were gone!

The Skouras Brothers, owners of the New Grand Central Theatre, hired Gene Rodemich and his orchestra, and offered him $325 a week personally for his services. Gene, now billed as "The Ragtime Paderewski," testified in a 1925 tax case that he was only paid $200, as he had to offset the salaries of two other musicians and buy music, but still his income tax records for the 1924 year showed an $18,000 salary.

Gene hired Tram to perform with his band. The band consisted of: Jules Blattner (trumpet); Allister Wylie, Julius Robb, Frank Trumbauer (saxes); Otto Reinert, Gus Schmitt (violins); Bill Bailey (xylophone); Paul Spor (born: Spoerloder) (drums); and Gene Rodemich (piano/leader).

I was sitting at home, going over the breaks of the music business and wondering what to do next, when I heard a knock at the door. I opened and there stood a good looking, well-dressed man.

"Are you Frank Trumbauer?" he asked.

"I am," I replied.

"May I come in? My name is Ray Miller. I used to have the Black and White Melody Boys."

Tram recognized Ray. Miller had quite a name in the East. He had started out as a singing waiter in Chicago at Harry James's Casino Gardens when the Original Dixieland Jazz Band (ODJB) was appearing there. The Gardens was a hangout for the theatrical groups that came through Chicago. Al Jolson was appearing at the Garrick Theatre at the end of December 1916, doing a tour of the stage production of *Robinson Crusoe, Jr.,* when he came into the cafe. The ODJB just knocked him over! Jolson telephoned his agent, Max Hart, and raved about the band, insisting that Max find a booking for them in New York. Max figured that they must really be something if Jolson was telling him how good someone else was, so he took a chance and booked them into Reisenweber's Restaurant for two weeks in January 1917. The engagement stretched into months, set record attendance, and resulted in their recording "Livery Stable Blues" in February—the rest is history.

Ray felt that there might be a place in New York for him, so he boarded a train and, upon arriving, discovered that every spot wanted this new style, a "jazz band." Ray was able to convince one cafe owner that while this was the current fad, it would not last, and things needed to be slowed down a bit. He was hired, leading a waltz band!

The jazz style did last, and with Ray on drums, he got his first break in 1920. Ed Wynn was putting together a big musical show for the New Amsterdam Theatre to be called *Ed Wynn's Carnival.* Ted Lewis's band was set for the spot, but Ray was able to convince Ed Wynn that he had a better band. Ray hired some men from the musicians' union hall, auditioned, and was awarded the job, which opened on April 5th and ran for a year. During the run, he was billed as "The Black And White Melody Boys."

For the past couple of years, Ray had played the vaudeville circuit, did a few club dates in New York, and made a few recordings. He wanted to add two new men to his band and go after some of the better jobs. He informed Tram that he had already hired Miff Mole.

Of course I had heard of Miff Mole. He was getting the reputation as the best trombonist in the East. No make that the world! He was recording with the biggest names in New York, and he was on his way up!

"Now when can you leave?" Ray asked.

Not a word about salary.

"But, Mr. Miller . . . "

"Call me Ray," he interrupted. "That's the way it is going to be from now on. What were you going to say, Frank?"

"Well, I was going to say that I could leave on Thursday, if you would tell me the salary—and give me some travel money."

He apologized for not mentioning money before, and suggested "would one hundred and fifty dollars a week be all right, with raises from time to time?"

He handed me a hundred dollar bill for travelling and left to catch a train. That was Ray Miller's way of doing things. He could sell anything to anyone!

William "Red" McKenzie was forever telling me to get out of St. Louis, and I guess, indirectly, he was responsible

for my joining Ray Miller's Orchestra. I had offers to leave before, but never felt that I was quite ready.

That reminds me of one offer. It was in 1920 when I was playing at Cicardi's Cafe. Wallace Reid, the famous silent film star, dined there one night. He called me to his table and told me that he was sure that he could get me into pictures. Me—in pictures! He even offered to pay my expenses to Hollywood. That idea scared me so much that I refused right on the spot.

I'd known Red a long time. He loved music, had been around a lot and knew the score. Red loved a small group that I had and came around whenever we played and sang with us. He had a comb trick. He'd put tissue paper around the comb and sing through it. That guy could get more out of that comb than a lot of musicians got with their instruments. He had organized the famed "Mound City Blue Blowers" (St. Louis is known as the Mound City), a three piece sensation. Jack Bland played guitar and ukulele, Dick Slevin played kazoo with a glass for a mute, and Red had his comb.

Gus Haenschen of Brunswick Records was in St. Louis during March 1924 in search of new talent to record. Tram pursued Gus to record the Mound City Blue Blowers, but his requests were met with Gus's belief that the recording of "Arkansas Blues" they had made in Chicago during February was sufficient. Tram held fast to persuading Gus to record the unit again, and finally Haenschen said that he'd do so with the stipulation that Tram be on the recording date. This resulted in the Brunswick recording of "San" and "Red Hot." Years later, Red returned the favor by convincing Tommy Rockwell of Okeh Records to record Frank Trumbauer and his band.

Friday, March 21, 1924, I arrived in Newark, New Jersey, and went directly to the Paradise Club, with my horns, to look over the situation.

Newark was Benny Krueger's home town and he was about as hot as a depot stove. He was sitting-in on saxophone, and it wasn't long before everyone crowded around him, including me.

Ray Miller spotted me and took me into his office. He asked if I was game enough to sit-in with Krueger.

"You hired me, Mr. Miller," I answered. "If my work starts tonight, I might as well get to earning my salary."

Benny would play a chorus and then I'd play one. One and then the other until the crowd went crazy. I'd had plenty of experience at this sort of thing so I saved my best for last.

When Benny left that night, the boys in the band said, "he'll never come back here again and sit-in." And, he never did!

Miff Mole and Tram became friends almost immediately. Their music background was somewhat similar. At eleven, Miff began violin lessons for three years, then at fourteen switched to piano and soon was accompanying silent movies at the nickelodeons. He switched to trombone after watching a parading brass band and noticing the glissando that the horn displayed. His first trombone came by mail order. Miff taught himself to play by striking each note on the piano and finding the appropriate position on the trombone. His violin technique was applied to his development, and he was soon way ahead of other contemporaries.

Ray Miller's Orchestra had the following personnel: Charles Rocco, Roy Johnston (trumpets); Miff Mole, Andy Sindelar (trombones); Andy Sannella, Frank Trumbauer, Bernie Daly (reeds); Dan Yates (violin and assistant director); Tommy Satterfield (piano and arranger); Harry Parella (piano); Louis Chassagne (tuba/string bass); Frank DiPrima (banjo); Ward Archer (drums). Andy Sindelar acted as librarian, and Ray conducted the band. The boys dressed in light gray suits of the latest English cut, wore soft white shirts and blue foulard bat ties.

The band started recording almost immediately, and Ray must have felt pleased with Tram's work, because on Tram's birthday, May 30, he presented him with a gold watch, inscribed: "To O.F.T. From the Boys And Ray Miller."

On May 31, the band opened at the Beaux Arts Cafe, on the corner of St. James Place and Boardwalk, in Atlantic City, and Tram sent for Bill and Mitzi to join him.

There appeared an article in the *Clipper* (June 7 edition), that reviewed the opening night. In referring to Trumbauer, they cited ". . . . a western youth, who is part Indian. . . . This boy produces both legit and blues on his horns, and the latter is where he glitters."

Upon Mitzi's arrival with their son, Tram took his family for a tour of the famed Boardwalk, and he was wearing a gun and holster strapped to his side.

Andy Sindelar recalled talking to Frank during that jaunt on the Boardwalk, in a letter of November 1968:

> "Hey, Frank, are you a cowboy today?" I laughed at my own remark and then it dawned on me, "Frank, is that gun loaded? That's not a real one, is it?"
>
> "Sure is," Trumbauer replied. "Let me tell you why I wear it." Frank liked to tell these tall stories and you never knew if they were truth or fiction.
>
> Tram went on to say: "There was this time, back home, when Mitzi and I took little Bill with us to a picnic. Now I was involved in a championship horse shoe game, and Mitzi was busy helping out with lunch. Bill was too little to walk, so we sat him off to the side where he could watch us, and we could watch him. Lo and behold! Right in the middle of this championship horse shoe game, Bill came face to face with a rattlesnake that had slithered through the grass, and now was staring our son right in the eye, with his tongue out, ready to strike! Luckily I was wearing my holster and gun, so I just whipped out my trusty six-shooter, aimed hip high, and shot that rattler right between the eyes. I don't know if there are any rattlers in New Jersey, but if Bill comes across one, I want to be ready."

Cliff Edwards (Ukulele Ike) and Tess Gardella (the original Aunt Jemima) headed the floor show. The local newspapers displayed ads almost weekly of a giveaway night and business was booming. Ray later confided to Trumbauer that this engagement was one of the happiest and most successful that he ever had.

> **I tried to get Ray to bring the Mound City Blue Blowers to Atlantic City as an added attraction, but he wasn't interested. It wasn't until I offered to pay their transportation and expenses that he realized how serious I was and that they must be great.**
>
> **Ray sent for them, and they were an absolute smash! He was so enthusiastic about them that he wanted to give me something for bringing the boys to his attention. I wasn't interested in making money on three guys from my home town, so I turned him down.**

A review on the Mound City Blue Blowers stated: . . . working before a musically wise audience, their weird indigo modulations and ''blues'' simply ''ruined'' em. . . . the boys are the last word in this sort of musical endeavor . . . . they are a musical treat and as a novelty, either for dance or for ''straight'' appreciation as a unit, they are undeniable. . . . [5]

> **It was here that Miller's gambling hit a new high. He asked me to accompany him to crap games, every Friday night. As he would win, he'd occasionally pass me a roll of bills, which I would tuck into my shirt. I never knew how much he won until I got home that night. Sometimes I'd have as much as four or five thousand dollars. It never occurred to me to keep any of the money, or to ask for a small percentage. The next day, when I'd give Ray his winnings, he was always surprised at how much there was.**

It was rumored that Ray won sixty-five thousand dollars that summer.

CAFE BEAUX ARTS
Next Thursday
August twenty-eight
(Our Famous Clown Night)
The Prize Of The Evening Will Be
A Pair Of
GOLDEN SLIPPERS
of the newest style
Given to the Lady with the smallest foot

That night, many of the ladies stood in line, as each foot was measured and inspected. Finally a winner was declared. Abe Lyman, well known orchestra leader, acting as ''Prince Charming,'' called ''Cinderella'' to the bandstand to accept her Golden Slippers. Mitzi was both proud and a little embarrassed, but she came forth to claim her prize. Her size four foot was the winner.

---

[5]**Jazz: A History Of The New York Scene** (published 1962), by permission of the authors, Samuel B. Charters and Leonard Kunstadt.

Well, now, there's always another guy who is a little smarter than the smart guy. A bunch of sharpies got together when we ended the season on September 1, and told Ray that he could double his winnings by buying a whole carload of Scotch Whiskey and transporting it to New York for resale. Atlantic City was one of the important points for illicit liquor.

Ray bought the liquor and personally sealed the door of the boxcar after inspecting the entire carload of Scotch. When the unloading took place in New York, all of the cases around the door were illegally imported bottles of Scotch but the beautifully labeled bottles in the rest of the car contained vinegar!

Naturally Ray had paid cash on a deal like that—what with prohibition and all—so what could he do?

Yeah, he'd had it!

The band opened the first week in September at the Hippodrome Theatre billed as ''Ray Miller And His Arcadia Orchestra.'' True, they were scheduled to open the Arcadia Ballroom the following month, but Ray decided to bill them as such ''for a little advanced publicity.''

''Limehouse Blues'' opened the program and when Tram took his solo, it was greeted with loud applause from one section of the theatre, so he nodded in appreciation. Miff followed with a chorus and when he finished, the same group started to whistle, clap, shout, and stamp their feet! When the tune ended, Tram leaned over towards Miff and asked ''What's that all about?''

Miff wiped his glasses, pushed the perspiration from his brow, and replied: ''Beats me, Tram! They must be giving us the razzberry!''

The same procedure took place over the next couple of numbers, as the small group was ''hootin' '' and ''hollerin',''when the ushers came down and escorted them from the theatre. It was seven boys that had been making all of the commotion. When the stage appearance ended, the band exited to the backstage and was surprised to find the same seven youths awaiting them. The young men apologized for their enthusiasm and were sorry for any disturbance that they might have caused. They explained that it was just appreciation that they were showing and they just were unable to contain the excitement of hearing the band.

Miff reprimanded them with, "You know, boys, the first time that I heard 'Daddy' Edwards play trombone with the Original Dixieland Jazz Band, I was excited as I could be. I was probably more thrilled than anyone, but I think that I was able to contain myself more than you displayed tonight. In the future, learn to 'hold it down' just a bit."

The youths explained that they had just arrived in New York from the midwest and were set to open on the 12th. They called themselves the Wolverines Orchestra, and they pleaded with Tram and Miff to come hear them at the Cinderella Dance Hall, located at 48th and Broadway. In later years, Paul Whiteman purchased the building and called it the Paul Whiteman Club, but for now, it was a dancers' haven. True to their promise, Tram and Miff attended the opening night at the Cinderella.

> **This was the first time that I heard Bix play! That tone just went right through us! I know we waited until intermission before going up to the bandstand. Unfortunately, as we approached the bandstand to heap our praise on the band, we witnessed an incident between Bix and pianist Dick Voynow, the leader.**
>
> **We later found out that they had been feuding for some time and Bix had given his notice. The friction had now resulted in the name calling stages, and we clearly heard Bix say:**
>
> **"Voynow, you're an old bastard! And, a lousy piano player to boot!"**
>
> **"That goes for you, too, and just double it," Voynow replied, and now his voice trailed off with, "But, unfortunately, you are the best cornet player in the world!"**

After their experience, Tram and Miff headed for a speakeasy that Miff knew, and once inside spotted Alfie Evans at a table, and they invited themselves to join him. At the time, Alfie was playing sax with the Sam Lanin Orchestra at Roseland and rooming at a nearby hotel with cornetist Red Nichols. The two men told Alfie of the events and asked if he knew Bix. Alfie recalled his response in a 1990 letter:

> Sure do, not much range, maybe a tenth, but what a tone. He has ideas that will take him six years to catch up to them. He

> roomed with Red and me for a while. He'd sit up all hours of the night, listening to my recordings of "Petrochka," then drool over some of Stravinsky's chords. Soft spoken, but interesting.
>
> Now you're not going to believe this, in the morning, he would sit on the edge of the bed, and swing his legs a few times. Then he would reach for a barrel shaped glass that he had in his suitcase. He'd pour four healthy ounces of gin, drink it "as is," and say that he drank his "orange juice" every morning. He'd splash water on his face, comb his hair, and was ready for the new day.
>
> Now then for Frank Trumbauer, I fell in love with his work long before I met him. Sax men, in those early days spent much time and effort in trying to develop a tone that did not sound like a buzz-saw going through a pine knot. But the young bloods of today are pretty close to that quality again. But along came "Tram" with his easy flowing way of playing a tune full of interesting little turns without destroying the tune that he was playing. Just a beautiful tone!
>
> We knew Frank had Indian blood in him, and that he was from out west, and some of those Indians down in Oklahoma really hit it big with oil wells, and I asked if this had happened to any of Frank's relatives.
>
> "My grandfather," Tram replied, "has his wigwam right on top of an oil dome. Ergo, a marble home on a big estate. I went to visit my grandfather and found him rolled up in a blanket, on the lawn under a tree—sound asleep! He had given in to one little concession to modern ingenuity and technology. He had a long extension chord from the house to where he was sleeping. He had a small electric fan blowing on his bare feet."
>
> Frank may of had a touch of Welsh blood in his veins. My daddy told me an old Welsh proverb I liked, "Never let the truth interfere with the telling of a good tale." Frank told the story and it sounded honest, but I wondered about it, and my daddy's proverb.

Ray's band was becoming one of New York's favorites, and when they were booked into the Palace Theatre during the latter part of September, *Billboard Magazine* featured an article on them in the September 27 issue, page 23:

> The Miller combination is what is known as a "hot" band. In fact they are so "hot" that they sound and act as if they all

> wore flannel underwear. When they get steamed up the temperature begins to sizzle. . . . In fact his combination compares very favorably with the best.

The Faggen Brothers, John and Jay, spent an entire year building the Arcadia Ballroom which was designed for a capacity of 4,000. Initially set to open on September 24, 1924, last minute delays pushed it back a few days. The final inspection was open to members of the press and invited guests for a conducted tour on October 1.

The ballroom opened to the public on October 2 to a crowd of 2,000 patrons. The Faggen Brothers wanted a special dedication and offered supporting bands behind the Ray Miller Orchestra. Cliff Edwards acted as master of ceremonies, and the additional bands were Harry Reser and Carl Fenton (Gus Haenschen), with special appearances by the DeMarcos and the Musical Sheiks.

On October 9, Tram gathered Miff Mole and Rube Bloom, and persuaded Bix to bring along Min Leibrook and Victor Moore from the Wolverines for a recording date for Gennett Records. They had scheduled ''Flock O' Blues'' and ''I'm Glad'' as their numbers.

> **We slipped away from the Ray Miller Band to make these recordings for Gennett. Ordinarily this would have been a perfectly harmless procedure, but it so happened that the Ray Miller Orchestra was under exclusive contract to Brunswick. The recording session was getting along quite nicely when in walked Gus Haenschen, recording director of Brunswick, to buy a sound box. When he spotted me, his face dropped, and when I saw him, I retaliated with equal lowering of the jaw. He merely looked at me and said nothing. As he walked out, I felt an empty feeling in my stomach. I was ''out'' for the rest of that recording session.**

1924 was an election year, and Calvin Coolidge, who had assumed the presidency upon the death of Warren Harding, was now being urged to run. The Actors' Guild in New York had pledged full support for Coolidge, and they hired some of the top names in the entertainment business to make an appearance in Washington, D.C., to confirm that support. The troupe boarded the train in New York the night before, and appeared on the White House lawn on October 17. Al Jolson, with backing from the Ray Miller Orchestra, sang "Keep Cool With Coolidge." Others that offered their talents were The Dolly Sisters, Raymond Hitchcock, all backed by Miller's musicians.

The President invited the troupe to breakfast in the White House.

> **President Coolidge, after spending considerable time with us, stood up and said, "And now will you please excuse me? My cabinet is waiting." I never forgot those words!**
>
> **Miff Mole had a contract with Brunswick Records to produce some small band numbers, usually six or seven musicians, billed as The Cotton Pickers, and I made several records with them. "Jimtown Blues," "Mishawaka Blues," and "Jacksonville Gal" are but a few that come to my memory.**

Andy Sindelar's 1968 letter recalled:

> About the middle of 1925, Roger Wolfe Kahn made an offer to Miff and Frank to join his band. Roger paid fabulous salaries to get the best musicians. Roger, who was a New York socialite, and very wealthy, loved music and he wanted his own orchestra billed under his own name. His offer was a solid one. They would be on full salary, all year, and when Roger took trips abroad, although he didn't have any work for the musicians, they'd still be on full salary. Paid for not working? Sounded good to me!

Miff and Tram rejected Roger's generous offer. Red Nichols persuaded Miff to go with him into Ross Gorman's Band that opened at the Earl Carroll Theatre on June 29, 1925, for the "Earl Carroll Vanities." Tram received an offer from the Arcadia Ballroom in St. Louis to open with his own orchestra, and he accepted.

> **I had heard Bix in the old Wolverines Band and I said to myself, if I ever had my own band again, that's my boy!**
>
> **When I tried to locate Bix, by asking around, I always got the same answer, "Look out, he's trouble. He drinks**

> **and you'll have a hard time handling him." That didn't stop me. I was determined. Finally I got a lead that he was working with the Jean Goldkette office in Detroit.**

After a series of telephone calls, Tram was able to learn that Bix was working at Island Lake, Michigan, and he placed a telephone call to Bix there and made the offer. Bix informed Tram that Jimmy Dorsey was leaving their band, and he felt that he could arrange for him to be the replacement. Bix further suggested that they could use the summer months to become acquainted and to discuss the St. Louis job. Tram agreed and arrived in Detroit, joined the Musicians Local #5 on July 6, verified that he had the job with the Goldkette Office, and headed for Island Lake.

Andy Sindelar's 1968 letter continued:

> Bix met Frank when he arrived and advised him that Don Murray was a joker, thus putting him on guard. When Frank took his place on the bandstand that night, the conversation went like this . . .
>
> "You the replacement for Jimmy?" Don Murray inquired.
>
> "Yeah! Frank Trumbauer's the name."
>
> "Where're you from, Frank Trumbauer."
>
> "St. Louis. Originally from Carbondale . . . "
>
> "Carbondale?" said Murray. "Do they like music in Carbondale?"
>
> Tram seized the opportunity to tell one of his tall tales. "Like music? They are crazy about it! There was this New Year's Eve Dance and Breakfast that my band played, and it lasted until 8 o'clock in the morning. Now my grandparents had this neighbor, a Dutchman, who had three daughters who attended the affair. This Dutchman was a coal miner and he had to get up early in the morning and go to work.
>
> "When he got up, the daughters were not home! Well, when he came home from work, he was as mad as could be at his daughters. Supper was ready and the three girls were seated at the dinner table. He blew his top! He said: 'The three of you is a pair. Last night you don't come home until this morning. I know, I was on the whistle when the bridge blew six. You're no good and you always will be. Now if you want to stay home, you got to get the hell out'."

> Don just looked at Tram with a blank stare. He had some thinking to do.

The band, playing at Island Lake at the Blue Lantern Inn and billed as Jean Goldkette's ''Breeze Blowers,'' consisted of: Ray Lodwig (trumpet/leader); Bix (cornet); Bill Rank (trombone); Frank Trumbauer, Don Murray, Stanley ''Doc'' Ryker (reeds); Howdy Quicksell (banjo); Fred Bergin (piano); Steve Brown (string bass); Chauncey Morehouse (drums).

Tram's stay was a bit longer than a month, and by mid-August he left for St. Louis. Bix had agreed to join his band, and he soon followed.

Finally, Mitzi and Tram could spend time together. St. Louis was their home. The next few weeks found Tram seeking musicians, rehearsing, and setting arrangements. He was busier than ever, but one special arrangement that he wrote was of ''Tea For Two,'' a hit song, from the Broadway stage production *No, No, Nanette,* that Tram and Mitzi had adopted as ''their song''—and which, for the years that followed, he would always play for her when she came into the club or ballroom where his band was appearing.

CHAPTER FIVE

BIX
1925–1926

ADVERTISED TO OPEN IN LATE AUGUST, the band finally (according to Ray Thurston's date book) opened on September 8. The Arcadia Ballroom was a one-story, lengthy dance hall, located at 3515–3523 Olive Street.

The basic personnel included, after the typical changes: Bix Beiderbecke (cornet); Ray Thurston, later Vernon Brown (trombone); Charles "Pee Wee" Russell (clarinet/alto sax); Damon "Bud" Hassler (tenor sax/arranger); Frank Trumbauer (alto sax/C-melody sax/leader); Louis Feldman (piano); Dan Gaebe (bass); Wayne Jacobson (banjo); Dee Orr (drums); Marty Livingston (vocalist).

> **It was here that Bix and I got to know each other. When I hired him, he told me that he was a poor reader and he hesitated taking the job. Bix had a screwy way of picking out notes from a violin part, playing them in the key of "C" on a "B flat" cornet. It was confusing to everyone, even Bix! We fixed up a book of regular trumpet parts and for hours on end, I would work with Bix. I would teach him a tune, note for note, and then hand him the part and we would follow it. Bix was a brilliant boy and it wasn't long before he could follow new parts. No one but Bix and I shall ever know the hard work and patience it took to accomplish this. We would take down some of Bix's choruses, note for note, and then hand them to him to play in an ensemble. He would take one look at the notes and say, "man, this is impossible!"**
>
> **Many nights we sat in the back room of a little cafe with an old upright piano, going over things we both loved. Contrary to the belief of most people, Bix didn't care much**

for other bands. Oh, we both loved Louis Armstrong. But, our favorites were: Delius, Debussy, Ravel and Stravinsky.

You piano men, go out and get a copy of Eastwood Lane's "Woodland Sketches." Play "Land Of The Loon" and others, and hear the tremendous influence Lane had on Bix.

By now, Bix and I were thinking alike. I could stop on any note and Bix could pick it up and finish the phrase perfectly, and he could do the same with me. We could play simultaneous choruses and never clash. I want to say, right here, for the record, that this was the happiest and healthiest period in our lives. I made him assistant leader of the band. We played golf, rode horses, and he didn't have a drink for months at a time. To my knowledge, it was here that Bix met the only girl that he ever loved. I have since read some of the letters he wrote to her, and they were beautiful. Her name is Ruth. We'll let it go at that!

Ruth Shaffner Sweeney has pointed out, during a November 1989 conversation, that:

> Frank never liked the name of Frankie. He considered that name to belong to a little boy, and he actually resented being called Frankie. He preferred Frank, but would accept "Tram." His main interest was his family. He never cared much about going out after hours. When Bix, Pee Wee, and the other members of the band went out with my sisters and me, Frank would always go home. He had an adorable wife and little son, and he was a homebody-type.

A typical homebody-type with typical homebody-type family problems, such as the night young Bill put a scare into Tram and Mitzi, right after the Arcadia opened, by drinking a bottle of Mitzi's perfume. Bill was sick for days!

One publication in 1926 described the band as "a hell for leather playing group." Bix was so proud of the band that he wrote to Hoagy Carmichael at Indiana University, asking Hoagy to book the band for a campus date. In part, Bix wrote: "we have absolutely the hottest band in the country. We're playing at the Arcadia nightly and are panicking the town."

Hoagy booked the band for the April 16, 1926 junior prom.

Upon arriving in Bloomington, we were met at the train by Charles "Bud" Dant, who later conducted for singer Dennis Day on the west coast, the fabled Bill Moenkhaus, and the third member of the party who was introduced to me as Hogwash McCorkle. Bix quickly pointed out that his real name was Hoagy Carmichael to us, but students used a variety of names to identify him.

As a result of this dance, and additional dates at the university, I can say that I shared the warm spot that Bix had in his heart for Indiana. That entire college thought with a beat! They knew their music—and what dancing! In all of my years in the music business, I have never found a school so sharp. We literally knocked each other out—the school and the band!

The Music Corporation of America was just getting started and when we closed at the Arcadia on May 3, they offered us a job in Mansfield, Ohio. Somehow I felt that we should have taken the offer. But, about this time, Charles Horvath came to town and asked me to take over the leadership of the Jean Goldkette Orchestra in Detroit. Some of my men didn't want to go on the road, so I accepted the Goldkette offer, but only one condition—that I take Bix with me!

"I admit that Bix is a great cornet player," stated Horvath, "but I don't know if Jean will take a chance on him. He was in our band, for a short stay, and we let him go because he couldn't really read music! Then there was that time when we added him for a college date. We sent the band by train, and this really impressed Bix. Russ Morgan, who was leading the band, said that Bix kept repeating, over and over, how impressed he was with riding a train to the date. Russ said they pulled into a depot, and after a minute or two, he looked out the window and saw Bix seated on a bench. Russ rushed off the train, grabbed Bix by the arm, and got back on the train just as it was pulling out. Morgan asked Bix what was he doing outside on the bench. Bix said that he was so thrilled with riding the train to the date that he had seen all that he wanted of the train inside, so he wanted to see how the train looked outside."

"Charles," I persisted, "Bix has changed. He has matured. He can read an arrangement now. Tell you what! Bix will be my responsibility and I won't accept the job without him!"

Horvath told Jean of Tram's position, and Jean accepted the conditions.

Jean Goldkette was born in Patras, Greece, on March 18, 1893. His father died when Jean was a child, and his mother, a professional singer, married again, during her tour of Europe in 1900, to a Russian journalist, John Poliakoff, necessitating a move to Moscow. At age 10, Jean was accepted, after a thirty-day examination, at the Moscow Music Conservatory as one of fifty students selected from over a thousand applicants. He completed seven years of study (nine years being necessary to qualify for a diploma), before his family moved to America and settled in Chicago. In 1913, Jean continued as a student at the Lewis Institute in Chicago and studied music on a scholarship awarded by the American Conservatory of Music.

Jean's piano work dealt mostly with the classics, but he found work in Chicago playing at smart restaurants and an occasional concert hall. In 1914, he accepted a dinner music job at the Lamb's Cafe as pianist with an ensemble headed by Stephen Horvath (cello); George Lipschultz (violin); and a now-forgotten flutist and drummer. The engagement lasted until May 15, 1915, when they were replaced by "Tom Brown's Band From Dixie Land" of New Orleans. His next move was with the Edgar Benson Office, learning the business side of the music world. In 1918 he served in the Army.

Following the war, Jean first returned to Chicago but soon moved to Detroit. He became musical director at the Detroit Athletic Club in 1921, with a five-piece group, but in 1922, he took a larger band into the Graystone Ballroom and worked through 1923. During this engagement, Jean learned that the owners, unable to meet payroll and mortgage payments, had to default on the building. Jean was able to finance the purchase of the building, and in the next couple of years, built an empire to rival the Benson Office. His personal favorite was the Graystone Ballroom Band, to which he devoted his attention, paying for topnotch musicians to mold the band into one of the leading orchestras in the Midwest.

When Tram arrived, with Bix by his side, in Detroit on May 12, 1926, it was at the Graystone that Jean Goldkette[6] had asked them

[6]Jean Goldkette information from Jean, during correspondence and conversations (1957–1962). Additional background information provided by Stan Kuwik (October 25, 1991), via Clarita Goldkette.

to meet with him. Upon entering the main door, they saw Jean seated near the bandstand, and walked over to him.

"Gentlemen," said Jean, in his heavy Russian accent, "come over here." During the next half hour, he explained what he expected from Tram, and from Bix.

"Charles [Horvath] tells me that you are a new man, Bix," said an inquisitive Jean, "is this true?" Before Bix could clear his throat and give his answer, Jean continued, "Charles tells me of your wanting to be a member of my band again. I'm willing to forget 1924 and start over again. They tell me that you can read music now."

Again Bix started to answer, but Jean continued again, "Tell me, Frank, do you think that you can take over my band? Russ Morgan is leaving us, and Charles tells me that you can step right in and take over my group of young men. What do you say?"

"Yes, I can!" Tram spoke right up before Jean had a chance to cut off his reply.

Jean smiled, adjusted his glasses, and said, "I know you can, too. You wouldn't be here if I didn't think that you could. I've agreed to allow some of your St. Louis men to play Hudson Lake with you, but when the summer is over, they have to return to St. Louis. When the bands come back in September, you will have the Graystone Band. Now I have tickets for you and Bix. The train will take you to Terre Haute and you can finish the tour with the band, get a feel of the set up, and then head for Hudson Lake."

During the next few days, Tram discussed the band with Russ Morgan and got some valuable insights into the musicians, Jean's thinking, and the rest. When Jean Goldkette hired Russ Morgan in 1925 to lead his Graystone Orchestra, he surprised Russ by stating that his goal was to become known as "The Paul Whiteman Orchestra of the West." Russ asked why he didn't seek individuality and become known as the "Jean Goldkette Orchestra of the World?" Russ provided the needed direction, contributed many arrangements, and formed one of the finer bands in the Midwest. When they appeared in New York in January 1926, musicians and patrons alike heaped praise upon them, but the New York critics wrote about "The Paul Whiteman Orchestra of Detroit." Russ assured Tram that, once he could get by the critics in New York, the band had a chance to be recognized as one of the best in the country.

On May 22, 1926, the band started the summer job at Hudson Lake, Indiana, ninety miles east of Chicago on the South Shore

Electric Railroad between South Bend and Michigan City. Jean had hung a blue painted glass lantern atop the entrance of the former "The Casino" and renamed it "The Blue Lantern Inn." This dance hall was a wooden frame, one-story, building located right at the shoreline, and had surrounding wood framed cottages that housed the musicians and their wives.

During a July 27, 1974, conversation, Norma Ryker clearly recalled the events of that summer and sketched a map of the housing arrangements:

> Just to the right of the dance hall, a group of cottages had Fred Farrar and his wife, with Tram and Mitzi in the first one; Charles Horvath, his wife, Edith, and two sons, Charles Junior, and Allen, occupied the second. "Doc" and I had the third cottage. Directly across from the ballroom, Irving Riskin, Dan Gaebe, Pee Wee Russell and Bix shared the first one; Sonny Lee, Dee Orr, and Frank DiPrima shared the other one. None of them contained a bath. That was at the nearby hotel, and it cost us 25 cents a person.

> **You can imagine how happy we were to find Hoagy Carmichael at a ringside table the night that we opened. Later on that night, we really got to kicking. Bix and I took a series of choruses and Hoagy started banging his head on the railing near the bandstand. He was carried away to the local bastille as the local citizens didn't understand his musical enthusiasm.**
>
> **Another amusing incident occurred during that summer. Pee Wee and I were in the men's room, during intermission, and he asked me if I had noticed that beautiful girl in the white organdy dress dancing around in front of the bandstand.**
>
> **"Boy," he said, "I could just about flip my lid for her from here. I wonder if she would care for a short romance with me."**
>
> **A man, well over six feet tall and weighing every bit of two hundred pounds, stepped up and said, "I don't think so, but I'll ask her. She's my wife."**
>
> **Pee Wee looked around for a hole to crawl into but they were all in use, so he turned to me and said, "Boy, you wouldn't let a big brute like that hit your grandfather, would you?"**
>
> **That broke the tension. We all laughed, had a drink from the stranger's flask, and went back to work.**

Chicago was only ninety miles away, so it wasn't uncommon for musicians to drive down to hear the band. The more that came, the more the word was spread. Most of the musicians drove down and then back, after a night's engagement was over.

Matty Matlock's 1969 letter has offered a glimpse of that summer:

> I believe that Frank Trumbauer deserves possibly more credit than anyone ever, for his influence on jazz saxophone. This was expressed by the late Lester Young. I am absolutely sure that the great Eddie Miller would agree to this belief.
>
> I had the pleasure of meeting Frank that summer at Hudson Lake. Ray McKinley and I were playing at Paw Paw Lake with Beasley Smith's Orchestra. We had heard that Frank was leading a band out of the Jean Goldkette Office at Hudson Lake. What a thrill hearing Frank and Bix. One tune that impressed me was ''The Girl Friend.''
>
> A certain amount of corn whiskey was consumed that evening. I spent the night in the cottage with Bix and Pee Wee and a couple more of the members of the band.

The next morning, Matty found Norma and Mitzi. ''I told them that they would not believe that cottage. There were things crawling in there. Like a living swamp.''

In an April 25, 1972, letter, Irving Riskin stated:

> What a cottage! There was an old square piano in one room and another room that could have been for anything. Two rooms. That summer, they divided us up into two groups. The ''solid ones,'' meaning the families, such as Frank and Mitzi, Charles and Edith, were located in one area. I was with the other group they called ''the wild ones,'' relegated to this old broken down cottage. I was in the group because we were all single guys, not because of any bad social habits because I neither smoked nor drank, so you can be certain who did the cooking and cleaning up after each meal.

''Oh yes, I remember the incident,'' Norma Ryker has added:

> I rounded up Mitzi and Edith Horvath, a couple of buckets and mops, lots of soap, and headed for that cottage! Mitzi was throwing things out when the sleepy-headed boys realized what was happening and called out, ''Aw, Mitzi,

> come on, not that!'' or ''Mitzi, I was saving that!'' Everything went. Mitzi marched the four boys, in almost single file, towards the hotel. As she passed Frank, she asked for four quarters. She marched the boys right into the bath house, plunked down the four quarters, and told the bath house attendant to make them sparkle.
>
> When we finished with the cleaning job, I sort of felt proud of our efforts, but I can still remember Edith's comment, ''I think we should have just burned the place down.''

The Lake closed on August 29th, and Tram and Mitzi loaded the car with their belongings. Tram wanted to drive to Chicago, where he could pay his union dues, and Bix decided to go along with them. While at the Musicians Union, Bix learned that Louis Armstrong was appearing with Carroll Dickerson at the Sunset Cafe. Bix suggested to stop by and hear Louis, to which Tram readily agreed with one condition—Bix must introduce him to Louis!

Mitzi's letter, written ''on a cold day in November'' 1968, glowingly remembered the meeting with Louis:

> Frank had heard Louis when he was in New York, but never met him. Bix took us to this club, and Louis was playing when we walked in, so we headed for a table. What I remember was all of the cheering and whistling and applause when Louis would take a solo. Finally intermission came, and Louis spotted Bix and made a beeline for our table. Both were genuinely happy to see one another.
>
> Then comes the funny part. Bix spoke to Louis, and nodded to Frank, and said, ''Louis, this is my good friend, Frank Trumbauer.''
>
> Tram reached out his hand to Louis for a handshake, but a quizzing Louis said, ''How's that? Frank Trrrr . . . what?''
>
> ''Trumbauer,'' Bix repeated, ''Frank Trumbauer.''
>
> A giant smile crossed Louis' face. He reached for Tram's hand with both of his, gave Tram a warm grasp, and said ''Glad to know ya, Mr. Trambone.''
>
> It was ''Mr. Trambone'' then, and whenever Louis saw Tram again, over the years, it was always ''Mr. Trambone.''

CHAPTER SIX

JEAN GOLDKETTE
1926–1927

"THE GRAYSTONE BALLROOM WAS LOCATED on Woodward Avenue, near Canfield," stated Jean Goldkette in his May 22, 1960, letter:

> I had Frank report to me, when the band finished at the Lake, at the Graystone, for some last minute instructions. We walked across the dance floor and Frank repeated his dreams that he had for my band. I told him if you need anything just see Charlie Horvath, who was my trusted lieutenant. He'll solve any problems that Frank might have. Once the band was playing on the bandstand, he needed to meet those two muscular men, Charles Stanton and "Handsome Pat," the Irishman. If any of the customers get out of line or gave him a hard time, he just needed to give a call! They were the bouncers. I told Frank that I wished him good luck, and I was looking forward to great things from him.

Aside from Trumbauer and Bix Beiderbecke, the new Jean Goldkette orchestra consisted of:

FRED "FUZZY" FARRAR, trumpet, came from Pennsylvania from the band known as "The Scranton Sirens." Jean heard him in the summer of 1923 and hired him along with Irving Riskin and the Dorsey Brothers. His tone was beautiful and full. His favorite saying was "How's the kid?" no matter who he met!

RAY LODWIG, trumpet, left the Ray Williams Band to join Jean in 1923. Originally he was a member of the St. Louis Musicians' Local, and, when his music days were ended, he became a plumber.

Bill Rank started playing trombone in 1915 and joined his first band in 1921, the Collins Jazz Band in Florida. They played in the style of The Original Dixieland Jazz Band. Bill moved on to Tade Dolan's Singing Orchestra in Indianapolis, and in 1923 joined Jean Goldkette in time for the recording session that produced "In The Evening."

Newell "Spiegle" Willcox, second trombone, was from Cortland, New York. Fuzzy recommended Spiegle after hearing him play with the Paul Whiteman Collegians, basically made up of eight musicians from Cornell University. They had recorded "I Cried For You" and "That Red Headed Girl"; Spiegle told of the music stands suspended from the ceiling so the racks would not get in the way of the soloist, who ducked under them to approach the large and long horn, extending from the wall of the recording booth.

Stanley "Doc" Ryker, first alto saxophone, was one of two original members to play with the band during their entire existence. Doc was one of several that auditioned for the band and almost withdrew his name when he saw all of the sax men ahead of him, but decided that, since he had come this far, he owed it to himself to try. He was hired in 1922.

Don Murray played baritone saxophone, clarinet, and tenor saxophone. Don knew Bix from his earlier days around Chicago. Jean hired him based on his reputation and was surprised at his poor reading ability. But because of his wonderful solo work, and because he could duplicate anyone's sound on clarinet, Jean kept him with the band, and Doc worked with Don on improving his reading ability. He was the practical joker of the band.

Howdy Quicksell, banjo, was the other original member who played with the band from their beginning in 1922 until their end in 1927. He, too, passed the audition with Doc.

Irving Riskin, pianist, was hired by Jean when he hired Fuzzy and Jimmy and Tommy Dorsey.

Paul Mertz, who would often find himself in the Graystone Band, joined Jean's organization in 1923. This multitalented musician, composer, and arranger, served Jean in many capacities with a variety of his bands. He often played piano with the band when Irving was shifted to other groups.

Chauncey Morehouse, drummer, was hired by Russ Morgan. Russ wired Chauncey in Canton, Ohio, the very night that

Ted Weems's band folded. Chauncey had five dollars in his pocket, so he purchased a railroad ticket for his wife and himself and headed for Detroit. He went directly to the Graystone Ballroom, contacted Russ and Charlie Horvath, and Horvath immediately stepped down as the band's drummer, turning to becoming Jean's assistant. (Horvath now became part of management, giving up playing.)

STEVE BROWN, string bass, was a bit older than the others, and his slow talking and movements were just the opposite of his slap-bass playing. After the band recorded "Dinah" (28 January 1926), he received a number of job offers from various recording companies while the band was in New York, and he played on several sessions. His jazz training with the New Orleans Rhythm Kings was the reason Jean hired him.

Now that the summer was over, the Hudson Lake group (Bix-Tram-Riskin, etc.) was united with the musicians from Island Lake (Murray-Brown-etc.) in an attempt to form the one Graystone Orchestra. Irving Riskin's letter of July 6, 1962 has offered background information on the Goldkette Orchestra:

> I really think that it was Charles Horvath that revamped the band. I really don't think that Jean realized what kind of band we had. When we went to New York in January 1926 to record, Jean decided to bring in some New York arrangers, and we rehearsed arrangements by Phil Boutelje and Don Voorhees, which I think Jean felt would broaden our style, but I remember how dull and uninspired they were. I, for one, felt insulted that Jean should try and pawn off these arrangements on us. If I remember, we never played them in performance. They were stiff! Luckily Charles Horvath played the important role in bringing together what we now had.

Reflecting on the recording sessions in 1926, Irving recalled:

> I remember when we were doing "Dinah" [January 28], I had a piano vamp intro and Eddie King [recording director] came over and told me that it wasn't crisp enough for him. He played the piano intro, ever so corny, and insisted that I play it that exact way. Then when we did "Lonesome And Sorry" [April 23] Eddie was annoyed because we did not play it as he visualized it. He was annoyed with us. He let us

know that he was doing us a special favor by letting us record. Was he corny!

When Tram came on as our director, he brought in these fine arrangements that his band in St. Louis had been using. I think ''Fud'' Livingston did a couple. These were simply outstanding arrangements.

Although I was the leader of the band, I had difficulty controlling some of the men. There were some big names in the band, and some of them were prima donnas who constantly ran to Goldkette or Horvath with petty problems when they didn't feel like following logical instructions.

Don Murray and Howdy Quicksell always brought a picnic lunch and a case of beer to rehearsals. When I would request a cut in an arrangement to shorten it for a recording or a radio broadcast, Don and Howdy would actually take scissors and cut the part from the music. If any attempt was made to replace these cuts, Don would hold up his part and say, ''Oh no, you don't. Look!'' His parts looked like he had been cutting out paper dolls.

Irving Riskin's June 24, 1960, letter offers a bit of an insight to the problem:

There was a coolness in the band. Tram was a newcomer, and there was this clique that included Don and Howdy, and it boiled down to whose style would be predominate, the old Goldkette style, or the new Tram style! Bix was able to help because he was a friend of Don's, and Ray had been a friend of Frank's, so these two acted as go-betweens and soon got the matter straightened out. Of course, matters came to a complete understanding when Jean let it be known, in no uncertain terms, that Frank was his new director and if anybody didn't like it, well. . . .

Jean had booked a New England tour for September 1926, and as the band headed east, Spiegle received word of the impending birth of his first child, so he left the band, having made arrangements for Tommy Dorsey to replace him at Nutting's-On-The-Charles. But instead he had Tommy seeking the band at the nonexistent town of Muttins-on-the-Crow!

Spiegle has recalled, in an interview on September 11, 1989:

> I'll tell you what I remember most about that trip. Chauncey told us the story to alert us about our eventual destination, New York. There was this rube who went to New York and decided to stay in a hotel. The desk clerk asked him to register. "Not me," said the rube, "I'm not signing any unofficial documents." "And," said the rube, "the desk clerk knew I was right. I could tell by the way he was laughing." So, the moral of the story was, that Chauncey didn't want any of us guys signing any hotel registers when we got to New York.

The band checked into the Hillcrest Inn at Southboro, Massachusetts on September 21. The tour was to start in four days, and it gave them a chance to rest and rehearse.

Bill Challis had played four years with a band while attending Bucknell College, and during this time, he did the band's arrangements. After graduation, he joined a band from Williamsport which traveled as far west as Toledo. Bill knew about the Jean Goldkette Orchestra and drove to Detroit to hear them. He pestered Charles Horvath to allow him to do an arrangement for the band. "Sure, kid," was the reply. Later Bill sent the arrangement to Charles, but Horvath didn't feel that it was right for the Graystone band, so he gave it to Owen Bartlett for the Book Cadillac Hotel Band.

When Challis learned of the band's eastern tour, he again approached the band about doing arrangements, but this time he talked with Ray Lodwig and informed him of the past experience. Ray suggested that Bill submit several more arrangements, and Ray said that he would make certain that Charles heard them played by the band! Bill sent "Baby Face" and "Blue Room." True to his word, Ray got the band to play them, and Horvath was on the telephone, almost immediately, to Challis, offering him a job as arranger.

The eastern bus trips ended on October 2. Next stop—New York! Roseland Ballroom! October 6!

> **The night before we opened at Roseland, we arrived in New York and checked into the 44th Street Hotel. Joe Venuti put in a frantic telephone call, saying that he needed me, and to bring Bix over immediately to the Silver Slipper, Broadway at 48th.**

Bix and I made a dash for the club and found Joe waiting for us outside the club.

"Red Nichols and Jimmy Dorsey were to do the floor show," stated Joe, "but they are both out cold. The show is about to start, and I need you to take their places."

We said that we would. Joe grabbed the music—took us into a back room and gave us a fast fifteen-minute rehearsal for a forty-five-minute floor show. The buzzer sounded and we ran for the bandstand.

We played the fanfare and the lights went out! Even the lights on our music stands! The only illumination in the whole cafe was a spot light on the dancers.

Bix yelled to Joe, "Hey, mastermind, what the hell do we do now?"

Well, Joe laughed until tears ran down his face. "Fake it, boys, it'll sound better anyway."

Bix and I always thought that Joe had planned that well in advance.

After the show, the three of us joined friends in the club. A small relief band was playing and a couple danced by in formal attire. They bumped into Bix's chair and knocked him flat onto the floor. Bix was so mad that he bounced up like a tennis ball.

The gentleman saw Bix coming toward him with a big roundhouse swing, tied him up, picked up Bix's chair, and sat him upon it. "Very bad with your left, young man," he said, as he and his lady danced away.

Bix looked at Venuti. "Who the hell was that?"

"Just the French boxing champion, Georges Carpentier," answered Joe.

When the Goldkette band came in October 1926, it was playing opposite Fletcher Henderson's large, exciting orchestra, and the musical duel was the talk of Broadway. Not only did Goldkette have a great band but he had a very talented arranger, Bill Challis, who was one of the most original and imaginative arrangers of the twenties. They were a sensation at Roseland, opening in a lavish musical program that included not only themselves and Henderson, but groups led by Fats Waller and Miff Mole.[7]

[7]*Jazz: A History Of The New York Scene* (1962), cited by permission of its authors, Samuel B. Charters and Leonard Kunstadt.

During a November 1969 interview, Irving Riskin recalled the events at Roseland:

> Opening night, here were all these musicians in the audience to hear us, and when the Fletcher Henderson Orchestra finished playing, they remained on the bandstand. Reports were made that we had a great band, and everyone was anxiously awaiting us. Tram had a marvelous sense of humor, and it was never more evident that night. He opened with ''Valencia'' in 6/8 march tempo. At first, the audience was stunned, then they realized what we were doing, and it brought down the house. After that, we went into our ''hot'' numbers, and before long, the place was a near riot with cheering.
>
> Everyone wanted to get to know us, during our stay. Harry Akst, famous songwriter, sat in at the piano and was amazed at our beat (he referred to it as ''tempo''). Roger Wolfe Kahn, son of the famous banker and art connoisseur, asked to direct one number, and not knowing the arrangement, conducted on the after beat as we played on the strong beat (for a few bars at least). It struck me funny how he kept a straight, confident face through this wrong directional beat.

From an Irving Riskin letter of July 1962:

> Why didn't we do well on records? I think one of the reasons is that they muddied our new fresh sound and drive with dull, name singers, who had much experience in recording but were out of place with us. The Keller Sisters and Lynch might have been good on their own vaudeville routines but were rather dry with us. Frank Bessinger and Frank Marvin were guys who might have been very dependable when the down beat was given, and came in on the right beat, but as I said, D-U-L-L! Being sensitive, I feel that Eddie King might have done it on purpose. I suppose that Jean was so thrilled to get a chance to record for Victor Records that he'd accept most anything.

During a July 1974 interview, Bill Challis was asked his opinion of the 1926 recordings:

> These were tunes selected by Eddie King and Victor Records. These were not in our library. Imagine! ''Hush-A-

> Bye,'' ''I'd Rather Be The Girl In Your Arms.'' These were dogs! Even if Victor Records thought they were good tunes, they were dogs! I was given the tunes just a couple of days prior to the recording dates, and I did what I could with arranging them, but they were helpless tunes.

The Goldkette unit returned to Detroit and reopened at the Graystone on November 5, 1926. Riskin's 1962 letter recalled:

> One thing that I'll always remember, was when we opened at Roseland, here was this great negro band, Fletcher Henderson, who we admired. Shortly after we returned to Detroit, Henderson's Orchestra played the Graystone and then it struck me, as I listened to them, they were trying to sound like us![8]

Jean was ecstatic at the reports on the Roseland Ballroom engagement, but he could read the disappointment in the faces of the musicians over their treatment by Victor Records. The proverbial ''Things will be different next time'' was his promise. Jean booked the band for January 1927 at the Roseland.

> **We had worked hard for our next New York engagement and decided to have a big party before we left. In the early hours we retired to a nice, quiet speakeasy near the Graystone. Some of the boys played poker in the back room and I noticed Bix with a stack of money in front of him and two cards—one face up and one face down!**
>
> **The game was stud poker. Murray nudged Bix, ''What do you say, boy?''**
>
> **''How much? How much?'' asked Bix as he shoved money into the middle of the table.**
>
> **They had to wake him up each time a card was dealt. After the fifth card was dealt, Don said, ''Oh, come on, dopey, play cards or go home to bed.''**
>
> **Again Bix asked, ''How much? How much?''**
>
> **Don replied, ''Look at your cards. What do you do? Stay or what?''**

---

[8]Paul Mertz accompanied the Goldkette Orchestra, replacing Irving Riskin who remained in Detroit, when they opened at Roseland on January 24, 1927. Fletcher Henderson Band came to the Graystone on January 25, and this is when Irving Riskin heard them, during this engagement.

> **Bix peeked at his hole card and said, "By God, I'm game! Hit me again!"**
>
> **Poor Bix had been playing blackjack while the others were playing poker! You can imagine the poker hand that he must of had!**

The 1927 trip to New York was important for the Goldkette Orchestra's return to the Roseland Ballroom, opening on January 24, but also for jazz recording history.

> **For some time Bix and I had plans to make some recordings, and here was our chance. Through Red McKenzie, we met Tom Rockwell, then head of the Okeh Record Company. That was the beginning. Our first date was February 4, 1927. We made "Singin' The Blues" and "Clarinet Marmalade."**

Nuncio "Toots" Mondello, in a letter dated July 1990, offered an explanation on the impact of "Singin' The Blues":

> When this record was released, I think that every sax man in America bought a copy. I know that I did! It was as if a sax man could duplicate Tram's solo, then he felt he had passed a test. This was the greatest solo ever put on records.

Joe Urso interviewed Lester Young and asked if he felt that Tram was an inspiration to him. Just four months short of his death, Lester replied that a number of saxophone players have been credited over the years as having been an influence on him, "but their only association with me is that we belonged to the same New York Local."

"Tram was my man!" confirmed Lester. "When Tram made that recording of 'Singin' The Blues,' it just wounded my heart. It got me right there. From then on it was Tram!"

Fifty years later, Dinah Shore announced on the **Grammy Awards** program of February 19, 1977 that the **National Academy Of Recording Arts And Sciences** selected the famed recording for induction into their Hall of Fame at Universal Studios, Universal City, California.

The band returned to Detroit on February 11, 1927, and "Uncle Ray" Lodwig discovered that Bill Trumbauer had taken care of things for him. Bill had bathed both of his dogs, Tipper and Peggy, and proceeded to use Ray's razor to give them a shave. He dyed Ray's Gotham Hotel bath towels pink, and for good measure, ate Ray's delicious fruit cake Christmas gift. It was several days before young Bill could sit down again, after Tram found out what happened!

The next trip for the band commenced on April 10 when they closed at the Graystone. Irving Riskin recalled several dates in a November 1969 interview:

> I think one of our first stops was Indiana University [*Ed. note: April 22*]. As one would expect, the dance floor was overcrowded and every table filled with both dancers and listeners. Hoagy Carmichael had a table with about eight friends that were caught up early with our music!
>
> I called over to Tram, "What are they doing?"
>
> Hoagy and his contingent were half standing, with their arms lifted in sort of a "hallelujah" stance, moaning and "wheeing" as they heard and felt the music. The band shifted to an up tempo number and the "gang" raced onto the dance floor. Hoagy just collapsed at the feet of the dancers and yelled with enthusiasm.
>
> "Aw, don't pay any mind to it," Tram said. "Hoagy's just trying out a new dance craze!"
>
> I knew that we had a great band and everyone that heard it simply raved about the music, that is, except one place—Pennsylvania State University [*Ed. note: April 29*]. We were booked there along with Jan Garber's Orchestra. The applause went to the Garber Band. They had musical numbers where they wore funny hats, pulled out all sort of antics, and simply wowed the crowd! They entertained the masses. Our band was ignored by all but some of the more "hep" students. We left the campus talking to ourselves on "how this could have happened?" We were a musicians' band and we played for ourselves. I guess we had a lot to learn about the public's interest.

On May 9, Trumbauer led a smaller unit that recorded "Riverboat Shuffle" and "Ostrich Walk" for Okeh Records. **Melody Maker**'s pages offered glowing words:

> . . . two of the "hottest" but at the same time artistic performances of really inspiring dance music. . . . I would

> like to have given a detailed report of this record, movement by movement, but there is so much to say that if I once start, I'll never stop.[9]

Yet there was one review, written June 11 from the law offices of Bingham, Mendall, and Bingham, located at 3037 North Graceland Avenue in Indianapolis. It read:

> Dear Frank:
>
> Just heard RIVERBOAT on Okeh and wish to reprimand you severly [sic] for singing through your horn. If there is anyone crazier than you, I would like to know who it is, unless it's Bix Bite-A-Becker. Accept my deep appreciation and sincerest gratitude for rendering LARDBOAT and accept my congratulations, felicitations and fumble-bugs for getting through it allright without sopping your bread in it. I've been wanting a nice base-burner but my father's cow won't hold still. Now I want to ween [sic] the trombone and take a chorus on the baby. I can't wait till the fourth of July comes. I want to blow up. Tell Don Birdsong that he's a comer on clarinet and I liked his first break on HOP SKIP AND A BOAT very much even if he did loose his place.
>
> Now, why don't we get together on MARCH OF THE HOODLUMS? I think it would make a whaling [sic] good number. Someone can spit upside down and the rest of you blow at it. Blow each other out and then have some one read the gas-meter. Let me know about this before I go floating.
>
> Tell Bix that Harry Hostetter is back and he fainted when he heard "Singin' The Blues" so I had to give him a pole-vault for Christmas. Also tell him I'm a heel.
>
> Very fart, Hogwash McCorkle.

Spiegle decided that he wanted a home life and served notice. Lloyd Turner eagerly accepted his trombone chair, leaving a band that he was leading in Chicago at the Hotel Edison at the time, and

[9]Quoted from June 1927 issue of **The Melody Maker** by permission of David Smith, Associate Publisher (September 14, 1990).

joined on May 24. In a September 1973 letter, Chris Fletcher stated:

> Eddy Sheasby had written some fine arrangements that called for three violins when the band was last in Detroit. Eddy was directing the band on this trip, and he wanted Jean to send "Red" Ingle and me down when they opened Castle Farms [*Ed. note: May 29*]. In addition to the violin work, Red sang the "hot" tunes, and I sang the ballads. As I recall, when the engagement ended, Eddy disappeared. Red and I returned to Detroit, and the band went on to St. Louis.

Eddy did, indeed, "disappear," and so did the trunk with the music arrangements! There has been much speculation on why he did not show at their next stop, St. Louis, and while there always will be rumors, Irving Riskin's letter of July 1962 suggested that Eddy, behind in his alimony payments, had received word that an angry ex-wife and the police were awaiting him.

Tram telephoned Goldkette to advise him of the situation. Jean told them to do the best they could, cancelled the remainder of the tour, and returned the band to Detroit. Jean then booked the band in Young's Million Dollar Pier on August 8. Fletcher continued:

> I went with the band to Atlantic City, and Eddy was again our director. Paul Whiteman showed up one night, after hearing rumors about the band ready to break up, and said, "I'm not here vulturing! I know that you are set for New York. If anything happens after that, contact Jimmy Gillespie at my New York office, and let him know if any of you would like to join my band."

Whiteman's appearance was not without reason. He was seeking a replacement for Red Nichols, and his eye was on Bix Beiderbecke. To understand Whiteman's quest, it is important to note Nichols' role. Ernest Loring "Red" Nichols was clearly the most outstanding musician in New York in 1927. His cornet work was in constant demand among radio and recording studios. To list all of the recordings made under his own name and as a sideman would be nearly impossible. The noted Nichols collector, Stan Hester, estimates that Red cut 4,000 sides during the twenties. Typical of the applause of these recordings are these excerpts from **Melody Maker** reviews: " He has always had a marvelous tone and technique and many people consider him the last word in 'hot style,' " or " . . . Red has always been clever, and whatever he did, he did it perfectly," or, " . . . Red, whose perfection always makes me think of the majesty of the snow-clad mountains."

Red had one creed when it came to recording: he surrounded himself with the best musicians available, because he believed it made him play better. Whatever praise came his way, it was clearly earned, and clearly deserved!

Whiteman offered Red a job in his band and extended the offer to include the musicians that usually made up the bulk of Red Nichols And His Five Pennies recordings: Miff Mole, Jimmy Dorsey, Arthur Schutt, Eddie Lang, and Victor Berton. Only Dorsey and Berton accepted the offer. Whiteman planned to feature Red And The Five Pennies within the full Orchestra, a band within a band. This offer certainly appealed to Red, but when the others did not follow Red's entry into the band, the idea collapsed.

Whiteman kept his word and featured Red, and Nichols responded by giving the band a fresh, new sound that added a dimension to the band. His full tone and clean notes, offered a stark contrast to Henry Busse's muted work that had been the main feature of the trumpets. It was as if Red developed a new sound for the band. To compare the Whiteman recordings prior to Red's presence to the handful of recordings made during his brief stay is startling. Nichols had left the Don Voorhees Orchestra on April 18, 1927, to join Whiteman. Before rejoining Voorhees on May 28, he left an indelible mark. The recordings made, for example, on April 29 of "Side By Side" and "I'm Coming, Virginia" added an excitement to the band. Whiteman understood Red's disappointment with the others not joining the band, and agreed to tear up his contract. Red showed his appreciation by asking Whiteman to act as his best man when, on May 8, he married Willa Stutesman, then appearing with the "Earl Carroll Vanities."

Red's tone and style were his own. Almost never were his recordings incorrectly identified as Bix's (and vice-versa), yet in later years critics, particularly during the thirties and forties, would review Nichols recordings with reference to the "Bixian" sound, rather than the legitimate ''Nicholish'' sound. In all probability, these same reviewers could not distinguish between apples and oranges!

Whiteman wanted to maintain the sound that Nichols had given the band, and it was Jimmy Dorsey who suggested that he listen to Bix Beiderbecke. This was the main reason for Whiteman's appearance at Atlantic City. Chris Fletcher's recollections of that night concluded with ''Paul directed the band for a full hour, then, after we finished work, he had the whole band over to Vince Martini's speakeasy for fried chicken and free drinks.''

During the impromptu party, Whiteman acted as a congenial host, but he spent most of his time huddled with Trumbauer. It was obvious to everyone that Whiteman was trying to persuade Tram to join his band. Whiteman was a difficult person to refuse, but Tram wanted to see whether things turned out well in New York; and if they didn't, he'd contact Whiteman about his offer.

The Goldkette Orchestra closed in Atlantic City on September 5 and opened three days later at Roseland. Chris returned to Detroit.

> **Back in St. Louis, Bix used to play a piano solo for me and I suggested that he record it on one of our dates. He just laughed and said it wasn't good enough, but I was determined to get it on record, somehow, if only for my own collection.**
>
> **I herded him into a recording studio on September 9 and suggested that he make a test record of the piano solo.**
>
> **He played it once, and it was too short. He consented to try again, and this time it was too long. Bix never played it the same way twice.**
>
> **''That's all, brother. I just can't do it,'' he said as he started to walk out of the studio.**
>
> **''Just once more, Bix,'' I begged. ''This time, we'll record it. Okay?''**
>
> **We tried a ''take'' but the same problem persisted, Bix went too long.**
>
> **''This time,'' I said, ''just keep playing until I tap you on the shoulder, then make an ending and stop.''**
>
> **At two minutes and fifty seconds, I tapped him on the shoulder.**
>
> **I then convinced Tommy Rockwell that he should release the composition.**

"Okay," said Tom. "But what will we call it?"

Well, I thought to myself, Bix was certainly in a fog when he made it. And then it hit me. Fog. Mist. In A Mist. That's it—"In A Mist."

Yes, that's the true story of how it got its title. The success of this composition is musical history.

Again our Roseland engagement met with great success and again rave reviews. I believe that every musician in town heard that band at one time or another.

But, one day, out of a clear blue sky, Jean called the entire band into the office. He just could not continue to make the payroll. This would be our last engagement.

There were tears in Jean's eyes when he finished! He loved that band even though he never appeared with us on tour.

I immediately called a meeting and asked the boys to get work elsewhere for six months. At the end of that time we would meet, go to Jean and give him a chance to reorganize. Everyone agreed but one. Even though it was our idea, Jean would not accept it. He was too regular to tie us down.

Many have presumed that Jean was having financial trouble, thus the reason for discontinuing the Graystone Band, or as it was now known, The Victor Band. It was strictly a financial decision.[10] The band was costing more than he could obtain contractually for their services, so he cut his losses. At the time, Jean was president of five corporations, including a finance company, and he was operating three lake resorts in Michigan, in addition to his Detroit music organizations.

The Roseland engagement, the Victor Orchestra, and the balloon burst on September 18, 1927, a night remembered by Irving Riskin during his 1969 interview:

> That night, we took our seats on the bandstand and looked at the ropes that had been placed to keep the dancers at a distance from where we played, because of the usual excitement that our music caused. We asked the management to take down the barriers. We confused the capacity crowd by playing old arrangements by George Crozier, Russ Morgan,

[10]The weekly payroll during the Atlantic City engagement was $2096.

Dewey Bergman, and the rest that made up the original orchestra. We were playing our tribute to the years that the band had lived and to the musicians that had performed in the band.

Musicians numbering at least two hundred were standing, lining the dance floor, and soon the information of this being our final night circulated among the patrons. The spotlights were on the musicians, and soon almost everyone, except Howdy, had tears in their eyes. The information spread and the customers knew that one of the great bands of all time were playing their final numbers.

We cut loose, for one last time, with every member taking a solo on every tune. We were saying goodbye to one another. Finally the hour had arrived and it was time for Cinderella to go home.

But, then a truly amazing thing happened. The crowd had encircled the bandstand and refused to allow us off the stage. Cries of "more, more," rang out. We could not get down the steps nor even attempt to work our way through the chanting crowd. We started up again, and played to almost frenzied cries and shouts from the audience. Many of them now had tears streaming down their cheeks. No one wanted this night to end.

The Roseland management had put in a call for the riot squad, and soon dozens of policemen were pushing their way through the masses, making a lane for us to depart from the dance hall. Even as we scurried through the long line of police officers, patrons tried to reach through and around the blue barrier just to touch us, one more time, as we raced out of the building.

They say when we opened at the Roseland in 1926, it was a "Riot Of Glory." I think that our last night would have been the correct description of "Riot of Glory."

The band now scrambled for jobs. Bill Challis had left the band in Atlantic City and joined Paul Whiteman. Steve Brown now joined Paul. Fred Farrar made five or six trips to Detroit before joining the Nat Shilkret Orchestra at the Strand Theatre. He would later work with Don Voorhees in the stage production, **Rain Or Shine**. Ray Lodwig jobbed around New York and eventually ended in **Rain Or Shine**, too.

Doc Ryker decided to study clarinet with an eye towards being a teacher and later was personally selected by George Gershwin to do the play **Funny Face** with Fred and Adele Astaire; this led to additional shows with the Shuberts before studying with Meryl Johnson.

Irving Riskin immediately joined the B. A. Rolfe Orchestra as pianist and arranger on their Lucky Strike radio program and remained for years. Howdy Quicksell returned to Detroit, and then eventually to Saginaw, Michigan, where he settled down, married, and raised a family. Lloyd Turner, also jobbed around town, returned to Chicago, made his way back to New York and played with some of the leading bands of the era.

> **Our records were selling, we were creating a lot of talk, and yet we were out of work! But not for long, though, because Adrian Rollini walked into our lives. He had a line on a new club in New York, The New Yorker, and he took along Bix, Bill Rank, Don Murray, Chauncey Morehouse, and myself, in addition to some outstanding musicians that he already had. Frank Faye was to head the floor show with Patsy Kelly as his stooge. And contracts for us to double with Faye at the Strand Theatre across the street. How could we miss?**
>
> **Strangely enough, though, the public didn't take to Frank Faye. Perhaps his material was too fast for them, I don't know. It was just one of those screwy breaks in show business. He fractured the band and played most of his shows to us.**

Jack Benny, the noted comedian, closed the Club Alabam and arranged with Adrian Rollini to use the band in the act that he was taking into the Audubon Theatre on 14th Street. Jack, who repeated this performance for years, would open with Joe Venuti directing the band in a number. Jack would appear, take the baton from Joe, and proceed to conduct the band into total disarray. He'd return the baton to Joe, and produce his violin, asking the band to accompany him on popular songs of the day. Jack would forever play off key, lapse into disgust with the band not being able to keep up with him, and generally have the whole audience, and musicians, too, in fits of laughter. The engagement ran from October 15 through the 26th.

Tram showed up for work on the 18th with a "shiner," the result of showing his young son "how to protect himself."

CHAPTER SEVEN

PAUL WHITEMAN—THE VICTOR YEARS 1927–1928

WHEN THE ROLLINI JOB FOLDED, Bix and I met with Jimmy Gillespie[11] and we were told that the old man wanted us.

The year—1927. The pinnacle of success for a country boy was to have Paul Whiteman put his arm around him and say, "Boy, we're happy to have you with us!"

The whole country was talking about Paul Whiteman, "The King Of Jazz." Paul had acquired the nickname in 1923 when his orchestra appeared in England. The London newspapers began to refer to Paul as "The Jazz King From America," and Paul's publicity manager seized on that title and translated it to "King Of Jazz." When the band returned to America in August 1923, Victor Records' public relations department proclaimed his forthcoming recordings with "Paul Whiteman is back from Europe to the high delight of American dancers. He has been crowned 'King Of Jazz' by American dance musicians, and now boasts an actual crown, which he wears on convivial occasions. His American triumphs were easily repeated abroad, and then some.[12]" In later years, Paul seemed more comfortable with the title, "The Dean Of Modern American Music," but in 1927 he was, "The King Of Jazz."

That was the era when the Whiteman baton was almost like a magic wand—a downbeat from Paul brought great success wherever he played.

---

[11]Jimmy Gillespie and Paul Whiteman's Offices located at 33 West 42nd Street, New York.

[12]1923 Victor Records Phonograph Catalog, by permission of BMG Music/RCA Records.

Many of the greatest musicians came out of that organization. Those were colorful and exciting years and will never be forgotten.

Whiteman was clearly a king in the "Roaring Twenties." His name meant the pinnacle for musicians to reach, but only a few reached it. Whiteman's fame was such that when Stutz Automobile Company advertised their latest model, they were pleased to have the world renowned auto body designer's name in their advertisement: "A New Creation By Derham." But the ad also noted: "Paul Whiteman Owns Two Stutz Cars."

Whiteman had signed a contract to appear at the Paramount-Publix Theatres during an extended tour in 1927. Initially, he opened with a six-week run at the Paramount Theatre in New York during June and July. He offered three consecutive shows, two weeks each, of: "Jazz a La Carte" (featuring Ruth Etting); "Ali Baby" (featuring Mildred Vanderhoff Whiteman, Paul's wife, under her stage name of "Vanda Hoff," making a comeback as a dancer); and "Your America" (featuring "unknown" talent). Weekly payroll of $10,500.

Then the band did a string of one-nighters in ballrooms and concert halls, with Whiteman returning to New York, prior to a 40-week tour from September 1927 through July 1928 for Paramount-Publix. The fee was announced at $16,250 per week. It is interesting to note that when Whiteman played the larger cities, such as Chicago and New York, the shows were put together by John Murray Anderson. Some of the top acts were featured: Gilda Gray, Joe Penner, Mae Murray, Bobby Clark, and some of the top women vocalists of the day. At the smaller stops, usually Whiteman featured five acts of vaudeville and 12 female dancers.

Bix and I flew to Indianapolis, Indiana, and landed on October 27, tired as hell, with an uneasy feeling in the pit of our stomachs. We were headed for the Indiana Theatre where Paul Whiteman was appearing when Bix leaned over and said, "Tram, if the big guy tries to knock our price down, let's cut out quick."

"Bix," I said, "this is the beginning of the greatest period in our lives. Well, uh, let's stay a week, at least."

We found the theatre, entered the stage door and stopped. The stage show was on. Never had we heard

music like this before in our lives. We just stood there, like two kids. Oh, we had played with some good bands, that's true, but listening to the King made everything else seem small.

Jimmy Gillespie saw us, and rushed us through a stage door into a packed house, so we could see the show.

"What music," cried Bix. "Aw, Tram, what the hell are we doing here, anyway."

I wondered too. We were completely knocked out by the magnitude of it all.

We made our way backstage after the first show. There was the famous Paul Whiteman, towel around his shoulders. Perspiration literally running off his massive body, which tipped the scales at 300 pounds.

Gillespie said, "Paul, here they are."

"Dammit," yelled Paul. "Come here, you punks. Let the old man hug you!"

He sat Bix on one knee, and me on the other. I think we both felt that the King was a great guy, but little did we know then how great he really was. He could get more out of a score than most composers put into it. I wonder if "Rhapsody In Blue" would have been as successful if Paul played it as Gershwin intended it to be played when he composed it. And—that goes for many works Paul commissioned composers to write for the orchestra.

While Bix and I were introduced to some of the boys, a voice yelled "fifteen." Fifteen minutes before the next performance.

Pops shouted, "Where are your horns? Get those men some clothes. Come on, get out those horns. You're going on with us!"

Lucky for us that he didn't give us time to think it over because I doubt if we could have made it!

There were eight men in the sax section and they took me in charge. I just sat next to Jimmy Dorsey. The "brass men" grabbed Bix. We wore red Eton jackets like the others. Bix sat on the edge of the platform directly in back of me.

There we sat, no music, and all the men glancing our way, now and then, to see what was going to happen. As if we knew! There was Paul, down in front of the band, giving us that big, reassuring smile. I sat there with my mouth open, like a farm boy at his first fair.

Jimmy Dorsey reached over and poked me with that old Albert system clarinet. I came to with a start when I heard him say, "Hey, Tram, the old man wants you to take the next chorus."

Me? Oh, no! How did I get into this? What's the tune? The key? Where the hell's my horn? Oh yes, I'm holding it! Where's Bix? He'll understand if I don't make it, but what about the others? What'll I play?

About that time, a great searing javelin of light from afar, away up from somewhere, hit me in the face and I was on my feet, playing. I played the first half of the chorus and took the break. The band yelled! It broke up Paul, too. I felt a little better then and looked around at Bix. He was laughing but I don't think he meant it, because he knew that he was next. I gave him a familiar lead-in on the ending, and he picked up my phrase and carried on with a beautiful chorus. I dropped to my chair, amid the applause of the audience, and the band. Well, what do you know!

Bix finished and the ovation was deafening! We both took bows. Whiteman introduced us and we took more bows.

After the performance we stood in the wings, exhausted from the excitement. Someone said, "I'll bet you guys could stand a drink."

That was one bet that guy easily won. A far cry from the river boats for Bix, and the Westminister Hall in St. Louis for me.

After the show, Whiteman took us out to eat. What a day for us. The three of us talked of many things and made lots of plans. Then Paul brought up the subject of recording.

"Listen," Whiteman said, "I know you boys have plans for recordings. Go ahead and make them. If your records go over, we'll all benefit by them. I'll give each of you fifty dollars a side for all the records that you want to make with the band, our band, that is! If you're sick, your pay goes right on, and if you need any money, see Gillespie. I'm tired and I'm going to bed. It's been a big day. See you tomorrow."

We just sat there, speechless. What a statement! Brief, but to the point. All of a sudden, Bix let out a whoop and

> **everyone in the restaurant looked at us. We felt a little embarrassed and left quickly.**
>
> **We walked for blocks, talking, planning, and discussing our good fortune. Back in the hotel room, we had a few drinks and just sat and watched the sun come up. I have often wondered what would have happened if we had been able to look into the future. Bix just sat there with the toes of his shoes turned up, looking out the window, saying, over and over, "Boy, that Whiteman! What a guy! What a guy!"**

The next day, as the boys entered the Indiana Theatre, they were pleasantly surprised to find, waiting in the wings, Hoagy Carmichael!

Hoagy, in a conversation of June 1974, related how Bix and Tram introduced him to Paul Whiteman, who both surprised and flattered Hoagy with a reply of "Yes, I've heard of you." Both young men gave Hoagy a big build up to Paul, pointing out that they had recorded one of his tunes ("Riverboat Shuffle") and Red Nichols had recorded both "Riverboat Shuffle" and "Washboard Blues." They convinced Paul to listen to Hoagy play, and he sat down at the piano and offered "Washboard Blues." The maestro listened intently and, when Hoagy was finished, surprised him with the announcement that Paul wanted to record the number with his orchestra. "I thought that he was just being polite," recalled Hoagy, "but he was serious. I couldn't say 'yes' fast enough. Then Whiteman said that he'd like me to be on the recording with his band. Wow!"

Hoagy offered the reason behind his visit to Indianapolis in a September 1962 letter. He was there to talk with Bill Challis about a couple of arrangements that he planned to record for Gennett Records.

> I had a couple of tunes. Bill Challis did try to put the notes down for "One Night in Havana" and "Waltz Supreme." Tommy and Jimmy Dorsey, and a couple of others of the guys in the Whiteman band, did go to Richmond with me on a bus, and I had a guitar player come from Toledo to join us. The guitar player froze on the date and it was a bust, musically. We tried to play rhumba music in "One Night In

Havana'' but it did not come around. It was calypso—this was the first attempt at rhumba music in the United States. We did not know how to use the percussion instruments properly to get the desired effect. Actually, these were pretty bad recordings we did there.

When asked at the June 18, 1974, interview, as to why Bix and Tram were not on these recordings, Hoagy replied, ''I really can't tell you now. Probably because they had just joined Whiteman and were tired. Then again, there was always, 'next time.' As I look back, I wish that I had been able to persuade them to make the date. But that's hindsight now.''

Next stop, St. Louis. Ambassador Theatre. October 29—November 4, 1927.

A friend of mine invited Bix and me to go pheasant hunting on his farm. He told us that he had all of the equipment that he would need.

After we arrived, he outfitted us with guns, ammunition, and even trotted out his prize dog, ''Red.'' He told us where the best hunting would be and started us off in the right direction.

In short time, ''Red'' made a beautiful point, and we flushed out a big cock bird. Oh boy, here I go! I shot away—both barrels at once! Bix didn't even get to shoot. The bird sailed right on into the next field, unharmed!

This happened again and again, only I was careful with the triggers on subsequent tries. Firing both barrels at once, is quite a jolt from a 12-gauge shotgun!

Bix and I finally fired at the same bird and were rewarded with a few feathers. This gave us fresh courage.

I noticed ''Red'' ahead of us. I called out, ''Careful, Bix, here's another. Steady Boy! Steady, 'Red,' steady!''

Two birds flew up in the air. Naturally I fired between them. I think Bix fired in front of them.

Well, ''Red'' looked at Bix and then at me, and took off for home in a slow trot. He ignored our calls and whistles and continued over the hill and out of sight.

We returned to find our farmer friend waiting for us near the barn.

''You know,'' he said, ''when 'Red' came back all alone, I knew how many birds you had. I forgot to tell

you, 'Red' won't hunt long for guys who can't hit the birds that he locates!"

Bix stayed behind for a few days, to spend some time with Ruth, while the Paul Whiteman Orchestra headed for Chicago. He rejoined them on November 7 at the Chicago Theatre.

Bing Crosby, Harry Barris, and Al Rinker were known as "Paul Whiteman's Rhythm Boys." Whiteman had placed them on the Keith-Albee-Orpheum circuit for most of 1927, and now they had rejoined the Whiteman troupe for the Chicago engagements.

Bing and Rinker had left Spokane, Washington, in 1926, bound for Los Angeles seeking their fame and fortune. They chose Los Angeles to start because Rinker's sister, Mildred Bailey (then Mrs. Benny Stafford), was living there and they could be assured of lodgings. After a series of hits and misses, they were booked as "Two Boys and a Piano" at $150 per week for Will Morrisey's Music Hall Revue. Matty Malneck had heard the boys and recommended them to Whiteman, as the Whiteman Orchestra was then appearing in Los Angeles. Whiteman hired them, and they joined his organization in December 1926.

Harry Barris was playing piano with the band, and Whiteman had decided to let him go, but Matty intervened. He pointed out to Whiteman that Barris had written a couple of songs, and maybe something could be worked out with Crosby and Rinker, so why not give it a try? The trio worked out an arrangement on Barris' "Mississippi Mud" offering three-part harmony, and included another tune, "Ain't She Sweet," to sing for Whiteman's approval. He liked what he heard and christened them, "The Rhythm Boys." They became a feature with the band, when Whiteman could secure the money for their services, or else he would find additional employment for them, such as the Keith-Albee-Orpheum Theatre circuit.

While Barris played the piano, Rinker and Crosby would keep time with a drum stick on a cymbal or simply open and shut the lid of Barris' piano in rhythmic time. Their styling was a caricature of the music of the day, humorous in its own way, but definitely unique. At times, a second piano was added with Rinker at the keys; as Bing did not play any musical instrument, he usually was the one that announced the tunes and offered playful patter to the audience, setting the tone for their variety of songs.

Bing well remembered the Whiteman days, during an interview in November 1969:

> In those days, the vocalists of the big bands were not seated alongside the musicians, but were placed in the band. We actually held instruments. Whiteman gave me a peck horn ("a rain catcher"), and pretty soon I got this thing going, and I found a note or two that would work, and I'd blow along with the band. Apparently I found more notes that didn't work because Whiteman took it away from me and handed me a violin with rubber strings. I faked it, and here I was bowing with the best of them. But this didn't suit Whiteman either. The band had a big production number on "1812 Overture," and I was put off stage and told to bang on the chimes. Well, I did! I was beating the hell out of them when the stage manager informed Whiteman that if this continued, we'd probably go through six or seven sets of chimes a season. Whiteman decided that it would be best not to give me an instrument. I was given a chair and told to sit!

Whiteman had a change of heart, seeing Bing just sitting there all alone, so he started giving him solo spots to sing with the band. Slowly a definite singing style started to emerge, and Bing was soon to become the featured singer with the band. Bing's good looks, easygoing nature, and stage presence all presented an impressive figure to a most receptive audience. In addition to his spot with "The Rhythm Boys," he was now billed on the marquee with the other headliners, i.e., Mike Pingitore and his specialty banjo numbers; the muted trumpet of Henry Busse; the fine tenor voice of Jack Fulton, who set many a woman's heart aflutter; and Wilbur Hall's antics.

Wilbur would come on stage, dressed in a rube's outfit, wearing a derby with his hair combed forward so that it hung from under the hat. He then wore two oversized shoes onto which he had attached boards of about three feet in length that allowed him to raise himself upwards to the tip of his toes, and then lean at almost any angle, and all the time playing his violin to "Pop! Goes The Weasel!" His bow would shift positions from behind his back, under his leg, etc., and he never missed a note. Next, he'd produce a trombone and triple tongue the novelty tune, "Nola." He'd finish his act with a bicycle pump, using the hose pressed against the palm of his left hand, while his right hand pumped away! By pressing the hose against his palm, he could control the flow of air, thus producing sounds and wowed the audience with his rendition of "Stars And Stripes Forever."

Hoagy Carmichael showed up as scheduled for the November 18 recording session with the Whiteman Orchestra. Hoagy was now becoming a somber young man, perhaps realizing that there was a place for his songs and his talent in the music business. Hoagy felt that his music might find a place with the smaller groups for recordings, but he never dared to dream that the great Whiteman Orchestra would record his compositions.

Bill Challis had made an arrangement of "Washboard Blues" to be used that day. Bill often discussed arrangement with the musicians that he planned to feature, getting their ideas and input. He worked closely with them, making everyone feel a part of the tune. Challis usually left the solo parts open, relying on the musicians' ability to create a phrase that would complement the arrangement.

The arrangement of "Washboard Blues" was for a scaled down orchestra, without Henry Busse and Mike Pingitore, two of the original musicians from Whiteman's first band. Pingitore, whom Whiteman called the first member of the band because he was the first to show up at the initial rehearsal, could not have cared less about not being on the recording, but not so Henry Busse! Busse let Whiteman know that his contract called for him to make every recording; he felt that he should be doing the record date. It was a decision that Whiteman had to make. He didn't like the idea of having to omit Busse from the date, but he agreed with Bill Challis that an arranger had to have a freedom of expression. Busse soon simmered down, but while he forgave the slight, he never forgot it!

Ferde Grofé tried to make peace. Grofé, who had studied orchestration with Pietro Florida and conducting with Ricardo Dallera, was the granddaddy of all arrangers; Roy Bargy believed Grofé to be the first to put introductions, endings, breaks and other special effects down on paper. As Whiteman's chief arranger, whose arrangements had done more to establish the band's style, Grofé tried to comfort Busse by pointing out that he would include the old guard in all of his offerings. He explained to Busse that Challis was writing for the newer musicians to give them exposure and recognition, while Busse was well established. He urged Busse to give the younger and newer musicians a chance.

Tram's first recording with the Paul Whiteman Orchestra was on November 22, "Among My Souvenirs." He now felt accepted as a member, and when he was presented with an old steamer trunk, just like those all of the musicians had, he knew he was "in." The trunk proclaimed:

FRANK TRUMBAUER
MUSICAL INSTRUMENTS
DON'T DROP
PAUL WHITEMAN'S ORCH. THEATRE

Whiteman concluded his Chicago recording sessions for Victor on November 23 ("Changes") and November 25 ("Mary"). Tram and Bix had stamped their mark on the Whiteman Orchestra, and the trade papers were soon to take notice of that fact.

Trumbauer took his first flying lessons from "Pop" Keller on the south side of Chicago. As was the case throughout his early years of flying, Trumbauer made arrangements to receive instructions from various pilots, depending on the cities that the band was then appearing.

In early December, Whiteman decided to replace Tommy Dorsey. It had become apparent that Tommy was a disrupting force. He had several personality clashes with other members, including his brother, Jimmy. The two were known as "The Battling Dorseys" and often engaged in fist fights at the drop of a hat, but they were the first to defend one another if any of the other musicians had a critical thing to say about one of them.

Bill Challis suggested to Whiteman that he hire Bill Rank. Whiteman sent a wire to Rank at the Strand Theatre in New York, where he was working with Nat Shilkret, and made an offer which Rank immediately accepted. He joined the band in Pittsburgh on December 12.

Robert Mayhew had joined the Whiteman Orchestra replacing Red Nichols, who left in late May. Mayhew's two brothers, Nye and Jack, then members of the Whiteman Orchestra, persuaded Whiteman "to at least listen" to their kid brother, and once given the green light, sent for Bob and told him to report directly to Whiteman. Robert Mayhew, barely into his teens, arrived at Whiteman's hotel and knocked on the door. Whiteman thought that Mayhew was a messenger due to his being dressed in short pants and looking younger than his age. When he realized that this was the trumpet replacement, he reached into his pocket and pulled out a few dollars:

''Here, buy some long pants. I don't talk to kids in short pants about joining my band. Come back when you have some new britches.'' Mayhew got the job.

On closing night in Pittsburgh, Mayhew decided to go down to the nearby newsstand to purchase some comic books to read on the train. He could hardly contain his amusement, when he repeated the story during a June 1956 interview:

> A short while after my trip to the newsstand, I was banging on Bix's hotel room and calling his name. He opened the door, and I rushed in, and told him what had happened to me. Bix about collapsed in hysterical laughter. Trumbauer entered the room, and Bix, trying to get the words out between laughs, said ''Tell Frank what you just told me.''
>
> I decided to go down to the corner and buy some comic books, and when I got there, this woman was just standing there, looking me over. She asked if I was with the Whiteman Band, and I told her that I was. She asked, ''How about a little fun?'' and I told her that I had all of the fun that I could handle being a member of the band. She smiled and said that wasn't what she had in mind. I crossed the street, but she crossed it right after me. Well, I took off running. When I got back to the hotel, I looked back and I didn't see her. I made a bee-line for your room, and if she showed up here, I wanted Bix to tell her to stay away from me.
>
> Do you know what Bix and Tram did for the rest of the tour? Trumbauer would hold open the front door of the hotel, look up and down the street, making certain that the coast was clear, and then he'd wave to Bix, and Bix would escort me out into the street. I really took a ribbing over the incident.

Let me say that the Whiteman Orchestra had their share of practical jokers. Chester Hazlett, a great artist, was first saxophone. He was a practical joker that decided to pick on me, but soon found out that this country boy had a few tricks of his own, so we teamed up, pooled our talents, and went to work on some of the other boys. More about this later on!

Jack Fulton started early in the music business, and as he reflected upon his career during an interview with Jim Gordon in July 1990, he pointed out that the bands of the early days did not have vocalists. He was a pioneer in this area, in addition to being the trombonist with the band, and the earliest tune that he can recall singing with the band was "I'll See You In C-U-B-A." During a later stay with the Mason-Dixon Orchestra, made up of students from West Virginia and Ohio State Universities, Jack formed a vocal trio with future Whiteman members Charles Gaylord and Austin "Skin" Young.

George Olson's 1925 Victor recording of "Who" featured Jack in a vocal trio with Bob Rice and Frank Frey. It was this recording that attracted Whiteman's attention, and he made an offer to Fulton in 1926 to join his band. Whiteman's offer was less money than Fulton was then making with George Olson but he accepted the job based on two factors. Fulton felt that every musician wanted to be a member of Whiteman's Orchestra, and he knew that Whiteman had scheduled a tour to Europe in March 1926, which Fulton could use as a honeymoon trip with his recent bride, Thelma.

The morning of January 1, 1928, the Whiteman Orchestra was en route to New York.

Fulton asked Bill Rank if Bix could take a joke. Rank not only assured Fulton that he could, but he volunteered to assist.[13]

As the train roared towards New York, Bix was asleep in the passenger chair, half bent over but slowly straightened up by Fulton and Rank as they applied stage makeup of rouge, mascara, and powder to Bix's face. They didn't stop with the ordinary heavy beard but added heavy eyebrows and a dab, here and there, for good measure.

When the train arrived in New York, Bix got off in his usual way, completely oblivious to his appearance. As he walked up the street from the station, bags in hand, everyone he passed stopped to gape at him. One lady remarked, "You look pretty funny," to which Bix replied, "you don't look so hot yourself." The more stares that he got, the more he stared back. Finally Bix hailed a taxi for transportation to the hotel. The driver gaped at him in such openmouthed amazement that Bix leered back at him, "Well, do

[13]Story told by Jack Fulton March 27, 1966, during an interview at Ferde Grofés home.

you want to make something of it?'' Bix was prepared to engage the inquisitive driver when he told Bix to look into the mirror. When Bix saw how funny he looked, he fairly howled!

> **There were times when some of the boys got their drinks mixed up with the shows and caused Whiteman many headaches. There was the night when Harry Parella was trying his very best at the piano. The old man was furious with Parella for having that extra drink and gave him a little help with the tempos. Parella was a quarter of a beat behind and in a bad way. Finally, Whiteman looked over at Parella and yelled loud enough for the whole band to hear, "Harry, for God's sake, reach out about even with your navel and you'll find the keyboard."**
>
> **That broke up the band, and needless to say, it never happened again.**
>
> **Harry Parella was walking down the street in Newark, in mid-January, in a dense fog. Parella wore very thick glasses and they became fogged over. This annoyed him, and he jerked them off, just as two men passed by. Unaware of anyone's presence, he muttered "Son of a bitch!" Well, the men thought that he was addressing them and just beat the Be-Jesus out of poor Harry. Parella couldn't fight his way out of a wet paper bag. It just goes to show you what you have to put up with in the music business sometimes.**

The entry of Tram and Bix into the Whiteman Orchestra was clearly hailed by England's **The Melody Maker** in its "Gramophone Review," in early 1928:[14]

> In the course of his career as leader of the world of modern rhythmic music, it has often been said of Paul Whiteman: "Oh! He's finished." And Whiteman quietly laughing up his sleeve has promptly brought out something new which has made his name ring again throughout the civilised universe.
>
> These two dance records ("Changes" and "Mary") are quite different from any of Whiteman's which have so far been issued over here. From a rather "straight" style in

[14]Quoted from 1928 issues of **The Melody Maker** by permission of David Smith, Associate Publisher (September 14, 1990).

which tone colour and more orthodox dance rhythm have been the predominating features, the band has become "red hot," the really wonderful orchestrations catering much more for "hot" individuality.

In both the above titles the irrepressible Bix and Tram are given full score to display their inimitable stylishness, sometimes in solos, at others in "hot" obbligatos, while yet often as playing lead in "hot" movements scored for their respective sections.

The Melody Maker also reviewed Tram's recording date for Okeh on January 9, 1928:

In "There'll Come A Time," Frank Trumbauer's chorus is at his very best, never before have such marvelous breaks for saxophone and cornet been heard as on this side. Listen to the double break by Bix Beiderbecke in the cornet chorus, and to the final sax break by Frank Trumbauer just before the coda. Note here how the last two notes of this are miraculously taken up by Bix from Tram playing sax.

Bing Crosby's recollections of that era, during his November 1969 interview, revealed:

There was a pub, a bistro, on 48th or 49th, just off Broadway, where all of the guys went. The one quality the place had was a piano on the balcony. Bix and all the rest would play and exchange ideas on the piano. With all the noise going on, I don't know how they heard themselves, but they did. I didn't contribute anything, but I listened and I learned. I felt my style then was a cross between Al Jolson and a musical instrument. I was now being influenced by these musicians, particularly horn men. I could hum and sing all of the jazz choruses from the recordings made by Bix, Phil Napoleon, and the rest. Bix, Bill Challis, even Frank Trumbauer, would make suggestions to me for my vocalizing and I'd give it a try. After all, these were the giants of our day, and they knew their music.

One of the greatest records I ever made with Bix was "Mississippi Mud" with Bing Crosby on the vocal. Bix played a chorus that just won't quit! The collectors and record enthusiasts never said much about it, but I always felt it was one of Bix's best!

The January 20, 1928 recording session for Okeh Records began with:

> TRAM: Say there, now now, how come there's ain't no singing in this here record?
> BING: Mister Tram, there's gonna be singing presently of the song.
> TRAM: You-you-you know, I ain't heard no singing yet!
> BING: Well, you just get a load of this song.

In 1969, when asked for his memories on this particular recording, Bing was quite certain that he never sang with Trumbauer on a record. After listening to the recording, he commented, with great humor, "I had a lot of nerve in those days. Me, singing with Tram. I should have been arrested."

> **Yes, by now my dream of returning to New York had come true. I was a featured member of the best band in the world, so the critics said; I had my own recording contract and plenty of money in my pocket.**
>
> **I had now developed a tone that was smooth and close to the human voice.**

February 1928 brought a great many changes into the Whiteman Orchestra. The band now consisted of:

CHARLES MARGULIS: Trumpet, fluegelhorn, melophone.
HENRY BUSSE: Trumpet, fluegelhorn, melophone.
BIX BEIDERBECKE: Cornet, fluegelhorn, melophone.
EDDIE PINDER: Trumpet, fluegelhorn, melophone.
BOYCE CULLEN: Trombone, euphonium.
WILBUR HALL: Trombone, euphonium.
JOHN "JACK" FULTON: Trombone, euphonium, vocalist.
WILLIAM RANK: Trombone, euphonium.
CHESTER HAZLETT: E-flat alto saxophone, B-flat clarinet, E-flat clarinet, bass clarinet, B-flat soprano saxophone.
FRANK TRUMBAUER: C-melody saxophone, E-flat alto saxophone, B-flat soprano saxophone, B-flat clarinet, bass saxophone, bassoon.
CHARLES STRICKFADEN: B-flat tenor saxophone, E-flat alto saxophone, B-flat soprano saxophone, E-flat soprano

saxophone, E-flat baritone saxophone, B-flat clarinet, English horn, oboe, heckelphone.

ROY MAYER: B-flat tenor saxophone, E-flat alto saxophone, B-flat soprano saxophone, E-flat baritone saxophone, B- flat clarinet, flute, piccolo, oboe, English horn, bassoon.

RUPERT CROZIER: E-flat alto saxophone, E-flat tenor saxophone, E-flat baritone saxophone, B-flat soprano saxophone, flute, English horn, B-flat clarinet, contra-bassoon, bassoon, piccolo.

IRVING FRIEDMAN: B-flat tenor saxophone, E-flat alto saxophone, B-flat soprano saxophone, B-flat baritone saxophone, B-flat clarinet.

KURT DIETERLE: Violin. (concertmaster)

MISCHA RUSSELL: Violin.

MATTHEW MALNECK: Violin, arranger.

CHARLES GAYLORD: Violin, vocalist.

MARIO PERRY: Violin, accordion.

JOHN BOWMAN: Violin, librarian.

MICHAEL PINGITORE: Tenor banjo, guitar.

AUSTIN YOUNG: Guitar, vocalist.

MICHAEL TRAFFICANTE: String bass, tuba.

WILFORD LEIBROOK: Tuba, bass saxophone.

ROY BARGY: Piano, arranger.

LENNIE HAYTON: Piano, celeste, arranger.

HAL MAC DONALD: Drums, tympani, traps.

FERDE GROFÉ: Chief arranger.

WILLIAM CHALLIS: Arranger.

THOMAS SATTERFIELD: Arranger.

HARRY "BING" CROSBY: Vocalist.

ALTON RINKER: Vocalist.

HARRY BARRIS: Vocalist.

Irving Friedman's arrival into the Whiteman Orchestra was welcomed with open arms by both Bix and Tram, who used him on their recordings. ''Izzy'' was a very talented clarinet player. As a youth, he played the Indianapolis-Terre Haute area, starting out with a carnival, moving to a stock company, and then playing with a band in a combination motion picture and vaudeville house.

In the mid twenties, he played with the bands of Ross Reynolds and Willard Robison before settling down in Chicago at the

Moulin Rouge, with a band fronted by Eddie Richmond and Eddie Rothchild, former musicians with Sophie Tucker. While in Chicago, he listened to, sat in with, and relieved clarinetist Volle De Faut at the Friar's Inn. Izzy was with Isham Jones when he received an offer from Paul Whiteman, which he accepted in December 1927.

The month of March started off sadly for Tram. He learned of his grandfather's death on the fifth and took the news hard. Even sadder, a few months later, his grandmother passed away. Trumbauer felt that medical science put some statement on her death certificate, but he confided that he felt that Parolee died of a broken heart, grieving for Henry's loss.

Paul Whiteman reopened at the Paramount Theatre on the final day of March, and settled in for four new shows during their three-week stay: "Rainbow Rhapsody" with The Lenora Dancers; "Knick Knacks" with The Foster Girls; "Say It With Music" with The Albertina Rasch Dancers; and, "Broadway Blues" with a dance company billed as "The Ingenues." John Murray Anderson, who wound up his career as Musical Director for Ringling Brothers, Barnum and Bailey Circus, put the shows together.

During an engagement at the Paramount Theatre in April 1928, Chet and I placed a firecracker in a pound can of cold cream in our dressing room. We lit it and stood back to see what would happen.

The explosion tore the can to bits, showered the room and ceiling with cold cream and left a fine mist of grease all over our uniforms. It cost us fifty dollars to clean up the debris. We didn't repeat the trick, ever again.

Whiteman decided to end his eight-year association with Victor Records. Trumbauer's C-melody saxophone remains a part of the legacy Whiteman left in that catalog. Among many examples, Tram had sixteen-bar solos on "Ol' Man River" and "There Ain't No Sweet Man," and eight-bar solos on "Dardanella," "Sugar," "When," and "My Pet." He is heard on bassoon in "Chloe" and "High Water." And the final recording of "You Took Advantage of Me" contains a classic chase chorus of 32 bars with Bix, which Tram described as "sort of an extraneous tune that makes for easy listening."

Henry Busse, still unhappy about the decreasing number of

solos given to him on the recordings, felt uncertain about the move to Columbia Records. It was, at best, an open secret that Busse had negotiated with Frank Cromwell to take over his entire band at Jansen's Hafbrau, a restaurant on Broadway, and lead the band into the Club Richman, owned by Harry Richman, noted Brunswick recording artist. Busse honestly believed that Whiteman would not let him out of his contract, so during the next-to-last Victor recording session, April 24, he engaged Whiteman in a heated argument, which resulted in the boss firing him right on the spot! Busse must have felt that he put one over on the old man, but Whiteman had heard the same rumors and had already discussed with Jan Garber the prospect of hiring Harry Goldfield from his band. When Busse left, "Goldie" was a telephone call away, and played on the recording session the very next day!

Harry "Goldie" Goldfield was very similar to Whiteman in build and moustache, and Whiteman would often joke to the audience that Goldie had been in his band so long that he was starting to look like him. Goldie was hired to assume the role that Busse had fulfilled since the beginning of the band. Whiteman wanted to maintain the tunes associated with Busse, and Goldie adapted the Busse style and continued the sound so familiar on "Hot Lips," "Wang Wang Blues," "When Day Is Done," and other Busse features. The public had these recordings in their collections; and when they heard the band in person, they wanted to hear these tunes, played exactly as they sounded on the recordings, and Whiteman obliged.

> **Goldie had trouble sleeping when he first joined the band because of the noise in the hotels, so he brought some sleeping pills. Chet and I replaced the sleeping pills with No-Doze pills.**
>
> **Goldie would take a pill and go to bed. In an hour, he'd be so wide awake that he'd take another pill. Still no sleep!**
>
> **"Paul, I feel like a zombie," Goldie said. "I take these pills and go to bed. I'm asleep but I can't get my eyes to close. There's something wrong with me. I know it!"**
>
> **It was two days before Goldie found out what we had done. Man, was he really on the warpath then!**

The Melody Maker, of June 1928, commented on the move from Victor to Columbia:

> . . . Whiteman has today what is considered by practically all the most competent authorities to be the finest and most stylish dance band extant.
>
> Though Whiteman has always been a leading figure in the world of rhythmic music, like most others, he has had his ups and downs. But never has his band been finer than it is at the moment. And Whiteman is playing "hot"!
>
> . . . Not only is the individual musicianship of a class which is beyond compare, but the orchestrations and the mode of the using vocal effects mark yet another era in a type of music which having outgrown the crudeness of its youth, now moves from one stage of excellence to another so rapidly that it has left the big-wigs of "straight" music in a state of complete bewilderment.[15]

[15]Quoted from June 1928 issue of **The Melody Maker** by permission of David Smith, Associate Publisher (September 14, 1990).

CHAPTER EIGHT

PAUL WHITEMAN—THE COLUMBIA YEARS 1928–1929

WHITEMAN'S CONTRACT WITH COLUMBIA RECORDS called for a yearly guarantee of $50,000 and contained a two-year extension clause, beginning May 1, 1928.

More than one of Whiteman's musicians grumbled when it was learned that recording director Eddie King had switched from Victor Records to Columbia Records.

Columbia Records was eager to build a reserve of Whiteman recordings and had the band in the studios as quickly as possible. Some of the early selections turned out to be the best: "The Man I Love," on which Tram had 16 bars (he remarked that this was one of his best recordings); "Felix The Cat," on which Tram had 14 bars; and "'Tain't So," with 16 bars on bassoon. Quickly the band filled the sales departments with their recordings.

The band was booked into the Capitol Theatre in Detroit, for a week, starting May 26.

> **Bix had a front tooth that was false. A pivot tooth. On opening night, the tooth became very loose. There wasn't any time to see a dentist, so for several days Bix was careful not to lose it.**
>
> **It was almost showtime and we were taking our places on the stage when something funny happened. Bix let out a big laugh and out popped the tooth!**
>
> **"Hold the curtain," yelled Bix.**
>
> **Everyone fell to the floor and began looking for Bix's tooth.**
>
> **"I can't hold this curtain any longer," the stage manager said. "Here she goes!"**

Bix ran for his chair as the curtains parted. At that instant, I spied the tooth. "Catch, Bix," I said, as I tossed the found item to him.

Bix caught the tooth, snapped it into place just in time to play the introduction.

Without the tooth, Bix couldn't have played a single note!

July found the band booked into Chicago for short stays at the Chicago Theatre (2–8), Uptown Theatre (9–15), and Tivoli Theatre (16–22).

In one of our stage shows, Goldie had a featured number that he did in front of the band. Roy Bargy and I bought a large supply of firecrackers that sounded like a four inch field gun when discharged. We timed it so that at the exact moment Goldie delivered his punch line, the lighted firecrackers went off behind him. It almost blew him into the orchestra pit. The band got a big laugh out of it, but I don't think the audience thought that it was funny. Nevertheless, we kept this up until Goldie's punch line was a total loss.

Whiteman gave the band a much deserved vacation, with Trumbauer taking time to return to St. Louis and spend time with Mitzi and their son, Bill. The vacation ended with all members returning to New York for a brief eastern tour and recordings. Whiteman had arranged a Transcontinental Concert Tour, starting in October, that would cover half of the United States. This one-nighters tour was booked over the next few months; realizing that the members needed proper rest, they were booked into a hotel in each city to assure a good night's sleep. Before they left, Whiteman arranged a farewell party.

Paul gave a costume party and invited the band. The bar was four deep, and I noticed a nice looking guy in a cowboy outfit trying to get a glass of beer. I went to his rescue.

"Look, Jack," I said. "You go get the sandwiches—I'll get the beer and meet you over there in the corner."

"Okay," he said and left.

We had a nice chat over our beer and sandwiches. I noticed that everyone spoke to my new friend as they passed us.

Finally he said, "I know you'll excuse me. I have to join some of my friends."

I had been talking with Jimmy Walker, the mayor of New York.

We started the tour the next day, and we had a very early morning jump to make. Johnny Fulton and I were standing on the railroad station platform when Bix appeared with the huge English bag that he always carried. He looked like he'd had a rough night.

"Watch my bag while I get some coffee," Bix said as he left for the coffee shop.

It was then that Johnny noticed a brake shoe on the tracks in front of us. Apparently it had fallen from a railroad car. Brake shoes weigh about twenty-five pounds.

Johnny and I looked at each other. Without saying a word, we picked up the shoe, wrapped it in a newspaper, and placed it in the bottom of Bix's bag, underneath his clothes.

When we got on the train, we found Whiteman and told him the story. We walked through the cars until we found Bix.

"Hi, Bix, how you feeling, boy?" Whiteman asked him.

"Paul, I'm gonna have to see a doctor in the next town. I'm so weak I can hardly lift my bag!"

Well, Whiteman laughed until he cried before he finally told Bix what had happened.

Bix seldom paid much attention to the country that we passed through. One day, however, he decided to sit next to the window and look out—a rare occasion for Bix. Just about that time a freight train that seemed miles long passed his window, obstructing his view.

"How do you like that?" Bix said. "The first time I look out the window and what do I see? Nothin'! There's a million square miles of space in this country and they had to drag that damn freight train past my window. Nuts!"

And with that, he pulled down the shade.

The tour started down the East Coast, then into the Deep South, over to Texas, and then up through the Midwest. Each day a different city.

> **One night, on one of our longer jumps, "Skin" Young became very uppity. We always had two pullman cars for those trips. "The cattle car" and "the longhair car." The latter was for the boys who didn't play poker or drink and had a silly idea that sleep was more important. Many times since, I've wished I'd taken up quarters in "the longhair car."**
>
> **On this particular night, both cars were "cooking" strongly.**
>
> **Finally, Skin put on his robe and slippers and went through the train until he found an empty berth, crawled into it, and went to sleep.**
>
> **The next morning, everyone was in his berth but Skin. Paul started a search of the entire train but he could not find a trace of him! He finally learned that the car Skin was sleeping in had been removed from the train during the night.**
>
> **Now Skin didn't have any clothes with him, that was for sure, and he didn't have any money or identification. And, we had no way of knowing where to wire or call him.**
>
> **We reached the town where we were to play, and checked into our hotel. No word from Skin.**
>
> **Very late that night, there was a knock at Paul's door. He opened it and there stood Skin. He was wearing bedroom slippers without any socks, pants three sizes too big, and an old topcoat over his pajamas and robe, with a pullman porter's cap that was so large that it fell down over his ears.**
>
> **"I quit!" he shouted. "I'm through running around the country dressed like this. I wish you'd get these railroads straightened out."**
>
> **Paul laughed as only he could. He finally broke up Skin, too!**

The lengthy stay on the train was very trying on everyone, and suddenly it was becoming evident that Bix was drinking far too much. Trumbauer spoke to him and Bix assured Tram that it wasn't anything that he couldn't handle. Four days prior to their concert in Sioux City, Iowa, Bix stopped drinking.

As expected, Bix's family members and a large group of friends from Davenport attended the concert. Bix acted like a schoolboy, after the performance, ushering his family and friends backstage to meet all of the musicians, and was proud as he could be when Whiteman remarked to Bix's parents of how important Bix was to the band.

Unfortunately, within the next couple of days, the illness returned to Bix, and he was drinking more heavily than before.

> **Bix was now getting out of hand, and Paul asked me to try and straighten him out. I promised that I would do my best, but that wasn't enough. What influence I ever had with Bix was now gone!**

Bix suffered a breakdown in Cleveland, November 30, and the band left him behind in a hospital. Whiteman was assured that it was best for Bix, and he'd received the best of care. Reluctantly, Whiteman agreed. What other choice did he have?

The band played Detroit on December 3, and were guests afterwards at a party hosted by famed aviator, Eddie Rickenbacker. Trumbauer was able to get Rickenbacker to autograph a copy of his book: **Fighting the Flying Circus.** The inscription read: "With my very best wishes to Frank Trumbauer. (signed) Capt. Eddie Rickenbacker, 1928."

> **During the evening, Eddie sold Paul two Cadillacs. And Paul with a custom built Stutz on order at the time. He later offered to sell me the Stutz—payments to be made from my recording dates. How could I turn down an offer like that? A $5,600 car with racing tires and special body that could go over a hundred miles an hour. Paul had already sold his Stutz Blackhawk to Jimmy Gillespie.[16]**

---

[16]On January 1, 1928, Eddie Rickenbacker went to work as a spokesman for General Motors to help market their new LaSalle automobile, but he was also promoting Cadillacs. It was considered a coup when Eddie was able to get Paul to switch from the Stutz to the Cadillac automobile.

The tour concluded in December, and the band, once again, returned to the recording studios. Bix rejoined the band for the session of December 11.

> **At one of these dates, Bix was trying to get a nap between numbers. Someone gave him a "hot foot." Bix jumped up and said, "Okay, school boy, pass me a clam."**
>
> **Eddie King, somewhat of a nemesis for Bix, during his recording career, had a lengthy discussion with Paul about Bix's stability. Paul defended Bix as a father would a son. Paul could clearly see what was happening to Bix, but he was still a member of the band, and he was one of Paul's musicians. Paul never wavered in his loyalty to his musicians!**
>
> **Remembering Bix's remark about the clam, the boys started calling our recording dates, "clambakes!"**

Roy Bargy's interview of November 1969, discussed that "damn train trip," and added:

> I approached Paul about doing an arrangement of "Liebestraum" for a recording date.
>
> "Sure, Roy," said Paul. "I encourage all of my musicians to submit arrangements that we might use. I pay a standard fee of $75 for every one that we use."
>
> Paul set up a rehearsal for the tune and told me that he would not be conducting the tune, as he had business elsewhere. He suggested that I conduct the arrangement. Unbeknown to me, Paul had set up this gag with the other musicians.
>
> I gave the down beat and what resulted was a few of the guys started blowing sour notes, a handful of arrangements were tossed into the air, and a barrage of spit-balls showered down on me.
>
> Once order was restored, I said, "let's take it from the top again. This time play the tune as arranged! I don't remember assigning any spit balls to the sections."
>
> We got through the number and ended up recording it—minus spit balls!

On December 29, the band opened Flo Ziegfeld's "Whoopee," at the new Amsterdam Theatre with Eddie Cantor, and played the famous Ziegfeld Roof Cafe after the show, closing on January 11,

1929. They did double duty by playing the Palace Theatre from December 30 to January 5.

The New Amsterdam Theatre was located at 214 West 42nd Street and was built by Abe Erlanger. When it officially opened on September 4, 1906, it was the marvel of its day. The lobby consisted of new chrome, mirrors, original paintings and sculptures. The auditorium featured a huge stage. Flo Ziegfeld opened his first ''Follies'' at the theatre in 1913 but felt something was missing. He decided that the stage needed a new look, and he sought a room on the roof where he could provide entertainment before and after the show. Gene Buck, Ziegfeld's chief lieutenant, persuaded Ziegfeld to accompany him to a 1914 play entitled ''The Garden Of Paradise.'' Flo was so impressed with designer Joseph Urban's work that he hired him to design both his stage productions and ''The Roof.''

Urban had come to America in 1912, when he was appointed stage director of the Boston Opera. His reputation in Europe was unequaled; between 1904 and 1912, Urban had designed over 50 productions for the foremost theatres abroad.

For the ''Follies,'' Urban applied paints to the canvas backdrops of the stage by use of a technique used by many artists of the Impressionist School but new to scenic design. He avoided dark colors, preferring pastels, and achieved effects that he wanted with lighting.

Ziegfeld's Follies were designed with the American Woman being featured in all her glory, but each show featured an outstanding star of the day, such as Bert Williams (1914), W. C. Fields (1915), Fanny Brice (1916), Will Rogers (1917), and Marilyn Miller (1918).

''The Roof'' (as it was widely known) was not actually on the roof of the theatre, but a room at the top of the building. Urban turned this into a glittering night club with a moveable stage, glass balconies, and cross-lighting to create a stunning rainbow effect. The room featured intertable telephones, dancing, and after dinner supper with fine wines.

Helen Morgan, currently appearing in the stage production of ''Show Boat'' as Julie, was the featured attraction now. She would appear after the closing of the Broadway show, and sing one number with the Whiteman Band. Then she'd oblige the audience with *one* encore.

Dudley Field Malone gave a cocktail party for the Whiteman Band before the opening of "Whoopee" and some of the boys had that "extra drink."

Showtime came and we took our places on stage. The air was filled with excitement! All those beautiful Ziegfeld beauties running around backstage made it pretty hard for me to concentrate on my music.

Paul said, "Fellows, let's make a good showing tonight. Ziegfeld is out front."

The curtains opened and the famous Tamara Geva entered from the wings. Paul gave the downbeat for her number. Something was wrong!

Paul started screaming, "Follow me! Follow me!"

Too late, though. Charlie Margulis, our first trumpet player had the wrong music. He thought that he was right, and we were wrong. I guess he thought he would be a hero and save the day because he began to play twice as loud. We followed Paul, but trying to drown out Margulis was like trying to drown out a locomotive whistle with three flutes and an oboe.

Fortunately Geva's dance was short. But Paul was livid!

"Get me a pistol. Somebody kill that son-of-a-bitch. I'll tear him apart with my hands!"

During the finale, the stage was supposed to roll out over the orchestra pit. Paul was still in a violent rage as the stage started to move forward. He thought something was wrong and ran off the stage into the wings. He then realized what had happened and tried to get back on but once the platform was out it was impossible to get on or off stage.

Eddie Cantor climbed up over the back of the set and came down through the orchestra to the front of the stage, grabbing a drum stick on the way and swinging it in every direction.

About that time, Ziegfeld was seen running up the aisle, pulling his hair!

The audience seemed to think it was part of the act.

The stage rolled back into place, and Paul came out and took bows with the other stars, and everyone was happy.

No one but the fabulous Paul Whiteman, could have gotten away with that one.

After the show, we appeared on "The Roof." Each

elevator was packed with celebrities ascending to hear our band. Opening night was a star-studded event with Helen Morgan, Eddie Cantor, and such ravishing beauties as Hazel Forbes, Gladys Glad, and Jane Ackerman performing with the band.

The cover charge for this special night was $16.50 per person. The tables were going between $500 to $1,000. Everyone in New York seemed to be present. Mayor Jimmy Walker, George Gershwin, Peggy Joyce, Jim Barton, Moran and Mack, and Fanny Brice, who was coaxed onto the stage to sing her famous rendition of ''Rose Of Washington Square.''

Bee Palmer, one of the Ziegfeld girls, was a beautiful blond who possessed a most unusual voice. Her phrasing and interpretation of a song was just about fifteen years ahead of the times. Strange as it may seem, Bee turned down various offers to record, and sang in her own apartment among friends. Lennie Hayton was always there to play piano for Bee.

Ted Koehler, the lyricist who wrote such great hits as ''Stormy Weather'' and ''Wrap Your Troubles In Dreams,'' wrote two choruses of special lyrics to ''Singin' The Blues'' for Bee. Lyrics for Bix's chorus and my chorus.

Bix and I were invited to her apartment to hear them. As always, Bee sat on the floor in the middle of the room, and sang to us. That girl held everyone spellbound.

Bee did record with Trumbauer on January 10, 1929, for Columbia Records, but the tunes were never issued. In later years, Vince Giordano was able to purchase unissued tests of the two tunes recorded that day, ''Singin' The Blues'' and ''Don't Leave Me, Daddy'' and the results were very disappointing, as the microphones failed to capture her talent fully.

Whiteman had sent Bix to a rest spot on Long Island in December and felt that it had helped, but Whiteman was really clouding his judgment with wishful thinking. A second breakdown resulted in Whiteman sending Bix to Davenport for as much rest as he needed.

CHAPTER NINE

OLD GOLD BROADCASTS 1929

UPON CLOSING IN NEW YORK, the band's next engagement was at the Music Hall in Cincinnati, January 13–19, 1929.

> **We were firecracker happy in those days. One time in Cincinnati, Johnny Fulton was vocalizing in a huge marble ballroom. There was a wide crack under the door. Chet and I saw it at the same time. We grabbed a firecracker, lit it, and threw it under the door. What a blast! Poor Johnny couldn't hear anything for a week. Everyone wondered why he sang out of tune, and we realized then that it should never be repeated as the results could have been serious.**
>
> **For some reason, Johnny blamed Chet for the incident and vowed to get even, if it was the last thing he did.**
>
> **One day, Chet had just taken a shower and had no clothes on. We heard a knock at the door. Johnny opened it and, quick as a flash, he pushed Chet out into the corridor.**
>
> **About that time the elevator door opened and several men and women got out and started down the hall in Chet's direction.**
>
> **Luckily there was a trunk in the hall and Chet jumped behind it. He began yelling, "Don't come any closer. I don't have any clothes on!"**
>
> **They must have thought that he was insane and retreated.**
>
> **After a truce had been made, Johnny opened the door and let Chet back in. After that, Johnny joined up with us.**

Next stop—Detroit, Michigan—January 27 to February 2.

Whiteman discussed hiring one of Jean Goldkette's musicians, a cornetist from Muncie, Indiana, Andy Secrest. Whiteman told Goldkette that it would be for a short time, until Bix returned. Secrest, quick to admit that he did not copy Bix, note-for-note, still produced "Bixian" sound that was good enough for Whiteman. Whiteman felt that Secrest could step right in and handle Bix's tunes, that the "sound" would still be there. He regarded Secrest as an insurance policy. As Whiteman had replaced Busse with Goldfield and kept "the Busse sound," so did he replace Nichols with Bix, and now Secrest, to maintain that same "hot style!"

Charlie Margulis was known as "The Great Gabbo" to me, and the boys were identifying him with the nickname I had selected. During our stay in Detroit, a young lad came to see "Gabbo," during an intermission. He identified himself as a student of the trumpet and he wondered if Mr. Margulis would show him a few things? Gabbo was all puffed up with pride and told the kid to come into the dressing room. The boy produced a music book for trumpet methods and selected a page for them to play. Pretty soon it was obvious that this young man could really play the trumpet. He kept turning the pages to more difficult selections, and it was all that Margulis could do to keep up with him. He asked the boy his name and was told that it was Raphael Mendez! Margulis told the boy to keep practicing and someday he would make the big time, too.

As the Whiteman Orchestra returned to New York, Whiteman was discussing the party that he and Kurt Dieterle had attended one night during their Cincinnati engagement. Whiteman went on to tell Tram that he met an aviator there and discussed the possibility of purchasing an airplane, if that aviator would fly it to a hangar on Long Island. Whiteman said if the deal went through, Tram could use the airplane at times. Tram further learned that the pilot had flown during World War I, and Tram felt that maybe he might coax him into some instructions and possible "war stories."

Dieterle continued the story in a November 1989 letter:

Charles Gaylord and Skin Young called Tram aside, and asked, "Tram, what are you doing? Haven't you any respect for Kurt Dieterle's feelings?" The two went on to tell Tram of attending a film, **Wings,** with Dieterle some time before, and they were surprised to learn that Dieterle had been a flyer for the United States during the war. Charlie Strickfaden was so impressed with the news that he wanted to send to Washington for Dieterle's service record.

"It was then," continued Skin, "that we found out a tragic thing happened. In one of the dog fights over Germany, Dieterle shot down a German airplane. He later learned that it was a cousin of his that he killed, and it upset him so much that to this day, Dieterle cannot talk about it."

"And you, Tram," picked up Gaylord, "you start talking about flying, the war, and we could just see Dieterle's face reliving those days and recalling that horrible incident. You should really be proud of yourself."

"Believe me, fellows," Tram pleaded, "I didn't know anything about it."

Tram summoned up his courage and came over and sat down beside me.

"Kurt," Tram said, "I want to apologize for any embarrassment that I might have caused you. I didn't know about your shooting down your cousin during the war. I know that you don't want to talk about it, but maybe you could make an exception now."

"Where did you get that idea?" I asked. "I was never in the war."

We spotted Gaylord and Young, seated across the aisle, and when we shot a glance at them, all they did was shrug their shoulders and look innocent.

On February 5, Whiteman signed a contract with the P. Lorillard Company, makers of Old Gold cigarettes, for a weekly radio program to be broadcast nationwide every Tuesday night. Whiteman received the sum of $5,000 weekly for the series, and it was designed to offset the strong influence that Lucky Strike cigarettes had exerted over America's smokers with their Saturday night programs featuring the B. A. Rolfe Orchestra.

The sponsor wanted Whiteman to be involved with announcing the tunes on the program, but Whiteman felt that the announcer hired for the broadcasts, Ted Husing, would better serve that purpose. The sponsor argued that they were paying Whiteman a good deal of money and that his voice would be welcomed by the listening public and help with the value of the program. Although he was against it, Whiteman summoned his courage and, with the help of his valet and a few sips of scotch from a flask, got over his opening night jitters, did a good job on the initial broadcast, and continued to do an outstanding job thereafter. The old man learned to speak to the microphone as if he was just telling his story to another person, and his opening night fears completely disappeared.

The next night, the band reopened at the New Amsterdam Theatre, playing on "The Roof" for "Ziegfeld's Midnight Frolics." Ziegfeld envisioned the "Midnight Frolics" as a training ground for potential stars and a source of ideas to try out for the major production downstairs.

During a March 1966 interview, Andy Secrest well remembered opening night:

> The Duncan Sisters were set to do a number with the band. Whiteman gave the downbeat and nothing happened. The girls were next to Roy Bargy's piano, but they simply missed their cue. Whiteman gave an annoying look at them, and started again. This time, Bargy gave a piano arpeggio, running his hands from the left side of the keys to the right, and when he finished he reached over and "goosed" one of the sisters. Startled, they both jumped forward on cue. All through their number, they kept an eye on Bargy.
>
> **The newspaper said that Whiteman had to struggle along with a mere $13,000 a week.[17]**
>
> **Skin Young showed up, as a gag, wearing an opera cape and gold-handled cane. He felt if the newspapers said that we were making all of that money, we should dress the part.**
>
> **Paul took one look at Skin and yelled, "Get the hell out of that rig, and get on stage, or else you'll have a chance to show it to the folks back home!"**

Skin took deep offense to Whiteman's remark and served his notice, right on the spot!

---

[17]Paulette Ziegfeld was unable to locate any of Flo Ziegfeld's ledgers that showed the amount of money paid to the band, but Whiteman, himself, received $1500 weekly.

> During all this glamour, Charlie Strickfaden and I spent our intermissions in a back room, practicing knife throwing. I might add that we were pretty good, too. We repeatedly hit playing cards from a great distance, much to the amazement and amusement of the bus boys.
>
> A "fine" system was put into effect in an attempt to stop the boys from being late. One dollar a minute. Proceeds to be used for parties.
>
> Lennie Hayton contributed one hundred and fifty dollars to that fund in short order. He just couldn't make it on time.
>
> Mike Pingitore recorded all the fines in a little black book. "The Devil," as Venuti and Lang were later to call him, and his little black book drove everyone crazy.
>
> "The Devil" never put a penny into the fund, so we decided to try and catch him.
>
> Where Strick and I were throwing knives, there was a small staircase. During one intermission, Pingitore was watching us. We suddenly ran up the stairs for the bandstand, leaving Pingitore behind. Now Pingitore had a bad leg and couldn't make those as fast, and he was two minutes late. But, although we tried like hell, that was the best we could do!
>
> Poor Pingitore! We really gave him a bad time but he always laughed it off. Periodically we would steal his cane, remove the tip, cut off a quarter of an inch and replace the tip.
>
> "I must be growing," Pingitore said one day. "My cane's getting so short I can hardly touch the ground. Eventually Pingitore caught us in the act.

Bix returned to the band in March 1929. Eddie Pinder was let go.

> There comes the question of strangulation of men like Bix in a great band such as the Whiteman organization. A very unfair and cruel article, and to my knowledge, the only one of its kind, was written in subsequent years by an attorney in England. It appeared in a magazine called Swing.[18] Apparently this man's sole knowledge on the subject came from listening to a few recordings.

---

[18]Trumbauer was referring to the December 1940 issue of **Swing.**

I was accused of being responsible for the failure of Bix Beiderbecke. It was stated that after six months with Whiteman, Bix found himself, more and more in the background; that his only chance to express his musical emotions was through his recordings with his friend, Frank Trumbauer. But, the story went on, Tram used less and less of Bix's abilities on those Okeh dates.

As if anyone could have caused Bix's failure! Bix was consulted about every single record date. We discussed these dates well in advance and Bix even helped me make many of our arrangements.

Bix had the complete facilities and financial backing of the Whiteman Band. Months after Bix decided, in his own mind, that he was not playing up to standard, we tried, again and again, to get him to record on some of our dates. He did not want to record with prominent names because he felt that he wasn't playing well. That alone shows how intelligent he was. He decided, after April 1929, not to make any more recordings with Okeh Records until he felt that he was returning to his old form.

I honestly feel that Bix made constant progress from the time he joined my band in St. Louis in 1925, and on through the Whiteman days until the end of 1928.

It is true that playing with a large orchestra of twenty-five to thirty men had its drawbacks for men like Bix and me. However, if Whiteman had permitted the band to jam constantly in order to satisfy a few people who wanted to hear Bix and me, his success as a leader would have been jeopardized.

Bix loved Whiteman as much as I did, and was proud of his association with the band.

Even though Bix and I went on different paths at the end of 1928, we were still closer than most people thought. Whenever there was trouble, he always found me, and I tried to help in every way possible. And, that went for Whiteman, too! But when Bix departed on that voyage that was to take him out of this world, neither Whiteman nor I could have helped him!

Carl Laemmle, president of Universal Studios in Hollywood, first approached Whiteman about his doing a musical in November 1928. He assured Whiteman that this would be the ''biggest'' and "finest" of all talking musicals that were put on film as a result of the success of Jolson's **The Jazz Singer,** which sent all of the Hollywood Studios searching for just the right talent for their own musicals to match Warner Brothers' bonanza. The talks heated up during January and February 1929, and finally Whiteman put his name on the dotted line. Laemmle agreed to build two sound stages on the Universal lot for the film.

On April 28, 1929, the post of General Manager of Universal Studios was awarded to Carl Laemmle, Jr., on his twenty-first birthday. Carl Jr. inherited the decision-making on the Whiteman film. He decided to send Paul Fejos, who was to direct the film, and screenwriter Edmund Lowe to New York for discussions with Whiteman.

Fejos was a bit concerned about doing the film and welcomed suggestions from Whiteman. Fejos suggested a film showing the history of the band, but Whiteman nixed the idea. Fejos next suggested a history of the band, but with studio musicians. The old man turned that idea down quickly, saying "Any film about me includes my band!"

Finally Fejos sold Whiteman on a musical variety film featuring the entire band. L. Wolfe Gilbert and Abel Baer had been signed to compose new songs for the film, and Whiteman agreed to send Ferde Grofé back with them, so he could begin arranging the new tunes into the band's style. Whiteman was given a $50,000 "good will offer," a handshake, a pat on the back, and "We'll see you in Hollywood" by Paul Fejos.[19]

Bix's final recording date with Trumbauer on the Okeh label, occurred on April 30, when they cut two numbers: "No One Can Take Your Place" and "I Like That." Bix's embouchure betrayed him a bit, and he used a derby mute on the final tune to hide the imperfections.

The critics of **The Melody Maker** were generous in their praise of Trumbauer's work during Whiteman's May recordings: Of "Reaching For Someone": "There is a marvelous hot saxophone chorus by Frank Trumbauer and an equally marvelous vocal chorus by Bing Crosby . . . Trumbauer excels himself . . . a great chorus and a great record." Of "When Dreams Come True": "There is a really beautiful vocal by Jack Fulton which should be

[19]For details of contract, see chronology section: 28 June 1929.

studied by all singers of dance music. . . . Chester Hazlett shines with a sub-tone clarinet passage, which is taken up from him in marvelous style by Trumbauer.''

Any doubts Whiteman might have had about taking Bix to Hollywood were quickly dismissed after the recordings made that first week in May. The tunes were ''China Boy'' and ''Oh! Miss Hannah.'' Both were big hits for the band, and Bix sounded like his old self, taking 16 bars on each recording, as did Trumbauer. Whiteman was convinced that everything was set for their trip west.

Joe Venuti and Eddie Lang were added to the band, and it was a party of seventy that boarded the Union Pacific train on May 24. When they left the Pennsylvania Station, they had nine cars, thirty-five musicians, vocalists and arrangers, and Whiteman's own staff of electricians, plus Jimmy Gillespie and Hugo Hass from the Whiteman Office. The P. Lorillard Company sent along their vice president, E. G. Weymouth, to cash in on the publicity and to tell one and all of how the Old Gold Cigarette Company was working hand-in-hand with the Whiteman Orchestra and Universal Studios. Rounding out the troupe were some friends and several newspapermen.

''The Old Gold Special'' (as the train was called) was colorfully decorated and adorned with the familiar Paul Whiteman caricature.[20] Arrangements were made to do their weekly radio program en route to Hollywood, in addition to a few public appearances.

Joe Venuti well remembered the trip, during a February 1966 interview:

> Our train was crossing the Utah desert when I came upon a sleeping Bix. At the end of each passenger car was a bucket of sand to be used in case of fire. This was long before fire extinguishers. I went through the cars, gathering up as many as I could, and carefully dumped the sand onto Bix, the seat next to him, and all around the floor. Then I sat back and waited for him to awake.
>
> Finally Bix awoke, noticed all of the sand around him, and was startled by it!

[20]The caricature was that of Whiteman's head, as appeared on his Columbia Records and elsewhere. The musicians referred to it as ''The Potato Head.''

> "What happened?" Bix shouted. "Where did all of this sand come from?"
>
> I rushed over to calm him. "Don't worry, Bix," I assured him, "we've got most of it cleaned up. I don't know how you do it. The conductor said it was the worst sand storm that he'd ever seen, and you slept right through it all!"
>
> "Why didn't someone wake me up?" panicked Bix. "I could have suffocated."

The transcontinental journey stopped long enough in San Bernardino to pick up director Paul Fejos and starlet Evelyn Pierce. The train arrived in Los Angeles on June 6, and were met by executives from Universal Studios. The stop was brief, and they continued to San Francisco for a week's engagement at the Pantages Theatre.

Upon arriving at the San Francisco station, the entourage was driven to the hotel, where an army of reporters awaited Whiteman.[21] Whiteman tried to push past them to the desk, but was halted several feet short by a surrounding press.

"Boys," he shouted, "get your news from Gillespie. He has our itinerary and he knows all the details. Talk to him."

Whiteman spotted the desk clerk and shouted over the questioning reporters. "Hey, make certain that my room is a big one. I'm a big man, and I need a lot of space!" The flashes from cameras temporarily blinded Whiteman, and one reporter pursued the subject that Whiteman had just brought up:

"Just how big are you . . . Paul?"

The old man decided that he might as well answer a few questions. "A couple of years ago," Whiteman said, "when I got back from Germany, I'd lost 87 pounds. I know that my weight then was 262. I also know that I didn't feel right at that weight, and I am certain that I've gained most of it back. But if you mugs think that I'm getting on a scale for you, you're crazy!"

"One more question, Paul. This movie that you're doing. Is it about jazz music?"

"I haven't seen the script yet," answered Whiteman, "but I can tell you one thing. Jazz is losing out to the slower rhythms. You might print that and quote me!"

Following the San Francisco stay, the band boarded a train for

[21]Information compiled from pages of the *Los Angeles Examiner,* June 6, 7, 8, 1929.

Los Angeles. Their "official" arrival was June 15. They were met by a host of convertible automobiles and paraded to city hall,where Mayor Creyer presented Whiteman with the key to the city.

Universal studios turned out movie stars Reginald Denny, Laura La Plante, Kathryn Crawford, and John Boles, and notable musical directors such as Rube Wolf, Jack Dunn, and Gus Arnheim, all with prepared speeches of welcome to Whiteman and the band. When the speeches ended, the band was motored to the Los Angeles Pantages Theatre, where Alexander Pantages delivered yet another speech, welcoming them to their week's engagement.

Then Universal Studios rolled out the red carpet. They escorted the band to a new clubhouse, called the Whiteman Lodge, built especially for the band, right on their studio lot. It consisted of a large room with a complete library, huge fireplace, bar and kitchen, and a dressing table and locker for each member of the band.

Whiteman ordered thirty-five new Ford roadsters for the band. Each musician could select his own model, not to exceed $900 in purchase price, which would be taken out of their pay checks. Whiteman had his caricature painted on the covering of the spare tire on the back of each automobile.

Whiteman reported to Universal on June 28 for his first day of work and received a severe shock! The studio had not worked out a script, nor had any of the musical score been completed. Grofé explained to his boss that he had been presented with tunes, but each time he started to arrange them to fit the band, he was told that they had changed their mind—and that tune was out! Grofé told Whiteman that this happened several times, and finally he informed the executives that when they made up their minds on a set score, he would set to arranging it, but not until a final decision was made.

Aside from weekly Old Gold radio broadcasts, the band was inactive. Ted Husing asked Whiteman to help him secure a release from his announcer's role, so he could return to New York and pursue his radio work as a sports announcer. Whiteman was able to comply, and Harry Von Zell was hired as the new announcer.

R. W. Murray's letter of October 1957 offered an insight into the Old Gold broadcasts:

> The program originated on the coast during 1929 and 1930. I am more familiar with the originations in 1929 since the show originated in the old KMTR studios.

The 1929 series of broadcasts originated in Studio A. Our station was not equipped with recording facilities at the time of these broadcasts, and I doubt whether CBS was at this early date; therefore, it is doubtful whether any transcriptions were made of these broadcasts.[22]

The show itself was fed live to KMTR Studios and the CBS net east from 5:00–6:00 PM, PST.

The sponsor for the program was Old Gold and they sent out their own producer and sound engineer from New York. The producer was Burt McMurtrie, and the engineer was Mr. Louis Sumner Brookwalter. The sound engineer set up his own facilities since this orchestra was blended or mixed in a completely different method than was standard practice at this time. Incidentally, a lot of setups years later were basically the same as used by Mr. Whiteman's mixer.

Regarding the second series of shows for Old Gold, origination in 1930, I am not exactly familiar with these, but it seems a series of shows later originated at the Universal Studio which was rather unusual at this early date.[23]

Only The Rhythm Boys sought employment, and the *Los Angeles Examiner* reviewed their July 3 opening at the Montmartre Club with: "A trio of young gentlemen in blue flannel coats and tan flannel trousers, sing warm and gibberish songs to the flipping of the lids of miniature pianos."

That tire cover was easily spotted by the local gendarmes, who immediately began to follow us, knowing that sooner or later we would get into some kind of trouble.

Mischa Russell got into a jam of some kind and landed in jail! The local police would bring Mischa to our radio rehearsals and shows, and then return him to jail.

One night, we decided to take some cigarettes and candy to Mischa, only to find out that the turnkey had taken him to the movies. Figure that one out. We were asked if we wanted to wait.

---

[22]Despite rumors to contrary, a complete and exhaustive search has been made by CBS Radio, the P. Lorillard Company, and other leads supplied by collectors. Not one single broadcast has been found.

[23]Roy Bargy's letter of August 21, 1965, states that the second series of broadcasts were from the studio's rehearsal halls, during the filming.

Weeks went by and boys had nothing to do but wait. At first they reported to the studios every day and then left, but eventually they only showed up once a week to pick up their paychecks. Chester Hazlett, Roy Bargy, Bing Crosby, Al Rinker, and Kurt Dieterle joined the Lakeside Golf Club and played almost every day. Tram joined them at times, but his real interest was in learning to fly, and he took advantage of the free time to spend every possible moment at the airports.

On July 31, a terrible accident happened. A car, driven by Joe Venuti, collided with an automobile driven by two vacationing school teachers from Illinois. Venuti's passenger, Mario Perry, was badly hurt and later died in the hospital. Venuti's bowing arm was broken with the bone actually protruding from his wrist. The two women sued Venuti and named Paul Whiteman in their action. They sought $32,112 in damages. Whiteman's legal firm of Loeb, Walker, and Loeb handled the matter, and it was settled out of court.

Bing Crosby recalled during a November 1969 interview:

> Paul was not hiring any more musicians, but Al Rinker lured him to a party that was given by Mildred Bailey, Al's sister. The whole thing was planned to get her into the band. Paul didn't realize it at the time, but he was a goner when he walked into the house. She sang a song, of course, at the insistence of the boys, and Paul gave a listen. When she finished, Mildred said, "Okay, 'Pops,' that one was for you."
>
> Poor Paul, he had a new nickname and a new singer. She easily fit into the band, as her style was unique, and she was recognized as a sister to us all.

> **We played the beautiful Santa Barbara Fiesta on August 16, a gay, colorful yearly affair. We arrived by bus and were greeted by the welcoming committee. Each member of the band was given a bottle of wine.**
>
> **In the entrance of the building where we were to play, stood an old Indian. He was wearing a straight brimmed hat, yellow fringed buckskin shirt and pants and beautifully beaded moccasins. I later learned that he was about ninety years old and walked many, many miles from the hills to see this exciting Fiesta.**
>
> **Goldie, our jovial trumpet player, was trying to manage the wine and his instrument cases. He noticed the old**

Indian in the doorway, and handed him his bottle of wine. "A present for you, Pop."

The old boy accepted the wine with a big smile. During intermissions, Goldie was closely followed by the old Indian and his jug, the contents of which were rapidly disappearing.

Goldie finally became a little annoyed and, pointing to me, he said, "See that saxophone player over there? Full blooded Cherokee!"

Right then and there, I acquired a new friend. He never left me. He never spoke, just a smile whenever I looked his way. And the wine kept going down and down.

I realized that it was impossible to lose this majestic shadow, so I decided to accept the situation. I smiled at him and he smiled back. This continued throughout the afternoon and evening.

Finally, our instruments were packed and in the bus. I looked over at my friend, smile and wine were now gone. He was a lonely little character.

When the driver said, "All aboard," I smiled at my friend and raised my hand in a friendly salute. The old Indian, who had not spoken a single word all day, came over to me, put his arm around my shoulders, looked me squarely in the face and said, "You know, they didn't treat us Indians right!"

The love bug nipped two of the members of the band—Bing Crosby and Paul Whiteman. When The Rhythm Boys appeared at the Montmartre Club, it was known as a hangout for the film colony people. Bing was introduced to Wilma Wyatt, and became immediately interested in the attractive blond. It was some time before Bing learned that her "movie name" was Dixie Lee. She was one of the rising starlets at Fox Movietone Pictures, having just received billing in the recently released **Fox Movietone Follies** and **Why Leave Home?**

Whiteman met Margaret Livingston. She too was appearing in the movies and was just now receiving feature billing. Her big break came in **The Canary Murder** for Paramount Pictures. The film starred Louise Brooks but with the coming of sound, the studio decided to make it a "talkie" and asked Margaret to dub in the voice for Louise. It meant twice her usual studio salary, an offer she readily accepted, and she used the money for real estate investments. Whiteman had met Margaret in New York, but it wasn't until he was given a tour of the Universal Studios that he became acquainted with her. She was working on the film **Tonight At Twelve.** Margaret was a very attractive woman; though she seemed a bit out of place in films, she certainly was suited to the society life of California. She soon became a constant escort for Whiteman, and the relationship quickly became serious, but there were two strikes against Whiteman. She let it be known that she did not find fat orchestra leaders very becoming, but she offered to help solve this problem with a supervised diet, in which she expected Whiteman to lose the unheard of amount of one hundred pounds! The second problem, Whiteman had to solve by himself. He was still married to Mildred Vanderhoff.

Finally a script was ready and given to Whiteman to read.

> **Paul read the script and flatly refused to have any part of it. It was a love story with Pops as the romantic hero. The whole concept was so wrong for Paul and the boys.**
>
> **After much consideration, it was decided that a big mistake had been made! We decided to return to New York to fulfill previous engagements.**

The Whiteman Orchestra opened at the Pavilion Royale in Valley Stream, Long Island, on August 31, 1929. A week later, September 6, they returned to the recording studios for Columbia Records. When they returned on September 13, Bix was only able to get through the first number, ''Waiting At The End Of The Road,'' contributing an eight-bar solo, and then he asked Andy Secrest to take over for the rest of the session.

Whiteman had to make a difficult decision, and, after talking to Bix, they agreed that it would be best for Bix to return to Davenport for a brief rest. Whiteman kept Bix on full salary and kept his chair open, expecting him to return for the film.

In his January 1963 letter, Roy Bargy recalled:

> In the meantime, the sponsors of the radio show wanted some changes. Whiteman added one of the city's more popular singing duos, The Ponce Sisters (they featured two part harmony with Ethel carrying the high notes, and Dorothea the low ones), to appear during our New York stay.
>
> Still one of the wives of the sponsor's decision makers felt

that "a sweet trio" would be nice. Burt McMurtrie, the producer, asked me for any suggestions. We rounded up a new "sweet trio" that consisted of Bing Crosby, Jack Fulton, and Al Rinker. The sponsor liked what they heard and asked "how much?" Burt suggested $300 per broadcast, and got an okay! The three singers got $50 each, I got $75 because I did the arrangements, and McMurtrie took $75. The little deception was carried on for the duration of the show, and Old Gold never caught on.

CHAPTER TEN

THE KING OF JAZZ
1929–1932

UNIVERSAL STUDIOS RECALLED WHITEMAN to Hollywood on October 15, 1929. He left New York by train, and the band followed a few days later, arriving just as the depression hit!

> **When I returned to Hollywood, the second time, a stock broker nailed me. "Make a fortune, son. Why work all your life? Get in on this easy money."**
>
> **Well, that sounded all right to me. No work. I'll just play golf and fly the rest of the time.**
>
> **The morning of October 29, my friend phoned me. "Get right over here right away with margin money," he said.**
>
> **"What's that?" I asked.**
>
> **"Never mind! Just get over here!"**
>
> **I had bought all my stock on margin and in three days used up all my cash covering it, so I had to be sold out. That, my friends, is the short story of how I lost all of my money.[24]**
>
> **But I was young, healthy and had a good job, so I decided not to worry about it.**
>
> **Universal Studios not only had a new script, they had an entire new team assigned to the film.**

Paul Fejos had been dismissed. John Murray Anderson, who five months earlier admitted that he knew absolutely nothing about filmmaking, was selected to replace him. Anderson was one

[24]Trumbauer's tax record for 1930 showed that he had purchased Standard Oil stock for $500, and he declared a loss of $333 due to the stock market crash.

of the outstanding stage revue producers of this age, and he was now handed the job of bringing in one of the studio's higher budgeted efforts.

During the first two months, the band did the soundtrack to the film. A musical score was presented by Milton Ager and Jack Yellen, with a couple of added songs by Mable Wayne and Billy Rose. "It Happened In Monterey," and "Ragamuffin Romeo" were by Mable Wayne and Harry De Costa. George Gershwin was reportedly paid $10,000 for use of "Rhapsody In Blue." Whiteman continued to use it as his theme song in later years.

John Murray Anderson decided to shoot the soundtrack first. Whiteman felt that it would be best to do all of the recordings under the most perfect possible conditions, and that, he decided, was on a closed set. He felt that trying to record the numbers as they filmed would result in poor sound. Anderson agreed with him and went a step further by following the same procedure with the dialogue. In effect, Anderson directed the film as a silent picture, having the soundtrack later matched to the action, which would be considered doing the film backwards. Anderson felt that it was his first film, and he could call out directions, camera positions, and the workers could make as much noise as they wanted without hampering productions.

Irving Friedman disclosed in his 1962 correspondence with David Kingsbaker[25] that he was asked to do both his part and that of Chester Hazlett, who became ill during the filming. On the big production number of "Rhapsody In Blue," Friedman's clarinet is heard. He also doubled Hazlett's alto saxophone work and then jumped back over to his own solos. Not only did Izzy do this for the picture, but for the radio shows as well!

Hazlett was paid a larger salary than Izzy and, when he was able to return to the band, Whiteman asked Izzy if he'd accept the money that Hazlett would normally have received. Izzy told Whiteman that he'd only accept his regular salary for the twelve weeks that he doubled for Hazlett, and for Whiteman to give Hazlett the full payment. When Hazlett returned to the band, he was most profuse in his gratitude and asked Friedman how he could show his appreciation.

The band received instruments free from manufacturers in exchange for endorsements, and as a result, usually every musician had two of each instrument in his trunk. Friedman told

[25]Correspondence made available by John W. Miner.

Hazlett that he rather liked the feel of his alto and Hazlett literally jumped at the chance of giving it to him. In a gesture of appreciation, Friedman gave Hazlett one of his altos. Eleven years later, Hazlett sent Friedman a bill for $35, stating that it cost him that much to rebalance the alto that Izzy had given to him. The "bill" was most certainly a practical joke by Hazlett, but Friedman failed to see the humor and never answered the letter.

Most of the musicians were able to rent the apartments that they had left a few months earlier, and they reclaimed the Ford automobiles that they had left in storage on the Universal lot.

In a February 1966 interview, Joe Venuti recalled that Whiteman rented the home of silent film star Clara Bow. He left strict orders for none of the musicians to come within miles of the place for fear that someone would break something. It was nearing Christmas, and Whiteman had a tree decorated with candles. One toppled off the branch and started a fire. The fire was quickly subdued and not much damage was done except to Whiteman's pride. Venuti taunted Whiteman as to how Pops tried to burn down the home, but, in keeping with the spirit of Christmas, gave Whiteman a metal tree.

Venuti also confirmed a story about Charles King, star of **Broadway Melody** and **The Hollywood Revue,** who made a guest appearance on the January 15, 1930, radio broadcast. During the rehearsals, his style of singing annoyed Venuti no end. King was a ricky-tick singer, far from what Venuti had been used to with Bing Crosby and Jack Fulton. Shortly before the broadcast, Venuti disappeared, returning just as the red light was about to go on. As the band opened with their theme song, Venuti opened his violin case and displayed a huge pistol. Charlie King made his way to the microphone, and Venuti put the gun on his lap, looked at King and said, "You'd better be good!" The broadcast was live, coast to coast, and Whiteman simply went into a state of shock, as Venuti kept a bead on poor Charlie King with the gun. For all the musicians knew, Venuti actually planned to shoot King if he disliked the vocal. The number concluded, Venuti remarked, "good enough" and returned the gun to his violin case. Whiteman was furious, the guys in the band were laughing nervously, and Charlie King left in a huff!

The next week, Whiteman, bent on revenge, decided to teach Venuti a lesson. Following the rehearsal, Whiteman arranged for Venuti's violin, which he left on the music stand, to be taken and have wax rubbed across both his bow and violin strings. As the broadcast approached, Whiteman kept Venuti from returning to his chair with some "last minute instructions." Finally the light went on, the theme opened the program, and Venuti reached his chair just in time. Whiteman had set the arrangements to open with Venuti having a 16-bar solo right after an 8-bar introduction, so he quickly announced the tune and gave a down beat. Venuti realized what had happened to his violin immediately, but by now the tune was being played, and Whiteman just folded his arms and gave a "now what are you going to do, hot shot?" look at Venuti. Venuti did the 16 bars, but not with his violin. He sang! The musicians went into fits of uncontrolled laughter, and it was all they could do to finish the tune.

Whiteman wanted Jack Fulton for the "It Happened In Monterey" number in **The King Of Jazz** but lost the argument to the studio who wanted John Boles to sing it. Boles was well known in films, and he would be a plus to the film. He had just finished **The Desert Song** for Warner Brothers, and Universal wanted to cash in on his marquee value. Whiteman reluctantly gave in, but held firm on Bing Crosby for the film's big production number, "Song Of The Dawn." Whiteman lost that argument when Bing was arrested and sentenced to thirty days.

While the film was described as in Technicolor, only three colors were used: red, blue, and green.

Universal paraded their own stars into the film: Jeanne Loff, Jeanie Lang, The Sisters G (imported from France), The Russell Market Dancers, Grace Hayes, and a supporting cast that included "Slim" Summcrvillc and Walter Brennan.

The band was featured in almost every scene, with specialty numbers given to The Rhythm Boys, Venuti and Lang, Wilbur Hall, Roy Bargy, et al, and even Whiteman surprised the audience with a hot dance number until it was revealed to be his dancing double, Paul Small.[26]

March 20, 1930 was the final day of shooting at Universal. The boys sold their Fords for what they could salvage and began packing.

Trumbauer used every available day during this trip to pursue

---

[26]Though uncredited in the film, the dancing double is Paul Small. Some film historians have suggested that it was Dick Rich, who mimicked Whiteman in some Vitaphone shorts, but if they will give closer examination, they will agree that it is Small.

flying lessons, and was able to obtain a Limited Commercial Pilot's license. There were others within the band who shared his enthusiasm; and Trumbauer, Jack Fulton, Bill Rank, Harry Goldfield, and Wilbur Hall became known as "The Paul Whiteman Air Force."

Hall decided to remain in California and served his notice. Irving Friedman also decided to remain behind and get married.

On April 1, 1930 the band left Hollywood to play several dates on the coast and Canada.

> **Jimmy Gillespie and Billy Gibson, a big showman, started ahead of us in Gillespie's Stutz. A farewell party had been given for us the night before our departure and during the evening, just for a laugh, Gillespie borrowed a diamond-studded badge from the Los Angeles Chief of Police.**
>
> **Gillespie was about fifty miles out of town when he discovered that he still had the badge, and decided to turn back and return it to the Chief. He must have been traveling at a fast clip because state troopers caught up with him.**
>
> **Gillespie showed them various police and press cards.**
>
> **"No good," they told him.**
>
> **Then he brought out the badge. That didn't improve his status one bit. The troopers just couldn't understand how that badge came to be in his possession. Gillespie was then showing them everything, a letter from the Governor of California, more press passes, but nothing worked. Then Whiteman drove up and saved the day. He told the troopers that the band would be appearing in San Francisco, and if they could make it, there'd be a party afterwards and they would be more than welcome. Gillespie was allowed to continue on his way.**

PAUL WHITEMAN SAYS HE WILL SUE

That headline made the front page of the Vancouver *Daily Providence* newspaper on April 4.

The band was hired for three engagements in Vancouver: a concert at the Van-Theatre and a dance at the Hotel Vancouver on Friday, and a dance at the Danman Street Auditorium on Saturday. The Canadian Immigration Officials informed Whiteman that due to the worldwide depression, Canadian laws prohibited the employment of non-Canadian musicians at any dances. They would allow Whiteman to present the concert but not the two dance dates.

Whiteman called a press conference for that Friday morning, held in his hotel room. One newspaper noted that Whiteman was wearing a green bathrobe over his tweed trousers, had left open his collar, and appeared very comfortable. Whiteman might have appeared comfortable, but he was enraged. He quickly pointed out the following to the press:

> Gentleman, I have thirty three musicians and two car loads of scenery en route at this very minute. They should arrive sometime today. If the Canadian officials planned to enforce their regulations, they could have told me before now.
>
> First off, we advertised our engagement ten days in advance and none of the immigration officials made any protests. Secondly, I came across the border yesterday and no one offered any protest. Thirdly, the management of the Hotel Vancouver was given permission for our dance to run until 2 a.m., and still no protests.
>
> I have brought my organization to Canada at great expense, and if I cannot play the dance dates then I prefer not to play the concert. All or nothing!

The officials shrugged their shoulders. That was the law and nothing could be done about it.[27]

Universal Studios presented a private showing ("sneak preview") of **The King Of Jazz** on April 5 in Los Angeles. John Murray Anderson was very generous in his remarks to the press following the showing. He heaped praise upon the film. "What the screen will bring us in the future—pictures, colors, sound—is unimaginable. We can only guess at it."

Anderson went on to state: "The legitimate stage, except in New York, will die! For who in the world will pay five or six dollars to see a revue done on the stage with shoddy scenery, second-rate actors, and second-rate musicians, when for less than a dollar, they can see a show like **The King Of Jazz**—and greater ones in the future? The stage will die because it won't be able to compete."

The press called the final release, "the film ignoramus," and

---

[27]Information culled from several newspapers over the period of April 4–7, 1930.

cited a price tag of two million dollars spent on the production. "But," stated the Universal Studios press release, "we'll get our money back, and much more."

And then the Canadian Labor Ministry called upon Whiteman to inform him that he would not be permitted to perform in Vancouver.

Whiteman blew his top. Whiteman was so furious that he decided to go all out and give a party to end all parties.

I shared Paul's suite and we dreamed up a little publicity stunt. We didn't realize then the size it was going to take.

We called all the newspapers to inform them of a press meeting to take place in Whiteman's hotel suite. At the meeting, Paul announced that since the Labor Ministry would not permit him to play an engagement for money, he was going to give a benefit performance and the proceeds would go to the local milk fund.

He added, "In that way, we won't disappoint the people that want to hear our band."

Now, the monkey was on the back of the Labor Ministry. For three days the newspapers carried stories of Whiteman's plans and all the details of the labor situation.

During all this, we remained in Whiteman's hotel suite and the party continued in full swing. What laughs we had—Venuti and Whiteman trying to top each other. I think Venuti won, though, when he put salt on some flowers and ate them, stems and all!

The final outcome was the refusal of the Labor Ministry to grant us permission to play in Vancouver under any circumstances. The publicity in the papers was really sensational then.

Meanwhile, the party continued.

One of the boys in the band, to whom Whiteman had been especially wonderful, was very drunk. He became noisy, abusive and said some pretty nasty things to Whiteman. But Whiteman, in his fatherly way, chose to ignore them. Billy Gibson, however, did not know the full details and finally said, "Look, one more crack out of you, and I'll let you have it!"

The boy repeated the remark, adding, "And that goes for you too, Gibson!"

With that Billy banged him right on the snout. As our

friend left, I heard him mumble something about, "I'll fix you guys."

I don't know why but I decided to follow him. I went to his room and he wasn't there. I looked all over the hotel for him and walking through the lobby when I saw two of the reporters present at Whiteman's press meeting, enter the hotel. I followed them. They went to a room occupied by another member of the band and knocked on the door. Sure enough, our boy opened the door. I followed the two reporters into the room.

"Whiteman had me slugged," he yelled. "The whole thing is a scheme to get some publicity. I'll give you the story."

He began to talk, incoherently, and most of his information was incorrect. His nose did show evidence of some mishap, though.

I left with the reporters, took them into the bar and told them the true story. I was sober, thank heavens, and they listened. When I finished they tore up their notes. "That guy's just drunk and mad."

What a narrow escape for Whiteman and our organization. Whiteman never knew about this; at least, I never told him. It made me feel good to be able to repay him for some of the wonderful things he did for me.

The band continued concert dates in Washington and Oregon, with the final performance in Portland on April 15, and then headed back to New York.

Bing and I were now rooming together at the Belvedere Hotel, and decided to do the town one night. As the evening wore on, Bing suddenly realized that he had to call Dixie in Hollywood, and he rushed back to the hotel to make the call.

Sometime later that night, I walked into our hotel room and found Bing sound asleep with the receiver in his hand. I shook him and he began, "hello, hello."

I never really knew that happened except that the telephone call cost me $130.75! I still have the bill.

May 2 had been selected as the opening presentation of **The King Of Jazz** at the Roxy Theatre in New York. Whiteman's Orchestra was booked for a stage show, between showings of the film, for three weeks with the expectation of an extended run. Five-a-day performances! George Gershwin appeared with the Whiteman Orchestra and the Roxy Symphony Orchestra (125 musicians) on stage, performing his "Rhapsody In Blue." Mildred Bailey was featured with the Roxy Chorus. The Roxy Ballet, due to lack of space, was sent over to the Palace Theatre for the first week at least!

The recording companies were hard hit by the Depression, and sales had declined, but Tram's gang was able to record "I Like To Do Things For You" on May 8, using Mildred Bailey in a Betty Boop-type vocal. **The Melody Maker** reviewed the record: "This is a commercial rendering except for one complete chorus by Trumbauer, which is as good as anything he has done. . ." and "This chorus is a masterpiece and sticks out from the rest of the record like a beacon."

Two days later, Tram's unit recorded "Get Happy" and "Deep Harlem." He sang on both tunes. In March 1991, Warren Scholl recalled a February 1934 interview with Tram:

> Frank willingly and good naturedly admitted he did not even pretend to be a vocalist. Frank said the hired vocalist failed to show up. The records had to be made, or they would lose several hundred dollars. So, Frank volunteered.

Paul Whiteman ended the Old Gold radio programs on May 6 and the engagement at the Roxy Theatre on May 13. The band settled for a well-deserved vacation.

To economize Whiteman cut the band to 18 men. Those that did remain took a pay cut. The orchestra now consisted of: Nat Natolie, Harry Goldfield (trumpets); Andy Secrest (cornet); Herb Winfield, Jack Fulton, Bill Rank (trombones); Chester Hazlett, Walter "Fud" Livingston, Frank Trumbauer, Charles Strickfaden (reeds); Kurt Dieterle, Mischa Russell, Matty Malneck, John Bowman (violins); Mike Pingitore (banjo/guitar); Mike Trafficante (bass); Roy Bargy (piano); and George Marsh (drums).

The June 1930 newspapers offered readers details of the Florida officials' padlocking Al Capone's mansion in Miami. People commented on this with "Wow!" Tram noticed in those same June newspapers that aviator Boris Sergievsky set an altitude record by flying a seaplane to 30,000 feet above Long Island. Tram said, "Wow!"

An interview by Kenneth Porter, of Hearst's Universal News Service, with Carl Laemmle, Jr., appeared in the June 14 papers. Laemmle felt that the press had been unfair to **The King Of Jazz.** He pointed out that 16 publications had reviewed the film when it premiered in New York and that ten had been favorable, one lukewarm, and only five were unfavorable. Laemmle felt the film glorified the Whiteman Orchestra and if, given time, people would realize the high standard that was given to each production number. He set the final price tag at two million dollars but felt they would, in time, show a profit.

On the same date, the band opened at Pelham, New York, at the Hollywood Gardens.

> **It was late afternoon and Chet, Jack Fulton and I walked out on the pier. We started tossing firecrackers off the end of the pier and watched them kick up mud some distance away.**
>
> **Paul came sauntering out on the pier, dressed in a light blue jacket and stiff shirt with special studs. He really looked wonderful!**
>
> **"What-cha doin', guys?" Paul asked.**
>
> **We tossed a couple firecrackers to show him.**
>
> **"Give me one. I want to see what happens."**
>
> **The tide was out and there was nothing but blue black mud beneath the pier where Paul stood. He lit the firecracker and threw it straight down into the mud—making a small crater.**
>
> **"Aw, it didn't go off," he mumbled as he walked over to the edge of the pier to get a better look.**
>
> **And then there was a muffled noise—and a shower of black sticky mud shot high into the air!**
>
> **Paul turned to run but headed right into mud particles as they descended. His beautiful blue jacket and white shirt—everything—was completely covered with mud.**
>
> **We were due to start shortly, and Paul's nearest change of clothes was back in New York, about thirty miles away.**
>
> **Paul kept his back to the audience the entire evening. To say that he was furious would be an understatement. He kept repeating, over and over, "I'll kill the next bastard that I find with firecrackers!"**
>
> **So ended our "firecracker days."**

Whiteman's Orchestra played the racing season (July 30 to August 30) at the Arrowhead Hotel in Saratoga, New York. All of the high rollers invaded the town during this period, and gambling was conducted in almost every hotel and establishment.

> **One day, during rehearsal, Charlie Strickfaden made a noise like a train on his baritone saxophone. It gave me an idea. Matty Malneck and I wrote a tune around the idea and called it, "Choo Choo." My group recorded it on September 8 for Okeh Records.**
>
> **The London Press reviewed the record. They used such blazing statements as, " . . . the most descriptive piece of music written since the Overture of 1812 . . . " and " . . . a definite musical form in that it tells a story."**
>
> **They gave us credit for writing something that would go down in musical history—". . . a piece of immortal music born to a dance band."**
>
> **We were utterly amazed to read these comments. The number was primarily written as a gag in order to use the train sound Strick had played that day. I wrote the lyrics and I remember the first line, "I want you to go, too, with me on the Choo Choo," which probably indicated that I should have gone back to railroading.**

From the middle of October through the end of the year, the band spent their days in Chicago at the Casa Granada Cafe, reportedly owned by Al Capone, but managed by Al Quadbach.

An "outside" band was simply not welcomed to Chicago by the Musicians' Union. They wanted *their* musicians to get the work and made no bones about it. It was all right to do a concert and move on, but a lengthy stay was resented by the unemployed members of Local #10. Much to Whiteman's surprise, opening night, Jimmy Petrillo, president of Chicago Musicians' Local #10, appeared at a ringside table. Whiteman introduced Petrillo to the audience and called him to the bandstand to say a few words. Whiteman almost went into shock when Petrillo said how pleased he was to have the Whiteman Orchestra in Chicago and extended a warm Chicago welcome to Whiteman and the band. As Petrillo started to return to his chair, Mildred Bailey asked him for his favorite tune, which she proceeded to sing, through her new rhinestone megaphone.

One night at the Casa Granada Cafe, a tipsy guest knocked over a clarinet belonging to Fud Livingston, and broke it in half. The patron offered to pay ten dollars for the damage, no more! Al Quadbach came over and surveyed the damage and ushered the man into his office. One of the bouncers later told us what happened.

"Pay the boy for the clarinet," Al said quietly, but firmly.

By now the guy was sore. "Ten bucks. Take it or leave it!" And, he called Al a dirty name.

Now to call Al a dirty name was like looking into the muzzle of a loaded .45 automatic. This wasn't exactly the safe thing to do.

When the patron came to, Al asked if he was now ready to pay the clarinet player the true value of the instrument.

"Hell no," was the answer, and he started to take a swing at Al.

When the tipsy patron came to, the second time, he was ready to pay for the horn.

Al later told me that he had to make a visit to the fellow's house when he entertained thoughts of a lawsuit and convince him of how useless that would have been.

That's the way Al took care of his boys—and the Whiteman musicians were his boys!

Shortly after this, I had an offer to conduct a small staff band in a New York radio station, but Pops didn't like the idea, so I turned it down. Andy Sanella, from the old Ray Miller band, took the job.

We had some wonderful times in Chicago, and Al kept us on long after our original scheduled engagement. He tore up the original contract and told Paul to "stay on as long as you want."

Al was crazy about the way that Jack Fulton sang "Trees," and requested it over and over. I can still see Al in front of the band, straddling a straight back chair, as he listened to Jack sing "Trees." If anyone in the cafe made any noise during Al's favorite number, he was thrown out.

Royal Howell recalled, in an October 1968 interview:

I had lost track of Frank, then I heard that he was the number one saxophone player with Paul Whiteman. So around

> Thanksgiving time, I had business in Chicago, and decided to see old Frank. I waltzed myself down and told the doorman that I had an appointment with Frank and he let me into their dressing room. The band was playing, and the first thing that I saw was a case of gin on the table. I helped myself to a bottle.
>
> Frank was really happy to see me. He started to ask about all of the guys when Paul and Roy Bargy entered the dressing room in a heated argument. Roy had purchased some tight fitting Italian gloves and wore them during the performance because he said the cafe was cold. He refused to take them off.
>
> "Either take off those gloves," said an enraged Paul, "or get out of the band! You're not playing piano with those gloves on, and that's final!"
>
> Frank and I couldn't hear above the heated words, so we went out into the backstage area. "Tell me, Royal," Tram insisted, "tell me about the guys. What's new?"
>
> I said, "Clarie Carr's family moved to Chicago. He went to the university there and now's he's a baby doctor. Glenn Banuum went on to be the director of music at the University of Illinois. Bill Ashley was living somewhere in Chicago, but I didn't know what he was doing."
>
> Paul Whiteman came out of the dressing room, carrying a pair of Italian gloves.
>
> "I see you won that argument," Tram said to Paul.
>
> "You won't believe it, Tram," said Paul. "When I told Roy that either the gloves go or he goes, he actually gave the matter some thought. For a moment there, I thought he was going to quit. How would I have ever replaced him?"
>
> I told Frank that it was too bad that the old hometown gang couldn't see him now, being with Whiteman and all. He really made it to the top.

This suggestion gave rise to Tram's discussing the idea with Whiteman. The Music Corporation of America (MCA) was handling Whiteman's bookings, and Tram wondered if there was a chance that the band could play Carbondale.

Just before Christmas, 1930, Tram received the following letter:

> Dear Frank:
>
> How are you, boy? I've been having a hell of a time. I am writing this flat on my back as I have been since my arrival

home. The rest is sure making a new man of me, I'm in good shape, all but my knees. It seems I had a touch of pneumonia at one time and that our doctor thinks it wasn't discernable because of its slightness. He also said that because of the wonderful doctor and care that Paul arranged for me in New York, the pneumonia didn't get a chance to show itself. But here at home, he noticed a slight infection in the lower right lobe of my lung. It seems that after all this trouble, the poison in my system has settled in my knees and legs—I guess I am a minus quality. I have never suffered so continually without a letup in my life. The doctor says the heart and everything is okay, but I am not worth a dime. My knees don't work. I try to stand and fall right on my face. I am taking walking lessons and I am improving every day, but with great pain. I haven't had a drink for so long I'd pass on one. I'm strictly gleaming above the boys on the big wagon and I am sticking there.

Tram, you probably know better than anyone my financial status after going through a grand of my own and I am really broke and now is when I need money the most. So I wonder if you could see fit to send me some money. Try like hell, boy.

Itzy[28] said in a wire that Paul said to hurry and come back when I am able.

Say, Tram, see what you can about having Bob Stevens[29] send me that cornet. I could practice some if I had it.

Well, Happy New Year, Tram. I'll be back with you soon as my knees will work—if Paul will have me. Regards to any of the boys that may be interested and the best of everything in the world to you.

Your pal,
Bix

General Motors sponsored the longest commercial radio program (four hours) on New Year's Eve, but when the radio audience heard Whiteman's Orchestra broadcasting from Chicago, they would never have believed what was transpiring during the program.

Federal agents, enforcing the prohibition laws, decided to raid

[28]While Bix did write "Itzy," he obviously meant "Izzy," referring to Irving Friedman.

[29]Bix probably meant Bob Stephens, former trumpet player, who was then selling musical instruments, and later became A&R man at Decca Records in 1934.

two of Chicago's leading clubs. When they entered the Lincoln Club, on the North Side, many of the patrons hurled bottles to the floor and dumped their glasses and tea cups from their tables to the floor, breaking as much evidence as possible. Just the opposite happened on the South Side, at the Casa Granada Cafe. As the agents entered, Whiteman's band was in the midst of a radio program, so they quietly went from table to table confiscating the liquor, as everyone remained silent so as not to disturb the broadcast. The agents did return the next day to padlock the Casa Granada Cafe for a short while.

January 1931 opened with a two-week vacation period for the band.

Tram flew his new present, N.C. 801K Cirrus III, to Cleveland to see his old friend, Dr. Leonard Samartini, and have some work done on his teeth.

Paul Whiteman caught the train to California, after he announced that he was making a business trip to confer with the officials of Universal Studios, and arrived in Santa Barbara on January 7, where he was met at the depot by Margaret Livingston.

Universal Studios had taken an option in February 1930 for a second motion picture to be made, and had even discussed a third film, but nothing had been made final. The studio now was hesitant to pursue it's options, in view of the panning that **The King Of Jazz** had received, and wanted to work out a definite decision with Whiteman. The studio was firm that a third film would not be made.

Whiteman was very hesitant about the possibilities of another film because, as he told reporters, "Sure, I'd like to do another motion picture. I'm considering their offers, but they want to do the same thing as before. I want some originality. I really don't want to repeat what we already filmed."

Carl Laemmle, Jr., suggested a series of novelty shorts, released as two-reel musical films, running about 20 minutes each, to feature various musicians and singers in Whiteman's organization. Whiteman liked the idea, and January 20 was the scheduled date for a press release that contracts had been signed.

Then came a shocker. Whiteman called a press conference[30] to announce his engagement to Margaret Livingston.

---

[30]Whiteman's press conference was reported in Los Angeles newspapers and nationwide, but the *Los Angeles Examiner* was the primary source here.

The first and obvious question was: ''Paul, aren't you still married to Mildred [nee Vanda Hoff]?''

''Yes,'' admitted Whiteman, ''but we are going to have a friendly divorce. I think she's wonderful. We have been practically separated for three years, and actually for two. We tried married life on the road for seven years and it just isn't a go.''

''What about your son, Paul?''

''Van will keep the boy, but I'll have opportunities to have him with me for periods of time. Right after he was born, Van quit dancing to be with Paul, Jr., and I feel that she should continue with his upbringing.''

''What do you think caused the marriage to go sour?''

''It's hard for two people to be in show business and be happily married,'' replied Whiteman. ''Anyway, I found it impossible. It isn't a normal existence. Van always said that I took more interest in other people's affairs than I did in hers. For instance, the boys in my band. My work is my life and I can't allow anything to interfere with it.''

After some deliberation, Whiteman continued, ''I can't ever remember having a home. I haven't lived more than two months in any one place for years. How to be happy though successful—that's been my problem. I've been a flop in my private life and I'm not blaming anyone, but still I can't blame myself, either.''

The band regrouped in Chicago and headed on a brief tour. In a March 1966 interview, Andy Secrest remembered January 17, 1931, in Davenport, Iowa:

> Our train pulled into the station, and we didn't know if we'd see Bix at the dance or even if he was still in town. Our doubts were quickly put to rest when a familiar figure awaited us at the depot. It was Bix.
>
> He looked like a million dollars to all of us. Tram threw his arms around Bix and hugged him as someone would a long lost son who had just returned home. They didn't say a word. They didn't have to, you could see their feelings in their eyes. By now, all of the guys were pushing towards Bix, reaching out to slap him on the back, mess up his hair, or just touch him to show their affection.
>
> Paul got off the rear of the train, and stood on the platform, just beaming with happiness at the sight of Bix.

"Come here, Bix," Paul commanded. "Come here, you lovable son-of-a-gun. Let the old man hug you."

It was an emotional reunion, and Paul insisted that Bix sit in when the band played that night at Danceland.

"It will seem like old times," Whiteman said. Bix seemed a bit reluctant, but he was not about to deny Whiteman any request.

True to his word, Bix showed up, and after an introduction to the crowd by Whiteman, Bix took his seat. I didn't know what we expected. We knew that Bix had been ill, but because he looked so well, I guess we expected the old fire to be in his cornet. It wasn't! We played one of the tunes that would give Bix some solo spot, and when he stood and played, you could see the hurt in Paul's eyes. Pops didn't let on, nor did any of us. Tram later said to Paul that all Bix needed was a bit more time and he'd be back. We all agreed. Just give Bix a bit more time and the old pizzazz would be there. Paul told Bix that his chair was still open, and Bix assured Pops that he'd be back in a couple more months.

We said our farewell at the railroad station, and both Paul and Tram gave Bix one last hug, and we all said our goodbyes to Bix as we boarded. We waved until the depot was out of sight.

Paul turned to Frank and asked if Tram thought Bix would be back. Frank told Paul that he was uncertain. He didn't know what to think, but he hoped that he would be back, very soon.

Paul said, "You know that I love Bix like a son, but, deep down inside, I don't think Bix will ever be with us again."

On January 28, in Red Oak, Iowa, Tram had news of his long-departed father, as related in Harold Hossle's letter to Mary Trumbauer, Tram's daughter-in-law in 1990. Hossle met Tram at this engagement:

We had Frank at my mother's for a chicken dinner. I had met his dad, Fred Trumbauer, and he was anxious to hear all about him.

When Frank's parents divorced, Fred went up into Canada. He had operated a steam stiff-legged crane, building a large water-powered electric power plant on the St. Lawrence River. He sat the big water turbines in the dam with this crane.

In about 1914 or 1915, he lived with us for about three months. He helped gather corn on our farm. I guess that I got to know him as well as anyone.

I kept in touch with Fred after that, and was able to tell Frank that his dad admired him from afar. He often referred to how proud he was of Frank, and he kept up with his career through the radio and recordings, and what he could read about him, but he never made any effort to try and be present at any of the places that Frank played.

Apparently Tram was content with what he learned that night, as we do not believe that Tram ever attempted to locate his father, who passed away on April 22, 1943.

The band ended their tour, and reopened at the Casa Granada Cafe on February 9, 1931. A couple of nights later, the band had a surprise guest. Bix! Secrest's recollection was still fresh on that visit:

Bix stopped off en route to New York, where he said he had a few business deals brewing. Bix now confirmed what Whiteman had already concluded, he wouldn't be returning to the band, at least, not any time soon.

"Bix," Whiteman said, "if you ever need a job . . . "

"Yeah, Paul," Bix replied, "I know."

Bix turned to Tram, half kidding, and said, "And you, Frank, all I have to do is give a call and you'll be there for me. Right?" Bix flashed a big smile at Tram.

Tram reached out, grabbed Bix, gave him a hug, and said "You know it." That was the last time we ever saw Bix.

Mildred Vanderhoff Whiteman broke her silence on the divorce in late February 1931 from her apartment in New York. The syndicated news story carried on the 27th stated:

I was just informed of the divorce suit today, but let me say that the divorce has already been granted, secretly, and with my consent.

I left Palm Beach a few weeks ago and went to Hollywood. On the way back, I stopped off in Chicago and saw Paul and agreed to let him get a divorce there, his having an

> Illinois residence. I was served with papers and he got the decree. I didn't want to bring suit in New York because it's so messy the way you have to do it here.
>
> I guess, we couldn't make a go of matrimony because his band business kept him away from home, and now Paul has transferred his interest to a film actress named Margaret Livingston.

Although Whiteman denied to the press that there had been a secret divorce, he did admit that his attorneys had filed suit and cited the reason as being desertion by Mildred on January 15, 1929. Whiteman was quick to explain, ''There is no venom in this action whatsoever. The law demands a reason for dissolving the marriage and that is what we listed. I still think that Van is a wonderful girl.'' Superior Court Judge Sullivan granted the divorce on March 1, 1931, in Chicago, ending the marriage that started in 1922.

Tram purchased a Moth N.C. 22V Gypsy III airplane in March. He conducted flying lessons for a few students and even offered a few chartered flights during April to such towns as Toledo, Ohio.

Ever since Royal Howell planted the idea of Tram appearing in Carbondale with the Whiteman Orchestra, Tram had begun pestering Jimmy Gillespie to include the date on a tour. Jimmy put together a deal for the band to appear at Carbondale on April 29. They had a concert set for 7:30 P.M. at the teachers college, and then a three-and-a-half-hour dance at the shoe factory, beginning at 9:30 P.M.

The American Legion was underwriting the appearance, hoping the proceeds would go towards the costs of their bringing the National Legion Commander to their May 30 program. They agreed to pay $2,200 for the band. Whiteman was dubious about the date, and grew even more so when he learned that the price that he was receiving was $700 more than John Philip Sousa had received last fall for his band and that the town had lost money on that program. When Whiteman learned the population of Carbondale, he wondered how they could make any money. Even if one thousand people attended at a dollar a ticket, they would lose money. The matter really bothered him.

The band had a special car attached to the regular railroad run, and Whiteman instructed the engineers to decouple the car a little way from the station. Whiteman kept repeating that he had never played an engagement this small before, and it was all Tram's fault.

A local group of officials of the American Legion greeted the private railroad car, and as Whiteman looked out the window and saw them approaching, he cried, "I knew it! A lynch mob!" Once assured that it was a welcoming committee, he ventured out of the train to exchange handshakes. Whiteman learned that the concert had already sold 1700 tickets and the dance was nearing 1500. They fully expected to be sold out when the band started playing. The welcoming committee invited the entire band to a picnic that they had prepared, with corn on the cob and chicken as the main course. The boys dug in with both hands!

> **From the moment that I stepped off the train, it seemed that I was surrounded with people that had been my friends for years. I recognized some of the boys that I used to ditch school with and head for the ole swimmin' hole, and those girls that used to wear gingham aprons and had their hair in braids, well, they were all grown up now!**
>
> **"Hey, Frank," someone would call out, "do you remember me?"**
>
> **"Sure I do," I'd reply. "How's old so and so these days?"**
>
> **Sometimes soft replies would come back of "oh, he's dead now," but for the most part, it was a thrill to hear what the old gang was doing now that they had grown up.**
>
> **There was time before the concert, so I walked through the streets again, covering ground that was so familiar to my youth. I walked by the school and the words to the old school song started to return to me. I guess that every kid spends a lot of time in school dreaming. I did. I can remember how I wanted to grow up and come back to town as a big man, something like a president or something. Now I was back as a member of the best orchestra in the world. Boyhood dreams can come true.**

The *Carbondale Free Press* reported on the dance:

> Whiteman introduced Frank at the dance, and he made his bow. The audience cheered enthusiastically when he stood. At the dance, Frank was in the front row of the band where

> he was the attraction of scores of admiring dancers who continually grouped around him.
>
> The dance, which attracted 2,000 people, was well handled. The floor was in good condition. The little crack in the floor was not serious and in no way endangered anyone.

Brunswick Records had contracted for two recording dates with Tram, April 10 and June 24, 1931. The second date offered a bit of concern for Andy Secrest, who was to play the excellent solo on "Georgia On My Mind." Tram had decided that the tune needed a featured singer, and he was giving thoughts to being the vocalist. Joe Rushton, as he stated in 1962, "was hanging around the Whiteman Band at this time," and heard Secrest's remarks:

> I happened to be over at Art Jarrett's home when the guys asked if he would do the date. He consented and I drove him to the studio. Of course, Tram agreed that Jarrett would be a better choice to sing the tunes. I watched from the control booth, and when they were doing "Georgia," Jarrett looked at me, then Tram, and back to me and smiled. I wiped my hand across my forehead, as if to convey a sign of relief that Jarrett was doing the vocal, and Jarrett started to laugh, but contained it. If you listen to the recording, the last few lines, where he sings, ". . . leads back to you. Georgia. Georgia . . . " It is the second time that he sings "Georgia" that he starts the laugh.

Andy Secrest's discussion of March 1966, clearly recalled the fateful day when a telephone call came for Whiteman at the Edgewater Beach Hotel[31] in Chicago:

> Whiteman came rushing over and called for Tram. "Come quickly, Tram," he said. "It's Bix!"
>
> Whiteman told us that a doctor in New York had called in a frantic attempt to locate a relative of Bix's. Bix was in need of immediate medical care and refused to enter a hospital so the doctor was hopeful that Whiteman could give him information on who in the Beiderbecke family could give

[31]During this 1931 period, when the band was at the Edgewater Beach Hotel, Joe Rushton filmed the band during a rehearsal. Silent. No sound. Harry Goldfield, thought that Joe had a box camera, and stood motionless. The annoyance showed on Goldie's face as he glanced around and saw other musicians moving about. The film has been lost with the passing years.

the needed permission. Tram put in a call to the Beiderbecke home in Davenport, and advised them of the seriousness of the situation, and Bix's brother and mother caught the first train to New York.

Then we waited for word.

Finally the telephone call came. The one that we never wanted to receive. The family did not reach New York in time. Bix was dead! August 6, 1931, of lobar pneumonia.

When Paul gave us the news, Tram went out back. I didn't know whether to leave him alone, or whether he needed comfort, but I elected to go out and see if he was all right. All Tram could do was ask, "Andy, why didn't Bix call? I've always been there for him. Why didn't he call?" Of course, I did not have an answer. No one did.

In New York, a stunned Hoagy Carmichael heard the news, when Bix's girlfriend, Helen Weiss, telephoned him. Carmichael clearly recounted the events during a July 1974 interview:

I asked her why she hadn't called. I was then working with S. W. Strauss Company, on Fifth Avenue, and only making $25 a week, but I told her if I had to go out into the streets and beg for money, we could have gotten him an oxygen tent, and the best of care, anything! She said that it all happened too fast.

A few days later when she came by I was still in shock. I know we talked about Bix, but I don't remember a thing we said. All I could think about was that he had been up to see me a couple of weeks earlier, and he looked great. How could it have happened? She gave me some of Bix's effects: cuff links, a couple of handkerchiefs, and his mouthpiece.[32]

John Steiner's June 1990 interview with Warren Smith had Smith saying that Bix's death really hit the music world hard. Yet most could not accept it, and the only person that could confirm the sad news was Frank Trumbauer. If Tram said Bix had died, that put the final stamp on the matter. "I approached Frank, during intermission, at the Edgewater to ask him about it," said Smith. "It was all Frank could do to keep from crying." Bix was now "officially" dead!

[32]Hoagy Carmichael donated Bix's handkerchiefs and cuff links to the New Orleans Jazz Museum in November 1963, accompanied by a letter verifying their authenticity. The mouthpiece, a Holton, he had gilded in gold, and placed upon his fireplace mantel.

If ever there was an American musician in the field of hot jazz to whom the over-worked word "genius" could be justifiably applied, it was Bix Beiderbecke.

This is the all of Bix. What he left us musically had to be given within a little more than half a decade. The best of what he produced on records came out at a time when the public's interest for this kind of music was beginning to decline. We are very fortunate then to have our Okeh Records, a few made with Jean Goldkette, and the records where Bix's cornet climbs high above the whole Whiteman organization. Without them, Bix's horn would be more or less hearsay!

Enough anecdotal material has grown up around Bix to make him a legendary figure. Great men in the music field are happy just to have shared in his glory. Musicians are proud to have played in the same bands with him.

I can remember his greeting to those that would say "hello" to him as he came off the bandstand. "How ya', boy? How you doin'? You still down there?" Then he would close with "Well, I'll see you down there." Chances are that he never knew where "down there" was, but he just wanted to be nice to everyone.

To this day, musicians and fans get together and swap yarns about Bix. How much truth and how much myth these stories contain is of little importance. What Bix left behind is important!

Very few musicians leave anything to be remembered. Bix was different. What he created will live forever.

Well, as you might realize, this could go on and on. However, this seems to be a spot to review and correct, if possible, many of the statements made about Bix.

Bix's greatest admirer, next to me, was Paul Whiteman. Whiteman said, "Bix was not only one of the greatest natural musicians I have ever known, but also the greatest gentleman I have ever known."

Whiteman should know because he has probably known more musicians and gentlemen than anyone around.

Bix was not the young man with a horn! He was not responsible for the many literary attempts to describe the beat-it-down, jivin' cat, that everyone might think constituted the immortal personality. Bix was an intelligent young man, a fast thinker, and well versed in many things. To describe in print the work of Bix is almost like trying to describe the color in the beautiful flowers that we see all around us, or the beautiful clouds we see in the sky, or the varicolored leaves in the fall which make an impression so indelible on our minds. Still, these things relatively have an association with anything artistic. You just can't measure it with a yardstick.

One writer commented on an eight dollar cornet Bix always played. What some writers will say just to see their names in print. This was an erroneous article if there ever was one!

About that eight dollar cornet, let me just say, right here, that Bix had the finest Clarke cornet that could be had. It was made to order for Bix at the Holton Instrument Factory and he was extremely proud of it. Many of the better cornet players of the day followed Bix's example and played this particular type of instrument.

Hughes Panassié, the author of Le Jazz Hot, claimed that Bix achieved a tone and quality that has never been equalled.

Bix never bothered much about his horn or embouchure as most trumpet players do. His only thought was what came out of the front end of that horn. He never worried much about his lip or how high he could play or how long he could play. In fact, he was always surprised when some of the boys told him he had just hit high "C." That didn't make much different to Bix when he was improvising. How it sounded was his main concern.

Panassié wrote of Bix's imagination and improving and mentioned his superb chorus on "Sweet Sue" with the Whiteman Orchestra as a striking example. I certainly agree with him. Bix's chorus on "Sweet Sue" is a masterpiece, but he has many other records with wonderful choruses on them that collectors and critics have said little about. Our Okeh Record of "Mississippi Mud" is one.

Panassié stated that Bix's phrases were never thrown together haphazardly. They were organized into a tonality as solid as that of the original tune and that his improvisations were constructed in such perfect proportions that he would be quite ready to think that he had plotted them out in advance were they not so obviously spontaneous.

Bix worked out his choruses and each time he played them he tried to improve them! Paul Whiteman would verify the fact that Bix never played a chorus the same way twice, until he got just what he wanted and then he stuck to that chorus! Once in a while, Bix would try to improve on the finished product but most of the time he did not distort his own composition. This brings out the fact that it was not extemporaneous music! When a great artist plays a chorus of a new tune, he draws from the great supply of knowledge and ideas he has stored in his subconscious mind. If he didn't have this background of phrases and intervals he couldn't play a chorus at all!

To analyze Bix's style is beyond the words of most writers. About all I can say is that Bix had the tone and the ability to impart the ideas that came into his head from, shall we say, another world. Therefore, Bix became immortal.

Bix and I often talked of the early influence in life with regard to music. It always brought to mind the first three-piece band that interested me. They were three colored boys playing on the levee in Memphis. Trombone, a jug, and a guitar. The boy who played the guitar would get a most unusual effect with the neck of a pop bottle on his little finger which he applied to the strings. I especially remember something called "Sweet Potato Pie."

Many men have taken credit, or should I say, have attempted to take credit for teaching Bix cornet. As far as I know, Bix had no instruction on trumpet or cornet. He probably did about the same thing that I did—learned the fingering and from there on handled the situation.

Whether Bix was influenced by other great trumpet men is unimportant because he played like Bix! Sure, he was inspired by some of them, but teaching Bix would have been pretty much like teaching a sea gull to fly.

Emmett Hardy might have said, "Boy, you got feathers—why don't you fly?"

Satchmo might have said, "Boy, your wings is so big—go on and sail some."

Red Nichols could have said, "You've left the nest, son, you're flyin' alone and good."

Hoagy Carmichael did say, "From here out, you're my boy!"

In that incomparable jazz band of the Great Beyond

> **there are a few chairs being held open. Save a chair for me, Bix. I'll see you up there, sometime.**

Paul Whiteman and Margaret Livingston were married in Denver, Colorado on August 18, 1931, at the home of Whiteman's parents, Wilberforce and Elfrida Whiteman. Dr. George Vosburgh officiated at the ceremony that was restricted to members of the family and close friends. The honeymoon was brief, and the couple returned to Chicago and set up residency in a suite at the Edgewater Beach Hotel.

Whiteman now discovered that while he had gained a wife, he was to lose a close friend and business manager. Jimmy Gillespie and Margaret Livingston clashed at the outset over the way that the band should be handled, and Gillespie offered his resignation, effective September 1. Jack Lavin was hired as the new business manager.

Jane Vance was attending Northwestern University, and had applied in September for membership to the Gamma Pi Beta Sorority. She was told that before she could become accepted she had to pass an initiation task. She was informed that she was to become a contestant on one of Paul Whiteman's weekly Friday ''College Nights,'' a promotional feature that allowed local college students to perform with his band. Jane agreed to the initiation stunt with the stipulation that two other girls would accompany her. This was agreed. The trio rehearsed by singing along with Boswell Sisters recordings and adapting their stylings. All three girls, and another friend that they persuaded to play piano, headed for the Edgewater Beach Hotel on Friday night.

During a September 1990 interview, Jane Vance clearly remembered the events that followed:

> Roy Bargy gave up his piano to our group, and after the introduction of the song, my two partners ''froze,'' and left me, *alone,* to sing ''Honeysuckle Rose.''
>
> The applause that followed was more than the usual polite appreciation shown by the crowd, it was more sincere and enthusiastic.
>
> ''Young lady,'' said Paul Whiteman, ''I want to see you!''
>
> I tried to tell Paul that I was singing the number only as a

prank, due to the sorority initiation, and that I realized that I couldn't sing, but . . .

"What are you talking about?" Paul said. "You sounded great! Can you come down tomorrow? I'd like to hear you at the NBC Studio, behind a proper microphone, and really give you a chance to sing."

I couldn't believe what was happening. I eagerly told my parents about the chance of a job with Whiteman's band, but I never dreamed it would happen. My family were long time friends with the Rushtons, and it was decided that their son, Joe, would drive me to the audition.

The next day, Joe sat next to Whiteman, in the control room, listening to me sing. "She's a great little singer," Joe told Whiteman, without a hint of modesty. "I know that you'll enjoy having her in your band."

Whiteman listened to me sing about a half dozen tunes, and then asked, "When can you start?"

In those days, Joe knew practically every musician in Chicago, often hosting an entire band for dinner at his parent's home, who were wealthy in their own way. Rushton was a bit older than most of the gang, so we nicknamed him "Mother Rushton," as he always seemed to be around to help and advise us. Rushton did not follow into his dad's business at the stock exchange, but devoted his life to music, and became one of the all time greats on the bass-saxophone.

I arranged a meeting for my parents with Paul and Margaret in their hotel suite. My parents were given assurances by Paul Whiteman that either Margaret or Jack Lavin would keep an eye on me, and make certain that I was taken care of, and Paul simply gave all the correct answers to my parents' questions. Perhaps a bit reluctantly, they consented to allow me to sing with the band at the Edgewater Beach Hotel.

Victor Records re-signed the Whiteman Orchestra and after an absence of a year from the recording studio, they returned in late September and early October 1931.

November found the band in New York, but they returned to Chicago in December, and again played at the Edgewater Beach Hotel. While the band was in the East, Whiteman had arranged to have Jane Vance sing with the band that had performed at the Edgewater Beach Hotel in their absence, and now he felt that she was ready to become a regular member of his band.

Mildred Bailey was the featured singer, and Jane Vance learned to admire her talent and friendship deeply. ''I was a big fan of Mildred's,'' Jane remarked. ''We hit it off right from the start.''

On January 2, 1932, the band started a nine-week tour that eventually took them to New York. Jane remembered some advice:

> Mike Pingitore appointed himself as my guardian angel. ''Now when you get on the train,'' Pingitore explained to me, ''there are two cars. One for 'The Gents,' and the other for 'The Bums.' You'll find the nondrinkers, like Kurt, Rank, Goldie, and Strict, in The 'Gents.' The crew that drinks, plays cards, and are a bit rowdy, like Roy, Andy, Mischa, they will be in The 'Bums' car. It would be best for you to ride in The 'Gents' car.
>
> I asked Mike, ''Will you be in 'The Gents,' too?''
>
> ''Oh no,'' Pingitore replied. ''I'll be in the other car. More fun there!''
>
> Pingitore's lucky number was five, and he insisted upon always having berth number five in the sleeper car. He explained it to me and suggested that he could take the upper berth and I could have the lower one. ''Maybe,'' he said, ''the number five will bring you as much luck as it has brought me over the years.''

Red Norvo, in a September 1990 interview, said:

> I met Mildred Bailey when she was doing a fifteen-minute radio broadcast, two or three times a week, over the NBC network in Chicago. I was on staff then, and got to know her pretty well, and we started dating.
>
> I believe that Whiteman heard me when I was with Ben Bernie, and hired me as a result. When he left on that January 1932 tour, I shared dressing room space with Tram at the various theatres that we played. Whiteman had me featured in a bit where I played slap hammers, as they were called, and I'd end up breaking these on a regular basis. They were tympani sticks with felt and then covered with leather. I was always popping them out, and Tram would sew them up and have them ready for the next show.
>
> Tram decided that he was going to design a pair that wouldn't break. He took two steel golf shafts, cut them down, and placed washers on the end and another one back about three inches. He wrapped the sticks with string,

> building them up, and covered them with felt. He had a harness maker make the covering. Things went great for the first couple of shows, but by the last show, the washers had worked their way through the covering and as a result, I chipped 6 or 7 bars on the xylophone. The next day, things were back to Tram sewing them.

Whiteman had booked the band into four and five shows a day, plus recordings, radio programs, and public appearances for charity, and the work was starting to take a toll on Tram. On April 17, he received another job offer.

> **Along came Charlie Horvath, my old boss from the Goldkette Band. He tried to sell me on the idea of organizing my own band, but I didn't think too much of the idea.**

Ferde Grofé had composed one of his outstanding contributions to American music, with his "Grand Canyon Suite." The band recorded it over a three-day period in late April, just before vacation time. Victor Records noted Jack Fulton as being on vocaphone for this session, in addition to his regular trombone work, and for many years, researchers have often wondered just what this was. During the "On The Trail" section, Fulton hummed through a megaphone, giving the passage an added effect. This was the "vocaphone" that Victor listed.

> **I had forgotten about our talks when Charlie Horvath arrived on May 3 with a contract for eight weeks at the Bellerive Hotel in Kansas City at $1,850 a week!**
>
> **Now this was something I didn't want to turn down. Even though Whiteman was against it, I was determined to give it a whirl. Paul told me that my chair would never be occupied, and I could always come back if things didn't work out.**
>
> **Off to Chicago to organize my band.**[33]

Paul and Margaret took the Los Angeles Limited to California and found an army of reporters awaiting them. Whiteman assured the newsmen that they were tired, but if they would come around the next day to the Ambassador Hotel, the Whitemans would host an informal breakfast and they could ask all the questions they wanted.

---

[33]Vacation period started after May 5 closing at the Stanley Theatre in Pittsburgh.

The number one topic was Whiteman's diet.[34]

Margaret started the discussion: "To begin with, it was done without costly dietitians. I read every book that I could on diets and then discovered the secret. It is simply this: Starches and proteins should never be mixed at the same meal. It is alright to mix proteins and sweets, and sweets and starches, but never proteins and starches." She continued, "Nearly every meal I start with a huge bowl of fruit salad or vegetable salad, loaded with lettuce, or sometimes, for a change, a salad of fruits and vegetables."

"Then," Margaret admitted, "once a week we will go on a sugar jag and eat a box of candy, but we never eat the candy until three or four hours after a meal."

Margaret concluded with, "Now we start the day with a light breakfast, and have a light lunch, and a heavy dinner."

"Paul," asked one of the reporters, "when you were out here, last time, you told us that your weight was 287. Did you lose the 100 pounds that you promised Margaret that you'd lose prior to your marriage?"

"You bet I did," stated Whiteman. "I am now at 186 pounds, and trying to stay there. I feel like a new person. Me for diets and more diets."

"You mugs really wanted to hear about this diet," Whiteman asked, "and what I think of it."

"When I first started to lose weight, it wasn't so bad. But then I started to worry. In the first place, my suits began to get much too large for me. I took the problem up with my tailor and he started to cut them down. Soon he couldn't cut them down any more. This meant that I had to buy new suits."

"Next my feet started to shrink and my shoes got too large. My boot maker was able to shorten them by manipulating the seams on the heels. But my feet started to hurt, so I had to buy new shoes."

"My head shrank, too, and consequently new hats were in order."

"This diet certainly wasn't an economic move. It cost me more than $2,400 for a new wardrobe. But I kept my word to Margaret, and with her help I plan to stay at my present weight. Besides, I'm able to do something that I haven't done in some time. Every now and then, I get out the old violin and play a number or two with my band. Now there is room for me to tuck it under my chin."

---

[34]Compiled from *Los Angeles Times* newspapers with permission of Renee Nembhard, Public Information Department (August 3, 1990).

CHAPTER ELEVEN

FRANK TRUMBAUER & HIS ORCHESTRA 1932–1933

TRAM'S ARRIVAL IN CHICAGO, and subsequent meeting with Charles Horvath on May 7, 1932, resulted in a bit of a surprise. Horvath had not hired a single musician. That task of putting together arrangements and hiring musicians fell to Tram, and by the 12th he had his first rehearsal, with disastrous results. He was to note in his diary "the band was sure sad but it will be better with better men."

In the meantime, perhaps having second thoughts about hiring an unknown band, the Bellerive Hotel was reconsidering their offer, lowering it first to $1750, then to $1600, and then considering cancelling the engagement.

Pierre André, one of the backers of the band, made the trip to Kansas City to confront the management of the hotel and inform them that Tram was putting his band together and that he would honor the contract. Management suggested a May 24 opening, which Pierre relayed to Tram. Tram turned it down, being firm on the agreed upon date, June 9.

Max Connett was hired on May 17th, not only as the first trumpet chair, but as the business manager as well. Tram presented Connett with a small caliber revolver that he felt Connett needed to protect the cash receipts from various engagements the band would play.[35]

One of the first hirings was the popular singing trio from radio

[35]The pistol given to Connett was never fired. "I probably would have shot myself if I had fired it," Connett remarked. In 1991, Connett gave the pistol to Tram's grandson, Bill. Connett had kept it, all these years, and he returned it intact, including a full chamber of the original bullets.

station WMAQ, who substituted for the **Amos 'n Andy** radio program on Sunday nights, their night off. The trio consisted of Cedric Spring, Harold Jones, and LeRoy Buck. All doubled on instruments.

The band rehearsed on the top floor of the Furniture Mart, and before long, they had: Max Connett (first trumpet); Vance "Chick" Rice (second trumpet); Hal Matthews (trombone); Gale Stout (first alto saxophone); Harold Jones (tenor saxophone); Malcolm Elstead[36] (third alto saxophone); Craig Leitch (guitar); Cedric Spring (guitar/violin/accordion); Leon Kaplan (violin/guitar); LeRoy Buck (drums); Charles McConnell (bass); Herm Crone (piano); Frank Trumbauer (saxophones/leader). Vocals were by Craig Leitch (tenor), Hal Redus (baritone), and Elinor Sherry, plus the trio.

Leitch, who had been with Whiteman, decided to join Tram's band. As a youth, he once gave a "canned" audition to a radio station. The station was holding auditions for a new staff singer, so Leitch called the station manager and told him that due to his present job, he could not appear in person, but he asked if he might send a demonstration recording of his voice to be considered. He was told that they would accept this audition. Leitch, with the imp of youth in his veins, soaked the red label off a Caruso record and sent it to the auditioning staff. "Nice" came back the station manager's note with the record, "but the quality of your voice isn't rich enough."[37]

The band's theme song was a short arrangement, utilizing Tram's chorus from the 1927 recording of "Singin' The Blues."

Jack Kapp, then of Brunswick Records, was anxious to produce some Bing Crosby recordings. He flew from New York to Chicago, contacted Dick Voynow, then head of their Chicago branch, and discussed the matter. Bing was appearing at the Oriental Theatre in a stage production, backed by his own men, Eddie Lang and Lennie Hayton, and the house orchestra. The dates of May 25 and May 26 were chosen to record.

Tram was contacted about backing Bing, and he included a few men from his band to be augmented with Lang and Hayton. Hayton

[36]Malcolm Elstad's duties also included driving the small rented truck that carried their instruments and luggage during their engagements.

[37]Press release offered to various cities that were on Tram's itinerary. A few newspapers reprinted the story.

acted as the arranger and manager, and he talked through each arrangement with the musicians, hoping to achieve the desired results. The tunes recorded were "Cabin In The Cotton," "With Summer Coming On," "Love Me Tonight," and "Some Of These Days," the latter containing a Bing "scat vocal" improvised in the manner that Crosby felt Bix would have played it. After the recording sessions, Bing told Tram that he felt the future was in motion pictures and he was hopeful of getting into that medium.

A week before our opening date, I received a wire from the Bellerive Hotel stating that I could not open. It seemed that the manager who hired the band did not have the authority to do so and therefore my contract was no good.

Brother, this was a big blow! In addition to all the hard work, I had spent a lot of money organizing the band, paying for arrangements, uniforms, etc. And, besides, there was my pride!

I wired the hotel at once: "Arriving on date previously set. Unless you want two bands on the stand, you'd better not hire anyone else."

We arrived at the Bellerive on schedule. I couldn't find the manager, nor could I find out who had any authority.

I finally rounded up the publicity man and instructed him to get some ads in the local papers about our opening. I contacted the radio stations about our broadcasts.

Finally the owner of the hotel called me into his office.

"Now look here," he said, "I can't let you play here for nothing. The union will get me and you, too."

I was so damn mad I could have punched him in the nose.

"Tell you what I'll do," he said at last. "I'll pay you scale, deduct your rooms, and you can have all the cover charge. Nobody knows you here—you don't draw much of a crowd, so we'll both be safe."

"I don't give a damn what it is—just write it out and this time, you sign it," I replied. And, he did!

But strange things happen! Opening night was a complete sellout. Telegrams poured in from all around the country. Everyone in the music business, big and small, sent their good wishes for our success. They were posted all over the lobby, and guests tore them down for souvenirs.

> **The first week we took in $1,650 for our share. The second week was the same. Now the shoe was on the other foot.**
> **I was given two weeks' notice because I refused to turn back the cover charge to the big boss, and the coverage was reduced.**
> **The last two weeks I only averaged $950 a week.**
> **By now I was completely disillusioned about the band business. Horvath had nothing for me, so I signed with Fredericks Brothers.**

The first engagement? The Bellerive Hotel. ''Brought back by popular demand'' on July 10. The hotel advertisement read: ''The musical organization included: Elinor Sherry, a well-known radio and vaudeville star who has a sensational contralto voice; Craig Leitch, tenor, another of the original Burtnett Biltmore Trio and Whiteman's ''King's Jesters''; Hal Redus, baritone, former Whiteman soloist; ''The Three Spooks'', vocal trio comprising Spring, Jones, and Buck, who also double on nine instruments; the ''Little Gypsy'' string ensemble, a six-piece group boasting three guitars, an accordion, string bass, and Trumbauer's saxophone, headed by ''Cappy'' Kaplan, a talented Russian addition; a banjo trio and a guitar quartet.''

The ads also noted the ''cool dry-ice air'' in the Terrace Cafe, where they played. Max Connett well remembers that this atmosphere consisted of huge blocks of dry-ice, placed at various spots in the room, each backed with a fan blowing on the dry-ice, pointed towards the dance floor!

Herman Crone reminisced about joining Trumbauer just before the Crosby recording date.

> Frank was priceless and probably one of the greatest story tellers I've ever heard. It was so hot at the Bellerive that we would go out on the front lawn or veranda of the hotel, where it was a bit cooler, and he would regale us with endless stories about legendary figures, like Bix, Miff Mole, Joe Venuti, etc.
> In my humble opinion, Tram's venture into the big bands, well in advance of the other swing bands to follow (including Goodman) was, in his mind, one of the more important periods in his life. He was a man whose name, if not revered, was certainly respected by all musicians of that era. To me, he was a giant—as a musician and a man!

> Tram, fronting a band, was a novel thing in those days. Here was a great virtuoso, instead of some personality guy (who was a better businessman than musician), as a leader. It is my belief that had he been handled in a smart manner, he would have emerged as the *big* band of the 30s. The scope of his appeal was beyond imagination. The young or the old, the dancers or the listeners, the squares or the heps. He was one of the all time greats in the music business and way too few ever mention him or recall his tremendous contribution to jazz and popular music. He stood alone—and what's more, his saxophone would be just as acceptable today as it was 60 years ago.

Upon closing at the hotel, the band was booked through a series of one-nighters throughout the Middle West. Following a Saturday night dance at the Frog Hop (ballroom), a case containing Tram's two saxophones and clarinet was stolen. This crime wave also included "hits" on Jacob Lazriowich's grocery store, where $42 in merchandise was stolen (including $4 in pennies, and $1.50 in stamps), and a filling station at Thirty-Seventh Street and Mitchell, where a radio was taken.[38] Tram offered a reward of $100 for the return of his clarinet and two saxophones with "no questions asked." The Jenkins Music Company of Kansas City acted as the go-between, and his stolen instruments were returned.

Herm Crone's August 1968 letter recalled an incident at Riverview Park, "about a week before we were to record":

> My only unhappy memory of playing with Tram was a tragic accident that took place. When Tram was at the peak of his popularity as a jazzman, he helped design and set up the mold for a pair of C-melody saxophones. When they were finished, one of them became his pet. It was perfect in all respects.
>
> Tram had a habit of laying the sax down on a light control box, about a foot in diameter and about three feet tall, and it was me that brushed by it and knocked it down. It landed on the bell of the horn, and to outward appearances didn't seem to be damaged, but when he picked it up and tried to play it, all he could get was a sound like a fish horn. I don't believe that I've ever seen a man with a more hurt expression. He took it to his room and worked on it—not for hours, but for days!

[38]Reports on file, St. Joseph, Missouri, Police Department.

> We were recording in Chicago the following week and of course, he had the twin to the sax, but to him it did not play the same. I even went with him up to Elkhart, where the horns had been made, but even they were unable to restore it to its original form. I think only a musician can appreciate the loss, and I hope that wherever he is today, he has forgiven me.

The Chicago recording date for Columbia Records was on August 17, 1932. Among the selections recorded were ''Cinderella's Wedding Day,'' ''Bass Drum Dan,'' and a novelty arrangement of ''The Newest St. Louis Blues,'' in which arranger Cedric Spring had the vocal sung in pig Latin. Columbia Records described ''Business in Q'' as ''a dance musician's delight,'' and ''I Think You're a Honey'' as ''completely performed for the primary rhythmic purpose for which its originality intended.''

Cedric Spring's August 1969 letter well remembered the final number recorded that day:

> Frank told me to leave it all blank. He told me to sing the vocal, and then make way because he wanted to just let himself go on the tune. I left it all up to Tram, it was his recording. Anyone that has this recording will have one of the finest that Tram ever did. After it was released, it was one of the most requested numbers by the patrons at our dances.
>
> I once asked Tram why, when he played our theme song, ''Singin' The Blues,'' he always played his solo note-for-note from the 1927 Okeh Recording. He said the customers were acquainted with the recording, knew the solo, and expected him to play it, and he didn't want to disappoint them.

After their engagement at the Golden Pheasant in Cleveland (September 3–10), their next stop was in Chicago at The Lincoln Tavern.

Tram decided to pilot his own plane from Cleveland to Chicago, and he ran low on gas. Darkness was fast approaching, and there was a rain-like mist so thick and low that he could not see the ground. Then he discovered that his landing lights wouldn't function because the batteries were low. He spotted the Pal-Waukee Airport's beacon through the fog, and zoomed over what he thought was the hangar, hoping to attract enough attention to have the field's landing lights turned on. He zoomed a second time. Still no lights! On the third try, the engine began to sputter and he knew a forced landing was necessary. Tram headed straight into the wind, straightened his stick, and turned off the ignition (and later admitted that he prayed that an ambulance would be handy), and started his descent. His experience as a flyer came into focus and he was able to make a safe landing on the Pal-Waukee runway. Then the field's landing lights came on!

"I remember that incident well," Herm Crone stated in his August 1968 letter. "In those days there were few instruments and Tram flew 'by the seat of his pants.' He told me at one point, when he was out over the lake, he discovered that he was upside down!"

Gale Stout recounted in a November 1968 letter:

> When we ended the engagement at The Lincoln Tavern, I talked to Tram about accepting an offer from Paul Whiteman. Frank was a man you loved, admired, and copied. Those of us that were privileged to play with him, day by day, heard Tram play such wonderful things at times, things so musical and sensitive.
>
> Frank was a great salesman, a spellbinder, and he could sell you on most anything. He sold me on staying, which I did for a few more weeks. There never was anyone quite like Frank Trumbauer.

October and November 1932 found the band on tour through Southern Illinois, Texas, and Oklahoma. En route from Dallas to Galveston, they stopped in Conroe on November 14 for fuel and something to eat. Cedric spotted a movie house across the street and made the suggestion that they take a break from the long trip to watch **Grand Hotel.** The idea met with full approval, and each member purchased a ticket for 25 cents at the ticket booth, and was handed a folding chair. Once inside the theatre, they discovered that they could set their folding chairs anywhere they felt offered the best view of the screen.

The band opened November 16 at the Sui Jen in Galveston, Texas (Sui Jen means "crystal" in Chinese). The club had a flickering dragon draped over the doorway, Chinese lights illuminated the interior, and the menu highlighted chop suey. Their slogan was: "Like A Purple Chinese Night under the lambent light of stars. . . . America's shrine of the smart to dine and dance."

Tram felt the bookings Fredericks Brothers had arranged were too far away from the cities that he wanted to play, Chicago and New York.

> **When MCA[39] heard that I had been booked into the Sui Jen Cafe in Galveston, Texas, they offered Sam Macio, the owner, two week stands for the best bands they had. Naturally they succeeded in getting me out of the place.**

Tram felt that the switch to MCA was a good move because of the radio broadcast exposure. They advertised their bands as "On The Air—Everywhere." MCA suggested Tram add a female vocalist to the band, Frances Kerr, an acclaimed radio star for the NBC network.

MCA booked Tram into the Baker Hotel in Dallas (December 24–January 14, 1933), and, true to their slogan, arranged radio broadcasts of 7:45–8:15 P.M. over WFAA, and added broadcasts on Tuesday and Thursday from 10 to 10:30 P.M., and on Saturday from 10:15 P.M. to midnight. Local newspapers gave rave reviews to the Trumbauer Orchestra, and one singled out Hal Redus, formerly with the St. Louis Municipal Opera Company: "when he sings, one forgets nearly everything else except a beautiful voice, extremely well cultured and capably handled."

MCA booked the band in Chicago, with a few one-nighters along the way. The January 20 appearance in Murphysboro was noted in the newspaper and cited "Frank's unique rendition of . . . 'Strange Interlude' . . . ." The musicians well remember Tram "experimenting" with that tune, and felt that he was preparing it for a recording date, but Tram never recorded it. Musicians remembered these bookings. Cedric Spring stated:

> When we were playing those clubs in Texas, they all had a gambling room. We'd see these Texans come in there with large rolls of money, and you'd never know that the country was in the midst of a depression. Here we were coming from Texas, where money was plentiful and we drove into Chicago and saw the many, long bread lines. It was like

[39]Music Corporation of America, booking agency.

> coming into another time and place. Everywhere we looked, we could see the effects of the Depression.

And LeRoy Buck recalled in February 1969:

> I personally think Frank made a mistake switching to MCA. We had been asked to go to New Orleans in January by Mills-Rockwell, but Frank took the MCA booking at the Moulin Rouge in Chicago, where we were to follow Frankie Masters' Orchestra. We arrived, and found the club had folded, and Masters was en route to New Orleans to fill the job. MCA did not have anything further for us.

Tram had to face his musicians and ask them to accept whatever work they could find in the Chicago area, and promised that he would try and reorganize the band with some definite dates. Tram returned home to Mitzi, completely discouraged and ready to forget the entire venture, but her strong will persuaded Tram to "keep trying, something will turn up." A couple of dates, late in February 1933 were booked, and Mitzi drove Tram to the dances to render moral support. When Tram took his turn driving, Mitzi would sing lullabies to their son, Bill, who accompanied them, putting him to sleep in the car's back seat. Cedric Spring cited reminders of Beiderbecke:

> You have to remember, every time we played a dance, someone would come up and tell Frank about a local trumpet player that sounded just like Bix. Tram would try and be polite about it, but sometimes he got roped in to hearing some young boy that just graduated from high school and no more sounded like Bix than anything.
>
> When we played Davenport [*Ed. note: February 26*], Tram was told about this local trumpet player that he had to hear. Frank and Mitzi had already made arrangements, after the dance, to have dinner with Bix's mother, so LeRoy Buck and some of the guys and I went to hear him. He impressed us, not that he played like Bix because he really didn't, but he had made some of the band's arrangements that knocked us out. We told Tram, and he suggested that Russ Case send us an arrangement and he'd decide for himself.

Tram's low ebb, due to the lack of jobs, was evident when he jotted a note to a friend:

> **We've been banging through the woods and it's breaking my heart.**
>
> **Roy Bargy had the Maytag Washing Machine radio show, and Paul had the Allied Quality Paint program. I played both radio shows and the Edgewater Beach Hotel job. All of this helped me get well from the stock market losses that I suffered in the crash of 1929.**
>
> **I managed to accumulate around $12,000 which I deposited in a Chicago bank.**
>
> **One night, one of Paul's friends told me that I should buy Johns-Manville stock at 14 and hang on to it. Now he should have known that I wouldn't buy stock in the United States Mint. I had been burned once and that was enough!**
>
> **While I sat around and watched that stock go up to 156, President Franklin Roosevelt took office on March 4, 1933, and one of the first things that he did was declare a "Bank Holiday" on March 6. There had been many rumors circulating around the country which caused many investors to withdraw their funds and forced banks into bankruptcy. The president decided to put a stop to the bank runs, and determine which banks were solvent, and just how much money this country had in accounts.**
>
> **You guessed it! My bank wasn't solvent and I lost all of my money.**
>
> **Now going broke was becoming a bit monotonous! Right then and there, I decided to spend everything I made. No more worrying about losing my money.**

Still no work, and on March 10, Tram wrote: **"Just plain nothing."**

On March 13, the Blackhawk Restaurant in Chicago contacted Tram and asked if he could have a band for an engagement on the 16th. They discussed the possibility of additional jobs, and once a deal was set, Tram reorganized his band, with the following personnel: Max Connett, Vance Rice (trumpets); Joe Harris (trombone); Frank Trumbauer (C-melody/alto saxophones); Ken Mild (first alto saxophone); Hugh Doyle (tenor saxophone); Mal Elstad (third alto saxophone); Cedric Spring (violin/accordion/

guitar); Leon Kaplan (violin/guitar); Craig Leitch (guitar); Herman Crone (piano); Charles McConnell (bass); LeRoy Buck (drums); Frances Kerr, Hal Redus (vocalists).

Russ Case, acting upon the suggestion of LeRoy Buck and Cedric Spring, sent an arrangement to Tram in late March. It was a full band treatment of "In A Mist."

> **I wired Russ to join us in Chicago. I offered him twenty-five dollars a week for any arrangements that he made for the band. He had been playing in a band in Iowa for twelve dollars a week. He made some pretty good arrangements, he was a good kid, and we hit it off just fine.**

In mid-April 1933, the band did a two-week tour through the Midwest before returning to Chicago. In July 1990, Cedric Spring told John Steiner of the stop in Omaha:

> I played mainly violin with the band, but I did double on accordion. While we were playing there, I noticed some fellow in the audience, watching me and he said, "when you going to play that accordion?" I told him that we had some tunes where I played it a few times. When we got back to the hotel, there was this same fellow, sitting in the lobby, and he wanted me to show him my accordion. He had a little six-piece band, travelling around the country, and he persuaded me to get Max Connett to dig it out of the truck. He played it in the lobby of the hotel and he about woke everyone up. The instrument made so much noise, what with the marble walls, and he played until about two in the morning. He really liked my accordion. I was playing an Excellisor at the time. His name? Lawrence Welk!

In Sioux City, Iowa, directly across the street from their engagement, the marquee proclaimed, "Mildred Bailey."

> **Mildred started before our engagement, so I purchased a ticket, found a seat, and sat back and enjoyed her singing: "Rockin' Chair," "Don't Take Your Love From Me," "Honeysuckle Rose," and so many more.**
>
> **Mildred didn't know that I was in the audience until I yelled out: "Hoss, sing one for me!"**
>
> **That broke her up! She stopped right in the middle of**

her performance, put her hand up to her forehead to shield the spot lights, and said, "Trammy, where is you?"

I told her that we were playing right across the street and suggested that she come over when her show was finished.

"It's a date," she said.

Everyone loved Millie. She's no longer with us, but her memory will live forever.

Red Norvo explained the circumstances, during his September 1990 interview, of Mildred's leaving Paul Whiteman:

> When Paul relocated from Chicago to New York, it left me without a job. His band were all card carriers from the New York Local, but I wasn't, I was a member of the Chicago Local. When we went into the Biltmore Hotel in 1932 for an extended stay, it meant that I had to have a lengthy waiting period as a transfer musician before I could work in New York. Paul and I decided that this would not work out, so I left the band.
>
> Mildred found out, when they were playing the Paramount Theatre, that he was getting an extra $1500 a week for her as a top attraction with the band. She felt that Paul should compensate her, but he refused. When they settled in the Biltmore, she persisted in her demands, telling Paul that what he was paying her didn't cover the gowns that she had to buy, and she felt that since he was getting extra money for her, he should raise her salary. Both felt their positions were right, and Mildred felt it best to quit in August 1932, and she did.

The boys in Tram's band well remember Mildred's appearance that night with them. She sang some of the tunes associated with her, and then the evening ended with her singing requests, with Tram's sax softly backing her every chorus.

In the months that followed, Tram centered his activities around the Chicago area, and the midwest, finally realizing that his dream of hitting it "big" wasn't to be.

Former Paul Whiteman cornetist, Andy Secrest, contacted Tram and asked if there might be an opening for him. Whiteman had let Secrest go and hired Bunny Berigan. He was in Chicago due to Jane Vance's persuading Ben Bernie to hire Secrest, but

Secrest told Tram that his heart just wasn't in playing with this band. Tram hired him as a replacement for Vance Rice.

> **In spite of the many heartaches, I was playing better than I had ever played, but unfortunately there weren't many places to play. I finally decided that the band had to go.**
>
> **I was saturated in the Paul Whiteman beliefs of getting a top man for every post in the band and ignore the costs. In this way, I was ahead of the public. Dancers weren't yet ready for the swing music that we offered. It cost me $7,000 before I called it a day! My main downfall was that I insisted on hiring only the best musicians that I could get!**

Harold Jones's views were presented in a December 1968 letter:

> This was a fine band! It had about everything—well-trained professionals, playing well-rehearsed fine arrangements, excellent vocals, good entertainment value for stage and floor shows, and above all, Frank! As the kids say nowadays, "he was something else!" It is too bad that the band was organized at the depths of the Depression.

Max Connett and Tram decided to try their luck in New York.

> **Russ had no money to go anywhere, and as a matter of fact, had nowhere to go. I told him all about New York and how I thought he could make a go of it with us.**
>
> **"What do you say, Russ?" I asked.**
>
> **Russ didn't even think it over. "Let's use my car and we'll save some money."**
>
> **His car was really a clunker. We bought two used tires and among numerous repairs we fixed thirteen flats on our way to New York, but we finally made it.**

Max Connett remembered the trip during a January 1991 interview:

> **None of us had enough money for separate rooms, so we pooled our resources, and Tram was chosen to register for the cheapest room at the old Paramount Hotel. It turned out to have one bed in which all three of us slept. Our breakfast, lunch, and dinner consisted of rolls and coffee.**

Since Frank was registered, he didn't have any trouble with the desk clerk, but Russ and I had to dodge him at every turn and make our way up to our room. After a week of this routine, I received an offer from Vincent Lopez to join his band at the Chez Paree in Chicago, and I accepted.

I found that I still had a good reputation in New York. Somehow or other, I had to get some money. I didn't have the nerve to go to Paul, after my failure, or what I felt was my failure, so I went to some of the booking offices and offered to do single dates until I got started again.

"Sorry, Tram," they said, "we'd like nothing better to use you but we can't stand your price. We just can't pay fifty to seventy-five dollars a night."

I left—too proud to say that I needed the work.

The next day, I went back. I had an idea!

"Tell you what I'll do. I'll work your jobs for scale if you'll use a kid I have with me on trumpet."

A deal was made and I went home with some dates booked.

Russ had found a small apartment where we cooked, slept, and practiced.

After two weeks of constant practicing, we heard a knock on the door. We opened it and there stood a man who towered over us.

"Please, fellas," he said in a plaintive voice, "won't you be a little quieter? I have to get up at four in the morning. I'm a policeman and I have to have my sleep, so hold it down a little, please, fellas."

We made the rounds of the cafes where the good men were playing. I introduced Russ to all of them, and we bought drinks just like we had money.

One of the music publishers[40] asked me to write some solos for saxophone and also an instrumentation book for saxophone. When we weren't jobbing, I worked for them.

I was thinking seriously of joining Rudy Vallee and, as always, I decided to ask Paul what he thought about it. We met for lunch and I asked his advice.

"Tram, if you work anywhere you'd better come back to work with me," the Great man said. "Let's say rehearsal on Tuesday?"

---

[40]Most certainly, Robbins Music Publishers.

CHAPTER TWELVE

THE THREE T's
1933–1934

THERE HAD BEEN MANY CHANGES in the Paul Whiteman Organization during Tram's absence. As a result of the January 20, 1931, joint announcement by Whiteman and Universal, a series of 20–25 minute musical shorts were made in 1932. These two-reelers were filmed in New York, produced by William Rowland and Monte Brice, and distributed by Universal Studios.

Each two reeler was tied in with a recognized personality of that day. The famous radio columnist, Nick Kenny, featured Mildred Bailey in two films. **The Radio Mystery Murder,** one film in the **Down Memory Lane** series, hosted by Broadway columnist Louis Sobol, had John Fulton singing "A Boy And A Girl Dancing" and (as announced in the film) Paul Whiteman's latest protege, Peggy Healy singing "Fit As A Fiddle." Whiteman's entire orchestra, with solo spots for John Fulton and "The New Rhythm Boys," were featured in **I Know Everybody And Everybody's Racket,** starring critic and columnist Walter Winchell. [*Ed. note: A 1990 telephone conversation with an official at the UCLA Film-Television Archives, confirmed that they own a print of the Winchell short. They estimated a price tag of $4,000 to completely restore the print for satisfactory viewing but added that this was not among their immediate priorities.*] Unfortunately these and other shorts did not include Trumbauer. Victor Records issued a promotional short in 1933 that showed the Paul Whiteman recording session of November 25, 1932, with John Fulton singing "Turn Out The Lights."

Kraft-Phenix was now sponsoring Whiteman's weekly radio program, **The Kraft Music Hall.** Whiteman was initially signed as the headliner, but on June 26, 1933, Al Jolson guest-starred and became an instant hit with the audience and sponsors when he sang "Cantor On The Sabbath," "My Gal Sal," and "Sonny Boy." Jolson was signed, as a result, to co-star with Whiteman when he was available. Jolson was under contract to Warner Brothers and scheduled for the film **Wonder Bar** to begin production in late 1933. When Trumbauer joined the Whiteman Orchestra at the Paradise Cafe, Jolson was in Hollywood filming **Wonder Bar.**

Whiteman's Orchestra offered a varied listening program for the variety hour. Featured were medleys from Victor Herbert, "An American In Paris," a variety of vocalists, and, for the younger crowd, "swing music" (as it was now called)!

> **Well, naturally I felt pretty happy about rejoining Paul and I guess I floored Russ Case when I told him the good news? I was a little dumbfounded myself.**
>
> **Rehearsals were under way for a concert and I was asked to prepare a solo. [Ed. note: December 15, 1933, concert].**
>
> **I told my publishers that I wouldn't give them my numbers unless Russ arranged them. A sort of take it or leave it deal. They agreed but warned me that for my own good, I should use a more experienced arranger. They were partly right, I guess, because Case's arrangements were so tough that the boys in the smaller bands couldn't cut them.**
>
> **I convinced Paul that Russ should make the arrangements for my solos, and he also did some other work in the band.**
>
> **My next move was to set Russ in radio. This was practically impossible for a newcomer in New York. I introduced him to all of my friends and personally guaranteed his work and conduct.**
>
> **Charlie Margulis, no longer with Whiteman, and Mannie Klein, were two of the top boys in radio. They began to use Russ as a substitute and he lived up to all I had said about him.**
>
> **Mannie Klein left for Hollywood and not long after that Charlie Margulis left town. That put Russ in the number one spot. He soon had every show he could possibly play. After that he had his own radio show**

sponsored by Seven Up. Later Russ became Musical Director for RCA-Victor Records. Case worked hard. He made a lot of money, and he spent a lot of money.

A few years later, Russ was a guest on a coast to coast radio program. When he was asked how he got to New York, he replied "Oh, by playing with bands and such."

How could he possibly have forgotten our trip to New York in that beat-up car? And eating beans and fried potatoes so we could spend our money putting up a front for the boys who could help Russ? Maybe he did forget it? And then maybe it wouldn't have sounded right? Nevertheless, he was still my boy, good or bad. A great artist with a tremendous amount of talent. Russ was kind of like Bix in a lot of ways.

The December 1933 issue of *Orchestra World* interviewed Tram and asked for his reaction to rejoining Whiteman. He said: "I intend to continue playing with the greatest leader in the business, help with arranging, and produce the things that are possible only under the able hands of Mr. Whiteman."

Tram officially rejoined Whiteman on December 14, although he had unofficially been playing radio dates,and attending rehearsals, for two weeks prior to that date. One radio date, November 30, had Bunny Berigan and Tram taking solos on "Blue Room" on **The Kraft Music Hall** program. Bunny had been hired as a replacement for Andy Secrest in late 1932, but now was out of favor with Margaret Whiteman, mainly for his refusal to keep the gin bottles off the bandstand. He soon was replaced by Dave Wade and then eventually by Charlie Teagarden. In spite of his shortcomings, Jane Vance had deep admiration for Bunny. As she explained during a 1990 interview:

> Late at night, after we'd have done four or five shows, a radio date, recordings, and what have you, most of the guys would be tired and their lips started to hurt, so some of them laid off the last set. Not Bunny! He played a strong support with that magnificent trumpet of his. Words can't express how much his presence meant when I sang a tune, knowing he was there to back me.

Chester Hazlett left the band in January 1933, and, as Jane Vance remembered:

Benny Goodman called Roy Bargy and said that he heard that Chester was leaving, and he wondered if he might replace him. Roy said, ''Sure, come down for an audition!'' ''Audition?'' Benny cried! Roy told him, ''We know that you can play jazz, but can you play the ''Rhapsody in Blue?'' Apparently Benny decided against the audition, because Benny Bonacio replaced Hazlett.

What I remember best, about these days was the NBC radio studios. NBC purchased all of the land on a city block, but could not budge Hurley's. Apparently this bar had a 99-year lease or something, and NBC could not buy the land and tear down the place, so they built the studio around it! Remember, Prohibition was now repealed. One of Hurley's main features was this huge clock that all of the musicians relied on. The guys would have a drink in the bar, watch that clock, and be able to time, to the second, what it took the elevator to reach the floor of the studio where they were working. It got comical when something went wrong, like someone getting off on the wrong floor, and since the floors with their studios all looked alike, unsuspecting musicians would walk into the studio, sit down, and then discover they were on the wrong radio program!

I made a lot of records and everyone thought they were great but somehow they didn't suit me. I felt that I didn't have the spark to make anything really sensational. Bix was gone! Eddie Lang was gone!

Then Paul added two exciting names in the music business: The Teagarden Brothers! We were featured as ''The Three Ts'': ''Big T'' (Jack), ''Middle T'' (me), and ''Little T'' (Charlie).

The Paul Whiteman Orchestra now offered: Nat Natolie, Harry Goldfield, Charlie Teagarden (trumpets); Bill Rank, Jack Fulton, Jack Teagarden (trombones); Bennie Bonacio, Jack Cordaro, Frank Trumbauer, Charles Strickfaden (reeds); Kurt Dieterle, Mischa Russell, Matty Malneck, Harry Strubel (violins); Roy Bargy, Ramona Davies (pianos); Artie Miller (string bass); Norman McPherson (tuba); Mike Pingitore (guitar/banjo); Herb Quigley (drums); Strubel was also the librarian. Male vocalists were Johnny Mercer, John Fulton, Jack Teagarden, John Hauser and Bob Lawrence; female vocalists, Ramona Davies, Peggy Healy and Jane Vance.

The December 15, 1933, concert at the Metropolitan Opera

House was billed as "The Sixth Experiment In Modern Music," and Whiteman augmented the band to seventy-five musicians. This also served as a benefit concert for the Church Mission of Help of the Diocese of New York.

The program opened with "An American in Paris," using a new arrangement scored by Carroll Huxley. Only a couple of the reviewers noted the absence of any Grofé offerings, and one magazine tossed it away with "maybe Ferde has been too busy?" Actually Whiteman and Grofé ended their relationship early in 1933. The match that started the fire was Grofé's conducting his own composition "Grand Canyon Suite," at the New York premiere performance in the spring of 1932 with another concert orchestra. Whiteman had anticipated presenting the work with his own band that fall. The newspapers publicized the feud towards the end, and Whiteman's last recorded arrangements from Grofé were made on February 7, 1933: "You Are The Song" and "I'd Write A Song."

Roy Bargy revealed on March 18, 1962, that Joe Rushton arranged a 70th birthday party for Ferde Grofé and invited several former Whiteman alumni. At the end of the evening, the party moved to Ferde's home in Santa Monica, and the musicians placed a telephone call to Whiteman at his residence in New Jersey. Ferde, after some urging, talked with Paul. "Any bad feelings that resulted from that 1932 'Grand Canyon Suite' incident were now long since forgotten," reported Bargy. The wounds of many years standing were healed with a single telephone call.

The December 1933 concert offered a "Blues Trilogy" danced by Felicia Sorel, with piano and recital accompaniment by Ramona Davies. A pantomime set to music, this story related the story of a black girl who escapes from her father, who beat her, and crosses the river to go to her lover, only to find him with another woman. She then walks into the cold river and disappears. William Grant Still, one of the most gifted of black composers, offered "Deserted Plantation," a musical picture of Uncle Josh, an old black man who is the sole occupant of the dying plantation, and who dreams of past glories.

Dana Suesse, at the piano, played her own composition, "Eight Valses," orchestrated by Dana and Adolph Deutsch. This was skillfully varied between piano and orchestra, offering "jazzy" parts (as one reviewer put it) and colorful variations in rhythm.

''Waltzing Through The Ages'' was a clever arrangement by Adolph Deutsch, showing waltzes from Beethoven and Tschaikovsky's works to ''In The Good Old Summertime'' and ''The Sidewalks Of New York.'' Mike Pingitore played an organ grinder's hurdy-gurdy at the conclusion of this selection, and Whiteman walked over and dropped a coin in a tin cup that Pingitore held up. The audience roared with laughter!

Matt Malneck and Frank Signorelli's offering was ''Park Avenue Fantasy,'' a musical depiction of a penthouse cocktail party. Al Rinker, formerly with the band, submitted a symphonic piece out of a nursery rhyme entitled: ''Peter, Peter, Pumpkin Eater.'' Mike Pingitore did his banjo specially on ''Wabash Blues'' and received loud applause. Russ Case arranged Tram's number, ''Bouncing Ball,'' and it was well received by the audience, and the next day newspaper reviews singled out the presentation. Joseph Livingston's concert arrangement of ''St. Louis Blues'' was next. The program concluded with Roy Bargy featured on ''Rhapsody in Blue.'' Bargy's work on this Gershwin composition has always been nothing short of sensational.

Backstage, following the concert, Whiteman was hosting a number of newspaper reporters. The polite level of conversation was shattered when Whiteman yelled, ''I mean it!'' He then smashed his baton across the back of a chair to emphasize his point. Everyone was hushed, as he lectured the reporters:

> You mugs don't know what these Experiments in Music are all about! I'll tell you! These are openings that I offer to the talent of our nation. This is a showplace for our music creators to present their work. In eight years, we have almost exhausted a music library that took eight hundred years to build. Our Congress gives millions of dollars for foreign aid, but not one cent is spent for the creation of American music. American music is our culture, our history. Why can't government provide centers for our composers and musicians to study, so we can produce the best music possible? That is a question that needs an answer, and needs results.

Whiteman's outcry did some good. The *New York Sun* headlined: ''Opera Doffs Hat To Paul Whiteman,'' and offered a review on the concert that included:

> Mr. Whiteman deserves the thanks of all who give any thought to the music of our native soil for arranging his good program of American works and for giving the young composers of this time who are trying to find a distinctly national musical language, opportunity to bring their creations before the public.

On January 7, 1934, Mitzi presented the family with a baby daughter, Lynne. Tram and Mitzi now realized that the arrangement of Tram's always living in hotels in New York and her living at their Chicago residence raising Bill, and now Lynne, simply was not working. They decided that, since Tram's work was in New York, they would locate a home and be united as a family.

> **On January 12, under my name, we recorded for Brunswick Records. I believe there was not one spot that could be improved upon on those records. As the period and demand for hot music had changed, I had changed with them. ''Juba Dance'' and ''Break It Down'' were our first release. On these records I was trying to produce something that the trade would accept, and the public would buy at the same time. From time to time, I plan to drop brasses, pick up strings or reeds, and vice versa, depending on the type of number being recorded. Both of these arrangements were by Russ Case.**
>
> **You can imagine my displeasure when Nathaniel Dett later requested Brunswick to withdraw this recording from their catalog because he was displeased with Russ Case's interpretation of his ''Juba Dance.''**

New York Symphony Musicians, 100 strong, was augmented by the Whiteman Orchestra for a concert on February 1. The program listed Whiteman as ''The King of Syncopation.'' Among the numbers used was, Tram featured on ''Bouncing Ball.'' This time, Whiteman used a Grofé arrangement of ''Going To Press'' (fourth movement from his ''Tabloid'' composition), and closed, with Grofé's arrangement of ''Rhapsody in Blue.''

Al Jolson returned to rehearsals on February 14 for the **Kraft Music Hall** radio programs, and while many of the Whiteman musicians felt that Jolson was a bit too cocky, Jack Fulton remarked, in an October 1986 letter:

> Al had a right to have an ego. He was a great talent, and a fine performer. We had no trouble working with him nor did he with us. To my way of thinking, you had to see Jolson to really enjoy him. There's no doubt in my mind as to what he would be like in t.v. today—great! As you know I was featured on the show at the same time, and he and I got along very well, ego or no ego. He was something and I feel very honored to have known him and to have worked with him.

Whiteman was asked to conduct the Cincinnati Symphony Orchestra, numbering 125 musicians, on March 6, as part of the Cincinnati Musicians' Association Grand Concert, featuring a total of 400 musicians, for the relief of unemployed Cincinnati musicians. Whiteman augmented the symphony orchestra with some of his own men: Adolph Deutsch, Kurt Dieterle, Roy Bargy, Benny Bonacio, Nat Natolie, Mike Pingitore, Herb Quigley, Bill Rank, Charlie Strickfaden, Charlie Teagarden, and Tram. Tram always claimed his soloing, that night, on "Bouncing Ball," with the symphony, as one of the highlights of his career in music!

Warren Scholl had previously written a nice story for the November 23, 1933 issue of **The Melody Maker** entitled: "Bix, Frankie and Company." He requested an interview with Tram for an article he planned that would appear in the March 17 issue of **The Melody Maker.** When Scholl asked Tram about his recordings, Tram replied:

> **My favorite was a record nobody paid much attention to. It was a tune from "Dynamite" entitled "How Am I To Know?" The arrangement was by Lennie Hayton and the vocal chorus by Smith Ballew. You'll probably think this is a bit unusual because it is the only straight dance record that I ever recorded.**
>
> **The most successful disc that I ever made was our first Okeh Record "Singin' The Blues" and "Clarinet Marmalade" in 1927. This was a classic. Did you know that Fletcher Henderson made a Victor Record of "Singin' The Blues," years ago, and it was arranged note for note from our original recording?**

Tram and Mitzi purchased a home on March 16, at 8814 62nd Drive, Rego Park, Long Island.

Nat Natolie and John Fulton decided to leave the band in August 1934, leaving Tram with a sense of sad feelings and sentimental memories. His two partners in pranks, first Chet Hazlett, and now John Fulton, had decided to pursue other avenues. Fulton left the boys with a final prank, placing sneezing powder in the ventilator directly in back of the bandstand.

In 1968 Roy Bargy wrote in a letter:

> I don't think today's modern musicians know what work is compared to our schedule then. Our routine went something like this: 9 A.M. rehearsal for the weekly radio show; 11:45 A.M. first stage show (usually Roxy, Capitol, or Paramount) which ran about 50 minutes. Then two more shows with rehearsals. Radio show at NBC. Short session at the Biltmore Hotel. Final supper session show. All of this sandwiched around recording dates. On weekends and holidays, at the theatres we'd do six stage shows.
>
> Frank and I usually shared a dressing room in the theatres, also a liking for Hennessy's Brandy. A little nip of same was a big help before the last show after a hard day and supper session at some hotel coming up.

> **I got to drinking too much for my own good. I guess I was considered one of the regulars with the jug? What in the hell was wrong with me? Just saw off so much music for so much money. That must be the brandy talking. I couldn't be that tired already. I hadn't been back in the band long enough.**
>
> **Eddie Wade, who replaced Nat Natolie, was my drinking partner. We did it up brown! I had a bad hurt inside and drinking seemed to help. I don't remember much except getting paid and always being broke.**
>
> **I decided to straighten myself out a bit. I had gained some weight and was flying right. I bought a custom Waco cabin plane which I kept at Roosevelt Field for an occasional hop when I had time.**

John Fulton had gone on to become a popular radio singer with programs both in New York and Chicago, necessitating weekly commuter trips by airplane, but when Pops asked a favor, Fulton could not refuse. Whiteman needed Fulton to fill in for Jack Teagarden, who had become indisposed for a **Kraft Music Hall** radio program. Fulton knew the band's book, and Whiteman immediately thought of him, yet Fulton was reluctant because he had discarded his trombone when he landed his radio spots.

Fulton confided to Jim Gordon in July 1990:

> I told Paul that I hadn't touched the trombone in a long time and my embouchure isn't what it should be. To be honest, I told him that I didn't think that I could reach the low notes. Paul put a fatherly arm around me, and half kidding, said, "Think nothing of it John, you never could reach the low notes."

> **We went to Canada to play a special date at the Mount Royal Hotel** [Ed. note: December 28, 1934–January 2, 1935]. **Now leaving for Montreal is no different than leaving for Florida. There's the same luggage with perhaps a few more stickers, and the same eagerness to get started.**
>
> **It was the tradition of the band that all new members occupy the upper berths, and it was only when a class of old members graduated that new members were entitled to the upper class men distinction of the lower berths.**
>
> **Some of the boys told me of an almost identical trip in 1924, during Prohibition. When the boys left Montreal they took many bottles of liquor with them. On the train those bottles were cleverly deposited in unusual places, such as the water coolers, in the springs under the seats and in the ventilators near the ceiling of the cars.**
>
> **Once the train reached the border, custom officers went to work. Their scrutinizing eyes discovered every single bottle of liquor!**
>
> **Ten years brought many changes. There were many new faces in the band. Prohibition ended. The merchandise we brought back with us consisted mostly of Hudson Bay woolen blankets. Maybe we anticipated a poor year in the music business?**

CHAPTER THIRTEEN

"JUMBO" TO THE TEXAS ENDING 1935–1937

JANUARY 26, THROUGH 31, 1935, the Whiteman Orchestra appeared at Shea's Buffalo (New York) Theatre. The owner, Michael Shea, was the first man to realize that an orchestra like Whiteman's would be a big attraction in his movie house, and Whiteman never forgot the faith shown in him by Michael, and tried to appear at the theatre as often as his schedule allowed.

> **Paul next booked a tour through the southern states and I asked if I might not accompany the band on the bus, but fly my own airplane to each engagement. Paul was hesitant but ended up giving permission with the understanding that I not miss a single date or else it would cost me $100. I turned that around to a bet of $100 that I could make every engagement. A handshake, and the bet was on!**
>
> **I almost killed myself doing it—but I won the $100. I slipped into cow pastures that I couldn't fly out of; landed on beaches and tied the plane to rocks; and flew in all kinds of weather. I think Paul purposely picked towns without airports. Sometimes I would have to hire for the plane to be hauled to a bigger field, so I could fly on to the next job.**

Whiteman added several of his musicians to the Philadelphia Orchestra for a July 29–30, presentation at the Robin Hood Dell. The opening number consisted of "Dance Types," those represented being "Hollywood" (Conrad), "Buenos Aires" (Cugat), and "London" (Forsythe). Next came "Deep Purple" by De Rose. The opening half of the concert offered such selections as William Grant Still's "Land Of Superstition" from his symphony

"Darkest Africa," which one reviewer placed on the borderline between classical and jazz and convincing from neither angle. The band did two movements from Ferde Grofé's "Grand Canyon Suite," entitled "On The Trail" and "Cloudburst."

The second half opened with "Park Avenue Fantasy," and then the crowd was thrilled when Whiteman announced, "The rest of the concert is for the members of my band."

The *Philadelphia Ledger* described the second half with:

> Mr. Whiteman has gathered around him a group of artists whose abilities in their particular lines have few rivals but no superiors. Space does not admit a detailed discussion of these numbers, but mention must be made of Frank Trumbauer, a "demon" saxophonist; the male quartet known as The King's Men, Ramona, Goldie, and Mike Pingitore, the banjoist. . . .
>
> So many encores were demanded that the concert almost got out of Mr. Whiteman's skillful hands. The last number was Gershwin's "Rhapsody in Blue" in an abbreviated version, the solo piano being brilliantly played by Roy Bargy. An encore number, "The Flight From The Divorcee" by Forsythe was given before Mr. Whiteman summoned the orchestra from the stage.

Tram continued with his flying, and gave lessons to fellow musicians. "The Paul Whiteman Air Force" now consisted of Bill Rank, Roy Bargy, Rad Robinson, Bob Lawrence, Charlie Teagarden, and Tram. Charlie Teagarden purchased a commercial two-seater airplane Waco ASO (NC 8538), on August 7, 1935. During the shakedown flight he managed to come too close to the tops of some trees while landing, necessitating some repair work by Tram on the landing gear.

During August the band reported to the movie studios in Astoria for their brief film appearance in the Twentieth Century-Fox film **Thanks A Million,** which featured Dick Powell running for governor, with the help of wise-cracking manager Fred Allen and sweetheart Ann Dvorak. The band's sequence was added to the film, which was shot in Hollywood (August 19–October 4).

The Magic Key Of Radio program, featuring the Paul Whiteman Orchestra as guests, debuted on September 29. This popular radio show would switch to music and personalities all around the world for their listening audience. The Whiteman Orchestra was heard in the first half of the program offering a bit from "Rhapsody In Blue" and Bob Lawrence, Ramona, and The King's Men singing "Belle Of New O'Leans." The second half, Johnny Hauser sang, after a brief theme of "Rhapsody in Blue," "I'm Sitting High Up on a Hilltop." Both selections were featured in the forthcoming movie.

Tram became impressed with the articles that Warren Scholl was preparing for publication in **The Melody Maker** entitled "Trumbauer Still Greatest White Alto Sax Man In The Business" for the November issue, and "Bix's Tragic Death Marred Brilliant Career" for the December issue. Tram apparently contacted Glenn Burrs' of **Down Beat** about Warren, suggesting that Scholl would be a real acquisition for their publication. Burrs agreed and hired Scholl.

Scholl's correspondence of April 1990, remembered the incident:

> Frank gave me Glenn Burrs' name and told me I should contact him by mail because he was looking for someone to write from New York. They were apparently friends, and at that time Burrs was toying with the idea of the magazine as sort of puff sheet and a tool for selling insurance to musicians. As the magazine took off, he gave up that idea and let it stand on its own merit.

The November 16 opening of **Jumbo** at the Hippodrome Theatre was the attraction of the year in New York. Billy Rose spared no expense in converting the theatre into an arena where he presented his circus masterpiece, starring the elephant, Jumbo. Raoul Pene du Bois designed the costumes, while Albert Johnson set the stage to decorations of red, white, blue, and gold. A giant ring upon the stage enclosed the animals, while trapeze artists and other aerial acts performed high above the center ring, without the aid of a net, daring to fall among the confined lions and tigers. Richard Rodgers and Lorenz Hart wrote such outstanding tunes as "My Romance" and "The Most Beautiful Girl In The World." John Murray Anderson and George Abbott shared the roles as directors.

Charles MacArthur and Ben Hecht wrote the script, which had this plot: The Considine Circus and the Mulligan Troupe are deadly rivals, but the Considine daughter (Gloria Grafton) and the Mulligan heir (Donald Novis) become lovers. Their families openly fight, and the tax collector attempts to take away the Considine Show. The press agent, Jimmy Durante, burns down the circus, gains the insurance money, and starts anew with Jumbo as the star. The lovers unite, and everyone lives happily ever after!

Whiteman's Orchestra made the opening entrance with Whiteman atop a white horse named "Popcorn," and paraded around the ring. A November 1957 letter from Roy Bargy set the scene:

> Whiteman rode a horse in the opening parade around the ring, and I played bass drum in that, with Tram next to me playing cymbals, the violinists and other string players played bells, peckhorns (altos), etc. After the parade, our band ascended to the bandstand over the entrance to play the show. Whiteman conducted only the opening number, "Over And Over Again," and the entree act preceding the second act, then back on the horse for the finale. I conducted the rest of the show.

The band spent ten weeks rehearsing the show, which ran for 233 performances. The opening night audience included Ed Wynn, Ben Bernie, Fannie Brice, Fanny Hurst, Marion Davies, and George Burns and Gracie Allen. The critics loved it, and Rose had a hit.

Whiteman continued to appear at the Paradise Restaurant and broadcast its weekly program, but the Kraft-Phenix Company announced on December 5 that Bing Crosby would share the final four weeks with them, his portion originating from the West Coast, and then he would take over the program starting in January 1936.

> **Everything about the show was different. Even the tickets were nine times the ordinary size.**
>
> **One day a chorus girl approached me backstage at the Hippodrome. "Have you read Butterfield 8 by John O'Hara?" she asked.**
>
> **"No, should I?"**
>
> **"Well, you're in the book."**
>
> **Now I read the whole book to find one line where the character said he liked to listen to my records.**

Deems Taylor said I was the world's greatest C-melody saxophonist, but I don't think he really believed it—probably just read it in the script. It helped my record sales a lot, anyway. My weekly solos at the Biltmore Hotel concerts hadn't hurt them, either.

Whiteman started off 1936 with a new sponsor, Woodbury Soap and Cosmetics, for a 45-minute variety program commencing on January 5 and continuing as a weekly Sunday night program.

Warren Scholl, who met Tram in December 1933, while Tram was staying with Bill Rank[41] and his wife in Astoria, became better acquainted over the following months, and learned of Tram's notebook kept over the years, pertaining to recordings. Scholl's letter of March 1990 mentioned the notebook:

> It was the famous Trumbauer diary where I got first hand the exact dates of Paul Whiteman's "Dardanella." Once I knew "Dardanella" existed, I checked it out directly to the recording pages at RCA Victor in the 24th Street Studio, located the master number and talked to Bob Wetherald in Camden about issuing it.[42] We got some publicity about this and while doing other research, discovered that alternate masters might still exist on much of the Paul Whiteman 1928 stuff on which Bix and Tram were featured.

We had been in the Jumbo show a short while when Roy Bargy looked out of our dressing room window at all the snow and slush. "I could really go for a game of golf about now. Why don't we take a few days off and fly to Florida in your plane?"

"Roy," I said, "that's a sound suggestion. All we need are two more players and the permission from Paul for about three days off."

Bargy's smile resembled a cut in my golf ball after I attempted to come out of a trap with a sand wedge.

In two weeks our plans were set—with about six extra passengers left over. The lucky foursome finally turned out to be Roy Bargy, Carl Kress, Johnny Hauser, and me!

---

[41] Scholl interviewed Bill Rank during his first meeting with Tram for an article that later appeared in the April 21, 1934, issue of **The Melody Maker.**

[42] "Dardanella" was issued on Victor 25238, released on January 29, 1936.

Now due to the importance of my passenger list, I telephoned Roosevelt Field and had my mechanics install an additional compass. I didn't know just where we were going and I wanted all the necessary aid. You see, our plans were to fly south until we hit sunshine.

We arrived at the field at three o'clock in the morning. My plane was already on the field, warmed up and ready to go. There was high overcast with a favorable day ahead, so everything seemed satisfactory for us to take off.

I decided to call the Mitchell Field Weather Bureau for another check.

"If you fellows want to get out you'd better take off right now," my friend told me. "There's a ground fog rolling in across the east side of the field here at about eight miles an hour—it's practically zero zero here at present!"

I rushed back and told the boys to pile in the plane at once. I taxied into position for a take off. I opened the throttle on my trusty Wright engine and started down the runway using only about half the available space for our heavily loaded ship to take off. By now we could see that the fog was already around the water tank between Roosevelt and Mitchell Fields. It was reported to be 300 feet thick. By staying low, we had plenty of speed at the end of the runway, but the fog was bad so we turned to the left and started to climb up to look over the situation. Another circle and we decided to land and forget the trip only to find that the field had disappeared from under us. Old Man Fog had spread a gauzy mantle over the entire world.

It then dawned on me that high tension wires were still around airports and that Roosevelt Field was no exception, so we started a slow climb of two or three hundred feet. The hand on my altimeter approached the thousand foot mark. Where was the top of this three hundred foot ground fog I had heard about?

I knew a little about instrument flying but certainly not enough to barge into anything like that.

At twelve hundred feet we came out on top of a new world. By now we could see the approaching dawn in the east, but under this thick fog on the ground it was still night. I doubt if this impressed any of the passengers because Carl reached up and tapped me on the shoulder.

"Man, where's the nearest saloon?"

Now the task of flying our course. Both compasses were

checked—they read the same—so away we went! About forty minutes later the clouds began to break below us. I glanced down to find nothing but water—just plain ocean.

I came down through one of the clouds and saw a strip of land off to the right. Compasses, maps and all my navigation training were tossed aside as I headed for this land at full speed.

I reached the shore line and off to my left I recognized the larger hangar. It was Lakehurst. Something was definitely wrong with the compasses—no mistake about that! But I had a landmark now and headed for Washington, D.C.

In about two-and-a-half hours the weather was fine. I signaled Erskine Caldwell's favorite airport, came in over the river, skipped the fence and used a good part of the field in landing with the heavy load.

I called the weather bureau and found that bad weather was expected all along our proposed destination.

"How about Norfolk?" they asked. "Still good weather there."

What a bring down. But it was Norfolk or nothing so we gassed up, taxied down past the big hangar and made a turn for a cross wind take off.

Our compasses didn't work but with the aid of maps we had no trouble getting to Norfolk. We landed at the airport and started to unload.

The sun shining on the steel shafts of our golf clubs hit me like a bomb! There was our compass trouble. Those four sets of steel clubs had caused the compasses to deviate.

We were at the golf course in twenty minutes. I forgot to mention that while we were in Norfolk, Carl found that saloon that he was looking for. By the time we started our game, he was trying to get the busboy at the club to take his place so that he could caddy for Roy Bargy.

The bad weather we had been told about closed in on us at the 18th hole.

The next day it rained so we contented ourselves with shooting galleries and pool rooms.

The following morning it cleared a bit so we decided to start back. No more compass trouble for us. Our golf clubs had been deposited at the Express Office.

We stopped at Camden for a weather report and

learned that New York had only a thousand feet. A thousand foot ceiling in New York didn't mean much to me in those days. I thought we could make it, so we took off!

It had been four hours since a report from Trenton, which is between Camden and New York. Outside of Camden we spotted an airport—checked our maps and found it to be Hightstown.

As we approached Trenton we found it to be a wall of milk. The clouds were right down on the ground.

It was a cinch that we couldn't land there so we started back to Camden, only to find it closed in, too. Nothing to do but try and land in Hightstown.

I looked over the airport, deliberated for about one tenth of a second and signaled that I was coming in. I noticed several people on the field waving their arms. Maybe it was just a friendly salutation.

We hit the ground and stopped in practically 70 to 100 feet. The last few feet I could feel the tailing coming up. I'll never know what caused me to push the throttle open and hold the stick back, but that kept us from going over on our back. We stepped out of the plane and noticed the lower wing resting in the mud.

The people who had waved at us came running up to tell us that the airport was closed.

Carl found that precious jug of brandy in his duffel bag. We were all set for a much needed drink when the belle of the airport stepped up to Carl and said, "Sir, fliers don't drink—and you can't drink on an airport, Sir!"

"Well, it's a cinch an airport can't drink on me, so here goes!" And he took a healthy slug.

My plane was really stuck. All the manpower on the field couldn't budge it. By the time we got it back to New York that holiday turned out to be an expensive one.

We finally arrived in New York by bus and just made it to the Hippodrome and into our uniforms in time for the show.

Whiteman was about to bring down his baton to open the show when Bargy looked over at me and said, "When do we go again?"

Down Beat magazine's April 1936 issue asked the readers to pick "A Real Musician's Band," and offered their choice of the following: Bix Beiderbecke (cornet); Louis Armstrong, Henry

''Red'' Allen (trumpets); Tommy Dorsey, Jack Teagarden, Miff Mole (trombones); Coleman Hawkins (tenor saxophone); Frank Trumbauer (alto saxophone); Adrian Rollini (bass saxophone); Benny Goodman (saxophone and clarinet); Eddie Lang (guitar); George ''Pops'' Foster (string bass); Gene Krupa (drums); and Earl Hines (piano).

April also brought to a close the stage production of **Jumbo** on the 18th.[43] The band continued on tour through the next two months before arriving in Philadelphia to again be with the Philadelphia Orchestra for an appearance at the Robin Hood Dell on June 23–24. Paul would conduct the ''Seventh Experiment In Modern American Music.''[44] The concert opened with ''An American In Paris'' and then offered ''Dance Group'' selections of ''Chinatown'' (Schwartz), ''Thank You, Mr. Bach'' (Van Phillips), and ''Havana'' (Blond), but the evening's spotlight was on David Diamond's ''Sinfonietta'' which had won first place in the first annual Elfrida Whiteman Scholarship Award, established by Whiteman in memory of his late mother. Unfortunately, local critic Samuel Lacair panned the number, writing ''the composition has only the slightest musical value'', a remark that caused Whiteman to shake his head and repeat his high praise of the work.

''Tales From The Vienna Woods'' and Ferde Grofé's ''Tabloid'' concluded the opening half. Following intermission, Gershwin's ''Wintergreen for President'' from **Of Thee I Sing** was

[43]During the run of the stage production of **Jumbo** (1935–1936), Billy Rose was able to promote a radio production also called **Jumbo,** heard each Tuesday night, NBC, 9:30 P.M., sponsored by Texaco. The artists who appeared in the stage show were featured. The band was conducted by Adolph Deutsch, but none of the Whiteman musicians were used.

[44]Whiteman presented a total of eight in the series, each featuring the work of an outstanding composer and including a concert of Whiteman selections. The main features offered:

1. February 12, 1924, Aeolion Hall. George Gershwin's ''Rhapsody in Blue.''
2. December 29, 1925, Carnegie Hall. George Gershwin's jazz opera ''135th Street'' and Ferde Grofé's ''Mississippi Suite.''
3. October 7, 1928, Carnegie Hall. George Gershwin's ''Concerto In F.''
4. November 4, 1932, Carnegie Hall. Dana Suesse's ''Concerto In Three Rhythms'' and George Gershwin's ''An American In Paris.''
5. January 25, 1933, Carnegie Hall. Johnny Green's ''Night Club.''
6. December 15, 1933, Metropolitan Opera House. Dana Suesse's ''Eight Valses'' and William Grant Still's ''A Deserted Plantation.''
7. June 23–24, 1936, Robin Hood Dell. David Diamond's ''Sinfonietta.''
8. December 25, 1938, Carnegie Hall. 40-minute selection, ''Those Bells,'' and Artie Shaw featured on ''The Blues.'' Louis Armstrong was a guest in the second half of the program.

followed by Fischer's "Dardanella"; Ken Darby's suite "Ebony", a work in three connected movements, "Safari," "Jungle Night," and "Ebony"; and Walter Freed's "Fiesta."

Whiteman then turned to the vast audience (over 8,000) and announced, "Now I want you to hear 'my personalities'." Applause dominated the rest of the program as The King's Men had to sing three encores; Tram received demands for encore numbers; as did Ramona, Jack Teagarden, Bob Lawrence, Harry Goldfield, and Mike Pingitore. Roy Bargy brought the evening to a close with "Rhapsody in Blue." A reviewer wrote "Roy Bargy played the piano part brilliantly". Critic Lacair wrote "If Mr. Whiteman hadn't ended the program, due to the late hour, the 'personalities' would probably still be performing."

Victor Records was pleased with the sales from their "Dardanella" issue in January, and commissioned Warren Scholl to produce an album. Scholl responded with a July 1936 album of six recordings: Victor 25366–25371. Originally issued without an album number, the set sold for $5, and, when they sold out, Victor Records issued them as P-4 "Bix Beiderbecke Memorial Album."[45] The recordings were basically drawn from the Paul Whiteman recordings, but did add a couple of numbers that Bix did in 1930 without Tram.

Whiteman heard Judy Canova on the Rudy Vallee radio program and inquired about her being available to appear with his band. Canova was then doing a solo in the Ziegfeld Follies of 1936 at the Winter Garden Theatre, portraying her famed role as an American hillbilly. Canova was featured in what J. Russell Robinson once described as the greatest novelty number ever written, "The Music Goes Round And Round." The Follies, which opened on January 30, 1936, ran for 115 performances.

Canova was hired, along with her brother, Zeke, and sister, Anne, for the summer months. A typical Whiteman radio program, featuring the Canovas, would have Judy discussing things with Whiteman, commenting on her hillbilly upbringing, and conclude with the singing by Judy of a popular tune, joined by her brother and sister.

---

[45]Scholl did another album for Victor, P-100 Paul Whiteman Souvenir Album, in 1941, again featuring Bix and Tram from 1928. The five-record set covered from Victor 27685–27689. The P-4 and P-100 albums produced by Scholl were as a result of information provided by Tram through his personal papers.

This typical dialogue is from the July 5, 1936, radio program:

Judy: Mr. P.W., you've got more men in that band than you can shake a stick at.

or,

Judy: My brother, Zeke, has decided to join up with your band.

Whiteman: I didn't know that Zeke was a musician.

Judy: He's no musician. He's a band leader.

The offbeat style easily won over the audience and the Canovas continued with the band during the move to Texas. Canova even spoofed the sponsor's products, by announcing that her sister had written a song entitled "Soap On The Range" or "Woodbury Me Not On The Lone Prairie."

Amon Carter, publisher and owner of the *Fort Worth Star-Telegram* spearheaded a drive among the city fathers to promote the Texas Centennial as one of the biggest events ever seen in the United States. They wanted it "BIG"—"Texas Style Big!" They hired Billy Rose, upon the conclusion of **Jumbo,** and gave him an open checkbook to offer an exposition that the country had never seen the like of before! Rose brought along John Murray Anderson, Raoul Pene du Bois, and Albert Johnson. Using 162 acres, the group transformed Texas into an illumination of lights that filled the night air and attracted crowds of 25,000 per day. "Fort Worth—Where Broadway Crosses The Sunset Trail" was the way that the Fort Worth Frontier Centennial was described.

The Texas Centennial offered the following attractions: "The Last Frontier" presented a musical dealing with the early West and featuring an array of cowboys and Indians, concluding with a rousing climax of "Sashay All." Rosie, the featured elephant in **Jumbo,** was imported as a sideshow. "The Pioneer Palace" offered a look at the early West, complete with dancing girls and ten-cent beer.

The center-piece of the event was the Casa Mañana, listed as the most celebrated cafe-theatre in the world, with a huge circular stage floating in water and revolving before the eyes of 4,000 spectators. This "House of Tomorrow" featured beauty pageants and showcased Fay Cotton, the Borger girl, wearing a $5,000 gold dress.

Whiteman was to open on July 18, 1936 at the Casa Mañana, but arrived a few days early to settle in with the accommodations.

> **I remember arriving at the Worth Hotel. Roy Bargy and I were on our way to the desk to register when we passed Frank Libuse, a comedian from Chicago and an old friend of ours. He mumbled something about "don't crack that you know me."**
>
> **Now Roy and I knew that something was up so we stayed around to watch.**
>
> **In Texas you can do anything you are big enough to do. It's more or less an unwritten law.**
>
> **Libuse sat down in a chair in the lobby and began to read a newspaper. After a while he got up, yawned and stretched, and removed his coat and shoes.**
>
> **He sat down and wiggled his toes as he resumed his reading. A few people were now watching him.**
>
> **A few minutes later he stood up again. This time he removed his shirt, tie, and undershirt and draped them over the back of his chair. He yawned and stretched and ruffled his hair.**
>
> **Again he sat down and picked up the paper. By now his audience had increased.**
>
> **Finally he got up and removed his pants. He stood there in his shorts and looked around the lobby at all the people who were watching him. He lifted up the edge of the rug on the lobby floor and crawled under it.**
>
> **Well, you could have heard a pin drop. The wide-eyed clerk leaned over the desk to look at the lump in the carpet. In a few moments Libuse worked his way over to the edge of the rug and looked up at the astonished desk clerk. In a voice you could have heard a block away, he said, "I say, son, give me an eight o'clock call!"**
>
> **Well, that did it! A couple of ranchers grabbed Libuse and literally carried him into the bar to welcome a real guy to Texas.**
>
> **Later that night, we went out to dinner. After we had finished eating, Libuse picked up a plate filled with scraps of food and started in the direction of the kitchen.**
>
> **As he walked to the back of the restaurant he kept talking about the lousy food and that he was going to find the chef and tell him about it.**

> **Everyone in the restaurant watched him as he disappeared through the swinging door.**
>
> **''Don't hit me again. No! No!'' Libuse screamed as he ran out of the restaurant.**
>
> **About that time the chef came out from the kitchen with a big knife in his hand. The women gasped!**
>
> **The poor guy hadn't even seen Libuse—he just wanted to know what all the shouting was about—but he was blamed for the incident.**
>
> **Two days passed before we saw Libuse again. And again it was in a crowded hotel lobby. He ran up to us, clapped his hands together and then put one hand over his face and fell to the floor.**
>
> **''Roy,'' he yelled. ''Don't hit me again. That's a helluva way to greet an old friend!''**
>
> **We got a big laugh out of it but from the looks the people gave us I guess they thought we really hit the guy.**

Mary Jane and Frances Watkins, sisters, were enrolled at Stephens College in Columbia, Missouri, when they met Virginia MacLean, also a student, at a school party. Before the evening was over, they had teamed up and were singing together. They sang that summer at the Coconut Grove in Chicago, billed as ''The Dixie Deb Trio.'' All were capable musicians. Mary Jane studied piano and voice for five years, Virginia studied voice and dancing, and Frances devoted her time to voice alone. All had studied the violin.

The trio were visiting a friend in Zanesville, Ohio, when Whiteman came through town. They contacted him about an audition, which resulted in Whiteman signing them to a five-year contract. The girls were now featured with his band, on the opening number of their Texas, July 19, 1936, radio program, ''Chicago 1933,'' depicting the World's Fair of 1933. They also sang semi-classical and sweet popular songs.

Sally Rand, exotic fan/bubble dancer, who achieved notoriety during the Chicago Century of Progress Exposition, was hired to perform at the Casa Mañana. She chose to use a large bubble. Backstage was cleared before every performance. ''Poor Roy,'' Virginia MacLean Bargy stated in June 1990, ''who as her musical director, went over any changes that Sally might want in the orchestrations. Roy, forever the gentleman, tried to keep his eyes fixed on the manuscript paper, as Sally, completely naked, discussed the music with him."

The weekly Sunday night Woodbury programs came from the nearby Ringside Club. This club was used because the perfect acoustics blended well for the band's music. The house band provided the piano for Bargy, and Artie Miller was able to use Roland Evans's string bass. All doors and windows had to be closed against traffic noise, and this was before air conditioning, so the temperature actually climbed above 100 degrees. Goldie had the perfect solution. He played the show with an ice bag tied onto his head!

Billy Rose decided that he wanted continual dancing at the Casa Mañana and asked Whiteman to suggest another band. Whiteman did. He suggested Joe Venuti, and, as Virginia MacLean put it, "this resulted in fun and games during that summer."

Paul and Margaret had leased the 400-acre Van Zandt farm outside of Fort Worth and hosted many parties for dignitaries and members of his orchestra. Margaret left her friend, Jane Vance, in charge when she had to return to New York on business, with full instructions to make certain that Whiteman made every show! Whiteman, increasingly acting as a leisured gentleman, felt that Bargy could conduct the band. True to her promise, Vance, at times, had as many as four ranch hands hold Whiteman down, shave and dress him, and get him to the performance on time.

During the summer months, Tram became a close friend of John Rushing, a prominent Dallas surgeon. "Doc" owned a large hospital and several oil wells, and as he told Tram, "whenever I want some money, I just turn on the spigot on an oil well or two." Tram began giving Doc flying lessons, and he soon reached the stage of soloing.

While the band was in Texas, a party was given in honor of Paul Whiteman. James V. Allred, Governor of Texas, was present. He was as regular as they came. A great guy.

Posing as a waiter was, yes, you guessed it, Frank Libuse! He served soup and made sure that the Governor saw his thumb in the bowl as he placed it in front of him. Allred pushed the bowl aside and said nothing.

Several times Libuse reached in front of the Governor

to serve someone else, rubbing his elbow over the Governor's head. Now and then Libuse glared at him, as if to say, "wanna make something of it, bub?"

The Governor maintained his dignity through all of this, that is, until Libuse served him a glass of water and then poured what water remained on the tray into his glass. With that, Allred jumped to his feet and the whole room roared with laughter. Then he caught on and laughed along with everyone else. He was a good sport and enjoyed Libuse as much as the rest of the party.

Stories about Frank Libuse could go on and on. He was such a great comedian—on and off the stage!

The contract called for Whiteman's services only to September 1, but, due to record crowds, Billy Rose first extended the contract to October 15, and then on October 9 extended it to November 3. Whiteman, the city boy, had now become a born-again Texan! He rode horses almost daily, dressed in western attire, and was proud of the nickname the wranglers had given to him, "Dog-ass!"

As a result of the first extension, Whiteman stated in a publicity release for all of the local newspapers, "I'm happy to stay in Texas with my horses, fancy Mexican saddle, sombrero, and all the rest of the trimmings that go with my country life here. Never have I been among people who extended such wonderful hospitality or who went out of their way so much to make a visitor feel at home as the Texans have done."

Comfortably quartered for the next few months, The King's Men sent for their wives. Ken, Rad, and Bud rented a cottage on the edge of Lake Worth, forcing bachelor Jon Dobson to move into the Worth Hotel, but the quartet joined for swimming and boating.

Ramona devoted her time to sun-tanning, and Durelle Alexander, a native Texan, found not only water sports to her liking, but loved to dance. This was her first visit home after signing with Whiteman in 1935 as a replacement for Peggy Healy.

Roy Bargy, who enjoyed swimming and accompanying the Whitemans on horseback rides, now was casting an eye towards Virginia MacLean, whom he would wed in 1937. Virginia and the other two Dixie Debs, lived in an apartment at 2256 Fifth Avenue, and shared a rattletrap of a car they nicknamed "Buckaroo—a 1492 model," breathing a sigh of relief when the car delivered them to their destinations. All three girls were devoted sailboat lovers.

Jackson Teagarden, upon hearing the news of the extra weeks, sent to New York for his beloved Stanley Steamer. His first trip, when it arrived, was to his hometown, Vernon, Texas.

Goldie preferred "good old 42nd Street and Broadway" but found contentment in just relaxing, for the time being.

Whiteman often turned over his baton to Bargy, and slipped away from the Casa Mañana over to "The Last Frontier," and mounted a horse for a late night ride.

In Texas everyone had a horse so I had to have one, too. Paul had several and we rode together a lot.

I bought my horse from Walter McAllister, an airline pilot friend of mine. Mac didn't tell me much about the horse except that his name was Joe and that he had been highly trained by a former owner.

After the sale was completed, I started to lead Joe home. I turned my head away for a second and Joe wheeled around and bit my left leg just above the knee! I was sure my leg was broken.

I put Joe in the stall and went back to see McAllister.

"Mac, that damn horse is a cannibal. Why didn't you tell me?"

Well, Mac started laughing and pulled up his right pants leg to show me a bruise much larger than mine.

"I meant to—but I forgot," he told me.

Then Mac started telling me all about Joe. "Look, Tram, never go into the stall with Joe, and never, never approach him from the right side. He'll buck a while in the morning after he's been saddled but he could do a lot of tricks for the right owner. You know, he's been trained by a circus man. He can tell his age by pawing the ground. He'll play dead, roll over, lie down and kneel. And, oh yes, he's been taught to scream when touched under the left foreleg."

"To hell with that stuff—I want my money back," I told him.

"My friend," replied Mac, as he again showed me the black and blue mark on his leg, "you just bought yourself a horse!"

He gave me a loaded riding crop and advised me to use it if I didn't want to get killed.

It was three days before I could get a bridle on that

horse. I finally got him saddled after a few sharp encounters with the loaded crop.

I put my left foot in the stirrup and started to swing up. Joe whirled to his left, throwing me in the saddle and away we went like a Panther Jet.

Joe jumped a six foot ditch that was handy and landed on the other side bucking. The vertebrae in my spine seemed to go together like an exhausted accordion and stars danced in front of my eyes. I pulled plenty of leather and was glad it was there to pull.

I was everywhere on that horse but in the saddle. I guess the only reason I wasn't thrown was because each time I went into the air Joe seemed to wait for me to land before tossing me again.

I could hardly get out of bed for the next three days but during that time I put Joe on a training program that helped both of us. With the aid of my crop I got him to do all of his tricks, taking extra care, of course, not to turn my back on him.

There was a dude round-up of horses at the Van Zandt ranch nearby and Paul invited me to bring my horse and come out.

I borrowed two ranch hands and a trailer for the occasion. For a half hour the three of us tried to get Joe in that trailer. No luck! We went around the barn for a drink of water and returned for another try. Well, what do you think — that damn horse had walked up into the trailer all by himself!

At the edge of town, I stopped at a small tavern to ask directions. Dressed in my levis, boots, and Stetson hat, I opened the door and walked in. The place was packed with cowboys.

In the deepest voice I could muster I said, "Can any of you gents tell me how to get to the Van Zandt ranch?"

You should have heard them laugh. Without saying a word, a couple of cowboys picked me up by my arms and sat me on the bar.

"Have a drink, son," and one of them handed me about three ounces of bourbon in a water glass.

I thought I might as well die happy so down it went—no chaser!

They all cheered. Guess they were surprised that my eyes didn't pop out.

Then came the questions.

"How long you been off the range? What outfit do you belong to, son? Where'd you get those Sears-Roebuck boots? How are things in New York? How many cattle do ya brand a day back there? Where's your horse?"

And then they all joined in on the chorus, "Yeah, where's your horse?"

When the noise subsided I repeated my request. "How do you get to the Van Zandt ranch?"

I offered to buy a drink for everybody and explained that my horse was outside in a trailer.

Ignoring my request and offer, they swarmed through the door and made a dash for the trailer.

Someone climbed up on the right side of the trailer. Mistake Number One. Joe's right side—he couldn't stand for that! He started kicking and bucking and tried his best to tear up that trailer.

Mistake Number Two. Someone reached in and touched Joe's left foreleg and he screamed like an elephant and tried to bite the cowboy's hand.

I had a fine saddle and bridle on Joe and I think it helped my status somewhat.

They all backed away from the trailer and returned to the bar.

"Mighty fine little horse you got there, pardner. Wanna sell him? Here, have another drink."

I guess they thought I was okay because I had a wild horse.

You know, some of those fellows became my good friends. They just thought they'd have some good, clean fun with a tenderfoot.

I invited all of them to see our show and Paul reserved a special section for them. They really had a wonderful time.

Well, now all of a sudden I was proud of Joe. He weighed nine hundred pounds, short coupled and from the Morgan string, solid black with a white star on his forehead.

Two of the boys escorted me to the Van Zandt ranch. When we arrived they noticed a friend of theirs and called me over to meet him. He was Chet Whiteman, champion cowboy, and a relative of Paul Whiteman.

Chet told me he would like to ride my horse and that I

could ride his. We unloaded Joe, and Chet swung aboard. Sure enough, Joe bucked a few times just for fun and then answered the commands of this great cowboy. And much better, I might say, than he ever did for me.

That settled it—the boys knew I had a good horse then.

I mounted Chet's horse and was told to cut out and bring in a certain horse from the string. The horse cut him out and brought him in—I just went along for the ride. The hands expected me to take a spill but luckily I remained in the saddle.

I was taught how to hold a rope and then how to throw it to get a colt that had never before had a halter on. I threw the rope several times before I finally landed it over the colt's neck. The minute that rope hit him, he took off—with me on the other end of it! It seemed that I took steps ten feet long trying to keep up with that horse, but I finally fell on my face and was dragged about fifty feet. I didn't have sense enough to let go of that damn rope. The cowhands laughed until they cried!

Then I was taken to another barn. One of the boys said, "Like to have you try my horse."

I took one look at this horse and knew something was up. Ears back flat, nostrils flared out, and eyes as big as a teacup. What a wild look.

I thought to myself—should I be bold and get killed or a sissy and live? While I was pondering over this, Paul Whiteman came riding by. When he saw what was going on, he really raised hell with those boys!

"You guys cut out this horse play," Paul said. "I don't mind a little fun, but, by God, I don't want one of my boys killed—just for laughs!"

Then Paul turned to me, "And, Tram, you'd better get rid of that damn crazy Joe horse or else. He just snapped at me a minute ago!"

In the next few days, I realized that Paul was right so I started to look around for a buyer. Tom Cole, of the Cosden Oil Company, finally bought Joe for $150.

A week later, I called on Tom to see how he liked Joe. "You know," Tom said, "I was showing that damn horse to some friends of mine and he ran me right up on my front porch. He's out in pasture now and that's where he's going to stay—that is, unless you want him back."

Paul Whiteman closed at the Casa Mañana on November 3, 1936.

Billy Rose announced that the Centennial would continue to the 14th and that Joe Venuti's Band, and Ben Young's, heard at the Pioneer Palace, would carry on at the Casa Mañana. Billy revealed that during Whiteman's stay, the Centennial showed a handsome profit, going "in the red" only one week, during which time it rained four days.

> **I tried every conceivable way to get Paul to take Joe back east in the private horse car he was transporting his famous walking horses in, but he'd have no part of that suggestion. He was afraid Joe might kill some of his fine horses. Maybe he was right—but I'm sure I could have sold Joe for a thousand dollars in New York.**
>
> **After that episode I went back to golf. It was much easier on the back.**

The Whiteman Orchestra returned to New York in early November 1936.

> **There was also competition for jazz musicians in big bands. One night, Jack and Charlie Teagarden and I were in the Hickory House. Mike Riley was playing there. During the evening, someone suggested that the three of us get a small band together to take over when Riley left. This sounded great to us. The Whiteman band was only doing a weekly radio program and the idea hit a vibrant chord.**
>
> **We talked it over with Paul and he gave his okay, and so the Three T's were set for an engagement at the Hickory House. At last we could play to our hearts' content until three o'clock in the morning. After playing the same choruses over and over, this would be a kick for us. Five coast to coast broadcasts each week. No dancing—the people had to listen!**

In 1968 Herman Crone recalled:

> Frank called me in Chicago, from New York, and asked if I would come up and write a slew of arrangements for this particular combination. He wanted many of the hit recordings made by both him and Jack Teagarden (with various

> groups) cut to the Three T's size. This I did, and the band rehearsed every night at Tram's house. Jack Russin was supposed to go in on piano, but at the last minute, begged out and took a Broadway show. I filled in on rehearsals and Frank was trying to get me set with the Musicians' Union. I was a transfer member then in #802.
>
> **There was very little time to rehearse. We tried jamming and something was missing. We were stiff from playing in big bands so long it was hard to relax. Only four or five arrangements were set by the time we opened.**

Crone further remembered:

> Jack Teagarden hired Frank Signorelli and we both showed up for opening night. It was decided that I would get the job. Frank Froeba played intermission piano. I was there till the finish, when Frank went back to Whiteman.

December 2, 1936, opening night at the Hickory House, 144 West 52nd Street. The Three T's band consisted of: Jack ''Big T'' Teagarden (trombone); Frank ''Middle T'' Trumbauer (C-melody and alto saxophones); Charlie ''Little T'' Teagarden (trumpet); Min Leibrook (bass saxophone); Casper Reardon (harp); Herm Crone (piano); and Stan King (drums).

The theme song was basically ''Singin' The Blues,'' with Charlie opening the number, doing Bix's solo from the 1927 Okeh recording, then Tram duplicating his solo from the same recording, and Jack closing the theme singing a refrain from ''Basin Street Blues.''

Newspapers reported that the club was ''jammed,'' and among the guests were Roger Wolfe Kahn, Mal Hallett, Dick Stabile, Red McKenzie, and a ''slimmed down'' Paul Whiteman, who attributed his weight loss to months of horseback riding during his recent stay in Texas.

One reporter observed Whiteman drinking milk and inquired about it. Whiteman replied, ''I'm on the wagon. When you're sober, and hear the jokes that you thought were so hilarious when you're drunk, and realize how dumb they were, then you realize it is time to give up the stuff.''

Jack Teagarden introduced Pops to the crowd, and the band paid tribute to him by playing his ''Three O'Clock In The

Morning." The Whiteman recording had sold three million copies.

During intermission, one of the patrons asked me if we planned to play the popular songs of the day. I replied that the best thing about most popular songs is that they are not popular long. No, we planned on playing standards and our own favorites.

The big night arrived before we knew it. It turned out to be one of the greatest opening nights the Hickory House ever had. After a few sets, we began "to get away," and before the night was over, we knew that it would only take us a week to become completely flexible.

Adele Girard replaced Casper Reardon on harp December 9th.

We continued to do the Whiteman radio programs for Woodbury, and one night I had just finished a show and returned to the Hickory House, where I was invited to sit at Dutch Brown's table. After a few minutes, I excused myself to go and shave before the job.

"Oh, sit still!" Dutch said. "Have a drink and relax. Why don't you shave right here?"

"You don't know me very well, do you Dutch?" I replied.

"Okay," he said, reaching into his pocket. "Here's ten bucks that you haven't got the nerve to do it."

The necessary supplies were ordered from the wash room, and I shaved at the table while Dutch finished his dinner. The surrounding guests watched with amazement and applauded when Dutch handed me the ten dollar bill.

Another time I was riding across town in a cab with Dutch. I was on my way to do Whiteman's last program for Woodbury on December 27 at the NBC Studios. I was feeling a little down and Dutch sensed it.

"What's bothering you son? Are you having trouble?"

I mumbled something about being a little short but I'd be okay on pay day.

With that, Dutch put some folded bills in my hand. "Here, get yourself straightened out. Give it back when you can, and believe me, there's no hurry."

I started to look at the bills but Dutch made me pocket the money.

I arrived at the studio, hung up my overcoat and pulled out the bills to see what Dutch had given me. The damn fool had handed me ten one thousand dollar bills!

I almost flipped. Couldn't play. Couldn't think. I just wanted to get those bills back to Dutch. I was afraid to leave the studio alone, so a couple of the boys took me back to the Hickory House.

No Dutch. I called everywhere trying to find him. I was almost out of my mind by the time he strolled in at 3 a.m. Before he had a chance to take off his hat, I nailed him and returned the ten grand.

Dutch laughed. "Well, take what you want, then."

Oh, no. I didn't want any part of it. I went to the cashier and drew twenty dollars. That's all I needed.

We were getting into a good groove when Whiteman announced in January 1937 that some dates had been booked and that we were to rejoin the band.

The management[46] of the Hickory House blew their top. They didn't want to let us go because we were packing the place every night. But Whiteman had something to say, too. Why should he ruin his own back by letting three of his boys stay behind in New York? We were really brought down about it, but Whiteman came first, and that was that.

Dutch Brown finally asked Whiteman to let me stay behind until they could get another band set. Lo and behold, Paul consented.

Jack and Charlie Teagarden left on January 15, 1937. I was lost without those two. Charlie was about the most underrated trumpet player that I knew, and Jackson, he was just the end!

A lot of the boys around town came over and helped out. First Johnny "Scat" Davis, from the Fred Waring Band, played a week, and then Bunny Berigan finished the month.

Bunny had been around but it was several years before the boys started to notice him. There's one fellow you just can't leave off the "great" list. Misunderstood

[46]The three partners were: John Popkin (nee, Zelig Pupko), Jack Goldman, who acted as official host, and Dutch Brown. Following the Teagardens' departure, Tram's new contract was negotiated by Jack Lavin, of Paul Whiteman's office, and signed by Jack Goldman.

and misquoted so much that he just gave up trying, and played when and where he could.

Late one night, after we had both played several choruses on a good tune, we sat at the bar, having a drink.

"Tram," he said suddenly, "I think you belong. I think you know."

Well, that was quite a statement and it made me very proud. All the words in the world couldn't explain how he felt. He must have sensed that I knew the internal anguish he was going through, and that it could only be relieved by playing the way that he wanted to play.

Musicians like Bunny are strange to everyone but great musicians. They have a language all their own and it does not involve the spoken word. It was a great honor and wonderful experience to have known Bunny Berigan.

Al Stuart (trumpet) and Ford Leary (trombone) joined the band in February, along with Frances Lane (vocalist). The band was billed as "Frank Trumbauer and his ensemble." Johnny Spragge, in reviewing the band, wrote an article for the March **Down Beat.** He referred to Tram as a man who caressed chords and his phrasing as voiced with finesse.

The Hickory House engagement ended February 16, 1937, and Tram headed south to rejoin Paul Whiteman in Florida. Whiteman had booked the band from February 10 through March 5 at the Biscayne Kennel Club, where he was advertised as: "Mammoth Attraction . . . Top Of the Music World . . . In Person . . . Paul Whiteman."

During the hiatus in New York, both Durrell Alexander and Ramona Davies left the band. Davies married Ken Hopkins, and started off on her own career, feeling that her exposure to the radio audience and her appearances with Whiteman, would be in her favor. Linda Lee was hired as featured female singer.

The NBC network offered a salute to Paul Whiteman on March 24, 1937 in New York. This combined Whiteman's Orchestra and members of the NBC Symphony Orchestra, a total of 50 musicians, performing for one hour. It was described as "Paul Whiteman's Birthday Party."[47] Graham MacNamee opened the broadcast by quoting Whiteman on the reasons behind his various

[47]Paul Whiteman, March 28, 1890–December 29, 1967.

concerts devoted to "Experiments in Modern Music." MacNamee said:

> No one man has done more for modern American music than Paul Whiteman. Paul has worked diligently towards what has long been a dream of his. In Paul's own words, "to create a center which can be used by composers, both for inspiration and research to interpret musically the life of our country. To instill in America a consciousness of her own music and one of the great arts."

Upon being introduced and asked how he felt about another birthday, Whiteman replied:

> I've always had my own ideas about birthdays. To a certain extent it should be like New Year's Eve. By that I mean, instead of just being a day in the year when people say congratulations and felicitations and so forth, it should be a day on which you can look back on the past year and give thanks to all the pleasant things that have happened.

The band spent the next several weeks on tour, dividing their time between New York and the Midwest. On June 26, the band returned to Fort Worth and an engagement at the Casa Mañana, and Whiteman had just signed a radio contract with NBC for a summer series to be performed from the auditorium at the Frontier Fiesta. But hard times once again beset Whiteman. He gathered the band together and explained his financial situation. He was asking the band to take a pay cut, so he could meet the payroll. He explained that the money that he had been receiving in past years was no longer available. He found himself considering bookings at theatres and clubs that he would have sneered at before, but it was a case of having to maintain his financial obligation to every member.

Tram discussed the situation with Mitzi and it was decided that it might be time to start fresh in Los Angeles. Most of the musicians were finding work in the motion picture and radio studios. The move was definitely west to Hollywood. Tram informed Whiteman of his decision, and in spite of Whiteman trying to persuade Tram to stay, the decision was final.

Tram left Paul Whiteman on July 1, 1937.

Charlie Teagarden described Paul as having more charisma than anyone that he ever met. Most of the former members of the Whiteman Orchestra considered Whiteman a father figure rather than a boss. Their relationship was more than that of an employee and employer, it was more one of having a friend to turn to in time of need. There were several whom he underwrote when they left the band to go into private business, others that he helped with their careers. Paul informed each musician that he was a welcome addition to the Whiteman family, and this remained true to the end of Whiteman's life. Whiteman reunion parties were held at Ferde Grofé's home in March during the 1960s, until Paul passed away. Each party resulted in a large gathering of alumni, all proud that they were once employed by "the old man." Each musician had his favorite story of his days with the band, and every story was told with genuine affection.

Whiteman's Orchestra is one that history cannot forget. His band could offer some of the greatest names of jazz, provide weekly dance music, perform variety shows on weekends, and top it off with a Sunday night concert. The versatility of both his music and musicians have never been duplicated.

Whiteman has been called "The King Of Jazz," "The Dean Of Modern American Music," and other titles, but whatever title he was assigned, his music was admired by the public and musicians alike. There will never be another Paul Whiteman.

CHAPTER FOURTEEN

FROM TROMBAR TO RETIREMENT 1937–1940

MUSICIANS' LOCAL #47 IN LOS ANGELES had a three-month waiting period for transferring musicians. When Tram was awarded his union card on July 13, 1937, he had to wait until mid-October before finding full employment. He used this time to establish a residence at 1873 Midvale in West Los Angeles, and sent for Mitzi and the children.

He sold his Puss Moth airplane, as the money was needed. Trumbauer continued to hang around the Cloverfield Airport, where he was hired to provide schooling for prospective pilots.

Down Beat reported in November 1937 that Tram had retired from the music business, a report that amused him. During his probation time with Local #47, Tram was experimenting with an idea that combined musical instruction books with record illustrations from leading soloists, who could demonstrate on the discs the tone and technique styling of the selection found in that particular instrumental instruction book.

Georgie Stoll hired Tram for the band supporting a CBS radio show, "Jack Oakie's College," for Camel Cigarettes, following Tram's probation period. Having found work as a studio musician, Tram contacted Mannie and Dave Klein about organizing their own band.

The Klein brothers agreed, and they set out hiring fellow studio musicians, and putting together a library. By the end of 1937, they had hired Lennie Conn and Oliver Suderman to work up some "hot" arrangements, and were able to hire Al Goering to do some "sweet" ones, filling their book with 75 arrangements. In December, they recorded the first of seven sessions for Standard Transcriptions at the RCA Victor Studios in Los Angeles.

John Zentner remembered during a 1991 interview, Tram telling him of an idea the band had:

> Frank told the guys to pool all their money, and they would hire a boat, and take out some prospective employers, for a day of ''wining and dining'', in order to influence someone to hire the band.
>
> Everyone agreed, and the money was raised. Trumbauer went down to rent a yacht and had just enough money for the boat and crew. He was asked who the pilot would be. He thought for a moment, flashed his wallet, showing his pilot's license. Apparently they did not notice that it was a pilot's license for an airplane. The deal was set.
>
> The day of the big event they pulled away from the dock in fine fashion, and spent the day according to plans, but then a big problem began when they had to return to the harbor. Trumbauer felt they were coming in too fast, and called down to the engine room for a reduction in speed, and the crew cut it to half-speed. Still the harbor was coming upon them too quickly, and he called down again for a slow down, and received a further reduction in speed. Finally Trumbauer realized that they were on a collision course with the pier, and called down, frantically, for a ''complete stop'' or ''backwards'' or whatever commands came to his immediate cry for help! Too late, the ship hit the dock, tore out the planks of the landing site, and tore away some of the siding of the yacht. The boys were quite a while in paying for the damages.
>
> I can still see Tram telling that story, wearing a hat. He'd had the brim on the front of his head as he relayed his part of the story, and then turned the hat with the brim towards the back of his head, as he relayed the response that he was given by the engine room.

Tram found work in 1938 with the Leonid Leonardi Orchestra at the KFWB radio studios, in addition to his job with Jack Oakie, and he subbed on the Jack Haley radio program.

Then came the big break!

Jimmie Grier handed in his notice at the Biltmore Hotel, and owner Baron Long decided that he wanted "something fresh," and sent out the word that he would be holding auditions for any orchestra interested in the job. Long spent the month of February 1938 trimming the 35 competing bands down to a final few, and then decided upon Tram's band. On March 8, 1938, the band signed with (Tom) Rockwell and ("Corky") O'Keefe Booking Agency, and Tram and his family moved to 166 Barlock.

The Frank Trombar Orchestra opened on March 18, and consisted of Mannie Klein, Joe Meyer, Bill Shaw (trumpets); Frank Trumbauer (C-melody/alto saxophones); Len Kavash, Lyall Bowen (alto saxophones); Lennie Conn (tenor saxophone); Jimmy Oliver (clarinet/tenor saxophone); Al Goering (piano); Bob Hemphill (guitar); Russ Morhoff (bass); Ward Archer (drums); Deane Janis[48] and Dave Saxon (vocalists).

> **I was selected as the leader, and stood in front of the band, giving the tempos and usual hand signals (three fingers up meant heavy on the brass, etc.), and since it was a new beginning, I felt that I owed myself a new name, so we used: Frank Trombar and his Orchestra.**

Dave Saxon, during a January 1991 interview, stated that he believed that Tram changed the last name spelling to Trombar because that was the way that people pronounced it, and he felt the spelling easier for them to remember.

Opening night found the place packed. Many of the local orchestra leaders came by to offer congratulations, such as: Rudy Vallee, Joe Venuti, Lou Bring, Jimmie Grier, and Eddy Duchin. Phil Harris also dropped by, and in April 1990 remembered the night, ending the thought with, "Man, those were the good ole days—even when we were busted" (broke).

An April review in **Tempo** (periodical publication of AFM local 47) stated: "Song pluggers reported that the USC and UCLA collegians who frequent the Biltmore had accepted the new Trombar Band as top stuff, and most musicians were willing to admit it was a good band with commercial possibilities."

Other reviews referred to the band as "The Sweet Swingsters," and as "Musical Masters." One Los Angeles newspaper gave

---

[48]Deane Janis was the niece of Elsie Janis (1889–1956), a vaudeville headliner.

such a glowing review that they suggested Tram could direct the band with a feather. Barney McDevitt, the publicity man for Rockwell-O'Keefe seized on that remark and had a photo taken of Tram actually leading the band with a feather, and later distributed it to the newspapers, and it appeared in several publications.

Dave Saxon continued about the opening week of the Biltmore Hotel. ''Baron told Frank that on Sundays he wanted the music softly presented for the 7 o'clock crowd, as he felt was appropriate music for what he termed 'afternoon tea dances.' Tram decided no one was going to tell him what to play, so we opened with 'Flight Of A Haybag' and 'Semper Fidelis'. Baron got the idea, and never made any suggestions again on the music.''

The band was broadcast from coast to coast and continued with the recording sessions for Standard Transcriptions, recording 129 titles in all.

> **Many years ago, when I was down in New Orleans, I noticed that some of the bands down there, playing parades, would get a little enthused and get a little swing into their march tempo, and it gave me an idea. We developed several arrangements for the band of popular marches with swing tempos, i.e., ''Stars And Stripes Forever'' and ''Semper Fidelis,'' and it went over so well that we started presenting it on records and appearances around the country. Well, it didn't quite catch on. I think that we were a little ahead of our time with our idea.**
>
> **We had ideas and if the record sold then the idea was good, but if the record didn't sell then the idea wasn't any good.**
>
> **We were experimenting. We felt these things. We wanted to see what would happen. We'd write the music, record it, and then sit home and listen to it. We got all of the kicks out of it because the recordings didn't sell very well. I'm referring to a couple of titles like ''Beetle At Large'' and ''Portrait Of A Pretzel.'' I don't know why we called them that. Those are titles that the guys in the band came up with, sitting around late at night, attempting to put a title to the music.**

Alice King, whom Tram knew from working with Leonid Leonardi, replaced Deane Janis. As Dave Saxon recalled, ''Deane had a chance for her own radio show, and wanted to go into a new direction with her career." And Charlie LaVere came aboard on piano. Charlie's son, Stephen, noted in a February 1991 letter:

> I'd like to relate to you a story that my father told me. The guys in the Trumbauer Band got caught stealing silverware out of the Biltmore. Everyone was lifting silverware and smaller items—one musician furnished his boat out of the Biltmore coffers, but it was another one that was the cause of the whole band almost being arrested. It seems that he left his trumpet on the stand one night, yet he carried his case out the back door. Someone in authority noticed that something was awry and stopped him to see what was in the case. When he opened it, there was a beautiful silver urn! Tram told the whole band, "OK, boys, bring it all back!" Some of the guys did bring back some of the stuff; however, I've still got quite a few pieces of Biltmore silverware among my kitchen utensil collection.

Baron Long stated the bad news on August 20 that he wanted to bring in another band. He expressed satisfaction with Tram's band and felt that at a later time he would use them again. Rockwell-O'Keefe started lining up a road trip for the band.

Paul Whiteman selected his "All American Swing Band" for the September 10 issue of **Collier's** magazine. Whiteman offered these musicians for his selections: Mannie Klein, Charlie Teagarden, Roy Eldridge, Louis Armstrong (trumpets); Tommy Dorsey, Jack Teagarden, Jack Jenny (trombones); Benny Goodman, Artie Shaw (clarinets); Jimmy Dorsey, Benny Carter (alto saxophones); Chu Berry, Eddie Miller (tenor saxophones); Frank Trumbauer (C-melody saxophone); Joe Venuti, Al Duffy, Matty Malneck, Eddie South (violins); Tito (accordion); Carl Kress (guitar); Art Tatum, Bob Zurke (pianos); Adrian Rollini (vibraphones); Bob Haggart (bass); Gene Krupa, Ray Bauduc (drums).

> **I was interviewed about being selected to this elite orchestra and asked to offer some comments. I felt that it would be something to get that group together. Why couldn't the combination be brought together for one or two concerts in New York? It would be the biggest thing in the history of modern music, and while there would be some obstacles, they would not be insurmountable. Most of the men that Whiteman selected were leaders. They**

could get others to front their bands for the few days needed to put over the idea. A couple of days of rehearsals, say four all told.

Baseball capitalized on an annual all star game, so why not the music world?

The event could be made a benefit affair, with the proceeds going to worthy entertainment and musical organizations. Vast revenue would be assured for the actual performance and radio rights.

Unfortunately the idea was not adopted.

The Biltmore Hotel engagement closed on September 14. Shep Fields's band followed Tram's band. Many of the musicians[49] decided to remain in Los Angeles for studio jobs, so Tram had to reorganize the band for the forthcoming road tour. Tram changed the spelling back to Trumbauer. The road band's personnel was: Eddie Wade (first trumpet); Matt Hendrickson (second trumpet); Harold Trumbia, who was replaced after one night by Max Tiff (third trumpet); John Smith (first trombone); Santo ''Pec'' Pecora (second trombone); Johnny Ross (first alto saxophone); Johnny Hamilton (tenor saxophone); Don Bonnee (third alto saxophone/clarinet); Jimmy Oliver (baritone saxophone/clarinet); Frank Trumbauer (C-melody/alto saxophone); Edwin ''Buddy'' Cole (piano); Russ Soule (guitar); Bill Jones (bass); John ''Doc'' Zenor (drums); Vonnie King, Jo (Mrs. Johnny Hamilton) Hopkins (vocalists). Jo was a gorgeous blond who had started singing seven years earlier, using the name Jewell Hopkins. Vonnie was Alice King's sister, and replaced her when Alice decided to join Alvino Rey in New York.

A string of one-nighters began on September 16 in Fresno, California, and continued through the second week of October, when the band landed for three weeks at the Century Room of the Adolphus Hotel in Dallas, October 14–November 8, 1938. The **Dallas Morning News** offered an opening night review:

> Trumbauer's ability to bring out the full body tone of his brass without blowing his customers out of the room, stamp him as the smartest maestro to blow in at the Adolphus in

[49]Dave Saxon decided against going on the road with Tram. At the time, there was a possibility of a job with Twentieth Century-Fox, so he left the band. Eventually Saxon joined Ben Bernie's Orchestra, and at Bernie's insistence, changed his name to Don Saxon.

many a day. Other bands on the brassy side just tossed up their hands, asserted the room was too harsh acoustically and let it go at that. But not Trumbauer. He overcame the poor acoustics by instructing his men to blow their instruments into their stands, the interior of which have been heavily matted. The result is good, solid dance music without the punches pulled and at the same time isn't blasting to the ears. Trumbauer's crew is somewhat of a rarity at that. It's good enough so that the supercritical musicians can't pick it to pieces, yet commercial enough to please the crowd.

One reporter asked about my sax, noting its age. This is a custom built job that took me three years of experimenting until I got it this way, I told him. I have a special device inside which keeps water off the pads. It may not look like much, but it has been my meal ticket for many years past, and it will be for many years to come.

Then, on closing night, the **Dallas Morning News** reported:

The Dallasites have found Mr. Trumbauer can give them tempo for dancing feet. While he has an orchestra that is well manned at all spots, Mr. Trumbauer is one expert musician who is not too snobbish to cater to the customer. He is an alumnus of the swing school, yet he modulates the volume of the band enough to permit table conversation.

The reviews continued to be favorable—for example this November 25, item from San Antonio, Texas:

Frank Trumbauer, one of the best saxophone players in the business, brought his orchestra to the Rainbow Terrace at the St. Anthony Hotel last night, and played to a record crowd, whose enthusiasm mounted steadily as the Trumbauer rhythm increased in tempo.

The Trumbauer Orchestra closed at the St. Anthony Hotel on December 8, but it was an editorial written eight days later for the **San Antonio Register,** that caught Lawrence Brown's eye. It read:

My memory is far too short to recall an incident that compares with the friendly gesture pulled by Frankie Trumbauer, ofay band leader, and one of the world's leading saxophonists, who, with his entire band still in uniforms, trekked to the Valon Grill following completion of the last night of his engagement, and proceeded to play a serenade in honor of the St. Anthony waiters. Often some of the members of an ofay ork make the trip for an informal session, but this is the first time a leader had brought his entire troupe and played music as they play them on the job. And listeners were told by Mr. Trumbauer just why, and for what, he came. My wish is that he and his band go on forever.

We had quite a time in Texas. I rented a Ken Royce, took it up, blew off a little steam, squashed down over the hangar, sat down past the runway and rolled about 60 feet, taxied back to the hangar, and next time I came out, the man said he would just as soon I didn't fly his airplane anymore, and I really thought I was flying very safely.

The reviews continued to be favorable, wherever the band appeared. Here are two examples:

Maestro Frankie Trumbauer and his band are now to be seen and heard on the stage at the Grant Theatre in a show that snaps and crackles with top-flight entertainment . . . the patrons craned their necks and asked for more. (December 15, Evansville, Indiana.)

A champion of the world returned to his native St. Louis . . . . Frank has gained worldwide recognition as the greatest saxophone blower of them all. (December 18, St. Louis, Missouri.)

Tram's band closed the year on December 30 and 31 at the Congress Hotel in Chicago. The New Year's Eve price of $7.50 provided admission, supper, show, and party favors. Vonnie had left the band on December 1, and now Jo Hopkins was the featured singer. Her rendition of "Night And Day" stopped the show, and she received three encore requests. Tram thereafter included that number as a regular feature.

The band continued their set routine for 1939. When they played a ballroom or hotel, it was straight dance music, with a few specialty numbers from the boys. But when they played a theatre, it usually followed a more theatrical scenario. First, all house lights were turned off. A single spotlight was trained on the stage, illuminating Tram, as he played the band's theme, his solo from the 1927 Okeh recording, "Singin' The Blues." The lights would slowly come up as the curtain parted, and Johnny Hamilton opened with his rendition of "Three Blind Mice." Next came John Philip Sousa's "Stars And Stripes Forever." Then a medley of "I Cried For You," "Lady Be Good," and a full rendition of "Blue Holiday" (a renaming of "Singin' The Blues"). The boys would be featured in a novelty number, leading to a five-piece dixieland arrangement of "Ding Dong Daddy From Dumas." Don Bonnee, who had a fine singing voice, would offer "Stormy Weather." Jo Hopkins would then slay the audience with "Night And Day," and would sing an encore, usually "Gypsy In My Soul." The final band encore number was usually "Tempo Takes A Holiday."

Jo Hopkins and her husband, John Hamilton, left the band after the January 22, 1939 engagement in Vincennes, Indiana, date. Bob McCracken replaced Hamilton.

Fred Seymour and I were discussing where we might find a replacement for Jo, as we drove through the lonely darkness of the countryside. Our caravan of automobiles often carried us as far as six hundred miles between one-nighters, and on this particular night, I decided to turn on the car radio and break the monotony. I located a station that offered some music and stopped the dial, and as the refrains of a popular tune filled the car, a girl's voice, clear, sharp, and with a touch of the blues rang out.

"Boy, oh boy!" I yelled. "Just what we need."

We listened for the station identification and learned that the broadcast was coming from St. Louis, a good two hundred miles off of our course. We pulled over and I instructed the other automobiles to continue on to Bloomington, Indiana. We had a few days before our date at the university, and this allowed Fred and me time to drive to St. Louis and find out who this singer, Jean Webb, might be.

We arrived at the KMOX radio station in St. Louis and made inquiries.

"Oh, you mean the poster girl," we were told. "Jean Webb is the young miss that wears those scotch plaids for the national gasoline advertisements. She sings with Ben Feld's band, but nothing on a regular basis."

Tram and Seymour located Jean Webb, and found her to be a very beautiful blond, who could easily have found employment as a model. Tram offered her a two-year contract with the band, and she accepted, but she insisted, because of her youth (she was 16), that her mother accompany her on the road. Tram agreed.

The University of Nebraska booked both Anson Weeks's Band and Tram's band for their February 1, 1939, Interfraternity Ball, billing the event as "A Battle Of Bands."

> **Before the job, we were at the hotel and heard some of the boys tell Anson, "This Trumbauer guy is as tough as the back end of a shooting gallery." Anson said, "I'm not worried!" Well, he changed his mind after the first set because we blew him out of town.**

Neil Messick, manager of the Nichollet Hotel in Minneapolis, booked the band for a run of February 10 through March 9, 1939, at The Terrace Room of the hotel.

One of the first things that Tram decided to do was get his golf game back in shape. He had been shooting in the low 80s but the continual one-nighters left little time for golf. During the band's October 1939 engagement at the Adolphus Hotel, orchestra leader Jimmy Joy (originally: Maloney), a Texan, offered a golf challenge to Tram's band. "The next time you foreigners come to Texas," Joy boasted, "you'd better be prepared for a Texas style round of golf and the stakes will be high!" Russell Soule, Russ Morrison, Fred Seymour, and Tram located Arnold Chester's Golf School at 803 Thorp Building and enrolled as students. Much to their surprise, he had nets on one end of his studio, with setups at the other end for placing tees and driving the balls. In addition, he had Pete Hauenstein, head of the Northern Photo Supply Company (521 Second Avenue South) come over and take slow-motion pictures of their swings. The guys could then study their swings, as they hoped for an early spring and a chance to rout the Jimmy Joy Band. Unfortunately, while Tram's band returned to Texas, the two bands did not cross paths again.

While the reviews were more than kind to the band, the musician who caught the eye of the crowd was John Smith. The film "Alexander's Ragtime Band" with Tyrone Power and Alice Faye had just been released, and people were continually coming up to John and asking whether he was the one in the movie. John had been a studio musician at 20th Century-Fox, working on such films as "Wake Up And Live," but this was his first featured role. Smith's December 1991 interview recalled an incident during this engagement:

> One night, Tram and I had a disagreement right on the stand. He felt that he was right, and of course, I felt that I was right. When you work together as closely as we were, these disagreements do arise. Frank decided that we should step out back and settle it "man to man." That was okay with me! Off the bandstand we went, across the dance floor, and into the kitchen. Frank pointed to a table and told me to sit down. He then put his arm on the table and challenged me to an arm wrestling contest. I held my own, but don't let that slender build that he had fool you. He was strong!

Tram wrote to Charlie LaVere on February 23, 1939 and offered him a job as arranger and cited "waiting patiently" for "Riverboat Shuffle." In part, his letter read:

> **Some lady came up last night and requested "You're A Sweet Little Headache" from the headache of the same name!**
>
> **The band went to see Tyrone Power in "Jesse James" and liked the picture so well that we went right outside and held up the box office.**

Ralph Hitz owned the Nichollet hotel, among others, and Tram went to him with an idea. Monday nights were normally slow nights on any orchestra schedule, and, to liven things up a bit, Tram suggested that Hitz offer a special rate to the local musicians. There would not be a "minimum" number of drinks placed on attendance; in fact, Tram suggested they knock off on the drinks altogether. If the local musicians came by, it afforded them a chance to have a complete night of just jamming. Tram felt that the local people would like the idea and come out and hear their favorite musicians playing with the band, or just jamming with a few of the guys. Permission was given, and it was tried during the final half of the band's stay, and went over well. March 10 concluded the Nichollet Hotel stay, and it was back on the road.

By April, the band consisted of Eddie Wade, Matt Hendrickson,

Max Tiff (trumpets); John Smith, John Reynolds (trombones); Guy Anderson, Bob McCracken, John Ross, Jimmy Oliver, Frank Trumbauer (reeds); Arnold Bliesner (piano); Russ Soule (guitar); Bill Jones (bass); Carl Maus (drums); Jean Webb (vocalist).

The tour through the Southwest ended that month, and the band opened on May 9 in St. Louis at Tune Town (formerly the Arcadia Ballroom).

> **Benny Goodman was appearing at the Fox Theatre with his orchestra, and after his night's work, he came by and sat-in with our band. BG and I traded solos, and it was a kick playing with him. The crowd loved it, too!**

The band headed east in June, and ended up at Hamid's Million Dollar Pier in Atlantic City, July 5 through 10. They arrived in time for the promotion that the *Atlantic City Daily World* newspaper was having: a contest to pick the resort's most beautiful waitress. Tram was given the honor of crowning the winner, Miss Stella Stacey.

Their next stop was a lengthy one: July 16 through August 5 at the Lake Worth Casino in Fort Worth. This proved to be the final engagement for the band. Tram was negotiating a date with Topsy's in Los Angeles, but when it fell through, as John Smith remembers:

> There just didn't seem to be any further bookings, so Tram called it quits! We didn't have a bus, so when he paid off the guys, some of us, like me, got a little extra for using our own cars to haul the others around from town to town.
>
> How was Frank's playing? Over the years, the word "great" was attached to his name. He earned that respect, and his playing matched the title. He was truly one of the all time great musicians.
>
> In 1939, we played the large hotels and main theatres in the country. Theatre work had always been my favorite since entering the music business. Radio work was swell and easy, but there is no thrill like the applause of a theatre crowd at the end of a number.

All America was edgy as they watched Hitler's German Army march across Europe. Hitler had already taken Austria and

Czechoslovakia in 1938, and when he attacked Poland on September 1, 1939, the world braced itself for a Second World War. England and France declared war on Germany on September 3. Tram spent September nervously pacing the floor of their Los Angeles residence on Barlow Street, eagerly reading the newspapers and assuring Mitzi that the country would soon be involved. The month passed without incident.

Perhaps America would remain neutral? Tram needed work, and decided to return to St. Louis in October and try to round up a band. He stayed at his mother's home, 6842 Arthur, as he put the pieces together. William Herrick acted as the band manager, working out of his room at the Great Northern Hotel in St. Louis. Tram and Herrick contacted General Amusement Corporation in Chicago, 32 West Randolph Street, about bookings. Tommy Rockwell owned this agency and assigned Joe Shribman to handle the forthcoming tour. Tram returned to Los Angeles and contracted Golden State Van Company of Los Angeles to pick up his equipment and arrangements on October 16 and transport them to St. Louis in eight days. Tram then returned to St. Louis and proceeded to hire the musicians.

Things started off on a bad note for the band. On November 3, Tram was still trying to track down the shipment he expected by October 24. It finally arrived on November 11.

A scrics of letters from Herrick, now staying at the Mark Twain Hotel (Eighth and Pine), to Golden State Van Company resulted in the Company's position that a time limit was not agreed to and that they were blameless for the delay. Mr. Herrick pointed out that such an understanding did exist, and as a result of the delay, the band lost playing dates in the amount of $3,000 for the band, and $600 personal profit for Tram. Eventually an out-of-court settlement was reached.

Tram's band now consisted of the following personnel, known as Frank Trumbauer and his Orchestra: Howard Lamont, Dick Dunne, Wayne Williams (trumpets); Del Melton, Bernie Bahr (trombones); Frank Trumbauer (C-melody/alto saxophones); Johnnie Ross (first alto saxophone); Rudy Boyer (tenor saxophone); Connie Blessing (third alto saxophone); Joe Schles (baritone saxophone); Joseph Levin (piano); Jesse Bourgoise (bass); Joe Becker (drums). The band did not have a female singer.

Their tour started in Lansing, Michigan (November 22) and

Green Bay, Wisconsin (November 25 and 26). Because Herrick remained in St. Louis, Tram needed a road manager. Johnnie Ross's letter of November 1990 offered:

> Frank decided to make me the manager. The very first night he said, before having dinner, let's have a martini. I had never had one before, but we sat at the bar and had one, after which he said let's have another. Well, they tasted good to me. When we got up off the stool, I fell right on my face. You can imagine the jokes Frank made of that. To top that off, he brought two bottles of beer, and set one next to my bed and one next to his. We roomed together for a few nights. He wouldn't let me out of bed the next morning until I drank that warm beer. His hangover cure!

Herrick's letter of December 4 to the General Amusement Corporation, frantically pointed out that they only had December engagements set for the sixth, eighth, ninth, eleventh, and sixteenth, and they required a long jump between cities. Herrick pleaded with the agency, "We appreciate the fact that you haven't had a great deal of time on these bookings but at the same time it seems as tho' you could have done a little better than you have." He went on to point out that he had personal contacts from various hotels inquiring into Tram's availability, and he urged the agency to contact these prospective dates. Subsequent letters from Herrick stated that he had been contacted for Tram's band by: Pat Miller of the Adolphus Hotel in Dallas; Bruce Carter of the Rice Hotel in Houston; and Mr. Meeker of the Coronado Hotel in St. Louis. The suggestion apparently was ignored by the booking agency, but they arranged for Tram to open at the Moana Ballroom in Tulsa, Oklahoma, for one week at $1,500 on December 22, 1939.

Tram arrived in Tulsa and was shocked to discover that the 100-by-150 foot ballroom was still being remodeled. Owner Charles Goltry had planned for an opening on December 22, but he was financially unable to pay for a carload of flooring and powerless to finish the interior due to his partner's withdrawal from their investment. Mr. Goltry persuaded Tram to go on that evening, assuring him that the advertisements would bring patrons to the dance. It did—all 150 of them! Tram received $21 for his night's work.

Tram took the matter to the Tulsa Musicians' Local #94 and Secretary G. J. Fox. Fox informed Tram that an identical situation had occurred earlier in the month, when Mr. Fox was able to raise funds to send the band back to Chicago. He advised Chicago Musicians' President, James C. Petrillo, about the incident and requested that Petrillo inform the General Amusement Corporation to refrain from sending any further bands until the building was completed. He then advised Tram to file a claim with the Musicians' Union for the full amount of the contract.

Two personnel changes were made as the band ended 1939. Rene Favre took over on piano, and bass player Herman Alpert (who got his nickname ''Trigger'' from playing ''cops and robbers'' as a child) replaced Jesse Bourgoise.

> **I took the profits from the various jobs we played and paid all the boys but four[50] in full, for the Tulsa engagement. General Amusement had done nothing for me and apparently did not anticipate doing anything for me. January the office booked four days, and the following month of February they had eight days booked for me, and as our progress was questionable, I went to Chicago [Ed. note: January 4, 1940] to visit with Mr. Petrillo, so he could readily see what might happen with thirteen people on the road with bookings such as I mentioned.**

Tram followed Petrillo's advice and went to New York in early January 1940.

> **I went to New York and asked for, and obtained my release from Tommy Rockwell [Ed. note: President of General Amusement Corporation], upon signing a note for the amount of commissions allegedly due Rockwell's Booking Agency.**
>
> **I tried, following that, to make a connection with another office, only to find that all contracts were approximately the same. They want your left eye and they give you their best efforts in return, which was not quite enough, using my past experience as a criterion.**
>
> **I made arrangements, personally to make some re-**

[50]While noting owing four musicians, Tram only listed the names of Bernie Bahr, Del Melton, and Dick Dunne. Perhaps he felt that he was owed money, thus the fourth name.

> **cords for a flat scale in New York, thinking this might promote the band to a better berth, having been told by Rockwell that they were setting record dates for me, but they never did happen. I personally set record dates for my organization with very little trouble.**

Cosmopolitan Magazine's February 1940 issue carried an article by noted columnist Dorothy Kilgallen, entitled "Swing Set." Kilgallen picked her "Dream Band Of All Time": Louis Armstrong, Bix Beiderbecke, King Oliver (trumpets); Miff Mole, Jimmy Harrison, Tommy Dorsey (trombones); Benny Goodman (clarinet); Frank Trumbauer, Coleman Hawkins, Benny Carter, Jimmy Dorsey (saxes); Earl Hines (piano); Eddie Lang (guitar); George "Pops" Foster (bass); Warren "Baby" Dodds (drums).

Tram signed the contract with Varsity Records on February 15 and mailed it ahead, as the band started its motorcade from Cincinnati. Just outside of Cadiz, Ohio, they were hit by a snowstorm that buried their automobiles for two days before the snowplows could dig them out. Johnnie Ross well remembered what happened once they were free from the snow. "Wayne Williams's tires were so bald, we watched him skid to a near fatal accident. Wayne flatly refused to drive any further. It was scary!" Tram decided to store the automobiles, and continue to New York by train. Tram's contract called for a flat fee of $900 for two days of recording for Varsity Records. The company, owned by U. S. Record Corporation, was located at 1780 Broadway in New York. Their Varsity label was used for the pop and jazz music and their Royale label for concert music. Warren Scholl's March 1990 letter recalled:

> Eli Oberstein was vice-president and chief A&R man for the company, which had New England bankers as the principal owners. My job was working as assistant under Oberstein, but I still supervised the actual recording session. Things were going along nicely in 1939, but by fall 1940, it became apparent it was going to be tough sledding for a newcomer to get all the raw materials they needed, so the backers got cold feet and decided to retrench entirely. Oberstein carried on by himself after that.
>
> A couple of interesting notes. Irving Berlin's nephew (he went by the original name Milt Baline) was in charge of

> publicity. We used Fredda Gibson, as Georgia Gibbs, on the vocals. I seem to recall that we used her on jazz dates by the Varsity Seven.
>
> Getting back to Frank. I didn't have anything to do with the tune picking on this date. I do recall though, he was very easy to work with, completely cooperative and open to suggestions when there was a question of balance, etc.

The band recorded eight selections (including: ''A Ghost Of A Chance,'' ''Jimtown Blues,'' and ''I Surrender Dear'') on February 22, and nine selections (including: ''Lady Be Good,'' ''Wrap Your Troubles In Dreams,'' ''Sugar Foot Stomp'') on February 23.

Down Beat panned the selections, while *Metronome* reviewed the recordings very favorably and were high in their praise of Tram's playing.

> **Mr. Oberstein seemed to think that there might be a market for a few of the numbers that I had played during my extensive tours since leaving the Biltmore Hotel in Los Angeles. We had played towns of 300 population and in the same breath the great New York City, where the maze of sidewalk intellect frighten a boy from the hills. We also played a few one nighters so far north a few Russian shells came over.**

Orchestra World's March 1940 issue carried an unsupported remark about Tram's band: ''Reports drift back from the road about Frankie Trombar beating around the mid-west band bush, playing honky-tonk dates and not caring particularly how well he plays or how the band looks. We hope that these reports aren't so, because Frankie is one of the finest men in the business, and certainly deserves a break. There are few better musicians than Frankie.''

Tram was outraged by this and immediately wrote to the editor, Syde Berman, who replied and admitted that he was the one responsible for the report. He went on to state that the source (whom he did not name) was one of the sax men in Tommy Dorsey's Band. In way of an apology, he asked Tram to submit a 500–800 word article for their April issue that they would ''be glad to feature.'' Tram did, and the results were that Tram set the record straight for all to read. His letter to Berman bears repeating here:

> **I would like to take this opportunity to express my gratitude and enjoyment in seeing the great strides you are making with your magazine. I agree with you entirely on your procedure of more intelligent criticism and comments on our great music business. So many critics, because they had an opportunity of seeing their name in print, wrote biased opinions, influencing the youth which will turn out to be your audience of tomorrow. How can a critic criticize when he doesn't know the facts and is not well versed in the subject?**
>
> **In the first place, how can one man be smart enough to actually issue an ultimatum that will build or distract the artistry of the various individuals about whom they are writing, which took years in the building and some youngster gets a typewriter, writes a controversial article. Bang! He's a critic!**
>
> **How many people know what constitutes immortality in our business? I'm just a saxophone player and my own sheets do not carry the caption "The World's Greatest" because that's a hell of a lot of territory, and I would like to go on record as saying that I have known and played with the greatest musicians that have ever lived; respected them, and they respected me. This, however, is something no one could ever buy at any price, speaking in a monetary vernacular.**
>
> **Here is my ultimatum: If it's played in a melodic vein with good tone quality, good construction, creative and with that God-given touch for phrasing that only a few have been chosen for, it will live.**
>
> **You can't measure artistry with a yard stick. So many hours for so much money. The competitive spirit in our business has been hacked down to a point that it is destroying the animation of our greater musicians to whom the entire bulk of our industry looks to, to set a representative precedent.**
>
> **I don't propose a cure-all or even an antidote, but I do believe that we have today the greatest crop of talent we have ever had, and that the more talented ones in this group should not let down, but should continue to be creative at any cost.**

There is plenty of room on the top shelf and don't get hacked when they say you can't take it with you—just remember the entry blanks for that band that Bix and Lang are playing in will have a lot of funny questions I betcha. Here's hoping I can at least turn the music!

Tram decided not to sign with any booking agency, but to seek jobs through his own personal contacts by telephone and correspondence during March.

Meanwhile, in a surprise move, Charles Goltry wrote to the Musicians' Union National Secretary, Fred Birnbach, and suggested a plan to pay off the money that the union informed him that he owed Tram from the December 1939 engagement. Goltry's letter stated that he had finished his dance hall at a cost of $100,000, and "I would like to have Frank Trumbauer's Band back here again to open my place of business. I believe I would be able to not only make his salary, but also the deficit I owe him, in two weeks time, presuming that the band would not cost me as much money during this off season of the year as it did during the Xmas Holidays."

Needless to say, the month of March 1940 we had no bookings whatever and up until April 15th, at which time, through the sanction of the National, we booked another week in Tulsa for the International Oil Show, for the same man [Ed. note: Goltry] for whom we played previously and didn't get paid, assuming that with the International Oil show we would do land office business and Mr. Fox of Tulsa had power of attorney to collect our money so that we could be paid for our previous engagement, plus the salaries for this present engagement.

Naturally, during the time off, most of my men had accepted jobs in other organizations which left me as the only nucleus of a band. I accepted the job and hired Bobby Pope and his band from Kansas City.

Upon our arrival in Tulsa, we found the establishment in which we were to play, unfinished—nothing completed but the dance floor itself. We played to very poor crowds and after five days, realized there would be no money forthcoming, decided, with the sanction of Mr. Fox of the Tulsa Local, not to play any more. You understand we did not get paid for this engagement either.

Eventually the Musicians' Local in Tulsa was able to collect $600. They paid the band $450 for the April 1940 date, and gave Tram the $150 balance towards payment of his December 1939 claim. Tram felt that he was owed $1,500 for December 1939, and $850 for April 1940, and he authorized the National to collect it for him, minus a 10% collection fee. Finally on August 30, 1944, the National advised Tram that they were unable to collect the money.[51] Goltry had filed for bankruptcy, and the dance hall was now a skating rink.

Tram had taken a physical examination on March 15 with the purpose of determining his fitness for a commercial pilot's job. Germany had now invaded Denmark, Norway, The Netherlands, Luxembourg, Belgium, and France. He returned to his mother's home in St. Louis and awaited word on the appointment he sought when he wrote to the United States Civil Service Commission:

> **Since 1930 to date I have been an active pilot having approximately 2,000 hours to my credit. I first obtained my transport license in 1930, which is still active today. During the past ten years I have engaged in considerable cross-country flying, instruction work and flying for pleasure. During the time period, 1930 to 1940, I have obtained considerable knowledge in connection with airplane engines and aircraft.**

The appointment came on June 10. He was assigned to the Fifth Region of the Civil Aeronautics Authority in Kansas City, Missouri, and given a position of Private Flying Specialist, salary of $3,200 per annum.

One national magazine reported the reason that Tram retired from the music business and stored his $20,000 music library, instruments, and uniforms, was due to tiring of one-night stands. This was only part of the reason.

> **Numerous offers came for $75 for me and $35 for the men. I made the rule to myself when I joined the Union in the first place, if I didn't get my price I'd quit—which is just what I did!**

---

[51]The National was also unable to collect money due other band leaders by Goltry: Paul Page ($1,240.75); Carle Decon Moore ($1,800); and Ben Pollack ($847.67).

CHAPTER FIFTEEN

CIVIL AERONAUTICS AUTHORITY—THE WAR YEARS 1941–1946

I HELD AN INSTRUCTOR'S RATING up to my last pilot's license renewal but due to my music interests, I had discontinued instruction during the past year. I have been in the category of a private flyer since receiving my transport license (1930), and I made sufficient money in the music business to buy and maintain, at different times, eight airplanes which I wanted to fly.

My retirement from the music business didn't mean that I was tired or I thought that the business was through, it just meant that I was more interested in the new program that meant so much to America's defense. We needed all the pilots that we could get and I wanted to do my part in seeing that we got them.

Tram accepted the June 1940 position in the Fifth Regional Office of the CAA as an assistant to Jess Green. Their assignment was the summer Civilian Pilot Training program that covered a seven-state area which had about 2,200 students. They were to check on the enrollment in the flying schools and use their abilities to promote a smooth operation of the programs. When any trouble arose, their job was to fly to the scene and quickly find a solution.

Teaching new pilots must have reminded Tram of 1929, when he was learning to fly at Curtiss Field in New York with his instructor, Bob Grabenhoffer, who flew with German Baron Von Richthofen's Flying Circus during World War I. Grabenhoffer continually told him that it took a good deal of patience to learn to fly, and now Tram had to apply that rule with these new recruits.

In August 1940, Tram sent for Mitzi and the children who were in California. He moved from his room at the Boulevard Manor Hotel to a home they leased at 5538 Park Avenue in Kansas City.

His job was now listed as Flying Development Division and Ground School Supervisor, and Tram was assigned an office on the ninth floor of City Hall. Tram received a probation appointment in January 1941, sending him to Des Moines, Iowa, as an Assistant Aeronautics Inspector. He remained there until May, when he was able to return to Kansas City with the title of Aeronautics Inspector. He resumed his office space in City Hall.

The anticipated war arrived when the Japanese attacked Pearl Harbor on December 7, 1941. Four days later, Germany declared war on the United States.

Tram generated a letter-writing campaign to every person imaginable, trying "to get into the war," but due to his age and position, which the government deemed necessary to the war effort, his letters were all answered with discouraging results.

On September 1, 1942, Tram was transferred to Washington, D.C. serving as an assistant to Fred Lanter, chief of the CAA Division, until November 3.

> **After a short time in Washington, due to conditions beyond my control, I elected to return to Kansas City. During this reassignment, I was very active in safety work, covering the region extensively on an educational basis for flying in general. I gave hundreds of flight tests of all types of light aircraft and a great many instrument and multi-engine tests.**

Don Ingle's letter of November 1989 offered the following information on his dad, Ernest "Red" Ingle:

> Red had begun music as a violinist, and had a solid conservatory training, but he took up the sax when a cousin gave him a C-melody. Another cousin traded him an alto for it, and Red got a book on fingering and self-taught himself the saxophone. His training in solfeggio and reading made it an easy transition, but there were gaps in technique, one was tonguing.
>
> So, at the age of 19, while touring with the Jean Goldkette Band in 1927, he had many one-on-one sessions with Tram, who taught him the elements of fast, articulate tonguing.

> Those who have played "Trumbology" will understand how he mastered that technique. He also showed Red many alternate fingerings and how to control vibrato. Red's sax work, later with Spike Jones, showed how much that training paid off as Red made his tenor sax do things that most people never heard of, or thought possible.
>
> In 1943, Red got a phone call from Tram. He was in town and recruiting instructors for the CAA. He got Red at a time when a steady non-playing job looked good. Red had a talent for drawing, cartooning especially, and he did a series of highly successful AV slides to help students learn the complicated federal aviation rules and regulations. This led to Red being sent to Washington to head a new Office of Flying Safety, as an art director for a number of projects. But the bureauracy was strongly entrenched and a lot of back biting and envy over the "new kid in town" got to be too much. By the spring of 1943, Red announced that he was resigning to take an air force commission being offered to him.
>
> Bailey Wright, a friend of both Tram's and Red's in the CAA, tried to talk him out of it. Finally, through Wright's intervention, Red got a call from Tram asking him to reconsider.
>
> "Hell, no! I've had it with these back-biting bastards. If I wanted to take this much abuse, Tram, I would have worked for Horace Heidt!" was my father's answer.
>
> Red's eyesight caused him to flunk the air force final physical, he was just over the age for the draft, so he went to work for Spike Jones, and you know the rest of the story.

A ray of hope for Tram came from the War Department, in a letter from Lt. Col. George C. Price, Air Corps, Director of Flight Control. On May 19, he advised Tram that, if he could obtain his release from the CAA, Price would recommend him for a commission as captain, based on his qualifications and experience.

> **I applied for military leave to get into active service. I was refused as I had no reserve commission. I resigned on June 1, 1943 to take a position with North American Aviation for which I expected to get a release to take a captaincy in the safety command as my entire file had been accepted which included 64 physicals, flight test and 14 letters of reference from high ranking air corps officers.**

The commission that Tram had hoped for never materialized. In the meantime, he was assigned as a test pilot by North American Aviation on their Mitchell B-25 bombers and P-51 fighter planes.

> **After six months at NAA, I had charge of all instrument work and was assigned to all special technical situations, when calls came to the company for assistance in the maintenance and operation of aircraft built by North American. I was appointed multi-engine and instrument examiner by safety regulation and gave many flight tests during that time.**
>
> **During this period of time, I had an opportunity to further study aviation in general, and through our efforts many T.O.'s issued by the army were the results of our diligent research. I was assigned to several British OTU (Operational Training Units) bases at which time I was placed in complete charge of all flight operations.**

Lt. Col. Henry W. Dickerson, Army Air Force, with headquarters at Patterson Field, Ohio, sent an order dated May 8, 1944:

> The services of Mr. Frank Trumbauer, technical representative of the North American Aviation, Inc., are to be utilized by the Royal Air Force, No. 5, Operational Training Unit, Boundary Bay, British Columbia, Canada in assisting in the maintenance and operation of equipment manufactured by the North American Aviation, Inc.

This Royal Canadian Air Force base opened on April 1, 1944 and closed October 31, 1945. At the time of Tram's arrival, it had 1,629 personnel. The aircraft consisted of 37 Mitchell bombers, 21 Liberators, 6 Bolingbrokes, for a total of 64 planes. Temperatures ranged from an average of 60 degrees high to 40 degrees low, with a continual overcast in the morning, with clearings in the afternoons, and variable winds of 15–20 mph.

Tram arrived in Vancouver, and was provided with a room (#673) at the Hotel Vancouver on May 14, 1944. His written report to R. H. Rice on May 23 included:

> **I proceeded to Boundary Bay and reported to the Commanding Officer, Group Captain D. A. R. Bradshaw. The Commanding Officer was very cooperative**

> **and placed the entire base at my disposal for any suggestions that might be offered.**
>
> **It was determined immediately that no exterior inspection of the aircraft prior to flight by pilot personnel was being accomplished. Aircraft were being accepted as air-worthy with various malfunctions. One generator out, one oil pressure out, one at minimum, and one above maximum, improper idling and gear indicators not functioning. Numerous aircraft were found with cowl fasteners damaged and no replacements available. Several aircraft had Phillips screws missing in the stress plate at the wing butt. One aircraft in particular had eight screws snapped and a number of others loose.**
>
> **In view of the above conditions complete inspection was instigated by pilot personnel prior to flight. The first day this procedure was in effect it was necessary to inspect four aircraft before one that was air-worthy would be found for demonstration purposes.**
>
> **I arrived in Vancouver expecting to conduct winterization tests in the Far North and was immediately requested to demonstrate the complete capabilities of a B-25 to the entire staff. I have reasons to believe that the demonstrations of the B-25 which included evasive action, all emergency procedures and all standard maneuvers were completely successful. The maintenance seemed to be the paramount problem.**

Tram's report of June 1, 1944 to R. H. Rice suggested that the aircraft be accompanied by 10 sets of the ''Pilot's Handbook,'' the small version issued by the Kansas City plant, which included fuel consumption, manifold, r.p.m. and horsepower charts. He further suggested that when the aircraft were delivered that they be accompanied by a pilot, who could answer the many questions that pilots might have, plus a maintenance representative, who would instruct the crew chiefs.

He also submitted a voucher for a dinner party he hosted for Squadron Leader Gray, Squadron Leader Stroud, Wing Commander Malcolm, Flight Lieutenant Gallant, and Flight Leader Farot. The cost, including tips and beverages, came to $27.50. Tram used this dinner party to discuss the upkeep of the Mitchell B-25 bombers, and he felt the relaxed atmosphere of the evening helped to lead to a better understanding of the workings of the airplane.

On June 4th, Tram left Vancouver. D. M. Smith, Acting Commander of the Royal Canadian Air Force (Western Air Command), wrote to North American Aviation on June 12, 1944, and stated:

> Your test pilot, Mr. Frank Trumbauer, who has recently returned to the United States after spending 20 days with No. 5 OTU at Boundary Bay, did a very excellent job whilst he was with this unit.
>
> His services were exceedingly valuable to the potential instructors at this new school and all ranks spoke of his work in highest terms.
>
> Would you please convey to Mr. Trumbauer our very sincere appreciation of his efforts as we are sure that they will bear fruit during the training which is being carried on at this unit.

As the months rolled into 1945, the advances of the allied armies served notice that World War II was soon to come to a conclusion. With this in mind, Tram wrote on March 15, 1945, to National Secretary, Leo Cluesmann, of the American Federation of Musicians:

> **I would like to be reinstated in Locals #802-#2-#4-#10 and #47.**
>
> **I believe I am correct in the fact that the Locals to which I reinstate should by necessity have a letter of authority from your office.**
>
> **Please bear in mind that I left the profession as a leader and shall return as a side man and needs of my family should have some consideration in the over all plan.**
>
> **At present I am employed in the war effort by North American Aviation as a test pilot. Having this secondary vocation has served a two-fold purpose and now I feel that I would like to return to my rightful place in the professional field.**

Fred Joste, Secretary of Local #34 in Kansas City, worked closely with Tram in his efforts for reinstatement, and all the locals granted his reinstatement. A typical response would be from Local #2, St. Louis, Clarence Ermanauer, recording secretary, written on March 28, 1945:

> Your request for terms of reinstatement was referred to our Board of Directors on the 26th, and in view of your misfortunes as a result of the indifference of your booking agent for your interests, before giving up the music business a few years ago, our board agreed to offer you reinstatement.

Tram continued to work during the duration of the war for North American Aviation. When the war was "officially declared ended" on September 1, 1945,[52] he was very proud of the record he had established.

> **Kansas City North American produced over 6,000 Mitchell B-25 bombers with 30,000 landings and only two minor accidents, no loss of life. We were rated by the army as the only organization in the United States having every pilot rated properly and completely on the aircraft they were flying. Each pilot was required to check through my office and was never released solo until extensive checks were made under actual instrument conditions plus a complete knowledge of all safety procedures. My experience with the CAA aided materially in assisting with the above safety program.**

Tram can be seen in a group photograph of the employees at North American Aviation taken on October 31, 1945. Tram was unable to obtain an immediate release from the company due to Colonel Slagle, Commanding Officer, who protested Tram's request, and did all he could to retain Tram's employment. Finally, Tram's request was granted in November 1945, and he left North American.

Now unemployed, Tram decided to travel to New York and see what possibilities existed in the music business. Raymond Paige found work for him on the radio program, "The RCA Victor Show," and Russ Case was able to use him on some recording dates.

After spending about 6 weeks in New York, Tram returned to Kansas City, and suggested to Mitzi that they try their luck in Hollywood. They waited for the Christmas school break, moved to Santa Monica, and rented a house at 833 17th Street in January

[52]The war in Europe ended on May 8, 1945, and the war with Japan ended in late August 1945.

1946. Lynne was enrolled in the sixth grade and while her memory is sketchy of this period, she remembers her dad taking her to visit with Benny Goodman. Goodman's band was appearing at Meadowbrook Gardens in Culver City, and one afternoon, they went by Goodman's house.

Red Norvo vividly recalled Tram coming by his home on Alta Avenue in Santa Monica:

> Frank was hoping to find work as a studio musician, and had been making the rounds of the various movie studios and radio shows, but without much luck. He said that he was spending a good deal of time with Charlie Strickfaden. Charlie was now into building shopping centers, and Frank renewed his friendship; his family even stayed with Charlie's family until they got situated, and Tram spent a good deal of time co-piloting Charlie's airplane.

Apparently nothing turned up for Tram, and he decided to return to New York in late February 1946. He was again hired by Raymond Paige for his NBC radio program, "The RCA Victor Show," and by Russ Case for many of his recording sessions, notably with Perry Como. Toots Mondello returned from the Army at this time and was hired by Russ for a couple of radio shows. "Imagine my surprise when I showed up at one sponsored by 7-Up, and found Tram seated next to me. I found Frank to be a great gentleman, and it was just a honor to be working with him."

Conrad Janis, during a 1991 discussion, recalled that time:

> Frank was in town and the word was out! Bands would try to get him to come by the clubs and sit in, and, whenever he did, word seemed to spread like wildfire and soon the place was packed with musicians trying to get in to hear him play. Tram was still top man on sax!

On March 25, Tram arranged a recording session with Capitol Records and cut three sides: "You Took Advantage Of Me," "Between The Deep Blue Sea," and "China Boy."

> **I approached Johnny Mercer** [Ed. note: Then A & R man for Capitol] **with an idea to organize a small band and re-do some of the famous records that were made in the**

20s and early 30s, using the same or very similar solo passages for a matter of record, and supplying a more modern accompaniment which would make the records more or less current. Johnny thought this was a grand idea, and we set our first date for Capitol, and as this was to be an event, we naturally hired the best men available. When the record date actually started, I was the only one there. About thirty minutes later a few of the men showed up, and after another thirty minutes the remainder of the band appeared so fractured that they couldn't play even the simple passages.

I pleaded with the Capitol representative on the date to call it off, and in desperation he said he must have something to present to the home office to substantiate payment of the date. Needless to say, I was heartsick, as a large file of explanation was to no avail, and naturally these records were so bad they couldn't possibly be released. I am positive Johnny Mercer was never aware of what happened to what we both thought was an excellent idea.

But, lo and behold, in 1952 I picked up an album that Capitol had released titled "Sax Stylists" which included many of the "greats," and heading the list of these sax stylists was my name; and I found that they dug into their archives and pressed one of these rejects with no consideration for my reputation, and pressed a record that was extremely bad by comparison with all other presentations in the album.

George "Pee Wee" Erwin confirmed Tram's recollection in a December 1968 letter: The date you mentioned for Capitol [some] were so drunk (not Tram but others), it was a disgrace. One other musician from that session, who asked anonymity, remarked, "Not all of the guys showed up bombed, but there were several that did. It was really an insult to this great musician, and no matter how many apologies were given after the date, the damage was done. You could just see the hurt in Frank's eyes. He didn't deserve that at all!"

Tram left New York very shortly after the recording session and returned to Santa Monica. He told Mitzi that he was finished with the music business, and now started a letter writing campaign for a job in the Kansas City area. Now that the war had ended, the returning servicemen flooded the job market, but Tram persisted in his search for employment, and in May, Robert Laurie of Insurance Research Service, Kansas City, offered Tram an agency job as manager of their aviation division.

> **I accepted a position with Insurance Research Service, Inc., as manager of the aviation division. I was appointed aviation underwriter for Lloyd's of London through D. K. MacDonald and Company of Seattle, Washington, and completed several national surveys, the principal ones being for Employers Mutual Insurance Company on aviation, and Fleet Aircraft Company of Canada.**

Upon the completion of Lynne's schooling in Santa Monica, Mitzi and the children rejoined Tram in Kansas City. At the time, Tram was living in a cottage on the grounds of the Unity School of Christianity, and here the family was reunited. Until later in the year, they purchased a house at 14 East Navajo Lane.

CHAPTER SIXTEEN

JOHN ZENTNER
1947–1952

AFTER HAVING SPENT A YEAR WITH Robert Laurie's Insurance Research Service, Trumbauer applied for reinstatement to the Civil Aeronautics Authority in Kansas City. His July 15, 1947, request was approved on August 18.

> **My reinstatement to permanent status with CAA was effective August 1947, when I accepted the position of Assistant to the Regional Administrator (Personal Flying Development).**

Leonard Jurden, regional administrator, sent a memo to Trumbauer on August 18: "It is a pleasure to have you again as an employee in this region. We wish you success in your new job and hope that you will enjoy, as we do, the satisfaction of doing worth-while work with congenial associates, many of whom will become your firm friends."

John Zentner began flying in 1933 and upon being mustered out of the Air Corps in 1946, became involved in flying safety as an aeronautical inspector for the CAA, assigned to Wichita, Kansas, under the supervision of Kansas City. In 1990, a Zentner letter recalled the postwar scene:

> Leonard Jurden was a tall, lean, kind man, whose background had been in building the airway communications system. He was not an aviator per se, and he needed the expertise of men like Frank to introduce an aviation education program within his region. So, they came together, and Mr. Jurden immediately latched onto Frank and made him

an assistant to his own position as Administrator. Frank set up shop in a small cubicle on the 9th floor of the City Hall building.

Frank recruited the services of an Oklahoma educator, John Patterson. John was looking for new challenges in his field, and having a keen interest in aviation, teamed up with Frank in developing an aviation education program for schools at all grade levels.

The concept was simple, Post War Aviation was booming. It was commonly understood that before long, people would go to their jobs in airborne paraphernalia of some sorts.

I guess I was among the first to hold up a hand and volunteer. There were others in other offices, and under Frank's tutelage we made appointments with our local school officials, school board folks, and most importantly, the media.

At the beginning it was necessary to induce some of the text book people to use aviation as a backdrop to their material. It took several years, but with the arm twisting of educators who were seeking new ways to motivate both teachers and students, this part of the program began to bear fruition. It wasn't long before schools were competing among themselves with regard to the scope and timing of their respective programs. And then there was the really big day. This was planned well in advance, well publicized in the media for miles around. This was a school's chance to show off its program to the community. Frank and I would attend. Included in the day long program were classroom sessions with teachers and principals in which successes and failures were discussed. The afternoon was spent at the airport. Flight operators donated aircraft and pilots so that each teacher could have a free flight over the area, ask questions, and get good answers. Sometimes a major airline would volunteer a large aircraft for this activity, and would include an attractive flight attendant and one of their top P.R. men as part of the crew.

The evening was devoted to the attendance at a big banquet with the food purveyor absorbing part of the cost. The main speaker of the evening, introduced by Johnny Patterson as "The Bob Hope Of Aviation," was Frank. Frank's talks were real bellringers, combining a lot of fact, fiction, and an abundance of humor. The word of these

> special days got around, and soon schools throughout the seven state area of the CAA 5th Region were clamoring to climb on board.

Harry Troxell, in his April 1991 letter, added,

> In 1947 I was Supervisor Inspector of the Des Moines, Iowa district office. I was really flabbergasted when I heard Frank was working in our Regional Office, and on my next trip to the R.O., I went directly to Frank's office. I was aware of Frank's musical background, as I first heard him with Paul Whiteman, and I told him that I was proud to have him aboard. He grinned and said I was one of the few around that knew he was a musician and he asked to please keep it quiet. He wanted to be known as a good pilot. All the time I was around him, Frank never talked about his music or background unless asked—and then he was very brief.

Warner Brothers Motion Pictures Studio announced in February 1948 their forthcoming production of **Young Man With A Horn** and their plans to star Gene Kelly in the role.[53] Tram wrote to Chic Cowpland, a friend with connections in the studio business, about the planned film. Excerpts of Tram's February 11, 1948, letter are as follows:

> **The brother of Bix** [Ed. note: Charles B. Beiderbecke] **and myself are the two most qualified people in the country today to help them in a proper interpretation. If "Young Man With A Horn" is followed conclusively, the interpretation will be erroneous, as the writer of "Young Man With A Horn" did not know Beiderbecke as we knew him. A great portion of the material I have already written deals with this subject.** [Ed. note: All material written by

[53]Warner Brothers released **Young Man With A Horn** in 1950, starring Kirk Douglas, and featuring the trumpet work of Harry James. The film, based on Dorothy Baker's best-selling book of the same name, was incorrectly thought by many to be based on Bix's life. Ms. Baker presented a disclaimer in her book that while Bix's music may have inspired the book, it was not written about Bix's life. Many West Coast musicians believe that Ms. Baker's 1938 book could have been inspired by Los Angeles trumpet player, Jimmy Briggs. In 1953, Charles Beiderbecke was contacted by producer Sidney Skolsky about possible movie interest by Universal Studios in filming Bix's story, but the discussions ended when the studio decided to film **The Glenn Miller Story,** starring James Stewart. In neither case was Tram contacted by Warner Brothers or Universal Studios.

Tram on Bix, is included in this book] **This would not only help the production in being correct, but it would also be a great advantage to me both from a publicity standpoint and financially; and I believe details could be arranged.**

Bobby Hackett is probably the logical musician to play the proper passages for the picture. However, I believe Mannie Klein could do a representative job. This particular item is one that should be given considerable thought.

On March 3, 1948, the formation of the Flying Farmers of Wyoming took place in Laramie, Wyoming. Tram was sent to represent the CAA in his first of many conventions. John Zentner was able to offer background on an association that Tram would maintain with the Flying Farmers of America through the remainder of his life:

> The Civil Aeronautics Act of 1938, in plain language, required us [CAA] to ''foster and promote'' aviation, and we were just doing our job. Time-wise, this activity commenced in 1948, and continued on through the early fifties. It gathered momentum with each passing year, and garnered support from outside pure educational circles. One of these organizations was The Flying Farmers.
>
> In a general sense, farmers throughout the nation were benefitting from the postwar recovery, and none more so than those in the Midwest. Crops were good, and prices were right. The organization of Flying Farmers became a voice to be reckoned with in political circles, to say nothing when their members began to be the best customers of the burgeoning light aircraft industry. Cessna, Beech, Piper, Stinson, and all the others that were springing up, wooed them incessantly through advertising and through attendance at their meetings. And the farmers responded. Landing strips were drilled in on many farms, and individually they began to vie for the best airstrip, the best aircraft, and who might be the best pilot. The CAA was called upon to assist in some of these activities, and we began to prepare safety seminars and to attend these gatherings.
>
> Invitations increased to the point where we couldn't accommodate them all. Again, Frank became the leader in CAA's activity with this group, and he was in great demand. As in the school program, I was frequently called on to accompany Frank to many of the Flying Farmers gatherings.

> We'd join the farmers by flying into some airport, put on our "dog and pony" safety show, and then join them in their fun. Most of these people knew Frank's past as a musician and entertainer, and they were always pressuring him to bring his horn and play for them. Frank continued to resist their pressure until events that occurred on a trip to Mexico in January 1950 changed him!

In his April 1991 letter, Harry Troxell remembered an event that took place about this time that illustrated Tram's humor when presenting a talk on aviation:

> Frank opened the talk on the topic: "What You See Is Not Always What You Get." As always, Frank was neatly dressed. Nice collar and tie, and beautiful cuffs. He wore a nice blue jacket with brass buttons. Really neat! After his talk, he took off his jacket and revealed that, except for the nice collar and cuffs, his shirt was all cut to hell! He said "See!"
>
> Frank was a real gentleman in every sense of the word. quiet, neatly dressed and always paid his own way. In the winter time, he had a peculiar habit of wearing a dark blue stocking cap to and from work. All dressed up, wearing a nice top coat, and that stocking cap!

Helen Leighow's interview of April 1991 accounted for Tram's finally agreeing to perform:

> Boone School had purchased a new stage curtain for the auditorium in 1949 and couldn't come up with enough money to pay for it. Someone remembered that when Lynne attended school, last year [Ed. note: She was now enrolled at Southwest High School], mention was made that her dad used to play with Paul Whiteman. A group approached Frank about putting on a show to help raise the money to pay off the debt. Frank telephoned me, and discussed the idea.

Leighow formerly taught dance classes in Kansas City, under the name of Helen Crandall, and now worked with the CAA as an administrative assistant, in the same building as Tram. The April 22, 1949 event at Boone School was entitled "Funajumpin'," Leighow recalled:

> We worked out a real cute show. I taught the fathers (8 man ballet) a scarf dance which was hilarious. I made them practice this routine and insisted that they do it right, and not just act silly like some people do. It was much funnier than if they had acted stupid. There were quite a few sketches, sort of a blackout. Frank's mother played the piano, and Frank was on sax. Mitzi worked the opening and closing of the curtain. My daughter, Sandra, and I did a tap dance routine. It has been so long that I can't remember the rest, but I do remember that the curtain was bright red velvet, trimmed in gold fringe.

> **I believe that I was more excited about giving a good show out at Boone, Friday night, than I used to be when I was with Whiteman's Band and we had The Rhythm Boys, including one Bing Crosby, as singers.**
>
> **After all, you can play dance music every night of your life, but only once in years and years does a guy get a chance to take out his saxophone to play for a school curtain.**

Tram continued in his duties with the CAA, representing them at various functions, including the Manhattan, Kansas, conference (November 30–December 1), called by The National Flying Farmers. The organization reviewed experience gained during the previous season; in the last growing season 1,200,000 acres were covered: 800,000 by airplanes and 400,000 by ground spraying. It was pointed out that there was a need for research leading toward production of adequate spraying, fertilizing, and seeding equipment. It was agreed that there was a need for research into all phases of aerial agriculture. Trumbauer pointed out that as many as 2,000 grasshoppers to the square yard were eliminated by aerial control methods. He figured that 16 million pounds of beef could be fed on the grass saved by spraying.

John Zentner and Trumbauer were asked to lay the groundwork, i.e., plan the fuel stops, the route, alert the customs officials, the Mexican CAA, and to an extent "ride herd" on the National Flying Farmers group of more than 100, as they crossed the border into Mexico on January 17, 1950, for a vacation trip and tour of Mexico's historic countryside. Taking part in this trip was Kansas Governor Frank Carlson. Though not a pilot, he was appointed as an honorary member of the group, due to his using the airplane in keeping with his many official appointments. Zentner's recollection of the event stated:

> Frank rented a Beech Bonanza from Dan Meisinger in Topeka, and picked me up in Grand Junction, Colorado, my duty station at the time.
>
> We took off and climbed out over the mountains of southeastern Colorado, sunshine, and a tail wind. Not for long, however. We began to have misgivings before we crossed into Texas. Rain, sleet, and lowering visibilities demanded a landing at Midland, Texas. We remained there overnight, worrying all the while the Farmers would have encountered the same storm, and would they have had the judgement to get back on the ground. The fury of the storm passed during the night, and following an early morning breakfast of ham and eggs, we taxied to the airport, refueled, checked the airplane, and took off in good weather.
>
> My turn to fly. Frank would note the time of take-off and would continue to use the fuel in one tank until the engine coughed, sputtered, or as often happened, quit. He would then note the time that had elapsed, and simple calculation would lead to how long the aircraft could remain aloft on the other tank, since it contained the same amount of fuel. All the while making a restart of the engine by furiously activating the wobble pump and changing tanks. It was on this leg of the flight that I think Frank changed his thinking, only a little bit.
>
> I have never ever believed in starving an engine from fuel, especially when flying. It's possible that a fuel tank that has a residue of sediment to have it sucked out into the fuel lines as the fuel pump discharges the very last ounce of fuel from the tank.
>
> Anyway, approaching Alice, Texas, at 6,000 feet, I began to switch tanks from left to right. Frank stopped me, counselling that he wanted to wait until the fuel pressure began to drop. I reluctantly obeyed, nervously. Sure enough, right over the Alice Municipal the fuel pressure dropped rapidly and the engine quit! I switched tanks and began the vertical up and down motion on the wobble pump which was supposed to and most often did recharge the fuel system. Not this time, though. Having an airport underneath me, I began a shallow circle, and we began to lose altitude. The only sound came from a rather faint swishing of air as it passed over the top of the cabin. Frank maintained his cool, and

> though I might have faked it, I was mad and embarrassed inwardly that two CAA types would dead stick on an airport, out of fuel, but with a full tank that couldn't be used!
>
> At about 1,500 feet above ground, Frank leaned across me and grabbed the wobble pump. And even before he began to wobble the engine started to cough, backfire a couple of times, and take off with a roar. We continued a heading for Laredo and landed for refueling. On to Monterrey, and as we landed, Bill Janssen, from McPherson, Kansas, asked where we'd been? We were the last to arrive in Monterrey. The Farmers, using road maps, flew underneath the storm, down close to the highways, and had arrived the previous afternoon.

The first night, January 17, 1950, their host, José Maguerza, who owned two breweries in Mexico and the Columbia Hotel where they stayed, entertained with a banquet for the entire group. A good Mexican band provided the music. Lillian Janssen's letter of January 1991 recalled the events of that night:

> My husband, Bill, was president of the Flying Farmers that year, and he acted as the master of ceremonies. He asked Governor Carlson to prove himself eligible for honorary membership.
>
> It was here that the Governor proved that he could take a joke. In order to prove his prowess as a farmer, they provided him with a sombrero and serape and asked him to milk a goat that had just been led into the room. He obliged, to much applause and laughter.
>
> After that, Bill turned to Frank and asked him to choose an instrument from the musicians and play a number for the group. Frank hesitated for a moment or so, then went over to the troubadours and choose a saxophone—played 2 or 3 bars, returned the instrument and sat down. One knew something was wrong! Bill later asked John Zentner about the incident, and was informed that Frank had given up the music business, and just didn't want to play the sax any longer.

On January 19, the party split up in Monterrey. Trumbauer and Zentner went to Mexico City and found accommodation at the Hotel de la Reforma, a luxury hotel on the Paseo de la Reforma Boulevard. Zentner's account continued:

> We were assigned the Chief of Police of Mexico City, a full Mexican General, to show us about. "General Jessie," as we called him, had spent some of his early years in Chicago where he worked for the Al Capone organization. His job had been to "visit" the various speakeasies in Chicago, and take a reading as to the percentage of beer and bootleg booze supplied by Capone and his gang, as compared to that being supplied by the other two major gangs.
>
> Jessie took us all about, chauffeured in a big Packard sedan. We visited the tombs underneath the famous Victory Monument, saw the skeletons of some of the most famous Mexican fighters and leaders, the famous floating gardens, and we entered and went through Maximillian's and Carlotta's palace. These places, aside from the gardens, were entered with special keys that Jessie carried. At one point in the palace, I spied a very old dusty harpsichord, and I pressed a key and heard a faint, scratchy sound. Jessie admonished me rather severely, telling me that it was probably the first time in a hundred years or so that anyone had touched it.
>
> The early evening was spent accepting an invitation to accompany Governor Carlson as he and his wife were being honored at a reception at the Presidential Palace. It was a gala affair, and Frank and I were in the receiving line as the guests were being greeted by first, the President's wife, and then the President. Señora de Aleman, the President's wife, was a very pretty lady, a bit on the heavy side. I had not been briefed on what to say, so I decided to say in Spanish what would ordinarily be at least acceptable, "buenos dias" (good day). All well and good, but my gringo pronunciation was faulty, and I said "buenos dios," which means "good God." She laughed and laughed, so much so, that I was kind of glad that I'd made the error. What was worse, she spoke very good English. Frank and I didn't stay long. We were out of our element. Jessie returned us to the hotel, where we spent an hour or so telling our farmer friends what had happened to us during the day.

The Flying Farmers split into various groups, with Zentner and Trumbauer heading to Acapulco, January 21–26, and then returning to Monterrey for two days. On January 29, most of the group left Mexico to return home. John Zentner's final recollection:

Our trip back to the states was routine, except for a few moments of sheer panic. As we were crossing the International Border near Brownsville, Texas, we noted a distinct weather front approaching the Gulf from the west. I was flying this leg. We were both tired, and agreed that we could get around the front by turning seaward and maintaining a north easterly heading for 30 minutes, then swing back to the west toward land. Weather reports in that area were good.

We were soon flying on instruments, both of us inwardly edgy about being over water, one engine, and no "water wings." We both kept looking at our watches, and the 30 minutes went by ever so slowly. Finally, we took up the westerly heading, still on instruments, but the overcast was getting lighter, and we could occasionally see the water below us.

We dropped down to about 200 feet, and our forward visibility began to increase somewhat. Suddenly, within a space of thirty seconds, we were in the clear, and just as suddenly we were dodging airplanes that seemed to be going in every direction. It didn't take us long to realize that we had made land right smack dab over the U. S. Navy's Primary Flight School at Corpus Christi.

We played dodge 'em for about sixty seconds, all the time scared to death that even though we didn't have a midair collision ahead of us, we'd probably have been identified and would have to pay the consequences. This latter aspect could mean severe disciplinary action, since flying into restricted airspace, without a clearance, is severely frowned on. Once out of the mess, we tuned up the volume on Corpus Christi tower frequency and were astounded that not a single report of our transiting their airspace had been made. Frank allowed as how we were probably too low to be picked up by their radar.

We concluded the trip without further incident. Frank dropped me off in Grand Junction, and continued on to Kansas City.

All Scout Dads presented a second "Funzajumpin' " at the Boone School on March 17, 1950, which according to the program, was "Dedicated To The Lovers Of Stuff." The three listed directors of the two-part production, were: "Hap Paulsen, Ed Wilson, and Frank Trumbauer." Helen Leighow again offered her services as a tap dancer, with her daughter Sandra, and as director of "Artistry and Grace In Ballet," a repeat of the eight-man ballet of the previous year. The presentation was again a huge success, but Tram did not play his saxophone. He had "retired" his instrument following last year's program.

Trumbauer's duties with the CAA were bringing him in closer contact with the National Flying Farmers Organization. He was becoming an accepted friend, rather than a government official identified with red tape that was put in their way. They found Trumbauer attempting to help them lift the regulations and solve problems that did not seem to be in phase with their efforts.

In mid-1950, the conflict in Korea represented a possible danger of escalating, possibly into a World War. This concern was paramount on the minds of the National Flying Farmers Convention, held September 4–7. They anticipated rationing of gasoline, thus reducing unrestricted use of their airplanes in planting their fields.

Setting aside their possible production problems, the convention focused on how they could assist the nation should the need arise. Such proposals as patrolling shorelines, protecting water supplies, pipe lines, communications lines, railroads, and inland waterways were discussed. Should an atomic war come to our shores, they felt it would be necessary to stand by to transport hundreds of doctors to the scene of a bombing in short time. A quick call for blood plasma, and numerous other light cargo movements, were considered. No other group in America had such a national organization, with qualified pilots and airplanes to assist their government. A spirit of pride swelled in Trumbauer at this convention, knowing that if home defenses were needed, the Flying Farmers were ready to answer the call!

The results of the September Convention did not go unnoticed by the Civil Air Patrol, an auxiliary unit of the Air Force, who volunteered their services and equipment in their civilian defense of their country. Colonel J. Roy McGuire, Commanding Officer of the Ohio Wing, and a member of the National Board of the Civil Air Patrol, showed deep interest in the possible alliance with the Flying Farmers. He suggested that the membership consider joining the CAP and the two organizations could assist each other. It was proposed that the Flying Farmers would be in an excellent position to act as spotters, fly on search missions, etc., in time of civilian defense efforts. In turn, as members of the CAP they could be issued radio and radio-telephone equipment to report on assistance to isolated and strategic communities. While some individuals did join the CAP, the two organizations did not merge.

Trumbauer spent the better part of a year promoting a tour to California for the midwestern Flying Farmers. His suggestion was one that could combine business (trips to the Sacramento Valley and San Joaquin Valley to study agricultural methods), with pleasure (a tour of Los Angeles, Hollywood, and surrounding places of interest). Approval came during the Flying Farmers meeting in June, and William Janssen was assigned to make the necessary arrangements for the October 2–7 tour. Ninety-one members, using fifty airplanes, from Kansas, Nebraska, Colorado, Texas, and Oklahoma, took part.

The trip was a new experience for many of the plains farmers, as the Rockies, with down drafts, high peaks, threats of icing, and countless thousands of miles of area unfamiliar to them caused grave concern. Fortunately, the trip presented an accident-free holiday. Radio stations along the way provided weather tips and other needed information to the flyers. Many of the stations dubbed the tour "Operations Farmer" and went all out to help guide the contingent to their destination in California.

All of the planes gathered in El Paso, Texas on October 2. During their overnight stay, many of the tourists crossed the Rio Grande and visited Mexico. They were told to keep eating the fine Mexican steaks, but some felt venturous and tried Mexican dishes. Trumbauer overheard one visitor, who had ordered Mexican food, comment "I know just how that man feels," as they watched a floor show actor eat razor blades!

"On To California" (the selected slogan) resumed without incident, and the flyers were thankful for the clear weather and navigational assistance when they met with their biggest challenge. Their destination was Santa Monica, a city among hundreds of miles dotted with numerous cities that made up the greater Los Angeles area. It became difficult to locate the airport because of a huge overcast of smog. Experienced personnel in the towers of the airport were able to direct safe landings for all aircraft through the dense smog hindrance. The pilots and companions boarded the busses at the airport for their journey to the hotel when National Vice-President "Tex" Anderson took note of the surrounding hilltop covered with oil derricks. "Geez, those things were in my final approach," he groaned for the better part of an hour.

Social activities included a trip to several movie studios and movie stars' homes by bus and a boat trip to Catalina Island. Many brought their bathing suits and were treated to sun-drenched days at the beaches. The highlight was a trip to the Farmer's Market, where produce of all varieties could be purchased. The final day was spent at the University of California Agriculture College at Davis, with a side trip to the Fiorini Farm. The returning tourists all marveled at the special courtesies they were shown at all stops, and many felt that these pleasant memories would lure them back for future visits.

John Zentner resumed his recollections of Trumbauer during 1951:

> The annual CAA Inspector conference was ahead, and while it was all daytime business, the nighttime was mostly fun. The regional Administrator and his staff would usually arrange for a banquet of sorts at a good hotel, and would invite some nationally known aviation personality to give us all the word via a speech.
>
> This time, they wanted something a little different, and since all the men throughout the Region knew Frank, and were aware of his music background, Leonard Jurden got a half way commitment from Frank to get out his horn and play for the men.
>
> Frank called me and asked what I thought. I gave it a resounding OK. Frank said that hc would practice and he wanted me to accompany him. [Ed note: Zentner studied piano for about ten years, enabling him to play dance jobs while in college, and still regarded himself as a "half-ass" piano player.] I didn't hesitate long after he assured me that whatever we played wouldn't be in six sharps or flats, and we would have time to rehearse before going on stage.
>
> I arrived in Kansas City a day ahead of time, and though I remember our rehearsing, I have forgotten where it took place. Frank had spent some time boning up on a very difficult saxophone solo which he had used with the Whiteman Band, and during intermissions when he had his own outfits. Fortunately for me, the accompaniment was quite simple, since the whole idea was to feature the soloist.
>
> Between some beer and a little hard liquor, the guys were in an extremely receptive mood for our performance. Frank not only played for the men, but he told several priceless yarns about his days with Paul Whiteman, with Bix, and

> with what he called his "studio orchestra" out in California. I doubt that I've ever had more fun than I had that night listening to Frank. Incidentally, the special solo that Frank played was "Hejre Kati," which Frank pronounced as "Hairy Kitty." It was a real toughy to play, but Frank didn't miss a lick! Now, at last, Frank didn't put his horn back into mothballs!

Harry Troxell's letter of August 1990, recalled an event during this 1951 period:

> Frank used to come up to Des Moines from Kansas City on week-ends to play golf with me and my wife. He was a pretty good golfer. Shot between 85 and 90.
>
> This time, I got a kick out of the way that he came off the airplane at Des Moines. He was carrying his clubs, but no bag! He had a white clothes line wrapped around his clubs. That's all. I had an extra bag for him.
>
> We played a muni-course. The eleventh hole was a par 3, 140 yards. No fairway. Just a lake between the tee and the green. I always used an old ball (water ball) off the tee for obvious reasons.
>
> This one Sunday, he bugged me about using an old ball. He teed up a new ball. Used an iron and promptly dumped it into the water. He repeated this act 3 more times! Frank then asked if he could borrow a water ball from me, which he hit onto the green. He made some comment about my golf ball knowing the course better than the ones that he was using.

John Zentner met Trumbauer in Kansas City just prior to the February 1952 International Flying Farmers trip to Mexico. He recalls:

> Frank's saxophone was among his luggage items, and I had brought along a small piano accordion that I had borrowed from a music store friend. After spending several weeks figuring out some of the bass chord changes, I felt that I could attempt to accompany Frank on some of his favorite tunes.
>
> Prior to taking off for Dallas, Frank and I performed the financial ritual that we had adopted in previous trips. I took a paper sack and put all the money that I had in it, handed the

> sack to Frank, and he did likewise. He never knew nor did he ever ask how much I put in, nor did I ever ask or know how much Frank's offering was. From that moment on, we financed the trip out of the sack— food, fuel, and whatever. Until now we have never run out of funds, and on the return, we just divided up whatever was left.

Laredo, Texas, was again chosen as the rallying site, and on February 4, 196 tourists and airplanes from 24 states gathered for the pleasure-and-business trip to Mexico. One of the main points of interest was to study "patch farming" techniques by which crops could be grown and harvested on some of the precipitous slopes of the mountain areas. Another concern was the control of hoof and mouth disease, and the method that had been developed to combat this dreaded disease by the Mexican ranchers.

As before, the tourists were hosted by the Muguerza family, owners of the Carta Blanca Brewery, on February 5 at the swank Monterrey Casino Club. The dinner was hosted by the two Muguerza brothers, José "Pepe" Muguerza, who was vice-president of American Airlines of Mexico, and Fernando Muguerza, owner of a butane distributorship in northern Mexico.

The evening's entertainment was highlighted by Señor Frank Trumbauer and Señor John Zentner (or as some of the flyers called them, "Frankie and Johnny"), who were introduced as "The last of the Mexican Indians in Monterrey," and proceeded to entertain by playing a variety of tunes, including Mexican numbers, for the appreciative audience.

After leaving Monterrey on February 5, there were brief stops in Tampico, Tuxpan, and Tulancingo, before heading for Acapulco on February 9. Zentner remembered:

> Four days of Acapulco were ahead of us. We spent most of our afternoons on the patios watching the water activity, the sailboats and the fishing boats and the occasional large, luxurious cruise ships that had begun to make Acapulco a port of call. Evenings never ended until well past midnight, and days never began before ten in the morning. A swim suit was the costume, and we'd all lay around on beach towels and soak up the sun.
>
> One event that sticks out in my memory was an evening when Frank and I decided to attend a Jai-Alai (pronounced

Hi-Li) match.[54] There everyone was, even in an atmosphere where we didn't know a soul.

The game finally ended. Since we still had no idea as to the intricacies of the game, and how it was scored, or even who won, we were pleased that our elderly friend was climbing up the bleacher steps and approaching us. ''Mucho buenos, señors,'' he exclaimed as he dumped a pile of pesos in my lap. All the time he had waved to us, and we'd wave back, we had been betting on the next point without the slightest hint of what we were doing!

Trumbauer and Zentner left on February 12, after dividing their time in Acapulco between the homes owned by ''Doc'' and Marie, and by Jimmy and Dorothy Staton. Next stop, Mexico City on February 13 and 15, as Zentner recounted:

We landed in the city mid-morning and checked into our hotel on the Paseo, after the usual wild taxi ride. Frank and I both agreed that it was to our best interest to take stock of our finances. The sack was brought out, and the contents dumped on the bed. A quick calculation regarding hotel expense, food, fuel for the aircraft, plus incidentals would probably result in a negative cash flow before we returned home.

Our hotel was almost adjacent to a Sanborn's restaurant, a favorite of the Norte Americanos, as we were referred to. It was about midmorning when Frank and I walked in. Most of these folks were having the time of their lives, making friends with one another, comparing notes about their Mexican excursions, and really living it up. Frank and I were in a somber mood because of our financial situation until I suggested a possible way out, plus maybe have some fun!

I suggested that we return to our hotel, get the horn and the accordion, and return to Sanborn's where we could borrow a couple of big sombreros, a couple of serapes, find a tin cup, and go down on the street, outside the restaurant, and pretend that we were blind. Frank resisted the idea, but I could see by the gleam in his eye that it wouldn't take much to win him over.

---

[54]Jai-Alai was adopted from the Basque game. It was played on a court with high walls on each end. The players have clawlike wicker rackets strapped to their wrists, and alternate catching and propelling the ball (''pelota'') against the wall.

"Just a gag," I said, "and if we get thrown in the pokey, we can always call for General Jessie to get us out."

That did it! We got the music stuff, returned, and it was easy to borrow the trappings for disguise. The tin cup came harder, but we got one from the Sanborn kitchen. We found a ledge on the store side of the street in front of Sanborn's. Frank put on his dark aviator glasses, my sombrero shaded my face, the cup was in front of us, and we began to play some old American jazz tunes. It was hard to keep from laughing, particularly when it became evident that we were fooling the Americanos, and they began to drop pesos in the tin cup.

This went on for about fifteen minutes, at which time Frank played "Herje Kati," and sure enough, there was one gringo in the crowd who contributed that recognized Frank. By that time, we were laughing so hard we couldn't continue to play. We gave back the disguises, offered to give back any of the money that we had obtained under false pretenses, but there were no takers!

Counting the silver pesos, along with our paper money, we had just about the right amount to fill the fuel tanks of the Bonanza airplane the following morning. Nobody but Frank Trumbauer would have gone along with a stunt like that one!

From Sanborn's we went down the Paseo until we came to a music store. I wanted to buy a recording of the "Mexican Hat Dance." At least that is what we called it stateside. The folks in the store couldn't or wouldn't admit that they could speak English. So I asked for the record by translating "Mexican Hat Dance" into Spanish, something like "Baile de Sombrero Mexicano." They didn't know what I was talking about. There were several people in the store by now, and they along with the four or five store clerks, were gathering closely around, curious about what was happening. Suddenly Frank saved the day, as he usually did. "Da da da da da-dada dada dada dada," he sang in his scratchy voice, and everyone in the store cheered! "Jarabe Tapatio" is the Mexican name of the record I bought.

Frank could get along fine in any country, without knowing a word of their language. He could improvise, make his needs known by facial expressions, and his Spanish most often was simply adding an "ero" to an English word. The Mexicans rarely understood his verbal sounds, but it was a rare occasion when they were stumped after he

> acted something out by screwing up his face, gesturing, or by inventing a word. For example, a dog was a "dogero," a hotel was a "hotelero," the men's room in the hotel was a "crapero."

The contingent of flyers left Mexico on February 18, 1952. Trumbauer and Zentner flew to Dallas and stayed overnight at Jimmy Staton's home, before returning to their homes. Zentner added:

> But before going to his home, he took us to a very exclusive private club to introduce us to some of his friends. It was a cold night, and we were checking our gear, when the lady behind the counter literally leaped across it, let out a muffled yell, and embraced Frank. Frank backed off, looking baffled, until he recognized her. He introduced her as "Miss Georgia Gibbs" that had recorded with him. Between music and airplanes, it is indeed a small world.

Zentner next heard from Trumbauer when he telephoned and asked Zentner to attend the Flying Farmers safety seminar in Douglas, Wyoming, during June 22–26, 1952:

> Frank said that he would pick me up in Denver. He had finally coerced his mother, Gertrude Stevenson, into taking an airplane ride, and the three of us would fly to the convention together.

The Chamber of Commerce hosted a Friday night (June 21) dinner for their guests attending the convention, and while Trumbauer had been razzed for not bringing his saxophone before, he was now prepared to entertain the members, and had brought his mother to accompany him. Tram introduced his mother as a former pianist for the silent pictures theatre, and as she played various musical pieces associated with the screening of a silent film, Tram narrated what the viewers might be seeing on the screen. The piano music of "the chase," "hearts and flowers," "the villain," and "the hero," was cued to Tram's explanation of the story, and resulted in laughter. Following the presentation, Tram's mother played one of her own melodic compositions, and then Zentner took over at the piano and "Frankie and Johnny" played some high entertaining old time favorites on saxophone and piano.

The weekend went without incident, but as the trio prepared to board their airplane on the final day, a "close call" occurred. Zentner clearly remembered the events of that day:

> The above sea level elevation of Douglas was about 4,900 feet, and those of us who flew aircraft in those days knew that as you operated above sea level, engine power was reduced in proportion to the increase in altitude. The Navion aircraft was not noted for anything but sea level kind of flying.
>
> Frank is flying, and his mom is seated beside him, and I am in the rear seat. Take-off is to the south, toward a rising hill that is about 1,500 feet above the airport elevation. As we approach the rising terrain, it quickly became apparent that our rate of climb was not going to match that of the clearance of the hill. We were too low to turn, since any turn would result in some loss of lift, and we certainly had none of that to lose.
>
> The ground underneath us had been planted in wheat, was relatively smooth, and off to our right was a major north-south highway, with cars cruising along without any care.
>
> We managed to clear the hill with about 50 feet to spare! I'll never forget Mrs. Stevenson's comment as we were trying to make it over the crest of the hill, throttle to the firewall, prop in high RPM, and Frank and I rising up in our seats (as if that would help):
>
> "Gee, it was certainly nice of you boys to fly so nice and close to the ground so that I could enjoy all of the scenery."
>
> Frank's backward look towards me said it all for the both of us.

Elliott Hammond's March 1991 letter revealed that the antics of the Whiteman era still lingered:

> It had to be July or August 1952. It was at a Regional Office Meeting of approximately 3 to 5 district offices closest to Indianapolis ASDO (Aviation Safety District Office).
>
> We were going out to lunch and Tom Murphy, who was conducting the meeting, went ahead of us when Frank spied Murphy's new Stetson hat on the coat tree. Frank went and picked up the hat and sliced the front brim down to the crown

with a paper cutter. He put the hat back on the coat tree and joined the rest of us for lunch. When we returned, Tom spotted his hat and just about flipped! The veins in his neck swelled and turned red. That's how he got the nickname "Turkey Neck." He was really miffed but none of us let on who did it.
At Christmas time, Frank returned the piece of the brim in a Christmas Card; however, I'm quite sure it was an anonymous card.

John Zentner next saw Tram a couple of months after their Douglas experience:

He spent the night with us in Grand Junction. We'll never forget his visit.
Our "little Johnny" was about four years old. Frank would get down on his hands and knees in our living room, and he'd play horse. Johnny would ride on his back. The following morning, when both were outside before breakfast, Frank spied a grasshopper. "What dat?" asked Frank. "Dat's a hooperdropper," replied Johnny. Now Frank had another homespun yarn that he embellished and often used as he was charming another audience.

It was in September that I learned of a Columbia Records release called "The Bix Beiderbecke Story" in three albums: First: "Bix And Gang", Second "Bix And Tram", and then "Whiteman Days". All of the material in the second album, "Bix And Tram", was recorded with my band, and half of the material in "Whiteman Days".
The information appearing on the back of these albums is ridiculous in many aspects. With a complete course of information available it would be almost impossible for a writer to be as far off base as some of the statements indicated in the discography accompanying these albums, even to the physical stature of the individuals involved. He tells how Bix looked, and how I looked, with a reference to my being shorter than Bix with "Mephistophelian[55]" features, and specific reference to my bad "Rudy Vallee" type vocals, plus other deroga-

[55]It is easy to understand Tram being upset with the reference to his "Mephistophelian" features. Tram was a devoted member of the Kansas City Church of the Unity Society of Practical Christianity.

tory remarks aided in prompting me to give you this information.

He apparently didn't know that most of the vocals I made were recorded in desperation, and some of them strictly as gags. In several cases the soloist engaged didn't show up, and to keep from cancelling the date, members of our band encouraged me to do the lyrics. The side patter on "Take Your Tomorrow And Give Me Today" was done by Marlin Hurt, the famous "Beulah" character of radio in later years, and I believe almost everyone credits this to Scrappy Lambert.

The writer also states that Bix never got to play with the people he should have played with, and he mentions those people in his review. He doesn't take into account that the finest things Bix ever did was in that period of time that we were associated with each other, and also the fact that there are certain restrictions that recording managers and recórding companies give you to work with after a given period of time that are sometimes hard to handle, plus the fact that we were very young and thought it was cute to try and make every record different. We had no idea of following a given style to please a public fancy for a mere monetary gain. It was all a big, happy game, and apparently this was never determined in research. If we didn't like a tune the company wanted us to make we just didn't level on it.

Paul Mertz suggested to Frank Bull and Gene Norman that they dedicate their forthcoming Fifth Annual Jazz Concert, set for October at the Shrine Auditorium in Los Angeles, to the memory of Bix Beiderbecke. They liked the idea, and gave Mertz the go-ahead to contact Tram about appearing at the tribute. Mertz corresponded with Tram, and was able to persuade him to perform.

I agreed to do a "comeback", if only a one night stand. I still had my tone, but my digits were of course creaky. I flew out a week early and sat-in with Red Nichols And His Five Pennies at Mike Lyman's on Vine Street in Hollywood.

Red's group was playing "Manhattan Rag," "Riverboat Shuffle," and all the tunes that I had recorded in the

> **twenties, and in most cases playing them better than we did.**
>
> **For the first four nights, I sat behind the band, out of sight, trying to sharpen my timing. On the fifth night, Red moved me out front so the customers could see me.**
>
> **Red told me to stop being so skeptical, and just be myself. He assured me that I hadn't lost any of my ability. I guess his pep talk did the trick. I know that I had a great time that night, and the audience seemed to enjoy it.**

The eagerly awaited night of the Dixieland Jubilee arrived on October 10, and the Shrine Auditorium Box Office displayed a ''sold out'' sign for their 6,700 seating capacity.

Joe Rushton (long time bass-saxist with Red Nichols' Pennies) offered to pick Tram up at his hotel and drive him to the concert. Rushton, whom Red Nichols acclaimed as the greatest personality that he had ever met, in or out of the music business, was to become one of the most beloved legends in his profession. Possibly only Joe Venuti had more stories told about him by fellow musicians and associates. One of Rushton's habits was to give every object a name, that is, except his cat. As Rushton explained it, ''It didn't have any personality, and until it develops one, it was not getting a name.'' He called the pet, simply, ''cat.''

As Tram rode to the auditorium in Rushton's car (named ''Freddie Ford''), Rushton commented on Tram's calmness. Tram replied that during rehearsal with the musicians that Paul Mertz had assembled to make up his band, several of them mentioned that they expected Tram to be nervous, but as he told them, and explained to Rushton, he was always at ease prior to a performance. Rushton went on to express his feelings about concerts of this type, and told Tram how much it annoyed him to hear listeners applaud a soloist immediately after his playing, because it often drowned out the next soloist, who might be doing a pickup, as some solos overlap, and the listeners could miss something special. ''I wish that everyone would only applaud at the end of every tune,'' concluded Rushton, and to which Tram, and countless other musicians, readily agreed.

The first half of the presentation featured Pete Daily's Chicagoans; Nick Fatool's Friends (including Joe Rushton); Bob Scobey's San Francisco Jazz Band; and Jack Teagarden's group, featuring his brother Charlie and, as an added attraction, their mother Helen, playing ''Possum & Tater Rag'' on piano. The second half offered Eddie Skrivanek's Sextette From Hunger; Rosy McHargue's Rag-Timers; George Lewis's New Orleans Jazz Band; and as the closing group, Frank Bull proudly announced: ''And Now, Ladies And Gentlemen, Frank Trumbauer!''

The huge crowd rose in a standing ovation as Tram and his fellow musicians came on stage. Tram adjusted the microphone, waved to the crowd, and awaited the conclusion of their applause by both nodding and saying ''Thank You,'' as the people resumed their seats. Tram turned to his band and started a count off for the opening number, ''Singin' The Blues.'' When Tram completed his famed solo, the crowd rose again, as if electrified by the moment, and offered tremendous applause in salute to Tram. The band came to a stop until the crowd's enthusiasm subsided, and then Dick Cathcart continued the number by playing Bix's famed 32-bar solo.

Tram next spoke of his association with Bix, telling a couple of anecdotes, and then a hush fell over the auditorium, as the lights dimmed, and a single spotlight beamed onto a wooden framed chair upon the stage, displaying a cornet. Paul Mertz's piano offered his effective rendition of Bix's ''In A Mist. '' The music continued with Tram leading the band into such numbers as ''Ostrich Walk'' and ''My Pretty Girl.''

Tram's appearance concluded, and Frank Bull came forth to share the microphone with Tram.

''How'd it feel?'' Bull asked.

''Seems mighty strange'' replied Tram.

''But it sounded mighty nice,'' commented Bull, sharing the crowd's appreciation.

Tram then announced that this was probably his final public appearance. Scattered cries of ''No,'' ''No,'' were heard throughout the audience, as if begging Tram to reconsider. Tram started for the stage exit and waved, one last time, as the audience gave him a final standing ovation.

''Frank did say that he was never nervous,'' stated Rushton, ''but as he came off that stage, he displayed an emotional side of himself. He had tears in his eyes. Tears of appreciation, and tears from a musical legend marking an end to his final appearance.''

Following the concert, Rushton suggested they stop by his home (which he had dubbed ''Weird Manor'') at 1740 North

Dillon for a quick snack. Tram agreed, and it gave Tram the chance to visit the home of Rushton's two bass-saxophones, "Beatrice" (the gold plated one) and "Buster" (the silver plated one). They headed for the kitchen and the refrigerator. Rushton, who had taken a course in shorthand, would always leave a note for his wife, Priscilla, in shorthand, on the refrigerator that read, "I Love You." Priscilla, who could not write in shorthand, always left a note with a lot of curlicues that was supposed to read, "I Love You," but ended being deciphered by former Nichols's vocalist, Modie Da Costa, for Joe Rushton as "Narchoosh!" In subsequent years, in writing to close friends, Priscilla often closed her correspondence with Narchoosh, Priscilla.

Rushton then drove Tram to Lindy's on Wilshire Boulevard, where Joe Venuti's group was playing, before taking him back to his hotel. Venuti was able to prevail upon Tram to come up and sit in, and as Tram later remarked, in the vernacular of that era, "Those that heard us that night were lucky enough to hear some real-gone jammin'."

Less than ten days later, Tram returned to Los Angeles to fulfill a speaking engagement, and received a telephone call at this hotel which extended an invitation to lunch. Bing Crosby called and invited Tram to join him at the Paramount Studio commissary, for a quick bite, where they were joined by former announcer, now actor, Paul Douglas.

Years earlier, when Jane Vance had joined the Paul Whiteman Orchestra, Dick Stabile prevailed upon her to deliver a saxophone that he wanted Tram to have. "On the money that he was then making," recalled Jane, "Dick could little afford to do this, but he wanted Frank to have it." Now, Tram sought out Stabile, who was musical director for the Dean Martin and Jerry Lewis films being made at Paramount, and presented him with one of Tram's saxophones.

"I had a spare sax that I had been carrying around for years," commented Tram, "and I wanted to return an earlier favor. Besides the horn that Dick was playing is older than the hills. Time for a change to another one."

CHAPTER SEVENTEEN

THE FINAL YEARS 1953–1956

TRUMBAUER STARTED 1953 WITH A SUMMARY of his association with the CAA.

> **My reinstatement to permanent status with the CAA was effective August 1947, when I accepted the position of Assistant to the Regional Administrator (Personal Flying Development). Since that time a very comprehensive public relations program has been initiated through this office in Region 5. Also, a program to increase training proficiency is currently being actuated. Public Relations is a very important function of this office at the present time, as we are in constant contact with leading officials of the industry and the public in general. Evidence of the anticipated success of this program is apparent throughout the region. The cooperation of Mr. Jurden, Regional Administrator, and all regional personnel has been most gratifying.**
>
> **As assistant to the Regional Administrator, the past five years have been devoted to the development of general aviation, working closely with the agricultural segment and the manufacturers. Personal and public relations are an important factor in this activity, plus a good working knowledge of public speaking.**
>
> **I have a rather extensive working knowledge of the CAA, and am personally acquainted and have worked with most of the ranking personnel. It is also gratifying to know that all segments of aviation have gained through the intelligent efforts of the past twelve years in development aspects.**
>
> **I started my aviation career in 1927. I have an instrument and instructor's rating, single and multiengine, A**

> **and E certificate and third class radio. I have considerable practical engineering experience and have flown approximately 200 hours per year for the past six years; prior to that time, approximately 500 hours per year, in all types of aircraft including B-25s, C-46s, C-47s, AT-6s, BT-13, and P-51 pursuits, and I have also been through the school of the P-80 pursuits. My total time—8,000 hours plus. I have approximately 175 hours of link time, plus some 250 hours on actual instruments. I have flown almost every type of commercial aircraft manufactured.**
>
> **Activities in the past five years are too extensive to relate; however, we have twenty-one major accomplishments and several that have been accepted on a national basis for the good of aviation within and outside of the CAA.**

Glenn Tabor, Director, Division of Aeronautics, Kansas Industrial Development Commission, took note of Trumbauer's work with the CAA and started a letter-writing campaign in seeking Trumbauer's appointment to the National Civil Aeronautics Board. His initial letter met with favorable response from Al Cole, Congressman from the First District of Kansas, and he forwarded Glenn's recommendation to the Kansas Republican State Committee on February 3, 1953. State Chairman C. I. Moyer, wrote to Glenn on February 9 and assured him that the recommendation would result in serious consideration for Trumbauer for the position. The thrill of the possibility that existed during February came to a disappointing fate with a March letter from Governor Frank Carlson of Kansas. He informed Glenn that the White House had made a selection to the position in Mr. Denny of Pittsburgh, Pennsylvania.

Dr. Dave Palmer, President of the Davenport (Iowa) Chamber of Commerce, in conjunction with radio and television station WOC, presented a salute to Bix Beiderbecke in connection with his birth date of March 10. A committee was formed and a formal request was sent to Trumbauer to partake in the festivities, and he accepted. Miff Mole drove down from Chicago, where he was currently appearing, and joined Tram for a radio broadcast devoted to Bix.

The WOC radio host asked if they had ever worked together:

> *Tram:* Yes, in 1924. Ray Miller came to St. Louis and hired me for his band. I guess that the main reason that I joined

was because he told me that Miff would be in the band, and I welcomed the opportunity to work with him.

Miff: That was the same story that Ray gave me, when he asked me to join, that Tram would be in the band. I decided to wait and see if Tram was in that band before I joined.

Tram: You mean that he told each of us that the other person was in the band, in order to get us to join? No wonder when I joined Miff wasn't in the band. I thought that he was away on business or something. He was there a few days after I joined, and no one said anything about the situation.

Miff: As I said, I wanted to be certain of things. Ray had a reputation of being a real salesman.

The radio program included recordings and comments by Tram and Miff about them and their association with Bix. "I'm Glad," a 1924 recording made by The Sioux City Six for Gennett Records, was placed on the turntable and spun. Tram asked that Miff's solo be played again. "That solo is well conceived, has good intonation, and Miff has command of his instrument," noted Tram. "That portion he plays actually tells a musical story, and it will live forever." Tram's asides as the recording was being played offered high praise to Miff with "very intelligent" and "how great it is!" audible to the studio personnel only.

Tram was prevailed upon to host a program and spin some of Bix's recordings and comment upon them or reflect on his association with Beiderbecke. Red Nichols sent along a forthcoming record release of "Candlelights" that Tram played and thanked Red for contributing.

Telegrams arrived from Paul Whiteman, Bing Crosby, and countless others. Dave Garroway had his NBC television show devote time to the festivities, having television cameras switching to Davenport for an interview, calling all of America's attention to Bix and the tribute being paid to him. Trumbauer spent three days in Davenport (March 9–11) and then returned to Kansas City, where he resumed his duties with the CAA.

President Dwight Eisenhower ordered a reduction in government forces, and this resulted in a "domino effect" of upper positions being eliminated and personnel having to scramble for lower positions. Such was the case with Trumbauer in July when he was ''bumped'' from Assistant to the Regional Administrator to Supervisor of Flight Operations. He accepted the new position without complaint and was assigned an office in the Federal Building, 911 Walnut Street, on the twenty-seventh floor.

On September 24, during the eighth annual meeting of the National Flying Farmers Association held at the Broadview Hotel in Wichita, Kansas, President E. M. Anderson announced: ''At this time, I would like to ask Mr. Frank Trumbauer, who you all know, and this office has worked with for quite a few years, and who has been with the Fifth Region of the CAA, to say a few words. He has an idea he is working on and he talked to me about it this morning, and I asked Frank to tell you that in a few short words. So, at this time, if Frank will come up here minus his saxophone . . .'' A round of applause accompanied Trumbauer.

> **My good friend here said ''Pilots are never lost, they are just confused''. I think a better word is ''misplaced''.**
>
> **You know, as I look around the room, I see so many familiar faces and I believe I have attended a lot of your meetings; probably the last five years, I have gained a friendship with some of you people that I feel sure will be lasting because not too many of you hold it against me because I happened to be a member of the CAA.**
>
> **I see faces here that I have had arguments with. Friendly arguments, I am happy to say. Mr. Hansen, Mr. John Phifer, John Kirk, E. M. ''Tex'' Anderson—they have all racked me over my poor back, but through all of this, we have come up with something constructive.**
>
> **What I want to tell you. We are always dreaming up something that I think might have some merit, so if you don't like it, throw it out, because then it does not have any place in your operations.**
>
> **We are now in the process of opening what we call a Flight Clinic! A local deal in a local community where all you people can come in when you have problems, or a question, whether it is maintenance, or flight, we will try to have some people there that will have the answer for you. We will have some flight personnel that will be tickled to death to ride with you. Probably just to take a little check. For instance, you all know coming into a landing field, if you have to turn sharp it requires quite a**

little bank but if you don't like to bank, you come in shallow, but you must make the turn on the rudder, so you hold the arrow on the high side and see where you are going. Heavenly days, isn't that a beautiful site to spin in? [Ed note: Then Tram laughed over the next remark] **And it does happen!**

We'd like to have you recognize the value of the clinic, come in and ask your questions and tell us what you would like to have at that clinic and then we will do it. If you don't like it, what is happening at the clinic, we wouldn't know it until you tell us. And if you don't like it, let's throw it out!

Then we'll know where we are going. If you people will advocate to all your friends where you hear of one of those clinics, join up and have all the people in the neighborhood to come to the clinic. If you don't get the answer there, it must be somewhere, we will find it for you!

We have many requests for such sort of a thing. We believe it is very healthy. We would like to improve the progress of the organization. We can't improve the safety record, we feel that is pretty good already, but we think if you talk to some of the people in your community, that don't have good records like yours, they will soon have as good a record as yours.

I was talking to Johnny Phifer and he kept begging me to come and see him, and finally I decided to accept his invitation. I found his strip, and I drove to the little hangar and I made a very careful approach and went down the hilly approach and over another hill and down another, and up another. When I got out at the hangar, and got out of the airplane, Johnny said, "I don't believe it! I didn't think you could ever come in here. Matter of fact, I haven't been using this strip myself. I keep my airplane up town."

Nevertheless that night, Johnny and I had a very interesting meeting and he told me all the things he thought were wrong and strange as it may seem, we got a lot of them fixed.

One of the things I want to do is thank all of you for your favors shown to me in the past. I don't know how many meetings I will be able to attend in the future, but one of the proudest possessions I have is the sincere friendships I have made with you people and regardless of whatever you

hear about me: I have learned some good logic and understanding in aviation from you. If you don't think we are making progress, just look around because we are, and please keep the clinics in mind.

Thank you.

E. M. "Tex" Anderson then called John Kirk to the microphone. John asked Trumbauer to come forth and accept a plaque. Kirk said in part:

Throughout the experience of the past 18 months, I have never worked with a finer group of people in my life than the people of the CAA and I have reference to the Future Farmers of America program, we took on as sponsorship in the board meeting at Kansas City. We had to have help and the only people we could get to give us that help were you people close to us, CAA, and we called on our good friend, Frank Trumbauer, and Frank and his assistant up there, his partner in crime, Johnny Patterson, came down to Wichita and we got John Paul Jones from Fort Worth and he got Howard Taylor from Ohio down here, and we sat in the hotel for two days and drafted the program that we thought you would like to have, and present to the youth of America and give it to the Future Farmers of America.

A concrete, sound program that couldn't have been devised and written without the help of Frank Trumbauer and Johnny Patterson. Every time the office has been in trouble, in the past year, and needed to know some answers we got them. When I first took over as Executive Secretary at the last convention, I had to find out a lot of things the hard way and that is my experience. I had to find that if you want to know the answer about a certain thing, go to the people who have those answers.

Frank, I personally want to shake your hand and say "Thanks" to you for all the help you have given us, and for all the help you gave us on the Future Farmers of America Program.

This is a most pleasant surprise but I feel reluctant to accept it on a personal basis because it isn't true. Actually everything that has happened has been a result of your requests and your efforts, and believe me, all of

my colleagues in the CAA have worked diligently toward the success of aviation in general because I think most of them believe in it sincerely.

We have many fellows that could make much more money in other walks of life as I am sure you know, but they remain in the CAA because they like it. I frankly wish this had been presented to a group of people. However, you have given it to me, and I will cherish it all my life.

It is a great moment and one of the few times in my life I have been at a loss for words. "Tex" has always said, "Don't ever ask this guy to talk because he will fool you. He will!" However, the head of our Department under which I have served for a number of years, who has given me the most able assistance and backed me completely in all projects we had in our region is here, and the gentleman who has recently assumed the position that I had for a number of years in our region. They are both in the room and I think this should be jointly presented to them and "Tex." I think it would be very appropriate if we could have Mr. Willirith, who so ably took these projects from the Washington level, and Mr. Carl Voelter, who is now in charge of all these activities in our region.

I hardly know how to thank you. Thank you, so much.

The National Flying Farmers Association had one more award for Tram. In a letter dated November 16, Secretary Locke Norton stated:

> The National Flying Farmers wish to express their sincere appreciation for your participation in the Building Fund Program. By your contribution you have indicated that you join the advancement of rural aviation.
>
> Along with this letter is a Certificate of Appreciation for your contribution. It is presented to you on behalf of the entire membership. In closing I would like to express my personal appreciation and cordially invite you to come in and enjoy your new "home" in which you truly had a part.

The new "home" of The National Flying Farmers Association was constructed at the Mid-Continental Airport in Wichita, Kansas. Trumbauer continued with his duties at the CAA and it was in January 1954 that he received a strange request. He was invited by Don Molmberg, on behalf of Ralph Edwards, to be a guest on their national television program, **This Is Your Life.** They planned to honor guest ''Doc'' Rando and requested that Tram be a participant and offer some words of praise earned during their association. Tram's reply of February 2 stated:

> **I just can't remember any early incident that I feel would be of value to you in doing the life of ''Doc'' Rando.**
>
> **Having retired from professional activity about eight years ago, I have been out of contact completely with one exception. In October 1952, I was the featured guest in the Jazz Jubilee in Hollywood.**
>
> **After the show, I went to Lindy's on Wilshire where Joe Venuti was playing with a small group. I sat in with Joe unannounced and to say we upset the place is a mild statement.**
>
> **After the session, Joe took me to a table to meet a fellow, as he said, ''who has admired and followed your work all his life''. I haven't seen him in years and it was ''Doc'' Rando. He just happened to be there and I just happened to sit in.**

Tram was not contacted any further by Molmberg.

Major General Lucas V. Beau, National Commander of the Civil Air Patrol, approved the request submitted by Colonel Emmett Rushing, Director of the Southwestern Region of the CAP to have Trumbauer appointed to the rank of Lieutenant Colonel on June 28 and assigned to his command. Trumbauer's duties would be as an advisor to the Regional Director.

At this time, Columbia Records contacted Tram about a proposed album they wanted to produce and suggested a ''show business type'' album, with Tram providing information on his career, using recordings they released plus private radio broadcasts that Tram had in his possession of his various bands during the late Nineteen Thirties.

> **The interest in the project was most refreshing but I have very little time to think about it.**
>
> **On July 12, I expected to land in New York with reservations at the Biltmore Hotel. Then a conference with the Under Secretary for Defense, Bob Anderson, in Washington, D.C. on July 15.**

> **I did not feel satisfied in my own mind to send material to Columbia as I was in the process of registering it with the Writers Guild, which has not been done to date.**
>
> **This entire show business type album was their idea. I don't think I want Columbia to get the idea I'm selling something. If they want to do it, O.K., if not, I won't miss a beat!**

Neither Tram nor Columbia Records could agree on the proposal, and the project ended.

Tram's comments about registering his material with the Writers Guild pertained to his plans to write his own autobiography. For years, Trumbauer had received letters from all around the world seeking his comments on pending articles, answers to questions, and comments on his days in the music business. Tram decided that he could best answer all the requests by preparing his own life story, and he started making notations, as they came to mind, in preparing for the day when he would write his memoirs. In the meantime, Tram politely said "no" when requests for further information arrived, pointing out that he was preparing his own book. All of his notations are included in this book, exactly as he jotted them down.

Colonel Rushing's letter to Trumbauer on July 19 outlined plans for teaching CAP cadets to fly: "The primary purpose of the program is to supply cadet pilot material for the armed services. The instruction will be done by CAA approved schools and operators. We plan on turning out 5,000 such pilots the first year, 10,000 the second and up to 25,000 in subsequent years, depending on the demand of the services." Colonel Rushing requested that Trumbauer serve as the fourth member of the committee "to perfect such a program." In addition to Rushing, General Robert Harper, USAF Retired, and Gill Robb Wilson, editor of *Flying* magazine, had accepted appointments. Trumbauer turned the matter over to his boss, Leonard Jurden of the CAA, for his approval and received permission to serve as an advisor to the CAP as requested, on August 20.

Maggie Pickett's interview during 1991 recalled the 1950–1955 period when she lived next door to the Trumbauers:

> My husband, Bob, and I were a bit younger than Frank and Mitzi—they were about my parents' age—but this didn't

> detract from our friendship. We often had a barbecue or shared dinner or had a few drinks together. At that time, I was a jazz aficionado and I tried to get Frank to talk about his days in the music business, but he seemed rather hesitant to do so, often changing the topic to the weather or something else. My birthday is in November, and in either 1952 or 1953, Frank gave me a special birthday present—the recording of "Singin' The Blues" from his personal collection. He talked briefly about Bix, that night, and I remember his saying that he often had to tuck Bix into bed. I asked him why he gave up the music business and he said that he preferred the normal life that he was now leading. You know, get up and go to work, come home and have dinner with the family, and just enjoy the daily routines of life.

Maggie recalled the summer of 1954:

> My mother had just lost her mother and she and my dad, [Duvall Strother] who was a circuit court judge, were over for a visit, and we were sitting around the backyard when the subject of a trip to Mexico came up. Frank and Mitzi decided that it was a great idea and were all set to go. My mom felt it would do her good to get away for awhile, but my dad had to clear his court calendar before he could go.
>
> The trip finally came about right after Thanksgiving. I went down to the airport to see my parents off, and then I saw the airplane that Frank planned to fly. It looked like the one Lindbergh flew. It held four people, but it had only one propeller! Frank just laughed and assured me that it was safe and more than adequate to make the trip.

(Bill Trumbauer, Jr., has noted that Tram had taught Mitzi some basics on flying, in the event that he suffered a heart attack while in the air. She could take control and have some idea of being able to pilot and land the aircraft.)

Trumbauer did pilot the quartet to Mexico but the holiday ended abruptly when Judge Strother forgot the basic warning about drinking the water. He acquired "Montezuma's Revenge" when he added an ice cube to the drink that he had the first night. His illness became so severe that the decision was made to return to Kansas City, but due to the judge's upset stomach, the Strothers returned by train, and the Trumbauers by airplane.

Under 1955 orders to cut back, the CAA decided to not maintain a film library. Trumbauer often used the film library in his presentations on behalf of the CAA, and when some of his friends learned of his plight, they set out to assist him. John Smith wrote a personal and confidential letter to W. T. Raymond, assistant to the vice president of Eastern Air Lines, on January 27. John cited the Eastern Air Lines showing of a public relations film, featuring Arthur Godfrey, that had received very flattering and gratifying comments during a recent Kansas Aviation Trades meeting.

In part, John wrote:

> Trumbauer is called upon to attend many general aviation conventions in the mid-west and does one of the most effective public relations jobs done by the CAA. The National Flying Farmers always include an invitation to Frank to take part in their programs. I would venture to say that he is probably better known to everyone connected with fixed-base operation and private airplanes than any other single guy I know.

A copy of the film was made available to John, on an indefinite basis, for Trumbauer to use, a kindness that Tram never forgot.

Paul Flanary, Paul Cannom, and Frank Trumbauer collaborated on a tongue-in-cheek proposal in keeping with the reductions ordered by the government, and submitted a proposal on February 18 to the Chief, Air Carrier Division. They submitted their plans for a newly organized company known as the ''Upright and Downright Airline,'' a commuter service between Kansas City Municipal Airport and the Mid-Continent International Airport in Platte County, Missouri. Their letter said:

> We have equipped a DC-3 with a tricycle landing gear for passenger comfort while on the ground. The passenger cabin is equipped with 60 sets of alternate pink and blue wooden shower sandals securely fastened to the floor and approved by Welling's outfit. Convenient straps with sanitary hand grips are fastened to the ceiling above each sandal. Passengers stand face to face so they may ''chat'' while en route. We chose this arrangement over one having them all face the front in order to reduce the possibility of anyone inadvertently getting goosed during takeoff or landing, and for passenger convenience. Cabin will be placarded against ''passenger acrobatics.''

> We have increased the pay load by installing only one 55 gallon drum, properly vented, since more than that will not be required for this run. Further we have removed all navigational equipment since we plan to stretch a steel cable from one airport to the other and to equip the DC-3 with a loop mounted on top of the fuselage at a correct CG location for good fore and aft balance in flight. The cable will pass through the loop as the aircraft proceeds on course. There will be no necessity for holding an instrument weather which is another reason why it was necessary to install only one 55 gallon drum properly vented.
>
> Our flight crews are being trained at the present time and will be ready to walk the wire by the time you can get this application processed and approved in 1960. In our training program, we are stressing pilot proficiency. At no time are they to permit the cable to touch the sides of the loop. We have a cable stretcher to keep it taut and our passengers at no time will ever hear the ring sing. The pilots all hold non-zing ratings which, we are sure you will have to admit, far exceed the usual air carrier requirements.
>
> Since the flight will be of short duration, no rest rooms are provided. They will just have to wait. Placards to this effect will be placed in plain view in the cabin.
>
> We anticipate that this application and operation will not be handled by the regular Air Carrier Branch but will come under the jurisdiction of the new Special Operations Branch proposed for Region Three.
>
> We would appreciate your early consideration and approval.
>
> P. S. The little building which you see standing on the new International Airport, which is now under construction, is not our ticket office.

The routine of daily duties with the CAA and of conferences throughout the nation was broken by an assignment to Washington. Tram and John Zentner were dispatched to put together a Pilot's Information Manual, focusing on safety for the CAA. Upon reporting, they were asked the usual questions by government officials, i.e. "Who sent you?", "Why are you here?" and "Who said what?". Once they established their mission and produced the orders that accompanied their assignment, they were shown an office in the old CAA General Safety Division sans furniture and personnel.

As John Zentner recalled in 1992:

> These buildings were "war surplus" temporary kind of structures, and they were close by the Washington National Airport. The buildings were still being identified by their old World War II numbers, and ours was T-4. Our area was commonly referred to as the "coal mines," since all of our buildings were heated with coal furnaces which not only didn't do the job, but were also very dirty.

Tram's and John's first priority was office furniture. They arrived early, awaited the opening of their new headquarters, and when the janitor opened the front door for a day of business, Tram button-holed him, mentioned the name of a high official, and told the janitor that they were there to pick up the furniture assigned to them. It resulted in a basement search, which produced a desk, chair, etc. that were transported to their office. Then came the problem of a secretary. As the employees came to work that same morning, Trumbauer picked out a likely secretary, put his arms around her, and escorted her to their office, informing the bewildered girl that she had been transferred to their unit and was their new secretary. In the meantime, the "powers that be" came to check on Trumbauer and Zentner, and were surprised to find that they had acquired both furniture and a secretary, and commented on how well they were organized. Trumbauer and Zentner finished their assignment and left Washington with a sense of pride in their newly prepared book and a sense of amusement at what they had experienced with the Washington bureaucracy.

When Trumbauer joined the CAA, he was given a qualifications sheet prepared by other members in jest, and in reviewing it, he could now see how his years had closely related to the initial suggestions. In part the sheet read:

> You must be a man of vision and ambition, an after-dinner speaker, night owl, able to fly all day and make out reports all night and appear fresh the next day! Learn to sleep on the floor and eat two meals a day to economize on traveling expenses so you can entertain friends in the next room.
>
> You must attend all meetings, air shows, funerals, visit pilots in hospitals and jails, contact and smooth feelings of every operator, student and instructor in your district, and in

> spare time do missionary work and good will work; drive a Government Ford with a poop-sheet strapped to your knee and be readily able to compute mileage, drift, ground speed, gas consumption per-block-per-mile, wear and tear on tires and depreciation on paint job.
>
> You must be able to stick your neck out by answering all questions of operations and then pull it back in before it's chopped off. You must be an expert talker, liar, dancer, traveler, bridge player, poker hound, golf player, diplomat, financier, capitalist, philanthropist, and an authority on palmistry, chemistry, physiology, psychology, cats, dogs, horses, engines, airplanes, students, and still make your expense voucher stick the first time it is submitted.

Perhaps due to government cutbacks or his advancing age, as 1955 grew to a close, he began expressing an interest in seeking employment outside of the CAA, perhaps in the private sector. Ralph Piper of Monsanto Chemical Company suggested that he might have some influence and contacted Henry Boggess of the National Business Aircraft Association, suggesting that Boggess would find an outstanding employee in Trumbauer. Boggess's confidential letter to Trumbauer of February 7, 1956 stated, in part:

> NBAA anticipates decentralization to a regional basis, expansion of membership, and greatly increased activities in the not too distant future. Such plans will, of course, entail staff expansion which may put us in the market for someone possessing a thorough knowledge and background in aviation and requisite qualifications in administrative public relations work. If you would be interested in being considered for such a post, I would appreciate your writing me in full as to your qualifications and experience including earliest date of your availability, expected salary, and other pertinent information and data which will indicate to us whether or not you will be in a position to entertain the idea of your possible employment.

Trumbauer replied immediately, submitting some ideas in a February 14, 1956, letter here quoted in part:

> **I have been vitally interested in your organization since it was conceived and its natural planned growth has been very gratifying.**

> **One of the plans that I have in mind would necessitate a visit of a committee from your Operations Division with the Administrator of the Civil Aeronautics Administration in Washington, D.C. The objective would be to get higher level sanction for the selection of a highly qualified CAA representative in each of the four regions to work with NBAA and to assume the responsibility of liaison through the Regional Administrators.**
>
> **I have served in numerous operational capacities within the CAA including Assistant to the Regional Administrator. Administrative and public relations present no problem and being in a supervisory capacity involving twenty-two district offices in the mid-western states afford various experience. My latest effort was the preparation of text material for the psychology of accident investigation. Public Speaking has been a strong point and a Toastmaster's Club, of which I am a past president, originated in our office to aid our people in presenting their technical knowledge.**
>
> **My work is productive in nature. I like what I am doing and I'm doing what I like, "working with aviation."**
>
> **It is only natural that I should consider bettering my position if that is possible.**

Henry Boggess's confidential letter to Trumbauer on March 21, 1956, said in part:

> Your background and experience well qualifies you to fit into the NBAA administrative staff. The type of work you have conducted with the CAA and your natural interests and your extracurricular activities in flight safety, as well as your apparent recognition of the big job to be done in education, fits well into our thinking as to the type of person who may do us the greatest service.
>
> . . . the program may not be in position for a few more months. . . . Perhaps at such time we will request your meeting with the Board if you are then still interested.

Trumbauer replied and assured them of his interest and willingness to arrange an interview at their convenience.

Mary Freeman began dating Bill Trumbauer in February 1956, and they would later marry. Mary Trumbauer's letter of February 1991 states:

> For the few short months I was acquainted with Frank, I found him to be a kind, considerate and wonderful man. He had a great sense of humor and was extremely easy to talk to. Bill and Frank had an excellent father/son, musician/musician relationship. They understood each other probably like no other father/son. Musicians usually understand each other best. They were the best of friends. They jammed together, they wrote songs together. They played golf whenever weather permitted and were pretty good golfers. Bill could go to his dad with any problem and they usually were able to solve it. I am extremely proud to have known Frank if only for a short time. He was always kind to me and to everyone. I knew him as a wonderful husband to his wife, Mitzi; a loving father to Lynne and Bill; a proud grandfather of Roger's and Lynne's son, Larry; and a true friend to all that he met.
>
> I was included in their nights out for dinner. This was usually to Luigi's Restaurant at about 45th and Main. The atmosphere was very relaxing—fire in the fireplace, comfortable chairs, the works. Frank would usually order a steak. Sometimes on Sunday, we would all get together, including his mother, and go to Putsch's Cafeteria on the Plaza.
>
> I was employed in a building not too far from the Federal Building where Frank worked, and I remember, one day at lunch time, I heard someone give this "wolf whistle" at me from across the street. I hesitated to look, but I did, and saw Frank smiling and waving. Whenever possible, Frank and Mitzi would drive to visit with Lynne and Roger [Ed. note: Mr. and Mrs. Johnson] and their son, Larry. During these drives, Frank would love to soak up the sun with the top down on their convertible. Frank loved it, but it was hard on Mitzi with her light skin, but she never complained.

One of Trumbauer's last appearances with The National Flying Farmers Organization was as a guest speaker at the Eleventh Annual Convention on May 4 at Great Bend, Kansas. Alberta Reed Brinkman was then serving as Kansas and National Flying Farmers Queen, and she was seated at the same table with Trumbauer. The highlight of the evening was the final presentation on the agenda, the selection of a new state queen. Lillian Janssen was so chosen. When asked if Tram might have known of her selection in advance, and due to his friendship with her and her husband, attended the convention to witness the award, Lillian did not think so. ''But,'' Lillian reflected, ''it would have been nice to think that Frank knew in advance, and made the trip especially for the crowning; however the voting was done secretly and the winner was only notified at the conclusion of the program.''

Frank Trumbauer's last days have been remembered by friends and family members.

Harry Troxell, in a 1990 letter:

> I had dinner with Frank on June 8, Friday night, in Des Moines. He appeared to be in good physical condition at that time. As I said, over the years Frank often came up to Des Moines and we'd get together. Through Frank, I met the Dorsey Brothers, my favorite piano player Frankie Carle, and Nat ''King'' Cole. We'd go see them, and they'd take a ''break'' and have a drink with us. All seemed really glad to see Frank. That June night was the last time that I saw Frank.

Maggie Pickett:

> I guess that it was about this same time that I last saw Frank. He had just had a complete physical and he was so proud that a man of his age had passed with flying colors. When I think about it now, I get angry. He passed a complete physical and they found nothing wrong. I just can't forget it.

Helen Leighow:

> Frank showed up at work on Monday, but he didn't look too well, and I told him that it might be a good idea to take the day off and check with his doctor. Frank said that he didn't feel too well but he thought that he could finish the day's work. It was our habit when the job was finished to wait until the building cleared of personnel. We were located on the twenty-seventh floor and it was easier to find a less crowded elevator. During our wait, I kept pressing Frank to check with his doctor. After we left the elevator and walked onto the street, I made Frank promise me that he would check with a doctor. He had planned to visit his mother, who had a recent heart attack, at St. Mary's Hospital, and he promised to have a doctor check him over while he was there. I reminded him, as he left, that I was going to hold him to that promise.

Mary Trumbauer:

> My father was the last one in the family to see Frank alive. They were both on the same elevator leaving work. Dad [*Ed. note: Dave Freeman*] later mentioned that Frank did not look well but he did not say anything to dad about it. I still wish Frank would have said something because dad would have taken him to the hospital.

Tram left Helen and headed for St. Mary's Hospital. According to the information that Mitzi was given, Tram entered the hospital and collapsed in the lobby. Immediate help was rushed to him, but it was too late. Death due to coronary occlusion was instantaneous. The time was recorded as 5:20 P.M.

Trumbauer's body was removed to D. W. Newcomer's Sons Funeral Home, 1331 Brush Creek, in Kansas City, on June 12. Mitzi decided on a quick and limited service that would include only close friends and relatives. Memorial services were held on June 13 at 12:30 P.M. in the chapel of the funeral home with the Reverend Louis E. Meyer, Unity Society of Practical Christianity, officiating. Music was provided by The Newcomer Quartet with Philip Stevens at the organ. Leonard Jurden, Fred Regan, Charles German, Joe Shumate, Judge Duvall Strother, Jack Ross, and H. A. Paulsen served as honorary pallbearers.

Cremation followed the services, and Mitzi later scattered Tram's ashes from an airplane that flew above the grounds of his beloved church, The Unity Society of Practical Christianity, located about 15 miles south of Kansas City.

At the time of Trumbauer's passing, he was one of 167 associates—including Paul Cannom, Joe Shumate, Paul Flanary, and John Zentner—who made up the pilots' organization known as Members of the Gentleman's Agreement. Upon the death of a member or spouse, the organization donated a check to help defer the expenses of the funeral. Such a contribution was sent to Mitzi, and she duly noted her appreciation in a reply that stated:

> Dear Gentlemen of Gentleman's Agreement:
>
> I've tried more than once to express what is in my heart in a letter to you—so please try to understand when I say I'm so grateful and appreciative for the generous gift from each of

> you which helped so very much with expenses—but most of all your sincere friendship. I believe it was the writer "Gibran" who so wisely said "Your friends are your needs answered and let there be no purpose in friendship save the deepening of the Spirit.
>
> Surely Frank knows of your kindness to me and no doubt smiles knowing that individually and collectively the Spirit of Friendship dwells in rhythmic silence among you.
>
> Of course, it is a challenge to me now to readjust to this strange new road of life I must travel and try to find a happy normal solution to my question "Why?". I'll continue to do my very best and know "I'll never walk alone."
>
> Frank was a truly dedicated man to aviation and its many interesting facets. He always spoke well of all when he came in contact whether in business or pleasure. In fact, he lived by words of wisdom handed down from his great, great grandfather who said "Never judge your brother until you've walked in his moccasins for many moons."
>
> So—again, Gentlemen, thank you and may His Blessings be upon you always.

A pilot's toast given to a departed flyer would conclude with his having "Gone West," in reference to clear flying with the sun at his back and blue skies before him.

Tram's memory will always be with us as long as a phonograph rccord can be played. We may be deprived of the pleasure of his company, but he left us his music to enjoy.

So let us now listen to a recording of Frank Trumbauer and when it is ended raise our glass on high in a final toast, remembering the words expressed by John Zentner: "Frank's heart, from which he had given so much to so many, finally gave out. God bless Frank Trumbauer—always!"

INDEX OF ABBREVIATIONS OF INSTRUMENTS, RECORD LABELS AND COUNTRIES

All recordings in the Discography are listed alphabetically by Group name/or last name of leader. Each group is then listed Chronologically utilizing the abbreviations listed below.

The abbreviations listed below are used in the Discography, Chronology and the Song Titles as needed.

INSTRUMENTS

acc	-Accordion	h	-Harp
alto	-Alto Saxophone	ldr	-Leader
arr	-Arranger	org	-Organ
bjo	-Banjo	pcs	-Percussion
bar-sx	-Baritone Saxophone	p	-Piano
bs	-Bass	sx	-Saxophone
bs-sx	-Bass Saxophone	sop-sx	-Soprano Saxophone
bsn	-Bassoon	st-bs	-String Bass
br-bs	-Brass bass	ten-sx	-Tenor Saxophone
C-mel	-C-Melody Saxophone	tbn	-Trombone
cel	-Celeste	tpt	-Trumpet
co	-Cello	uke	-Ukulele
clt	-Clarinet	vb	-Vibraphones
cnt	-Cornet	va	-Viola
dir	-Director	vn	-Violin
dms	-Drums	vc	-Vocal
gtr	-Guitar	xyl	-Xylophone

RECORD LABELS

Ban	-Banner	Mel	-Meltone
Blt	-Biltmore	MW	-Montgomery Ward
Brun	-Brunswick	Od	-Odeon
Bwy	-Broadway	OK	-Okeh
Cap	-Capitol	Par	-Parlophone
Col	-Columbia	Pat	-Pathe
Clx	-Claxtonola	Per	-Perfect
Dav	-Davon	P-A	-Pro-Arte
Dec	-Decca	Riv	-Riverside
Ed	-Edison	Sil	-Silvertone
Ele	-Electrola	Sb	-Sunbeam
Gnt	-Gennett	Tpl	-Temple
Gra	-Gramola	UHCA	-United Hot Clubs Of America
Har	-Harmony		
HMV	-His Master's Voice	Var	-Varsity
HRS	-Hot Record Society	Vel	-Velvetone
JK	-Joker	Vic	-Victor
Jz	-Jonzo	Voc	-Vocalion
MOJ	-Masters Of Jazz	Zon	-Zonophone

COUNTRIES

Arg	-Argentina	Eng	-England/English
Aus	-Australian	Fr	-France/French
Cnd	-Canada/Canadian	Ger	-Germany/German
Cch	-Czechoslavakian	Ita	-Italy/Italian

THE DISCOGRAPHY

ARKANSAS TRAVELERS

20 MAY 1924 (Tue): New York, NY.
ARKANSAS TRAVELERS: Roy Johnston (tpt); Miff Mole (tbn); Chuck Miller (clt); **Frank Trumbauer** (C-mel/alto); Rube Bloom (p); Ward Archer (dms).

S-72553-C **GEORGIA BLUES**
10″-78 Okeh 40124

S-72554-A **LOST MY BABY BLUES**
10″-78 Okeh 40124

S-72554-C **LOST MY BABY BLUES**
10″-78 Okeh 40124

BENSON ORCHESTRA OF CHICAGO
(Under the direction of Don Bestor)

29 JANUARY 1923 (Mon): Victor Studios, Camden, NJ.
BENSON ORCHESTRA OF CHICAGO: Walter Zurawski (first tpt); Myles Vanderauer (second tpt); Sig Berendsohn (tbn); Stuart Williams (clt/alto); **Frank Trumbauer** (C-mel/alto); Marvin T. Thatcher (ten-sx); Myron Fischer (vn); Don Bestor (p); Joseph Miller (bjo); Pierre Olker (br-bs); George Brommerberg (dms).

27513-1 **DOWN IN MARYLAND**
10″-78 Victor 19022

27514 **TROT ALONG**
Rejected. Remade 30 January 1923.

30 JANUARY 1923 (Tue): Victor Studios, Camden, NJ.
BENSON ORCHESTRA OF CHICAGO: Walter Zurawski (first tpt); Myles Vanderauer (second tpt); Sig Berendsohn (tbn); Stuart Williams (clt/alto); **Frank Trumbauer** (C-mel/alto); Marvin T. Thatcher (ten-sx); Myron Fischer (vn); Don Bestor (p); Joseph Miller (bjo); Pierre Olker (br-bs); George Brommerberg (dms).

27515-3 **STARLIGHT BAY**
10″-78 Victor 19031

27516-3 **GEORGIA CABIN DOOR**
10″-78 Victor 19022

27514-7 **TROT ALONG**
10″-78 Victor 19044

27517 **SOMEDAY YOU'LL CRY OVER SOMEONE**
Rejected

27518-1 **THINK OF ME**
10″-78 Victor 19031
10″-78 Eng HMV B-1672

31 JANUARY 1923 (Wed): Victor Studios, Camden, NJ.
BENSON ORCHESTRA OF CHICAGO: Walter Zurawski (first tpt); Myles Vanderauer (second tpt); Sig Berendsohn (tbn); Stuart Williams (clt/alto); **Frank Trumbauer** (C-mel/alto); Marvin T. Thatcher (ten-sx); Myron Fischer (vn); Don Bestor (p); Joseph Miller (bjo); Pierre Olker (br-bs); George Brommerberg (dms).

27519-4 **LOOSE FEET**
10″-78 Victor 19045
10″-78 Eng HMV B-1662
10″-78 Eng Zon 3577

LOOSE FEET was originally issued on Victor 19045 as the ''B'' side. It was then withdrawn by Victor and replaced by another title. LOOSE FEET was not issued again.

27524 **SWEET ONE**
Rejected

27525 Old Time Medley:
(arrangement by Don Bestor)
a. **WHEN YOU AND I WERE YOUNG MAGGIE**
b. **TAMMANY**
c. **THE BOWERY**
d. **ON THE BANKS OF THE WABASH**
e. **AFTER THE BALL**
f. **JUST ONE GIRL**
g. **WAITING AT THE CHURCH**
h. **LITTLE ANNIE ROONEY**
Rejected

13 JUNE 1923 (Wed): Victor Studios, Camden, NJ.
BENSON ORCHESTRA OF CHICAGO: Walter Zurawski (first tpt); Herb Carlin (second tpt); Art Weiss (tbn); **Frank Trumbauer** (C-mel/alto); Stuart Williams (clt/alto); Marvin T. Thatcher (ten-sx); Myron L. Fischer (vn); Don Bestor (p); Joseph Miller (bjo); Pierre Olker (br-bs); George W. Brommerberg (dms).

28114-4 **IN A TENT**
10″-78 Victor 19103

28115-2 **LOVE IS JUST A FLOWER**
10″-78 Victor 19129

28116 **I'M DRIFTING BACK TO DREAMLAND**
Rejected. Remade 15 June 1923.

14 JUNE 1923 (Thu): Victor Studios, Camden, NJ.
BENSON ORCHESTRA OF CHICAGO: Walter Zurawski (first tpt); Herb Carlin (second tpt); Art Weiss (tbn); **Frank Trumbauer** (C-mel/alto); Stuart Williams (clt/alto); Marvin T. Thatcher (ten-sx); Myron L. Fischer (vn); Don Bestor (p); Joseph Miller (bjo); Pierre Olker (br-bs); George W. Brommerberg (dms).

28117-2 **JUST FOR TONIGHT**
10″-78 Victor 19101

28118-3 **NOBODY KNOWS BUT MY PILLOW AND ME**
10″-78 Victor 19102

28124-3 **I NEVER MISS THE SUNSHINE** (I'M SO USED TO THE RAIN)
10″-78 Victor 19102
10″-78 Eng HMV B-1712
10″-78 Eng Zon 3601

Matrixes 28119-28123 are by other artists.

15 JUNE 1923 (Fri): Victor Studios, Camden, NJ.
BENSON ORCHESTRA OF CHICAGO: Walter Zurawski (first tpt); Herb Carlin (second tpt); Art Weiss (tbn); **Frank Trumbauer** (C-mel/alto); Stuart Williams (clt/alto); Marvin T. Thatcher (ten-sx); Myron L. Fischer (vn); Don Bestor (p); Joseph Miller (bjo); Pierre Olker (br-bs); George W. Brommerberg (dms).

28116-5 **I'M DRIFTING BACK TO DREAMLAND**
10″-78 Victor 19101

28125-2 **DREAMS OF INDIA**
10″-78 Victor 19106

28126-4 **MARCH OF THE MANNIKINS**
10″-78 Victor 19183
10″-78 Cch HMV AH-381

28127-2 **THE CAT'S WHISKERS**
10″-78 Victor 19103
10″-78 Eng HMV B-1717
10″-78 Eng Zon 3679

20 JULY 1923 (Fri): Victor Studios, Camden, NJ.
BENSON ORCHESTRA OF CHICAGO: Walter Zurawski (first tpt); Herb Carlin (second tpt); Art Weiss (tbn); **Frank**

Trumbauer (C-mel/alto); Stuart Williams (clt/alto); Marvin T. Thatcher (ten sx); Myron L. Fischer (vn); Don Bestor (p); Joseph Miller (bjo); Pierre Olker (br-bs); George W. Brommerberg (dms).

28406-5 **NO NO NORA**
10″-78 Victor 19121
10″-78 Cch HMV AH-188

28407 **WHO COULD BE SWEETER?**
Rejected

25 JULY 1923 (Wed): Victor Studios, Camden, NJ.
BENSON ORCHESTRA OF CHICAGO: Walter Zurawski (first tpt); Herb Carlin (second tpt); Art Weiss (tbn); **Frank Trumbauer** (C-mel/alto); Stuart Williams (clt/alto); Marvin T. Thatcher (ten-sx); Myron L. Fischer (vn); Don Bestor (p); Joseph Miller (bjo); Pierre Olker (br-bs); George W. Brommerberg (dms).

28145-3 **SOMEBODY'S WRONG**
10″-78 Victor 19122
10″-78 Cch Gramola B-1740
10″-78 Eng HMV B-1740
10″-78 Fr HMV K-2423

28146 **OTHER LIPS**
Rejected

17 AUGUST 1923 (Fri): Victor Studios, Camden, NJ.
BENSON ORCHESTRA OF CHICAGO: Walter Zurawski (first tpt); Herb Carlin (second tpt); Art Weiss (tbn); **Frank Trumbauer** (C-mel/alto); Stuart Williams (clt/alto); Marvin T. Thatcher (ten-sx); Myron L. Fischer (vn); Don Bestor (p); Joseph Miller (bjo); Pierre Olker (br-bs); George W. Brommerberg (dms).

28432-2 **SOBBIN' BLUES**
10″-78 Victor 19130

28433 **ROYAL GARDEN BLUES**
Rejected

21 AUGUST 1923 (Tue): Victor Studios, Camden, NJ.
BENSON ORCHESTRA OF CHICAGO: Walter Zurawski (first tpt); Herb Carlin (second tpt); Art Weiss (tbn); **Frank Trumbauer** (C-mel/alto); Stuart Williams (clt/alto); Marvin T. Thatcher (ten-sx); Myron L. Fischer (vn); Don Bestor (p); Joseph Miller (bjo); Pierre Olker (br-bs); George W. Brommerberg (dms).

28436-3 **MEAN, MEAN, MAMA**
10″-78 Victor 19138
10″-78 Eng HMV B-1718
10″-78 Eng Zon 3635

28437 **SHIM-ME-SHA-WABBLE**
Rejected

27 AUGUST 1923 (Mon): Victor Studios, Camden, NJ.
BENSON ORCHESTRA OF CHICAGO: Walter Zurawski (first tpt); Herb Carlin (second tpt); Art Weiss (tbn); **Frank Trumbauer** (C-mel/alto); Stuart Williams (clt/alto); Marvin T. Thatcher (ten-sx); Myron L. Fischer (vn); Don Bestor (p); Joseph Miller (bjo); Pierre Olker (br-bs); George W. Brommerberg (dms).

28447-2 **FOOLISH CHILD**
10″-78 Victor 19136

28448-4 **THAT OLD GANG OF MINE**
10″-78 Victor 19136

10 SEPTEMBER 1923 (Mon): Victor Studios, Camden, NJ.
BENSON ORCHESTRA OF CHICAGO: Walter Zurawski (first tpt); Herb Carlin (second tpt); Art Weiss (tbn); **Frank Trumbauer** (C-mel/alto); Stuart Williams (clt/alto); Marvin T. Thatcher (ten-sx); Myron L. Fischer (vn); Don Bestor (p); Joseph Miller (bjo); Pierre Olker (br-bs); George W. Brommerberg (dms).

28459-2 **WOLVERINE BLUES**
10″-78 Victor 19140

28460 **THE THRILL OF LOVE**
Rejected

17 SEPTEMBER 1923 (Mon): Victor Studios, Camden, NJ.
BENSON ORCHESTRA OF CHICAGO: Walter Zurawski (first tpt); Herb Carlin (second tpt); Art Weiss (tbn); **Frank Trumbauer** (C-mel/alto); Stuart Williams (clt/alto); Marvin T. Thatcher (ten-sx); Myron L. Fischer (vn); Don Bestor (p); Joseph Miller (bjo); Pierre Olker (br-bs); George W. Brommerberg (dms).

28474-5 **EASY MELODY**
10″-78 Victor 19147

28475-1 **ARE YOU LONELY**
10″-78 Victor 19263

28476-2 **IN A COVERED WAGON WITH YOU**
10″-78 Victor 19147

28477-5 **MIDNIGHT ROSE**
10″-78 Victor 19148

28478-3 **OH YOU LITTLE SUN-UV-ER-GUN**
10″-78 Victor 19155

BROADWAY BELLHOPS

29 SEPTEMBER 1927 (Thu):
BROADWAY BELLHOPS: Bix Beiderbecke (crt); Herman ''Hymie'' Farberman (tpt); Bill Rank (tbn); Don Murray (clt); Bobby Davis (alto); **Frank Trumbauer** (C-mel); Joe Venuti (vn); Frank Signorelli (p); John Cali (bjo); Joe Tarto (tuba); Vic Berton, Sam Lanin (pcs).

144809-2 **THERE AIN'T NO LAND LIKE DIXIELAND TO ME**
(vc by Irving Kaufman)
10″-78 Davon 104
10″-78 Diva 2504-D
10″-78 Harmony 504-H
10″-78 Temple 547
10″-78 Velvetone 1504-V
12″-LP Sb Bix Vol 5 ''Sincerely, Bix Beiderbecke''

12″-LP Eng Par EMI PMC-7113
C-DISC Eng JSP CD-316 "Bix & Tram-Vol 1"

144810-2 **THERE'S A CRADLE IN CAROLINE** (vc by Irving Kaufman)
10″-78 Davon 104
10″-78 Diva 2504-D
10″-78 Harmony 504-H
10″-78 Temple 547
10″-78 Velvetone 1504-V
12″-LP Sb Bix Vol 5 "Sincerely, Bix Beiderbecke"
12″-LP Eng Par EMI PMC-7113
C-DISC Eng JSP CD-316 "Bix & Tram-Vol 1"

BROADWAY BELLHOPS: Herman "Hymie" Farberman (tpt); Chuck Campbell (tbn); Don Murray (clt); Bobby Davis (alto); **Frank Trumbauer** (C-mel); Joe Venuti (vn); Frank Signorelli (p); John Cali (bjo); Joe Tarto (tuba); Vic Berton, Sam Lanin (pcs).

144811-2 **RAINBOW OF LOVE** (waltz)
10″-78 Harmony 508-H

All sides acoustically recorded. No "W" prefix to matrix numbers.

THE CHICAGO LOOPERS

20 OCTOBER 1927 (Thu): New York, NY.
THE CHICAGO LOOPERS: Bix Beiderbecke (crt); **Frank Trumbauer** (C-mel); Don Murray (clt); Frank Signorelli (p); Eddie Lang (gtr); Vic Berton (dms). (Personnel as listed in Trumbauer's ledger.)

Matrix<?-1 **I'M MORE THAN SATISFIED** (vc by Deep River Quintet)
10″-78 Perfect 14905 (as by "Willard Robison & His Orchestra")
12″-LP Sb Bix Vol 6 "Sincerely, Bix Beiderbecke"

Matrix<?-2 I'M MORE THAN SATISFIED
(vc by Deep River Quintet)
10″-78 Perfect 14905 (as by "Willard Robison & His Orchestra")
10″-78 Pathe Actuelle 36724 (as by "Willard Robison & His Orchestra")
12″-LP Sb Bix Vol 6 "Sincerely, Bix Beiderbecke"
12″-LP Ita Joker SM-3562 "Bixology Vol 6"

Matrix<?-3 I'M MORE THAN SATISFIED
Presume to be rejected; details unknown

Matrix<?-4 I'M MORE THAN SATISFIED
Presume to be rejected; details unknown

Matrix<?-5 I'M MORE THAN SATISFIED
(vc by Deep River Quintet)
10″-78 Perfect 14905 (as by "Willard Robison & His Orchestra")
12″-LP Ita Joker SM-3562 "Bixology Vol 6"

All issued as by "Willard Robison and His Orchestra." Matrix numbers unknown. Takes 2 and 5 are the same take. Take 1 is unique.

Matrix<?-1 CLORINDA
(vc by Deep River Quintet)
10″-78 Perfect 14910
12″-LP Sb Bix Vol 6 "Sincerely, Bix Beiderbeckc"
12″-LP Ita Joker SM-3562 "Bixology Vol 6"

Matrix<?-2 CLORINDA
(vc by Deep River Quintet)
10″-78 Perfect 14910
10″-78 Pathe 36729
12″-LP Sb Bix Vol 6 "Sincerely, Bix Beiderbecke"
12″-LP Ita Joker SM-3562 "Bixology Vol 6"

Matrix<?-3 CLORINDA
Details unknown; presume rejected.

Matrix<?-4 CLORINDA
(vc by Deep River Quintet)

10″-78 Perfect 14910
10″-78 Pathe 36729

Matrix<?-5 CLORINDA
(vc by Deep River Quintet)
10″-78 Perfect 14910

Matrix numbers unknown. On CLORINDA takes 1 and 4 are same take. On CLORINDA takes 2 and 5 are same take.

Matrix<?-1 THREE BLIND MICE
10″-78 HRS 1
10″-78 Perfect 14910
10″-78 Pathe 36729
12″-LP Sb Bix Vol 6 ''Sincerely, Bix Beiderbecke''
12″-LP Ita Joker SM-3562 ''Bixology Vol 6''

Matrix<?-2 THREE BLIND MICE
10″-78 HRS 1
10″-78 Perfect 14910
10″-78 Temple 553
12″-LP Sb Bix Vol 6 ''Sincerely, Bix Beiderbecke''
12″-LP Ita Joker SM-3562 ''Bixology Vol 6''

Matrix<?-3 THREE BLIND MICE
10″-78 Perfect 14910

Matrix numbers unknown. On THREE BLIND MICE takes 1 and 3 are same take. On THREE BLIND MICE take 2 is unique.

PERRY COMO
(with Russ Case & His Orchestra)

18 DECEMBER 1945 (Tue): Studio #2; 1:30-4:45 P.M., Victor Record Co., New York, NY.

RUSS CASE ORCHESTRA: George ''Pee Wee'' Erwin, John Lausen, Anthony Natoli (tpts); Bill Rank, Will Bradley (tbns); **Frank Trumbauer,** Russell Banzer, Murray Cohan, Jess Carneol, Paul Ricci (reeds); Jacques Gasselin, Bertrand Hirsch, Harry Hoffman, Samuel Rand, Kurt Dieterle, Leo Kruczek (vns); Howard Kay, Henry Pakaln (vas); Maurice Brown (co); Zepp Moscher (harp); Sam Liner (p); Danny Perri (gtr); Bob Haggart (st-bs); John Williams (dms).

D5-VB-990-1 **ALL THROUGH THE DAY**
(vc by Perry Como)
10″-78 Victor 20-1814

D5-VB-990-1A **ALL THROUGH THE DAY**
(vc by Perry Como)
Unissued

D5-VB-991-1 **PRISONER OF LOVE**
(vc by Perry Como)
10″-78 Victor 20-1814

D5-VB-991-1A **PRISONER OF LOVE**
(vc by Perry Como)
Unissued

12 MARCH 1946 (Tue): Studio #2; 1:00-4:00 P.M., Victor Record Co., New York, NY.

RUSS CASE ORCHESTRA: George ''Pee Wee'' Erwin, John Lausen, Anthony Natoli (tpts); Jack Lacey, Bill Rank, Jack Satterfield (tbns); **Frank Trumbauer,** Russell Banzer, Murray Cohan, Jess Carneol, Nuncio ''Toots'' Mondello (reeds); Howard Kay, Max Pollikoff, Sylvan Kirsner, Jack Zayde, Irving Prager, Max Silverman (vns); Henry Pakaln, Isador Zir (vas); Maurice Brown (co); Reinhardt Elster (harp); David Bowman (p); Carl Kress (gtr); Bob Haggart (st-bs); Johnny Blowers Jr. (dms).

THE SATISFIERS: Unidentified male trio.

D6-VB-1343-1 **LITTLE MAN YOU'VE HAD A BUSY DAY**
(vc by Perry Como with The Satisfiers)
10″-78 Victor 20-1918

D6-VB-1343-1A **LITTLE MAN YOU'VE HAD A BUSY DAY**
(vc by Perry Como with The Satisfiers)
Unissued

D6-VB-1344-1 MORE THAN YOU KNOW
(vc by Perry Como)
10″-78 Victor 20-1877
12″-LP Victor CAE-410

D6-VB-1344-1A MORE THAN YOU KNOW
(vc by Perry Como)
Unissued.

14 MARCH 1946 (Thu): Studio #2; 1:15-4:15 P.M.; Victor Record Co., New York, NY.

RUSS CASE ORCHESTRA: George ''Pee Wee'' Erwin, John Lausen, Anthony Natoli (tpts); Muni Morrow, Bill Rank, Jack Satterfield (tbns); **Frank Trumbauer,** Russell Banzer, Murray Cohan, Larry Binyon, Nuncio ''Toots'' Mondello (reeds); Howard Kay, Max Pollikoff, Sylvan Kirsner, Max Silverman, Leo Kruczek, Jacques Gasselin (vns); Isador Zir, Henry Pakaln (vas); Maurice Brown (co); Reinhardt Elster (harp); David Bowman (p); Carl Kress (gtr); Bob Haggart (st-bs); Johnny Blowers Jr. (dms).

THE SATISFIERS: Unidentified male trio.

D6-VB-1345-1 KENTUCKY BABE
(vc by Perry Como with The Satisfiers)
10″-78 Victor 20-1918
12″-LP Victor CAS-2299
16″-ET AFRS Basic Musical Library P-727

D6-VB-1345-1A KENTUCKY BABE
(vc by Perry Como with The Satisfiers)
Unissued

D6-VB-1346-1 A GARDEN IN THE RAIN
(vc by Perry Como with The Satisfiers)
7″-45 Victor 47-4445
10″-78 Victor 20-1916
12″-LP Victor CAL-694

D6-VB-1346-1A A GARDEN IN THE RAIN
(vc by Perry Como with The Satisfiers)
Unissued

19 MARCH 1946 (Tue): Studio #2, 1:00-4:30 P.M., Victor Record Co., New York, NY.

RUSS CASE ORCHESTRA: George "Pee Wee" Erwin, John Lausen, Nat Natoli (tpts); Jack Lacey, Bill Rank, Jack Satterfield (tbns); **Frank Trumbauer,** Russell Banzer, Murray Cohan, Larry Binyon, Nuncio "Toots" Mondello (reeds); Leo Kruczek, Jack Zayde, Irving Prager, Sylvan Kirsner, Max Pollikoff, Jacques Gasselin (vns); Isador Zir, Henry Pakaln (vas); Maurice Brown (co); Reinhardt Elster (harp); Sam Liner (p); Carl Kress (gtr); Bob Haggart (st-bs); John Blowers Jr. (dms).

THE SATISFIERS: Unidentified male trio.

D6-VB-1698-1 **BLUE SKIES**
(vc by Perry Como with The Satisfiers)
10"-78 Victor 20-1917
12"-LP Victor CAS-403

D6-VB-1698-1A **BLUE SKIES**
(vc by Perry Como with The Satisfiers)

D6-VB-1699-1 **MY BLUE HEAVEN**
(vc by Perry Como with The Satisfiers)
Unissued

D6-VB-1699-1A **MY BLUE HEAVEN**
(vc by Perry Como with The Satisfiers)
Unissued

(The selection MY BLUE HEAVEN has a notation on Victor file card: "To be processed with Mr. Oberstein's approval.")

21 MARCH 1946 (Thu): Studio #2; 1:00-5:00 P.M.; Victor Record Co., New York, NY.

RUSS CASE ORCHESTRA: George "Pee Wee" Erwin, John Lausen, Nat Natoli (tpts); Muni Morrow, Bill Rank, Jack Satterfield (tbns); **Frank Trumbauer,** Russell Banzer, Jack Cressy, Arthur Rollini, Nuncio "Toots" Mondello (reeds); Leo Kruczek, Sylvan Kirsner, Bertrand Hirsch, Jacques Gasselin, Sidney Harris, Felix Giglio (vns); Isador Zir, Henry Pakaln

(vas); Maurice Brown (co); Reinhardt Elster (harp); Samuel Liner (p); Danny Perri (gtr); Bob Haggart (st-bs); Norris Shawker (dms).
THE SATISFIERS: Unidentified male trio.

D6-VB-1366-1 YOU MUST HAVE BEEN A BEAUTIFUL BABY
(vc by Perry Como with The Satisfiers)
10″-78 Victor 20-1916

D6-VB-1366-1A YOU MUST HAVE BEEN A BEAUTIFUL BABY
(vc by Perry Como with The Satisfiers)
Unissued

D6-VB-1367-1 IF YOU WERE THE ONLY GIRL
(vc by Perry Como)
10″-78 Victor 20-1857

D6-VB-1367-1A IF YOU WERE THE ONLY GIRL
(vc by Perry Como)
Unissued

D6-VB-1368-1 GIRL OF MY DREAMS
(vc by Perry Como)
10″-78 Victor 20-1917
12″-LP Victor CAS-403
16″-ET AFRS Basic Musical Library P-665

D6-VB-1368-1A GIRL OF MY DREAMS
(vc by Perry Como)
Unissued

In all cases, take ''1'' was selected to be released. Take ''1A'' served as the backup take in the event that reissues took a toll on the initial master's sound. This proved not to be the case as none of the ''1A'' takes were issued.

The reverse sides of Como recordings, Victor 20-1857 THEY SAY IT'S WONDERFUL, and Victor 20-1877 SURRENDER, do not have **Frank Trumbauer** in the orchestra.

THE COTTON PICKERS

4 DECEMBER 1924 (Thu): A.M. session; 3 hours; Brunswick Record Co., New York, NY.

THE COTTON PICKERS: Roy Johnston (tpt); Miff Mole (tbn); **Frank Trumbauer** (C-mel/alto); Larry Abbott (clt/alto); Rube Bloom (p); Frank DiPrima (bjo); Ward Archer (dms).

14382 **PRINCE OF WAILS**

14383 **PRINCE OF WAILS**

14384 **PRINCE OF WAILS**

14385 **PRINCE OF WAILS**
(arrangement by Elmer Schoebel)

10″-78 Brunswick 2766

The Brunswick files do not indicate which matrix was issued.

6 DECEMBER 1924 (Sat): A.M. session; 3 hours; Brunswick Record Co., New York, NY.

THE COTTON PICKERS: Roy Johnston (tpt); Miff Mole (tbn); **Frank Trumbauer** (C-mel/alto); Larry Abbott (clt/alto); Rube Bloom (p); Frank DiPrima (bjo); Louis Chassagne (br-bs); Ward Archer (dms).

14411 **JIMTOWN BLUES**

14412 **JIMTOWN BLUES**

14413 **JIMTOWN BLUES**

14414 **JIMTOWN BLUES**

10″-78 Brunswick 2766

The Brunswick files do not indicate which matrix was issued.

6 FEBRUARY 1925 (Fri): Brunswick Record Co., New York, NY.

THE COTTON PICKERS: Roy Johnston (tpt); Miff Mole (tbn); **Frank Trumbauer** (C-mel/alto); Larry Abbott (clt/alto); Rube Bloom (p); Frank DiPrima (bjo); Louis Chassagne (br-bs); Ward Archer (dms).

14833 **MISHAWAKA BLUES**
Unissued

14834 **MISHAWAKA BLUES**
Unissued

14835 **MISHAWAKA BLUES**
10″-78 Brunswick 2818

14836 **JACKSONVILLE GAL**
Unissued

14837 **JACKSONVILLE GAL**
Unissued

14838 **JACKSONVILLE GAL**
10″-78 Brunswick 2818

14839 **JACKSONVILLE GAL**
Unissued

9 APRIL 1925 (Thu): A.M. session; 3 hours; Brunswick Record Co., New York, NY.
THE COTTON PICKERS: Roy Johnston (tpt); Miff Mole (tbn); **Frank Trumbauer** (C-mel/alto); Larry Abbott (clt/alto); Rube Bloom (p); Frank DiPrima (bjo); Louis Chassagne (br-bs); Ward Archer (dms).

15490 **THOSE PANAMA MAMAS**
10″-78 Brunswick 2879
10″-78 Sil 3101 (as by ''Johnson's Jazz Band'')

15491 **THOSE PANAMA MAMAS**
Unissued

15492 **THOSE PANAMA MAMAS**
Unissued

15493 **DOWN AND OUT BLUES**
Unissued

15494 **DOWN AND OUT BLUES**
10″-78 Brunswick 2879
10″-78 Sil 3101 (as by ''Johnson's Jazz Band'')

Frank Trumbauer was not present on the 21 August 1925 Cotton Pickers recording session as has been suggested.

BING CROSBY

25 MAY 1932 (Wed): Brunswick Record Co., Chicago, IL.
STUDIO ORCHESTRA: Max Connett (tpt); **Frank Trumbauer** (C-mel/alto); Gale Stout (clt/alto); Harold Jones (ten-sx); Cedric Spring (vb); Herm Crone (p); Eddie Lang (gtr); Charles McConnell (st-bs); LeRoy Buck (dms).

JC-8635-1 **CABIN IN THE COTTON**
(vc by Bing Crosby)
10″-78 Brunswick 6329 (released 2 July 1932)
10″-78 Columbia C-2340
10″-78 Eng Brunswick 01326
10″-78 Eng Columbia DB-2030
12″-LP Eng Jz JZ-"The Chronological Bing Crosby"

JC-8636-1 **(I'M STILL WITHOUT A SWEETHEART) WITH SUMMER COMING ON**
(vc by Bing Crosby)
10″-78 Brunswick 6329 (released 2 July 1932)
10″-78 Columbia C-2340
10″-78 Cch Brunswick A-9727
10″-78 Eng Brunswick 01349
12″-LP Eng Jz JZ-"The Chronological Bing Crosby"

The Brunswick File Card lists "Lennie Hayton Orchestra."

26 MAY 1932 (Thu): Brunswick Record Co., Chicago, IL.
STUDIO ORCHESTRA: Max Connett (tpt); **Frank Trumbauer** (C-mel/alto); Gale Stout (clt/alto); Harold Jones (ten-sx); Cedric Spring (vb); Herm Crone (p); Eddie Lang (gtr); Charles McConnell (st-bs); LeRoy Buck (dms).

JC-8640-1 **LOVE ME TONIGHT**
(vc by Bing Crosby)
(arrangement by Victor Young)

10″-78 Brunswick 6351 (released 6 August 1932)
10″-78 Columbia C-2355
10″-78 Cch Brunswick A-9727
10″-78 Eng Brunswick 01349
12″-LP Eng Jz JZ-''The Chronological Bing Crosby''

JC-8641-1 **SOME OF THESE DAYS**
(vc by Bing Crosby)
(arrangement by Victor Young)

10″-78 Banner 33163
10″-78 Brunswick 6351 (released 6 August 1932)
10″-78 Brunswick 6635
10″-78 Columbia 4305-M
10″-78 Columbia 4421-M
10″-78 Conqueror 8366
10″-78 Melotone 13130
10″-78 Okeh 2869
10″-78 Eng Columbia DB-1845
10″-78 Eng Columbia DO-1431
12″-LP Eng Jz JZ-''The Chronological Bing Crosby''

The Brunswick File Card lists ''Isham Jones Orchestra.'' However, Jones was not present, due to illness. Victor Young replaced him.

JOHNNY DESMOND
(with Russ Case & His Orchestra)

20 DECEMBER 1945 (Thu): Victor Studio #2, 11:00 P.M.-3:30 A.M., Victor Record Co., New York, NY.

RUSS CASE ORCHESTRA: Robert Cusumano, John Lausen, Nat Natoli (tpts); William Rank, Will Bradley (tbns); **Frank Trumbauer,** Russell Banzer, Jess Carneol, Paul Ricci, Murray Cohan (reeds); Howard Kay, Sylvan Kirsner, Bertrand Hirsch, Kurt Dieterle, Leo Krucez, Jack Zayde (vns); Isador Zir, Henry Pakaln (vas); Maurice Brown (co); Zepp Moscher (harp); Sam Liner (p); Carl Kress (gtr); Bob Haggart (st-bs); John Williams (dms).

D5-V8-1308-1 **IN THE MOON MIST**

D5-V8-1308-1A IN THE MOON MIST
(vc by Johnny Desmond)
10″-78 Victor 20-1810

D5-V8-1309-1 DO YOU LOVE ME?

D5-V8-1309-1A DO YOU LOVE ME?
(vc by Johnny Desmond)
10″-78 Victor 20-1810

D5-V8-1310-1 DON'T YOU REMEMBER ME?

D5-V8-1310-1A DON'T YOU REMEMBER ME?
(vc by Johnny Desmond)
10″-78 Victor 20-1796
10″-78 Aus HMV EA-501

D5-V8-1311-1 IN THE EYES OF MY IRISH COLLEEN

D5-V8-1311-1A IN THE EYES OF MY IRISH COLLEEN
(vc by Johnny Desmond)
10″-78 Victor 20-1796
10″-78 Aus HMV EA-501

Take ''1'' released on all issued recordings.

JEAN GOLDKETTE & HIS ORCHESTRA

12 OCTOBER 1926 (Tue): Victor Record Co., New York, NY. JEAN GOLDKETTE ORCHESTRA: Bix Beiderbecke (crt); Fred Farrar, Ray Lodwig (tpts); Bill Rank, Newell ''Spiegle'' Willcox (tbns); Stanley ''Doc'' Ryker, **Frank Trumbauer,** Don Murray (reeds); Joe Venuti (vn); Irving Riskin (p); Howdy Quicksell (bjo); Eddie Lang (gtr); Steve Brown (st-bs); Chauncey Morehouse (dms).

BVE-36813-1 IDOLIZING
(vc by Frank Marvin)
(arrangement by Bill Challis)
7″-LP NAT WEP-804

12″-LP Broadway 102
12″-LP Sb Bix Vol 2 ''Sincerely, Bix Beiderbecke''
C-DISC Fr MOJ MJCD-5 ''Bix Beiderbecke— Vol 2''

BVE-36813-2 **IDOLIZING**
(vc by Frank Marvin)
(arrangement by Bill Challis)
10″-78 Victor 20270 (released 4 February 1927)
10″-78 Canadian Victor 20270
10″-78 Aus HMV EA-152
10″-78 Aus HMV EA-4910
12″-LP Sb Bix Vol 2 ''Sincerely, Bix Beiderbecke''
C-DISC Fr MOJ MJCD-5 ''Bix Beiderbecke—Vol 2''

BVE-36814-1 **I'D RATHER BE THE GIRL IN YOUR ARMS**
(vc by Joe Griffith, Frank Magine, and Frank Marvin)
(arrangement by Bill Challis)
Rejected

BVE-36814-2 **I'D RATHER BE THE GIRL IN YOUR ARMS**
(vc by Joe Griffith, Frank Magine, and Frank Marvin)
(arrangement by Bill Challis)
Rejected

BVE-36814-3 **I'D RATHER BE THE GIRL IN YOUR ARMS**
(vc by Joe Griffith, Frank Magine, and Frank Marvin)
(arrangement by Bill Challis)
Rejected

BVE-36814-4 **I'D RATHER BE THE GIRL IN YOUR ARMS**
(vc Frank Magine, Joe Griffith and Frank Marvin)
(arrangement by Bill Challis)
Rejected

The selection I'D RATHER BE THE GIRL IN YOUR ARMS was remade on 15 October 1926.

BVE-36815-2 **HUSH-A-BYE** (waltz)
(vc by Frank Bessinger)
(arrangement by Bill Challis)
10″-78 Victor 20270 (released 4 February 1927)
10″-78 Cnd Victor 20270
10″-78 Aus HMV EA-151
12″-LP Sb Bix Vol 2 ''Sincerely, Bix Beiderbecke''

15 OCTOBER 1926 (Fri): Victor Record Co., New York, NY.
JEAN GOLDKETTE ORCHESTRA: Bix Beiderbecke (crt); Fred Farrar, Ray Lodwig (tpts); Bill Rank, Newell ''Spiegle'' Willcox (tbns); Stanley ''Doc'' Ryker, **Frank Trumbauer,** Don Murray (reeds); Joe Venuti (vn); Irving Riskin (p); Howdy Quicksell (bjo); Eddie Lang (gtr); Steve Brown (st-bs); Chauncey Morehouse (dms).
Lang only on 36814 and 36829.
THE KELLER SISTERS: Nan, Taddy.

BVE-36829-2 **SUNDAY**
(vc by The Keller Sisters and Al Lynch)
(arrangement by Bill Challis)
12″-LP Sb Bix Vol 2 ''Sincerely, Bix Beiderbecke''
12″-LP Victor LPM-2323

BVE-36829-3 **SUNDAY**
(vc by The Keller Sisters and Al Lynch)
(arrangement by Bill Challis)
10″-78 Victor 20273 (released 3 December 1926)
10″-78 Cnd Victor 20273
10″-78 Aus HMV EA-174
10″-78 German Electrola EG-357
12″-LP Sb Bix Vol 2 ''Sincerely, Bix Beiderbecke''
C-DISC P-A CDD-490 ''Bix Beiderbecke—Jazz Me Blues''
C-DISC Fr MOJ MJCD-6 ''Bix Beiderbecke—Vol 2''

BVE-36830-2 **COVER ME UP WITH SUNSHINE (AND FEATHER MY NEST WITH LOVE)**

(vc by Frank Bessinger)
(arrangement by Eddy Sheasby)
10″-78 Victor 20588 (released 20 May 1927)
10″-78 Cnd Victor 20588
12″-LP Sb Bix Vol 2 ''Sincerely, Bix Beiderbecke''

BVE-36814-8 **I'D RATHER BE THE GIRL IN YOUR ARMS**
(vc by Frank Bessinger)
(arrangement by Bill Challis)
10″-78 Victor 20273 (released 3 December 1926)
10″-78 Eng HMV K-5095
10″-78 Cnd Victor 20273
10″-78 German Electrola EG-438
12″-LP Sb Bix Vol 2 ''Sincerely, Bix Beiderbecke''

BVE-36831-2 **JUST ONE MORE KISS**
(vc by Al Lynch)
(arrangement by Bill Challis)
12″-LP Sb Bix Vol 2 ''Sincerely, Bix Beiderbecke''

BVE-36831-4 **JUST ONE MORE KISS**
(vc by Al Lynch)
(arrangement by Eddy Sheasby)
10″-78 Victor 20300 (released 4 November 1926)
12″-LP Sb Bix Vol 2 ''Sincerely, Bix Beiderbecke''

28 JANUARY 1927 (Fri): Victor Record Co., New York, NY.
JEAN GOLDKETTE ORCHESTRA: Bix Beiderbecke (crt); Fred Farrar, Ray Lodwig (tpts); Bill Rank, Newell ''Spiegle'' Willcox (tbns); Stanley ''Doc'' Ryker, **Frank Trumbauer,** Jimmy Dorsey (reeds); Joe Venuti (vn); Paul Mertz (p); Howdy Quicksell (bjo); Steve Brown (st-bs); Chauncey Morehouse (dms).
THE KELLER SISTERS: Nan, Taddy.

BVE-37579-1 **PROUD OF A BABY LIKE YOU**
(vc by Keller Sisters & Al Lynch)
(arrangement by Bill Challis)
12″-LP Broadway 102
12″-LP Sb Bix Vol 2 ''Sincerely, Bix Beiderbecke''
12″-LP Victor ''X'' EVA-9

12″-LP Victor ''X'' LVA-3017
12″ LP Aus Swaggie JCS-33756
12″-LP Ita Joker SM-3559 ''Bixology Vol 3''
C-DISC Fr MOJ MJCD-6 ''Bix Beiderbecke—Vol 2''

BVE-37579-4 **PROUD OF A BABY LIKE YOU**
(vc by the Keller Sisters and Al Lynch)
(arrangement by Bill Challis)
10″-78 Victor 20469 (released 8 February 1927)
12″-LP Sb Bix Vol 2 ''Sincerely, Bix Beiderbecke''
12″-LP Ita Joker SM-3559 ''Bixology Volume 3''
C-DISC Fr MOJ MJCD-6 ''Bix Beiderbecke—Vol 2''

BVE-37580-1 **I'M LOOKING OVER A FOUR LEAF CLOVER**
(vc by Billy Murray)
(arrangement by Bill Challis)
10″-78 Victor Test Pressing
12″-LP Broadway 102
12″-LP Sb Bix Vol 3 ''Sincerely, Bix Beiderbecke''
12″-LP Ita Joker SM-3559 ''Bixology Vol 3''
C-DISC Fr MOJ MJCD-6 ''Bix Beiderbecke—Vol 2''

BVE-37580-4 **I'M LOOKING OVER A FOUR LEAF CLOVER**
(vc by Billy Murray)
(arrangement by Bill Challis)
10″-78 Victor 20466 (released 11 March 1927)
10″-78 Aus HMV EA-163
10″-78 Cnd Victor 20466
12″-LP Sb Bix Volume 3 ''Sincerely, Bix Beiderbecke''
12″-LP Ita Joker SM-3559 ''Bixology Volume 3''
C-DISC Fr MOJ MJCD-6 ''Bix Beiderbecke—Vol 2''

31 JANUARY 1927 (Mon): Victor Record Co., New York, NY. JEAN GOLDKETTE ORCHESTRA: Bix Beiderbecke (crt); Fred Farrar, Ray Lodwig (tpts); Bill Rank, Newell ''Spiegle'' Willcox (tbns); Stanley ''Doc'' Ryker, **Frank Trumbauer,** Jimmy Dorsey (reeds); Joe Venuti (vn); Paul Mertz (p); Howdy Quicksell (bjo); Steve Brown (st-bs); Chauncey Morehouse (dms).

BVE-37583-2 I'M GONNA MEET MY SWEETIE NOW
(arrangement by Bill Challis)
10″-78 Victor 20675 (released 8 December 1927)
10″-78 Cnd Victor 20675
10″-78 Eng HMV B-5363
12″-LP Sb Bix Vol 3 ''Sincerely, Bix Beiderbecke''
12″-LP Ita Joker SM-3559 ''Bixology Vol 3''
C-DISC Fr MOJ MJCD-6 ''Bix Beiderbecke—Vol 2''

BVE-37583-3 I'M GONNA MEET MY SWEETIE NOW
(arrangement by Bill Challis)
10″-78 Victor 25354 (released 1 July 1936)
12″-LP Sb Bix Vol 3 ''Sincerely, Bix Beiderbecke''
12″-LP Ita Joker SM-3559 ''Bixology Vol 3''

BVE-37584-2 HOOSIER SWEETHEART
(vc by Ray Muerer)
(arrangement by Bill Challis)
10″-78 Victor 20471 (released 18 March 1927)
10″-78 Aus HMV EA-157
10″-78 German Electrola EG-455
12″-LP Sb Bix Vol 3 ''Sincerely, Bix Beiderbecke''
12″-LP Ita Joker SM-3559 ''Bixology Vol 3''
C-DISC Fr MOJ MJCD-6 ''Bix Beiderbecke—Vol 2''

1 FEBRUARY 1927 (Tue): Victor Record Co., New York, NY.
JEAN GOLDKETTE ORCHESTRA: Bix Beiderbecke (crt); Fred Farrar, Ray Lodwig (tpts); Bill Rank, Newell ''Spiegle'' Willcox (tbns); Stanley ''Doc'' Ryker, **Frank Trumbauer,** Danny Polo (reeds); Joe Venuti, Eddy Sheasby (vns); Paul Mertz (p); Howdy Quicksell (bjo); Eddie Lang (gtr); Steve Brown (st-bs); Chauncey Morehouse (dms).
Lang and Sheasby on BVE-37586 only.

BVE-37586-1 LOOK AT THE WORLD AND SMILE
(arrangement by Eddy Sheasby)
10″-78 Victor Test Pressing
12″-LP Broadway 102

12″-LP Sb Bix Vol 3 "Sincerely, Bix Beiderbecke"
12″-LP Ita Joker SM-3559 "Bixology Vol 3"

BVE-37586-2 LOOK AT THE WORLD AND SMILE
(arrangement by Eddy Sheasby)
10″-78 Victor 20472 (released 18 March 1927)
12″-LP Sb Bix Vol 3 "Sincerely, Bix Beiderbecke"
12″-LP Ita Joker SM-3559 "Bixology Vol 3"
C-DISC Fr MOJ MJCD-6 "Bix Beiderbecke—Vol 2"

BVE-37586-3 LOOK AT THE WORLD AND SMILE
(arrangement by Eddy Sheasby)
10″-78 Victor Test Pressing
12″-LP Broadway 102
12″-LP Sb Bix Vol 3 "Sincerely, Bix Beiderbecke"
12″-LP Ita Joker SM-3559 "Bixology Vol 3"

BVE-37587-1 MY PRETTY GIRL
(arrangement by Bill Challis, Jimmy Dorsey, Don Murray, and Irving Riskin)
10″-78 Victor 20588 (released 20 May 1927)
10″-78 Victor 25283 (released 8 April 1936)
10″-78 Cnd Victor 20588
10″-78 Aus HMV EA-1706
10″-78 Aus HMV EA-3617
10″-78 Eng HMV B-5324
10″-78 Eng HMV B-9237
10″-78 Fr HMV K-121
10″-78 German Electrola EG-3856
12″-LP Sb Bix Vol 3 "Sincerely, Bix Beiderbecke"
12″-LP Eng Jazz Collector 531
12″-LP Ita Joker SM-3559 "Bixology Vol 3"
C-DISC Fr MOJ MJCD-6 "Bix Beiderbecke—Vol 2"

BVE-37587-2 MY PRETTY GIRL
(arrangement by Bill Challis, Jimmy Dorsey, Don Murray, and Irving Riskin)
12″-LP Sb Bix Vol 3 "Sincerely, Bix Beiderbecke"
12″-LP Victor LVA-3017
12″-LP Victor "X" EVA-10
12″-LP Aus Swaggie JCS-33756

12″-LP Ita Joker SM-3559 ‘‘Bixology Vol 3’’
C-DISC Fr MOJ MJCD-6 ‘‘Bix Beiderbecke—Vol 2’’

The original stock arrangement of MY PRETTY GIRL was reworked by Don Murray. Bill Challis added additional instrumentation, and Irving Riskin took Bix's chorus on the Murray arrangement and turned it into a three tpt chorus. Finally, Jimmy Dorsey did the ending, Bix faking harmony with a trombone lead.

BVE-37588 **STAMPEDE**
(arrangement by Don Redman)
Rejected

3 FEBRUARY 1927 (Thu): Victor Record Co., New York, NY.
JEAN GOLDKETTE ORCHESTRA: Bix Beiderbecke (crt); Fred Farrar, Ray Lodwig (tpts); Bill Rank, Newell ‘‘Spiegle’’ Willcox (tbns); Stanley ‘‘Doc’’ Ryker, **Frank Trumbauer,** Jimmy Dorsey (reeds); Joe Venuti (vn); Paul Mertz (p); Howdy Quicksell (bjo); Steve Brown (st-bs); Chauncey Morehouse (dms).
THE REVELERS: Charles Harrison (first tenor); Lewis James (second tenor); Elliott Shaw (baritone); Wilfred Glenn (bass).

BVE-37738-1 **A LANE IN SPAIN**
(vc by The Revelers)
(arrangement by Bill Challis)
10″-78 Victor Test Pressing
12″-LP Sb Bix Vol 3 ‘‘Sincerely, Bix Beiderbecke’’

BVE-37738-3 **A LANE IN SPAIN**
(vc by The Revelers)
(arrangement by Bill Challis)
10″-78 Victor 20491 (released 8 April 1927)
10″-78 Aus HMV EA-195
10″-78 Cnd Victor 20491
12″-LP Sb Bix Vol 3 ‘‘Sincerely, Bix Beiderbecke’’
12″-LP Ita Joker SM-3559 ‘‘Bixology Vol 3’’

BVE-37738 was originally assigned BVE-37598 in error. This duplicated a waltz by Nat Shilret & The Victor Orchestra. It was originally planned as a Jean Goldkette recording of RIO RITA, which Nat Shilkret had recorded four days later.

BVE-37599-2 **SUNNY DISPOSISH**
(vc by The Revelers)
(arrangement by Don Murray)
12″-LP RCA LPV-545
12″-LP Sb Bix Vol 3 ''Sincerely, Bix Beiderbecke''
12″-LP Ita Joker SM-3559 ''Bixology Vol 3''

BVE-37599-3 **SUNNY DISPOSISH**
(vc by The Revelers)
(arrangement by Don Murray)
10″-78 Victor 20493 (released 29 April 1927)
10″-78 Aus HMV EA-170
10″-78 Eng HMV B-5289
12″-LP Sb Bix Vol 3 ''Sincerely, Bix Beiderbecke''
12″-LP Ita Joker SM-3559 ''Bixology Vol 3''

6 MAY 1927 (Fri): Victor Record Co., New York, NY.
JEAN GOLDKETTE ORCHESTRA: Bix Beiderbecke (crt); Fred Farrar, Ray Lodwig (tpts); Bill Rank, Newell ''Spiegle'' Willcox (tbns); Stanley ''Doc'' Ryker, **Frank Trumbauer,** Don Murray (reeds); Irving Riskin (p); Howdy Quicksell (bjo); Steve Brown (st-bs); Chauncey Morehouse (dms).

BVE-38607-2 **SLOW RIVER**
(arrangement by Bill Challis)
10″-78 Victor 25354 (released 1 July 1936)
12″-LP Sb Bix Vol 4 ''Sincerely, Bix Beiderbecke''
12″-LP Ita Joker SM-3560 ''Bixology Vol 4''
C-DISC Fr MOJ MJCD-6 ''Bix Beiderbecke—Vol 2''

BVE-38607-4 **SLOW RIVER**
(arrangement by Bill Challis)
10″-78 Victor 20926 (released 28 October 1927)
10″-78 Eng HMV B-5397
12″-LP Sb Bix Vol 4 ''Sincerely, Bix Beiderbecke''
12″-LP Ita Joker SM-3560 ''Bixology Vol 4''
C-DISC Fr MOJ MJCD-6 ''Bix Beiderbecke—Vol 2''

16 MAY 1927 (Mon): Victor Record Co., New York, NY.
JEAN GOLDKETTE ORCHESTRA: Bix Beiderbecke (crt); Fred Farrar, Ray Lodwig (tpts); Bill Rank, Newell ''Spiegle'' Willcox (tbns); Stanley ''Doc'' Ryker, **Frank Trumbauer,** Don Murray (reeds); Eddy Sheasby (vn); Irving Riskin (p); Howdy Quicksell (bjo); Steve Brown (st-bs); Chauncey Morehouse (dms).
Beiderbecke on BVE-38263 only.

BVE-38263 **LILY**
(arrangement by Eddy Sheasby)
Rejected

BVE-38264-1 **IN MY MERRY OLDSMOBILE** (a waltz)
(arrangement by Eddy Sheasby)
10″-78 Biltmore 1012
10″-78 Victor Special (un-numbered)
12″-LP Sb Bix Vol 4 ''Sincerely, Bix Beiderbecke''
12″-LP Ita Joker SM-3560 ''Bixology Vol 4''

23 MAY 1927 (Mon): Victor Record Co., New York, NY.
JEAN GOLDKETTE ORCHESTRA: Bix Beiderbecke (crt); Fred Farrar, Ray Lodwig (tpts); Bill Rank, Newell ''Spiegle'' Willcox (tbns); Stanley ''Doc'' Ryker, **Frank Trumbauer,** Don Murray (reeds); Eddy Sheasby (vn); Irving Riskin (p); Howdy Quicksell (bjo); Steve Brown (st-bs); Chauncey Morehouse (dms).
Sheasby on BVE-38267 only.

BVE-38267 **PLAY IT RED**
(arrangement by Eddy Sheasby)
Rejected

BVE-38268-1 **IN MY MERRY OLDSMOBILE** (fox trot)
(vc by Ray Lodwig, Howdy Quicksell, and Doc Ryker)
(arrangement by Bill Challis)
10″-78 Biltmore 1012
10″-78 Victor Special (unnumbered)
12″-LP Broadway 102

12″-LP Sb Bix Vol 4 ''Sincerely, Bix Beiderbecke''
12″-LP Ita Joker SM-3560 ''Bixology Vol 4''
C-DISC Fr MOJ MJCD-6 ''Bix Beiderbecke—Vol 2''

BVE-38268-2 **IN MY MERRY OLDSMOBILE**
(vc by Ray Lodwig, Howdy Quicksell, Doc Ryker)
(arrangement by Bill Challis)
12″-LP Broadway 102
12″-LP RCA 741093
12″-LP Sb Bix Vol 4 ''Sincerely, Bix Beiderbecke''
C-DISC Fr MOJ MJCD-6 ''Bix Beiderbecke—Vol 2''

15 SEPTEMBER 1927 (Thu): Victor Record Co., New York, NY. JEAN GOLDKETTE ORCHESTRA: Bix Beiderbecke (crt); Fred Farrar, Ray Lodwig (tpts); Bill Rank, Lloyd Turner (tbns); Stanley ''Doc'' Ryker, **Frank Trumbauer,** Don Murray (reeds); Joe Venuti (vn); Irving Riskin (p); Eddie Lang (gtr); Howdy Quicksell (bjo); Steve Brown (st-bs); Chauncey Morehouse (dms). Victor file card refers to a second, unidentified, violin but it is not audible.

BVE-40211-3 **BLUE RIVER**
(vc by Lewis James)
(arrangement by Bill Challis)
10″-78 Victor 20981 (released 11 November 1927)
10″-78 Aus HMV EA-260
12″-LP Sb Bix Vol 5 ''Sincerely, Bix Beiderbecke''
12″-LP Ita Joker SM-3560 ''Bixology Vol 4''

BVE-40212-2 **CLEMENTINE** (FROM NEW ORLEANS)
(arrangement by Don Murray, Howdy Quicksell, Frank Trumbauer)
10″-78 Victor 20994 (released 18 November 1927)
10″-78 Victor 25283 (released 8 April 1936)
10″-78 Aus HMV EA-1706
10″-78 Aus HMV EA-3617
10″-78 Cnd Victor 20994
10″-78 Eng HMV B-5402
10″-78 Eng HMV B-9237

10″-78 German Electrola EG-3856
12″-LP Sb Bix Vol 4 "Sincerely, Bix Beiderbecke"
12″-LP Eng Jazz Collectors 531
12″-LP Ita Joker SM-3561 "Bixology Vol 5"
C-DISC P-A CDD-490 "Bix Beiderbecke—Jazz Me Blues"

On some foreign issues of BVE-40212, an apparent "take 1" appears in the runoff groove. This is not a genuine take 1, but a speeded-up take 2.

MARY HOWARD

18 February 1946 (Mon): 1:17 P.M. 37 East 49th Street NYC. Private recordings. **Frank Trumbauer** (. . . .); Charles Bourne (. . . .); Mary Howard (. . . .).

BODY AND SOUL

BETWEEN THE DEVIL AND THE DEEP BLUE SEA

HERJE KATI

AL JOLSON

15 OCTOBER 1924 (Wed): Brunswick Record Co., New York, NY.

RAY MILLER ORCHESTRA: Charles Rocco, Roy Johnston (tpts); Miff Mole, Andy Sindelar (tbns); Andy Sannella, **Frank Trumbauer,** Larry Abbott, Billy Richards (reeds); Dan Yates (vn); Rube Bloom, Tommy Satterfield (ps); Frank DiPrima (bjo); Louis Chassagne (br-bs); Ward Archer (dms); Ray Miller (dir).

The Brunswick file card states "Mr. Chapman added two musicians." One was Reubie Greenberg (vn); the other unidentified.

13954 **I'M GONNA TRAMP! TRAMP! TRAMP!**

13955 **I'M GONNA TRAMP! TRAMP! TRAMP!**

13956 **I'M GONNA TRAMP! TRAMP! TRAMP!**
(vc by Al Jolson)
10″-78 Brunswick 2743
12″-LP Eng Voc VLP-3

The Brunswick files do not indicate which matrix/take was used for the master/issued recording. Only one of the three was issued.

26 JULY 1934 (Thu): Radio Program, **The Kraft Music Hall,** NBC, New York, NY.

PAUL WHITEMAN ORCHESTRA: Nat Natoli, Harry "Goldie" Goldfield, Charles Teagarden (tpts); Bill Rank, Jack Fulton, Jack Teagarden (tbns); **Frank Trumbauer,** Charles Strickfaden, Bennie Bonacio, Jack Cordaro, (reeds); Kurt Dieterle, Matty Malneck, Mischa Russell, Harry Strubel (vns); Roy Bargy, Ramona Davies (ps); Artie Miller (st-bs); Mike Pingitore (bjo); Herb Quigley (dms).

DAMES
(vc by Al Jolson)
12″-LP Sandy Hook SH-2003 "Al Jolson 'On The Air' "
12″-LP Totem 1006 "Al Jolson 'On The Air' "

THE CALL OF THE SOUTH
(vc by Al Jolson)
12″-LP Sandy Hook SH-2003 "Al Jolson 'On The Air' "
12″-LP Totem 1006 "Al Jolson 'On The Air' "

Both Sandy Hook and Totem LPs issued DAMES and THE CALL OF THE SOUTH under Al Jolson's name. These selections will also be found under Paul Whiteman's name in the Discography.

RAY MILLER & HIS ORCHESTRA

28 MARCH 1924 (Mon): A.M. session; 3 hours, 15 minutes, Brunswick Record Co., New York, NY.

RAY MILLER ORCHESTRA: Charles Rocco, Roy Johnston (tpts); Miff Mole, Andy Sindelar (tbns); Andy Sannella, Bernie Daly, **Frank Trumbauer** (reeds); Dan Yates (vn); Tommy Satterfield, Harry Parella (ps); Frank DiPrima (bjo); Louis Chassagne (br-bs); Ward Archer (dms); . . . . . Helleberg (instrument unknown); Ray Miller (dir).

12750 **COME ON, RED** (YOU RED HOT DEVIL MAN)
Unissued

12751 **COME ON, RED** (YOU RED HOT DEVIL MAN)
10″-78 Brunswick 2606

12752 **COME ON, RED** (YOU RED HOT DEVIL MAN)
Unissued

12753 **MONAVANNA**

12754 **MONAVANNA**

12755 **MONAVANNA**

12756 **MONAVANNA**
10″-78 Brunswick 2606

The Brunswick files do not indicate which matrix/take was issued for the title MONAVANNA.

23 APRIL 1924 (Wed): A.M. session; 3 hours, 15 minutes; Brunswick Record Co., New York, NY.

RAY MILLER ORCHESTRA: Charles Rocco, Roy Johnston (tpts); Miff Mole, Andy Sindelar (tbns); Andy Sannella, Bernie Daly, **Frank Trumbauer** (reeds); Dan Yates (vn); Tommy Satterfield, Harry Parella (ps); Frank DiPrima (bjo); Louis Chassagne (br-bs); Ward Archer (dms); . . . . . Helleberg (instrument unknown).

12962 **LOTS O' MAMA**
Unissued

12963 **LOTS O' MAMA**
Unissued

12964 **LOTS O' MAMA**
10″-78 Brunswick 2613

12965 **FROM ONE TIL TWO** (I ALWAYS DREAM OF YOU)

12966 **FROM ONE TIL TWO** (I ALWAYS DREAM OF YOU)

12967 **FROM ONE TIL TWO** (I ALWAYS DREAM OF YOU)
10″-78 Brunswick 2613

The Brunswick files do not indicate which matrix/take was issued of FROM ONE TIL TWO (I ALWAYS DREAM OF YOU).

3 JUNE 1924 (Tue): P.M. session; Brunswick Record Co., New York, NY.

RAY MILLER ORCHESTRA: Charles Rocco, Roy Johnston (tpts); Miff Mole, Andy Sindelar (tbns); Andy Sannella, Bernie Daly, **Frank Trumbauer** (reeds); Dan Yates (vn); Tommy Satterfield, Harry Parella (ps); Frank DiPrima (bjo); Louis Chassagne (br-bs); Ward Archer (dms).

13204 **MAMA'S GONE, GOOD-BYE** (arrangement by W. C. Polla)
Unissued

13205 **MAMA'S GONE, GOOD-BYE** (arrangement by W. C. Polla)
10″-78 Brunswick 2632

6 JUNE 1924 (Fri): P.M. session; Brunswick Record Co., New York, NY.

RAY MILLER ORCHESTRA: Charles Rocco, Roy Johnston (tpts); Miff Mole, Andy Sindelar (tbns); Andy Sannella, Bernie

Daly, **Frank Trumbauer** (reeds); Dan Yates (vn); Tommy Satterfield, Harry Parella (ps); Frank DiPrima (bjo); Louis Chassagne (br-bs); Ward Archer (dms).

13227 **WHERE IS THAT OLD GIRL OF MINE?**
(vc by Billy Jones)
Unissued

13228 **WHERE IS THAT OLD GIRL OF MINE?**
(vc by Billy Jones)
Unissued

13229 **WHERE IS THAT OLD GIRL OF MINE?**
(vc by Billy Jones)
10″-78 Brunswick 2632

13230 **I DIDN'T CARE TILL I LOST YOU**
(arrangement by Ted Eastwood)
Rejected. Remade 22 July 1927.

13231 **I DIDN'T CARE TILL I LOST YOU**
(arrangement by Ted Eastwood)
Rejected. Remade 22 July 1927.

13232 **I DIDN'T CARE TILL I LOST YOU**
(arrangement by Ted Eastwood)
Rejected. Remade 22 July 1927.

10 JULY 1924 (Thu): P.M. session, 2 hours; Brunswick Record Co., New York, NY.

RAY MILLER ORCHESTRA: Charles Rocco, Roy Johnston (tpts); Miff Mole, Andy Sindelar (tbns); Andy Sannella, Bernie Daly, **Frank Trumbauer** (reeds); Dan Yates (vn); Tommy Satterfield, Harry Parella (ps); Frank DiPrima (bjo); Louis Chassagne (br-bs); Ward Archer (dms).

13494 **I CAN'T GET THE ONE I WANT**

13495 **I CAN'T GET THE ONE I WANT**

13496 **I CAN'T GET THE ONE I WANT**

13497 **I CAN'T GET THE ONE I WANT**
10″-78 Brunswick 2643

The Brunswick files do not indicate which matrix/take was issued.

13498 **SALLY LOU**

13499 **SALLY LOU**

13500 **SALLY LOU**
10″-78 Brunswick 2643

The Brunswick files do not indicate which matrix/take was issued.

13504 **LONELY, LITTLE MELODY**

13505 **LONELY, LITTLE MELODY**

13506 **LONELY, LITTLE MELODY**
(Orchestrated by Walter Paul)
10″-78 Brunswick 2669

The Brunswick files do not indicate which matrix/take was issued.

13507 **SOMEBODY LOVES ME**

13508 **SOMEBODY LOVES ME**

13509 **SOMEBODY LOVES ME**
10″-78 Brunswick 2669

The Brunswick files do not indicate which matrix/take was issued.
The missing matrix/take numbers 13491, 13492, 13493, BARB WIRE BLUES and 13501, 13502, 13503, YOU AIN'T GOT NOTHIN' I WANT were recorded in New York by the Mound City Blue Blowers. Frank Trumbauer is the composer of BARB WIRE BLUES.

22 JULY 1924 (Tue): P.M. session; 2 hours; Brunswick Record Co., New York, NY.

RAY MILLER ORCHESTRA: Charles Rocco, Roy Johnston (tpts); Miff Mole, Andy Sindelar (tbns); Andy Sannella, Bernie Daly, **Frank Trumbauer** (reeds); Dan Yates (vn); Tommy Satterfield, Harry Parella (ps); Frank DiPrima (bjo); Louis Chassagne (br-bs); Ward Archer (dms).

13580 **PLEASE**

13581 **PLEASE**

13582 **PLEASE**
(arrangement by Arthur Lange)
10″-78 Brunswick 2666

The Brunswick files do not indicate which matrix/take was issued.

13583 **CHARLESTON CABIN**

13584 **CHARLESTON CABIN**

13585 **CHARLESTON CABIN**

13586 **CHARLESTON CABIN**
(arrangement by Dave Kaplan)
10″-78 Brunswick 2666

The Brunswick files do not indicate which matrix/take was issued.

13587 **I DIDN'T CARE TILL I LOST YOU**

13588 **I DIDN'T CARE TILL I LOST YOU**
(arrangement by Ted Eastwood)
10″-78 Brunswick 1753

The Brunswick files do not indicate which matrix/take was issued.
The sheet music of I DIDN'T CARE, published by Stark & Cown, has a photograph of the Miller Orchestra on the cover and credits the arrangement to Tommy Satterfield.

5 AUGUST 1924 (Tue): First title-A.M. session; Rest-P.M. session; 2 hours; Brunswick Record Co., New York, NY.

RAY MILLER ORCHESTRA: Charles Rocco, Roy Johnston (tpts); Miff Mole, Andy Sindelar (tbns); Andy Sannella, Bernie Daly, **Frank Trumbauer** (reeds); Dan Yates (vn); Tommy Satterfield, Harry Parella (ps); Frank DiPrima (bjo); Louis Chassagne (br-bs); Ward Archer (dms).

13673 **BAGDAD**

13674 **BAGDAD**

13675 **BAGDAD**

13676 **BAGDAD**
10″-78 Brunswick 2681

The Brunswick files do not indicate which matrix/take was issued.

13677 **RED HOT MAMA**

13678 **RED HOT MAMA**

13679 **RED HOT MAMA**
(arrangement by Willie Creager)
10″-78 Brunswick 2681

The Brunswick files do not indicate which matrix/take was issued.

13680 **ARABIANNA** (An Oriental Fantasy)

13681 **ARABIANNA** (An Oriental Fantasy)

13682 **ARABIANNA** (An Oriental Fantasy)
(arrangement by Will Perry)
10″-78 Brunswick 2761

The Brunswick files do not indicate which matrix/take was issued.

27 SEPTEMBER 1924 (Sat): Brunswick Record Co., New York, NY.

RAY MILLER ORCHESTRA: Charles Rocco, Roy Johnston (tpts); Miff Mole, Andy Sindelar (tbns); **Frank Trumbauer,** Larry Abbott, Billy Richards, Andy Sannella (reeds); Dan

Yates (vn); Tommy Satterfield, Rube Bloom (ps); Frank DiPrima (bjo); Louis Chassagne (br-bs); Ward Archer (dms).

13856 **DOODLE-DOO-DOO**

13857 **DOODLE-DOO-DOO**

13858 **DOODLE-DOO-DOO**

13859 **DOODLE-DOO-DOO**
10″-78 Brunswick 2724

Two takes were issued. The Brunswick files do not indicate which matrix/takes were issued.

13860 **ADORING YOU**

13861 **ADORING YOU**

13862 **ADORING YOU**

13863 **ADORING YOU**
(arrangement by Frank E. Barry)
10″-78 Brunswick 2724

The Brunswick files do not indicate which matrix/take was issued.

13 OCTOBER 1924 (Mon): Brunswick Record Co., New York, NY.

RAY MILLER ORCHESTRA: Charles Rocco, Roy Johnston (tpts); Miff Mole, Andy Sindelar (tbns); **Frank Trumbauer,** Larry Abbott, Billy Richards, Andy Sannella (reeds); Dan Yates (vn); Tommy Satterfield, Rube Bloom (ps); Frank DiPrima (bjo); Louis Chassagne (br-bs); Ward Archer (dms); Ray Miller (dir).

13926 **ME AND THE BOY FRIEND**
(arrangement by Tommy Satterfield)
10″-78 Brunswick 2753

13927 **ME AND THE BOY FRIEND**
(arrangement by Tommy Satterfield)
Unissued

13928 **ME AND THE BOY FRIEND**
(arrangement by Tommy Satterfield)
Unissued

13929 **ME AND THE BOY FRIEND**
(arrangement by Tommy Satterfield)
Unissued

7 NOVEMBER 1924 (Fri): P.M. session; Brunswick Record Co., New York, NY.

RAY MILLER ORCHESTRA: Charles Rocco, Roy Johnston (tpts); Miff Mole, Andy Sindelar (tbns); **Frank Trumbauer,** Larry Abbott, Billy Richards, Andy Sannella (reeds); Dan Yates (vn); Rube Bloom (p); Frank DiPrima (bjo); Louis Chassagne (br-bs); Ward Archer (dms).

14151 **BY THE LAKE**

14152 **BY THE LAKE**

14153 **BY THE LAKE**
10″-78 Brunswick 2778

The Brunswick files do not indicate which matrix/take was issued.

4 DECEMBER 1924 (Thu): P.M. session; 5 hours; Brunswick Record Co., New York, NY.

RAY MILLER ORCHESTRA: Charles Rocco, Roy Johnston (tpts); Miff Mole, Andy Sindelar (tbns); **Frank Trumbauer,** Larry Abbott, Billy Richards, Andy Sannella (reeds); Dan Yates (vn); Rube Bloom (p); Frank DiPrima (bjo); Louis Chassagne (br-bs); Ward Archer (dms).

14386 **WHY COULDN'T IT BE POOR LITTLE ME?**

14387 **WHY COULDN'T IT BE POOR LITTLE ME?**

14388 **WHY COULDN'T IT BE POOR LITTLE ME?**
10″-78 Brunswick 2788

The Brunswick files do not indicate which matrix/take was issued.

14389 **I'LL SEE YOU IN MY DREAMS**

14390 **I'LL SEE YOU IN MY DREAMS**

14391 **I'LL SEE YOU IN MY DREAMS**
10″-78 Brunswick 2788

The Brunswick files do not indicate which matrix/take was issued.

14392 **I'LL SEE YOU IN MY DREAMS**
(vc by Frank Bessinger)
Unissued.

Both selections were composed by Isham Jones, who conducted this session.

5 DECEMBER 1924 (Fri): A.M. session; 3 hours; Brunswick Record Co., New York, NY.

RAY MILLER ORCHESTRA: Charles Rocco, Roy Johnston (tpts); Miff Mole, Andy Sindelar (tbns); **Frank Trumbauer,** Larry Abbott, Billy Richards, Andy Sannella (reeds); Dan Yates (vn); Tommy Satterfield, Rube Bloom (ps); Frank DiPrima (bjo); Louis Chassagne (br-bs); Ward Archer (dms).

14393 **INDIAN LOVE CALL**

14394 **INDIAN LOVE CALL**

14395 **INDIAN LOVE CALL**
(arrangement by Tommy Satterfield)
10″-78 Brunswick 2789

The Brunswick files do not indicate which matrix/take was issued.

10 DECEMBER 1924 (Wed): Brunswick Record Co., New York, NY. First title-A.M. session; second title-P.M. session.

RAY MILLER ORCHESTRA: Charles Rocco, Roy Johnston (tpts); Miff Mole, Andy Sindelar (tbns); **Frank Trumbauer,**

Larry Abbott, Billy Richards, Andy Sannella (reeds); Dan Yates (vn); Tommy Satterfield, Rube Bloom (ps); Frank DiPrima (bjo); Louis Chassagne (br-bs); Ward Archer (dms).

14428 **YOU AND I**

14429 **YOU AND I**

14430 **YOU AND I**
(arrangement by Tommy Satterfield)

Rejected. Remade 16 December 1924.

14432 **NOBODY KNOWS WHAT A RED-HEAD MAMA CAN DO**

14433 **NOBODY KNOWS WHAT A RED-HEAD MAMA CAN DO**

14434 **NOBODY KNOWS WHAT A RED-HEAD MAMA CAN DO**

14435 **NOBODY KNOWS WHAT A RED-HEAD MAMA CAN DO**
(arrangement by Tommy Satterfield)

Rejected. Remade 16 December 1924.

16 DECEMBER 1924 (Tue): A.M. session; 3 hours; Brunswick Record Co., New York, NY.

RAY MILLER ORCHESTRA: Charles Rocco, Roy Johnston (tpts); Miff Mole, Andy Sindelar (tbns); **Frank Trumbauer,** Larry Abbott, Billy Richards, Andy Sannella (reeds); Dan Yates (vn); Tommy Satterfield, Rube Bloom (ps); Frank DiPrima (bjo); Louis Chassagne (br-bs); Ward Archer (dms).

14494 **YOU AND I**

14495 **YOU AND I**

14496 **YOU AND I**
(arrangement by Tommy Satterfield)

10-78 Brunswick 2789

The Brunswick files do not indicate which matrix/take was issued.

14497 **NOBODY KNOWS WHAT A RED-HEAD MAMA CAN DO**

14498 **NOBODY KNOWS WHAT A RED-HEAD MAMA CAN DO**

14499 **NOBODY KNOWS WHAT A RED-HEAD MAMA CAN DO**
(arrangement by Tommy Satterfield)
10″-78 Brunswick 2778

The Brunswick files do not indicate which matrix/take was issued.

30 DECEMBER 1924 (Tues): A.M. session; 3-1/2 hours; Brunswick Record Co., New York, NY.
RAY MILLER ORCHESTRA: Charles Rocco, Roy Johnston (tpts); Miff Mole, Andy Sindelar (tbns); **Frank Trumbauer,** Larry Abbott, Billy Richards, Andy Sannella (reeds); Dan Yates (vn); Tommy Satterfield, Rube Bloom (ps); Frank DiPrima (bjo); Louis Chassagne (br-bs); Ward Archer (dms).
No masters were made. The band used the time in rehearsal.

7 JANUARY 1925 (Wed): P.M. session; 3-1/2 hours; Brunswick Record Co., New York, NY.
RAY MILLER ORCHESTRA: Personnel not listed, but instrumentation shown as 13 men. Perhaps Satterfield and Miller were deleted.

14588 **TESSIE** (STOP TEASIN' ME)

14589 **TESSIE** (STOP TEASIN' ME)

14590 **TESSIE** (STOP TEASIN' ME)

14591 **TESSIE** (STOP TEASIN' ME)
10-78 Brunswick 2830

The Brunswick files do not indicate which matrix/take was issued.

14592 **ME NEED YAH** (MY LITTLE ONE)

14593 **ME NEED YAH** (MY LITTLE ONE)

14594 **ME NEED YAH** (MY LITTLE ONE)

14595 **ME NEED YAH** (MY LITTLE ONE)
(arrangement by Andy Sannella)
Rejected. Not remade.

27 JANUARY 1925 (Tue): A.M. session; Brunswick Record Co., New York, NY.
RAY MILLER ORCHESTRA: Charles Rocco, Roy Johnston (tpts); Miff Mole, Andy Sindelar (tbns); Andy Sannella, **Frank Trumbauer,** Larry Abbott, Billy Richards (reeds); Dan Yates (vn); Rube Bloom, Tommy Satterfield (ps); Frank DiPrima (bjo); Louis Chassagne (br-bs); Ward Archer (dms).

14811 **ON THE WAY TO MONTEREY**

14812 **ON THE WAY TO MONTEREY**

14813 **ON THE WAY TO MONTEREY**
Rejected. Remade 5 February 1925.

14814 **THAT'S MY GIRL**

14815 **THAT'S MY GIRL**

14816 **THAT'S MY GIRL**

14817 **THAT'S MY GIRL**
Rejected. Remade 5 February 1925.

5 FEBRUARY 1925 (Thu): A.M. session; Brunswick Record Co., New York, NY.
RAY MILLER ORCHESTRA: Charles Rocco, Roy Johnston (tpts); Miff Mole, Andy Sindelar (tbns); Andy Sannella, **Frank Trumbauer,** Larry Abbott, Billy Richards (reeds); Dan Yates (vn); Rube Bloom, Tommy Satterfield (ps); Frank DiPrima (bjo); Louis Chassagne (br-bs); Ward Archer (dms).

14811 **ON THE WAY TO MONTEREY**

14812 **ON THE WAY TO MONTEREY**

14813 **ON THE WAY TO MONTEREY**
10″-78 Brunswick 2823

The Brunswick files do not indicate which matrix/take was issued.

14814 **THAT'S MY GIRL**

14815 **THAT'S MY GIRL**

14816 **THAT'S MY GIRL**

14817 **THAT'S MY GIRL**
10″-78 Brunswick 2823

The Brunswick files do not indicate which matrix/take was issued.

10 FEBRUARY 1925 (Tue): P.M. session; Brunswick Record Co., New York, NY.
RAY MILLER ORCHESTRA: Charles Rocco, Roy Johnston (tpts); Miff Mole, Andy Sindelar (tbns); Andy Sannella, **Frank Trumbauer,** Larry Abbott, Billy Richards (reeds); Dan Yates (vn); Rube Bloom, Tommy Satterfield (ps); Frank DiPrima (bjo); Louis Chassagne (br-bs); Ward Archer (dms).

14895 **WILL YOU REMEMBER ME?**

14896 **WILL YOU REMEMBER ME?**

14897 **WILL YOU REMEMBER ME?**

14898 **WILL YOU REMEMBER ME?**
10″-78 Brunswick 2830

27 FEBRUARY 1925 (Fri): A.M. session; Brunswick Record Co., New York, NY.
RAY MILLER ORCHESTRA: Charles Rocco, Roy Johnston (tpts); Miff Mole, Andy Sindelar (tbns); Andy Sannella, **Frank Trumbauer,** Larry Abbott, Billy Richards (reeds); Dan Yates (vn); Rube Bloom, Tommy Satterfield (ps); Frank DiPrima (bjo); Louis Chassagne (br-bs); Ward Archer (dms).

15007 **WE'RE BACK TOGETHER AGAIN**

15008 **WE'RE BACK TOGETHER AGAIN**

15009 **WE'RE BACK TOGETHER AGAIN**

15010 **WE'RE BACK TOGETHER AGAIN**
10″-78 Brunswick 2847

The Brunswick files do not indicate which matrix/take was issued.

15011 **I'LL TAKE HER BACK, IF SHE WANTS TO COME BACK**

15012 **I'LL TAKE HER BACK, IF SHE WANTS TO COME BACK**

15013 **I'LL TAKE HER BACK, IF SHE WANTS TO COME BACK**
(vc by Irving Kaufman)
10″-78 Brunswick 2847

The Brunswick files do not indicate which matrix/take was issued.

13 MARCH 1925 (Fri): A.M. session; Brunswick Record Co., New York, NY.
RAY MILLER ORCHESTRA: Personnel listed as 13 men, unidentified, and no indication of which musician was omitted.

15157 **JUST A LITTLE DRINK**

15158 **JUST A LITTLE DRINK**

15159 **JUST A LITTLE DRINK**
(vc by Frank Bessinger and Frank Wright)
10″-78 Brunswick 2866

The Brunswick files do not indicate which matrix/take was issued.

15160 **MOONLIGHT AND ROSES**

15161 **MOONLIGHT AND ROSES**

15162 **MOONLIGHT AND ROSES**
(vc by Frank Bessinger and Frank Wright)
10″-78 Brunswick 2866

The Brunswick files do not indicate which matrix/take was issued.

16 MARCH 1925 (Mon): A.M. session; 3 hours; Brunswick Record Co., New York, NY.

RAY MILLER ORCHESTRA: Personnel listed as 13 men, unidentified, and no indication of which musician was omitted.

15181 **RED HOT HENRY BROWN**
10″-78 Brunswick 2855

15182 **LET IT RAIN—LET IT POUR**

15183 **LET IT RAIN—LET IT POUR**

15184 **LET IT RAIN—LET IT POUR**
10″-78 Brunswick 2855

The Brunswick files do not indicate which matrix/take was issued.

11 APRIL 1925 (Sat): A.M. session; 3 hours; Brunswick Record Co., New York, NY.

RAY MILLER ORCHESTRA: Personnel listed only as 13 men, with no indication of which musician was omitted.

15512 **PHOEBE SNOW** (THAT ANTHRACITE MAMA)

15513 **PHOEBE SNOW** (THAT ANTHRACITE MAMA)
10″-78 Brunswick 2898

The Brunswick files do not indicate which matrix/take was issued.

15514 **HOLD ME IN YOUR ARMS**

15515 **HOLD ME IN YOUR ARMS**

15516 **HOLD ME IN YOUR ARMS**
10″-78 Brunswick 2898

The Brunswick files do not indicate which matrix/take was issued.

MOUND CITY BLUE BLOWERS

13 MARCH 1924 (Thu): Brunswick Record Co., Chicago, IL.
MOUND CITY BLUE BLOWERS: **Frank Trumbauer** (C-mel); William "Red" McKenzie (comb); Dick Slevin (kazoo); Jack Bland (bjo).

CH-103 **RED HOT!**
Unissued

CH-104 **RED HOT!**
Unissued

CH-105 **RED HOT!**
Unissued

CH-114 **RED HOT!**
Brunswick 2602

It would appear that RED HOT! was also recorded on 14 March (CH-114), but for convenience the entry was noted on the 13 March entries. **Frank Trumbauer** is one of the composers of RED HOT!

14 MARCH 1924 (Fri): Brunswick Record Co., Chicago, IL.
MOUND CITY BLUE BLOWERS: **Frank Trumbauer** (C-mel); William "Red" McKenzie (comb); Dick Slevin (kazoo); Jack Bland (bjo).

CH-111 **SAN**

CH-112 **SAN**

CH-113 **SAN**
10″-78 Brunswick 2602

The Brunswick files do not indicate which matrix/take was issued.

RED NICHOLS' STOMPERS

26 OCTOBER 1927 (Wed): Victor Record Co., New York, NY.
RED NICHOLS' STOMPERS: Loring "Red" Nichols (crt); Leo McConville, Bob Ashford (tpts); Bill Rank, Glenn Miller (tbns); Fud Livingston (clt/ten-sx); Max Farley, **Frank Trumbauer** (altos); Adrian Rollini (bs-sx); Arthur Schutt (p); Carl Kress (gtr/bjo); Jack Hansen (tuba); Chauncey Morehouse (dms).

BVE-40512-1 **SUGAR**
(vc by Jim Miller and Charles Farrell)
(arrangement by Arthur Schutt)
10″-78 Victor 21056
10″-78 Cch HMV AM-1211
10″-78 Eng HMV B-5433

BVE-40513-1 **MAKE MY COT WHERE THE COT-COT-COTTON GROWS**
(vc by Jim Miller and Charles Farrell)
(arrangement by Glenn Miller)
10″-78 Victor 21056
10″-78 Cch HMV AM-1211
10″-78 Eng HMV B-5433

BEE PALMER

10 JANUARY 1929 (Thu): Columbia Record Co., New York, NY.
FRANK TRUMBAUER ORCHESTRA: Bix Beiderbecke (crt); Bill Rank (tbn); **Frank Trumbauer** (C-mel/alto); Chester Hazlett (alto); Irving Friedman (clt/ten-sx); Min Leibrook (bs-sx); Roy Bargy (p); Edward "Snoozer" Quinn (gtr); George Marsh (dms).

W-147750 **DON'T LEAVE ME, DADDY**
(vc by Bee Palmer)
Rejected

W-147751 **SINGIN' THE BLUES**
(vc by Bee Palmer)
Rejected

The Columbia Records file card reads: ''Paul Whiteman Presents Bee Palmer with the **Frank Trumbauer Orchestra.** ''Bix's presence is confirmed by ''Snoozer'' Quinn. Bix is not audible on either tune. Bee, after singing the lyrics of SINGIN' THE BLUES, does a scat vocal trying to imitate the Tram and Bix solos from their 1927 recording.

RHYTHMODIC ORCHESTRA

(Under the direction of Carl Fenton)
(Carl Fenton was a professional pseudonymn for Gus Haenschen)

4 FEBRUARY 1925 (Wed): Brunswick Record Co., New York, NY.

RHYTHMODIC ORCHESTRA: Charles Rocco, Roy Johnston (tpts); Miff Mole, Andy Sindelar (tbns); Andy Sannella, **Frank Trumbauer,** Larry Abbott, Billy Richards (reeds); Dan Yates (vn); Rube Bloom, Tommy Satterfield (ps); Frank DiPrima (bjo); Louis Chassagne (br-bs); Ward Archer (dms).

14808 **HUNGARIA**

14809 **HUNGARIA**
(arrangement by Frank Black)
10″-78 Brunswick 2828

The Brunswick files do not indicate which matrix/take was issued.

14810 **EGYPTIAN ECHOES**
(arrangement by Frank Black)
10″-78 Brunswick 2828

WILLARD ROBISON

18 JANUARY 1928 (Wed): New York, NY.

Personnel unidentified.

An entry was made in Trumbauer's diary for a recording

session on this date with Willard Robison. Unfortunately, he failed to list any details.

See also under CHICAGO LOOPERS, 20 October 1927.

GENE RODEMICH ORCHESTRA

EARLY OCTOBER 1921: Brunswick Record Co., New York, NY.

GENE RODEMICH ORCHESTRA: Clarence Foster (tpt); Paul Vegna (tbn); **Frank Trumbauer** (C-mel/alto); Benny Krueger (alto); Jules Silberberg (vn/sx); Otto Reinert (vn); Gene Rodemich (p/ldr); Hammond Bailey (bjo/xyl); Paul Spoerloder (dms).

6461 **FANCIES**
10″-78 Brunswick 2152

6462 **FANCIES**
Status unknown

6474 **GYPSY BLUES**
Status unknown

6475 **GYPSY BLUES**
10″-78 Brunswick 2152

6479 **JUST LIKE A RAINBOW**
10″-78 Brunswick 2159 (coupled with matrix 6503)

6480 **JUST LIKE A RAINBOW**
10″-78 Brunswick 2159 (coupled with matrix 6504)

6495 **RIGHT OR WRONG**
10″-78 Brunswick 2183

6498 **BY THE PYRAMIDS**
10″-78 Brunswick 2183

6503 **CRY BABY BLUES**
10″-78 Brunswick 2159 (coupled with matrix 6479)

6504 **CRY BABY BLUES**
10″-78 Brunswick 2159 (coupled with matrix 6480)

6507 **SNOWFLAKE**
10″-78 Brunswick 2169

6516 **APRIL SHOWERS**
10″-78 Brunswick 2169

REFERENCE: **Brunswick 1922 Catalog,** p.71: ''GENE RODEMICH'S ORCHESTRA: The brilliant dance recordings of this orchestra are found wherever people dance to phonograph music. Full of unusual harmonizations, refreshing color and originality, they satisfy the public demand for something new and are ever new in stronger rhythms and more and more syncopation. This highly specialized and thoroughly trained group of instrumentalists has developed with the music of the modern dance and is looked to by a large personal following for the foremost interpretations of the dance hits of the hour. Gene Rodemich's Orchestra is exclusively Brunswick.''

SIOUX CITY SIX
(Under the direction of **Frank Trumbauer**)

9 OCTOBER 1924 (Thu): 9-11 East 37th Street, New York, NY. SIOUX CITY SIX: Bix Beiderbecke (crt); Miff Mole (tbn); **Frank Trumbauer** (C-mel); Rube Bloom (p); Min Leibrook (tuba); Vic Moore (dms).

9119 **FLOCK O' BLUES**
Unissued. Copper master made 11 October.

9119-A **FLOCK O' BLUES**
Copper master made 11 October.
10″-78 Gennett 5569
10″-78 Session 7
10″-78 Cch Decca BM-02207
10″-78 Eng Brunswick 02207
10″-LP Riverside RLP-1050
12″-LP Sb Bix Vol 1 ''Sincerely, Bix Beiderbecke''
12″-LP Ita Joker SM-3558 ''Bixology Vol 2''
C-DISC Milestone MCD-47019-2(H)
''Bix Beiderbecke & The Chicago Cornets''

9119-B FLOCK O' BLUES
Unissued. Copper master made 11 October.

File card lists as "Miff Moe *[Ed. note: should be Mole]* with Sioux City Six under direction of Frank Trumbauer."

9120 I'M GLAD
Unissued. Copper master made 11 October.

9120-A I'M GLAD
Unissued. Copper master made 11 October.

9120-B I'M GLAD
Unissued. Copper master made 11 October.

9120-C I'M GLAD
Copper master made 11 October.
10″-78 Gennett 5569
10″-78 Session 7
10″-78 Cch Decca BM-02207
10″-78 Eng Brunswick 02207
10″-LP Riverside RLP-1050
12″-LP Sb Bix Vol 1 "Sincerely, Bix Beiderbecke"
12″-LP Ita Joker SM-3558 "Bixology Vol 2"
C-DISC Milestone MCD-47019-2(H)
"Bix Beiderbecke & The Chicago Cornets"
C-DISC Eng Saville CDSVL-201 "The Beiderbecke File"

Gennett file card lists as "Bid *[Ed. note: Should be Bix]* with Sioux City Six under direction of Frank Trumbauer." The musicians were paid $87.50 for the recordings. Distribution of money not listed.

JACK TEAGARDEN & HIS ORCHESTRA

18 SEPTEMBER 1934 (Tue): Brunswick Record Co., New York, NY.

JACK TEAGARDEN ORCHESTRA: Charlie Teagarden (tpt); Jack Teagarden (tbn); Benny Goodman (clt); **Frank Trum-**

bauer (C-mel); Casper Reardon (harp); Terry Shand (p); Artie Miller (st-bs); Herb Quigley (dms).

B-15938-A JUNK MAN
10″-78 Brunswick 7652
10″-78 Eng Brunswick 01979
10″-78 Eng Parlophone R-2599
10″-78 Fr Brunswick A-500512
10″-78 Fr Odeon A-272291
10″-78 Fr Polydor 580014
10″-78 German Brunswick A-9843
10″-78 Japanese Lucky S-3
12″-LP Folkways FP-67
12″-LP Polish Poljazz Z-SX-0662

B-15939-A STARS FELL ON ALABAMA
(vc by Jack Teagarden)
10″-78 Brunswick 6993
10″-78 Eng Brunswick 01979
10″-78 Fr Brunswick A-500482
12″-LP Epic SN-6044

B-15940-A YOUR GUESS IS AS GOOD AS MINE
(vc by Jack Teagarden)
10″-78 Brunswick 6993
10″-78 Eng Brunswick 01979
10″-78 Fr Brunswick A-500482
12″-LP Epic SN-6044

THE THREE T'S

(Jack Teagarden, **Frank Trumbauer**, and Charlie Teagarden)

10 MARCH 1936 (Tue): Victor Record Co., New York, NY.
THE THREE T'S: Charlie Teagarden (tpt); Jack Teagarden (tbn); Frank Trumbauer (C-mel); Jack Cordaro (clt); Lawrence ''Bud'' Freeman (ten-sx); Roy Bargy (p); Carl Kress (gtr); Artie Miller (st-bs); Bob White (dms).

BS-99447-2 I'SE A MUGGIN' (part 1)
(vc by Jack Teagarden & ensemble)
10″-78 Victor 25273

10″-78 Aus HMV EA-1690
10″-78 Eng HMV BD-5063
10″-78 Japanese Victor A-1231

BS-99448-1 **I'SE A MUGGIN' (part 2)**
(vc by Jack Teagarden & ensemble)
10″-78 Victor 25273
10″-78 Aus HMV EA-1690
10″-78 Eng HMV BD-5063
10″-78 Japanese Victor A-1231
12″-LP East German Amiga 850445

The "The Three T's" are listed in the Victor files as "The Teagarden Boys & Trumbauer Swing Band."

4 DECEMBER 1936 (Fri): WEAF/NBC Radio, New York, NY.
THE THREE T'S: Charlie Teagarden (tpt); Jack Teagarden (tbn/vcs); **Frank Trumbauer** (C-mel); Min Leibrook (bs-sx); Casper Reardon (h); Herm Crone (p); Stan King (dms).

ANNOUNCER: Your introduction to the THREE T'S presented for the first time on the NBC network . . .

SINGIN' THE BLUES (opening theme)

YOU TURNED THE TABLES ON ME
(vc by Jack Teagarden)

'S WONDERFUL

DID YOU MEAN IT?
(vc by Jack Teagarden)

I'M AN OLD COWHAND
(vc by Jack Teagarden)

FARE THEE WELL TO HARLEM
(vc by Jack Teagarden and Frank Trumbauer)

WHERE THE LAZY RIVER FLOWS

Medley:
a. **YOU TOOK ADVANTAGE OF ME**
(featuring **Frank Trumbauer**)
b. **TEA FOR TWO**
(featuring Jack Teagarden)

SINGIN' THE BLUES (closing theme)

11 DECEMBER 1936 (Fri): WEAF/NBC Radio, New York, NY.
THE THREE T'S: Charlie Teagarden (tpt); Jack Teagarden (tbn/vcs); **Frank Trumbauer** (C-mel); Min Leibrook (bs-sx); Adele Girard (h); Herm Crone (p); Stan King (dms).

SINGIN' THE BLUES (opening theme)

'TAIN'T GOOD

'S WONDERFUL

DID YOU MEAN IT?

I'M AN OLD COWHAND

LIZA (ALL THE CLOUDS'LL ROLL AWAY)

FARE THEE WELL TO HARLEM
(vc by Jack Teagarden and **Frank Trumbauer**)

ECLIPSE
(featuring **Frank Trumbauer**)

MR. "T" FROM TENNESSEE

LITTLE OLD LADY

Medley:
a. **BETWEEN THE DEVIL AND THE DEEP BLUE SEA**
b. **I GOT RHYTHM**

SINGIN' THE BLUES (closing theme)

18 DECEMBER 1936 (Fri): WEAF/NBC Radio, New York, NY.
THE THREE T'S: Charlie Teagarden (tpt); Jack Teagarden

(tbn/vcs); **Frank Trumbauer** (C-mel); Min Leibrook (bs-sx); Adele Girard (h); Herm Crone (p); Stan King (dms).

SINGIN' THE BLUES (opening theme)

'TAIN'T GOOD
(vc by Jack Teagarden)

At this point in the program the selection MR. "T" FROM TENNESSEE was announced but a station break is heard instead.

LITTLE OLD LADY
(vc by **Frank Trumbauer**)

I'M AN OLD COWHAND
(vc by Jack Teagarden)

LIZA (ALL THE CLOUDS'LL ROLL AWAY)
(featuring Adele Girard, h)

WHERE THE LAZY RIVER FLOWS

Medley:
a. **YOU TOOK ADVANTAGE OF ME**
b. **TEA FOR TWO**

SINGIN' THE BLUES (closing theme, briefly)
(**Frank Trumbauer**, only)

25 DECEMBER 1936 (Fri): WEAF/NBC Radio, New York, NY. THE THREE T'S: Charlie Teagarden (tpt); Jack Teagarden (tbn/vcs); **Frank Trumbauer** (C-mel); Min Leibrook (bs-sx); Adele Girard (h); Herm Crone (p); Stan King (dms).

SINGIN' THE BLUES (opening theme)

'S WONDERFUL

WHERE THE LAZY RIVER FLOWS

CHRISTMAS NIGHT IN HARLEM

ODE TO A CHIMNEY SWEEPER

I GOT RHYTHM

HERJE KATI
(featuring **Frank Trumbauer**)

'WAY DOWN YONDER IN ORLEANS

YOU TOOK ADVANTAGE OF ME

TEA FOR TWO

SINGIN' THE BLUES (closing theme)

8 JANUARY 1937 (Fri): WEAF/NBC Radio, New York, NY.
THE THREE T'S: Charlie Teagarden (tpt); Jack Teagarden (tbn/vcs); **Frank Trumbauer** (C-mel); Min Leibrook (bs-sx); Adele Girard (h); Herm Crone (p); Stan King (dms).

SINGIN' THE BLUES (opening theme)

CHINA BOY

BEALE STREET BLUES
(vc by Al Jennings)

HONEYSUCKLE ROSE

Medley:
a. **BETWEEN THE DEVIL AND THE DEEP BLUE SEA**
b. **I GOT RHYTHM**
(vc by Johnny ''Scat'' Davis)

Medley:
a. **THE NIGHT IS YOUNG AND YOU'RE SO BEAUTIFUL**
b. **FOOLS**
c. **THE KID IN THE THREE CORNER PANTS**
d. **ECLIPSE**
(featuring **Frank Trumbauer**)

DRIFTING
(featuring Frank Dixon and Adrian Rollini)

Medley:
a. **BLUE SKIES**
b. **SONG OF THE ISLANDS**
c. **I NEVER KNEW**
d. **THE SHEIK OF ARABY**

SINGIN' THE BLUES (closing theme)

15 JANUARY 1937 (Fri): WEAF/NBC Radio, New York, NY.
THE THREE T'S: Charlie Teagarden (tpt); Jack Teagarden (tbn/vcs); **Frank Trumbauer** (C-mel); Min Leibrook (bs-sx); Adele Girard (h); Herm Crone (p); Stan King (dms).

SINGIN' THE BLUES (opening theme)

MR. GHOST GOES TO TOWN

AIN'T MISBEHAVIN'

WHEN IT'S SLEEPY TIME DOWN SOUTH

REBOUND
(featuring Adrian Rollini)

Medley:
a. **COQUETTE**
b. **LOVE AND LEARN**

SKITTER
(featuring Adrian Rollini)

NAGASAKI

THE PEANUT VENDOR

SINGIN' THE BLUES (closing theme)

During the closing, the announcer noted that this was the final broadcast of The Three T's.

DECEMBER 1936-JANUARY 1937: WEAF/NBC Radio, New York, NY.
THE THREE T'S: Charlie Teagarden (tpt); Jack Teagarden

(tbn/vcs); **Frank Trumbauer** (C-mel); Min Leibrook (bs-sx); Adele Girard (h); Herm Crone (p); Stan King (dms).

A recording of the following undated partial broadcasts exist in private collections:

Set 1: **I GOT RHYTHM**

WITH PLENTY OF MONEY AND YOU

FROST ON THE MOON

HERJE KATI

Set 2: **BETWEEN THE DEVIL AND THE DEEP BLUE SEA**
(featuring **Frank Trumbauer**)

I GOT RHYTHM
(featuring Jack Teagarden)

SINGIN' THE BLUES (closing theme)

Set 3: **'S WONDERFUL**

'WAY DOWN YONDER IN NEW ORLEANS
(vc by Jack Teagarden)

Medley:
a. **CHAPEL IN THE MOONLIGHT**
(featuring Charlie Teagarden)
b. **DIANE**
(featuring Jack Teagarden)

I GOT RHYTHM
(featuring **Frank Trumbauer**)

Set 4: **SINGIN' THE BLUES** (opening theme)

MR. "T" FROM TENNESSEE
(vc by Jack Teagarden)

'WAY DOWN YONDER IN NEW ORLEANS
(vc by Jack Teagarden)

Medley:
a. **CHAPEL IN THE MOONLIGHT**
b. **DIANE**
(featuring Jack Teagarden)

The selection LAZY RIVER was announced, but not played.

Set 5: **CHRISTMAS NIGHT IN HARLEM**
(vc by Jack Teagarden and **Frank Trumbauer**)

Medley:
a. **YOU TOOK ADVANTAGE OF ME**
(featuring Adele Girard)
b. **TEA FOR TWO**

Set 6: Medley:
a. **YOU TOOK ADVANTAGE OF ME**
(featuring Adele Girard)
b. **TEA FOR TWO**
(featuring Jack Teagarden)
c. **OH LADY BE GOOD**
(featuring **Frank Trumbauer**)

SINGIN' THE BLUES (closing thcmc)

FRANK TRUMBAUER & HIS ORCHESTRA

4 FEBRUARY 1927 (Thu): Columbia Record Co., New York, NY.

FRANK TRUMBAUER ORCHESTRA: Bix Beiderbecke (crt); Bill Rank (tbn); **Frank Trumbauer** (C-mel); Jimmy Dorsey (clt/alto); Stanley ''Doc'' Ryker (alto); Paul Mertz (p); Eddie Lang (gtr); Chauncey Morehouse (dms). **Ryker not on W-80391-C.**

W-80391-C **TRUMBOLOGY**
(arrangement by Paul Mertz)
10″-78 Columbia 36280
10″-78 Okeh 40871

10″-78 English Parlophone R-2465
10″-78 English Parlophone R-3419
10″-78 French Odeon 165171
10″-78 Swiss Parlophone PZ-11245
10″-78 German Odeon A-189128
12″-LP Sunbeam Bix Vol 4 "Sincerely, Bix Beiderbecke"
12″-LP English Parlophone EMI PMC-7113
12″-LP Italian Joker SM-3560 "Bixology Vol 4"
C-DISC Fr MOJ MJCD-6 "Bix Beiderbecke—Vol 2"
C-DISC English JSP CD-316 "Bix & Tram—Vol 1"

W-80392-A CLARINET MARMALADE

10″-78 Columbia 37804
10″-78 Okeh 40772
10″-78 Vocalion 3010
10″-78 Vocalion 4412
10″-78 Argentine Odeon 193001
10″-78 Argentine Odeon 194718
10″-78 Australian Parlophone A-7534
10″-78 German Odeon A-189019
10″-78 English Parlophone R-2304
10″-78 English Parlophone R-3323
10″-78 French Odeon 165093
10″-78 German Odeon A-286089
12″-LP Columbia GL-508
12″-LP Sunbeam Bix Vol 4 "Sincerely, Bix Beiderbecke"
12″-LP Czechoslovakian Supraphone 10153108
12″-LP English Parlophone EMI PMC-7064
12″-LP Italian Joker SM-3560 "Bixology Vol 4"
C-DISC Fr MOJ MJCD-6 "Bix Beiderbecke—Vol 2"
C-DISC English JSP CD-316 "Bix & Tram—Vol 1"
C-DISC Eng Pavilion/Pearl PAST-CD-9765 "The Genius Of Bix Beiderbecke"
C-DISC Eng Saville CDSVL-201 "The Beiderbecke File"

W-80393-B SINGIN' THE BLUES

10″-78 Brunswick 7703
10″-78 Columbia 37804
10″-78 Okeh 40822
10″-78 Argentine Odeon 295124
10″-78 Australian Odeon A-2409

10″-78 Australian Parlophone A-6235
10″-78 German Odeon A-189019
10″-78 English Parlophone R-1838
10″-78 English Parlophone R-3323
10″-78 French Odeon 165093
10″-78 German Odeon A-286085
10″-78 Italian Parlophone TT-9073
10″-78 Scandinavian Parlophone B-27597
12″-LP Columbia GL-508
12″-LP Sunbeam Bix Vol 4 ''Sincerely, Bix Beiderbecke''
12″-LP Czechoslovakian Supraphone 10153108
12″-LP Czechoslovakian Supraphone 0152111
12″-LP English Parlophone EMI PMC-7064
12″-LP Italian Joker SM-3560 ''Bixology Vol 4''
C-DISC Fr MOJ MJCD-6 ''Bix Beiderbecke—Vol 2''
C-DISC P-A CDD-490 ''Bix Beiderbecke—Jazz Me Blues''
C-DISC Eng JSP CD-316 ''Bix & Tram—Vol 1''
C-DISC Eng Saville CDSVL-201 ''The Beiderbecke File''

9 MAY 1927 (Mon): Columbia Record Co., New York, NY.
FRANK TRUMBAUER ORCHESTRA: Bix Beiderbecke (crt); Bill Rank (tbn); **Frank Trumbauer** (C-mel); Don Murray (clt/alto); Stanley ''Doc'' Ryker (alto); Irving Riskin (p); Eddie Lang (gtr); Chauncey Morehouse (dms).

W-81071-B **OSTRICH WALK**
(arrangement by Bill Challis)

10″-78 Columbia 37805
10″-78 Okeh 40822
10″-78 United Hot Clubs Of America 29
10″-78 Argentine Odeon 193015
10″-78 Argentine Odeon 194718
10″-78 Australian Parlophone A-7555
10″-78 German Odeon A-189048
10″-78 English Parlophone R-2492
10″-78 English Parlophone R-3349
10″-78 French Odeon 165126
10″-78 Italian Odeon A-2414
10″-78 Italian Parlophone B-12501

12″-LP Czechoslovakian Supraphone 10153108
12″ LP English Parlophone EMI PMC-7064
12″-LP Columbia GL-508
12″-LP Sunbeam Bix Vol 4 "Sincerely, Bix Beiderbecke"
12″-LP Italian Joker SM-3560 "Bixology Volume 4"
C-DISC Fr MOJ MJCD-6 "Bix Beiderbecke—Vol 2"
C-DISC Eng JSP CD-316 "Bix & Tram—Vol 1"
C-DISC Eng Saville CDSVL-201 "The Beiderbecke File"

W-81072-B **RIVERBOAT SHUFFLE**
(arrangement by Bill Challis)
10″-78 Columbia 37805
10″-78 Okeh 40822
10″-78 United Hot Clubs Of America 30
10″-78 Argentine Odeon 193015
10″-78 Argentine Odeon 194786
10″-78 Australian Parlophone A-7555
10″-78 German Odeon A-189048
10″-78 English Parlophone R-2492
10″-78 English Parlophone R-3349
10″-78 French Odeon 165126
10″-78 Italian Odeon A-2409
10″-78 Italian Parlophone B-12501
12″-LP Columbia GL-508
12″-LP Sunbeam Bix Vol 4 "Sincerely, Bix Beiderbecke"
12″-LP Czechoslovakian Supraphone 0152227
12″-LP English Parlophone EMI PMC-7064
12″-LP Italian Joker SM-3560 "Bixology Vol 4"
C-DISC Fr MOJ MJCD-6 "Bix Beiderbecke—Vol 2"
C-DISC Eng JSP CD-316 "Bix & Tram—Vol 1"
C-DISC Eng Pavilion/Pearl PAST-CD-9765 "The Genius Of Bix Beiderbecke"
C-DISC Eng Saville CDSVL-201 "The Bix Beiderbecke File"

13 MAY 1927 (Fri): Columbia Record Co., New York, NY.
FRANK TRUMBAUER ORCHESTRA: Bix Beiderbecke (crt); Bill Rank (tbn); **Frank Trumbauer** (C-mel); Jimmy Dorsey (clt/alto); Stanley "Doc" Ryker (alto); Irving Riskin (p); Eddie Lang (gtr); Chauncey Morehouse (dms).

W-81083-B I'M COMING, VIRGINIA
(arrangement by Irving Riskin)

10″-78 Brunswick 7703
10″-78 Columbia 36280
10″-78 Okeh 40843
10″-78 Australian Parlophone A-4923
10″-78 German Odeon A-189060
10″-78 English Parlophone R-2687
10″-78 English Parlophone R-3361
10″-78 French Odeon 165134
10″-78 Italian Odeon 193050
10″-78 Italian Odeon A-2354
12″-LP Columbia C-6179
12″-LP Columbia GL-508
12″-LP Columbia M-435
12″-LP Sunbeam Bix Vol 4 "Sincerely, Bix Beiderbecke"
12″-LP Czechoslovakian Supraphone 10153108
12″-LP English Parlophone EMI PMC-7064
12″-LP Italian Joker SM-3560 "Bixology Vol 4"
C-DISC Fr MOJ MJCD-6 "Bix Beiderbecke—Vol 2"
C-DISC P-A CDD-490 "Bix Beiderbecke—Jazz Me Blues"
C-DISC English JSP CD-316 "Bix & Tram—Vol 1"
C-DISC Eng Pavilion/Pearl PAST-CD-9765 "The Genius Of Bix Beiderbecke"
C-DISC Eng Saville CDSVL-201 "The Beiderbecke File"

W-81084-B 'WAY DOWN YONDER IN NEW ORLEANS
(arrangement by Don Murray)

10″-78 Columbia 37806
10″-78 Columbia 39581
10″-78 Okeh 40843
10″-78 Vocalion 3010
10″-78 Vocalion 4412
10″-78 Australian Parlophone A-4923
10″-78 German Odeon A-189060
10″-78 English Parlophone R-2687
10″-78 English Parlophone R-3361
10″-78 French Odeon 165134

10″-78 Italian Odeon 193050
10″-78 Italian Odeon 194865
10″-78 Italian Odeon A-2354
12″-LP Columbia GL-508
12″-LP Sunbeam Bix Vol 4 ''Sincerely, Bix Beiderbecke''
12″-LP English Parlophone EMI PMC-7064
12″-LP Italian Joker SM-3560 ''Bixology Vol 4''
C-DISC Fr MOJ MJCD-6 ''Bix Beiderbecke—Vol 2''
C-DISC English JSP CD-316 ''Bix & Tram—Vol 1''
C-DISC Eng Saville CDSVL-201 ''The Beiderbecke File''

Frank Trumbauer (C-mel); Bix Beiderbecke (p/crt); Eddie Lang (gtr):

W-81085-B FOR NO REASON AT ALL IN C
10″-78 Columbia 35667
10″-78 Okeh 40871 (as by ''Tram—Bix and Eddie'')
10″-78 Aus Par A-7459 (as by ''Tram, Bix & Lang'')
10″-78 German Odeon A-189128
10″-78 English Parlophone R-2532
10″-78 English Parlophone R-3419
10″-78 French Odeon 165171
10″-78 Italian Odeon A-2338
12″-LP Columbia GL-508
12″-LP Sunbeam Bix Vol 4 ''Sincerely, Bix Beiderbecke''
12″-LP Czechoslovakian Supraphone 10153108
12″-LP English Parlophone EMI PMC-7113
12″-LP Italian Joker SM-3560 ''Bixology Vol 4''
C-DISC Fr MOJ MJCD-6 ''Bix Beiderbecke—Vol 2''
C-DISC P-A CDD-490 ''Bix Beiderbecke—Jazz Me Blues''
C-DISC English JSP CD-316 ''Bix & Tram—Vol 1''

Some issues of FOR NO REASON AT ALL have Arthur Schutt's name on the label with a reference to ''their four piece orchestra''!

25 AUGUST 1927 (Thu): Okeh Record Co., New York, NY.
FRANK TRUMBAUER ORCHESTRA: Bix Beiderbecke (crt); Bill Rank (tbn); **Frank Trumbauer** (C-mel); Stanley

''Doc'' Ryker (alto); Don Murray (clt/bar-sx); Adrian Rollini (bs-sx); Irving Riskin (p); Eddie Lang (gtr); Chauncey Morehouse (dms).

W-81273-C **THREE BLIND MICE**
(arr by **Frank Trumbauer** and Bill Challis)

10″-78 Okeh 40903
10″-78 Temple 553
10″-78 Argentine Odeon 193090
10″-78 German Odeon A-189076
10″-78 English Parlophone R-105
10″-78 French Odeon 165223
10″-78 Scandinavian PO-56
12″-LP Sunbeam Bix Vol 4 ''Sincerely, Bix Beiderbecke''
12″-LP English Parlophone EMI PMC-7064
12″-LP Italian Joker SM-3560 ''Bixology Vol 4''
C-DISC Fr MOJ MJCD-6 ''Bix Beiderbecke—Vol 2''
C-DISC English JSP CD-316 ''Bix & Tram—Vol 1''
C-DISC Eng Saville CDSVL-201 ''The Bix Beiderbecke File''

W-81274-B **BLUE RIVER**
(vc by Seger Ellis)

10″-78 Okeh 40879
10″-78 Argentine Odeon 193090
10″-78 Australian Parlophone A-2335
10″-78 English Parlophone R-3440
10″-78 German Parlophone A-4904
10″-78 Italian Odeon 165173
12″-LP Sunbeam Bix Vol 4 ''Sincerely, Bix Beiderbecke''
12″-LP Cch Supraphone 10152748 (as ''Sautna Reka'')
12″-LP English Parlophone EMI PMC-7064
12″-LP Italian Joker SM-3560 ''Bixology Vol 4''
C-DISC Fr MOJ MJCD-6 ''Bix Beiderbecke— Vol 2''
C-DISC English JSP CD-316 ''Bix & Tram—Vol 1''

W-81275-D **THERE'S A CRADLE IN CAROLINE**
(vc by Seger Ellis)

10″-78 Okeh 40879
10″-78 Argentine Odeon 193101
10″-78 Australian Parlophone A-2335

10″-78 English Parlophone R-3440
10″-78 German Parlophone A-4904
10″-78 Italian Odeon 165173
12″-LP Sunbeam Bix Vol 4 "Sincerely, Bix Beiderbecke"
12″-LP English Parlophone EMI PMC-7064
12″-LP Italian Joker SM-3560 "Bixology Vol 4"
C-DISC Fr MOJ MJCD-6 "Bix Beiderbecke—Vol 2"
C-DISC English JSP CD-316 "Bix & Tram—Vol 1"

17 SEPTEMBER 1927 (Sat): Okeh Record Co., New York, NY.
Frank Trumbauer (C-mel); Bix Beiderbecke (p/crt); Eddie Lang (gtr).

W-81450-A WRINGIN' AND TWISTIN'
10″-78 Columbia 37806
10″-78 Okeh 40916 (as by "Tram—Bix and Lang")
10″-78 Vocalion 3150
10″-78 Argentine Odeon 193104
10″-78 English Parlophone R-2532
10″-78 English Parlophone R-3504
10″-78 Italian Odeon A-2338
12″-LP Columbia GL-508
12″-LP Sunbeam Bix Vol 5 "Sincerely, Bix Beiderbecke"
12″-LP Czechoslovakian Supraphone 10153108
12″-LP English Parlophone EMI PMC-7113
12″-LP Italian Joker SM-3561 "Bixology Vol 5"
C-DISC English JSP CD-316 "Bix & Tram—Vol 1"

Some issues have Arthur Schutt's name on the label with a reference to "their four piece orchestra"!

28 SEPTEMBER 1927 (Wed): Okeh Record Co., New York, NY.
FRANK TRUMBAUER ORCHESTRA: Bix Beiderbecke (crt); Bill Rank (tbn); **Frank Trumbauer** (C-mel); Bobby Davis (alto); Don Murray (clt/bar-sx); Adrian Rollini (bs-sx); Joe Venuti (vn); Frank Signorelli (p); Eddie Lang (gtr); Chauncey Morehouse (dms).

W-81488-A HUMPTY DUMPTY
(arrangement by Walter "Fud" Livingston)

10″-78 Okeh 40926
10″-78 German Odeon A-189075
10″-78 English Parlophone R-3464
10″-78 Italian Parlophone TT-9073
12″-LP Sunbeam Bix Vol 5 "Sincerely, Bix Beiderbecke"
12″-LP English Parlophone EMI PMC-7064
12″-LP Italian Joker SM-3561 "Bixology Vol 5"
C-DISC English JSP CD-316 "Bix & Tram—Vol 1"

W-81489-B KRAZY KAT
(arrangement by Don Murray)
10″-78 Okeh 40903
10″-78 German Odeon A-189076
10″-78 English Parlophone R-105
10″-78 French Odeon 193101
10″-78 Italian Odeon 165223
10″-78 Scandinavian Parlophone PO-56
12″-LP Sunbeam Bix Vol 5 "Sincerely, Bix Beiderbecke"
12″-LP English Parlophone EMI PMC-7064
12″-LP Italian Joker SM-3561 "Bixology Vol 5"
C-DISC English JSP CD-316 "Bix & Tram—Vol 1"

W-81490-B THE BALTIMORE
10″-78 Okeh 40926
10″-78 German Odeon A-189075
10″-78 English Parlophone R-3464
12″-LP Sunbeam Bix Vol 5 "Sincerely, Bix Beiderbecke"
12″-LP English Parlophone EMI PMC-7064
12″-LP Italian Joker SM-3561 "Bixology Vol 5"
C-DISC English JSP CD-316 "Bix & Tram—Vol 1"

30 SEPTEMBER 1927 (Fri): Okeh Record Co., New York, NY. FRANK TRUMBAUER ORCHESTRA: Bix Beiderbecke (crt); Sylvester Ahola (tpt); Bill Rank (tbn); **Frank Trumbauer** (C-mel); Bobby Davis (alto); Don Murray (clt/bar-sx); Adrian Rollini (bs-sx); Joe Venuti (vn); Frank Signorelli (p); Eddie Lang (gtr); Chauncey Morehouse (dms).

W-81499-A JUST AN HOUR OF LOVE
(vc by Irving Kaufman)

10″-78 Okeh 40912 (as by ''Benny Meroff & His Orchestra'')
10″-78 French Odeon A-189070
10″-78 English Parlophone R-3463
10″-78 German Parlophone A-4912
12″-LP Sunbeam Bix Vol 5 ''Sincerely, Bix Beiderbecke''
12″-LP English Parlophone EMI PMC-7064
12″-LP Italian Joker SM-3561 ''Bixology Vol 5''
C-DISC English JSP CD-316 ''Bix & Tram—Vol 1''

W-81500-A I'M WONDERIN' WHO
(vc by Irving Kaufman)
10″-78 Okeh 40912 (as by ''Benny Meroff & His Orchestra'')
10″-78 French Odeon A-189070
10″-78 English Parlophone R-3463
10″-78 German Parlophone A-4912
12″-LP Sunbeam Bix Vol 5 ''Sincerely, Bix Beiderbecke''
12″-LP English Parlophone EMI PMC-7064
12″-LP Italian Joker SM-3561 ''Bixology Vol 5''
C-DISC English JSP CD-316 ''Bix & Tram—Vol 1''

Most issued recordings carry ''Frank Trumbauer and his Orchestra'' or ''Frank Trumbauer's Augmented Orchestra.''

25 OCTOBER 1927 (Tue): Columbia Record Co., New York, NY.

FRANK TRUMBAUER ORCHESTRA: Bix Beiderbecke (crt); Bill Rank (tbn); **Frank Trumbauer** (C-mel); Don Murray, Charles ''Pee Wee'' Russell (clts/ten-sxs); Adrian Rollini (bs-sx); Joe Venuti (vn); Frank Signorelli (p); Eddie Lang (gtr); Chauncey Morehouse (dms).

W-81570-C CRYING ALL DAY
10″-78 Columbia 35956
10″-78 Hot Jazz Clubs Of America 601
10″-78 Okeh 40966
10″-78 Argentine Odeon 193217
10″-78 Australian Parlophone A-6449

10″-78 German Odeon A-189125
10″-78 English Parlophone R-2176
10″-78 French Odeon 279713
10″-78 Italian Odeon 165291
12″-LP Columbia GL-508
12″-LP Sunbeam Bix Vol 6 ''Sincerely, Bix Beiderbecke''
12″-LP Czechoslovakian Supraphone 10153108
12″-LP English Parlophone EMI PMC-7064
12″-LP Italian Joker SM-3562 ''Bixology Vol 6''
C-DISC English JSP CD-317 ''Bix & Tram—Vol 2''

W-81571-B A GOOD MAN IS HARD TO FIND
10″-78 Columbia 35956
10″-78 Hot Jazz Clubs Of America 601
10″-78 Okeh 40966
10″-78 Argentine Odeon 193217
10″-78 German Odeon A-189125
10″-78 English Parlophone R-3489
10″-78 Italian Odeon 165291
12″-LP Columbia GL-508
12″-LP Sunbeam Bix Vol 6 ''Sincerely, Bix Beiderbecke''
12″-LP Czechoslovakian Supraphone 10153108
12″-LP English Parlophone EMI PMC-7064
12″-LP Italian Joker SM-3562 ''Bixology Vol 6''
C-DISC P-A CDD-490 ''Bix Beiderbecke—Jazz Me Blues''
C-DISC English JSP CD-317 ''Bix & Tram—Vol 2''

26 OCTOBER 1927 (Wed): Okeh Record Co., New York, NY.
FRANK TRUMBAUER ORCHESTRA: Bix Beiderbecke (crt); Unidentified (tpt); Bill Rank (tbn); **Frank Trumbauer** (C-mel/alto); Charles ''Pee Wee'' Russell (clt/ten-sx); Max Farley (alto); Adrian Rollini (bs-sx); Arthur Schutt (p); Carl Kress (gtr); Jack Hansen (tuba); Chauncey Morehouse (dms).

W-81575-3 SUGAR
(vc by Ed Macy and John Ryan)
10″-78 Okeh 40938
10″-78 Arg Od 193134 (as by ''Russell Gray & His Orch.'')
10″-78 Ger Od A-189092 (as by ''Russell Gray & His Orch.'')
10″-78 English Parlophone R-3489

12″-LP Sunbeam Bix Vol 6 "Sincerely, Bix Beiderbecke"
12″-LP English Parlophone EMI PMC-7113
12″-LP Italian Joker SM-3562 "Bixology Vol 6"
C-DISC English JSP CD-317 "Bix & Tram—Vol 2"

The identity of the trumpet player may never be known. Often suggested was Edgar James "Boe" Ashford, but this was dismissed when Steve LaVere played the recording for him on 7 March 1991. "Boe" said the record did not contain his brother (as often suggested) or himself. He identified the solo as Bix. This would seem to agree with past opinions expressed by Bill Rank and Chauncey Morehouse. Morehouse felt it was Bix "playing under duress."

The initial release of Okeh 40938 is credited as by "Russell Gray and His Orchestra." Later issues credited "Frank Trumbauer and his Orchestra."

W-81576 **DO YOU MEAN IT?**
(vc by Les Reis)
Rejected.

9 JANUARY 1928 (Mon): Okeh Record Co., New York, NY.
FRANK TRUMBAUER ORCHESTRA: Bix Beiderbecke (crt); Charles Margulis (tpt); Bill Rank, Miff Mole (tbns); **Frank Trumbauer** (C-mel/alto); Jimmy Dorsey (clt/alto); Chester Hazlett (alto); Rube Crozier (ten-sx/bar-sx); Min Leibrook (bs-sx); Lennie Hayton (p); Carl Kress (gtr); Harold McDonald (dms).
Mole on W-400002 only.

W-400002 **TWO LETTERS FROM DIXIE**
Rejected.

W-400003-B **THERE'LL COME A TIME**
10″-78 Okeh 40979
10″-78 Argentine Odeon 193128
10″-78 Australian Parlophone A-6311
10″-78 Australian Parlophone A-7692

10″-78 German Odeon A-189143
10″-78 English Parlophone DP-255
10″-78 English Parlophone R-2097
10″-78 English Parlophone R-3526
10″-78 Italian Odeon 165330
10″-78 Italian Odeon A-2399
12″-LP Columbia GL-508
12″-LP Sunbeam Bix Vol 7 "Sincerely, Bix Beiderbecke"
12″-LP English Parlophone EMI PMC-7100
12″-LP Italian Joker SM-3563 "Bixology Vol 7"
C-DISC English JSP CD-317 "Bix & Tram—Vol 2"
C-DISC Ger Bauer ADD-3520 "Bix Beiderbecke—Wa-Da-Da"

W-400004-C **JUBILEE**
(arrangement by Willard Robison)
10″-78 Okeh 41044 (released 15 June 1928)
10″-78 English Parlophone R-161
10″-78 English Parlophone R-2054
10″-78 German Odeon A-286091
10″-78 Italian Odeon 165539
12″-LP Sunbeam Bix Vol 7 "Sincerely, Bix Beiderbecke"
12″-LP English Parlophone EMI PMC-7200
12″-LP Italian Joker SM-3563 "Bixology Vol 7"
C-DISC English JSP CD-317 "Bix & Tram—Vol 2"

Personnel are identified from Trumbauer's ledgers. Payment made to Bix of $50; Chet Hazlett, $30; and the rest of the musicians $25 each.

20 JANUARY 1928 (Fri): Columbia Record Co., New York, NY. FRANK TRUMBAUER ORCHESTRA: Bix Beiderbecke (crt); Charles Margulis (tpt); Bill Rank (tbn); **Frank Trumbauer** (C-mel/alto); Jimmy Dorsey (clt/alto); Chester Hazlett (alto); Adrian Rollini (bs-sx); Matty Malneck (vn); Lennie Hayton (p); Carl Kress (gtr); Harold McDonald (dms).

W-400033 **FROM MONDAY ON**
Rejected. Not remade.

The Columbia/Okeh ledgers are incomplete. Bing Crosby is a possible vocalist on FROM MONDAY ON.

W-400034-A **MISSISSIPPI MUD**
(vc by Bing Crosby and **Frank Trumbauer**)

10″-78 Biltmore 1029
10″-78 Okeh 40979
10″-78 Argentine Odeon 193128
10″-78 Australian Odeon A-2399
10″-78 Australian Parlophone A-6311
10″-78 Australian Parlophone A-7692
10″-78 German Odeon A-189143
10″-78 English Parlophone DP-255
10″-78 English Parlophone R-2097
10″-78 English Parlophone R-3526
10″-78 German Odeon 031816
10″-78 Italian Odeon 165330
10″-78 Norwegian ND-5040-S
12″-LP Columbia GL-508
12″-LP Sunbeam Bix Vol 7 ''Sincerely, Bix Beiderbecke''
12″-LP Czechoslovakian Supraphone 0152227
12″-LP Eng Jz JZ-3 ''The Chronological Bing Crosby''
12″-LP English Parlophone EMI PMC-7100
12″-LP Italian Joker SM-3564 ''Bixology Vol 8''
12″-LP Polish Poljazz Z-SX-0662
C-DISC CBS SP-A2-201 ''The Crosby Story—Vol 2''
C-DISC P-A CDD-490 ''Bix Beiderbecke—Jazz Me Blues''
C-DISC English JSP CD-317 ''Bix & Tram—Vol 2''
C-DISC Eng Pavilion/Pearl Past-CD-9765 ''The Genius Of Bix Beiderbecke''

The Columbia/Okeh ledgers are incomplete.

Trumbauer's ledgers do not list the titles, only ''Okeh date,'' and the personnel. Bix was paid $50; Hazlett, $30; and the rest of the musicians, $25 each.

Edgar Jackson was rumored to have a test pressing of the first title, but all trace of the test has now vanished. A rumor also exists that copies of Australian Parlophone A-6311 were pressed using copies of matrix W-400033 instead of W-400034-A. This has never been confirmed.

3 APRIL 1928 (Tue): Okeh Record Co., New York, NY.
FRANK TRUMBAUER ORCHESTRA: Bix Beiderbecke (crt); Charles Margulis (tpt); Bill Rank (tbn); **Frank Trumbauer** (C-mel/alto); Irving Friedman (clt/alto); Chester Hazlett (alto); Min Leibrook (bs-sx); Lennie Hayton (p); Eddie Lang (gtr); Harold McDonald (dms).

W-400188-A **OUR BUNGALOW OF DREAMS**
(vc by Irving Kaufman as ''Noel Taylor'')
10″-78 Okeh 41019
10″-78 Temple 542
10″-78 Argentine Odeon 193172
10″-78 German Odeon A-189148
10″-78 English Parlophone R-142
10″-78 German Odeon 04074
10″-78 German Parlophone A-4543
10″-78 Italian Odeon 165362
12″-LP Sunbeam Bix Vol 11 ''Sincerely, Bix Beiderbecke''
12″-LP English Parlophone EMI PMC-7100
12″-LP Italian Joker SM-3565 ''Bixology Vol 9''
C-DISC English JSP CD-317 ''Bix & Tram—Vol 2''

W-400189-B **LILA**
(vc by by Irving Kaufman as ''Noel Taylor'')
10″-78 Okeh 41019
10″-78 Temple 542
10″-78 Argentine Odeon 193172
10″-78 German Odeon A1-189148
10″-78 English Parlophone R-141
10″-78 Italian Odeon 165362
12″-LP Sunbeam Bix Vol 11 ''Sincerely, Bix Beiderbecke''
12″-LP English Parlophone EMI PMC-7100

12″-LP Italian Joker SM-3565 "Bixology Vol 9"
C-DISC English JSP CD-317 "Bix & Tram—Vol2"

Apparently Okeh Records used the name "Noel Taylor" to disguise several singers for a variety of unknown reasons.

Personnel are identified from Trumbauer's ledger. Payments for the full band are not shown. Only those for Irving Friedman, $20; Bill Rank and Harold McDonald, $23 each.

10 APRIL 1928 (Tue): Okeh Record Co., New York, NY.
FRANK TRUMBAUER ORCHESTRA: Bix Beiderbecke (crt); Charles Margulis (tpt); Bill Rank (tbn); **Frank Trumbauer** (C-mel/alto); Irving Friedman (clt/ten-sx); Chester Hazlett (alto); Min Leibrook (bs-sx); Lennie Hayton (p); Eddie Lang (gtr); Harold McDonald (dms).

W-400603-B **BORNEO**
(vc by Harold "Scrappy" Lambert)
(arrangement by Bill Challis)

10″-78 Columbia 20674
10″-78 Okeh 41039 (released 5 June 1928)
10″-78 Argentine 193190
10″-78 German Odeon A-189159
10″-78 Eng Par R-203 (as by "The Goofus Five & Their Orchestra")
10″-78 Italian Odeon 165360
12″-LP Columbia GL-509
12″-LP Sunbeam Bix Vol 11 "Sincerely, Bix Beiderbecke"
12″-LP English Parlophone EMI PMC-7100
12″-LP Italian Joker SM-3566 "Bixology Vol 10"
C-DISC English JSP CD-317 "Bix & Tram—Vol 2"

W-400604-C **MY PET**
(vc by Harold "Scrappy" Lambert)
(arrangement by Bill Challis)

10″-78 Okeh 41039 (released 5 June 1928)
10″-78 Argentine Odeon 193190

10″-78 German Odeon A-189159
10″-78 English Parlophone R-141
10″-78 Italian Odeon 165360
12″-LP Sunbeam Bix Vol 11 "Sincerely, Bix Beiderbecke"
12″-LP English Parlophone EMI PMC-7100
12″-LP Italian Joker SM-3566 "Bixology Vol 10"
C-DISC English JSP CD-317 "Bix & Tram—Vol 2"

Personnel are identified from Trumbauer's ledger. Full payments to musicians not listed. Irving Friedman and Harold McDonald received $23 each. Chester Hazlett was paid $85 for both the last date and this one.

5 JULY 1928 (Thu): Okeh Record Co., New York, NY.
FRANK TRUMBAUER ORCHESTRA: Bix Beiderbecke (crt); Bill Rank (tbn); Irving Friedman (clt/ten-sx); **Frank Trumbauer** (C-mel); Chester Hazlett (alto); Min Leibrook (bs-sx); Roy Bargy or Lennie Hayton (p); George Rose (gtr); Harry Gale (dms).

W-400989-C **BLESS YOU SISTER**
(vc by **Frank Trumbauer**, Dee Orr, Harry Barris, and Marlin Hurt)

10″-78 Okeh 41100 (released 25 September 1928)
10″-78 Argentine Odeon 193236
10″-78 Australian Parlophone A-3992
10″-78 German Odeon A-189190
10″-78 English Parlophone R-1882
10″-78 French Parlophone 22006
10″-78 French Parlophone 25293
10″-78 Italian Odeon 165488
10″-78 Italian Parlophone B-27597
10″-78 Italian Parlophone TT-9073
12″-LP Columbia GL-509
12″-LP Sunbeam Bix Vol 14 "Sincerely, Bix Beiderbecke"
12″-LP English Parlophone EMI PMC-7100
12″-LP Italian Joker SM-3567 "Bixology Vol 11"

W-400990-B **DUSKY STEVEDORE**
(vc by **Frank Trumbauer**, Dee Orr, Harry Barris, and Marlin Hurt)

10″-78 Okeh 41100 (released 25 September 1928)
10″-78 Argentine Odeon 193236
10″-78 German Odeon A-189190
10″-78 English Parlophone R-265
10″-78 French Parlophone 22006
10″-78 Italian Odeon 165488
10″-78 Italian Parlophone B-27597
12″-LP Sunbeam Bix Vol 14 "Sincerely, Bix Beiderbecke"
12″-LP English Parlophone EMI PMC-7100
12″-LP Italian Joker SM-3567 "Bixology Vol 11"

Trumbauer identified the vocalists in a September 1952 correspondence. The "back and forth" is between Marlin Hurt and Frank. The ledger does not list payments to musicians.

20 SEPTEMBER 1928 (Thu): Okeh Record Co., New York, NY. FRANK TRUMBAUER ORCHESTRA: Bix Beiderbecke (crt); Bill Rank (tbn); Irving Friedman (clt/ten-sx); **Frank Trumbauer** (C-mel/alto); Min Leibrook (bs-sx); Roy Bargy (p); Wilbur Hall (gtr); Lennie Hayton (dms).

W-401133-B **TAKE YOUR TOMORROW** (AND GIVE ME TODAY)
(vc by **Frank Trumbauer** and Marlin Hurt)
10″-78 Columbia 37807
10″-78 Okeh 41145 (released 15 December 1928)
10″-78 Argentine Odeon 193297
10″-78 Australian Parlophone A-7534
10″-78 Dutch Columbia DCH-339
10″-78 German Odeon A-189210
10″-78 English Parlophone R-265
10″-78 English Parlophone R-2564
10″-78 German Odeon 031816
10″-78 Italian Odeon 165526
10″-78 Spanish Odeon 182473
12″-LP Columbia GL-509
12″-LP Sunbeam Bix Vol 16 "Sincerely, Bix Beiderbecke"
12″-LP English Parlophone EMI PMC-7100
12″-LP Italian Joker SM-3568 "Bixology Vol 12"

C-DISC Ger Bauer ADD-3520 ''Bix Beiderbecke—Wa-Da-Da''

W-401134-C LOVE AFFAIRS
(vc by Marlin Hurt)
10″-78 Biltmore 1103
10″-78 Okeh 41145 (released 15 December 1928)
10″-78 Argentine Odeon 193288
10″-78 German Odeon A-189210
10″-78 Italian Odeon 165526
10″-78 Spanish Odeon 182473
12″-LP Sunbeam Bix Vol 16 ''Sincerely, Bix Beiderbecke''
12″-LP English Parlophone EMI PMC-7100
12″-LP Italian Joker SM-3568 ''Bixology Vol 12''

W-401135 SENTIMENTAL BABY
(vc by Marlin Hurt)
Rejected. Remade 5 October 1928.

Trumbauer's ledgers show payments made to Bix of $55 ($70 less a $15 advance); Roy Bargy, $30; Bill Rank, $50. The rest of the musicians were paid $25 each. It is curious that Lennie Hayton was paid $50 but his instrument is not listed. It has been suggested that he played drums for this session. It has also been suggested that Smith Ballew is the vocalist. He was not!

5 OCTOBER 1928 (Fri): Okeh Record Co., New York, NY.
FRANK TRUMBAUER ORCHESTRA: Bix Beiderbecke (crt); Charles Margulis (tpt); Bill Rank (tbn); Irving Friedman (clt/ten-sx); **Frank Trumbauer** (C-mel/alto); Rube Crozier (bsn/bar-sx); Lennie Hayton (p); Wilbur Hall (gtr); unidentified (dms).

W-401195-B THE LOVE NEST
(vc by Charles Gaylord)
10″-78 Decatur 501
10″-78 English Parlophone R-2645
12″-LP English Parlophone EMI PMC-7100
12″-LP Sunbeam Bix Vol 16 ''Sincerely, Bix Beiderbecke''
12″-LP Italian Joker SM-3568 ''Bixology Vol 12''

W-401196-C **THE JAPANESE SANDMAN**
(vc by **Frank Trumbauer**)
10″-78 Biltmore 1103
10″-78 Australian Parlophone A-6449
10″-78 English Parlophone R-2176
10″-78 English Parlophone R-2645
12″-LP Sunbeam Bix Vol 16 ''Sincerely, Bix Beiderbecke''
12″-LP English Parlophone EMI PMC-7100
12″-LP Italian Joker SM-3568 ''Bixology Vol 12''

W-401197-A **HIGH ON A HILLTOP**
(vc by Charles Gaylord)
10″-78 Okeh 41128 (released 15 November 1928)
10″-78 Argentine Odeon 193254
10″-78 Australian Parlophone A-2682
10″-78 German Odeon A-189241
10″-78 English Parlophone R-2644
10″-78 German Parlophone A-4573
12″-LP Sunbeam Bix Vol 16 ''Sincerely, Bix Beiderbecke''
12″-LP English Parlophone EMI PMC-7100
12″-LP Italian Joker SM-3568 ''Bixology Vol 12''

W-401198-A **SENTIMENTAL BABY**
(vc by Charles Gaylord)
10″-78 Decatur 501
10″-78 Okeh 41128 (released 15 November 1928)
10″-78 Argentine Odeon 193254
10″-78 German Odeon A-189241
10″-78 English Parlophone R-298
10″-78 German Parlophone A-4573
12″-LP Sunbeam Bix Vol 16 ''Sincerely, Bix Beiderbecke''
12″-LP Columbia JZ1 ''I Like Jazz''
12″-LP English Parlophone EMI PMC-7100
12″-LP Italian Joker SM-3568 ''Bixology Vol 12''
12″-LP Jugoslavian Radio-Televizije Beograd LPV-4301-Ph.

W-401198-B **SENTIMENTAL BABY**
(vc by **Frank Trumbauer**)
Unissued.

W-401198-C **SENTIMENTAL BABY**
(vc by **Frank Trumbauer**)
Unissued.

The personnel for the October 8, 1928 session are identified from Trumbauer's ledger. The drummer's name is illegible—looks like ''kits.'' Payments were made to Bix, $70; Bill Rank, Lennie Hayton, Irving Friedman, $50 each. The rest of the musicians were paid $25 each. Gaylord was also paid $25. Charles Gaylord always signed his name John, but was always referred to as Charles.

8 MARCH 1929 (Fri): Okeh Record Co., New York, NY.
FRANK TRUMBAUER ORCHESTRA: Bix Beiderbecke, Andy Secrest (crts); Bill Rank (tbn); **Frank Trumbauer** (C-mel/alto); Irving Friedman (clt/ten-sx); Chet Hazlett (alto); Min Leibrook (bs-sx); Matty Malneck (vn); Lennie Hayton (p); Eddie Lang (gtr); Stan King (dms).

W-401703-B **FUTURISTIC RHYTHM**
(vc by **Frank Trumbauer**)
(arrangement by Matty Malneck)
10″-78 Okeh 41209 (released 15 April 1929)
10″-78 Argentine Odeon 193308
10″-78 English Parlophone R-2625
10″-78 Italian Odeon 165685
10″-78 Italian Parlophone B-27002
12″-LP Sunbeam Bix Vol 17 ''Sincerely, Bix Beiderbecke''
12″-LP English Parlophone EMI PMC-7113
12″-LP Italian Joker SM-3569 ''Bixology Vol 13''

W-401704-D **RAISIN' THE ROOF**
(arrangement by Matty Malneck)
10″-78 Okeh 41209 (released 15 April 1929)
10″-78 Argentine Odeon 193308
10″-78 English Parlophone R-2644
10″-78 Italian Odeon 165685
10″-78 Italian Parlophone B-27002
12″-LP Sunbeam Bix Vol 17 ''Sincerely, Bix Beiderbecke''

12″-LP English Parlophone EMI PMC-7113
12″-LP Italian Joker SM-3569 "Bixology Vol 13"

17 APRIL 1929 (Wed): Okeh Record Co., New York, NY.
FRANK TRUMBAUER ORCHESTRA: Bix Beiderbecke, Andy Secrest (crts); Bill Rank (tbn); **Frank Trumbauer** (C-mel/alto); Irving Friedman (clt/ten-sx); Chet Hazlett (alto); Min Leibrook (bs-sx); Matty Malneck (vn); Roy Bargy (p); Eddie Lang (gtr); Stan King (dms).

W-401809-B **LOUISE**
(vc by Smith Ballew)
(arrangement by Matty Malneck)
10″-78 Okeh 41231 (released 25 May 1929)
10″-78 Parlophone PNY-41231 (released 25 May 1929)
10″-78 Argentine Odeon 193316
10″-78 German Odeon A-189282
10″-78 German Odeon A-189287
10″-78 Eng Par E-6209(as by "Will Parry's Orchestra")
10″-78 German Parlophone A-4948
10″-78 Italian Odeon 165736
10″-78 Italian Parlophone B-27029
12″-LP Sunbeam Bix Vol 17 "Sincerely, Bix Beiderbecke"
12″-LP English Parlophone EMI PMC-7113
12″-LP Italian Joker SM-3569 "Bixology Vol 13"

On LOUISE, Bix has an 8-bar solo; last chorus has Secrest (lead) and Bix (4-bar obligato).

W-401810-C **WAIT TILL YOU SEE "MA CHERIE"**
(vc by Smith Ballew)
(arrangement by Matty Malneck)
10″-78 Okeh 41231
10″-78 Parlophone PNY-41231 (as by "Joe Curran's Band")
10″-78 Argentine Odeon 193316
10″-78 German Odeon A-189282
10″-78 German Odeon A-189287
10″-78 English Parlophone R-398
10″-78 German Parlophone A-4948

10″-78 Italian Odeon 165736
10″-78 Italian Parlophone B-27029
12″-LP Sunbeam Bix Vol 17 ''Sincerely, Bix Beiderbecke''
12″-LP English Parlophone EMI PMC-7113
12″-LP Italian Joker SM-3569 ''Bixology Vol 13''

W-401811-C **BABY WON'T YOU PLEASE COME HOME**
(vc by **Frank Trumbauer**)
10″-78 Clarion 5469-C (as by ''Tennessee Music Men'')
10″-78 Columbia 37807
10″-78 Har 1422-H (as by ''Tennessee Music Men'')
10″-78 Odeon ONY-41286
10″-78 Okeh 41286 (released 25 September 1929)
10″-78 Vel 2529-V (as by ''Tennessee Music Men'')
10″-78 Dutch Columbia DCH-339
10″-78 English Parlophone R-1978
10″-78 French Odeon 025412
10″-78 French Parlophone 22523
10″-78 German Odeon A-286087
10″-78 Italian Odeon 165843
10″-78 Italian Odeon A-2336
12″-LP Columbia CL-5469-C
12″-LP Columbia GL-509
12″-LP Sunbeam Bix Vol 17 ''Sincerely, Bix Beiderbecke''
12″-LP English Parlophone EMI PMC-7113
12″-LP Italian Joker SM-3569 ''Bixology Vol 13''

On BABY WON'T YOU PLEASE COME HOME, Secrest has 16-bars in verse; Bix (first fill); Secrest (other fills); Bix 16-bar solo; Secrest lead (last chorus); Bix 16-bar solo; Secrest lead (last chorus); and, Bix muted obligato.

30 APRIL 1929 (Tue): Okeh Record Co., New York, NY.
FRANK TRUMBAUER ORCHESTRA: Bix Beiderbecke, Andy Secrest (crts); Charles Margulis (tpt); Bill Rank (tbn); **Frank Trumbauer** (C-mel/alto); Irving Friedman (clt/ten-sx); Chet Hazlett (alto); Min Leibrook (bs-sx); Mischa Russell, Kurt Dieterle, Matty Malneck (vns); Lennie Hayton (p); Eddie Lang (gtr); Stan King (dms).

Margulis on W-401841-C only; violins on W-401840-B only.

W-401480-B **NO ONE CAN TAKE YOUR PLACE**
(vc by Jack Fulton)
(arrangement by Matty Malneck)
10″-78 German Odeon A-189259
10″-78 English Parlophone R-420
10″-78 French Parlophone 22430
12″-LP Sunbeam Bix Vol 17 "Sincerely, Bix Beiderbecke"
12″-LP English Parlophone EMI PMC-7113
12″-LP Italian Joker SM-3569 "Bixology Vol 13"

W-401841-C **I LIKE THAT**
(arrangement by Lennie Hayton)
10″-78 Okeh 41286 (released 25 September 1929)
10″-78 Odeon ONY-41286
10″-78 English Parlophone R-714
10″-78 French Parlophone 22523
10″-78 German Odeon A-286019
10″-78 Italian Odeon 165843
10″-78 Italian Odeon A-2318
12″-LP Sunbeam Bix Vol 17 "Sincerely, Bix Beiderbecke"
12″-LP English Parlophone EMI PMC-7113
12″-LP Italian Joker SM-3569 "Bixology Vol 13"
C-DISC Ger Bauer ADD-3520 "Bix Beiderbecke—Wa-Da-Da"

15 MAY 1929 (Wed): Columbia Record Co., New York, NY.
FRANK TRUMBAUER ORCHESTRA: Andy Secrest (crt); Charles Margulis, Harry "Goldie" Goldfield (tpts); Bill Rank (tbn); Irving Friedman (ten-sx/clt); **Frank Trumbauer** (C-mel/alto); Chet Hazlett (alto); Min Leibrook (bs-sx); Lennie Hayton (p); Eddie Lang (gtr); George Marsh (dms).

W-148537-3 **WHAT A DAY!**
(arrangement by Lennie Hayton)
10″-78 Columbia 1861-D (as by "Mason-Dixon Orchestra")
12″-LP Broadway 104

W-148538-4 **ALABAMY SNOW**
(arrangement possibly by Lennie Hayton)
10″-78 Columbia 1861-D (as by "Mason-Dixon Orchestra")
12″-LP Broadway 104

21 MAY 1929 (Tue): Okeh Record Co., New York, NY.
FRANK TRUMBAUER ORCHESTRA: Andy Secrest (crt); Charles Margulis (tpt); Bill Rank (tbn); **Frank Trumbauer** (C-mel/alto); Irving Friedman (clt/ten-sx); Chet Hazlett (alto); Min Leibrook (bs-sx); Joe Venuti (vn); Lennie Hayton (p/cel); Eddie Lang (gtr); George Marsh (dms).

W-401952-C **NOBODY BUT YOU**
(vc by Smith Ballew)
10″-78 Okeh 41252 (released 5 July 1929)
10″-78 German Odeon A-189276
10″-78 Eng Ariel 4445 (as by "Ariel Dance Orch.")
10″-78 English Parlophone R-434
10″-78 French Odeon 238942
10″-78 French Parlophone 22407
10″-78 Italian/Scandinavian B-27028

W-401953-B **GOT A FEELING FOR YOU** (GOT A FEELIN' FOR YOU)
(vc by Smith Ballew)
10″-78 Okeh 41252 (released 5 July 1929)
10″-78 German Odeon A-189276
10″-78 English Parlophone R-434
10″-78 French Odeon 238942
10″-78 French Parlophone 22407
10″-78 Italian/Scandinavian B-27028
10″-78 Spanish Odeon 182754

22 MAY 1929 (Wed): Okeh Record Co., New York, NY.
FRANK TRUMBAUER ORCHESTRA: Andy Secrest (crt); Charles Margulis (tpt); Bill Rank (tbn); **Frank Trumbauer** (C-mel/alto); Irving Friedman (clt/ten-sx); Chet Hazlett (alto); Min Leibrook (bs-sx); Joe Venuti (vn); Lennie Hayton (p/cel); Eddie Lang (gtr); George Marsh (dms).

W-401961-B SHIVERY STOMP

10″-78 Okeh 41268 (released 15 August 1929)
10″-78 Dutch Odeon A-189272
10″-78 Dutch Odeon A-189303
10″-78 English Parlophone R-511
10″-78 French Odeon 238080
10″-78 German Odeon A-286012
10″-78 Italian Odeon A-2320
10″-78 Italian/Scandinavian B-27061

W-401962-C REACHING FOR SOMEONE
(vc by Smith Ballew)

10″-78 Okeh 41268 (released 15 August 1929)
10″-78 Dutch Odeon A-189259
10″-78 English Parlophone R-420
10″-78 French Odeon 238080
10″-78 French Parlophone 22430
10″-78 German Odeon A-286012
10″-78 Italian/Scandinavian B-27061

18 SEPTEMBER 1929 (Wed): Okeh Record Co., New York, NY. FRANK TRUMBAUER ORCHESTRA: Andy Secrest (crt); Charles Margulis (tpt); Bill Rank (tbn); **Frank Trumbauer** (C-mel/alto); Irving Friedman (clt/ten-sx); Chet Hazlett (alto); Min Leibrook (bs-sx); Joe Venuti (vn); Lennie Hayton (p/cel); Eddie Lang (gtr); George Marsh (dms).

W-402963-C LOVE AIN'T NOTHIN' BUT THE BLUES
(vc by Smith Ballew)

10″-78 Okeh 41301 (released 1 November 1929)
10″-78 Parlophone PNY-41301 (as by ''Joe Curran's Band'')
10″-78 Eng Ariel 4537 (as by ''Ariel Dance Orch.'')
10″-78 English Parlophone R-644
10″-78 English Parlophone R-2541
10″-78 French Odeon 165912
10″-78 French Parlophone 22565
10″-78 German Parlophone A-4968
12″-LP Sunbeam Bix Vol 19 ''Sincerely, Bix Beiderbecke''

W-402964-A HOW AM I TO KNOW?
(vc by Smith Ballew)
10″-78 Okeh 41301 (released 1 November 1929)
10″-78 Parlophone PNY-41301 (as by "Joe Curran's Band")
10″-78 Eng Ariel 4537 (as by "Ariel Dance Orch.")
10″-78 English Parlophone R-618
10″-78 French Odeon 165912
10″-78 French Parlophone 22565
10″-78 German Odeon A-286013
10″-78 Italian Odeon A-2327

10 OCTOBER 1929 (Thu): Okeh Record Co., New York, NY.
FRANK TRUMBAUER ORCHESTRA: Andy Secrest (crt); Charles Margulis (tpt); Bill Rank (tbn); **Frank Trumbauer** (C-mel/alto); Irving Friedman (clt/ten-sx); Chet Hazlett (alto); Min Leibrook (bs-sx); Joe Venuti, Matty Malneck, Kurt Dieterle (vns); Lennie Hayton (p/cel); Hoagy Carmichael (p); Eddie Lang (gtr); George Marsh (dms).
Carmichael on W-403051 only.

W-403050-B TURN ON THE HEAT
(vc by Smith Ballew and Joe Venuti)
10″-78 Okeh 41313 (released 1 December 1929)
10″-78 Par PNY-41313 (as by "Joe Curran's Band")
10″-78 Argentine Odeon 193426
10″-78 Australian Parlophone A-2916
10″-78 Dutch Odeon A-189302
10″-78 English Ariel 4483
10″-78 French Odeon A-221187
10″-78 English Parlophone R-499
10″-78 French Parlophone 22628
10″-78 Italian Odeon 165881

W-403050-C TURN ON THE HEAT
(vc by Smith Ballew and Joe Venuti)
10″-78 Parlophone PNY-41313

Some discographies suggest a third voice on W-403050 may be Hoagy Carmichael's.

W-403051-B MANHATTAN RAG
12″-LP Broadway 104

W-403051-C MANHATTAN RAG
10″-78 Okeh 41330 (released 15 December 1929)
10″-78 Argentine Odeon 193497
10″-78 Australian Parlophone A-6235
10″-78 English Parlophone R-1978
10″-78 German Odeon 025412
10″-78 German Odeon A-286087
10″-78 Italian Odeon 165949
10″-78 Italian Odeon A-2334
12″-LP English Parlophone EMI PMC-7113

W-403052-B SUNNY SIDE UP
(vc by Smith Ballew)
10″-78 Okeh 41313 (released 1 December 1929)
10″-78 Par PNY-41313 (as by ''Joe Curran's Band'')
10″-78 Argentine Odeon 193246
10″-78 Australian Parlophone A-2916
10″-78 Dutch Odeon A-189302
10″-78 English Ariel 4483
10″-78 English Parlophone R-499
10″-78 French Odeon A-221187
10″-78 French Parlophone 22628
10″-78 Italian Odeon 165881
10″-78 Italian/Scandinavian B-27129

15 OCTOBER 1929 (Fri): Okeh Record Co., New York, NY.
FRANK TRUMBAUER ORCHESTRA: Andy Secrest (crt); Charles Margulis (tpt); Bill Rank (tbn); **Frank Trumbauer** (C-mel/alto); Irving Friedman (clt/ten-sx); Chet Hazlett (alto); Min Leibrook (bs-sx); Joe Venuti, Matty Malneck, Kurt Dieterle (vns); Lennie Hayton (p); Eddie Lang (gtr); George Marsh (dms).

W-403068-A GREAT DAY!

W-403068-B GREAT DAY!

W-403068-C GREAT DAY!
(vc by Smith Ballew)
Rejected. Remade 19 October 1929.

19 OCTOBER 1929 (Tues): Okeh Record Co., New York, NY.
FRANK TRUMBAUER ORCHESTRA: Andy Secrest (crt); Charles Margulis (tpt); Bill Rank (tbn); **Frank Trumbauer** (Cmel/alto); Irving Friedman (clt/ten-sx); Chet Hazlett (alto); Min Leibrook (bs-sx); Joe Venuti, Matty Malneck, Kurt Dieterle (vns); Lennie Hayton (p); Eddie Lang (gtr); George Marsh (dms).

W-403068-D **GREAT DAY!**

W-403068-E **GREAT DAY!**
(vc by Smith Ballew)
Rejected. Never remade.

W-403082-A **MY SWEETER THAN SWEET**
(vc by Smith Ballew)
10″-78 Okeh 41326 (released 1 December 1926)
10″-78 Argentine Odeon 193515
10″-78 Australian Parlophone A-2915
10″-78 Dutch Odeon A-189298
10″-78 English Parlophone R-583
10″-78 English Parlophone R-2564
10″-78 Italian Odeon 165882

W-403083-B **WHAT WOULDN'T I DO FOR THAT MAN?**
(vc by Smith Ballew)
10″-78 Okeh 41330 (released 15 December 1929)
10″-89 Argentine Odeon 193515
10″-78 English Parlophone R-583
10″-78 Italian Odeon 165949

8 MAY 1930 (Thu): Okeh Record Co., New York, NY.
FRANK TRUMBAUER ORCHESTRA: Andy Secrest (crt); Harry ''Goldie'' Goldfield (tpt); Bill Rank (tbn); **Frank Trumbauer** (C-mel/alto); Chester Hazlett (alto); Charles Strickfaden (bar-sx); Min Leibrook (bs-sx); Matty Malneck (vn); Roy Bargy (p); Eddie Lang (gtr); George Marsh (dms).

W-404007-C **HAPPY FEET**
(vc by Smith Ballew)
10″-78 Odeon ONY-36091

10″-78 Okeh 41421 (released 10 June 1930)
10″-78 Par PNY-34084 (as by "Tom Barker & His Orch.")
10″-78 Argentine Odeon 193495
10″-78 English Parlophone R-701
10″-78 French Odeon 238286
10″-78 German Odeon A-286018
12″-LP Sunbeam Bix Vol 19 "Sincerely, Bix Beiderbecke"

W-404007-D **HAPPY FEET**
(vc by Smith Ballew)
10″-78 Okeh 41421 (released 10 June 1930)

W-404008-A **I LIKE TO DO THINGS FOR YOU**
(vc by Mildred Bailey)
10″-78 Odeon ONY-36091
10″-78 Okeh 41421
10″-78 Par PNY-34085 (as by "Tom Barker & His Orch.")
10″-78 Argentine Odeon 193495
10″-78 English Parlophone R-702
10″-78 French Odeon 238286

10 May 1930 (Sat): Okeh Record Co., New York, NY.
FRANK TRUMBAUER ORCHESTRA: Andy Secrest (crt); Harry "Goldie" Goldfield (tpt); Bill Rank (tbn); **Frank Trumbauer** (C-mel/alto); Chester Hazlett (alto); Charles Strickfaden (bar-sx); Min Leibrook (bs-sx); Matty Malneck (vn); Roy Bargy (p); Eddie Lang (gtr); George Marsh (dms).

W-404009-D **GET HAPPY**
(clt and vc by **Frank Trumbauer**)
10″-78 Okeh 41431 (released 25 July 1930)
10″-78 English Parlophone R-2625
10″-78 French Odeon 238121

W-404010-B **DEEP HARLEM**
(clt, crt and vc by **Frank Trumbauer**)
(arrangement by Matty Malneck)
10″-78 Clarion 5461-C (as by "Tennessee Music Men")
10″-78 Har 1415-H (as by "Tennessee Music Men")
10″-78 Okeh 41431 (released 25 July 1930)
10″-78 Vel 2521-V (as by "Tennessee Music Men")
10″-78 Australian Parlophone A-6266

10″-78 English Parlophone R-1946
10″-78 French Odeon 238121
10″-78 French Odeon A-272014

22 JULY 1930 (Tue): Okeh Record Co., New York, NY.
FRANK TRUMBAUER ORCHESTRA: Andy Secrest (crt); Nat Natoli, Harry "Goldie" Goldfield (tpts); Bill Rank, Jack Fulton (tbns); **Frank Trumbauer** (C-mel/alto); Walter "Fud" Livingston (clt/ten-sx); Chet Hazlett (alto); Min Leibrook (bs-sx); Matty Malneck (vn); Roy Bargy (p/cel); Eddie Lang (gtr); George Marsh (dms).

W-404268-D **WHAT'S THE USE?**
(vc by Jack Fulton)
10″-78 Odeon ONY-36128
10″-78 Okeh 41437 (released 25 August 1930)
10″-78 Par PNY-34119 (as by "Tom Barker & His Orch.")
10″-78 English Parlophone R-1013
10″-78 French Odeon 238187
10″-78 German Odeon A-286045

W-404269-C **HITTIN' THE BOTTLE**
(vc by Jack Fulton and **Frank Trumbauer**)
10″-78 Odeon ONY-36128
10″-78 Okeh 41437 (released 25 August 1930)
10″-78 Par PNY-34120 (as by "Tom Barker & His Orch.")
10″-78 English Parlophone R-795
10″-78 French Odeon 238187
10″-78 German Odeon A-286024
10″-78 Italian Odeon A-2322

8 SEPTEMBER 1930 (Mon): Okeh Record Co., New York, NY.
FRANK TRUMBAUER ORCHESTRA: Andy Secrest (crt); Nat Natoli, Harry "Goldie" Goldfield (tpts); Bill Rank (tbn); **Frank Trumbauer** (C-mel/alto); Walter "Fud" Livingston (clt/ten-sx); Chet Hazlett (alto); Min Leibrook (bs-sx); Matty Malneck (vn); Roy Bargy (p/cel); Eddie Lang (gtr); George Marsh (dms).

W-404433-B **BYE-BYE BLUES**
(vc by Harold "Scrappy" Lambert)

10″-78 Okeh 41450 (released 10 October 1930)
10″-78 English Parlophone R-796
10″-78 French Odeon 238228
10″-78 French Parlophone 80447
10″-78 German Odeon A-286025
10″-78 Italian Odeon A-2326

W-404434-B CHOO CHOO
10″-78 Clarion 5467-C (as by "Tennessee Music Men")
10″-78 Har 1420-H (as by "Tennessee Music Men")
10″-78 Okeh 41450 (released 10 October 1930)
10″-78 Vel 2527-V (as by "Tennessee Music Men")
10″-78 Czechoslovakian Brunswick A-9633
10″-78 English Parlophone R-821
10″-78 French Odeon 183240 (as EL TREN)
10″-78 French Odeon 238228
10″-78 German Odeon A-286026
10″-78 Italian Odeon A-2323
10″-78 Italian Parlophone TT-9010
10″-78 Italian/Scandinavian Parlophone B-27294

10 APRIL 1931 (Fri): Studio "B"; Brunswick Record Co., Chicago, IL. First title 1:00-2:35 PM; second title 2:35-3:45 PM; Third title 3:45-4:45 PM.

FRANK TRUMBAUER ORCHESTRA: Andy Secrest (crt); Nat Natoli (tpt); Bill Rank (tbn); **Frank Trumbauer** (C-mel/alto); James "Rosy" McHargue (clt/alto); Matty Malneck (vn); Dave Rose (p); Jack Tobin (bjo); Dan Gaebe (tuba); Bob Conzelman (dms).
THE KING'S JESTERS: John Ravenscroft, Ira Barstow, George Howard.

C-7693 GEORGIA ON MY MIND
(vc by The King's Jesters)
Rejected. Remade 24 June 1931.

C-7693-A GEORGIA ON MY MIND
(vc by The King's Jesters)
10″-78 Brunswick Test Pressing
Rejected. Remade 24 June 1931.

C-7693-B GEORGIA ON MY MIND

C-7693-C **GEORGIA ON MY MIND**
(vc by The King's Jesters)
Rejected. Remade 24 June 1931.

C-7694 **BASS DRUM DAN**

C-7694-A **BASS DRUM DAN**

C-7694-B **BASS DRUM DAN**

C-7694-C **BASS DRUM DAN**
(vc by The King's Jesters)
10″-78 English Brunswick 01225 (released early 1932)
12″-LP TOM LP-26

The Brunswick files do not indicate which matrix/take was issued.

C-7695 **HONEYSUCKLE ROSE**

C-7695-A **HONEYSUCKLE ROSE**

C-7695-B **HONEYSUCKLE ROSE**

C-7695-C **HONEYSUCKLE ROSE**
(vc by The King's Jester)
10″-78 Brunswick 6093 (released 14 May 1931)

The Brunswick files do not indicate which matrix/take was issued. The selection was issued on Brunswick 6093 on the West Coast, but then it was recalled and Brunswick 6093 was assigned to Duke Ellington's CREOLE RHAPSODY, parts 1 and 2.

The band was paid $200 for the session. Individual payments not listed.

24 JUNE 1931 (Wed): Studio "B"; Brunswick Record Co., Chicago, IL.
First title 10:00 AM-12:15 PM; second title 12:15-1:30 PM; Third title 2:00-3:00 PM; fourth title 3:00-4:00 PM.

FRANK TRUMBAUER ORCHESTRA: Andy Secrest (crt); Nat Natolie (tpt); Bill Rank (tbn); **Frank Trumbauer** (C-mel /alto); James "Rosy" McHargue (clt/alto); Matty Malneck (vn); Dave Rose (p); Jack Tobin (bjo); Dan Gaebe (bs-sx); Bob Conzelman (dms).
THE KING'S JESTERS: John Ravenscroft, Ira Barstow, George Howard.

C-7875 **IN THE MERRY MONTH OF MAYBE**

C-7875-A **IN THE MERRY MONTH OF MAYBE**

C-7875-B **IN THE MERRY MONTH OF MAYBE**
(vc by The King's Jesters)
10″-78 Brunswick 6146 (released 31 August 1931)
10″-78 English Brunswick 01261
12″-LP TOM LP-26

The Brunswick files do not indicate which matrix/take was issued.

C-7876 **IN THE MERRY MONTH OF MAYBE**
(vc by The King's Jesters)
10″-78 German Brunswick A-9110

C-7877 **CRAZY QUILT**

C-7877-A **CRAZY QUILT**

C-7877-B **CRAZY QUILT**

C-7877-C **CRAZY QUILT**
(vc by The King's Jesters)
10″-78 Brunswick 6146 (released 31 August 1931)
10″-78 English Brunswick 01261
12″-LP TOM LP-26

The Brunswick files do not indicate which matrix/take was issued.

C-7878 **CRAZY QUILT**
(vc by The King's Jesters)
10″-78 German Brunswick A-9110

C-7879 **GEORGIA ON MY MIND**

C-7879-A **GEORGIA ON MY MIND**

C-7879-b **GEORGIA ON MY MIND**
(vc by Art Jarrett and The King's Jesters)
10″-78 Brunswick 6159 (released 17 September 1931)
10″-78 English Brunswick 01192
10″-78 German Brunswick A-9116
12″-LP TOM LP-26

The Brunswick files do not indicate which matrix/take was issued.

C-7880 **HONEYSUCKLE ROSE**

C-7880-A **HONEYSUCKLE ROSE**

C-7880-B **HONEYSUCKLE ROSE**
(vc by Art Jarrett and The King's Jesters)
10″-78 Brunswick 6159 (released 17 September 1931)
10″-78 English Brunswick 01192
10″-78 German Brunswick A-9116
12″-LP TOM LP-26

The Brunswick files do not indicate which matrix/take was issued.

The band was paid $250. Individual payments unknown.

5 APRIL 1932 (Tue): Columbia Record Co., New York, NY.
FRANK TRUMBAUER ORCHESTRA: Andy Secrest (crt); Nat Natoli, Harry "Goldie" Goldfield (tpts); Hal Matthews, Jack Fulton, Bill Rank (tbns); **Frank Trumbauer**, Charles Strickfaden, Chet Hazlett, John Cordaro (reeds); Kurt Dieterle, Mischa Russell, Matty Malneck, John Bowman (vns); Roy Bargy (p); Carl Kress (gtr); Pierre Olker (st-bs); Red Norvo (xyl); Herb Quigley (dms).
THE NITECAPS: Unidentified trio.

255004-1 Sizzling One-Step Medley:
a. **DINAH**
(vc by Johnny Mercer amd The Nitecaps)
b. **MY HONEY'S LOVIN' ARMS**
(vc by Johnny Mercer)
c. **NOBODY'S SWEETHEART**
(vc by The Nitecaps)

10″-78 Columbia 18002-D (released 5 May 1932)
12″-LP TOM LP-26

255005-2 Medley of Isham Jones Hits
a. **ON THE ALAMO**
b. **SWINGING DOWN THE LANE**
(vc by Helen Rowland)
c. **I'LL SEE YOU IN MY DREAMS**
(vc by Johnny Blake)

10″-78 Columbia 18002-D (released 5 May 1932)
12″-LP TOM LP-26

17 AUGUST 1932 (Wed): Columbia Record Co., Chicago, IL.
FRANK TRUMBAUER ORCHESTRA: Max Connett, Vance ''Chink'' Rice (tpts); Hal Matthews (tbn); **Frank Trumbauer** (C-mel/alto); Gale Stout, Malcolm Elstad (altos); Harold Jones (ten-sx); Herm Crone (p); Craig Leitch (gtr); Cedric Spring (gtr/vn/acc); Cappy Kaplan (gtr/vn); Charles McConnell (st-bs); LeRoy Buck (dms).
THE THREE SPOOKS: Cedric Spring, Harold Jones, LeRoy Buck.

152280-2 **CINDERELLA'S WEDDING DAY**
(vc by LeRoy Buck)

10″-78 Columbia 2897-D (released 28 February 1934)
10″-78 English Columbia CB-542
12″-LP TOM LP-26

152281-2 **I THINK YOU'RE A HONEY**
(vc by The Three Spooks)

10″-78 Columbia 2710-D (released 15 October 1932)
10″-78 Australian Columbia DO-824
12″-LP TOM LP-26

152282-2 **BUSINESS IN Q**
10″-78 Columbia 2710-D (released 15 October 1932)
10″-78 English Columbia CB-542
12″-LP TOM LP-26

152283-2 **BASS DRUM DAN**
(vc by The Three Spooks)
10″-78 Columbia 2897-D (released 28 February 1934)
10″-78 English Columbia CB-580
12″-LP TOM LP-26

152284-2 **THE NEWEST ST. LOUIS BLUES** (aka ST. LOUIS BLUES)
(arrangement by Cedric Spring)
(vc by LeRoy Buck, in pig Latin, and the ensemble)
10″-78 Columbia 2729-D (released 23 December 1932)
10″-78 English Columbia CB-580 (as ST. LOUIS BLUES)
10″-78 English Columbia DB-867
12″-LP TOM LP-26

152285-2 **BETWEEN THE DEVIL AND THE DEEP BLUE SEA**
(arrangement by Cedric Spring)
(vc by LeRoy Buck)
10″-78 Columbia 2729-D (released 23 December 1932)
10″-78 English Columbia DB-5007
12″-LP TOM LP-26

Some discographies show a take -1 being released for matrix numbers 152282, 152283, and 152284. Columbia Records states that only take -2 was issued on each recording. Columbia Records further claims that the date of 17 August is correct. The previously listed date of 17 October, shown in other discographies, is in error.

12 JANUARY 1934 (Fri): Brunswick Record Co., New York, NY.

FRANK TRUMBAUER ORCHESTRA: Nat Natoli, Charlie Teagarden (tpts); Jack Teagarden (tbn); Bennie Bonacio,

Charles Strickfaden, Jack Cordaro, **Frank Trumbauer** (reeds); Mischa Russell (vn); Roy Bargy (p); Carl Kress (gtr); Artie Miller (st-bs); Herb Quigley (dms).

B-14586-A BREAK IT DOWN
10″-78 Brunswick 4929
10″-78 Brunswick 6763
10″-78 Brunswick 6912
10″-78 English Brunswick 01812
10″-78 French Brunswick A-500399
10″-78 German Brunswick A-9555
12″-LP Epic SN-6044
C-DISC Teagarden TCD-112291

B-14587-A JUBA DANCE
(arrangement by Russ Case)
10″-78 Brunswick 6763
10″-78 German Brunswick A-9555

B-14588 HOW AM I TO KNOW?
Rejected 24 February 1934. Not remade.

Personnel identified from Trumbauer's ledger. Cash received, $500. Trumbauer was paid $180; Roy Bargy, $35; other 10 musicians each received $28.

23 FEBRUARY 1934 (Fri): Brunswick Record Co., New York, NY.

FRANK TRUMBAUER ORCHESTRA: Nat Natoli, Charlie Teagarden (tpts); Jack Teagarden (tbn); Bennie Bonacio, Charles Strickfaden, Jack Cordaro, **Frank Trumbauer** (reeds); Matt Malneck, Mischa Russell (vn); Roy Bargy (p); Carl Kress (gtr); Artie Miller (st-bs); Herb Quigley (dms).

B-14848-A CHINA BOY
10″-78 Brunswick 4929
10″-78 Brunswick 6912
10″-78 Australian Columbia DO-1253
10″-78 Czechoslovakian Brunswick A-9633
10″-78 English Brunswick 01812
10″-78 French Brunswick A-500423

10″-78 German Brunswick A-9596
12″-LP Epic SN-6044
C-DISC Teagarden TCD-112291

B-14849-A **EMALINE**
(vc by Jack Teagarden)
10″-78 Brunswick 6788
10″-78 Australian Columbia DO-1253
10″-78 Czechoslovakian Brunswick A-9594
10″-78 English Brunswick 01767
10″-78 French Brunswick A-500424
10″-78 German Brunswick A-9594
C-DISC Teagarden TCD-112291

B-14850-A **IN A MIST**
(arrangement by Russ Case)
10″-78 Brunswick 6997
10″-78 English Brunswick 01979
10″-78 French Brunswick A-500423
10″-78 German Brunswick A-9596
C-DISC Teagarden TCD-112291

B-14851-A **'LONG ABOUT MIDNIGHT**
(vc by Jack Teagarden)
10″-78 Brunswick 6788
10″-78 English Brunswick 01767
10″-78 French Brunswick A-500424
10″-78 German Brunswick A-9594
C-DISC Teagarden TCD-112291

Personnel identified from Trumbauer's ledger. Cash received $448. Trumbauer paid $113; Roy Bargy, $35; Mischa Russell, $20; other 10 musicians each paid $28.

20 NOVEMBER 1934 (Tue): Victor Studio 2, 9:30-12:30 AM; Victor Record Co., New York, NY.

FRANK TRUMBAUER ORCHESTRA: Bunny Berigan, Nat Natoli (tpts); Glenn Miller (tbn); **Frank Trumbauer** (C-mel); Artie Shaw (clt/alto); Jack Shore (alto); Larry Binyon (ten-sx); Roy Bargy (p); Lionel Hall (gtr); Artie Bernstein (st-bs); Jack Williams (dms).

86219-1 **BLUE MOON**
(vc by Dick Robertson)
10″-78 Victor 24812
10″-78 English HMV BD-119
10″-78 French HMV K-7454
10″-78 Italian HMV GW-1098

86220-1 **PLANTATION MOODS**
10″-78 Victor 24834
10″-78 English HMV BD-158
10″-78 Swedish HMV X-4454

86221-1 **DOWN T' UNCLE BILL'S**
(vc by Dick Robertson and **Frank Trumbauer**)
10″-78 Victor 24812
10″-78 Australian HMV EA-1459
10″-78 English HMV BD-119
10″-78 Italian HMV GW-1098

86222-1 **TROUBLED**
10″-78 Decatur 512
10″-78 Victor 24834
10″-78 English HMV BD-158
10″-78 Swedish HMV X-4454

The band was paid $540. Individual payments are not listed in ledger.

29 JANUARY 1936 (Wed): Brunswick Record Co., New York, NY.

FRANK TRUMBAUER ORCHESTRA: Ed Wade, Charlie Teagarden (tpts); Jack Teagarden (tbn); Johnny Mince (clt); Jack Cordaro, Mutt Hayes, **Frank Trumbauer** (sxs); Roy Bargy (p); George Van Eps (gtr); Artie Miller (st-bs); Stan King (dms).

B-18600-1 **FLIGHT OF THE HAYBAG**
10″-78 Brunswick 7629
10″-78 Australian Columbia DO-1514
10″-78 English Brunswick 02197

10″-78 French Brunswick A-500638
10″-78 German Brunswick A-9988
C-DISC Teagarden TCD-112291

B-18601-1 BREAKIN' IN A PAIR OF SHOES
10″-78 Brunswick 7613
10″-78 Australian Columbia DO-1551
10″-78 French Brunswick A-500639
10″-78 German Brunwwick A-9979
10″-78 Japanese Lucky 60153
C-DISC Teagarden TCD-112291

B-18602-1 ANNOUNCER'S BLUES
10″-78 German Brunswick A-9988

B-18602-2 ANNOUNCER'S BLUES
10″-78 Brunswick 5030
10″-78 Brunswick 7629
10″-78 Australian Columbia DO-1514
10″-78 English Brunswick 02197
10″-78 French Brunswick A-500638
C-DISC Teagarden TCD-112291

5 FEBRUARY 1936 (Wed): Brunswick Record Co., New York, NY.

FRANK TRUMBAUER ORCHESTRA: Ed Wade, Charlie Teagarden (tpts); Jack Teagarden (tbn); Johnny Mince (clt); Jack Cordaro, Mutt Hayes, **Frank Trumbauer** (sxs); Roy Bargy (p); George Van Eps (gtr); Artie Miller (st-bs); Stan King (dms).

B-18630-1 I HOPE GABRIEL LIKES MY MUSIC
(vc by Jack Teagarden and **Frank Trumbauer**)
10″-78 Brunswick 7613
10″-78 Australian Columbia DO-1551
10″-78 French Brunswick A-500639
10″-78 German Brunswick A-9979
10″-78 Japanese Lucky 60190
12″-LP Epic SN-6044
C-DISC Teagarden TCD-112291

27 APRIL 1936 (Mon): Brunswick Record Co., New York, NY.
FRANK TRUMBAUER ORCHESTRA: Ed Wade, Charlie Teagarden (tpts); Jack Teagarden (tbn); Artie Shaw (clt); Jack Cordaro, Mutt Hayes, **Frank Trumbauer** (sxs); Roy Bargy (p); George Van Eps (gtr); Artie Miller (st-bs); Stan King (dms).

B-19113-1 **SOMEBODY LOVES ME**
(vc by Jack Teagarden)
10″-78 Brunswick 7665
10″-78 Australian Columbia DO-1572
10″-78 English Brunswick 02232
10″-78 French Brunswick A-500666
10″-78 German Brunswick A-81033
12″-LP Epic SN-6044
C-DISC Teagarden TCD-112291

B-19114-1 **THE MAYOR OF ALABAM'**
(vc by Jack Teagarden & ensemble)
10″-78 Brunswick 7663
10″-78 Australian Columbia DO-1571
10″-78 English Brunswick 02232
10″-78 French Brunswick A-500665
12″-LP Epic SN-6044
C-DISC Teagarden TCD-112291

B-19115-2 **AIN'T MISBEHAVIN'**
(vc by Jack Teagarden)
10″-78 Brunswick 7665
10″-78 Australian Columbia DO-1572
10″-78 French Brunswick A-500666
10″-78 German Brunswick A-81033
10″-78 Japanese Lucky 60153
12″-LP Epic SN-6044
C-DISC Teagarden TCD-112291

B-19116-1 **'S WONDERFUL**
10″-78 Brunswick 7663
10″-78 Australian Columbia DO-1571
10″-78 French Brunswick A-500665
10″-78 Japanese Lucky 60175
12″-LP Epic SN-6044
C-DISC Teagarden TCD-112291

15 JUNE 1936 (Mon): Brunswick Record Co., New York, NY.
FRANK TRUMBAUER ORCHESTRA: Russ Case, Charles Teagarden (tpts); Jack Teagarden (tbn); Matty Matlock (clt); Jack Cordaro, Eddie Miller, **Frank Trumbauer** (reeds); Roy Bargy (p); Carl Kress (gtr); Artie Miller (st-bs); Ray Bauduc (dms).

B-19442-1 **I'M AN OLD COWHAND**
(vc by Jack Teagarden)
10″-78 Brunswick 7687
10″-78 Australian Columbia DO-1590
10″-78 French Brunswick A-500683
10″-78 Japanese Lucky 60164
12″-LP Epic SN-6044
C-DISC Teagarden TCD-112291

B-19442-2 **I'M AN OLD COWHAND**
(vc by Jack Teagarden)
10″-78 Brunswick Test Pressing (marked ''best vc'')
C-DISC Teagarden TCD-112291

B-19443-1 **DIGA DIGA DOO**
10″-78 Brunswick 7687
10″-78 Australian Columbia DO-1590
10″-78 French Brunswick A-500683
10″-78 Japanese Lucky 60164
C-DISC Teagarden TCD-112291

B-19443-2 **DIGA DIGA DOO**
10″-78 Brunswick Test Pressing
C-DISC Teagarden TCD-112291

JANUARY 1937: Radio program, from the Hickory House, WEAF/NBC, New York, NY.
FRANK TRUMBAUER ORCHESTRA: Johnny ''Scat'' Davis (tpt); Ford Leary (tbn); **Frank Trumbauer** (C-mel/alto); Min Leibrook (bs-sx); Adele Girard (h); Herm Crone (p); Stan King (dms).

Set 1: **NAGASAKI**
(vc by Frances Lane)

THE PEANUT VENDOR
(unidentified vcist, sung in Spanish)

Set 2: **CHINA BOY**

Medley:
a. **BLUE SKIES**
b. **I NEVER KNEW**

THE SHEIK OF ARABY
(vc by Johnny ''Scat'' Davis)

SINGIN' THE BLUES (closing theme)
(Trumbauer reprises his 1927 Okeh Record solo)

3 FEBRUARY 1937 (Wed): Radio Program, from the Hickory House, WEAF/NBC, New York, NY.

FRANK TRUMBAUER ORCHESTRA: Al Stuart (tpt); Ford Leary (tbn); **Frank Trumbauer** (C-mel/alto); Min Leibrook (bs-sx); Adele Girard (h); Herm Crone (p); Stan King (dms).

SINGIN' THE BLUES (opening theme)
(Trumbauer reprises his 1927 Okeh Record solo)
12″-LP IAJRC LP-21

JAZZ ME BLUES
12″-LP IAJRC LP-21

YOU TOOK ADVANTAGE OF ME
12″-LP IAJRC LP-21

I'M COMING VIRGINIA
12″-LP IAJRC LP-21

THE SHEIK OF ARABY
12″-LP IAJRC LP-21

SINGIN' THE BLUES (closing theme)
(Trumbauer reprises his 1927 Okeh Record solo)
12″-LP IAJRC LP-21

The Modernaires were announced for the program, but did not appear.

10 FEBRUARY 1937 (Wed): Radio Program, from Hickory House, WEAF/NBC, New York, NY.

FRANK TRUMBAUER ORCHESTRA: Al Stuart (tpt); Ford Leary (tbn); **Frank Trumbauer** (C-mel/alto); Min Leibrook (bs-sx); Adele Girard (h); Herm Crone (p); Stan King (dms).
THE MODERNAIRES (Guests): Hal Dickinson, Chuck Goldstein, Bill Conway, Ralph Brewster.

SINGIN' THE BLUES (opening theme)
(Trumbauer reprises his 1927 Okeh Record solo)

MR. GHOST GOES TO TOWN

Medley:
a. **OH, SAY, CAN YOU SWING**
b. **THIS YEAR'S KISSES**
c. **TIL THE POPPIES BLOOM**
d. **FORTY-SECOND STREET**
(vc by Sammy Cahn, with Saul Chaplin, P)

WILLIAM TELL OVERTURE

'WAY DOWN YONDER IN NEW ORLEANS
(vc by The Modernaires)

NAGASAKI
(vc by Frances Lane)

SINGIN' THE BLUES (closing theme)
(Trumbauer reprises his 1927 Okeh Record solo)

12 FEBRUARY 1937 (Fri): Radio Program, from Hickory House, WEAF/NBC, New York, NY.

FRANK TRUMBAUER ORCHESTRA: Al Stuart (tpt); Ford Leary (tbn); **Frank Trumbauer** (C-mel/alto); Min Leibrook (bs-sx): Adele Girard (h); Herm Crone (p); Stan King (dms).
THE MODERNAIRES (Guests): Hal Dickinson, Chuck Goldstein, Bill Conway, Ralph Brewster.

SINGIN' THE BLUES (opening theme)
(Trumbauer reprises his 1927 Okeh Record solo)

I'D CLIMB THE HIGHEST MOUNTAIN

SLUMMIN' ON PARK AVENUE
(vc by The Modernaires)

BLUE ROOM

MY BLUE HEAVEN
(vc by Sammy Cahn)

FORTY-SECOND STREET

OH-YAZOO
(featuring Adele Girard)

I'M AN OLD COWHAND

SENTIMENTAL OVER YOU

SINGIN' THE BLUES (closing theme)
(Trumbauer reprises his 1927 Okeh Record solo)

15 DECEMBER 1937 (Wed): 10:00 AM-5:00 PM; Los Angeles, CA.

FRANK TRUMBAUER ORCHESTRA: Emanuel ''Mannie'' Klein, Al Famularo, Bruce Hudson (tpts); Joe Yukl (tbn); **Frank Trumbauer**, Phil Shuken, Jimmy Oliver, Leonard Kavash, Len Conn (reeds); Al Goering, Howard Davis (ps); Dick Roberts (gtr); Russ Morhoff (st-bs); Ward Archer (dms).

PMS-09878-1 ITCHOLA
12″-LP IAJRC LP-13
16″-ET Standard A-1485
16″-ET Standard A-1488
16″-ET Standard Z-119

IN A MIST
16″-ET Standard A-1485

16″-ET Standard A-1488
16″-ET Standard Z-119

TEMPO TAKES A HOLIDAY
12″-LP IAJRC LP-13
16″-ET Keystone 44 (as by "Frank Trombar & His Orch.")
16″-ET Keystone 119 (as by "Frank Trombar & His Orch.")
16″-ET Standard A-1485
16″-ET Standard A-1488
16″-ET Standard Z-119

BODY AND SOUL
16″-ET Standard A-1485
16″-ET Standard A-1488
16″-ET Standard Z-119

PMS-09879-1 WILDCAT
16″-ET Standard A-1405
16″-ET Standard A-1408
16″-ET Standard Z-118

TIGER RAG FANTASY
16″-ET Keystone Z-118 (as by "Frank Trombar & His Orch.")
16″-ET Standard A-1405
16″-ET Standard A-1408
16″-ET Standard Z-118

PUT ON YOUR OLD GRAY BONNET
16″-ET Keystone 428 (as by "Frank Trombar & His Orch.")
16″-ET Standard A-1405
16″-ET Standard A-1408
16″-ET Standard Z-118

BIG BUTTER AND EGG MAN
12″-LP IAJRC LP-13
16″-ET Standard A-1405
16″-ET Standard A-1408

PMS-09880-1 BOUNCING BALL
16″-ET Standard A-1489
16″-ET Standard A-1492
16″-ET Standard Z-119

NO RETARD

16″-ET Keystone 44 (as by "Frank Trombar & His Orch.")
16″-ET Keystone 119 (as by "Frank Trombar & His Orch.")
16″-ET Standard A-1489
16″-ET Standard A-1492
16″-ET Standard Z-119

SPAGENZE (as **HEAT WAVE** on Keystone)

16″-ET Keystone 44 (as by "Frank Trombar & His Orch.")
16″-ET Keystone 119 (as by "Frank Trombar & His Orch.")
16″-ET Standard A-1489
16″-ET Standard A-1492
16″-ET Standard Z-119

CHANSONETTE

16″-ET Standard A-1489
16″-ET Standard A-1492
16″-ET Standard Z-119

PMS-09881-1 **YOU'RE A SWEETHEART** (vc by Phil Stuart)

16″-ET Standard A-1397
16″-ET Standard A-1400
16″-ET Standard Y-108

I HIT A NEW HIGH

16″-ET Standard A-1397
16″-ET Standard A-1400
16″-ET Standard Y-1408

JUST A SWEET OLD GENT AND A QUAINT OLD LADY (vc by Phil Stuart)

16″-ET Standard A-1397
16″-ET Standard A-1400
16″-ET Standard Y-108

I DOUBLE DARE YOU

16″-ET Standard A-1397
16″-ET Standard A-1400
16″-ET Standard Y-108

PMS-09882-1 CAN'T TEACH MY OLD HEART NEW TRICKS

16″-ET Standard X-34

WHEN LIGHTS ARE LOW

16″-ET Standard X-34

MY DAY

(vc by Phil Stuart)

16″-ET Standard 34

NAUGHTY NAUGHTY

16″-ET Standard X-34

PMS-09883-1 MY FINE FEATHERED FRIEND

16″-ET Standard A-1401
16″-ET Standard A-1404
16″-ET Standard Y-108

YOU TOOK THE WORDS RIGHT OUT OF MY HEART

(vc by Phil Stuart)

16″-ET Standard A-1401
16″-ET Standard A-1404
16″-ET Standard Y-108

ROCKIN' THE TOWN

16″-ET Standard A-1401
16″-ET Standard A-1404
16″-ET Standard Y-108

A STRANGE LONELINESS

16″-ET Standard A-1401
16″-ET Standard A-1404
16″-ET Standard Y-108

The band was paid $750. Al Goering, also listed as contractor, and Frank Trumbauer each received $75. The rest of the musicians were paid $50 each. The vocalist was paid under a separate contract.

28 JANUARY 1938 (Fri): Los Angeles, CA.

FRANK TRUMBAUER ORCHESTRA: Emanuel ''Mannie'' Klein, Joe Meyer, Cal Clifford (tpts); Joe Yukl, Homer ''Lank'' Menge (tbns); **Frank Trumbauer**, Len Conn, Len Kavash, Lyall Bowen, Jimmy Oliver (reeds); Al Goering, Tom Chambers (ps); Bob Hemphill (gtr); Russ Morhoff (st-bs); Ward Archer (dms).

PMS-09974-1 **ODE TO A CHIMNEY SWEEPER**
16″-ET Standard Z-120

HOME LIFE OF THE SNORF
16″-ET Standard Z-120

HERJE KATI
16″-ET Standard Z-120

BLUE HOLIDAY (aka **SINGIN' THE BLUES**)
16″-ET Standard Z-120

PMS-09975-1 **THE JUBA**
16″-ET Standard Z-121

BRING BACK MY BONNIE TO ME
16″-ET Keystone 70 (as by ''Frank Trombar & His Orch.'')
16″-ET Keystone 121 (as by ''Frank Trombar & His Orch.'')
16″-ET Standard Z-121

SHAG ON DOWN
16″-ET Standard Z-121

HOT SPELL
16″-ET Standard Z-121

PMS-09976-1 **LOVE IS HERE TO STAY**
(vc by Dave Saxon)
16″-ET Standard A-1501
16″-ET Standard A-1504
16″-ET Standard X-43
16″-ET Standard Y-11

I WAS DOING ALL RIGHT
(vc by Dave Saxon)
16″-ET Keystone 428 (as by ''Frank Trombar & His Orch.'')

16″-ET Standard A-1501
16″-ET Standard A-1504
16″-ET Standard X-43
16″-ET Standard Y-11

ROMANCE IN THE RAIN
(vc by Dave Saxon)
16″-ET Standard A-1501
16″-ET Standard A-1504
16″-ET Standard X-43
16″-ET Standard Y-11

ON THE SENTIMENTAL SIDE
(vc by Dave Saxon)
16″-ET Standard A-1501
16″-ET Standard A-1504
16″-ET Standard X-43
16″-ET Standard Y-11

PMS-09977-1 TEA FOR TWO
16″-ET Standard Z-122

RAISIN' THE ROOF
12″-LP IAJRC LP-13
16″-ET Standard Z-122

OL' MAN RIVER
12″-LP IAJRC LP-13
16″-ET Standard Z-122

NIGHT WILL FALL
16″-ET Keystone 70 (as by ''Frank Trombar & His Orch.'')
16″-ET Keystone 121 (as by ''Frank Trombar & His Orch.'')
16″-ET Standard Z-122

Al Goering listed as contractor. The band was paid $635, but individual payments are not listed. The vocalist was paid under separate contract.

11 FEBRUARY 1938 (Fri): Los Angeles, CA.
FRANK TRUMBAUER ORCHESTRA: Bill Shaw, Joe

Meyer, Cal Clifford (tpts); Joe Yukl, Homer ''Lank'' Menge (tbns); **Frank Trumbauer**, Len Conn, Len Kavash, Lyall Bowen, Jimmy Oliver (reeds); Al Goering (p); Bob Hemphill (gtr); Russ Morhoff (st-bs); Ward Archer (dms).

PMS-019017-1 IT'S WONDERFUL
(vc by Jo Stafford)
16″-ET Standard A-1497
16″-ET Standard A-1500
16″-ET Standard Y-109

ALWAYS AND ALWAYS
(vc by Jo Stafford)
16″-ET Standard A-1497
16″-ET Standard A-1500
16″-ET Standard Y-109

OUTSIDE OF PARADISE
(vc by Jo Stafford)
16″-ET Standard A-1497
16″-ET Standard A-1500
16″-ET Standard Y-109

YOU APPEAL TO ME
(vc by Dave Saxon)
16″-ET Standard A-1497
16″-ET Standard A-1500
16″-ET Standard Y-109

PMS-019018-1 TABOO
12″-LP IAJRC LP-13
16″-ET Standard X-41

HOMETOWN
(vc by Dave Saxon)
16″-ET Standard X-41

CHUCK A BOOM
16″-ET Standard X-41

THE ONE I LOVE
(vc by Dave Saxon)
16″-ET Standard X-41

PMS-019019-1 **TONIGHT WE LOVE**
(vc by Dave Saxon)
16″-ET Standard A-1493
16″-ET Standard A-1496
16″-ET Standard Y-109

GOOD NIGHT, ANGEL
16″-ET Standard A-1493
16″-ET Standard A-1496
16″-ET Standard Y-109

THE GYPSY IN MY SOUL
16″-ET Standard A-1493
16″-ET Standard A-1496
16″-ET Standard Y-109

DID AN ANGEL KISS YOU?
(vc by Dave Saxon)
16″-ET Standard A-1493
16″-ET Standard A-1496
16″-ET Standard Y-109

PMS-019020-1 **MY HEART IS TAKING LESSONS**
(vc by Dave Saxon)
16″-ET Standard X-41

BY MYSELF
16″-ET Standard X-41

HILLBILLY FROM TENTH AVENUE
16″-ET Standard X-41

DON'T CRY, SWEETHEART, DON'T CRY
16″-ET Standard X-41

Al Goering listed as contractor. The band was paid $525, but individual payments are not listed. The vocalists were paid under separate contract.

30 MARCH 1938 (Wed): Los Angeles, CA.
FRANK TRUMBAUER ORCHESTRA: Emanuel ''Mannie''

Klein, Joe Meyer, Bill Shaw (tpts); Joe Yukl, Homer "Lank" Menge (tbns); **Frank Trumbauer**, Len Conn, Len Kavash, Lyall Bowen, Jimmy Oliver (reeds); Al Goering (p); Bob Hemphill (gtr); Russ Morhoff (st-bs); Ward Archer (dms).

PMS-019181-1 STARS AND STRIPES FOREVER
12″-LP IAJRC LP-13
16″-ET Standard Z-120

IRISH WASHER WOMAN
16″-ET Keystone 44 (as by "Frank Trombar & His Orch.")
16″-ET Keystone 119 (as by "Frank Trombar & His Orch.")
16″-ET Standard Z-120

FLIGHT OF A HAY BAG
16″-ET Standard Z-120

MIDNIGHT OIL
16″-ET Standard Z-120

PMS-019182-1 THIS TIME IT'S REAL
(vc by Deane Janis)
16″-ET Standard Y-112

MOMENTS LIKE THIS
(vc by Deane Janis)
16″-ET Standard Y-112

ROMANCE IN THE DARK
(vc by Dave Saxon)
16″-ET Standard Y-112

LOST AND FOUND
(vc by Dave Saxon)
16″-ET Standard Y-112

PMS-019183-1 SHADOWS ON THE MOON
(vc by Dave Saxon)
16″-ET Standard Y-112

DON'T BE THAT WAY
16″-ET Standard Y-112

CRY BABY CRY
16″-ET Standard Y-112

WHERE HAVE WE MET BEFORE?
16″-ET Standard Y-112

PMS-019184-1 HOW'DJA LIKE TO LOVE ME?
16″-ET Standard Y-111

IN A HAPPY FRAME OF MIND
(vc by Bill Shaw)

TWO SHADOWS
16″-ET Standard Y-111

WHO ARE WE TO SAY?
16″-ET Keystone 447 (as by ''Frank Trombar & His Orch.'')
16″-ET Standard Y-111

Frank Trumbauer listed as contractor. The band was paid $507.50, but individual payments are not listed. The vocalists were paid under separate contract.

20 APRIL 1938 (Wed): Los Angeles, CA.
FRANK TRUMBAUER ORCHESTRA: Emanuel ''Mannie'' Klein, Joe Meyer, Bill Shaw (tpts); ''Babe'' Bowman, Homer ''Lank'' Menge (tbns); **Frank Trumbauer**, Len Conn, Len Kavash, Lyall Bowen, Jimmy Oliver (reeds); Al Goering (p); Bob Hemphill (gtr); Russ Morhoff (st-bs); Ward Archer (dms).

PMS-019221-1 THERE'S A BOY IN HARLEM
(vc by Bill Shaw)
16″-ET Standard Y-113

HOW CAN YOU FORGET?
(vc by Dave Saxon)
16″-ET Standard Y-113

I CAN'T FACE THE MUSIC
16″-ET Standard Y-113

SOMETHING TELLS ME
(vc by Deane Janis)
16″-ET Standard Y-113

BLUE HOLIDAY (aka **SINGIN' THE BLUES**)
12″-LP IAJRC LP-13
16″-ET Standard Y-113

PMS-019222-1 DO YE KEN JOHN PEEL?
(vc by Dave Saxon)
16″-ET Standard Y-113

COLORADO SUNSET
(vc by Bill Shaw)
12″-LP IAJRC LP-13
16″-ET Standard Y-113

A HEAVENLY PARTY
(vc by Deane Janis)
16″-ET Standard Y-113

YOU'D BETTER CHANGE YOUR TUNE
16″-ET Standard Y-113

PMS-019223-1 IF DREAMS COME TRUE
16″-ET Standard Y-114

AT YOUR BECK AND CALL
(vc by Dave Saxon)
16″-ET Standard Y-114

AN OLD STRAW HAT
16″-ET Standard Y-114

YES, THERE AIN'T NO MOONLIGHT
(vc by Deane Janis and Dave Saxon)
16″-ET Standard Y-114

PMS-019224-1 WHEN THE STARS GO TO SLEEP
16″-ET Standard Y-114

JUST AN ERROR IN THE NEWS
16″-ET Standard Y-114

THE NIGHT YOU SAID GOODBYE
(vc by Deane Janis)
16″-ET Standard Y-114

SO LITTLE TIME
16″-ET Standard Y-114

PMS-019225-1 **TELEVISION** (as **I SAW YOU LAST NIGHT** on Keystone)
16″-ET Keystone 70 (as by "Frank Trombar & His Orch.")
16″-ET Keystone 121 (as by "Frank Trombar & His Orch.")
16″-ET Standard Z-120

NEVER-NEVER LAND FANTASY
16″-ET Keystone 70 (as by "Frank Trombar & His Orch.")
16″-ET Keystone 121 (as by "Frank Trombar & His Orch.")
16″-ET Standard Z-120

DIPPER MOUTH BLUES
12″-LP IAJRC LP-13
16″-ET Standard Z-120

PORTRAIT OF A PRETZEL
12″-LP IAJRC LP-13
16″-ET Keystone 44 (as by "Frank Trombar & His Orch.")
16″-ET Keystone 119 (as by "Frank Trombar & His Orch.")
16″-ET Standard Z-120

Frank Trumbauer listed as contractor. The band was paid $471.25, but individual payments are not listed. The vocalists were paid under separate contract.

25 APRIL 1938 (Mon): Electro-Vox Studios, Los Angeles, CA. FRANK TRUMBAUER ORCHESTRA: Emanuel "Mannie" Klein, Joe Meyer, Bill Shaw (tpts); Joe Yukl, Homer "Lank" Menge (tbns); **Frank Trumbauer**, Len Kavash, Lyall Bowen, Lennie Conn, Jimmy Oliver (reeds); Al Goering (p); Bob Hemphill (gtr); Russ Morhoff (st-bs); Ward Archer (dms).

E.V. M200 **THE NIGHT YOU SAID GOODBYE** (vc by Deane Janis)

The date is taken from souvenir recordings that Trumbauer gave out. Whether it is a new recording date, as listed, or whether he had a dubbing made from the 20 April 1938 session, is unknown at this time.

30 APRIL 1938 (Sat): **Saturday Night Swing Session**, KNX/ CCS Radio program; Los Angeles, CA.

FRANK TRUMBAUER ORCHESTRA: Emanuel ''Mannie'' Klein, Joe Meyer, Bill Shaw (tpts); ''Babe'' Bowman, Homer ''Lank'' Menge (tbns); **Frank Trumbauer**, Len Conn, Len Kavash, Lyall Bowen, Jimmy Oliver (reeds); Al Goering (p); Bob Hemphill (gtr); Russ Morhoff (st-bs); Ward Archer (dms). Bill Goodwin (announcer).

MINNIE HA HA

NICE WORK IF YOU CAN GET IT
(vc by Maxine Sullivan)

A BOY, A GIRL, AND A LAMPLIGHT
(vc by Skinnay Ennis)

PORTRAIT OF A PRETZEL

NOBODY'S SWEETHEART
(unidentified vocalist)

YOU TOOK ADVANTAGE OF ME
(vc by Johnny Mercer)

HAPPY BIRTHDAY TO C.B.S.

LOCH LOMOND
(vc by Maxine Sullivan)

STARS AND STRIPES FOREVER

TEMPO TAKES A HOLIDAY

A recording of the broadcast exists in a private collection.

25 MAY 1938 (Wed): Los Angeles, CA.

FRANK TRUMBAUER ORCHESTRA: Emanuel ''Mannie'' Klein, Joe Meyer, Bill Shaw (tpts); ''Babe'' Bowman, Homer ''Lank'' Menge (tbns); **Frank Trumbauer** (C-mel/alto); Len Kavash, Lyall Bowen (altos); Lennie Conn (ten-sx); Jimmy

Oliver (clt/ten-sx); Al Goering (p); Bob Hemphill (gtr); Russ Morhoff (st-bs); Ward Archer (dms).

PMS-019281-1 THERE'S RAIN IN MY EYES
(vc by Dave Saxon)
16″-ET Standard Y-115

SWINGING ANNIE LAURIE
16″-ET Standard Y-115

SAYS MY HEART
(vc by Deane Janis)
16″-ET Standard Y-115

IT'S THE LITTLE THINGS THAT COUNT
16″-ET Standard Y-115

PMS-019282-1 COWBOY FROM BROOKLYN
(vc by Ward Archer)
16″-ET Standard Y-115

YOU LEAVE ME BREATHLESS
(vc by Deane Janis)
16″-ET Keystone KBS-428
16″-ET Standard Y-115

CATHEDRAL IN THE PINES
16″-ET Standard Y-115

SKRONTCH
12″-LP IAJRC LP-13
16″-ET Standard Y-116

PMS-019283-1 SO YOU LEFT ME FOR THE LEADER OF A SWING BAND
(vc by Deane Janis and Dave Saxon)
16″-ET Standard Y-116

NEGLECTED
16″-ET Standard Y-116

NEIGHBORHOOD OF HEAVEN
(vc by Dave Saxon)
16″-ET Standard Y-116

C.A.A. War Training Service Class and Instructors
March 25, 1943—Kansas City, Missouri
Frank in front row—fourth in from right
Photo courtesy Trumbauer Family Collection

L–R Frank Trumbauer, William "Red" McKenzie, Paul Whiteman
Undated
Photo courtesy Trumbauer Family Collection

Vonnie King—Frank Trumbauer during Adolphus Hotel Engagement, October–November 1938
Photo courtesy Vonnie King

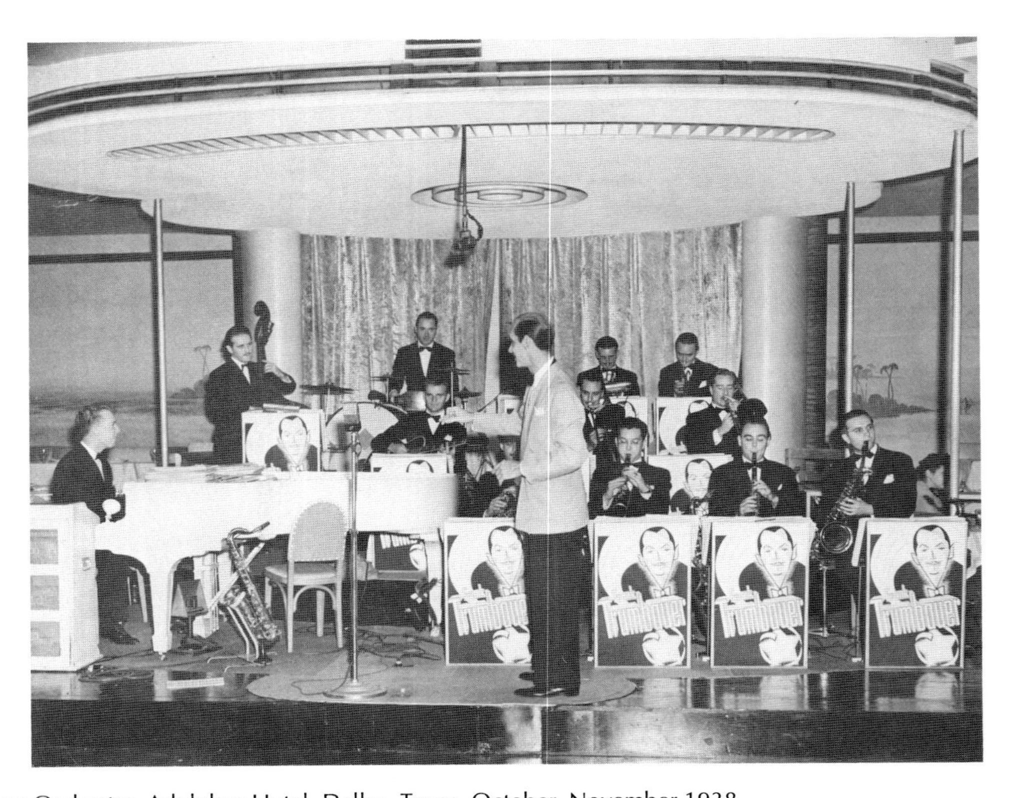

Frank Trumbauer Orchestra, Adolphus Hotel, Dallas, Texas. October–November 1938
Photo courtesy Trumbauer Family Collection

The Three "T's"—Jack Teagarden, Frank Trumbauer, Charles Teagarden
Dated 1936
Photo courtesy Trumbauer Family Collection

Billed as Frank Trumbar, Frank leads the band using a feather. Los Angeles—Biltmore Hotel, 1938
Photo courtesy Trumbauer Family Collection

Frank Trumbauer's Orchestra, Arcadia Ballroom St. Louis 1925
(L–R) Seated: Marty Livingston (vocals); Ray Thurston (Trombone); Charles Russell (Sax); Frank Trumbauer, holding Bass-Sax (Sax); Standing: Dee Orr (Drums); Bix Beiderbecke (Cornet); Seated: Damon Hassler (Sax); Louis Feldman (Piano); Standing: Dan Gaebe (Bass); Wayne Jacobson (Banjo) Seated
Photo courtesy Trumbauer Family Collection

Frank Trumbauer Orchestra 1933
Standing: Frank Trumbauer
(L–R) Front Row: Unidentified Sax; Craig Leitch, Guitar; Frances Kerr, Vocal; Hal Redus, Vocal; Max Connett, Trumpet; Chick Rice, Trumpet
Back Row: Unidentified Sax; Charles McConnell, Bass; Le Roy Buck, Drums; Cedric Spring, Violin; Leon Kaplan, Violin; Herman Crone, Piano; Joe Harris, Trombone
Photo courtesy Trumbauer Family Collection

Bill Trumbauer and father Frank
Kansas City 1950
Photo courtesy Trumbauer Family Collection

Frank and daughter Lynne, Christmas 1955
Photo courtesy Trumbauer Family Collection

April 1956
L–R Mitzi—Mary Freeman Trumbauer—Frank holding grandson Larry Johnson—Lynne Trumbauer Johnson
Photo courtesy Trumbauer Family Collection

May 1956 Last known photo of Frank, taken in his livingroom
Photo courtesy Trumbauer Family Collection

Ft. Worth, Texas—Summer, 1936
Frank with empty saddle
Photo courtesy Trumbauer Family Collection

Ft. Worth, Texas—Summer 1936
Frank on "Joe, the Horse"
Photo courtesy Trumbauer Family Collection

Frank's wife, Mitzi, and Frank's mother, Gertrude (Early 1950's)
Photo courtesy Trumbauer Family Collection

Sunday dinner—1955
(L–R) Mitzi Trumbauer; Frank's mother, Gertrude Stevenson; Frank Trumbauer
Photo courtesy Trumbauer Family Collection

Paul Whiteman's Air Force 1930.
L–R Bill Rank—Frank Trumbauer—Unidentified—Harry Goldfield—Wilbur Hall
Photo courtesy Trumbauer Family Collection

Paul Whiteman. Note caricature then referred to as "Potato Head" likeness of Paul. 1930.
Photo courtesy Trumbauer Family Collection

Paul Whiteman Sax Section 1932 L–R Chet Hazlett—John Cordaro—Frank Trumbauer—Charles Strickfaden
Photo courtesy Trumbauer Family Collection

Advertisement for Opening Night, September 11, 1932 at Lincoln Tavern—Chicago, Illinois
Photo courtesy Trumbauer Family Collection

Andy Sindelar and Frank Trumbauer, Ray Miller's Orchestra 1924
Photo courtesy Andy Sindelar

Ray Miller Orchestra appearing on the White House lawn, October 17, 1924. Third lady from left is Mrs. Calvin Coolidge, fifth from left is President Calvin Coolidge. Ray Miller (foreground) directs Al Jolson (front and center). Frank is third from right of photo.
Photo courtesy Trumbauer Family Collection

Wilbur Hall—Frank Trumbauer (1928 Paul Whiteman Orchestra)
Photo courtesy Trumbauer Family Collection

Irving Friedman—Bix Beiderbecke. Paul Whiteman en route to Hollywood
May 1929
Photo courtesy Trumbauer Family Collection

OH! MA-MA (THE BUTCHER BOY)
(vc by Deane Janis and Ensemble)
16″-ET Standard Y-116

PMS-019284 TONIGHT WILL LIVE
16″-ET Standard Y-116

IT'S THE DREAMER IN ME
16″-ET Standard Y-116

LITTLE LADY MAKE BELIEVE
(vc by Deane Janis)
16″-ET Standard Y-116

MOONSHINE OVER KENTUCKY
16″-ET Standard Y-116

Frank Trumbauer listed as contractor for the Standard session. The band was paid $435, but individual payments are not listed. The vocalists were paid under separate contract.

8 JULY 1938 (Fri): Los Angeles, CA.
FRANK TRUMBAUER ORCHESTRA: Emanuel ''Mannie'' Klein, Joe Meyer, Dave Klein (tpts); ''Babe'' Bowman, Homer ''Lank'' Menge (tbns); **Frank Trumbauer** (C-mel/alto); Len Kavash, Lyall Bowen (altos); Willie Martinez, Jimmy Oliver (clt/ ten-sxs); Charles LaVere (p); Russ Morhoff (st-bs); Ward Archer (dms).

PMS-019412-1 ONE KISS OF LOVE
16″-ET Standard X-56

LOST IN MEDITATION
(vc by Dave Saxon)
16″-ET Standard X-56

ISN'T IT WONDERFUL, ISN'T IT SWELL?
(vc by Deane Janis)
16″-ET Standard X-56

FLAT FOOT FLOOGIE
(vc by **Frank Trumbauer** and ensemble)
16″-ET Standard X-56

No vocal credit given on the label for FLAT FOOT FLOOGIE.

PMS-019413-1 NATIONAL EMBLEM MARCH
16″-ET Standard Z-121

BEETLE AT LARGE
12″-LP IAJRC LP-13
16″-ET Keystone KBS-70
16″-ET Keystone KBS-121
16″-ET Standard Z-121

ALEXANDER'S RAGTIME BAND
16″-ET Keystone KBS-447
16″-ET Standard Z-121

RUSTLE OF SPRING
12″-LP IAJRC LP-13
16″-ET Standard Z-121

PMS-019414-1 LATIN QUARTER
(vc by Dave Saxon)
16″-ET Standard X-56

SMALL FRY
(vc by Charles La Vere)
16″-ET Standard X-56

SPRING IS HERE
(vc by Deane Janis)
16″-ET Keystone KBS-447
16″-ET Standard X-56

I LIKE MUSIC
(vc by **Frank Trumbauer**)
12″-LP IAJRC LP-13
16″-ET Standard X-56

PMS-019415-1 MY WALKING STICK
(vc by Charles La Vere)
16″-ET Standard X-57

THERE'S A FAR AWAY LOOK IN YOUR EYES
(vc by Dave Saxon)

16″-ET Keystone KBS-447
16″-ET Standard X-57

NOW IT CAN BE TOLD
16″-ET Standard X-57

LET'S BREAK THE GOOD NEWS
16″-ET Standard X-57

PMS-019416-1 I'LL DREAM TONIGHT
(vc by Deane Janis)
16″-ET Standard X-57

YOU ARE MUSIC
(vc by Dave Saxon)
16″-ET Standard X-57

YOU AND ME
(vc by Deane Janis)
16″-ET Standard X-57

I'LL STILL BE LOVING YOU
(vc by Dave Saxon)
16″-ET Standard X-57

Frank Trumbauer listed as contractor. The band was paid $540, but individual payments are not listed. Vocalists were paid under separate contract.

9 JULY 1938 (Sat): NBC Radio; Los Angeles, CA.
FRANK TRUMBAUER ORCHESTRA: Emanuel "Mannie" Klein, Joe Meyer, Dave Klein (tpts); "Babe" Bowman, Homer "Lank" Menge (tbns); **Frank Trumbauer** (C-mel/alto); Len Kavash, Lyall Bowen (altos); Willie Martinez, Jimmy Oliver (clt/ten-sxs); Charles LaVere (p); Russ Morhoff (st-bs); Ward Archer (dms).

NATIONAL EMBLEM MARCH (2:23)

Announcer's voice over with introduction of program.

TEMPO TAKES A HOLIDAY (1:44)

PORTRAIT OF A PRETZEL (3:23)

TIGER RAG FANTASY (2:52)

BLUE HOLIDAY (aka **SINGIN' THE BLUES**) (closing theme)

Announcer's voice over with closing of program.

The broadcast was never issued. Program still in RCA Victor Records vaults (Box number 46—Disc number 6). Marked "Good Quality," with a "few ticks" on TIGER RAG FANTASY.

25 FEBRUARY 1939 (Sat): Radio; Minneapolis, MN.
FRANK TRUMBAUER ORCHESTRA: Eddie Wade, Matt Hendrickson, Max Tiff (tpts); John Smith, Santo "Pec" Pecora (tbns); **Frank Trumbauer** (C-mel/alto); Johnny Ross (alto); Don Bonnee (clt/alto); Jimmy McCracken (ten-sx); Jimmy Oliver (bar-sx); Arnold Bliesner (p); Russ Soule (gtr); Bill Jones (st-bs); Russ Morrison (dms).

BLUE HOLIDAY (aka **SINGIN' THE BLUES**)
(opening theme)

A STRANGER ON THE TRAIN

THEY SAY
(vc by Jean Webb)
(arrangement by Don Bonnee)

Medley:
a. **WEARING OF THE GREEN**
b. **IRISH WASHER WOMAN**

BEALE STREET BLUES

BLUE HOLIDAY (aka **SINGIN' THE BLUES**)
(closing theme)

A recording of the broadcast exists in a private collection.

22 FEBRUARY 1940 (Thu): United States Record Co., New York, NY.

FRANK TRUMBAUER ORCHESTRA: Howard Lamont, Dick Dunne, Wayne Williams (tpts); Del Melton, Bernie Bahr (tbns); **Frank Trumbauer**, Johnny Ross, Connie Blessing, Joe Schles, Rudy Boyer (reeds); René Favre (p); John Kreyer (gtr); Herman ''Trigger'' Alpert (st-bs); Joe Becker (dms).

US-1401-1 **WEARING OF THE GREEN** and **IRISH WASHERWOMAN**
10″-78 Davis 22-3
10″-78 Varsity 8215 (sales 2217)

US-1402-1 **NO RETARD**
10″-78 Davis 22-3
10″-78 Varsity 8215 (sales 2217)

US-1403-1 **I DON'T STAND A GHOST OF A CHANCE**
(vc by Fredda Gibson/Georgia Gibbs)
10″-78 Varsity 8256 (sales 1746)

US-1404-1 **I SURRENDER, DEAR**
(vc by Fredda Gibson/Georgia Gibbs)
10″-78 Davis 29-5
10″-78 Varsity 8239 (sales 2560)

US-1405-1 **SEMPER FIDELIS**
(arrangement by Wayne Williams)
10″-78 Davis 29-8
10″-78 Varsity 8253 (sales 2263)

US-1406-1 **JIMTOWN BLUES**
10″-78 Davis 29-1
10″-78 Varsity 8223 (sales 2263)

US-1406-2 **JIMTOWN BLUES**
10″-78 Varsity 8223 (sales 2263)

US-1407-1 **NOT ON THE FIRST NIGHT, BABY**
(vc by Fredda Gibson/Georgia Gibbs, Wayne Williams, and **Frank Trumbauer**)

10″-78 Juke Box 505 (as by ''Frankie & Her Hot Boys'')
10″-78 Varsity 8225 (sales 3175)

US-1408-1 **THE LAZIEST GAL IN TOWN**
(vc by Fredda Gibson/Georgia Gibbs)
10″-78 Juke Box 505 (as by ''Frankie & Her Hot Boys'')
10″-78 Varsity 8223 (sales 4526)

23 FEBRUARY 1940 (Fri): United States Record Co., New York, NY.

FRANK TRUMBAUER ORCHESTRA: Howard Lamont, Dick Dunne, Wayne Williams (tpts); Del Melton, Bernie Bahr (tbns); **Frank Trumbauer**, Johnny Ross, Connie Blessing, Joe Schles, Rudy Boyer (reeds); René Favre (p); John Kreyer (gtr); Herman ''Trigger'' Alpert (st-bs); Joe Becker (dms).

US-1415-2 **NEVER-NEVER LAND FANTASY**
10″-78 Varsity 8243 (sales 3737)

US-1416-1 **NATIONAL EMBLEM MARCH**
10″-78 Davis 29-3
10″-78 Varsity 8243 (sales 3737)

US-1417-1 **STARS AND STRIPES FOREVER**
10″-78 Varsity 8253 (sales 2263)

US-1418-1 **OH LADY BE GOOD**
10″-78 Varsity 8269 (as LADY BE GOOD) (sales 1598)

US-1419-1 **SUGAR FOOT STOMP**
10″-78 Davis 29-2
10″-78 Varsity 8256 (sales 1746)

US-1419-2 **SUGAR FOOT STOMP**
10″-78 Varsity Test Pressing

US-1420-1 **HONKY TONK TRAIN BLUES**
(arrangement by René Favre)
10″-78 Davis 29-4
10″-78 Varsity 8256 (sales 1746)

US-1421-1 **WALKIN' THE DOG**
(vc by Ensemble)

10″-78 Davis 29-6
10″-78 Varsity 8225 (sales 3175)

US-1422-1 **WRAP YOUR TROUBLES IN DREAMS**
10″-78 Davis 29-7
10″-78 Varsity 8269 (sales 1598)

US-1422-2 **WRAP YOUR TROUBLES IN DREAMS**
10″-78 Varsity Test Pressing

US-1423-1 **LITTLE ROCK GETAWAY**
(stock arrangement)
10″-78 Varsity 8236 (sales 2216)

Sales figures noted for the Varsity records are from the United States Record Company Statement of Sales dated 31 July 1940. Total sales reported was 27,038.

25 MARCH 1946 (Mon): File card session #257; Capitol Records Inc., New York, NY.

FRANK TRUMBAUER ORCHESTRA: George ''Pee Wee'' Erwin (tpt); Jack Lacey (tbn); **Frank Trumbauer** (C-mel/alto); Bill Stegmeyer (clt/ten-sx); Dave Bowman (p); Carl Kress (gtr); Herman ''Trigger'' Alpert, Bob Haggart (st-bses); John Blowers, Jr. (dms).

921 **YOU TOOK ADVANTAGE OF ME**
Unissued

922 **BETWEEN THE DEVIL AND THE DEEP BLUE SEA**
12″-LP Capitol W-2138 ''The Jazz Story—Vol 2''

923 **CHINA BOY**
10″-78 Capitol F-15857
10″-LP Capitol H-328 ''Sax Stylists''
10″-LP English Capitol LC-6582

"Trigger" Alpert believes that Bob Haggart does the bulk of the work on bass. On CHINA BOY both bassists can be heard on a duet break and both jam on the ending. "Trigger" could not offer any explanation as to why two basses were used.

FRANK TRUMBAUER HOME RECORDINGS

28 OCTOBER 1948 (Thu): Home recording in family collection.
Frank Trumbauer (C-mel); Bill Trumbauer (tpt); Gertrude Stevenson (p).

MY LOVE FOR YOU
(vc by Bill Trumbauer)

2 DECEMBER 1948 (Fri): Home recording in family collection.
Frank Trumbauer (C-mel); Bill Trumbauer (tpt); Gertrude Stevenson (p).

Take -1 **COULDN'T WE PRETEND?**
(vc by **Frank Trumbauer**)

Take -2 **COULDN'T WE PRETEND?**
(vc by Bill Trumbauer)

29 APRIL 1949 (Fri): Home recording in family collection.
Frank Trumbauer (C-mel); Bill Trumbauer (tpt); Gertrude Stevenson (p).

Take -1 **SUDDENLY**
(vc by **Frank Trumbauer**)

Take -2 **SUDDENLY**
(vc by Bill Trumbauer)

23 JUNE 1952 (Mon): Home recording in family collection.
Frank Trumbauer (C-mel); Bill Trumbauer (tpt); Gertrude Stevenson (p).

MY BABY SMILES
(vc by Bill Trumbauer)

29 SEPTEMBER 1952 (Mon): Home recording in family collection.
Frank Trumbauer (C-mel); Bill Trumbauer (tpt); Gertrude Stevenson (p).

THOMPSON'S BAND
(vc by Bill Trumbauer)

JOE VENUTI'S BLUE FOUR

18 OCTOBER 1929 (Fri): Okeh Record Co., New York, NY.
JOE VENUTI'S BLUE FOUR: **Frank Trumbauer** (C-mel); Joe Venuti (vn); Lennie Hayton (p); Eddie Lang (gtr).

W-403078-B **RUNNIN' RAGGED** (aka BAMBOOZLIN' THE BASSOON)
10″-78 Okeh 41361
10″-78 Argentine Odeon 193424
10″-78 English Parlophone R-531
10″-78 French Parlophone 22875
10″-78 German Odeon A-286005
10″-78 Italian Odeon A-2308
10″-78 Italian Parlophone TT-9048
10″-78 Italian/Scandinavian B-27793
12″-LP Columbia C2L-24

W-403079-B **APPLE BLOSSOMS**
10″-78 Okeh 41361
10″-78 Argentine Odeon 193424
10″-78 English Parlophone R-647
10″-78 German Odeon A-286015

PAUL WHITEMAN AND HIS ORCHESTRA

18 NOVEMBER 1927 (Fri): Victor Record Co., Chicago, IL.
Trumbauer was not present for the Whiteman recording of WASHBOARD BLUES, CVE-40901.

22 NOVEMBER 1927 (Tue): Victor Record Co., Chicago, IL.
PAUL WHITEMAN ORCHESTRA; Bob Mayhew (crt); Charles Margulis, Henry Busse(tpts); Boyce Cullen, Wilbur Hall, Jack Fulton, Tommy Dorsey (tbns); **Frank Trumbauer**, Chester Hazlett, Hal McLean, Jack Mayhew, Nye Mayhew, Rube Crozier, Jimmy Dorsey, Charles Strickfaden (reeds); Kurt Dieterle, Mischa Russell, Matty Malneck, Charles Gaylord, John Bowman, Mario Perry (vns); Harry Parella (p); Mike Pingitore (bjo); Mike Trafficante (tuba); Steve Brown (st-bs); Harold McDonald (dms).
THE PAUL WHITEMAN TRIO; John Fulton, Charles Gaylord, Austin ''Skin'' Young.

CVE-40934-4 **AMONG MY SOUVENIRS**
(vc by The Paul Whiteman Trio)
(arrangement by Tommy Satterfield)
12″-78 Victor 35877
12″-78 English HMV C-1472

23 NOVEMBER 1927 (Wed): Victor Record Co., Chicago, IL.
Trumbauer was not present for the Whiteman recording of CHANGES, BVE-40937.

25 NOVEMBER 1927 (Fri): 9:30 A.M.-12:00 P.M., Victor Record Co., Chicago, IL
PAUL WHITEMAN ORCHESTRA: Bix Beiderbecke (crt); Charles Margulis, Henry Busse (tpts); Wilbur Hall, Jack Fulton, Tommy Dorsey (tbns); **Frank Trumbauer** (C-mel); Chester Hazlett, Hal McLean, Jack Mayhew, Jimmy Dorsey (clts/alto); Charles Strickfaden (ten-sx); Kurt Dieterle, Mischa Russell, Matty Malneck, Mario Perry (vns); Harry Parella (p); Mike Pingitore (bjo); Mike Trafficante (tuba); Steve Brown (st-bs); Harold McDonald (dms).

BVE-40945-2 **MARY** (WHAT ARE YOU WAITING FOR?)
(vc by Bing Crosby)
(arrangement by Matty Malneck)
10″-78 Biltmore 1032
10″-78 Victor 21103 (released 20 January 1928)
10″-78 Australian HMV EA-291

10″-78 Canadian Victor 21103
10″-78 Czechoslovakian HMV AM-989
10″-78 English HMV B-5461
10″-78 German Electrola EG-771
12″-LP Sunbeam Bix Vol 7 ''Sincerely, Bix Beiderbecke''
12″-LP Eng Jz JZ-2 ''The Chronological Bing Crosby''
12″-LP Italian Joker SM-3563 ''Bixology Vol 7''

BVE-40945-4 **MARY** (WHAT ARE YOU WAITING FOR?)
(vc by Bing Crosby)
(arrangement by Matty Malneck)
10″-78 Victor 26415 (released 17 November 1939)
10″-78 Australian HMV EA-2764
12″-LP Sunbeam Bix Vol 7 ''Sincerely, Bix Beiderbecke''
12″-LP Eng Jz JZ-2 ''The Chronological Bing Crosby''
12″-LP Italian Joker SM-3563 ''Bixology Vol 7''

4 JANUARY 1928 (Wed): Victor Record Co., New York, NY.
PAUL WHITEMAN ORCHESTRA: Bix Beiderbecke (crt); Charles Margulis, Henry Busse (tpts); Wilbur Hall (tbn/gtr), Bill Rank (tbn); **Frank Trumbauer**, (C-mel/sop-sx); Chester Hazlett, Hal McLean, Jack or Nye Mayhew, Rube Crozier, Charles Strickfaden, Jimmy Dorsey (reeds); Kurt Dieterle, Mischa Russell, Matty Malneck, Charles Gaylord, Mario Perry (vns); Harry Parella, Tommy Satterfield (ps); Mike Pingitore (bjo); Mike Trafficante (tuba); Steve Brown (st-bs); Harold McDonald (dms).

BVE-41293-3 **RAMONA**
(vc by Austin ''Skin'' Young)
(arrangement by Ferde Grofé)
10″-78 Victor 21214 (released 16 March 1928)
10″-78 Victor 25436
10″-78 Czechoslovakian HMV AM-1202
10″-78 English HMV B-5476
10″-78 German Electrola EG-824
10″-78 Japanese Victor 21214
12″-LP Sunbeam Bix Vol 7 ''Sincerely, Bix Beiderbecke''

Trumbauer is not on BVE-41294, SMILE.

BVE-41295-1 LONELY MELODY
(arrangement by Bill Challis)
10″-78 Biltmore 1017
10″-78 Victor 21214 (released 16 March 1928)
10″-78 Argentine Victor 21214
10″-78 Australian HMV EAl-371
10″-78 Canadian Victor 21214
10″-78 English HMV B-5516
10″-78 Japanese Victor 21214
12″-LP Sunbeam Bix Vol 7 "Sincerely, Bix Beiderbecke"
12″-LP Italian Joker SM-3563 "Bixology Vol 7"
C-DISC Eng Saville CDSVL-201 "The Beiderbecke File"

BVE-41295-3 LONELY MELODY
(arrangement by Bill Challis)
10″-78 Victor 25366 (released 30 July 1936)
12″-LP Sunbeam Bix Vol 7 "Sincerely, Bix Beiderbecke"
12″-LP Italian Joker SM-3563 "Bixology Vol 7"

5 JANUARY 1928 (Thu): 9:30 A.M.-1:00 P.M., Victor Record Co., New York, NY.

PAUL WHITEMAN ORCHESTRA: Bix Beiderbecke (crt); Charles Margulis, Henry Busse (tpts); Boyce Cullen, Wilbur Hall, Bill Rank, Jack Fulton (tbn); **Frank Trumbauer**, Chester Hazlett, Hal McLean, Jack or Nye Mayhew, Rube Crozier, Charles Strickfaden, Jimmy Dorsey, (reeds); Kurt Dieterle, Mischa Russell, Matty Malneck, John Bowman, Charles Gaylord, Mario Perry (vns); Harry Parella (p); Mike Pingitore (bjo); Mike Trafficante (tuba); Steve Brown (st-bs); Harold McDonald (dms).

BVE-41296-2 O YA YA
(arrangement by Domenico Savino)
10″-78 Victor 21304 (released 27 April 1928)
10″-78 English HMV B-5488
12″-LP Sunbeam Bix Vol 7 "Sincerely, Bix Beiderbecke"

Trumbauer does not appear on BVE-41297, DOLLY DIMPLES.

11 JANUARY 1928 (Wed): 9:30 A.M.-1:45 P.M., Victor Record Co., Liederkranz Hall, New York, NY.

PAUL WHITEMAN ORCHESTRA: Bix Beiderbecke, Bob Mayhew (crt); Charles Margulis, Henry Busse (tpts); Boyce Cullen, Wilbur Hall, Bill Rank, Jack Fulton (tbn); **Frank Trumbauer**, (clt/C-mel/alto); Chester Hazlett, Hal McLean, Charles Strickfaden, Jimmy Dorsey (reeds); Kurt Dieterle, Mischa Russell, Matty Malneck, Mario Perry, John Bowman (vns); Harry Parella (p); Tommy Satterfield (cel); Mike Pingitore (bjo); Mike Trafficante (tuba); Steve Brown (st-bs); Harold McDonald (dms).

BVE-27268-11 **PARADE OF THE WOODEN SOLDIERS**
(arrangement by Ferde Grofé)
10″-78 Victor 21304 (released 27 April 1928)
10″-78 English HMV B-5488
12″-LP Sunbeam Bix Vol 7 "Sincerely, Bix Beiderbecke"

BVE-41607-2 **OL' MAN RIVER**
(vc by Bing Crosby)
(arrangement by Bill Challis)
10″-78 Sentry 4008
10″-78 Temple 4008
10″-78 Victor 21218 (released 9 March 1928)
10″-78 Victor 25249 (released 19 February 1936)
10″-78 Argentine Victor 21218, 25249
10″-78 English HMV B-5471; B-8929; BD-5066
10″-78 French Gramophone K-5448
10″-78 German Electrola EG-838
10″-78 Indian HMV B-8929, BD-5066
10″-78 Irish HMV IM-129
10″-78 Italian Gramophone R-4697
10″-78 Japanese Victor 21218, JA-766
10″-78 Swiss HMV JK-2822
12″-LP Sunbeam Bix Vol 7 "Sincerely, Bix Beiderbecke"
12″-LP Eng Jz JZ-2 "The Chronological Bing Crosby"
12″-LP Italian Joker SM-3563 "Bixology Vol 7"

12 JANUARY 1928 (Thu): 10:00 A.M.-1:20 P.M., Victor Record Co., Liederkranz Hall, New York, NY.

PAUL WHITEMAN ORCHESTRA: Bix Beiderbecke (crt); Charles Margulis (tpt); Bill Rank (tbn); **Frank Trumbauer** (C-mel); Jimmy Dorsey (clt/alto); Min Leibrook (bs-sx); Matty Malneck (vn); Bill Challis (p); Carl Kress (gtr); Hal McDonald (dms).

BVE-30172-6 **SAN**
(arrangement by Bill Challis)
10″-78 Biltmore 1031
10″-78 Victor 24078 (released 2 June 1933)
10″-78 Czechoslovakian HMV A.M.-1807
10″-78 English HMV B-5581
10″-78 Japanese Victor 24078
10″-78 Russian Melodija 33M60-41643-44
12″-LP Sunbeam Bix Vol 7 ''Sincerely, Bix Beiderbecke''
12″-LP Italian Joker SM-3563 ''Bixology Vol 7''
C-DISC P-A CDD-490 ''Bix Beiderbecke—Jazz Me Blues''
C-DISC Eng Saville CDSVL-201 ''The Beiderbecke File''

BVE-30172-7 **SAN**
(arrangement by Bill Challis)
10″-78 Victor 25367 (released 30 July 1936)
12″-LP Sunbeam Bix Vol 7 ''Sincerely, Bix Beiderbecke''
12″-LP Italian Joker SM-3563 ''Bixology Vol 7''

21 JANUARY 1928 (Sat): 9:30 A.M.-12:30 P.M., Victor Record Co., Church Studio, Camden, NJ.

PAUL WHITEMAN ORCHESTRA: Bix Beiderbecke, Bob Mayhew (crts); Charles Margulis, Henry Busse (tpts); Boyce Cullen, Wilbur Hall, Bill Rank, Jack Fulton (tbns); **Frank Trumbauer**, (C-mel/alto/bsn); Chester Hazlett, Hal McLean, Jack or Nye Mayhew, Rube Crozier, Charles Strickfaden, Jimmy Dorsey (reeds); Kurt Dieterle, Mischa Russell, Matty Malneck, Charles Gaylord, Mario Perry (vns); Harry Parella, Tommy Satterfield (ps); Mike Pingitore (bjo); Mike Trafficante (tuba); Steve Brown (st-bs); Harold McDonald (dms).

CVE-41653-3 **TOGETHER**
(vc by Jack Fulton)
(arrangement by Ferde Grofé)

12″-78 Victor 35883 (released 9 March 1928)
12″-78 English HMV C-1472
12″-LP Sunbeam Bix Vol 8 "Sincerely, Bix Beiderbecke"

24 JANUARY 1928 (Tue): 9:30-11:50 A.M., Victor Record Co., Church Studio, Camden, NJ.

PAUL WHITEMAN ORCHESTRA: Bix Beiderbecke, Bob Mayhew (crts); Charles Margulis, Henry Busse (tpts); Boyce Cullen, Wilbur Hall, Bill Rank, Jack Fulton (tbns); **Frank Trumbauer**, (C-mel/alto); Chester Hazlett, Hal McLean, Jack Mayhew, Nye Mayhew, Rube Crozier, Charles Strickfaden, Jimmy Dorsey (reeds); Kurt Dieterle, Mischa Russell, Matty Malneck, Charles Gaylord, Mario Perry (vns); Harry Parrella (p); Mike Pingitore (bjo); Mike Trafficante (tuba); Steve Brown (st-bs); Harold McDonald (dms).
No strings on 41294.

CVE-41465-1 **MY HEART STOOD STILL**
(vc by Jack Fulton, Charles Gaylord, Austin Young, and Al Rinker)
(arrangement by Bill Challis)
12″-LP Sunbeam Bix Vol 8 "Sincerely, Bix Beiderbecke"

CVE-41465-3 **MY HEART STOOD STILL**
(vc by Jack Fulton, Charles Gaylord, Austin Young, and Al Rinker)
(arrangement by Bill Challis)
12″-78 Victor 35883 (released 9 March 1928)
12″-LP Sunbeam Bix Vol 8 "Sincerely, Bix Beiderbecke"

BVE-41294-4 **SMILE**
(vc by Jack Fulton, Charles Gaylord, Austin Young, and Al Rinker)
(arrangement by Bill Challis)
10″-78 Victor Test Pressing
12″-LP Broadway 102
12″-LP Sunbeam Bix Vol 8 "Sincerely, Bix Beiderbecke"
12″-LP French RCA 741093
12″-LP Italian Joker SM-3564 "Bixology Vol 8"

BVE-41294-5 **SMILE**
(vc by Jack Fulton, Charles Gaylord, Austin Young, and Al Rinker)
(arrangement by Bill Challis)
10″-78 Biltmore 1017
10″-78 Victor 21228 (released 16 March 1928)
10″-78 English HMV B-5465
10″-78 Spanish HMV AE-2189
12″-LP Sunbeam Bix Vol 8 ''Sincerely, Bix Beiderbecke''
12″-LP Italian Joker SM-3564 ''Bixology Vol 8''

26 JANUARY 1928 (Thurs): Victor Record Co., Camden, NJ.
PAUL WHITEMAN ORCHESTRA: with Thomas ''Fats'' Waller at the organ, rehearsed the selection WHISPERING at the Victor Studios in Camden, New Jersey. A search by RCA Victor Records personnel failed to locate any evidence that any recordings or test pressings were made.

27 JANUARY 1928 (Fri): Victor Record Co., New York, NY.
PAUL WHITEMAN ORCHESTRA: Charles Margulis, Henry Busse (tpts); Boyce Cullen, Wilbur Hall, Bill Rank (tbns); **Frank Trumbauer** (clt/C-mel); Chester Hazlett, Hal McLean, Jack Mayhew, Nye Mayhew, Rube Crozier, Charles Strickfaden, Jimmy Dorsey (reeds); Kurt Dieterle, Mischa Russell, Matty Malneck, Charles Gaylord, Mario Perry (vns); Ferde Grofé (p); Mike Pingitore (bjo); Mike Trafficante (tuba); Steve Brown (st-bs); Harold McDonald (dms).

BVE-41470-5 **MAKE BELIEVE**
(vc by Bing Crosby)
(arrangement by Ferde Grofé)
10″-78 Victor 21218 (released 9 March 1928)
10″-78 Victor 25249 (released 19 February 1936)
10″-78 Czechoslovakian HMV AM-1194
10″-78 English HMV B-5471; BD-5066
12″-LP Eng Jz JZ-3 ''The Chronological Bing Crosby''
12″-LP Italian Joker SM-3564 ''Bixology Vol 8''

28 JANUARY 1928 (Sat): 9:30-11:25 A.M., Victor Record Co., Studio 3, Camden NJ.

PAUL WHITEMAN ORCHESTRA: Charles Margulis, Henry Busse (tpts); Boyce Cullen, Wilbur Hall, Bill Rank (tbns); **Frank Trumbauer** (clt/C-mel); Chester Hazlett, Hal McLean, Jack Mayhew, Nye Mayhew, Rube Crozier, Charles Strickfaden, Jimmy Dorsey (reeds); Kurt Dieterle, Mischa Russell, Matty Malneck, Charles Gaylord, Mario Perry (vns); Bill Challis, Ferde Grofé (p); Mike Pingitore (bjo); Mike Trafficante (tuba); Steve Brown (st-bs); Harold McDonald (dms).

BVE-41471-3 **BACK IN YOUR OWN BACKYARD**
(arrangement by Bill Challis)
10″-78 Victor 21240 (released 23 March 1928)
10″-78 Canadian Victor 21240
10″-78 English HMV B-5564
10″-78 French Gramophone K-5606
10″-78 German Electrola EG-1161
10″-78 Indian HMV B-5564
10″-78 Japanese Victor 21240
12″-LP Sunbeam Bix Vol 8 "Sincerely, Bix Beiderbecke"
12″-LP Italian Joker SM-3564 "Bixology Vol 8"

BVE-41471-4 **BACK IN YOUR OWN BACKYARD**
(arrangement by Bill Challis)
10″-78 Victor 27689 (released 12 December 1941)
12″-LP Sunbeam Bix Vol 8 "Sincerely, Bix Beiderbecke"
12″-LP Italian Joker SM-3564 "Bixology Vol 8"

7 FEBRUARY 1928 (Tue): Victor Record Co., New York, NY.
PAUL WHITEMAN ORCHESTRA: Bob Mayhew (crt); Charles Margulis, Henry Busse (tpts); Boyce Cullen, Wilbur Hall, Bill Rank (tbns); **Frank Trumbauer** (C-mel); Chet Hazlett, Hal McLean, Rube Crozier, Charles Strickfaden, Jimmy Dorsey (reeds); Kurt Dieterle, Mischa Russell, Matty Malneck, Charles Gaylord, Mario Perry (vns); Roy Bargy (p); Mike Pingitore (bjo); Mike Trafficante (tuba); Steve Brown (st-bs); Harold McDonald (dms).

BVE-41608-2 **POOR BUTTERFLY**
(Humming vc by Jack Fulton, Charles Gaylord, Austin Young, and Al Rinker)
(arrangement by Ferde Grofé)

10″-78 Victor 24078 (released 2 June 1933)
12″-LP Eng Jz JZ-3 ''The Chronological Bing Crosby''

Trumbauer did not appear on other selections made on this date: BVE-24390 THE JAPANESE SANDMAN, BVE-24392 AVALON and BVE-24393 WHISPERING.

8 FEBRUARY 1928 (Wed): 10:00 A.M.-12:05 P.M., Victor Record Co., Liederkranz Hall, New York, NY.

PAUL WHITEMAN ORCHESTRA: Bix Beiderbecke, Bob Mayhew (crts); Charles Margulis, Henry Busse (tpts); Boyce Cullen, Wilbur Hall, Bill Rank, Jack Fulton (tbns); **Frank Trumbauer** (C-mel); Chet Hazlett, Hal McLean, Rube Crozier, Charles Strickfaden, Jimmy Dorsey (reeds); Kurt Dieterle, Mischa Russell, Matty Malneck, Charles Gaylord, Mario Perry (vns); Roy Bargy (p); Mike Pingitore (bjo); Mike Trafficante (tuba); Steve Brown (st-bs); Harold McDonald (dms).

BVE-41681-2 **THERE AIN'T NO SWEET MAN THAT'S WORTH THE SALT OF MY TEARS**
(vc by Bing Crosby, Jack Fulton, Charles Gaylord, Al Rinker, Austin ''Skin'' Young, and Harry Barris)
(arrangement by Tommy Satterfield)

10″-78 Victor 25675 (released 22 September 1937)
10″-78 Czechoslovakian HMV AM-1623
10″-78 English HMV B-8929
10″-78 Indian HMV B-8929
10″-78 Swiss HMV JK-2822
12″-LP Sunbeam Bix Vol 8 ''Sincerely, Bix Beiderbecke''
12″-LP Eng Jz JZ-3 ''The Chronological Bing Crosby''
12″-LP Italian Joker SM-3564 ''Bixology Vol 8''
C-DISC Eng Pavilion/Pearl PAST-CD-9765-''The Genius Of Bix Beiderbecke''

BVE-41681-3 **THERE AIN'T NO SWEET MAN THAT'S WORTH THE SALT OF MY TEARS**
(vc by Bing Crosby, Jack Fulton, Charles

Gaylord, Al Rinker, Austin ''Skin'' Young, and Harry Barris)
(arrangement by Tommy Satterfield)
10″-78 Biltmore 1031
10″-78 Victor 21464 (released 20 July 1928)
10″-78 English HMV B-5515
10″-78 Indian HMV B-5515
12″-LP Sunbeam Bix Vol 8 ''Sincerely, Bix Beiderbecke''
12″-LP Eng Jz JZ-3 ''The Chronological Bing Crosby''
12″-LP Italian Joker SM-3564 ''Bixology Vol 8''

BVE-41682 **A SHADY TREE**
(vc by Jack Fulton; recitation by Austin Young)
(arrangement by Ferde Grofé)
Rejected. Remade 15 February 1928.

9 FEBRUARY 1928 (Thu): 10:00 A.M.-12:20 P.M. and 1:20-3:00 P.M., Victor Record Co., Liederkranz Hall, New York, NY.
PAUL WHITEMAN ORCHESTRA: Bix Beiderbecke (crt); Charles Margulis, Henry Busse (tpts); Bill Rank, Wilbur Hall, Boyce Cullen (tbns); **Frank Trumbauer** (C-mel); Chet Hazlett, Jimmy Dorsey, Hal McLean, Charles Strickfaden (reeds); Kurt Dieterle, Mischa Russell, Matty Malneck (vns); Roy Bargy (p); Mike Pingitore (bjo); Mike Trafficante (tuba); Steve Brown (st-bs); Hal McDonald (dms).
Beiderbecke on BVE-41683 only.

BVE-26377-22 **ORIENTAL**
(arrangement by Ferde Grofé)
10″-78 Victor 21599
10″-78 Czechoslovakian HMV AM-1807
10″-78 English HMV B-5581

BVE-30176-? **MEDITATION FROM ''THAÏS''**
(arrangement by Ferde Grofé)
10″-78 Victor 21796

BVE-30177-9 **BY THE WATERS OF THE MINNETONKA**
(arrangement by Ferde Grofé)

10″-78 Victor 21796
10″-78 English HMV B-5533

BVE-41683-2 **DARDANELLA**
(arrangement by Bill Challis)
10″-78 Victor 25238 (released 29 January 1936)
10″-78 Japanese Victor 25238, A-1281, JA-677
10″-78 English HMV B-8931
10″-78 Swiss HMV JK-2810
12″-LP Sunbeam Bix Vol 8 "Sincerely, Bix Beiderbecke"
12″-LP Italian Joker SM-3564 "Bixology Vol 8"

10 FEBRUARY 1928 (Fri): 10:00 A.M.-12:00 P.M., Victor Record Co., Liederkranz Hall, New York, NY.

PAUL WHITEMAN ORCHESTRA: Bix Beiderbecke (crt); Charles Margulis, Henry Busse (tpts); Bill Rank, Wilbur Hall, Boyce Cullen (tbns); **Frank Trumbauer** (alto); Chet Hazlett, Red Mayer, Hal McLean, Charles Strickfaden (reeds); Kurt Dieterle, Mischa Russell, Matty Malneck (vns); Roy Bargy (p); Mike Pingitore (bjo); Mike Trafficante (tuba); Steve Brown (st-bs); Hal McDonald (dms).

BVE-41684-2 **LOVE NEST**
(Humming by Jack Fulton, Charles Gaylord, Austin "Skin" Young)
(arrangement by Bill Challis)
10″-78 Victor 24105 (released 1 December 1932)
12″-LP Sunbeam Bix Vol 8 "Sincerely, Bix Beiderbecke"
12″-LP Italian Joker SM-3564 "Bixology Vol 8"

13 FEBRUARY 1928 (Mon): 1:15-4:00 P.M., Liederkranz Hall, Victor Record Co., New York, NY.

PAUL WHITEMAN ORCHESTRA: Bix Beiderbecke (crt); Charles Margulis (tpt); Bill Rank, Boyce Cullen (tbns); **Frank Trumbauer** (clt/alto/Eb clt); Chet Hazlett, Irving Friedman, Charles Strickfaden (reeds); Kurt Dieterle, Mischa Russell, Matty Malneck, Mario Perry, Charles Gaylord (vns); Roy Bargy (p); Wilbur Hall (gtr); Mike Pingitore (bjo); Mike Trafficante (tuba); Steve Brown (st-bs); Hal McDonald (dms). **Beiderbecke on BVE-41683 only.**

BVE-27432-14 WONDERFUL ONE
(arrangement by Ferde Grofé)
10″-78 Victor 24105 (released 1 December 1932)

CVE-41687-2 MIDNIGHT REFLECTIONS
(arrangement by Matty Malneck)
12″-78 Victor 35992 (released 29 November 1929)
12″-78 English HMV C-1652

BVE-41688-2 SUNSHINE
(vc by Bing Crosby, Jack Fulton, Charles Gaylord, Al Rinker, and Austin ''Skin'' Young)
(arrangement by Ferde Grofé)
10″-78 Victor Test Pressing
12″-LP Sunbeam Bix Vol 7 ''Sincerely, Bix Beiderbecke''

BVE-41688-3 SUNSHINE
(vc by Bing Crosby, Jack Fulton, Charles Gaylord, Al Rinker, and Austin ''Skin'' Young)
(arrangement by Ferde Grofé)
10″-78 Victor 21240 (released 23 March 1928)
10″-78 Canadian Victor 21240
10″-78 Japanese Victor 21240
10″-78 Spanish HMV AE-2236
12″-LP Sunbeam Bix Vol 8 ''Sincerely, Bix Beiderbecke''
12″-LP Eng Jz JZ-3 ''The Chronological Bing Crosby''

Trumbauer did not appear on the final selection from this session: BVE-41689 FROM MONDAY ON.

14 FEBRUARY 1928 (Tue): 9:30 A.M.-12:00 P.M., Victor Record Co., Liederkranz Hall, New York, NY.

PAUL WHITEMAN ORCHESTRA: Bix Beiderbecke (crt); Charles Margulis, Henry Busse, Eddie Pinder (tpts); Boyce Cullen, Wilbur Hall, Jack Fulton, Bill Rank (tbns); **Frank Trumbauer**, Chester Hazlett, Hal McLean, Jack Mayhew, Nye Mayhew, Rube Crozier, Charles Strickfaden, Roy ''Red'' Mayer, Irving Friedman (reeds); Kurt Dieterle, Mischa Russell,

Matty Malneck, Charles Gaylord, John Bowman, Mario Perry (vns); Roy Bargy (p); Mike Trafficante (tuba); Steve Brown (st-bs); Harold McDonald (dms); Herman Hand (dir).

CVE-41690-2 **GRAND FANTASIA FROM WAGNERIANA** (part 1)
(arrangment by Herman Hand)
12″-78 Victor 36065 (released 23 February 1928)
12″-LP Sunbeam Bix Vol 9 ''Sincerely, Bix Beiderbecke''

CVE-41691-4 **GRAND FANTASIA FROM WAGNERIANA** (part 2)
(arrangement by Herman Hand)
12″-78 Victor 36065 (released 23 February 1928)
12″-LP Sunbeam Bix Vol 9 ''Sincerely, Bix Beiderbecke''

15 FEBRUARY 1928 (Wed): Victor Record Co., New York, NY. PAUL WHITEMAN ORCHESTRA: Bix Beiderbecke (crt); Charles Margulis, Henry Busse, Eddie Pinder (tpts); Boyce Cullen, Wilbur Hall, Bill Rank (tbns); **Frank Trumbauer** (C-mel); Chester Hazlett, Rube Crozier, Charles Strickfaden, Roy ''Red'' Mayer, Irving Friedman (reeds); Kurt Dieterle, Mischa Russell, Matty Malneck, Mario Perry (vns); Roy Bargy (p); Mike Pingitore (bjo); Mike Trafficante (tuba); Harold McDonald (dms).
Beiderbecke on BVE-24391 only.

BVE-24391-5 **AVALON**
(arrangement by Ferde Grofé)
10″-78 Victor 25238 (released 29 January 1936)

CVE-41682-2 **A SHADY TREE**
(vc by Jack Fulton; recitation by Austin ''Skin'' Young)
(arrangement by Ferde Grofé)
10″-78 Victor Test Pressing
12″-LP Sunbeam Bix Vol 9 ''Sincerely, Bix Beiderbecke''

Trumbauer did not appear on the other selections of this session: BVE-24393 WHISPERING and BVE-27431 UNDERNEATH THE MELLOW MOON.

16 FEBRUARY 1928 (Thu): 10:15 A.M.–12:45 P.M. and 2:40–4:00 P.M., Victor Record Co., New York, NY.

PAUL WHITEMAN ORCHESTRA: Bix Beiderbecke (crt); Charles Margulis, Henry Busse, Eddie Pinder (tpts); Boyce Cullen, Wilbur Hall, Jack Fulton, Bill Rank (tbns); **Frank Trumbauer**, Chester Hazlett, Hal McLean, Rube Crozier, Charles Strickfaden, Roy ''Red'' Mayer, Irving Friedman (reeds); Milford ''Min'' Leibrook (bs-sx); Kurt Dieterle, Mischa Russell, Matty Malneck, Charles Gaylord, John Bowman, Mario Perry (vns); Roy Bargy (p); Mike Pingitore (bjo); Mike Trafficante (st-bs); Harold McDonald (dms).
Beiderbecke on 41692 only.

CVE-41692-3 **THREE SHADES OF BLUE** (part 1)
INDIGO
(arrangement by Ferde Grofé)
12″-78 Victor 35952 (released 28 December 1928)
12″-LP Sunbeam Bix Vol 9 ''Sincerely, Bix Beiderbecke''

CVE-41693-2 **THREE SHADES OF BLUE** (part 2)
ALICE BLUE and HELIOTROPE
(arrangement by Ferde Grofé)
12″-78 Victor 35952 (released 28 December 1928)
12″-LP Sunbeam Bix Vol 9 ''Sincerely, Bix Beiderbecke''

18 FEBRURY 1928 (Sat): 11:30 A.M.-12:40 P.M., Liederkranz Hall, Victor Record Co., New York, NY.

PAUL WHITEMAN ORCHESTRA: Charles Margulis, Henry Busse, Eddie Pinder (tpts); Boyce Cullen, Wilbur Hall, Jack Fulton, Bill Rank (tbns); **Frank Trumbauer**, Chester Hazlett, Hal McLean, Rube Crozier, Charles Strickfaden, Roy ''Red'' Mayer, Irving Friedman (reeds); Milford ''Min'' Leibrook (bs-sx); Kurt Dieterle, Mischa Russell, Matty Malneck, Charles Gaylord, John Bowman, Mario Perry (vns); Roy Bargy (p); Mike Pingitore (bjo); Mike Trafficante (st-bs); Harold McDonald (dms).

CVE-41695-2 **CAPRICE FUTURISTIC**
(arrangement by Ferde Grofé)
12″-78 Victor 36044 (released 18 December 1931)
12″-78 English HMV C-1607

BVE-41696-2 **MISSISSIPPI MUD**
(vc by Irene Taylor, Bing Crosby, Harry Barris, Al Rinker, Jack Fulton, Charles Gaylord, and Austin Young)
(arrangement by Tommy Satterfield)
10″-78 Biltmore 1029
10″-78 Victor 25366 (released 30 July 1936)
10″-78 Australian HMV EA-2764
12″-LP Sunbeam Bix Vol 9 "Sincerely, Bix Beiderbecke"
12″-LP Eng Jz JZ-3 "The Chronological Bing Crosby"
12″-LP Italian Joker SM-3564 "Bixology Vol 8"

BVE-41696-3 **MISSISSIPPI MUD**
(vc by Irene Taylor, Bing Crosby, Harry Barris, Al Rinker, Jack Fulton, Charles Gaylord, and Austin Young)
(arrangement by Tommy Satterfield)
10″-78 Victor 21274 (released 13 April 1928)
10″-78 Australian HMV EA-429
10″-78 Canadian Victor 21274
10″-78 Japanese Victor 21274
12″-LP Sunbeam Bix Vol 9 "Sincerely, Bix Beiderbecke"
12″-LP Eng Jz JZ-3 "The Chronological Bing Crosby"
12″-LP Italian Joker SM-3564 "Bixology Vol 8"
C-DISC Ger Bauer ADD-3520 "Bix Beiderbecke—Wa-Da-Da"

27 FEBRUARY 1928 (Mon): 12:00-3:15 P.M., Liederkranz Hall, Victor Record Co., New York, NY.

PAUL WHITEMAN ORCHESTRA: Bix Beiderbecke (crt); Charles Margulis, Henry Busse, Eddie Pinder (tpts); Boyce Cullen, Wilbur Hall, Jack Fulton, Bill Rank (tbns); **Frank Trumbauer** (bsn/alto); Chester Hazlett, Rube Crozier, Charles Strickfaden, Roy "Red" Mayer, Irving Friedman (reeds); Kurt Dieterle, Mischa Russell, Matty Malneck, Mario Perry (vns); Roy Bargy (p); Mike Pingitore (bjo); Milford "Min" Leibrook (tuba); Mike Trafficante (st-bs); Harold McDonald (dms).

CVE-43116-3 **CHLOE**
(vc by Austin "Skin" Young)
(arrangement by Ferde Grofé)

12″-78 Victor 35921 (released 29 June 1928)
12″ 78 English HMV C-1548
12″-LP Sunbeam Bix Vol 9 "Sincerely, Bix Beiderbecke"

28 FEBRUARY 1928 (Tue): 11:00 A.M.-2:30 P.M. and 2:30-3:45 P.M., Victor Record Co., New York, NY.

PAUL WHITEMAN ORCHESTRA: Bix Beiderbecke (crt); Charles Margulis, Henry Busse, Eddie Pinder (tpts); Boyce Cullen, Bill Rank, Wilbur Hall, Jack Fulton (tbns); **Frank Trumbauer**, Chester Hazlett, Rube Crozier, Charles Strickfaden, Roy "Red" Mayer, Irving Friedman (reeds); Kurt Dieterle, Mischa Russell, Matty Malneck, Mario Perry (vns); Roy Bargy (p); Mike Pingitore (bjo); Milford "Min" Leibrook (tuba); Mike Trafficante (st-bs); Harold McDonald (dms).

BVE-41689-4 **FROM MONDAY ON**
(vc by Bing Crosby, Austin Young, Al Rinker, Jack Fulton, and Charles Gaylord)
(arrangement by Matty Malneck)

10″-78 Victor 25368 (released 30 July 1936)
12″-LP Sunbeam Bix Vol 9 "Sincerely, Bix Beiderbecke"
12″-LP Eng Jz JZ-3 "The Chronological Bing Crosby"
12″-LP Italian Joker SM-3564 "Bixology Vol 8"

BVE-41689-6 **FROM MONDAY ON**
(vc by Bing Crosby, Austin Young, Al Rinker, Jack Fulton, and Charles Gaylord)
(arrangement by Matty Malneck)

10″-78 Biltmore 1017
10″-78 Victor 21274 (released 13 April 1928)
10″-78 Canadian Victor 21274
10″-78 English HMV B-5492
10″-78 Indian HMV B-5492
10″-78 Japanese Victor 21274
12″-LP Sunbeam Bix Vol 9 "Sincerely, Bix Beiderbecke"
12″-LP Eng Jz JZ-3 "The Chronological Bing Crosby"
12″-LP Italian Joker SM-3564 "Bixology Vol 8"
C-DISC P-A CDD-490 "Bix Beiderbecke—Jazz Me Blues"

Harry Barris replaced Roy Bargy (p) on matrix BVE-41689 only. Bargy overslept and arrived late.

CVE-43117-3 **HIGH WATER**
(vc by Bing Crosby)
(arrangement by Tommy Satterfield)
12″-78 Victor 35992 (released 29 November 1929)
12″-78 Victor 36186
12″-78 English HMV C-1607
12″-LP Sunbeam Bix Vol 9 ''Sincerely, Bix Beiderbecke''
12″-LP Eng Jz JZ-5 ''The Chronological Bing Crosby''

BVE-43118-1 **SUGAR**
(arrangement by Bill Challis)
10″-78 Victor 25368 (released 30 July 1936)
10″-78 English HMV B-8931
10″-78 Swiss HMV JK-2810
12″-LP Sunbeam Bix Vol 9 ''Sincerely, Bix Beiderbecke''
12″-LP Italian Joker SM-3565 ''Bixology Vol 9''

BVE-43118-2 **SUGAR**
(arrangement by Bill Challis)
10″-78 Victor 21464 (released 20 July 1928)
12″-LP Sunbeam Bix Vol 9 ''Sincerely, Bix Beiderbecke''
12″-LP Italian Joker SM-3565 ''Bixology Vol 9''

29 FEBRUARY 1928 (Wed): New York, NY.
Trumbauer was ill and not present for the Whiteman recordings of: BVE-43120 WHEN YOU'RE WITH SOMEBODY ELSE and, CVE-43119 SEA BURIAL.

1 MARCH 1928 (Thu): 10:15 A.M.-12:00 P.M. and 2:00-5:30 P.M., Victor Record Co., New York, NY.
PAUL WHITEMAN ORCHESTRA: Bix Beiderbecke (crt); Charles Margulis, Henry Busse, Eddie Pinder (tpts); Boyce Cullen, Wilbur Hall (tbns); **Frank Trumbauer** (clt/alto/bsn); Chester Hazlett, Irving Friedman, Red Mayer, Charles Strickfaden (reeds); Kurt Dieterle, Mischa Russell, Matty Malneck, Mario Perry (vns); Roy Bargy (p); Mike Pingitore (bjo); Milford ''Min'' Leibrook (tuba); Mike Trafficante (st-bs); Harold McDonald (dms).

Beiderbecke on 43123 only.
CHORUS: Olive Kline, Della Baker, V. Hold, Ruth Rogers (sopranos); Elsie Baker, Helen Clark, Ena Indermauer (contraltos); Lambert Murphy, Charles Harrison, Lewis James, John Hause (tenors); Elliott Shaw (baritone); Frank Croxton, Wilfred Glenn, ?? Kinsley (bs's).

CVE-30181-6 **SUITE OF SERENADES** (Spanish/Chinese)
(arrangement by Ferde Grofé)
12″-78 Victor 35926
12″-78 Eng HMV C-1600

CVE-43122-3 **OL' MAN RIVER**
(vc by Paul Robeson with Chorus)
(arrangement by Tommy Satterfield)
12″-78 Victor 35912 (released 20 April 1928)
12″-78 Czechoslovakian HMV AM-1194
12″-78 English HMV C-1505

CVE-43123-2 Selections From **Show Boat**
(arrangement by Tommy Satterfield)
a. **WHY DO I LOVE YOU?**
(vc by Olive Kline)
b. **CAN'T HELP LOVIN' DAT MAN**
(vc by Chorus)
c. **YOU ARE LOVE**
(vc by Lambert Murphy)
d. **MAKE BELIEVE**
(vc by Olive Kline, Lambert Murphy, and Chorus)
7″-LP Nat Wep 804 (excerpt of segment ''b'' only)
12″-78 Victor 35912 (released 20 April 1928)
12″-78 Argentine Victor 35912
12″-78 Canadian Victor 35912
12″-78 English HMV C-1505
12″-78 French Gramophone L-657
12″-78 German Electrola EH-225
12″-78 Indian HMV C-1505
12″-78 Italian Gramophone R-4697

12″-LP Sunbeam Bix Vol 10 ''Sincerely, Bix Beiderbecke''
12″-LP Italian Joker SM-3565 ''Bixology Vol 9''

CVE-43123-4 Selections From **Show Boat**
(arrangement by Tommy Satterfield)
a. **WHY DO I LOVE YOU?**
(vc by Olive Kline)
b. **CAN'T HELP LOVIN' DAT MAN**
(vc by Chorus)
c. **YOU ARE LOVE**
(vc by Lambert Murphy)
d. **MAKE BELIEVE**
(vc by Olive Kline, Lambert Murphy, and Chorus)

7″-LP Nat WEP-804 (excerpt of segement ''b'' only)
12″-LP Sunbeam Bix Vol 10 ''Sincerely, Bix Beiderbecke''
12″-LP Italian Joker SM-3565 ''Bixology Vol 9''

2 MARCH 1928 (Fri): 10:30 A.M.-12:10 P.M. and 1:15-3:50 P.M., Victor Record Co., New York, NY.

PAUL WHITEMAN ORCHESTRA: Bix Beiderbecke (crt); Charles Margulis, Henry Busse, Eddie Pinder (tpts); Boyce Cullen, Wilbur Hall (tbns); **Frank Trumbauer** (clt/alto/bsn); Chester Hazlett, Irving Friedman, Red Mayer, Charles Strickfaden (reeds); Kurt Dieterle, Mischa Russell, Matty Malneck, Mario Perry (vns); Roy Bargy (p); Mike Pingitore (bjo); Milford ''Min'' Leibrook (tuba); Mike Trafficante (st-bs); Harold McDonald (dms).

CVE-43124-3 **A STUDY IN BLUE**
(arrangement by Domenico Savino)

12″-78 Victor 36067 (released 21 October 1932)
12″-LP Sunbeam Bix Vol 10 ''Sincerely, Bix Beiderbecke''

Trumbauer did not appear on the other selections from this session: BVE-43125 COQUETTE and CVE-30180 SUITE OF SERENADES (Cuban/Oriental).

12 MARCH 1928 (Mon): 9:30 A.M.-12:00 P.M. and 2:00-3:00 P.M., Victor Record Co., Liederkranz Hall, New York, NY.

PAUL WHITEMAN ORCHESTRA: Bix Beiderbecke (crt); Charles Margulis, Henry Busse (tpts); Boyce Cullen, Bill Rank (tbns); **Frank Trumbauer** (C-mel); Chester Hazlett, Irving Friedman, Red Mayer, Rube Crozier, Charles Strickfaden (reeds); Roy Bargy (p); Mike Pingitore (bjo); Milford ''Min'' Leibrook (tuba); Mike Trafficante (st-bs); Harold McDonald (dms).
Beiderbecke on BVE-43138 only.

BVE-43138-2 **WHEN**
(vc by Jack Fulton, Charles Gaylord, Austin Young, Al Rinker and Harry Barris)
(arrangement by Tommy Saterfield)
10″-78 Victor 21338 (released 18 May 1928)
10″-78 Victor 25367
10″-78 English HMV B-5493
10″-78 French Gramophone K-5606
10″-78 Japanese Victor 21338
12″-LP Sunbeam Bix Vol 10 ''Sincerely, Bix Beiderbecke''
12″-LP Italian Joker SM-3565 ''Bixology Vol 9''

BVE-43138-3 **WHEN**
(vc by Jack Fulton, Charles Gaylord, Austin Young, Al Rinker, and Harry Barris)
(arrangement by Tommy Saterfield)
10″-78 Victor 21338 (released 18 May 1928)
12″-LP Broadway 102
12″-LP Sunbeam Bix Vol 10 ''Sincerely, Bix Beiderbecke''
12″-LP Italian Joker SM-3565 ''Bixology Vol 9''

BVE-43139-3 **DOWN IN OLD HAVANA TOWN**
(vc by Austin ''Skin'' Young)
(arrangement by Ferde Grofé)
10″-78 Victor 27687 (released 12 December 1941)

BVE-43140-2 **I'M WINGING HOME**
(vc by Bing Crosby with Al Rinker, Charles Gaylord, Jack Fulton, and Austin ''Skin'' Young)
(arrangement by Tommy Satterfield)
10″-78 Victor 21365 (released 25 May 1928)

10″-78 English HMV B-5497
12″-LP Eng Jz JZ-4 "The Chronological Bing Crosby"

BVE-43140-3 **I'M WINGING HOME**
(vc by Bing Crosby with Al Rinker, Charles Gaylord, Jack Fulton, and Austin "Skin" Young)
(arrangement by Tommy Satterfield)
12″-LP Eng Jz JZ-4 "The Chronological Bing Crosby"

13 MARCH 1928 (Tue): 9:30 A.M.-1:00 P.M. and 2:30-4:00 P.M., Victor Record Co., New York, NY.

PAUL WHITEMAN ORCHESTRA: Bix Beiderbecke (crt); Charles Margulis, Henry Busse, Eddie Pinder (tpts); Boyce Cullen, Wilbur Hall, Bill Rank, Jack Fulton (tbns); **Frank Trumbauer**, Chester Hazlett, Irving Friedman, Red Mayer, Rube Crozier, Charles Strickfaden (reeds); Kurt Dieterle, Mischa Russell, Matty Malneck, Mario Perry (vns); Roy Bargy (p); Mike Pingitore (bjo); Milford "Min" Leibrook (tuba); Mike Trafficante (st-bs); Harold McDonald (dms).

CVE-43141-4 **METROPOLIS** (part 1)
(arrangement by Ferde Grofé)
12″-78 Victor 35933 (released 26 October 1928)
12″-78 Argentine Victor 35933
12″-78 Australian HMV EB-31
12″-78 Canadian Victor 35933
12″-78 Japanese Victor 35933
12″-LP Sunbeam Bix Vol 10 "Sincerely, Bix Beiderbecke"
12″-LP Italian Joker SM-3565 "Bixology Vol 9"

CVE-43142-4 **METROPOLIS** (part 2)
(arrangement by Ferde Grofé)
12″-78 Victor 335933 (released 26 October 1928)
12″-78 Argentine Victor 35933
12″-78 Australian HMV EB-31
12″-78 Canadian Victor 35933
12″-78 Japanese Victor 35933
12″-LP Sunbeam Bix Vol 10 "Sincerely, Bix Beiderbecke"
12″-LP Italian Joker SM-3565 "Bixology Vol 9"

See 14 March 1928 for METROPOLIS (part 3); and, 17 March 1928 for METROPOLIS (part 4).

14 MARCH 1928 (Wed): 9:30 A.M.–12:00 P.M., Victor Record Co., Liederkranz Hall, New York, NY.

PAUL WHITEMAN ORCHESTRA: Same personnel as for 13 March 1928.

CVE-43143-3 **METROPOLIS** (part 3)
(incidental vcs by Bing Crosby, Boyce Cullen, Jack Fulton, Charles Gaylord, Al Rinker, and Austin ''Skin'' Young)
(arrangement by Ferde Grofé)

12″-78 Victor Test Pressing
12″-LP Sunbeam Bix Vol 10 ''Sincerely, Bix Beiderbecke''
12″-LP Eng Jz JZ-4 ''The Chronological Bing Crosby''

CVE-43143-4 **METROPOLIS** (part 3)
(incidental vcs by Bing Crosby, Jack Fulton, Charles Gaylord, Al Rinker, Boyce Cullen, and Austin ''Skin'' Young)
(arrangement by Ferde Grofé)

12″-78 Victor 35934 (released 26 October 1928)
12″-78 Argentine Victor 35934
12″-78 Australian HMV EB-32
12″-78 Canadian Victor 35934
12″-78 Japanese Victor 35934
12″-LP Sunbeam Bix Vol 10 ''Sincerely, Bix Beiderbecke''
12″-LP Eng Jz JZ-4 ''The Chronological Bing Crosby''

Frank Trumbauer did not appear on the other selection from this session: BVE-43144, MA BELLE.

15 MARCH 1928 (Thu): Victor Record Co., New York, NY.

Trumbauer did not appear on the Whiteman recordings of: BVE-43145, LOVABLE and BVE-43146, WHEN YOU'RE IN LOVE.

16 MARCH 1928 (Fri): Victor Record Co., New York, NY.

Trumbauer did not appear on the Whiteman recordings of:

BVE-43147, LITTLE LOG CABIN OF DREAMS, and BVE-43148, MARCH OF THE MUSKETEERS.

17 MARCH 1928 (Sat): Victor Record Co., Liederkranz Hall, New York, NY.

PAUL WHITEMAN ORCHESTRA: Personnel same as for 13 March 1928.

CVE-43149-3 **METROPOLIS** (part 4)
(arrangement by Ferde Grofé)
12″-78 Victor 35934 (released 26 October 1928)
12″-78 Argentine Victor 35934
12″-78 Australian HMV EB-32
12″-78 Canadian Victor 35934
12″-78 Japanese Victor 35934
12″-LP Sunbeam Bix Vol 10 ''Sincerely, Bix Beiderbecke''

21 APRIL 1928 (Sat): 10:00 A.M.–1:25 P.M. and 2:25–4:00 P.M., Victor Record Co., Liederkranz Hall, New York, NY.

PAUL WHITEMAN ORCHESTRA: Bix Beiderbecke (crt); Charles Margulis, Henry Busse, Eddie Pinder (tpts); Boyce Cullen, Wilbur Hall, Bill Rank, Jack Fulton (tbns); **Frank Trumbauer**, Chester Hazlett, Irving Friedman, Red Mayer, Rube Crozier, Charles Strickfaden (reeds); Kurt Dieterle, Mischa Russell, Matty Malneck, Mario Perry, John Bowman, Charles Gaylord (vns); Roy Bargy, Lennie Hayton (ps); Mike Pingitore (bjo); Milford ''Min'' Leibrook (tuba); Mike Trafficante (st-bs); Harold McDonald (dms).

BVE-43659-1 **IN MY BOUQUET OF MEMORIES**
(vc by Austin Young, Charles Gaylord, Al Rinker, and Jack Fulton)
(arrangement by Tommy Satterfield)
10″-78 Victor 21388 (released 15 June 1928)
10″-78 Czechoslovakian HMV AM-1657
10″-78 English HMV B-5510
10″-78 German Electrola EG-1000
12″-LP Sunbeam Bix Vol 11 ''Sincerely, Bix Beiderbecke''

BVE-43659-3 **IN MY BOUQUET OF MEMORIES**
(vc by Austin Young, Charles Gaylord, Al Rinker, and Jack Fulton)

(arrangement by Tommy Satterfield)
12"-LP Sunbeam Bix Vol 11 "Sincerely, Bix Beiderbecke"

BVE-43660-3 **I'M AFRAID OF YOU**
(vc by Bing Crosby)
(arrangement by Tommy Satterfield)
10"-78 Victor 27685 (released 12 December 1941)
12"-LP Sunbeam Bix Vol 11 "Sincerely, Bix Beiderbecke"
12"-LP Eng Jz JZ-4 "The Chronological Bing Crosby"

BVE-43660-4 **I'M AFRAID OF YOU**
(vc by Bing Crosby)
(arrangement by Tommy Satterfield)
10"-78 Victor 21389 (released 8 June 1928)
10"-78 Australian HMV EA-373
10"-78 English HMV B-5541
10"-78 German Electrola EG-979
12"-LP Sunbeam Bix Vol 11 "Sincerely, Bix Beiderbecke"
12"-LP Eng Jz JZ-4 "The Chronological Bing Crosby"

BVE-43661-1 **MY ANGEL**
(vc by Jack Fulton, Charles Gaylord, and Al Rinker)
(arrangement by Tommy Satterfield)
10"-78 Victor 21388 (released 15 June 1928)
10"-78 Czechoslovakian HMV AM-1657
10"-78 English HMV B-5510
10"-78 German Electrola EG-1000
12"-LP Sunbeam Bix Vol 11 "Sincerely, Bix Beiderbecke"

BVE-43661-2 **MY ANGEL**
(vc by Jack Fulton, Charles Gaylord, and Al Rinker)
(arrangement by Tommy Satterfield)
12"-LP Sunbeam Bix Vol 11 "Sincerely, Bix Beiderbecke"

22 APRIL 1928 (Sun): 10:00 A.M.–12:05 P.M. and 1:05–3:00 P.M., Victor Record Co., New York, NY.

PAUL WHITEMAN ORCHESTRA: Bix Beiderbecke (crt); Charles Margulis, Henry Busse, Eddie Pinder (tpts); Boyce Cullen, Wilbur Hall, Bill Rank, Jack Fulton (tbns); **Frank Trumbauer** (C-mel/alto), Chester Hazlett, Irving Friedman, Red

Mayer, Rube Crozier, Charles Strickfaden (reeds); Kurt Dieterle, Mischa Russell, Matty Malneck, Mario Perry, John Bowman, Charles Gaylord (vns); Roy Bargy, Lennie Hayton, Ferde Grofé (ps); Mike Pingitore (bjo); Milford "Min" Leibrook (bs-sx/tuba); Mike Trafficante (st-bs); Harold McDonald (dms).

BVE-43662-1 **MY PET**
(vc by Bing Crosby, Al Rinker, Austin Young, and Charles Gaylord)
(arrangement by Bill Challis)
10″-78 Victor 27686 (released 12 December 1941)
12″-LP Sunbeam Bix Vol 11 "Sincerely, Bix Beiderbecke"
12″-LP Eng Jz JZ-4 "The Chronological Bing Crosby"
12″-LP Italian Joker SM-3566 "Bixology Vol 10"

BVE-43662-2 **MY PET**
(vc by Bing Crosby, Al Rinker, Austin Young, and Charles Gaylord)
(arrangement by Bill Challis)
10″-78 Victor 21389 (released 8 June 1928)
10″-78 Australian HMV EA-373
10″-78 English HMV B-5504
10″-78 German Electrola EG-979
10″-78 Indian HMV B-5504
12″-LP Sunbeam Bix Vol 11 "Sincerely, Bix Beiderbecke"
12″-LP Eng Jz JZ-4 "The Chronological Bing Crosby"
12″-LP Italian Joker SM-3566 "Bixology Vol 10"

BVE-43662-3 **MY PET**
(vc by Bing Crosby, Al Rinker, Austin Young, and Charles Gaylord)
(arrangement by Bill Challis)
10″-78 Victor Test Pressing
12″-LP Broadway 102
12″-LP Sunbeam Bix Vol 11 "Sincerely, Bix Beiderbecke"
12″-LP Eng Jz JZ-4 "The Chronological Bing Crosby"
12″-LP Italian Joker SM-3566 "Bixology Vol 10"

BVE-43663-1 **IT WAS THE DAWN OF LOVE**
(vc by Bing Crosby, Charles Gaylord, Austin Young, and Al Rinker)
(arrangement by Tommy Satterfield)

10″-78 Victor Test Pressing
12″-LP Broadway 102
12″-LP Sunbeam Bix Vol 12 "Sincerely, Bix Beiderbecke"
12″-LP Eng Jz JZ-4 "The Chronological Bing Crosby"
12″-LP Italian Joker SM-3566 "Bixology Vol 10"

BVE-43663-2 **IT WAS THE DAWN OF LOVE**
(vc by Bing Crosby, Charles Gaylord, Austin Young, and Al Rinker)
(arrangement by Tommy Satterfield)
10″-78 Victor 21453 (released 13 July 1928)
10″-78 Australian HMV EA-381
10″-78 English HMV B-5522
10″-78 German Electrola EG-932
10″-78 Italian Gramophone R-14001
12″-LP Sunbeam Bix Vol 12 "Sincerely, Bix Beiderbecke"
12″-LP Eng Jz JZ-4 "The Chronological Bing Crosby"
12″-LP Italian Joker SM-3566 "Bixology Vol 10"

BVE-43663-3 **IT WAS THE DAWN OF LOVE**
(vc by Bing Crosby, Charles Gaylord, Austin Young, and Al Rinker)
(arrangement by Tommy Satterfield)
10″-78 Victor Test Pressing
12″-LP Broadway 102
12″-LP Sunbeam Bix Vol 12 "Sincerely, Bix Beiderbecke"
12″-LP Eng Jz JZ-4 "The Chronological Bing Crosby"
12″-LP Italian Joker SM-3566 "Bixology Vol 10"

BVE-43664-1 **DANCING SHADOWS**
(humming by Bing Crosby, Al Rinker, Charles Gaylord, and Austin Young)
(arrangement by Tommy Satterfield)
10″-78 Victor 21341 (released 22 June 1928)
10″-78 Victor 27687
10″-78 Australian HMV EA-367
10″-78 Czechoslovakian HMV AM-1656
10″-78 English HMV B-5511
12″-LP Sunbeam Bix Vol 12 "Sincerely, Bix Beiderbecke"
12″-LP Eng Jz JZ-4 "The Chronological Bing Crosby"

BVE-43665-2 **FORGET-ME-NOT**
(vc by Jack Fulton)
(arrangement by Bill Challis)
10″-78 Victor 27686 (released 12 December 1941)
12″-LP Sunbeam Bix Vol 12 "Sincerely, Bix Beiderbecke"
12″-LP Italian Joker SM-3566 "Bixology Vol 10"

BVE-43665-3 **FORGET-ME-NOT**
(vc by Jack Fulton)
(arrangement by Bill Challis)
12″-LP Sunbeam Bix Vol 12 "Sincerely, Bix Beiderbecke"
12″-LP French RCA 741093
12″-LP Italian Joker SM-3566 "Bixology Vol 10"

23 APRIL 1928 (Mon): 12:50-4:00 P.M., Liederkranz Hall, Victor Record Co., New York, NY.

PAUL WHITEMAN ORCHESTRA: Bix Beiderbecke (crt); Charles Margulis, Henry Busse, Eddie Pinder (tpts); Boyce Cullen, Wilbur Hall, Bill Rank, Jack Fulton (tbns); **Frank Trumbauer** (C-mel/alto); Chet Hazlett, Irving Friedman, Red Mayer, Rube Crozier (reeds); Kurt Dieterle, Mischa Russell, Matty Malneck, Mario Perry, John Bowman, Charles Gaylord (vns); Roy Bargy, Lennie Hayton (ps); Mike Pingitore (bjo); Min Leibrook (tuba); Mike Trafficante (st-bs); Hal McDonald (dms).

BVE-43666-1 **DIXIE DAWN**
(vc by Austin "Skin" Young)
(arrangement by Ferde Grofé)
10″-78 Victor Test Pressing
12″-LP Sunbeam Bix Vol 12 "Sincerely, Bix Beiderbecke"

BVE-43666-2 **DIXIE DAWN**
(vc by Austin "Skin" Young)
(arrangement by Ferde Grofé)
10″-78 Victor Test Pressing
12″-LP Sunbeam Bix Vol 12 "Sincerely, Bix Beiderbecke"

BVE-43666-3 **DIXIE DAWN**
(vc by Austin "Skin" Young)
(arrangement by Ferde Grofé)
10″-78 Victor 21438 (released 6 July 1928)
10″-78 English HMV B-5515

10″-78 German Electrola EG-933
12″-LP Sunbeam Bix Vol 12 "Sincerely, Bix Beiderbecke"

BVE-43667-1 **LOUISIANA**
(vc by Bing Crosby, Charles Gaylord, Jack Fulton, and Austin Young)
(arrangement by Bill Challis)
10″-78 Biltmore 1030
10″-78 Victor 21438 (released 6 July 1928)
10″-78 Australian HMV EA-386
10″-78 Canadian Victor 21438
10″-78 English HMV B-5522
10″-78 German Electrola EG-933
10″-78 Indian HMV N-4475
10″-78 Swiss HMV JK-2809
12″-LP Sunbeam Bix Vol 12 "Sincerely, Bix Beiderbecke"
12″-LP Eng Jz JZ-5 "The Chronological Bing Crosby"
12″-LP Italian Joker SM-3566 "Bixology Vol 10"
12″-LP Polish Poljazz Z-SX-0659 (excerpt)

BVE-43667-3 **LOUISIANA**
(vc by Bing Crosby, Charles Gaylord, Jack Fulton, and Austin Young)
(arrangement by Bill Challis)
10″-78 Victor 25369 (released 30 July 1936)
10″-78 English HMV B-8913
12″-LP Sunbeam Bix Vol 12 "Sincerely, Bix Beiderbecke"
12″-LP Eng Jz JZ-5 "The Chronological Bing Crosby"
12″-LP Italian Joker SM-3566 "Bixology Vol 10"

Note on file card: April 23, 1928. 10:00-11:30. Rehearsed and cut 3 tests (playbacks) of "Blue Danube Waltz"; Mr. Whiteman decided NG, that is should be done by string orchestra. Continued rehearsing "Louisiana."

24 APRIL 1928 (Tue): 10:00-11:45 A.M. and 1:00-2:30 P.M., Victor Record Co., Liederkranz Hall, New York, NY.

PAUL WHITEMAN ORCHESTRA: Bix Beiderbecke (crt); Charles Margulis, Henry Busse, Eddie Pinder (tpts); Boyce Cullen, Wilbur Hall, Bill Rank, Jack Fulton (tbns); **Frank**

Trumbauer (C-mel/alto/bsn), Chester Hazlett, Irving Friedman, Red Mayer, Rube Crozier, Charles Strickfaden (reeds); Kurt Dieterle, Mischa Russell, Matty Malneck, Mario Perry, John Bowman, Charles Gaylord (vns); Roy Bargy, Lennie Hayton (ps); Mike Pingitore (bjo); Milford ''Min'' Leibrook (tuba); Mike Trafficante (st-bs); Harold McDonald (dms).

BVE-43668-2 **GRIEVING**
(vc by Jack Fulton, Charles Gaylord, Al Rinker, and Bing Crosby)
(arrangement by Tommy Satterfield)
10″-78 Victor 21678 (released 26 October 1928)
10″-78 English HMV B-5541
12″-LP Sunbeam Bix Vol 12 ''Sincerely, Bix Beiderbecke''
12″-LP Eng Jz JZ-5 ''The Chronological Bing Crosby''

BVE-43669-2 **DO I HEAR YOU SAYING**
(vc by Bing Crosby, Al Rinker, and Charles Gaylord)
10″-78 Victor 21389 (released 29 June 1928)
10″-78 German Electrola EG-929
12″-LP Sunbeam Bix Vol 12 ''Sincerely, Bix Beiderbecke''
12″-LP Eng Jz JZ-5 ''The Chronological Bing Crosby''

25 APRIL 1928 (Wed): 10:00-11:30 A.M., Victor Record Co., Liederkranz Hall, New York, NY.

PAUL WHITEMAN ORCHESTRA: Bix Beiderbecke (crt); Charles Margulis, Harry ''Goldie'' Goldfield, Eddie Pinder (tpts); Boyce Cullen, Wilbur Hall, Bill Rank, Jack Fulton (tbns); **Frank Trumbauer** (C-mel/alto), Chester Hazlett, Irving Friedman, Red Mayer, Rube Crozier, Charles Strickfaden (reeds); Kurt Dieterle, Mischa Russell, Matty Malneck, Mario Perry, John Bowman, Charles Gaylord (vns); Roy Bargy, Lennie Hayton (ps); Mike Pingitore (bjo); Milford ''Min'' Leibrook (tuba); Mike Trafficante (st-bs); George Marsh (dms).

BVE-43760-1 **YOU TOOK ADVANTAGE OF ME**
(vc by Bing Crosby, Jack Fulton, Charles Gaylord, and Austin Young)
(arrangement by Tommy Satterfield)

10″-78 Biltmore 1030
10″-78 Collectors Item No. 2
10″-78 Victor 21398 (released 29 June 1928)
10″-78 Victor 25369 (released 30 July 1936)
10″-78 Australian HMV EA-816
10″-78 German Electrola EG-929
12″-LP Sunbeam Bix Vol 12 ‘‘Sincerely, Bix Beiderbecke’’
12″-LP Eng Jz JZ-5 ‘‘The Chronological Bing Crosby’’
12″-LP Italian Joker SM-3566 ‘‘Bixology Vol 10’’

On some foreign pressings a ‘‘2’’ appears in the runoff grooves. This is only a speeded-up version of take ‘‘1’’ and not a bonafide take ‘‘2’’ pressing.

12 May 1928 (Sat): Presumed date of Fox Movietone Newsreel. See Chronology Section. Whiteman Orchestra plays ‘‘My Ohio Home.’’

12 MAY 1928 (Sat): Columbia Record Co., New York, NY.
PAUL WHITEMAN ORCHESTRA: Bix Beiderbecke (crt); Charles Margulis, Harry ‘‘Goldie’’ Goldfield, Eddie Pinder (tpts); Boyce Cullen, Wilbur Hall, Bill Rank, Jack Fulton (tbns); **Frank Trumbauer** (C-mel/alto), Chester Hazlett, Irving Friedman, Red Mayer, Rube Crozier, Charles Strickfaden (reeds); Kurt Dieterle, Mischa Russell, Matty Malneck, Mario Perry, Charles Gaylord (vns); Roy Bargy, Lennie Hayton (ps); Mike Pingitore (bjo); Milford ‘‘Min’’ Leibrook (tuba); Mike Trafficante (st-bs); George Marsh (dms).
Beiderbecke not on W-98535.

W-98533-2 **LA PALOMA** (THE DOVE)
(unidentified vocalist incidental singing ‘‘dah-dah . . . ’’)
(arrangement by Ferde Grofé)
10″-78 Columbia Test Pressing
12″-LP Sunbeam Bix Vol 13 ‘‘Sincerely, Bix Beiderbecke’’
12″-LP Eng Jz JZ-5 ‘‘The Chronological Bing Crosby’’

LA PALOMA was remade 21 May 1928.

W-98534-3 **LA GOLONDRINA** (THE SWALLOW)
(unidentified vocalist incidental humming)
(arrangement by Ferde Grofé)
10″-78 Columbia 50070-D
10″-78 Australian Columbia 07501
10″-78 English Columbia 9459
12″-LP Sunbeam Bix Vol 13 "Sincerely, Bix Beiderbecke"
12″-LP Eng Jz JZ-5 "The Chronological Bing Crosby"

W-98535-2 **MY HERO**
(vc by Austin Young)
(arrangement by Tommy Satterfield)
10″-78 Columbia 50069-D
10″-78 English Columbia 9460

13 MAY 1928 (Sun): Columbia Record Co., New York, NY.
PAUL WHITEMAN ORCHESTRA: Charles Margulis, Harry "Goldie" Goldfield, Eddie Pinder (tpts); Boyce Cullen, Wilbur Hall, Bill Rank, Jack Fulton (tbns); **Frank Trumbauer** (C-mel/alto), Chester Hazlett, Irving Friedman, Red Mayer, Rube Crozier, Charles Strickfaden (reeds); Kurt Dieterle, Mischa Russell, Matty Malneck, Mario Perry, Charles Gaylord (vns); Roy Bargy, Lennie Hayton (ps); Mike Pingitore (bjo); Milford "Min" Leibrook (tuba); Mike Trafficante (st-bs); George Marsh (dms).

W-98536-2 **THE MERRY WIDOW**
(arrangement by Tommy Satterfield)
10″-78 Columbia 50069-D
10″-78 English Columbia 9460

W-146249 **LAST NIGHT I DREAMED YOU KISSED ME**
(vc by Jack Fulton)
(arrangement by Tommy Satterfield)
Rejected. Remade 21 May 1928.

W-146250 **EVENING STAR**
(vc by Bing Crosby, Jack Fulton, Charles Gaylord, and Austin Young)
(arrangement by Tommy Satterfield)
Rejected. Remade 21 May 1928.

15 MAY 1928 (Tue): Columbia Record Co., New York, NY.
PAUL WHITEMAN ORCHESTRA: Bix Beiderbecke (crt); Charles Margulis, Harry ''Goldie'' Goldfield, Eddie Pinder (tpts); Boyce Cullen, Wilbur Hall, Bill Rank, Jack Fulton (tbns); **Frank Trumbauer** (alto), Chester Hazlett, Irving Friedman, Red Mayer, Rube Crozier, Charles Strickfaden (reeds); Kurt Dieterle, Mischa Russell, Matty Malneck, Charles Gaylord (vns); Roy Bargy (p); Lennie Hayton (cel); Mike Pingitore (bjo); Milford ''Min'' Leibrook (tuba); Mike Trafficante (st-bs); George Marsh (dms).

W-98537-A **MY MELANCHOLY BABY**
(vc Austin ''Skin'' Young)
(arrangement by Tommy Satterfield)
10″-78 Columbia 50068-D
10″-78 Australian Columbia 07053
10″-78 English Columbia 9678
12″-LP Sunbeam Bix Vol 13 ''Sincerely, Bix Beiderbecke''
12″-LP Italian Joker SM-3567 ''Bixology Vol 11''

16 MAY 1928 (Wed): Columbia Record Co., New York, NY.
PAUL WHITEMAN ORCHESTRA: Bix Beiderbecke (crt); Charles Margulis, Harry ''Goldie'' Goldfield, Eddie Pinder (tpts); Boyce Cullen, Wilbur Hall, Bill Rank, Jack Fulton (tbns); **Frank Trumbauer** (C-mel/bsn), Chester Hazlett, Irving Friedman, Red Mayer, Rube Crozier, Charles Strickfaden (reeds); Kurt Dieterle, Mischa Russell, Matty Malneck, Charles Gaylord (vns); Roy Bargy, Lennie Hayton (ps); Mike Pingitore (bjo); Milford ''Min'' Leibrook (tuba); Mike Trafficante (st-bs); George Marsh (dms).

W-98538-2 **THE MAN I LOVE**
(vc by Vaughn De Leath)
(arrangement by Ferde Grofé)
10″-78 Columbia 50068-D
12″-LP Sunbeam Bix Vol 13 ''Sincerely, Bix Beiderbecke''

W-98538-4 **THE MAN I LOVE**
(vc by Vaughn De Leath)
(arrangement by Ferde Grofé)
10″-78 Columbia 50068-D

10″-78 Australian Columbia 07053
12″-LP Sunbeam Bix Vol 13 ''Sincerely, Bix Beiderbecke''

17 MAY 1928 (Thu): Columbia Record Co., New York, NY.
PAUL WHITEMAN ORCHESTRA: Bix Beiderbecke (crt); Charles Margulis, Harry ''Goldie'' Goldfield, Eddie Pinder (tpts); Boyce Cullen, Wilbur Hall, Bill Rank (tbns); **Frank Trumbauer** (bsn/C-mel/alto), Chester Hazlett, Irving Friedman, Rube Crozier, Charles Strickfaden (reeds); Kurt Dieterle, Mischa Russell, Matty Malneck (vns); Roy Bargy (p); Mike Pingitore (bjo); Milford ''Min'' Leibrook (tuba); Mike Trafficante (st-bs); George Marsh (dms).

W-146291-2 **C-O-N-S-T-A-N-T-I-N-O-P-L-E**
(vc by Austin ''Skin'' Young, Jack Fulton, Charles Gaylord, Al Rinker, Harry Barris, and Bing Crosby)
(arrangement by Tommy Satterfield)
10″-78 Columbia 1402-D (released 20 June 1928)
10″-78 Australian Columbia 07002
10″-78 English Columbia 4951
10″-78 German Columbia C-4951
12″-LP Sunbeam Bix Vol 13 ''Sincerely, Bix Beiderbecke''
12″-LP Eng Jz JZ-5 ''The Chronological Bing Crosby''

W-146291-3 **C-O-N-S-T-A-N-T-I-N-O-P-L-E**
(vc by Austin ''Skin'' Young, Jack Fulton, Charles Gaylord, Al Rinker, Harry Barris, and Bing Crosby)
(arrangement by Tommy Satterfield)
10″-78 Columbia 1402-D (released 20 June 1928)
12″-LP Sunbeam Bix Vol 13 ''Sincerely, Bix Beiderbecke''
12″-LP Eng Jz JZ-5 ''The Chronological Bing Crosby''

21 MAY 1928 (Mon): Columbia Record Co., New York, NY.
PAUL WHITEMAN ORCHESTRA: Bix Beiderbecke (crt); Charles Margulis, Harry ''Goldie'' Goldfield (tpts); Boyce Cullen, Wilbur Hall, Bill Rank (tbns); **Frank Trumbauer** (C-mel/bsn), Chester Hazlett, Irving Friedman, Red Mayer, Charles Strickfaden (reeds); Kurt Dieterle, Mischa Russell, Matty Malneck, Mario Perry (vns); Roy Bargy (p); Mike

Pingitore (bjo); Milford ''Min'' Leibrook (tuba); Mike Trafficante (st-bs); George Marsh (dms).
Beiderbecke on 98533 and 146316 only.

W-98533-6 **LA PALOMA** (THE DOVE)
(unidentified vocalist incidental singing ''dah-dah . . . '')
(arrangement by Ferde Grofé)
10″-78 Columbia 50070-D
10″-78 Australian Columbia 07501
10″-78 English Columbia 9459
12″-LP Sunbeam Bix Vol 13 ''Sincerely, Bix Beiderbecke''
12″-LP Eng Jz JZ-5 ''The Chronological Bing Crosby''

W-146249-5 **LAST NIGHT I DREAMED YOU KISSED ME**
(vc by Jack Fulton)
(arrangement by Tommy Satterfield)
10″-78 Columbia 1401-D (released 20 June 1928)
10″-78 English Columbia 4950

W-146250-6 **EVENING STAR**
(vc by Bing Crosby, Jack Fulton, Charles Gaylord, and Austin Young)
(arrangement by Tommy Satterfield)
10″-78 Columbia 1401-D (released 20 June 1928)
10″-78 English Columbia 4950
12″-LP Eng Jz JZ-5 ''The Chronological Bing Crosby''

W-146316-1 **'TAIN'T SO HONEY, 'TAIN'T SO**

W-146316-2 **'TAIN'T SO HONEY, 'TAIN'T SO**

W-146316-3 **'TAIN'T SO HONEY, 'TAIN'T SO**

W-146316-4 **'TAIN'T SO HONEY, 'TAIN'T SO**
(vc by Bing Crosby)
(arrangement by Bill Challis)
Rejected. Remade 23 May 1928.

22 MAY 1928 (Tue): Columbia Record Co., New York, NY.
PAUL WHITEMAN ORCHESTRA: Bix Beiderbecke (crt); Charles Margulis, Harry ''Goldie'' Goldfield, Eddie Pinder

(tpts); Boyce Cullen, Wilbur Hall, Bill Rank, Jack Fulton (tbns); **Frank Trumbauer** (C-mel/alto), Chester Hazlett, Irving Friedman, Red Mayer, Rube Crozier, Charles Strickfaden (reeds); Kurt Dieterle, Mischa Russell, Matty Malneck, Mario Perry (vns); Roy Bargy (p); Mike Pingitore (bjo); Milford ''Min'' Leibrook (tuba); Mike Trafficante (st-bs); George Marsh (dms).
Beiderbecke not on W-146319.

W-146317-3 IS IT GONNA BE LONG?
(arrangement by Bill Challis)
10″-78 Columbia 1496-D (released 30 August 1928)
10″-78 Argentine Columbia A-8002
10″-78 Australian Columbia 07004
10″-78 English Columbia 4956
10″-78 German Columbia C-4956
12″-LP Sunbeam Bix Vol 13 ''Sincerely, Bix Beiderbecke''
12″-LP Italian Joker SM-3567 ''Bixology Vol 11''

W-146318-1 JAPANESE MAMMY

W-146318-2 JAPANESE MAMMY

W-146318-3 JAPANESE MAMMY

W-146318-4 JAPANESE MAMMY
(vc by Austin Young and unidentified trio)
(arrangement by Ferde Grofé)
Rejected. Remade 10 June 1928.

W-146319-3 GET OUT AND GET UNDER THE MOON
(vc by Bing Crosby, Jack Fulton, Charles Gaylord, and Austin Young)
(arrangement by Tommy Satterfield)
10″-78 Columbia 1402 (released 20 June 1928)
10″-78 English Columbia 4951
10″-78 English Columbia 5161
12″-LP Eng Jz JZ-5 ''The Chronological Bing Crosby''
12″-LP Italian Joker SM-3567 ''Bixology Vol 11''

W-146320-1 I'D RATHER CRY OVER YOU

W-146320-2 I'D RATHER CRY OVER YOU

W-146320-3 **I'D RATHER CRY OVER YOU**
(vc by Bing Crosby, Harry Barris, Al Rinker, Jack Fulton, Charles Gaylord, and Austin Young.)
(vc by Charles Gaylord and an unidentified trio)
(arrangement by Bill Challis)
Rejected. Remade 10 June 1928.

Apparently two sets of vocals were used on the final title. The Columbia file card failed to note which group was assigned to which take.

23 MAY 1928 (Wed): Columbia Record Co., New York, NY.
PAUL WHITEMAN ORCHESTRA: Bix Beiderbecke (crt); Charles Margulis, Harry ''Goldie'' Goldfield, Eddie Pinder (tpts); Boyce Cullen, Wilbur Hall, Bill Rank (tbns); **Frank Trumbauer** (C-mel/alto), Chester Hazlett, Irving Friedman, Red Mayer, Rube Crozier, Charles Strickfaden (reeds); Kurt Dieterle, Mischa Russell, Matty Malneck, Mario Perry (vns); Roy Bargy (p); Mike Pingitore (bjo); Milford ''Min'' Leibrook (tuba); Mike Trafficante (st-bs); George Marsh (dms).
Beiderbecke not on W-146326 and W-146328.

W-146316-5 **'TAIN'T SO, HONEY, 'TAIN'T SO**

W-146316-6 **'TAIN'T SO, HONEY, 'TAIN'T SO**

W-146316-7 **'TAIN'T SO, HONEY, 'TAIN'T SO**
(vc by Bing Crosby)
(arrangement by Bill Challis)
Rejected. Remade 10 June 1928.

W-146326-1 **IN THE EVENING**

W-146326-2 **IN THE EVENING**

W-146326-3 **IN THE EVENING**

W-146326-4 **IN THE EVENING**
(vc by Jack Fulton, Charles Gaylord, and Austin Young)

(arrangement by Tommy Satterfield)
Rejected. Remade 10 June 1928.

W-146327-2 **OH! YOU HAVE NO IDEA**
(arrangement by Bill Challis)
10″-78 Columbia 1491-D (released 30 August 1928)
10″-78 Australian Columbia 07005
10″-78 English Columbia 4956
10″-78 German Columbia C-4956
10″-78 Japanese Columbia J-540
12″-LP Sunbeam Bix Vol 13 "Sincerely, Bix Beiderbecke"

W-146328-4 **MOTHER GOOSE PARADE**
(vc by Austin "Skin" Young)
(arrangement by Ferde Grofé)
10″-78 Columbia 1478-D (released 20 August 1928)

24 MAY 1928 (Thu): Columbia Record Co., New York, NY.
PAUL WHITEMAN ORCHESTRA: Bix Beiderbecke (crt); Charles Margulis, Harry "Goldie" Goldfield (tpts); Boyce Cullen, Bill Rank (tbns); **Frank Trumbauer** (C-mel/alto/bsn), Chester Hazlett, Red Mayer, Charles Strickfaden (reeds); Kurt Dieterle, Mischa Russell, Matty Malneck, Mario Perry (vns); Roy Bargy (p); Mike Pingitore (bjo); Milford "Min" Leibrook (tuba); Mike Trafficante (st-bs); George Marsh (dms).

W-146329-3 **BLUE NIGHT**
(vc by Jack Fulton)
(arrangement by Tommy Satterfield)
10″-78 Columbia 1553-D
10″-78 English Columbia 5204
10″-78 German Columbia C-5204
12″-LP Sunbeam Bix Vol 13 "Sincerely, Bix Beiderbecke"

25 MAY 1928 (Fri): Columbia Record Co., New York, NY.
PAUL WHITEMAN ORCHESTRA: Bix Beiderbecke (crt); Charles Margulis, Harry Goldfield (tpts); Boyce Cullen, Wilbur Hall, Bill Rank (tbns); **Frank Trumbauer** (C-mel); Chet Hazlett, Red Mayer (altos); Rube Crozier (ten-sx); Kurt Dieterle, Mischa Russell, Matty Malneck, Mario Perry (vns);

Roy Bargy (p); Mike Pingitore (bjo); Min Leibrook (tuba); Mike Trafficante (st-bs); George Marsh (dms).

W-146334-4 **FELIX THE CAT**
(vc by Austin ''Skin'' Young)
(arrangement by Tommy Satterfield)

10″-78 Columbia 1478-D (released 20 August 1928)
10″-78 Argentine Columbia A-8006
10″-78 Australian Columbia 07008
10″-78 English Columbia 5040
10″-78 German Columbia C-5040
10″-78 Japanese Columbia J-541
10″-78 Spanish RE 5040
12″-LP Sunbeam Bix Vol 13 ''Sincerely, Bix Beiderbecke''
12″-LP Italian Joker SM-3567 ''Bixology Vol 11''

W-146335-1 **CHIQUITA**

W-146335-2 **CHIQUITA**

W-146335-3 **CHIQUITA**

W-146335-4 **CHIQUITA**
(vc by Jack Fulton)
(arrangement by Ferde Grofé)

Rejected. Remade 10 June 1928.

10 JUNE 1928 (Sun): Columbia Record Co., New York, NY.
PAUL WHITEMAN ORCHESTRA: Bix Beiderbecke (crt); Charles Margulis, Harry Goldfield (tpts); Boyce Cullen, Wilbur Hall, Bill Rank, Jack Fulton (tbns); **Frank Trumbauer** (C-mel/alto/bsn); Chet Hazlett, Red Mayer, Rube Crozier, Irving Friedman, Charles Strickfaden (reeds); Kurt Dieterle, Mischa Russell, Matty Malneck, Mario Perry, John Bowman, Charles Gaylord (vns); Roy Bargy (p); Mike Pingitore (bjo); Min Leibrook (tuba); Mike Trafficante (st-bs); George Marsh (dms).
Beiderbecke not on W-146326.

W-146316-9 **'TAIN'T SO, HONEY, 'TAIN'T SO**
(vc by Bing Crosby)
(arrangement by Bill Challis)

10″-78 Columbia 1444-D (released 20 July 1928)
10″-78 Argentine Columbia A-8230
10″-78 Australian Columbia 07003
10″-78 English Columbia 4981
10″-78 German Columbia C-4981
10″-78 Japanese Columbia J-533
12″-LP Columbia GL-509
12″-LP Sunbeam Bix Vol 14 "Sincerely, Bix Beiderbecke"
12″-LP Czechoslovakian Columbia 4981
12″-LP Eng Jz JZ-6 "The Chronological Bing Crosby"
12″-LP Italian Joker SM-3567 "Bixology Vol 11"
12″-LP Russian Melodija 33M60-41643-44
C-DISC Eng Pavilion/Pearl PAST-CD-9765 "The Genius Of Bix Beiderbecke"

W-146318-6 **JAPANESE MAMMY**
(vc by Austin "Skin" Young and unidentified trio)
(arrangement by Ferde Grofé)
10″-78 Columbia 1701-D (released 15 February 1929)
12″-LP Sunbeam Bix Vol 14 "Sincerely, Bix Beiderbecke"

W-146320-5 **I'D RATHER CRY OVER YOU**
(vc by Bing Crosby, Jack Fulton, Charles Gaylord, and Austin Young)
(arrangement by Bill Challis)
10″-78 Columbia 1496-D (released 30 August 1928)
10″-78 Argentine Columbia A-8002
10″-78 Australian Columbia 07005
10″-78 English Columbia 4980
10″-78 German Columbia C-4980
10″-78 Japanese Columbia J-539
12″-LP Sunbeam Bix Vol 14 "Sincerely, Bix Beiderbecke"
12″-LP Eng Jz JZ-6 "The Chronological Bing Crosby"
12″-LP Italian Joker SM-3567 "Bixology Vol 11"

W-146326-5 **IN THE EVENING**
(vc by Jack Fulton, Charles Gaylord, and Austin Young)
(arrangement by Tommy Satterfield)
10″-78 Columbia 1484-D (released 20 August 1928)

W-146335-6 CHIQUITA
(vc by Jack Fulton)
(arrangement by Ferde Grofé)
10″-78 Columbia 1448-D (released 20 July 1928)
10″-78 English Columbia 4981
10″-78 German Columbia C-4981
12″-LP Sunbeam Bix Vol 14 ''Sincerely, Bix Beiderbecke''

17 JUNE 1928 (Sun): Columbia Record Co., New York, NY.
PAUL WHITEMAN ORCHESTRA: Bix Beiderbecke (crt); Charles Margulis, Harry Goldfield (tpts); Boyce Cullen, Wilbur Hall, Bill Rank, Jack Fulton (tbns); **Frank Trumbauer** (clt/C-mel/alto); Chet Hazlett, Red Mayer, Rube Crozier, Irving Friedman, Charles Strickfaden (reeds); Kurt Dieterle, Mischa Russell, Matty Malneck, Mario Perry (vns); Roy Bargy, Lennie Hayton (ps); Mike Pingitore (bjo); Min Leibrook (tuba); Mike Trafficante (st-bs); George Marsh (dms).
Beiderbecke not on W-146544, W-146545, and W-146546.

W-146541-3 I'M ON THE CREST OF A WAVE
(vc by Bing Crosby, Jack Fulton, Charles Gaylord, and Austin Young)
(arrangement by Ferde Grofé)
10″-78 Columbia 1465-D (released 10 August 1928)
10″-78 Australian Columbia 07012
10″-78 English Columbia 5241
12″-LP Sunbeam Bix Vol 14 ''Sincerely, Bix Beiderbecke''
12″-LP Eng Jz JZ-6 ''The Chronological Bing Crosby''

W-146542-3 THAT'S MY WEAKNESS NOW
(vc by Bing Crosby, Al Rinker, and Harry Barris)
(arrangement by Tommy Satterfield)
10″-78 Columbia 1444-D (released 20 July 1928)
10″-78 Argentine Columbia A-8230
10″-78 Australian Columbia 07008
10″-78 English Columbia 5006
10″-78 German Columbia C-5006
10″-78 Japanese Columbia J-533
12″-LP Sunbeam Bix Vol 14 ''Sincerely, Bix Beiderbecke''

12″-LP Eng Jz JZ-6 ''The Chronological Bing Crosby''
12″-LP Italian Joker SM-3567 ''Bixology Vol 11''

W-146543-3 **GEORGIE PORGIE**
(vc by Bing Crosby, Al Rinker, and Harry Barris)
(arrangement by Bill Challis)
10″-78 Columbia 1491-D (released 30 August 1928)
10″-78 Australian Columbia 07011
10″-78 English Columbia 5040
10″-78 German Columbia C-5040
10″-78 Japanese Columbia J-533
10″-78 Spanish RE 5040
12″-LP Sunbeam Bix Vol 14 ''Sincerely, Bix Beiderbecke''
12″-LP Eng Jz JZ-6 ''The Chronological Bing Crosby''
12″-LP Italian Joker SM-3567 ''Bixology Vol 11''

W-146544-1 **IF YOU DON'T LOVE ME**

W-146544-2 **IF YOU DON'T LOVE ME**

W-146544-3 **IF YOU DON'T LOVE ME**

W-146544-4 **IF YOU DON'T LOVE ME**
(vc by Bing Crosby)
(arrangement by Tommy Satterfield)
Rejected.

W-146545-4 **JUST LIKE A MELODY OUT OF THE SKY**
(vc by Jack Fulton, Charles Gaylord, and Austin Young)
(arrangement by Tommy Satterfield)
10″-78 Columbia 1441-D (released 20 July 1928)
10″-78 English Columbia 5007

W-146546-3 **LONESOME IN THE MOONLIGHT**
(incidental vc by Bing Crosby, Austin Young, and Jack Fulton)
(arrangement by Ferde Grofé)
10″-78 Columbia 1448-D (released 20 July 1928)
10″-78 English Columbia 5039
12″-LP Eng Jz JZ-6 ''The Chronological Bing Crosby''

18 JUNE 1928 (Mon): Columbia Record Co., New York, NY.
PAUL WHITEMAN ORCHESTRA: Bix Beiderbecke (crt); Charles Margulis, Harry Goldfield (tpts); Wilbur Hall, Bill Rank (tbns); **Frank Trumbauer**, Chet Hazlett (altos), Irving Friedman (ten-sx), Charles Strickfaden(bar-sx); Kurt Dieterle, Mischa Russell, Matty Malneck, Mario Perry (vns); Roy Bargy (p); Mike Pingitore (bjo); Min Leibrook (tuba); Mike Trafficante (st-bs); George Marsh (dms).
Beiderbecke not on W-146547 and W-146548.

W-146547-2 **JUST A LITTLE BIT OF DRIFTWOOD**
(vc by Austin Young)
(arrangement by Ferde Grofé)
10″-78 Columbia 1505-D (released 10 September 1928)
10″-78 English Columbia 5071

W-146548-1 **SORRY FOR ME**

W-146548-2 **SORRY FOR ME**

W-146548-3 **SORRY FOR ME**
(vocalist unidentified)
(arr unidentified)
Rejected.

W-146549-2 **BECAUSE MY BABY DON'T MEAN MAYBE NOW**
(vc by Bing Crosby, Charles Gaylord, Jack Fulton, and Austin Young)
(arrangement by Bill Challis)
10″-78 Columbia 1441-D (released 20 July 1928)
10″-78 Argentine Columbia A-8010
10″-78 Australian Columbia 07007
10″-78 English Columbia 5007
10″-78 German Columbia C-5007
10″-78 Japanese Columbia J-532
12″-LP Columbia CL-2830
12″-LP Columbia GL-509
12″-LP Sunbeam Bix Vol 14 "Sincerely, Bix Beiderbecke"
12″-LP Eng Jz JZ-6 "The Chronological Bing Crosby"
12″-LP Italian Joker SM-3567 "Bixology Vol 11"

146550-3 **OUT O' TOWN GAL**
(vc by The Rhythm Boys: Harry Barris, Bing Crosby, and Al Rinker)
(arrangement by Bill Challis)

10″-78 Columbia 1505-D (released 10 September 1928)
10″-78 Argentine Columbia A-8011
10″-78 Australian Columbia 07001
10″-78 English Columbia 5039
10″-78 German Columbia C-5039
10″-78 Japanese Columbia J-542
12″-LP Columbia CL-2830
12″-LP Sunbeam Bix Vol 14 "Sincerely, Bix Beiderbecke"
12″-LP Eng Jz JZ-6 "The Chronological Bing Crosby"
12″-LP Italian Joker SM-3567 "Bixology Vol 11"

19 JUNE 1928 (Tue): Columbia Record Co., New York, NY.
PAUL WHITEMAN ORCHESTRA: Bix Beiderbecke (crt); Charles Margulis, Harry Goldfield, Eddie Pinder (tpts); Boyce Cullen, Wilbur Hall, Bill Rank, Jack Fulton (tbns); **Frank Trumbauer** (C-mel/bsn/alto); Chet Hazlett, Red Mayer, Rube Crozier, Irving Friedman, Charles Strickfaden (reeds); Kurt Dieterle, Mischa Russell, Matty Malneck, Mario Perry, John Bowman, Charles Gaylord (vns); Roy Bargy, Lennie Hayton (ps); Mike Pingitore (bjo); Min Leibrook (tuba); Mike Trafficante (st-bs); George Marsh (dms).

W-146551-2 **AMERICAN TUNE**
(vc by Austin "Skin" Young)
(arrangement by Ferde Grofé)

10″-78 Columbia 1464-D (released 10 August 1928)
10″-78 English Columbia 5242
12″-LP Sunbeam Bix Vol 14 "Sincerely, Bix Beiderbecke"

20 JUNE 1928 (Wed): Columbia Record Co., New York, NY.
PAUL WHITEMAN ORCHESTRA: Bix Beiderbecke (crt); Charles Margulis, Harry Goldfield, Eddie Pinder (tpts); Boyce Cullen, Wilbur Hall, Bill Rank, Jack Fulton (tbns); **Frank Trumbauer**, Chet Hazlett, Red Mayer, Rube Crozier, Irving Friedman, Charles Strickfaden (reeds); Kurt Dieterle, Mischa Russell, Matty Malneck, Mario Perry, Charles Gaylord, John

Bowman (vns); Roy Bargy, Lennie Hayton (ps); Mike Pingitore (bjo); Min Leibrook (tuba); Mike Trafficante (st-bs); George Marsh (dms).

W-98556-3 **TCHAIKOWSKIANA** (part 1)
(A Fantasy On Tchaikowsky Themes)
(arrangement by Herman Hand)
10″-78 Columbia 50113-D
10″-78 English Columbia 9470
10″-78 German Columbia C-9470
12″-LP Sunbeam Bix Vol 14 "Sincerely, Bix Beiderbecke"

W-98557-4 **TCHAIKOWSKIANA** (part 2)
(A Fantasy On Tchaikowsky Themes)
(arrangement by Herman Hand)
10″-78 Columbia 50113-D
10″-78 English Columbia 9470
10″-78 German Columbia C-9470
12″-LP Sunbeam Bix Vol 14 "Sincerely, Bix Beiderbecke"

2 JULY 1928 (Mon):
The recordings, PICKIN' COTTON on Columbia 1464-D and WHAT D'YA SAY on Columbia 1465-d are by a studio orchestra conducted by Ben Selvin and not Whiteman.

20 JULY 1928 (Sat):
The recording, IF YOU DON'T LOVE ME on Columbia 1484-D is by a studio orchestra conducted by Ben Selvin.

All the recordings were issued as by Paul Whiteman and His Orchestra.

4 SEPTEMBER 1928 (Tue): Columbia Record Co., New York, NY.
PAUL WHITEMAN ORCHESTRA: Bix Beiderbecke (crt); Charles Margulis, Eddie Pinder, Harry Goldfield (tpts); Boyce Cullen, Wilbur Hall, Bill Rank, Jack Fulton (tbns); **Frank Trumbauer** (alto); Chet Hazlett, Red Mayer, Irving Friedman, Charles Strickfaden (reeds); Kurt Dieterle, Mischa Russell, Matty Malneck, John Bowman (vns); Roy Bargy (p); Lennie

Hayton (cel); Mike Pingitore (bjo); Min Leibrook (tuba); Mike Trafficante (st-bs); George Marsh (dms).

W-146945-1 **In The Good Old Summertime** (waltz medley)

W-146945-2 **In The Good Old Summertime** (waltz medley)

W-146945-3 **In The Good Old Summertime** (waltz medley)

W-146945-4 **In The Good Old Summertime** (waltz medley)
a. **IN THE GOOD OLD SUMMERTIME**
b. **LITTLE ANNIE ROONEY**
c. **COMRADES**
d. **SWEET ROSIE O'GRADY**
e. **YIP-I-ADDY-I-AY**
(vc by unidentified quartet)
(arrangement by Bill Challis)

Rejected. Remade 14 September 1928.

Columbia File Card refers to ''Miscellaneous Quartet.''

W-146946-1 **THE SIDEWALKS OF NEW YORK**

W-146946-2 **THE SIDEWALKS OF NEW YORK**

W-146946-3 **THE SIDEWALKS OF NEW YORK**

W-146946-4 **THE SIDEWALKS OF NEW YORK**
(vc by unidentified quartet)
(arrangement by Bill Challis)

Rejected. Remade 14 September 1928.

Columbia File Card refers to ''Miscellaneous Quartet.''

W-146947-3 **ROSES OF YESTERDAY**
(vc by Austin ''Skin'' Young)
(arrangement by Ferde Grofé)

10″-78 Columbia 1553-D
10″ 78 English Columbia 5161
12″-LP Sb Bix Vol 15 ‘‘Sincerely, Bix Beiderbecke’’

5 SEPTEMBER 1928 (Wed): Columbia Record Co., New York, NY.

PAUL WHITEMAN ORCHESTRA: Bix Beiderbecke (crt); Charles Margulis, Harry Goldfield, Eddie Pinder (tpts); Boyce Cullen, Wilbur Hall, Bill Rank, Jack Fulton (tbns); **Frank Trumbauer**, Chet Hazlett, Red Mayer, Rube Crozier, Irving Friedman, Charles Strickfaden (reeds); Kurt Dieterle, Mischa Russell, Matty Malneck, Mario Perry, John Bowman, Charles Gaylord (vns); Roy Bargy (p); Mike Pingitore (bjo); Min Leibrook (tuba); Mike Trafficante (st-bs); George Marsh (dms).

W-98568-1 **CONCERTO IN F** (part 1)

W-98568-2 **CONCERTO IN F** (part 1)

W-98568-3 **CONCERTO IN F** (part 1)

W-98568-4 **CONCERTO IN F** (part 1)
(First Movement—Allegro—Commencement)
(arrangement by Ferde Grofé)

Rejected. Remade 15 September 1928.

6 SEPTEMBER 1928 (Thu): Columbia Record Co., New York, NY.

PAUL WHITEMAN ORCHESTRA: Personnel same as for 5 September 1928.

W-98569-1 **CONCERTO IN F** (part 2)

W-98569-2 **CONCERTO IN F** (part 2)

W-98569-3 **CONCERTO IN F** (part 2)

W-98569-4 **CONCERTO IN F** (part 2)
(First Movement—Allegro—Continuation)
(arrangement by Ferde Grofé)

Rejected. Remade 15 September 1928.

W-98570-1 **CONCERTO IN F** (part 3)

W-98570-2 **CONCERTO IN F** (part 3)

W-98570-3 **CONCERTO IN F** (part 3)

W-98570-4 **CONCERTO IN F** (part 3)
(First Movement—Allegro—Completion)
(arrangement by Ferde Grofé)

Rejected. Remade 15 September 1928.

14 SEPTEMBER 1928 (Fri): Columbia Record Co., New York, NY.

PAUL WHITEMAN ORCHESTRA: Bix Beiderbecke (crt); Charles Margulis, Eddie Pinder (tpts); Boyce Cullen, Wilbur Hall, Bill Rank (tbns); **Frank Trumbauer** (alto); Chet Hazlett, Red Mayer, Irving Friedman, Charles Strickfaden (reeds); Kurt Dieterle, Mischa Russell, Matty Malneck, Mario Perry, John Bowman (vns); Roy Bargy (p); Lennie Hayton (cel); Mike Pingitore (bjo); Min Leibrook (tuba); Mike Trafficante (st-bs); George Marsh (dms).

W-146945-5 **In The Good Old Summertime** (waltz medley)
a. **IN THE GOOD OLD SUMMER-TIME**
b. **LITTLE ANNIE ROONEY**
c. **COMRADES**
d. **SWEET ROSIE O'GRADY**
e. **YIP-I-ADDY-I-AY**
(vc by unidentified quartet)
(arrangement by Bill Challis)

10″-78 Columbia 1558-D (released 20 October 1928)
12″-LP Sunbeam Bix Vol 15 ''Sincerely, Bix Beiderbecke''

W-146946-6 **THE SIDEWALKS OF NEW YORK**
(vc by unidentified quartet)
(arrangement by Bill Challis)

10″-78 Columbia 1558-D (released 20 October 1928)
12″-LP Sunbeam Bix Vol 15 ''Sincerely, Bix Beiderbecke''

The Columbia File Card lists ''Miscellaneous Quartet.''

15 SEPTEMBER 1928 (Sat): Columbia Record Co., New York, NY.

PAUL WHITEMAN ORCHESTRA: Bix Beiderbecke (crt); Charles Margulis, Harry Goldfield, Eddie Pinder (tpts); Boyce Cullen, Wilbur Hall, Bill Rank, Jack Fulton (tbns); **Frank Trumbauer**, Chet Hazlett, Red Mayer, Rube Crozier, Irving Friedman, Charles Strickfaden (reeds); Kurt Dieterle, Mischa Russell, Matty Malneck, Mario Perry, John Bowman, Charles Gaylord (vns); Roy Bargy (p); Mike Pingitore (bjo); Min Leibrook (tuba); Mike Trafficante (st-bs); George Marsh (dms).

W-98568-8 **CONCERTO IN F** (part 1)
(First Movement—Allegro—Commencement)
(arrangement by Ferde Grofé)

10″-78 Columbia 7170-M
10″-78 Columbia 50139-D
10″-78 Columbia ML-7315
10″-78 Argentine Columbia A-1157
10″-78 Australian Columbia 07506
10″-78 English Columbia 9665
10″-78 Italian Columbia GQX-10968
12″-LP Sunbeam Bix Vol 15 ''Sincerely, Bix Beiderbecke''
12″-LP Italian Joker SM-3568 ''Bixology Vol 12''

W-98569-5 **CONCERTO IN F** (part 2)
(First Movement—Allegro—Continuation)
(arrangement by Ferde Grofé)

10″-78 Columbia 7170-M
10″-78 Columbia 50139-D
10″-78 Columbia ML-7315
10″-78 Argentine Columbia A-1157
10″-78 Australian Columbia 07506
10″-78 English Columbia 9665
10″-78 Italian Columbia GQX-10968
12″-LP Sunbeam Bix Vol 15 ''Sincerely, Bix Beiderbecke''
12″-LP Italian Joker SM-3568 ''Bixology Vol 12''

W-98570-5 **CONCERTO IN F** (part 3)
(First Movement—Allegro—Completion)

(arrangement by Ferde Grofé)
10″-78 Columbia 7171-M
10″-78 Columbia 50140-D
10″-78 Columbia ML-7316
10″-78 Argentine Columbia A-1158
10″-78 Australian Columbia 07507
10″-78 English Columbia 9666
10″-78 Italian Columbia GQX-10969
12″-LP Sunbeam Bix Vol 15 "Sincerely, Bix Beiderbecke"
12″-LP Italian Joker SM-3568 "Bixology Vol 12"

W-98576-2 **CONCERTO IN F** (part 4)
(Second Movement—Andante Con Moto—First Half)
(arrangement by Ferde Grofé)
10″-78 Columbia 7171-M
10″-78 Columbia 50140-D
10″-78 Columbia ML-7316
10″-78 Columbia Argentine A-1158
10″-78 Australian Columbia 07507
10″-78 English Columbia 9666
10″-78 Italian Columbia GQX-10969
12″-LP Sunbeam Bix Vol 15 "Sincerely, Bix Beiderbecke"
12″-LP Italian Joker SM-3568 "Bixology Vol 12"

17 SEPTEMBER 1928 (Mon): Columbia Record Co., New York, NY.

PAUL WHITEMAN ORCHESTRA: Bix Beiderbecke (crt); Charles Margulis, Harry Goldfield, Eddie Pinder (tpts); Boyce Cullen, Wilbur Hall, Bill Rank, Jack Fulton (tbns); **Frank Trumbauer** (clt/bsn/alto); Chet Hazlett, Red Mayer, Rube Crozier, Irving Friedman, Charles Strickfaden (reeds); Kurt Dieterle, Mischa Russell, Matty Malneck, Mario Perry, John Bowman, Charles Gaylord (vns); Roy Bargy (p); Lennie Hayton (cel); Mike Pingitore (bjo); Min Leibrook (tuba); Mike Trafficante (st-bs); George Marsh (dms).

W-98577-3 **JEANNINE, I DREAM OF LILAC TIME**
(vc by Jack Fulton)
(arrangement by Ferde Grofé)

10″-78 Columbia 50095-D
10″-78 English Columbia 9578
12″-LP Sunbeam Bix Vol 15 "Sincerely, Bix Beiderbecke"

W-98578-4 **CONCERTO IN F** (part 5)
(Second Movement—Andante Con Moto—Completion)
(arrangement by Ferde Grofé)
10″-78 Columbia 7172-M
10″-78 Columbia 50141-D
10″-78 Columbia ML-7317
10″-78 Argentine Columbia A-1159
10″-78 Australian Columbia 07508
10″-78 English Columbia 9667
10″-78 Italian Columbia GQX-10970
12″-LP Sunbeam Bix Vol 15 "Sincerely, Bix Beiderbecke"
12″-LP Italian Joker SM-3568 "Bixology Vol 12"

W-98575-3 **CONCERTO IN F** (part 6)
(Finale—Allegro Con Brio)
(arrangement by Ferde Grofé)
10″-78 Columbia 7172-M
10″-78 English Columbia 9667
10″-78 Italian Columbia GQX-10970
12″-LP Sunbeam Bix Vol 15 "Sincerely, Bix Beiderbecke"
12″-LP Italian Joker SM-3568 "Bixology Vol 12"

W-98575, CONCERTO IN F (part 6), was later recalled and remade on 5 October 1928.

18 SEPTEMBER 1928 (Tue): Columbia Record Co., New York, NY.

PAUL WHITEMAN ORCHESTRA: Bix Beiderbecke (crt); Charles Margulis, Harry Goldfield, Eddie Pinder (tpts); Boyce Cullen, Wilbur Hall, Bill Rank, Jack Fulton (tbns); **Frank Trumbauer** (bsn/clt/C-mel); Chet Hazlett, Red Mayer, Rube Crozier, Irving Friedman, Charles Strickfaden (reeds); Kurt Dieterle, Mischa Russell, Matty Malneck, John Bowman, Charles Gaylord (vns); Roy Bargy, Lennie Hayton (ps); Mario

Perry (acc/vn); Mike Pingitore (bjo); Min Leibrook (tuba); Mike Trafficante (st-bs); George Marsh (dms).

W-98579-5 **GYPSY**
(vc by Austin ''Skin'' Young)
(arrangement by Ferde Grofé)
10″-78 Columbia 50095-D
12″-LP Columbia CSP-LP-16784
12″-LP Sunbeam Bix Vol 15 ''Sincerely, Bix Beiderbecke''
12″-LP Italian Joker SM-3568 ''Bixology Vol 12''

W-98584-1 **SWEET SUE, JUST YOU**
(vc by Jack Fulton)
(arrangement by Bill Challis)
10″-78 Columbia 35667 (edited to fit 10'' disc)
12″-78 Columbia 50103-D
12″-78 Argentine Columbia A-405
12″-78 Australian Columbia 07509
12″-78 English Columbia 9572
12″-LP Columbia GL-509
12″-LP Sunbeam Bix Vol 15 ''Sincerely, Bix Beiderbecke''
12″-LP Italian Joker SM-3568 ''Bixology Vol 12''

19 SEPTEMBER 1928 (Wed): Columbia Record Co., New York, NY.

PAUL WHITEMAN ORCHESTRA: Bix Beiderbecke (crt); Charles Margulis, Harry Goldfield, Eddie Pinder (tpts); Boyce Cullen, Wilbur Hall, Bill Rank, Jack Fulton (tbns); **Frank Trumbauer** (bsn/alto); Chet Hazlett, Red Mayer, Rube Crozier, Irving Friedman, Charles Strickfaden (reeds); Kurt Dieterle, Mischa Russell, Matty Malneck, Mario Perry (vns); Roy Bargy (p); Lennie Hayton (cel); Eddie King (sleighbells/org/p); unidentified (h); Mike Pingitore (bjo); Min Leibrook (tuba); Mike Trafficante (st-bs); George Marsh (dms).
Beiderbecke not on W-98585.

W-98585-2 **SILENT NIGHT, HOLY NIGHT**
(humming by Bing Crosby, Jack Fulton, Charles Gaylord, Austin Young)
(arrangement by Bill Challis)

12″-78 Columbia 50098-D
12″-78 English Columbia 9561
12″-LP Eng Jz JZ-6 "The Chronological Bing Crosby"

W-98586-3 CHRISTMAS MELODIES
(arrangement by Ferde Grofé)
a. **O HOLY NIGHT** (NOEL)
(humming by Bing Crosby, Jack Fulton, Charles Gaylord, Austin Young)
b. **ADESTE FIDELIS** (aka O COME ALL YE FAITHFUL)

12″-78 Columbia 50098-D
12″-78 Australian Columbia 07511
12″-78 English Columbia 9561
12″-LP Sunbeam Bix Vol 16 "Sincerely, Bix Beiderbecke"
12″-LP Eng Jz JZ-6 "The Chronological Bing Crosby"

21 SEPTEMBER 1928 (Fri): Columbia Record Co., New York, NY.

PAUL WHITEMAN ORCHESTRA: Bix Beiderbecke (crt); Charles Margulis, Harry Goldfield, Eddie Pinder (tpts); Boyce Cullen, Wilbur Hall, Bill Rank, Jack Fulton (tbns); **Frank Trumbauer** (clt/bsn/sop-sx/C-mel); Chet Hazlett, Red Mayer, Rube Crozier, Irving Friedman, Charles Strickfaden (reeds); Kurt Dieterle, Mischa Russell, Matty Malneck, Mario Perry, John Bowman, Charles Gaylord (vns); Roy Bargy (p); Lennie Hayton (cel); Mike Pingitore (bjo); Min Leibrook (tuba); Mike Trafficante (st-bs); George Marsh (dms).

W-98589-3 **I CAN'T GIVE YOU ANYTHING BUT LOVE**
(vc by Jack Fulton)
(arrangement by Ferde Grofé)

12″-78 Columbia 50103-D
12″-78 English Columbia 9572
12″-LP Sunbeam Bix Vol 16 "Sincerely, Bix Beiderbecke"

W-147032-1 **WHERE IS THE SONG OF SONGS FOR ME?**

W-147032-2 **WHERE IS THE SONG OF SONGS FOR ME?**

W-147032-3 **WHERE IS THE SONG OF SONGS FOR ME?**

W-147032-4 **WHERE IS THE SONG OF SONGS FOR ME?**
(vc by Jack Fulton)
(arrangement by Bill Challis)

Rejected. Remade 6 October 1928.

5 OCTOBER 1928 (Fri): Columbia Record Co., New York, NY. PAUL WHITEMAN ORCHESTRA: Bix Beiderbecke (crt); Charles Margulis, Harry Goldfield, Eddie Pinder (tpts); Boyce Cullen, Wilbur Hall, Bill Rank, Jack Fulton (tbns); **Frank Trumbauer**, Chet Hazlett, Rube Crozier, Red Mayer, Irving Friedman, Charles Strickfaden (reeds); Kurt Dieterle, Mischa Russell, Matty Malneck, John Bowman, Charles Gaylord, Mario Perry (vns); Roy Bargy (p); Mike Pingitore (bjo); Min Leibrook (tuba); Mike Trafficante (st-bs); George Marsh (dms).

W-98575-7 **CONCERTO IN F** (part 6)
(Finale—Allegro Con Brio)
(arrangement by Ferde Grofé)

12″-78 Columbia 7172-M
12″-78 Columbia 50141-D
12″-78 Columbia ML-7317
12″-78 Argentine Columbia A-1159
12″-78 Australian Columbia 07508
12″-78 English Columbia 9667
12″-78 Italian Columbia GQX-10970
12″-LP Sunbeam Bix Vol 16 ‘‘Sincerely, Bix Beiderbecke’’
12″-LP Italian Joker SM-3568 ‘‘Bixology Vol 12’’

6 OCTOBER 1928 (Sat): Columbia Record Co., New York, NY. PAUL WHITEMAN ORCHESTRA: Bix Beiderbecke or Eddie Pinder (crt); Charles Margulis, Harry Goldfield (tpts); Boyce Cullen, Wilbur Hall, Bill Rank (tbns); **Frank Trumbauer** (alto); Chet Hazlett, Red Mayer, Irving Friedman, Charles Strickfaden (reeds); Kurt Dieterle, Mischa Russell, Matty Malneck, Charles Gaylord (vns); Roy Bargy (p); Lennie Hayton (cel); Mike Pingitore (bjo); Min Leibrook (tuba); Mike Trafficante (st-bs); George Marsh (dms).

W-147032-8 **WHERE IS THE SONG OF SONGS FOR ME?**
(vc by Jack Fulton)
(arrangement by Ferde Grofé)
10″-78 Columbia 1630-D (released 20 December 1928)
10″-78 English Columbia 5204
10″-78 German Columbia C-5204
12″-LP Sunbeam Bix Vol 16 ''Sincerely, Bix Beiderbecke''

11 DECEMBER 1928 (Tue): Columbia Record Co., New York, NY.

PAUL WHITEMAN ORCHESTRA: Bix Beiderbecke (crt); Charles Margulis, Harry Goldfield, Eddie Pinder (tpts); Boyce Cullen, Wilbur Hall, Bill Rank, Jack Fulton (tbns); **Frank Trumbauer** (bsn/clt/C-mel/alto); Chet Hazlett, Rube Crozier, Red Mayer, Irving Friedman, Charles Strickfaden (reeds); Kurt Dieterle, Mischa Russell, Matty Malneck, John Bowman (vns); Roy Bargy, Lennie Hayton (ps); Mike Pingitore (bjo); Min Leibrook (tuba); Mike Trafficante (st-bs); George Marsh (dms).

Beiderbecke not on W-147539.

W-147539-1 **I'VE GOT A FEELING I'M FALLING**

W-147539-2 **I'VE GOT A FEELING I'M FALLING**

W-147539-3 **I'VE GOT A FEELING I'M FALLING**

W-147539-4 **I'VE GOT A FEELING I'M FALLING**
(vc by Jack Fulton)
Rejected. Remade 19 December 1928.

W-147540-1 **MAKIN' WHOOPEE**

W-147540-2 **MAKIN' WHOOPEE**

W-147540-3 **MAKIN' WHOOPEE**

W-147540-4 **MAKIN' WHOOPEE**
(vc by Bing Crosby, Jack Fulton, Charles Gaylord, and Austin Young)
(arrangement by Ferde Grofé)
Rejected. Remade 22 December 1928.

12 DECEMBER 1928 (Wed): Columbia Record Co., New York, NY.

PAUL WHITEMAN ORCHESTRA: Bix Beiderbecke (crt); Charles Margulis, Harry Goldfield, Eddie Pinder (tpts); Boyce Cullen, Wilbur Hall, Bill Rank, Jack Fulton (tbns); **Frank Trumbauer** (clt/C-mel); Chet Hazlett, Rube Crozier, Red Mayer, Irving Friedman, Charles Strickfaden (reeds); Kurt Dieterle, Mischa Russell, Matty Malneck, Charles Gaylord (vns); Roy Bargy, Lennie Hayton (ps); Mike Pingitore (bjo); Min Leibrook (tuba); Mike Trafficante (st-bs); George Marsh (dms).

Beiderbecke not on W-147535.

W-147534-1 **I'M BRINGING A RED, RED ROSE**

W-147534-2 **I'M BRINGING A RED, RED ROSE**

W-147534-3 **I'M BRINGING A RED, RED ROSE**

W-147534-4 **I'M BRINGING A RED, RED ROSE**
(vc by Jack Fulton)
(arrangement by Ferde Grofé)

Rejected. Remade 19 December 1928.

W-147535-1 **SWEET DREAMS**

W-147535-2 **SWEET DREAMS**

W-147535-3 **SWEET DREAMS**

W-147535-4 **SWEET DREAMS**
(vc by unidentified trio)
(arr unidentified)

Rejected. Remade 3 January 1929.

13 DECEMBER 1928 (Thu): Columbia Record Co., New York, NY.

PAUL WHITEMAN ORCHESTRA: Bix Beiderbecke (crt); Charles Margulis, Harry Goldfield, Eddie Pinder (tpts); Boyce Cullen, Wilbur Hall, Bill Rank, Jack Fulton (tbns); **Frank Trumbauer** (alto); Chet Hazlett, Rube Crozier, Red Mayer, Irving Friedman, Charles Strickfaden (reeds); Kurt Dieterle, Mischa Russell, Matty Malneck (vns); Roy Bargy (p); Mike

Pingitore (bjo); Min Leibrook (tuba); Mike Trafficante (st-bs); George Marsh (dms).

W-98610-2 **LIEBESTRAUM**
(arrangement by Roy Bargy)
12″-78 Columbia 50198-D
12″-78 Australian Columbia 07510
12″-78 English Columbia 9798
12″-78 German Columbia C-9798
12″-LP Sunbeam Bix Vol 16 ''Sincerely, Bix Beiderbecke''
12″-LP Russian Melodija 33M60-41643-44

14 DECEMBER 1928 (Fri): Columbia Record Co., New York, NY.

PAUL WHITEMAN ORCHESTRA: Charles Margulis, Harry Goldfield, Eddie Pinder (tpts); Boyce Cullen, Wilbur Hall, Bill Rank, Jack Fulton (tbns); **Frank Trumbauer** (clt/C-mel); Chet Hazlett, Rube Crozier, Red Mayer, Irving Friedman, Charles Strickfaden (reeds); Kurt Dieterle, Mischa Russell, Matty Malneck, Charles Gaylord (vns); Roy Bargy, Lennie Hayton (ps); Mike Pingitore (bjo); Min Leibrook (tuba); Mike Trafficante (st-bs); George Marsh (dms).

W-147536-1 **LET'S DO IT, LET'S FALL IN LOVE**

W-147536-2 **LET'S DO IT, LET'S FALL IN LOVE**

W-147536-3 **LET'S DO IT, LET'S FALL IN LOVE**
(vc by Jack Fulton, Charles Gaylord, and Austin Young)
(arrangement by Bill Challis)
Rejected. Remade 22 December 1928.

W-147537-1 **HOW ABOUT ME?**

W-147537-2 **HOW ABOUT ME?**

W-147537-3 **HOW ABOUT ME?**

W-147537-4 **HOW ABOUT ME?**
(vc by Austin ''Skin'' Young)
(arrangement by Bill Challis)
Rejected. Remade 19 December 1928.

19 DECEMBER 1928 (Wed): Columbia Record Co., New York, NY.

PAUL WHITEMAN ORCHESTRA: Personnel same as for 14 December 1928.

W-147534-6 I'M BRINGING A RED, RED ROSE
(vc by Jack Fulton)
(arrangement by Ferde Grofé)
10″-78 Columbia 1683-D (released 1 February 1929)
10″-78 English Columbia 5556
12″-LP Columbia CL-2830

W-147537-5 HOW ABOUT ME?

W-147537-6 HOW ABOUT ME?

W-147537-7 HOW ABOUT ME?
(vc by Austin ''Skin'' Young)
(arrangement by Bill Challis)
Rejected. Remade 11 January 1929.

W-147539-5 I'VE GOT A FEELING I'M FALLING

W-147539-6 I'VE GOT A FEELING I'M FALLING

W-147539-7 I'VE GOT A FEELING I'M FALLING
(vc by Jack Fulton)
(arr unidentified)
Rejected.

22 DECEMBER 1928 (Sat): Columbia Record Co., New York, NY.

PAUL WHITEMAN ORCHESTRA: Mannie Klein, Eddie Pinder (crts); Charles Margulis, Harry ''Goldie'' Goldfield (tpts); Boyce Cullen, Wilbur Hall, Jack Fulton, Bill Rank (tbns); **Frank Trumbauer**, Chester Hazlett, Hal McLean, Rube Crozier, Charles Strickfaden, Roy ''Red'' Mayer, Irving Friedman (reeds); Kurt Dieterle, Mischa Russell, Matty Malneck, Charles Gaylord, John Bowman (vns); Mario Perry (vn/acc); Roy Bargy, Lennie Hayton (ps); Mike Pingitore (bjo); Min Leibrook (tuba); Mike Trafficante (st-bs); George Marsh (dms).

W-147536-5 **LET'S DO IT, LET'S FALL IN LOVE**
(vc by Bing Crosby, Jack Fulton, Charles Gaylord, and Austin Young)
(arrangement by Bill Challis)

10″-78 Columbia 1701-D (released 15 February 1929)
10″-78 English Columbia 5331
12″-LP Eng Jz JZ-6 "The Chronological Bing Crosby"

W-147540-7 **MAKIN' WHOOPEE**
(vc by Bing Crosby, Jack Fulton, Al Rinker, and Austin Young)
(solo by Mannie Klein, crt)
(arrangement by Ferde Grofé)

10″-78 Columbia 1683-D (released 1 February 1929)
10″-78 English Columbia 5556
12″-LP Eng Jz JZ-6 "The Chronological Bing Crosby"

3 JANUARY 1929 (Thu): Columbia Record Co., New York, NY.
PAUL WHITEMAN ORCHESTRA: Bix Beiderbecke (crt); Eddie Pinder, Charles Margulis, Harry "Goldie" Goldfield (tpts); Boyce Cullen, Wilbur Hall, Jack Fulton, Bill Rank (tbns); **Frank Trumbauer**, Chester Hazlett, Hal McLean, Rube Crozier, Charles Strickfaden, Roy "Red" Mayer, Irving Friedman (reeds); Milford Kurt Dieterle; Mischa Russell, Matty Malneck, Charles Gaylord, John Bowman, Mario Perry (vns); Roy Bargy, Lennie Hayton (ps); Mike Pingitore (bjo); Mike Trafficante (st-bs); Min Leibrook (tuba); George Marsh (dms).

W-147535-5 **SWEET DREAMS**

W-147535-6 **SWEET DREAMS**

W-147535-7 **SWEET DREAMS**
(vc by unidentified trio)

Rejected.

10 JANUARY 1929 (Thu): Columbia Record Co., New York, NY.
PAUL WHITEMAN ORCHESTRA: Bix Beiderbecke (crt); Charles Margulis, Harry Goldfield, Eddie Pinder (tpts); Boyce

Cullen, Wilbur Hall, Bill Rank, Jack Fulton (tbns); **Frank Trumbauer** (bsn/clt/alto); Chet Hazlett, Rube Crozier, Red Mayer, Irving Friedman, Charles Strickfaden (reeds); Kurt Dieterle, Mischa Russell, Matty Malneck, Charles Gaylord, John Bowman, Mario Perry (vns); Roy Bargy (p); Lennie Hayton (cel); Mike Pingitore (bjo); Min Leibrook (tuba); Mike Trafficante (st-bs); George Marsh (dms).
Beiderbecke not on W-147749.

W-147749-1 **CRADLE OF LOVE**
(vc by Austin ''Skin'' Young)
(arrangement by Bill Challis)
10″-78 Columbia 1723-D (released 15 March 1929)
10″-78 Czechoslovakian Columbia 5411
10″-78 English Columbia 5411

W-147750-2 **CHINESE LULLABY**
(arrangement by Ferde Grofé)
10″-78 Columbia 2656-D
10″-78 Australian Columbia 07020
12″-LP Sunbeam Bix Vol 16 ''Sincerely, Bix Beiderbecke''

For other selections from this session see under ''Bee Palmer.''

11 JANUARY 1929 (Fri): Columbia Record Co., New York, NY. PAUL WHITEMAN ORCHESTRA: Eddie Pinder, Charles Margulis, Harry ''Goldie'' Goldfield (tpts); Boyce Cullen, Wilbur Hall, Jack Fulton, Bill Rank (tbns); **Frank Trumbauer** (C-mel/alto saxphone); Chester Hazlett, Hal McLean, Rube Crozier, Charles Strickfaden, Roy ''Red'' Mayer, Irving Friedman (reeds); Milford Kurt Dieterle; Mischa Russell, Matty Malneck, Charles Gaylord, John Bowman, Mario Perry (vns); Roy Bargy, Lennie Hayton (ps); Mike Pingitore (bjo); Mike Trafficante (st-bs); Min Leibrook (tuba); George Marsh (dms).

W-147537-9 **HOW ABOUT ME?**
(vc by Austin ''Skin'' Young)
(arrangement by Bill Challis)

10″-78 Columbia 1723-D (released 15 March 1929)
10″-78 English Columbia 5305

W-147551-1 **MY ANGELINE**

W-147551-2 **MY ANGELINE**

W-147551-3 **MY ANGELINE**

W-147551-4 **MY ANGELINE**
(vc by Jack Fulton)
(arrangement by Ferde Grofé)
Rejected. Remade 28 February 1929.

7 FEBRUARY 1929 (Thu): Columbia Record Co., New York, NY.
PAUL WHITEMAN ORCHESTRA: Personnel same as for 11 January 1929. Andy Secrest replaced Eddie Pinder (tpt).

W-147925-4 **LOVER, COME BACK TO ME**
(vc by Jack Fulton)
(arrangement by Ferde Grofé)
10″-78 Columbia 1731-D (released 22 March 1929)
10″-78 English Columbia 5377

W-147943-4 **MARIANNA**
(vc by Norman Clark)
(arrangement by Ferde Grofé)
10″-78 Columbia 1731-D (released 22 March 1929)
10″-78 English Columbia 5377

8 FEBRUARY 1929 (Fri): Columbia Record Co., New York, NY.
PAUL WHITEMAN ORCHESTRA: Personnel same as for 11 January 1929.

W-147926-3 **BUTTON UP YOUR OVERCOAT**
(vc by Vaughn DeLeath)
(arrangement by Ferde Grofé)
10″-78 Columbia 1736-D (released 29 March 1929)
10″-78 English Columbia 5550

W-147950-4 **MY LUCKY STAR**
(vc by Norman Clark)
(arrangement by Ferde Grofé)

10″-78 Columbia 1736-D (released 29 March 1929)
10″-78 English Columbia 5550

28 FEBRUARY 1929 (Thu): Columbia Record Co., New York, NY.
PAUL WHITEMAN ORCHESTRA: Personnel same as for 11 January 1929.

147751-5 **MY ANGELINE**

147751-6 **MY ANGELINE**

147751-7 **MY ANGELINE**
(vc by Jack Fulton)
(arrangement by Ferde Grofé)
Rejected. Remade 7 March 1929.

148013-3 **COQUETTE**
(vc by Bing Crosby)
(arrangement by William Grant Still)
10″-78 Columbia 1755-D (released 12 April 1929)
10″-78 English Columbia 5388
12″-LP Eng Jz JZ-7 ''The Chronological Bing Crosby''

7 MARCH 1929 (Thu): Columbia Record Co., New York, NY.
PAUL WHITEMAN ORCHESTRA: Charles Margulis, Harry ''Goldie'' Goldfield (tpts); Boyce Cullen, Wilbur Hall, Jack Fulton, Bill Rank (tbns); **Frank Trumbauer** (C-mel/alto saxphone); Chester Hazlett, Rube Crozier, Charles Strickfaden, Roy ''Red'' Mayer, Irving Friedman (reeds); Milford Kurt Dieterle; Mischa Russell, Matty Malneck, Charles Gaylord, John Bowman, Mario Perry (vns); Roy Bargy, Lennie Hayton (ps); Mike Pingitore (bjo); Mike Trafficante (st-bs); Min Leibrook (tuba); George Marsh (dms).

W-147751-11 **MY ANGELINE**
(vc by Bing Crosby)
(arrangement by Ferde Grofé)
10″-78 Columbia 1755-D (released 12 April 1929)
10″-78 English Columbia 5388
12″-LP Eng Jz JZ-7 ''The Chronological Bing Crosby''

W-148028-2 **NOLA**
(arrangement by Roy Bargy)
10″-78 Columbia 2277-D (released 30 September 1930)
10″-78 Czechoslovakian Columbia 5411
10″-78 English Columbia 5411

15 MARCH 1929 (Fri): Columbia Record Co., New York, NY.
PAUL WHITEMAN ORCHESTRA: Bix Beiderbecke, Andy Secrest (crts); Charles Margulis, Harry Goldfield (tpts); Boyce Cullen, Wilbur Hall, Bill Rank, Jack Fulton (tbns); **Frank Trumbauer** (bsn/clt/alto); Chet Hazlett, Rube Crozier, Red Mayer, Irving Friedman, Charles Strickfaden (reeds); Kurt Dieterle, Mischa Russell, Matty Malneck, Charles Gaylord (vns); Roy Bargy (p); Lennie Hayton (cel); Mike Pingitore (bjo); Min Leibrook (tuba); Mike Trafficante (st-bs); George Marsh (pcs).

W-148085-4 **BLUE HAWAII**
(vc by Charles Gaylord and Jack Fulton)
(arrangement by Ferde Grofé)
10″-78 Columbia 1771-D (released 26 April 1929)
10″-78 Australian Columbia 07021
10″-78 English Columbia 5456
10″-78 German Columbia C-5456
12″-LP Sunbeam Bix Vol 17 "Sincerely, Bix Beiderbecke"

W-148086-3 **LOUISE**
(vc by Bing Crosby)
(arrangement by Roy Bargy)
10″-78 Columbia 1771-D (released 26 April 1929)
10″-78 English Columbia 5456
12″-LP Eng Jz JZ-7 "The Chronological Bing Crosby"
12″-LP Italian Joker SM-3569 "Bixology Vol 13"
12″-LP Russian Melodija 33M60-41643-44

5 APRIL 1929 (Fri): Columbia Record Co., New York, NY.
PAUL WHITEMAN ORCHESTRA: Bix Beiderbecke, Andy Secrest (crts); Charles Margulis, Harry Goldfield (tpts); Boyce Cullen, Wilbur Hall, Bill Rank, Jack Fulton (tbns); **Frank Trumbauer** (clt/alto); Chet Hazlett, Rube Crozier, Red Mayer,

Irving Friedman, Charles Strickfaden (reeds); Kurt Dieterle, Mischa Russell, Matty Malneck, John Bowman, Charles Gaylord (vns); Roy Bargy (p); Lennie Hayton (cel); Mike Pingitore (bjo); Min Leibrook (tuba); Mike Trafficante (st-bs); George Marsh (pcs).

W-148183-3 **I'M IN SEVENTH HEAVEN**
(vc by The Rhythm Boys: Harry Barris, Bing Crosby, and Al Rinker)
(arrangement by Bill Challis)

10″-78 Columbia 1877-D (released 2 August 1929)
10″-78 Argentine Columbia A-8208
10″-78 Australian Columbia 07021
10″-78 English Columbia 5544
10″-78 German Columbia C-5544
10″-78 Japanese Columbia J-749
12″-LP Sunbeam Bix Vol 17 ''Sincerely, Bix Beiderbecke''
12″-LP Eng Jz JZ-7 ''The Chronological Bing Crosby''
12″-LP Italian Joker SM-3569 ''Bixology Vol 13''

W-148184-1 **LITTLE PAL**

W-148184-2 **LITTLE PAL**

W-148184-3 **LITTLE PAL**

W-148184-4 **LITTLE PAL**
(vc by Bing Crosby)
(arrangement by Ferde Grofé)

Rejected. Remade 25 April 1929.

25 APRIL 1929 (Thu): Columbia Record Co., New York, NY.
PAUL WHITEMAN ORCHESTRA: Bix Beiderbecke, Andy Secrest (crts); Charles Margulis, Harry Goldfield (tpts); Boyce Cullen, Wilbur Hall, Bill Rank, Jack Fulton (tbns); **Frank Trumbauer**, Chet Hazlett, Bernie Daly, Red Mayer, Irving Friedman, Charles Strickfaden (reeds); Kurt Dieterle, Mischa Russell, John Bowman, Charles Gaylord (vns); Roy Bargy (p); Lennie Hayton (cel); Mike Pingitore (bjo); Min Leibrook (tuba); Mike Trafficante (st-bs); George Marsh (pcs).

W-98653-4 **SONG OF INDIA**
(arrangement by Roy Bargy)

12″-78 Columbia 50198-D
12″-78 Australian Columbia 07510
12″-78 English Columbia 9798
12″-78 German Columbia C-9798
12″-LP Sunbeam Bix Vol 17 ''Sincerely, Bix Beiderbecke''

W-148184-8 **LITTLE PAL**
(vc by Bing Crosby)
(arrangement by Ferde Grofé)
10″-78 Columbia 1877-D (released 2 August 1929)
10″-78 Argentine Columbia A-8208
10″-78 Australian Columbia 07023
10″-78 English Columbia 5544
10″-78 German Columbia C-5544
12″-LP Sunbeam Bix Vol 17 ''Sincerely, Bix Beiderbecke''
12″-LP Eng Jz JZ-8 ''The Chronological Bing Crosby''

3 MAY 1929 (Fri): Columbia Record Co., New York, NY.
PAUL WHITEMAN ORCHESTRA: Bix Beiderbecke, Andy Secrest (crts); Charles Margulis, Harry Goldfield (tpts); Boyce Cullen, Wilbur Hall, Bill Rank, Jack Fulton (tbns); **Frank Trumbauer** (C-mel/alto); Chet Hazlett, Bernie Daly, Red Mayer, Irving Friedman, Charles Strickfaden (reeds); Kurt Dieterle, Mischa Russell, John Bowman, Charles Gaylord (vns); Roy Bargy (p); Lennie Hayton (cel); Mike Pingitore (bjo); Min Leibrook (tuba); Mike Trafficante (st-bs); George Marsh (pcs).

W-148407-4 **WHEN MY DREAMS COME TRUE**
(vc by Jack Fulton)
(arrangement by Roy Bargy)
10″-78 Columbia 1822-D (released 7 June 1929)
10″-78 Australian Columbia 07024
10″-78 English Columbia 5484
10″-78 Japanese Columbia J-711
12″-LP Sunbeam Bix Vol 17 ''Sincerely, Bix Beiderbecke''
12″-LP Italian Joker SM-3569 ''Bixology Vol 13''

W-148408-4 **REACHING FOR SOMEONE AND NOT FINDING ANYONE THERE**
(vc by Bing Crosby)

(arrangement by Bill Challis)
10″-78 Columbia 1822-D (released 7 June 1929)
10″-78 Australian Columbia 07024
10″-78 English Columbia 5484
10″-78 Japanese Columbia J-711
12″-LP Sunbeam Bix Vol 17 ''Sincerely, Bix Beiderbecke''
12″-LP Eng Jz JZ-8 ''The Chronological Bing Crosby''
12″-LP Italian Joker SM-3569 ''Bixology Vol 13''

W-148409-4 CHINA BOY
(arrangement by Lennie Hayton)
10″-78 Columbia 1945-D (released 4 October 1929)
10″-78 Temple 529
10″-78 Argentine Columbia A-8278
10″-78 Australian Columbia 07025
10″-78 English Columbia DC-177
10″-78 Japanese Columbia J-1518
12″-LP Columbia GL-509
12″-LP Columbia Special Products P-16784
12″-LP Sunbeam Bix Vol 18 ''Sincerely, Bix Beiderbecke''
12″-LP Italian Joker SM-3569 ''Bixology Vol 13''

4 MAY 1929 (Sat): Columbia Record Co., New York, NY.
PAUL WHITEMAN ORCHESTRA: Bix Beiderbecke, Andy Secrest (crts); Charles Margulis, Harry Goldfield (tpts); Boyce Cullen, Wilbur Hall, Bill Rank, Jack Fulton (tbns); **Frank Trumbauer** (bsn/alto); Chet Hazlett, Bernie Daly, Red Mayer, Irving Friedman, Charles Strickfaden (reeds); Kurt Dieterle, Mischa Russell, John Bowman, Charles Gaylord (vns); Roy Bargy (p); Lennie Hayton (cel); Mike Pingitore (bjo); Min Leibrook (tuba); Mike Trafficante (st-bs); George Marsh (pcs).

W-148421-4 OH! MISS HANNAH
(vc by Bing Crosby)
(arrangement by Bill Challis)
10″-78 Columbia 1945-D (released 4 October 1929)
10″-78 Temple 529
10″-78 Argentine Columbia A-8278
10″-78 Australian Columbia 07025
10″-78 English Columbia DC-176
10″-78 European Continental DC-176

10″-78 Japanese Columbia J-1518
12″-LP Sunbeam Bix Vol 18 ''Sincerely, Bix Beiderbecke''
12″-LP Eng Jz JZ-8 ''The Chronological Bing Crosby''
12″-LP Italian Joker SM-3569 ''Bixology Vol 13''

W-148422-1 YOUR MOTHER AND MINE

W-148422-2 YOUR MOTHER AND MINE

W-148422-3 YOUR MOTHER AND MINE

W-148422-4 YOUR MOTHER AND MINE
(vc by The Rhythm Boys: Harry Barris, Bing Crosby, and Al Rinker)
(arrangement by Roy Bargy)
Rejected. Remade 16 May 1929.

W-148423-4 ORANGE BLOSSOM TIME
(vc by Bing Crosby)
(arrangement by Ferde Grofé)
10″-78 Columbia 1845-D (released 28 June 1929)
10″-78 Australian Columbia 07026
10″-78 English Columbia 5560
12″-LP Sunbeam Bix Vol 18 ''Sincerely, Bix Beiderbecke''
12″-LP Eng Jz JZ-8 ''The Chronological Bing Crosby''

16 MAY 1929 (Thu): Columbia Record Co., New York, NY.
PAUL WHITEMAN ORCHESTRA: Bix Beiderbecke, Andy Secrest (crts); Charles Margulis, Harry Goldfield (tpts); Boyce Cullen, Wilbur Hall, Bill Rank, Jack Fulton (tbns); **Frank Trumbauer** (alto); Chet Hazlett, Bernie Daly, Red Mayer, Irving Friedman, Charles Strickfaden (reeds); Kurt Dieterle, Mischa Russell, John Bowman, Charles Gaylord (vns); Roy Bargy (p); Lennie Hayton (cel); Mike Pingitore (bjo); Min Leibrook (tuba); Mike Trafficante (st-bs); George Marsh (pcs).
Beiderbecke on W-148422 only.

W-148422-8 YOUR MOTHER AND MINE
(vc by The Rhythm Boys: Harry Barris, Bing Crosby, and Al Rinker)
(arrangement by Roy Bargy)
10″-78 Columbia 1845-D (released 28 June 1929)
10″-78 Australian Columbia 07026

10″-78 English Columbia 5560
12″-LP Sunbeam Bix Vol 18 "Sincerely, Bix Beiderbecke"
12″-LP Eng Jz JZ-8 "The Chronological Bing Crosby"

W-148544-3 **S'POSIN'**
(vc by Bing Crosby)
(arrangement by Roy Bargy)
10″-78 Columbia 1862-D (released 19 July 1929)
10″-78 English Columbia 5520
12″-LP Eng Jz JZ-8 "The Chronological Bing Crosby"

W-148545-4 **LAUGHING MARIONETTE**
(arrangement by Roy Bargy)
10″-78 Columbia 1862-D (released 19 July 1929)
10″-78 English Columbia 5520

6 SEPTEMBER 1929 (Fri): Columbia Record Co., New York, NY.

PAUL WHITEMAN ORCHESTRA: Bix Beiderbecke, Andy Secrest (crts); Charles Margulis, Harry Goldfield (tpts); Boyce Cullen, Wilbur Hall, Bill Rank, Jack Fulton (tbns); **Frank Trumbauer**, Chet Hazlett, Bernie Daly, Red Mayer, Irving Friedman, Charles Strickfaden (reeds); Kurt Dieterle, Mischa Russell, Matty Malneck, Otto Landau (vns); Roy Bargy (p); Lennie Hayton (cel); Mike Pingitore (bjo); Min Leibrook (tuba); Mike Trafficante (st-bs); George Marsh (dms).

W-148985-3 **AT TWILIGHT**
(vc by Bing Crosby, Al Rinker, Jack Fulton)
(arrangement by Ferde Grofé)
10″-78 Columbia 1993-D (released 15 November 1929)
10″-78 Australian Columbia 07028
10″-78 English Columbia 5655
10″-78 German Columbia C-5655
12″-LP Sunbeam Bix Vol 18 "Sincerely, Bix Beiderbecke"
12″-LP Eng Jz JZ-8 "The Chronological Bing Crosby"

W-148986-1 **WAITING AT THE END OF THE ROAD**

W-148986-2 **WAITING AT THE END OF THE ROAD**

W-148986-3 **WAITING AT THE END OF THE ROAD**

W-148986-4 **WAITING AT THE END OF THE ROAD**
(vc by Bing Crosby)
(arrangement by Ferde Grofé)

Rejected. Remade 13 September 1929.

13 SEPTEMBER 1929 (Fri): Columbia Record Co., New York, NY.

PAUL WHITEMAN ORCHESTRA: Bix Beiderbecke, Andy Secrest (crts); Charles Margulis, Harry Goldfield (tpts); Boyce Cullen, Wilbur Hall, Bill Rank, Jack Fulton (tbns); **Frank Trumbauer**, Chet Hazlett, Bernie Daly, Red Mayer, Irving Friedman, Charles Strickfaden (reeds); Kurt Dieterle, Mischa Russell, Matty Malneck, Otto Landau (vns); Roy Bargy (p); Lennie Hayton (cel); Mike Pingitore (bjo); Eddie Lang (gtr); Min Leibrook (tuba); Mike Trafficante (st-bs); George Marsh (dms). **Beiderbecke on W-148986 only.**

W-148986-8 **WAITING AT THE END OF THE ROAD**
(vc by Bing Crosby)
(arrangement by Ferde Grofé)

10″-78 Columbia 1974-D (released 25 October 1929)
10″-78 Australian Columbia 07032
10″-78 English Columbia 5675
10″-78 German Columbia C-5675
12″-LP Sunbeam Bix Vol 19 "Sincerely, Bix Beiderbecke"
12″-LP Eng Jz JZ-8 "The Chronological Bing Crosby"
12″-LP Italian Joker SM-3569 "Bixology Vol 13"

W-149005-3 **WHEN YOU'RE COUNTING THE STARS ALONE**
(vc by Bing Crosby, Jack Fulton, Al Rinker)
(arrangement by Bill Challis)

10″-78 Columbia 1993-D (released 15 November 1929)
10″-78 English Columbia 5675
12″-LP Eng Jz JZ-8 "The Chronological Bing Crosby"
12″-LP Italian Joker SM-3569 "Bixology Vol 13"

W-149006-2 **LOVE ME**
(vc by Jack Fulton)
(arrangement by Ferde Grofé)
10″-78 Columbia 1974-D (released 25 October 1929)
10″-78 English Columbia 5655

9 OCTOBER 1929 (Wed): Columbia Record Co., New York, NY.
PAUL WHITEMAN ORCHESTRA: Andy Secrest (crt); Charles Margulis, Harry ''Goldie'' Goldfield (tpts); Boyce Cullen, Wilbur Hall, Jack Fulton, Bill Rank (tbns); **Frank Trumbauer**, Chester Hazlett, Bernie Daly, Charles Strickfaden, Roy ''Red'' Mayer, Irving Friedman (reeds); Kurt Dieterle, Mischa Russell, Matty Malneck, Otto Landau, John Bowman, Joe Venuti (vns); Roy Bargy, Lennie Hayton (ps); Eddie Lang (gtr); Mike Pingitore (bjo); Mike Trafficante (st-bs); Min Leibrook (tuba); George Marsh (dms).

W-149123-2 **NOBODY'S SWEETHEART**
(arrangement by Lennie Hayton)
10″-78 Columbia 2098-D (released 28 February 1930)
10″-78 English Columbia 5702

W-149124-3 **GREAT DAY!**
(vc by Bing Crosby, Boyce Cullen, Jack Fulton, Al Rinker)
(arrangement by Bill Challis)
10″-78 Columbia 2023-D (released 13 December 1929)
10″-78 English Columbia CB-116
12″-LP Eng Jz JZ-8 ''The Chronological Bing Crosby''

W-149125-3 **WITHOUT A SONG**
(vc by Bing Crosby)
(arrangement by Bill Challis)
10″-78 Columbia 2023-D (released 13 December 1929)
10″-78 English Columbia CB-116
12″-LP Eng Jz JZ-8 ''The Chronological Bing Crosby''

16 OCTOBER 1929 (Wed): Columbia Record Co., New York, NY.
PAUL WHITEMAN ORCHESTRA: Personnel same as for 9 October 1929.

W-149149-4 **I'M A DREAMER, AREN'T WE ALL?**
(vc by Bing Crosby, Boyce Cullen, Jack Fulton, Al Rinker)
(arrangement by Ferde Grofé)
10″-78 Columbia 2010-D (released 29 November 1929)
12″-LP Eng Jz JZ-9 "The Chronological Bing Crosby"

W-149150-4 **IF I HAD A TALKING PICTURE OF YOU**
(vc by Bing Crosby)
(arrangement by Lennie Hayton)
10″-78 Columbia 2010-D (released 29 November 1929)
12″-LP Eng Jz JZ-9 "The Chronological Bing Crosby"

18 OCTOBER 1929 (Fri): Columbia Record Co., New York, NY.
PAUL WHITEMAN ORCHESTRA: Personnel same as for 9 October 1929.

W-91790-1 ***Moonlight And Roses*** Medley:
(arrangement by Ferde Grofé)
a. **MOONLIGHT AND ROSES**
b. **ON MOONLIGHT BAY** (chorus)
(vc by Bing Crosby, . . . ?)
12″-78 Columbia Test Pressing
12″-LP Eng Jz JZ-9 "The Chronological Bing Crosby"

W-91791-1 Southern Medley:
(arrangement by Ferde Grofé)
a. **OLD BLACK JOE**
(vc by Bing Crosby)
b. **MY OLD KENTUCKY HOME**
c. **CARRY ME BACK TO OLD VIRGINNY**
(vc by Bing Crosby)
d. **SWANEE RIVER**
12″-78 Columbia Test Pressing
12″-LP Pelican LP-104 "Soft Lights & Sweet Music"
12″-LP Eng Jz JZ-9 "The Chronological Bing Crosby"

W-149157-3 **SHOULD I?**
(vc by Jack Fulton)
(arrangement by Lennie Hayton)

10″-78 Columbia 2047-D (released 3 January 1930)
10″-78 English Columbia 5724

W-149158-3 **A BUNDLE OF OLD LOVE LETTERS**
(vc by Bing Crosby)
(arrangement by Ferde Grofé)
10″-78 Columbia 2047-D (released 3 January 1930)
10″-78 English Columbia 5724
12″-LP Eng Jz JZ-9 ''The Chronological Bing Crosby''

Columbia Records re-recorded W-149158, A BUNDLE OF OLD LOVE LETTERS, on 31 October 1929 and assigned matrix number W-194379. Take ''3'' was still the issued take.

W-149159-3 **AFTER YOU'VE GONE**
(vc by Bing Crosby)
(arrangement by Ferde Grofé)
10″-78 Columbia 2098-D (released 28 Februry 1930)
10″-78 English Columbia 5702
12″-LP Eng Jz JZ-9 ''The Chronological Bing Crosby''

November-December 1929: Motion Picture, ***King Of Jazz,***
UNIVERSAL PICTURES CORP: Production Number 4975. Twelve reels (105 minutes); color.
COPYRIGHT: 17 May 1930, LP-1318; renewed, R-211370, 26 March 1958.
REVIEWS: *New York Times,* 7 May 1930 (21:2); *Variety,* 3 May 1930 (23:1).
CREDITS: dir, John Murray Anderson; sketches, Harry Ruskin; cartoon sequence, Walter Lantz; musical score, Ferde Grofé.
CAST: Paul Whiteman & His Orchestra, The Rhythm Boys, The Brox Sisters, John Boles, Laura LaPlante, Glenn Tryon, Jeanette Loff, Merna Kennedy, Stanley Smith, Slim Summerville, Walter Brennan, Otis Harlan, William Kent, Jeannie Lang, George Chiles, Jacques Cartier, Wilbur Hall, Jack White, Grace Hayes, Kathryn Crawford, Frank Leslie, Charles Irwin (master of ceremonies), Al Norman, Paul Howard, Marion Statler & Don Rose, Nell O'Day Adagio Dancers, Russell Markert Dancers, Tommy Atkins Sextet.

SUMMARY: A series of sketches and musical specialities introduced as pages from ''Paul Whiteman's Scrapbook.''
PAUL WHITEMAN ORCHESTRA: Paul Whiteman (ldr); personnel same as for 10 February 1930.
THE RHYTHM BOYS: Harry Barris, Bing Crosby, Al Rinker.
THE BROX SISTERS: Lorayne (née Eunice), Patsy (née Kathleen), Bobby (née Josephine; aka Bobbie, Bobbi, Bobbe, and for a while, Dagmar).

RHAPSODY IN BLUE
16″-SD Universal 4975-1

MUSIC HATH CHARMS
(vc by Bing Crosby over opening credits)
12″-LP Fanfare 20120 ''Jazz 1929 Style''
12″-LP Australian Crosbyana PTH
16″-SD Universal 4975-1

MY BRIDAL VEIL
(vc by Jeanette Loff, girls chorus, and Jack Fulton)
16″-SD Universal 4975-2

MISSISSIPPI MUD
(vc by The Rhythm Boys)
16″-SD Universal 4975-3

SO THE BLUEBIRDS AND THE BLACKBIRDS GOT TOGETHER
(vc by The Rhythm Boys)
12″-LP Fanfare 20120 ''Jazz 1929 Style''
12″-LP Australian Crosbyana PTH
16″-SD Universal 4975-3

IT HAPPENED IN MONTEREY
(vc by John Boles and Jeanette Loff)
16″-SD Universal 4975-

A BENCH IN THE PARK
(vc Jack Fulton, Jeanette Loff, The Rhythm Boys and The Brox Sisters)
12″-LP Fanfare 20120 ''Jazz 1929 Style''
12″-LP Australian Crosbyana PTH
16″-SD Universal 4975-5

RAGAMUFFIN ROMEO
(vc by Jeanie Lang with George Chiles)
16″-SD Universal 4975-

HAPPY FEET
(vc by The Rhythm Boys)
12″-LP Fanfare 20120 ''Jazz 1929 Style''
12″-LP Australian Crosbyana PTH
16″-SD Universal 4975-9

I LIKE TO DO THINGS FOR YOU
(vc by Jeanie Lang, Grace Hayes and William Kent)
16″-SD Universal 4975-

SONG OF THE DAWN
(vc by John Boles)
16″-SD Universal 4975-

THE MELTING POT
16″-SD Universal 4975-12

The complete film is contained on the video tape:
V-BETA MCA Home Video BTA-55119 (93 minutes)
V-VHS MCA Home Video VTA-55119 (93 minutes)

10 FEBRUARY 1930 (Mon): Columbia Record Co., Los Angeles, CA.

PAUL WHITEMAN ORCHESTRA: Andy Secrest (crt); Charles Margulis, Harry ''Goldie'' Goldfield (tpts); Wilbur Hall, Boyce Cullen, Bill Rank, Jack Fulton (tbns); Chet Hazlett, Bernie Daly, Red Mayer, **Frank Trumbauer**, Irving Friedman, Charles Strickfaden (reeds); Kurt Dieterle, Mischa Russell, Matty Malneck, Otto Landau, Joe Venuti (vns); Roy Bargy, Lennie Hayton (ps); Eddie Lang (gtr); Mike Pingitore (bjo); Mike Trafficante (st-bs); Min Leibrook (tuba); George Marsh (dms).

W-149810-1 **HAPPY FEET**
(vc by Harry Barris, Bing Crosby, Al Rinker)
(arrangement by Ferde Grofé)

10″-78 Columbia 2164-D (released 30 April 1930)
10″-78 English Columbia CB-86
12″-LP Eng Jz JZ-9 ‘‘The Chronological Bing Crosby’’
12″-LP Russian Melodija 33M60-41643-44

W-149811-1 **IT HAPPENED IN MONTEREY**

W-149811-2 **IT HAPPENED IN MONTEREY**

W-149811-3 **IT HAPPENED IN MONTEREY**

W-149811-4 **IT HAPPENED IN MONTEREY**

W-149811-5 **IT HAPPENED IN MONTEREY**
(vc by Jack Fulton)
(arrangement by Ferde Grofé)
Rejected. Remade 21 March 1930.

21 MARCH 1930 (Fri): Columbia Record Co., Los Angeles, CA. PAUL WHITEMAN ORCHESTRA: Personnel same as for 10 February 1930.

W-149811-7 **IT HAPPENED IN MONTEREY**
(vc by Jack Fulton)
(arrangement by Ferde Grofé)
10″-78 Columbia 2163-D (released 30 April 1930)
10″-78 English Columbia CB-88

W-149822-2 **SONG OF THE DAWN**
(vc by Bing Crosby and unknown chorus)
(arrangement by Ferde Grofé)
10″-78 Columbia 2163-D (released 30 April 1930)
10″-78 English Columbia CB-87
12″-LP Eng Jz JZ-9 ‘‘The Chronological Bing Crosby’’

22 MARCH 1930 (Sat): Columbia Record Co., Los Angeles, CA. PAUL WHITEMAN ORCHESTRA: Personnel same as for 10 February 1930.

W-149823-2 **RAGAMUFFIN ROMEO**
(vc by Jeannie Lang)
(arrangement by Ferde Grofé)
10″-78 Columbia 2170-D (released 15 May 1930)
10″-78 English Columbia CB-88

W-149824-4 **LIVIN' IN THE SUNLIGHT, LOVIN' IN THE MOONLIGHT**
(vc by Bing Crosby)
(arrangement by Ferde Grofé)
10″-78 Columbia 2171-D (released 15 May 1930)
10″-78 English Columbia CB-117
12″-LP Eng Jz JZ-9 "The Chronological Bing Crosby"

W-149825-2 **A BENCH IN THE PARK**
(vc by The Rhythm Boys: Harry Barris, Bing Crosby, Al Rinker; and The Brox Sisters: Kathlyn, Dagmar, Lorraine)
(arrangement by Ferde Grofé)
10″-78 Columbia 2164-D (released 30 April 1930)
10″-78 English Columbia CB-86
12″-LP Eng Jz JZ-9 "The Chronological Bing Crosby"
12″-LP Russian Melodija 33M60-41643-44

23 MARCH 1930 (Sun): Columbia Record Co., Los Angeles, CA.
PAUL WHITEMAN ORCHESTRA: Personnel same as for 10 February 1930.

W-149826-2 **I LIKE TO DO THINGS FOR YOU**
(vc by The Rhythm Boys: Harry Barris, Bing Crosby, Al Rinker)
(arrangement by Ferde Grofé)
10″-78 Columbia 2170-D (released 15 May 1930)
10″-78 English Columbia CB-87
12″-LP Eng Jz JZ-9 "The Chronological Bing Crosby"

W-149827-4 **YOU BROUGHT A NEW KIND OF LOVE TO ME**
(vc by Bing Crosby)
(arrangement by Ferde Grofé)
10″-78 Columbia 2171-D (released 15 May 1930)
10″-78 English Columbia CB-117
12″-LP Eng Jz JZ-9 "The Chronological Bing Crosby"

9 JUNE 1930 (Mon): Columbia Record Co., New York, NY.
PAUL WHITEMAN ORCHESTRA: Andy Secrest (crt); Nat Natolie, Harry "Goldie" Goldfield (tpts); Jack Fulton, Bill

Rank, Herb Whinfield (tbns); **Frank Trumbauer**, Chester Hazlett, Walter "Fud" Livingston, Charles Strickfaden (reeds); Kurt Dieterle, Mischa Russell, Matty Malneck (vns); Mike Pingitore (bjo); Roy Bargy (p); Mike Trafficante (st-bs); George Marsh (dms).
THE KING'S JESTERS: John Ravenscroft, George Howard, Fritz Bastow.

W-150579-4 **SITTING ON A RAINBOW**
(vc by The King's Jesters)
(arrangement by Bill Challis)
10″-78 Columbia 2224-D (released 15 July 1930)
10″-78 English Columbia CB-120

W-150580-5 **OLD NEW ENGLAND MOON**
(vc by Jack Fulton)
10″-78 Columbia 2224-D (released 15 July 1930)
10″-78 English Columbia CB-120

25 JULY 1930 (Fri): Columbia Record Co., New York, NY.
PAUL WHITEMAN ORCHESTRA: Personnel same as for 9 June 1929.
THE KING'S JESTERS: John Ravenscroft, George Howard, Fritz Bastow.

W-150681-2 **SONG OF THE CONGO**
(vc by The King's Jesters)
(arrangement by Roy Bargy)
10″-78 Columbia 2263-D (released 15 September 1930)

W-150682-3 **THE WEDDING OF THE BIRDS**
(vc by Jack Fulton)
(arrangement by Roy Bargy)
10″-78 Columbia 2263-D (released 15 September 1930)
10″-78 English Columbia CB-163

W-150683-1 **THE NEW TIGER RAG**
(arrangement by Roy Bargy)
10″-78 Columbia 2277-D (released 30 September 1930)
10″-78 English Columbia CB-163
12″-LP Russian Melodija 33M60-41643-44

10 SEPTEMBER 1930 (Wed): Columbia Record Co., New York, NY.

PAUL WHITEMAN ORCHESTRA: Personnel same as for 9 June 1929.

THE KING'S JESTERS: John Ravenscroft, George Howard, Fritz Bastow.

W-150787-4 **A BIG BOUQUET FOR YOU**
(vc by Jack Fulton)
10″-78 Columbia 2289-D (released 15 October 1930)
10″-78 English Columbia CB-120

W-150788-3 **BODY AND SOUL**
(vc by Jack Fulton)
10″-78 Columbia 2297-D (released 31 October 1930)
10″-78 English Columbia DC-177

W-150789-3 **SOMETHING TO REMEMBER YOU BY**
(vc by The King's Jesters)
10″-78 Columbia 2297-D (released 31 October 1930)
10″-78 English Columbia DC-176

W-150790-3 **IN MY HEART IT'S YOU**
(vc by The King's Jesters)
10″-78 Columbia 2289-D (released 15 October 1930)
10″-78 English Columbia CB-210

W-150791-4 **CHOO CHOO**
(arr by Frank Trumbauer and Matty Malneck)
10″-78 Columbia 2491-D

30 SEPTEMBER 1930 (Tues): Victor Record Co.,New York, NY.

PAUL WHITEMAN ORCHESTRA: Andy Secrest (crt); Nat Natoli, Harry ''Goldie'' Goldfield (tpts); Jack Fulton, Fritz Hummel, Bill Rank (tbns); **Frank Trumbauer**, Chester Hazlett, Ray McDermott, Charles Strickfaden (reeds); Kurt Dieterle, Mischa Russell, Matty Malneck, John Bowman (vns); Mike Pingitore (bjo); Roy Bargy (p); Fritz Ciccone (gtr); Pierre Olker (st-bs); George Marsh (dms).

67591-1 **TANGO AMERICANO**
(arrangement by Matty Malneck)
10″-78 Victor 22913

67592-1 **VILIA**
(arrangement by Roy Bargy)
10″-78 Victor 22885

67593-1 **SYLVIA**
(vc by Jack Fulton)
(arrangement by Roy Bargy)
10″-78 Victor 22885

5 MAY 1931 (Tue): Radio Program, ***Allied Quality Paintsmen*** Station/Network; Chicago, IL.

PAUL WHITEMAN ORCHESTRA: Andy Secrest (crt); Nat Natoli, Harry ''Goldie'' Goldfield (tpts); Jack Fulton, Fritz Hummel, Bill Rank (tbns); Chester Hazlett, **Frank Trumbauer**, Fud Livingston, Charles Strickfaden (reeds); Kurt Dieterle, Mischa Russell, Matty Malneck, John Bowman (vns); Roy Bargy (p); Fritz Ciccone (gtr); Mike Pingitore (bjo); Pierre Okler (bs-sx); George Marsh (dms).

THE KING'S JESTERS: John Ravenscroft, George Howard, Fritz Bastow.

THAT'S A PLENTY
(solos by Frank Trumbauer, Fud Livingston, Andy Secrest)

WHEN I TAKE MY SUGAR TO TEA
(vc by The King's Jesters)

HOSANNA
(vc by Mildred Bailey)

WEARY BLUES

HAY, STRAW (incomplete)

A recording of this broadcast is in a private collection.

CIRCA JUNE 1931: Radio Program, ***Allied Quality Paintsmen*** Station/Network; Chicago, IL.
PAUL WHITEMAN ORCHESTRA: Personnel same as for 5 May 1931.

NEVERTHELESS

TIGER RAG
(Frank Trumbauer, Andy Secrest chase chorus)

TIGER RAG
(Frank Trumbauer full chorus solo)

TIGER RAG
(Andy Secrest full chorus solo)

A recording of these broadcast excerpts are in a private collection.

1 AUGUST 1931 (Sat): Radio Broadcast, Chicago, IL.
PAUL WHITEMAN ORCHESTRA: Personnel same as for 5 May 1931.

CRAZY QUILT
(Frank Trumbauer solo)

A recording of this broadcast excerpt is in a private collection.

3 AUGUST 1931 (Mon): Radio Program, Radio Station KWY, Chicago, IL.
PAUL WHITEMAN ORCHESTRA: Personnel same as for 5 May 1931.

TIGER RAG

A recording of this broadcast excerpt is in a private collection.

14 AUGUST 1931 (Fri): Radio Program, Radio Station KWY, Chicago, IL.

PAUL WHITEMAN ORCHESTRA: Personnel same as for 5 May 1931.
THE KING'S JESTERS: John Ravenscroft, George Howard, Fritz Bastow.

LOOK IN THE LOOKING GLASS
(vc by The King's Jesters)

LITTLE GIRL
(Frank Trumbauer solo)

A recording of this broadcast excerpt is in a private collection.

AUGUST 1931: Radio Program, ***Allied Quality Paintsmen*** Radio Station KWY, Chicago, IL.
PAUL WHITEMAN ORCHESTRA: Personnel same as for 5 May 1931.

LOOK IN THE LOOKING GLASS

PLEASE DON'T TALK ABOUT ME WHEN I'M GONE
(vc by Mildred Bailey)

SWEET SUE, JUST YOU
(Andy Secrest solo)

A recording of this broadcast excerpt is in a private collection.

1 OCTOBER 1931 (Thu): Victor Record Co., New York, NY.
PAUL WHITEMAN ORCHESTRA: Personnel same as for 30 September 1930.

67594-1 **OLD PLAYMATE**
(vc by Jack Fulton)
10″-78 Victor 22827
10″-78 English HMV B-6107

67595-1 **WHEN THE WORLD WAS NEW**
(vc by Jack Fulton)
10″-78 Victor 22849

67596-1 **GETTIN' SENTIMENTAL**
(vc by The Romancers: Jack Fulton, Craig Leitch, Bill Seckler)
10″-78 Victor 22876
10″-78 English HMV B-6148

4 OCTOBER 1931 (Sun): Victor Record Co., New York, NY.
PAUL WHITEMAN ORCHESTRA: Personnel same as for 30 September 1930.
THE ROMANCERS: Jack Fulton, Craig Leitch, Bill Seckler.

70611-1 **WHEN IT'S SLEEPY TIME DOWN SOUTH**
(vc by Mildred Bailey and The Romancers)
10″-78 Victor 22828
10″-78 English HMV B-6116
12″-LP Tono TJ-6002 ''Mildred Bailey—The Paul Whiteman Years''

70612-1 **CAN'T YOU SEE?**
(vc by Mildred Bailey)
10″-78 Victor 22828
12″-LP Tono TJ-6002 ''Mildred Bailey—The Paul Whiteman Years''

6 OCTOBER 1931 (Mon): Victor Record Co., New York, NY.
PAUL WHITEMAN ORCHESTRA: Personnel same as for 30 September 1930.
THE ROMANCERS: Jack Fulton, Craig Leitch, Bill Seckler.
THE KING'S JESTERS: John Ravenscroft, George Howard, Fritz Bastow.

70616-1 **CUBAN LOVE SONG**
(vc by Jack Fulton and The Romancers)
(arrangement by Ferde Grofé)
10″-78 Victor 22834

70617-1 **A FADED SUMMER LOVE**
(vc by Jack Fulton and The Romancers)
10″-78 Victor 22827
10″-78 English HMV B-6116

70618-1 **DANCE OF THE LITTLE DUTCH DOLLS**
(vc by The King's Jesters)
(arrangement by Ferde Grofé)
10″-78 Victor 22876
10″-78 English HMV B-6148

70619-1 **MY GOOD-BYE TO YOU**
(vc by Mildred Bailey)
10″-78 Victor 22876
10″-78 English HMV B-6148
12″-LP Tono TJ-6002 ''Mildred Bailey—The Paul Whiteman Years''

70620-1 **TELL ME WITH A LOVE SONG**
(vc by Jack Fulton and The Romancers)
(arrangement by Ferde Grofé)
10″-78 Victor 22834
10″-78 English HMV B-6186

30 NOVEMBER 1931 (Mon): Victor Record Co., New York, NY.
PAUL WHITEMAN ORCHESTRA: Personnel same as for 30 September 1930.
THE ROMANCERS: Jack Fulton, Craig Leitch, Bill Seckler.
THE KING'S JESTERS: John Ravenscroft, George Howard, Fritz Bastow.

70632-3 ***George White's Scandals*** Medley:
a. **MY SONG**
(vc by Jack Fulton)
b. **THIS IS THE MISSUS**
(vc by The King's Jesters)
c. **LIFE IS JUST A BOWL OF CHERRIES**
(vc by The King's Jesters)
d. **THAT'S WHY DARKIES WERE BORN**
(vc by Mildred Bailey)
10″-LP Victor L-16001
12″-LP Tono TJ-6002 ''Mildred Bailey—The Paul Whiteman Years'' (segment ''d'' of medley only)

70633-1 **'LEVEN POUNDS OF HEAVEN**
(vc by Mildred Bailey)
10″-78 Victor 22883
12″-LP Tono TJ-6002 "Mildred Bailey—The Paul Whiteman Years"

70634-1 **THERE'S A BLUE NOTE IN MY LOVE SONG**
(vc by Jack Fulton and The Romancers)
10″-78 Victor 22873
10″-78 English HMV B-6135

1 DECEMBER 1931 (Tue): Victor Record Co., New York, NY.
PAUL WHITEMAN ORCHESTRA: Personnel same as for 30 September 1930.
THE ROMANCERS: Jack Fulton, Craig Leitch, Bill Seckler.

70635 Popular Selections Medley:
a. **I'M SORRY DEAR**
(vc by Mildred Bailey)
b. **OLD PLAYMATE**
(vc by Jack Fulton)
c. **GOODNIGHT, SWEETHEART**
(vc by The Romancers)
10″-LP Victor L-16002
12″-LP Tono TJ-6002 "Mildred Bailey—The Paul Whiteman Years" (segment "a" of medley only)

70636-1 **ALL OF ME**
(vc by Mildred Bailey)
10″-78 Victor 22879
12″-LP Tono TJ-6002 "Mildred Bailey—The Paul Whiteman Years"

3 DECEMBER 1931 (Thu): Victor Record Co., New York, NY.
PAUL WHITEMAN ORCHESTRA: Personnel same as for 30 September 1930.

70642-1 **A ROSE AND A KISS**
(vc by Jack Fulton)
(arrangement by Ferde Grofé)
10″-78 Victor 22882

70643-1 **BY THE SYCAMORE TREE**
(vc by Jack Fulton)
10″-78 Victor 22879
10″-78 English HMV B-6160

70644-1 **I DON'T SUPPOSE**
(vc by Jack Fulton)
10″-78 Victor 22882

1 MARCH 1932 (Sun): Victor Record Co., New York, NY.
PAUL WHITEMAN ORCHESTRA: Personnel same as for 30 September 1930.
THE KING'S JESTERS: John Ravenscroft, George Howard, Fritz Bastow.

71905-1 ***Face The Music*** medley:
(arrangement by Roy Bargy)
a. **SOFT LIGHTS AND SWEET MUSIC**
(vc by Frank Munn)
b. **SAY URS SPINACH**
(vc by The King's Jesters)
c. **ON A ROOF IN MANHATTAN**
d. **LET'S HAVE ANOTHER CUP OF COFFEE**
(vc by William "Red" McKenzie)
12″-78 Victor 36050

71906-1 **DEAR OLD MOTHER DIXIE**
(arrangement by Matt Malneck)
(vc by Mildred Bailey with Frank Munn and The King's Jesters)
10″-78 Victor 24137
10″-78 English HMV B-7873
12″-78 Tono TJ-6002 "Mildred Bailey—The Paul Whiteman Years"

The Victor file card shows DEAR OLD MOTHER DIXIE: "Mildred Bailey, vocal, accompanied by Matt Malneck Orchestra, assisted by Frank Munn and The King's Jesters."

2 MARCH 1932 (Mon): Victor Record Co., New York, NY.
PAUL WHITEMAN ORCHESTRA: Personnel same as for 30 September 1931.

71907-1 *Hot Cha* medley:
(arrangement by Roy Bargy)
a. **WHO CAN MAKE MY LIFE A BED OF ROSES**
b. **THERE I GO DREAMING AGAIN**
(vc by Mildred Bailey)
c. **SAY**
(vc by William ''Red'' McKenzie)
d. **WHO CAN MAKE MY LIFE A BED OF ROSES**

12″-78 Victor 36050
12″-LP Tono TJ-6002 (segment ''b'' of medley only)

71908 *Face The Music* Medley
Hot Cha Medley

12″-78 Victor LP-16008

Matrix 71908 from the 1 March 1932 and 2 March 1932 matrices 71905-1 and 71907-1.

14 APRIL 1932 (Thu): Victor Record Co., New York, NY.
PAUL WHITEMAN ORCHESTRA: Andy Secrest (crt); Nat Natoli, Harry ''Goldie'' Goldfield (tpts); Hal Matthews, Jack Fulton, Bill Rank (tbns); **Frank Trumbauer**, Chet Hazlett, John Cordaro, Charles Strickfaden (reeds); Kurt Dieterle, Mischa Russell, Matty Malneck, John Bowman (vns); Roy Bargy (p); Mike Pingitore (bjo); Pierre Olker (st-bs); Herb Quigley (dms).

72283-1 **LAWD, YOU MADE THE NIGHT TOO LONG**
(vc by William ''Red'' McKenzie)

10″-78 Victor 22984

72284-1 **THE VOICE IN THE OLD VILLAGE CHOIR**
(vc by Jack Fulton)

10″-78 Victor 22998

72285-1 **DAYBREAK**
(vc by William ''Red'' McKenzie)
(arrangement by Roy Bargy)
10″-78 Victor 24017

26 APRIL 1932 (Tue): Victor Record Co., New York, NY.
PAUL WHITEMAN CONCERT ORCHESTRA: Andy Secrest (crt); Nat Natoli, Harry ''Goldie'' Goldfield (tpts); Hal Matthews, Jack Fulton, Bill Rank (tbns); **Frank Trumbauer**, Chet Hazlett, John Cordaro, Charles Strickfaden (reeds); Kurt Dieterle, Mischa Russell, Matty Malneck, John Bowman (vns); Roy Bargy (p); Mike Pingitore (bjo); Artie Miller (st-bs); Herb Quigley (dms). At least nine unidentified musicians were added for the recording of Ferde Grofé's GRAND CANYON SUITE.

72090-1 **GRAND CANYON SUITE** (SUNRISE-part 1)
(arrangement by Ferde Grofé)
10″-78 Victor 36052

72091-1 **GRAND CANYON SUITE** (SUNRISE-part 2)
(arrangement by Ferde Grofé)
10″-78 Victor 36052

72092-1 **GRAND CANYON SUITE** (SUNRISE-part 1)/(SUNRISE-part 2)
(arrangement by Ferde Grofé)
10″-LP Victor L-35001

Matrix 72093 and 72094 were special discs cut for sales talk sides.

27 APRIL 1932 (Wed): Victor Record Co., New York, NY.
PAUL WHITEMAN CONCERT ORCHESTRA: Personnel same as for 26 April 1932.

72095-1 **GRAND CANYON SUITE** (PAINTED DESERT)
(arrangement by Ferde Grofé)
10″-78 Victor 36053

72096-1 **GRAND CANYON SUITE** (ON THE TRAIL) (part 1)
(arrangement by Ferde Grofé)
(humming by Jack Fulton, through a megaphone)
10″-78 Victor 36053

72097-1 **GRAND CANYON SUITE**
a. PAINTED DESERT
b. ON THE TRAIL (part 1)
(humming by Jack Fulton)
(arrangement by Ferde Grofé)
10″-LP Victor L-35001

72098-1 **GRAND CANYON SUITE** (ON THE TRAIL-part 2)
(arrangement by Ferde Grofé)
10″-78 Victor 36054

72099-1 **GRAND CANYON SUITE** (SUNSET)
(arrangement by Ferde Grofé)
10″-78 Victor 36054

72100-1 **GRAND CANYON SUITE**
a. ON THE TRAIL (part 2)
b. SUNSET
(arrangement by Ferde Grofé)
10″-LP Victor L-35002

28 APRIL 1932 (Thu): Victor Record Co., New York, NY.
PAUL WHITEMAN CONCERT ORCHESTRA: Andy Secrest (crt); Nat Natoli, Harry ''Goldie'' Goldfield (tpts); Hal Matthews, Jack Fulton, Bill Rank (tbns); **Frank Trumbauer**, Chet Hazlett, John Cordaro, Charles Strickfaden (reeds); Kurt Dieterle, Mischa Russell, Matty Malneck, John Bowman (vns); Roy Bargy (p); Mike Pingitore (bjo); Artie Miller (st-bs); Pierre Olker (tuba); Herb Quigley (dms). At least nine unidentified musicians were added for the recordings of Ferde Grofé's GRAND CANYON SUITE.

72601-1 **GRAND CANYON SUITE** (CLOUDBURST-part 1)

(arrangement by Ferde Grofé)
10″-78 Victor 36055

72602-1 **GRAND CANYON SUITE**
(CLOUDBURST-part 2)
(arrangement by Ferde Grofé)
10″-78 Victor 36055

72603-1 **GRAND CANYON SUITE**
a. CLOUDBURST (part 1)
b. CLOUDBURST (part 2)
(arrangement by Ferde Grofé)
10″-LP Victor L-35002

72604-1 **TOSELLI'S SERENADE**
(arrangement by Roy Bargy)
10″-78 Victor 24017

30 NOVEMBER 1933 (Thu): ***The Kraft Music Hall,*** NBC Radio Program, New York, NY.

PAUL WHITEMAN ORCHESTRA: Bunny Berigan, Harry ''Goldie'' Goldfield, Nat Natoli (tpts); Jack Fulton, Vincent Grande, Bill Rank (tbns); **Frank Trumbauer**, Benny Bonacio, John Cordaro, Charles Strickfaden (reeds); Kurt Dieterle, Matty Malneck, Mischa Russell, Harry Strubel (vns); Roy Bargy, Ramona Davies (ps); Mike Pingitore (bjo/gtr); Norman McPherson (tuba); Artie Miller (st-bs); Herb Quigley (dms).
THE RHYTHM GIRLS: unidentified
THE ROLLICKERS: unidentified

RHAPSODY IN BLUE (opening theme)

PETER, PETER, PUMPKIN EATER

LITTLE WOMEN LIKE YOU
(vc by Jack Fulton)

BLUE ROOM
(solos by Bunny Berigan and Frank Trumbauer)

Going Hollywood Medley:
a. **TEMPTATION**
(vc by Bob Lawrence)

b. **WE'LL MAKE HAY WHILE THE SUN SHINES**
(vc by Ramona Davies)
c. **OUR BIG LOVE SCENE**
(vc by Jack Fulton)

ANNIE DOESN'T LIVE HERE ANYMORE
(vc by Ramona Davies)

Pilgrim's Progress 1933 Sketch-
(featuring The Rollickers, The Rhythm Girls, Johnny Mercer, and Harry ''Goldie'' Goldfield)

PUDDIN' HEAD JONES
(vc by Peggy Healy)
(muted solo by Bunny Berigan)

SMOKE GETS IN YOUR EYES
(vc by Bob Lawrence)
(featuring Chester Hazlett)

SMOKE RINGS
(vc by The Rhythm Girls)

BY THE WATERS OF THE MINNETONKA

RHAPSODY IN BLUE (closing theme)

The complete 60-minute program is available on:
CASS Cassettes Only and TAPE Nostalgia MT-3302

7 DECEMBER 1933 (Thu): ***The Kraft Music Hall,*** NBC Radio Program, New York, NY.

PAUL WHITEMAN ORCHESTRA: Charlie Teagarden, Harry ''Goldie'' Goldfield, Nat Natoli (tpts); Jack Fulton, Jack Teagarden, Bill Rank (tbns); **Frank Trumbauer**, Benny Bonacio, John Cordaro, Charles Strickfaden (reeds); Kurt Dieterle, Matty Malneck, Mischa Russell, Harry Strubel (vns); Roy

Bargy, Ramona Davies (ps); Mike Pingitore (bjo/gtr); Norman McPherson (tuba); Artie Miller (st-bs); Herb Quigley (dms).
THE RONDOLIERS: unidentified
THE THREE RHYTHM GIRLS: unidentified

RHAPSODY IN BLUE (opening theme)

LOVE IS SWEEPING THE COUNTRY
(vc by The Rondoliers)

BETTER THINK TWICE
(vc by Peggy Healy and Jerry Arlen)

HOME ON THE RANGE
(vc by Bob Lawrence)

BOUNCING BALL
(featuring Frank Trumbauer)
12″-LP Aircheck 9 ''Teagarden & Trumbauer''
12″-LP Totem 1001 ''Teagarden & Trumbauer''

Murder At The Poles (mystery sketch)
(also featuring Jack Teagarden and others, and)

a. **FOUR DETECTIVES**
(The Rondoliers)

b. **SIX SECRETARIES**
(vc by The Three Rhythm Girls)

c. **SPIRIT OF PROHIBITION**
(featuring Harry ''Goldie'' Goldfield)

d. **JOHN Q. PUBLIC**
(vc by Andy Love)

e. **DISTRICT ATTORNEY**
(vc by Johnny Mercer)

CLAMBAKE (PROHIBITION)
(featuring Frank Trumbauer)
12″-LP Aircheck 9 ''Teagarden & Trumbauer''
12″-LP Totem 1001 ''Teagarden & Trumbauer''

DID YOU EVER SEE A DREAM WALKING?
(vc by Peggy Healy)

Let's Fall In Love Medley

SAM, THE OLD ACCORDION MAN
(vc by Ramona Davies)

PETER, PETER, PUMPKIN EATER
(featuring Roy Bargy)

I'LL BE FAITHFUL
(vc by Jack Fulton)

THAT DALLAS MAN
(vc by Ramona Davies)

RHAPSODY IN BLUE (closing theme)

The complete 60-minute program is available on:
CASS Cassettes Only and TAPE Nostalgia MT-1176

14 DECEMBER 1933 (Thu): ***The Kraft Music Hall,*** NBC Radio Program, New York, NY.
PAUL WHITEMAN ORCHESTRA: Personnel same as for 7 December 1933.
THE RONDOLIERS: unidentified
THE RHYTHM GIRLS: unidentified

RHAPSODY IN BLUE (opening theme)

BAMBALINA

ONE MINUTE TO ONE
(vc by Bob Lawrence)

BOY AND GIRL ON THE SCOOTER
(vc by Peggy Healy and Jerry Arlen)

WILDCAT
(featuring Frank Trumbauer)
12″-LP Aircheck 9 ''Teagarden & Trumbauer''
12″-LP Totem 1001 ''Teagarden & Trumbauer''

PARK IN PAREE
(vc by The Rondoliers)

Blackbirds of 1934 Medley:
a. **TAPPING THE BARREL**
(vc by The Rondoliers)
b. **I JUST COULDN'T TAKE IT BABY**
(vc by Peggy Healy)
c. **I'M WALKIN' THE CHALK LINE**
(vc by Ramona Davies)
d. **ONE HUNDRED YEARS FROM TODAY**
(vc by Jack Fulton and The Rhythm Girls)
e. **MY MOTHER'S SON-IN-LAW**
(vc by Ramona Davies)

PARADE OF THE WOODEN SOLDIERS

THE OLD SPINNING WHEEL
(vc by Jack Fulton)

WALTZING THROUGH THE AGES

GOOPY GEER
(vc by Ramona Davies)

I'M JUST WILD ABOUT HARRY

RHAPSODY IN BLUE (closing theme)

The complete 60-minute program is available on:
CASS Cassettes Only and TAPE Nostalgia MT-1176

28 DECEMBER 1933 (Thu): ***The Kraft Music Hall,*** NBC Radio Program, New York, NY.

PAUL WHITEMAN ORCHESTRA: Personnel same as for 7 December 1933.
THE PICKENS SISTERS: Jane, Helen, Patti.
THE RONDOLIERS: unidentified

RHAPSODY IN BLUE (opening theme)

GREAT DAY!

DON'T YOU REMEMBER ME?
(vc by Bob Lawrence)

DOING THE UPTOWN LOWDOWN
(vc by The Pickens Sisters)

Joe Palooka Medley
(vc by Arthur Boron impersonating Jimmy Durante)

TURN BACK THE CLOCK
(vc by Ramona Davies)

SONG OF THE BAYOU
(vc by The Pickens Sisters and The Rondoliers)

"F" BLUES
(featuring Frank Trumbauer)
12″-LP Aircheck 9 "Teagarden & Trumbauer"
12″-LP Totem 1001 "Teagarden & Trumbauer"

OH! THAT KISS
(vc by The Rondoliers)

A STREET WHERE OLD FRIENDS MEET

THE BELLS OF ST. MARY'S

RHAPSODY IN BLUE (closing theme)

The complete 60-minute program is available on:
CASS Cassettes Only and TAPE Nostalgia MT-1177

4 January 1934 (Thu): ***The Kraft Music Hall,*** NBC Radio Program, New York, NY.
PAUL WHITEMAN ORCHESTRA: Personnel same as for 7 December 1933.
THE PICKENS SISTERS: Jane, Helen, Patti.
THE RONDOLIERS: unidentified

RHAPSODY IN BLUE (opening theme)

REVOLT IN CUBA

Song Hits Of 1933 Medley:
a. **THE BIG BAD WOLF**
b. **SHADOW WALTZ**
c. **VALLEY OF THE MOON**
d. **THE LAST ROUND-UP**

TWO HEARTS IN THREE QUARTER TIME

GOOD MORNING GLORY
(vc by The Pickens Sisters)

BEAUTIFUL GLORY
(vc by Bob Lawrence)

PETER IBBETSON (waltzes)
(featuring Roy Bargy, Ramona Davies, Deems Taylor—3 pianos)

ANNIE DOESN'T LIVE HERE ANYMORE

OH ME! OH MY! OH YOU!

WHEN THE MIGHTY ORGAN PLAYS
(vc by Jack Fulton and The Rondoliers)

RACHMANINOFF'S PRELUDES
(vc by The Pickens Sisters and The Rondoliers)

RHAPSODY IN BLUE (closing theme)

The complete 60-minute program is available on:
CASS Cassettes Only and TAPE Nostalgia MT-1177

11 JANUARY 1934 (Thu): ***The Kraft Music Hall,*** NBC Radio Program, New York, NY.
PAUL WHITEMAN ORCHESTRA: Personnel same as for 7 December 1933.
THE PICKENS SISTERS: Jane, Helen, Patti.

RHAPSODY IN BLUE (opening theme)

WHO

IN OTHER WORDS, WE'RE THROUGH
(vc by Ramona Davies)

CLARABELLE
(featuring Roy Bargy)

DIXIE LEE
(vc by Peggy Healy)
12″-LP Aircheck 9 "Teagarden & Trumbauer"
12″-LP Totem 1001 "Teagarden & Trumbauer"

SING A LOW-DOWN TUNE
(vc by The Pickens Sisters)

SPRING, BEAUTIFUL SPRING

CLAMBAKE: THE FUNNIES
(featuring Frank Trumbauer)
12″-LP Aircheck 9 "Teagarden & Trumbauer"
12″-LP Totem 1001 "Teagarden & Trumbauer"

Roman Scandals Medley:
a. **KEEP YOUNG AND BEAUTIFUL**
b. **NO MORE LOVE**
c. **BUILD A LITTLE HOME**

YOU HAVE TAKEN MY HEART
(vc by Jack Fulton)

YOU'RE AN OLD SMOOTHIE
(vc by Ramona Davies)

DANCE OF THE HOURS

RHAPSODY IN BLUE (closing theme)

The complete 60-minute program is available on:
CASS Cassettes Only CO-0873 and TAPE Nostalgia MT-1214.

16 JANUARY 1934 (Tue): Victor Record Co., New York, NY.
PAUL WHITEMAN ORCHESTRA: Nat Natoli, Harry ''Goldie'' Goldfield, Charlie Teagarden (tpts); Jack Fulton, Bill Rank, Jack Teagarden (tbns); **Frank Trumbauer**, John Cordaro, Charles Strickfaden, Bennie Bonacio (reeds); Kurt Dieterle, Mischa Russell, Matty Malneck, Harry Strubel (vns); Roy Bargy, Ramona Davies (ps); Mike Pingitore (gtr); Artie Miller (st-bs); Norman McPherson (tuba); Herb Quigley (dms).
THE VOCORDIANS: unidentified

BS-81061-1 **"G" BLUES**
Rejected. Remade 17 April 1934.
C-DISC Teagarden TCD-112291

BS-81062-1 **IF I LOVE AGAIN**
(vc by Bob Lawrence)
10″-78 Victor 24517
10″-78 English HMV B-6561

BS-81063-1 **MY LITTLE GRASS SHACK IN KEALUAKEKUA, HAWAII**
(vc by The Vocordians)
10″-78 Victor 24514
10″-78 Australian HMV EA-1332
12″-LP Russian Melodija 33M60-41643-44

BS-81064-1 **WAGON WHEELS**
(vc by Bob Lawrence)
10″-78 Victor 24517
10″-78 Australian HMV EA-1420

BS-81065-1 **IT'S AN OLD FASHIONED WORLD AFTER ALL**
(vc by Jack Fulton)
10″-78 Victor 24514

Trumbauer was paid $30.00 for this session.

25 JANUARY 1934 (Thu): ***The Kraft Music Hall,*** NBC Radio Program, New York, NY.

PAUL WHITEMAN ORCHESTRA: Personnel same as for 16 January 1934.
THE RONDOLIERS: unidentified

RHAPSODY IN BLUE (opening theme)

PETER, PETER, PUMPKIN EATER
(vc by The Rondoliers)

INKA DINKA DOO
(vc by Peggy Healy)

FARE-THEE-WELL TO HARLEM
(vc by Johnny Mercer and Jack Teagarden)
12″-LP Aircheck 9 ''Teagarden & Trumbauer''
12″-LP Totem 1001 ''Teagarden & Trumbauer''

HE RAISED HIS HAT
(vc by Ramona Davies)

DUSK (tango)

CLAMBAKE: THE FUNNIES

Alice In Wonderland (sketch):
(Entire cast in impressions of famous movie personalities)

Follies (medley)

SUDDENLY
(vc by Ramona Davies)

WHAT IS THERE TO SAY?
(vc by Jack Fulton)

I LIKE THE LIKES OF YOU
(vc by Peggy Healy)

MOON ABOUT TOWN
(vc by Ramona Davies)

THE TOREADOR SONG (from *Carmen*)
(vc by Bob Lawrence)

RHAPSODY IN BLUE (closing theme)

The complete 60-minute program is available on:
CASS Cassettes Only and TAPE Nostalgia MT-1214.

1 FEBRUARY 1934 (Thu): ***The Kraft Music Hall,*** NBC Radio Program, New York, NY.
PAUL WHITEMAN ORCHESTRA: Personnel same as for 16 January 1934.
THE RONDOLIERS: unidentified.

RHAPSODY IN BLUE (opening theme)

RAGGING THE SCALE

WHO WALKS IN WHEN I WALK OUT?
(vc by Ramona Davies)

WAGON WHEELS
(vc by Bob Lawrence)

I'M SO IN LOVE WITH YOU
(vc by Jack Teagarden)
12″-LP Aircheck 9 ''Teagarden & Trumbauer''
12″-LP Totem 1001 ''Teagarden & Trumbauer''

LET'S FALL IN LOVE
(vc by Jack Fulton)

LET'S FALL IN LOVE ANYWHERE
(vc by Peggy Healy)

CLAMBAKE: PASSION'S PLAYTHING

VIRGINIA REEL

PERFECT PARADISE
(vc by Jack Fulton)

MAURICE, LE GENDARME
(vc by The Rondoliers)

THAT'S LOVE
(vc by Ramona Davies)

RHAPSODY IN BLUE (closing theme)

The complete 60-minute program is available on:
CASS Cassettes Only and TAPE Nostalgia MT-1215/p21

16 FEBRUARY 1934 (Fri): Victor Record Co., New York, NY.
PAUL WHITEMAN ORCHESTRA: Personnel same as for 16 January 1934.

BS-81713-1 **THE MOONLIGHT WALTZ**
(vc by Jack Fulton)
10″-78 Victor 24566

BS-81714-1 **TRUE**
(vc by Jack Fulton)
10″-78 Victor 24566
10″-78 English HMV B-6481

BS-81715-1 **FARE-THEE-WELL TO HARLEM**
(vc by Jack Teagarden and Johnny Mercer)
10″-78 Bluebird B-10969
10″-78 Victor 24571

BS-81716-1 **SUN SPOTS**
10″-78 Victor 24574
10″-78 Australian HMV EA-1344

BS-81717-1 **THE BOUNCING BALL**
10″-78 Victor 24574
10″-78 Australian HMV EA-1344
10″-78 English HMV BD-187

BS-1076-1 **SUN SPOTS**
10″-78 Test Pressing

Trumbauer was paid $30.00 for this session.

The last matrix, BS-1076-1, is listed in the Victor files as an ''experimental'' item.

28 MARCH 1934 (Tue): 1:00-5:00 P.M., Studio #2, Victor Record Co., New York, NY.
PAUL WHITEMAN PRESENTS RAMONA AND HIS PARK

AVENUE BOYS: Nat Natoli, Harry ''Goldie'' Goldfield (tpts); Bill Rank (tbn); **Frank Trumbauer**, Jack Cordaro, Charles Strickfaden (reeds); Ramona Davies (p); Mike Pingitore (gtr); Artie Miller (st-bs); Herb Quigley (dms).

BS-81987-1 **THE BEAT O' MY HEART**
(vc by Ramona Davies)
10″-78 Victor 24597

BS-81987-2 **THE BEAT O' MY HEART**
(vc by Ramona Davies)
Victor unissued

BS-81988-1 **THE HOUSE IS HAUNTED**
(vc by Ramona Davies)
10″-78 Victor 24597

BS-81988-2 **THE HOUSE IS HAUNTED**
(vc by Ramona Davies)
Victor unissued

BS-81989-1 **BROADWAY'S GONE HILL-BILLY**
(vc by Ramona Davies)
10″-78 Victor 24598

BS-81989-2 **BROADWAY'S GONE HILL-BILLY**
(vc by Ramona Davies)
Victor unissued

BS-81990-1 **WE'RE OUT OF THE RED**
(vc by Ramona Davies)
10″-78 Victor 24598

Trumbauer was paid $28.00 for this session.

17 APRIL 1934 (Tue): Victor Record Co., New York, NY.
PAUL WHITEMAN ORCHESTRA: Personnel same as for 16 January 1934.

BS-81061-2 **''G'' BLUES**
(remake from 16 January 1934 session)
10″-78 Victor 24668
10″-78 Australian HMV EA-1407

BS-82319-1 **TAIL SPIN**
10″-78 Victor 24668

BS-82320-1 **CHRISTMAS NIGHT IN HARLEM**
(vc by Jack Teagarden and Johnny Mercer)
10″-78 Bluebird B-10969
10″-78 Victor 24615
10″-78 English His Master's Voice B-6549

BS-82321-1 **CARRY ME BACK TO GREEN PASTURES**
(vc by Bob Lawrence)
10″-78 Victor 24615

BS-82322-1 **ANNINA**
(vc by Bob Lawrence)
10″-78 Victor 24715

Trumbauer was paid $28.00 for this session.

19 APRIL 1934 (Tue): ***The Kraft Music Hall,*** NBC Radio Program, New York, NY.
PAUL WHITEMAN ORCHESTRA: Personnel same as for 16 January 1934.

RHAPSODY IN BLUE (opening theme)

MY, OH, MY

We're Not Dressing Medley:

I'M COMING VIRGINIA
(vc by Lee Wiley)
12″-LP Totem 1021 ''Lee Wiley 'On The Air' ''

A THOUSAND GOOD NIGHTS
(vc by Lee Wiley)
12″-LP Totem 1021 ''Lee Wiley 'On The Air' ''

MADAME BUTTERFLY
(vc by Helen Jepson and John Dunbar)

ILL WIND

PARADE OF MARCHES

RHAPSODY IN BLUE (closing theme)

The complete 60-minute program is available on:
CASS Cassettes Only and TAPE Nostalgia MT-3302.

24 MAY 1934 (Thu): ***The Kraft Music Hall,*** (partial) NBC Radio Program, New York, NY.

PAUL WHITEMAN ORCHESTRA: Personnel same as for 16 January 1934.

RHAPSODY IN BLUE (opening theme)

SUMMER ROMANCE (sketch)
(featuring Lee Wiley)

IF I LOVE AGAIN
(vc by Lee Wiley)

12″-LP Totem 1021 "Lee Wiley 'On The Air' "

CLARABELLE
(featuring Roy Bargy)

ITALIAN STREET SONG
(vc by Helen Jepson)

MEMORIAL DAY OVERTURE

THE MYSTERY SINGER

RHAPSODY IN BLUE (closing theme)

TAPE: Nostalgia MT-3302.

28 JUNE 1934 (Thu): ***The Kraft Music Hall,*** (partial) NBC Radio Program, New York, NY.

PAUL WHITEMAN ORCHESTRA: Personnel same as for 16 January 1934.

RHAPSODY IN BLUE (opening theme)

CLAP YO' HANDS
(vc by Johnny Mercer and Jack Teagarden)

JEWEL SONG (from Faust)
(vc by Helen Jepson)

DOWN TO THEIR LAST YACHT
(sketch)
(featuring Lee Wiley)

FUNNY LITTLE WORLD
(vc by Lee Wiley)
12″-LP Totem 1021 "Lee Wiley 'On The Air' "

BEACH BOY

RHAPSODY IN BLUE (closing theme)

TAPE: Nostalgia MT-3302.

29 JUNE 1934 (Fri): Victor Record Co., New York, NY.
PAUL WHITEMAN ORCHESTRA: Personnel same as for 16 January 1934.

BS-83350-1 **THERE'S NOTHING ELSE TO DO IN NA-LA-KA-MO-KA-LU** (BUT LOVE)
(vc by Johnny Hauser)
10″-78 Victor 24678
10″-78 English HMV BD-160

BS-83351-1 **BEACH BOY**
(vc by Bob Lawrence)
10″-78 Victor 24678
10″-78 English HMV BD-160

BS-83352-1 **BORN TO BE KISSED**
(vc by Ramona Davies)
10″-78 Victor 24670

BS-83353-1 **LOVE IN BLOOM**
(vc by Jack Fulton)
10″-78 Victor 24672
10″-78 English HMV B-6513

BS-83354-1 **I SAW YOU DANCING IN MY DREAMS**

(vc by Jack Fulton)
10″-78 Victor 24670

Trumbauer was paid $28.00 for this session.

26 JULY 1934 (Thu): ***The Kraft Music Hall,*** (partial) NBC Radio Program, New York, NY.
PAUL WHITEMAN ORCHESTRA: Personnel same as for 16 January 1934.

RHAPSODY IN BLUE (opening theme)

TIJUANA

DAMES
(vc by Al Jolson)
12″-LP Sandy Hook SH-2003 ‘‘Al Jolson ‘On The Air’ ’’
12″-LP Totem 1006 ‘‘Al Jolson ‘On The Air’ ’’

THE CALL OF THE SOUTH
(vc by Al Jolson)
12″-LP Sandy Hook SH-2003 ‘‘Al Jolson ‘On The Air’ ’’
12″-LP Totem 1006 ‘‘Al Jolson ‘On The Air’ ’’

RHAPSODY IN BLUE (closing theme)

Full details of program unknown at time of publication.

2 AUGUST 1934 (Thu): ***The Kraft Music Hall,*** (partial) NBC Radio Program, New York, NY.
PAUL WHITEMAN ORCHESTRA: Personnel same as for 16 January 1934.

RHAPSODY IN BLUE (opening theme)

TIJUANA

RHAPSODY IN BLUE (closing theme)

Full details of program unknown at time of publication.

9 AUGUST 1934 (Thu): ***The Kraft Music Hall,*** (partial) NBC Radio Program, New York, NY.

PAUL WHITEMAN ORCHESTRA: Personnel same as for 16 January 1934.

RHAPSODY IN BLUE (opening theme)

TAMBALINA

LA CUCARACHA
(vc by Ramona Davies)

MAMMY SINGER
(Whiteman's musical salute to Al Jolson)

RHAPSODY IN BLUE (closing theme)

Full details of program unknown at time of publication.

16 AUGUST 1934 (Thu): ***The Kraft Music Hall,*** (partial) NBC Radio Program, New York, NY.

PAUL WHITEMAN ORCHESTRA: Personnel same as for 16 January 1934.

RHAPSODY IN BLUE (opening theme)

PARADE OF MARCHES

MIRRORS

RHAPSODY IN BLUE (closing theme)

Full details of program unknown at time of publication.

18 AUGUST 1934 (Sat): Victor Record Co., New York, NY.

PAUL WHITEMAN ORCHESTRA: Nat Natoli, Harry ''Goldie'' Goldfield, Charlie Teagarden (tpts); Jack Fulton, Bill Rank, Jack Teagarden (tbns); **Frank Trumbauer**, John Cordaro, Charles Strickfaden, Bennie Bonacio (reeds); Roy Bargy, Ramona Davies (ps); Mike Pingitore (gtr); Artie Miller (st-bs); Norman McPherson (tuba); Herb Quigley (dms).

BS-84010-1 **PARDON MY SOUTHERN ACCENT**

(vc by Peggy Healy and Johnny Mercer)
10″-78 Victor 24704

BS-84011-1 **HERE COME THE BRITISH** (BANG! BANG!)
(vc by Peggy Healy, Johnny Mercer, and Johnny Hauser)
10″-78 Victor 24074

BS-84012-1 **ITCHOLA**
10″-78 Victor 24885

BS-84013-1 **I'M COUNTING ON YOU**
(vc by Ramona Davies)
10″-78 Victor 24705

BS-84014-1 **I SAW STARS**
(vc by Peggy Healy)
10″-78 Victor 24705
10″-78 English HMV B-6532
12″-LP Russian Melodija 33M60-41643-44

Trumbauer was paid $28.00 for this session.

23 AUGUST 1934 (Thu): ***The Kraft Music Hall,*** (partial) NBC Radio Program, New York, NY.
PAUL WHITEMAN ORCHESTRA: Personnel same as for 16 January 1934.

RHAPSODY IN BLUE (opening theme)

THE BIRTH OF THE BLUES

ONE NIGHT OF LOVE
(vc by Helen Jepson)

WE BROUGHT OUR HARP
(vc by The King's Men)

TALES FROM VIENNA WOODS
(arrangement by Adolph Deutsch)

RHAPSODY IN BLUE (closing theme)

Full details of program unknown at time of publication.
TAPE: Nostalgia MT-3303.

30 AUGUST 1934 (Thu): ***The Kraft Music Hall,*** (partial) NBC Radio Program, New York, NY.
PAUL WHITEMAN ORCHESTRA: Personnel same as for 16 January 1934.

RHAPSODY IN BLUE (opening theme)

ABE MCINTOSH (3-part suite)
(Meredith Willson's Composition
Honoring The New York Columnist)

RHAPSODY IN BLUE (closing theme)

Full details of program unknown at time of publication.

11 SEPTEMBER 1934 (Tue): Victor Record Co., New York, NY.
PAUL WHITEMAN ORCHESTRA: Nat Natoli, Harry ''Goldie'' Goldfield, Charlie Teagarden (tpts); Hal Matthews, Bill Rank, Jack Teagarden (tbns); **Frank Trumbauer**, John Cordaro, Charles Strickfaden, Bennie Bonacio (reeds); Kurt Dieterle, Mischa Russell, Matty Malneck, Harry Strubel, (vns); Vincent Pirro (acc); Roy Bargy, Ramona Davies, Dana Suesse (ps); Mike Pingitore (gtr); Artie Miller (st-bs); Norman McPherson (tuba); Herb Quigley (dms).

CS-84258-1 **PARK AVENUE FANTASY**
12″-78 Victor 36131

CS-84259-1 **DEEP PURPLE**
12″-78 Victor 36131

(Dana Suesse, guest pianist on CS-84258-1 and CS-84259-1 only.)

CS-84260-1 **PETER, PETER, PUMPKIN EATER**
(part 1)
12″-78 Victor 36143

CS-84261-1 **PETER, PETER, PUMPKIN EATER** (part 2)
12″-78 Victor 36143

Trumbauer was paid $20.00 for this session.

13 SEPTEMBER 1934 (Thu): ***The Kraft Music Hall,*** (partial) NBC Radio Program, New York, NY.
PAUL WHITEMAN ORCHESTRA: Personnel same as for 11 September 1934.

RHAPSODY IN BLUE (opening theme)

WINTERGREEN FOR PRESIDENT

RHAPSODY IN BLUE (closing theme)

Full details of program unknown at time of publication.

20 SEPTEMBER 1934 (Thu): ***The Kraft Music Hall,*** (partial) NBC Radio Program, New York, NY.
PAUL WHITEMAN ORCHESTRA: Personnel same as for 26 October 1934.

RHAPSODY IN BLUE (opening theme)

YOU'RE NOT THE ONLY OYSTER IN THE SEA
(vc by Johnny Mercer)

LULLABY OF THE LEAVES

RHAPSODY IN BLUE (closing theme)

Full details of program unknown at time of publication.

4 OCTOBER 1934 (Thu): ***The Kraft Music Hall,*** (partial) NBC Radio Program, New York, NY.
PAUL WHITEMAN ORCHESTRA: Personnel same as for 26 October 1934.

RHAPSODY IN BLUE (opening theme)

SERENADE FOR A WEALTHY WIDOW

RHAPSODY IN BLUE (closing theme)

Full details of program unknown at time of publication.

11 OCTOBER 1934 (Thu): ***The Kraft Music Hall,*** (partial) Radio Program, New York, NY.

PAUL WHITEMAN ORCHESTRA: Personnel same as for 26 October 1934.

RHAPSODY IN BLUE (opening theme)

HERBERTIANA
(A salute to Victor Herbert)

Irving Berlin Medley:
(vc by Ramona Davies)
(arrangement by Roy Bargy)
a. **SAY IT WITH MUSIC**
b. **BLUE SKIES**
c. **MANDY**

BLUE MOONLIGHT
(featuring Dana Suesse, guest pianist)

LOST IN A FOG
(vc by The King's Men)

BALLATELLA-LAGLIACI

A Connecticut Yankee In King Arthur's Court (sketch)
(featuring William Gaxton)

VIRGINIA REEL

RHAPSODY IN BLUE (closing theme)

TAPE: Nostalgia MT-3303.

26 OCTOBER 1934 (Fri): Victor Record Co., New York, NY.
PAUL WHITEMAN ORCHESTRA: Eddie Wade, Harry "Goldie" Goldfield, Charlie Teagarden (tpts); Hal Matthews, Bill Rank, Jack Teagarden (tbns); **Frank Trumbauer**, John Cordaro, Charles Strickfaden, Bennie Bonacio (reeds); Kurt Dieterle, Mischa Russell, Matty Malneck, Harry Strubel (vns); Vincent Pirro (acc); Roy Bargy, Ramona Davies, (ps); Mike Pingitore (gtr); Artie Miller (st-bs); Norman McPherson (tuba); Herb Quigley (dms).

CS-84770-1 *Anything Goes* Medley:
a. **ANYTHING GOES**
b. **I GET A KICK OUT OF YOU**
(vc by Ramona Davies)
c. **YOU'RE THE TOP**
(vc by Peggy Healy and John Hauser)
d. **WALTZING DOWN THE AISLE**
e. **ALL THROUGH THE NIGHT**
(vc by Bob Lawrence)

12″-78 Victor 36141
(as by "Paul Whiteman & His Concert Orchestra")

CS-84771-1 **I GET A KICK OUT OF YOU**
(vc by Ramona Davies)

10″-78 Victor 24769
10″-78 English HMV BD-171

CS-84772-3 **YOU'RE THE TOP**
(vc by Peggy Healy and Johnny Hauser)

10″-78 Victor 24769
10″-78 English HMV BD-171

CS-84773-1 **ALL THROUGH THE NIGHT**
(vc by Bob Lawrence)

10″-78 Victor 24770
10″-78 English HMV BD-170

CS-84774-1 **ANYTHING GOES**
(vc by Ramona Davies)

10″-78 Victor 24770
10″-78 English HMV BD-170

Trumbauer was paid $36.00 for this session.

22 NOVEMBER 1934 (Thu): ***The Kraft Music Hall,*** NBC Radio Program, New York, NY.

PAUL WHITEMAN ORCHESTRA: Personnel same as for 26 October 1934.

THE KING'S MEN: Ken Darby, Jon Dobson, Bud Linn, Rad Robinson.

RHAPSODY IN BLUE (opening theme)

French Cafe Medley

SHOULD I BE SWEET OR NOT?
(vc by Ramona Davies)

IN MY COUNTRY THAT MEANS LOVE
(vc by Ramona Davies)

DARK EYES

I LIKE A BALALAIKA
(vc by The King's Men)

Selection from *Manon*
(vc by Yvonne Gaul)

SI TU LE VEUX
(vc by Yvonne Gaul)

RUSSIAN SAILOR'S DANCE

ANYTHING GOES

VILIA

LE CHALANO
(vc by Yvonne Gaul)

L'AVE BLANC
(vc by Yvonne Gaul)

WALTZING THROUGH THE AGES

RHAPSODY IN BLUE (closing theme)

The complete program is available on:
CASS Cassettes Only and TAPE Nostalgia MT-1215.

29 NOVEMBER 1934 (Thu): ***The Kraft Music Hall,*** NBC Radio Program, New York, NY.

PAUL WHITEMAN ORCHESTRA: Personnel same as for 26 October 1934.

THE KING'S MEN: Ken Darby, Jon Dobson, Bud Linn, Rad Robinson.

RHAPSODY IN BLUE (opening theme)

President Franklin D Roosevelt Medley

THE BEE SONG
(vc by The King's Men)

LA CUCARACHA
(vc by Ramona Davies)

THE DAY OF THE LORD
(The Reading Chorus)

VISSI D'ARTE (from Tosca)
(vc by Yvonne Gaul)

L'HENRE EXQUISE
(vc by Yvonne Gaul and Va Peters)

HERBERTIANA
(A salute to Victor Herbert)

YOU'RE THE TOP
(vc by Peggy Healy and Johnny Hauser)

INVICTUS
(The Reading Chorus)

PHANTOM OF THE RUMBA

THE NILE and **FISHES**
(vc by Yvonne Gaul)

STARDUST
(vc by The King's Men)

YOUR HEAD ON MY SHOULDER
(vc by Ramona Davies)

BOUNCING BALL
12″-LP Aircheck 9 "Teagarden & Trumbauer"
12″-LP Totem 1001 "Teagarden & Trumbauer"

BATTLE HYMN (from *Rienzi*)
(The Reading Chorus)

RHAPSODY IN BLUE (closing theme)

The complete program available on TAPE Nostalgia MT-1298

6 DECEMBER 1934 (Thu): ***The Kraft Music Hall,*** NBC Radio Program, New York, NY.

PAUL WHITEMAN ORCHESTRA: Eddie Wade, Harry "Goldie" Goldfield, Charlie Teagarden (tpts); Hal Matthews, Bill Rank, Jack Teagarden (tbns); **Frank Trumbauer**, Benny Bonacio, John Cordaro, Charles Strickfaden, (reeds); Kurt Dieterle, Matty Malneck, Mischa Russell, Harry Strubel (vns); Vincent Pirro (acc); Roy Bargy, Ramona Davies (ps); Mike Pingitore (bjo/gtr); Norman McPherson (tuba); Artie Miller (st-bs); Chet Martin, Herman Fink (pcs).
THE KING'S MEN: Ken Darby, Jon Dobson, Bud Linn, Rad Robinson.

RHAPSODY IN BLUE (opening theme)

ESPANA RAPSODY

MUSIC IN MY FINGERS
(vc by Ramona Davies)

POP GOES YOUR HEART
(vc by Ramona Davies)

LISA LOU
(vc by The King's Men)

COWBOY WHERE ARE YOU RIDING?
(vc by The King's Men)

DEPUIS LE JOUR (from *Louise*)
(vc by Yvonne Gaul)

ELEGIE
(vc by Yvonne Gaul)

WHEN MY SHIP COMES IN
(vc by Peggy Healy and Johnny Hauser)

AN EARFUL OF MUSIC
(vc by Peggy Healy and Johnny Hauser)

I'M JUST WILD ABOUT HARRY

SLEIGH RIDE
(vc by The King's Men)

WINTER WONDERLAND
(vc by The King's men)

THE JEWEL SONG (from *Faust*)
(vc by Yvonne Gaul)

PRINTEMPS
(vc by Yvonne Gaul)

AN AMERICAN IN PARIS
12″-LP M. F. Distributing Company LP 94748X

RHAPSODY IN BLUE (closing theme)

The complete program available on TAPE: Nostalgia MT-1298

13 DECEMBER 1934 (Thu): ***The Kraft Music Hall,*** NBC Radio Program, New York, NY.
PAUL WHITEMAN ORCHESTRA: Personnel same as for 6 December 1934.
THE KING'S MEN: Ken Darby, Jon Dobson, Bud Linn, Rad Robinson.

RHAPSODY IN BLUE (opening theme)

ALEXANDER'S RAGTIME BAND

ONCE UPON A TIME
(vc by Ramona Davies)

THESE SACRED HALLS

Roberta Medley:
a. **SMOKE GETS IN YOUR EYES**
(vc by Bob Lawrence)
(featuring Kurt Dieterle, vn)
b. **LET'S BEGIN**
(vc by Ramona Davies)

WEAF experienced transmitter difficulties during the medley, causing considerable distortion during transmission.

SWEET AND LOVELY
(vc by The King's Men)

STAY AS SWEET AS YOU ARE
(vc by The King's Men)

A THOUSAND TIMES, NO!
(vc by The King's Men)

LOVE'S OLD SWEET SONG
(vc by Helen Jepson and Chorus)

WEAF transmitter cut off for adjustment, approximately one minute.

THE CONTINENTAL

THE OBJECT OF MY AFFECTION
(vc by Peggy Healy and John Hauser)

BASIN STREET BLUES
(vc by Jack Teagarden)
12″-LP Aircheck 9 "Teagarden & Trumbauer"
12″-LP Totem 1001 "Teagarden & Trumbauer"

TEA FOR TWO
(featuring Roy Bargy)
(arrangement by Roy Bargy)

LITTLE MUCHACHA
(vc by Ken Darby)

THE END OF A PERFECT DAY
(vc by Helen Jepson and Chorus)

RHAPSODY IN BLUE (closing theme)

The complete program available on TAPE: Nostalgia MT-1299

14 DECEMBER 1934 (Fri): Victor Record Co., New York, NY.
PAUL WHITEMAN ORCHESTRA: Eddie Wade, Harry ''Goldie'' Goldfield, Charlie Teagarden (tpts); Hal Matthews, Bill Rank, Jack Teagarden (tbns); **Frank Trumbauer**, John Cordaro, Charles Strickfaden, Bennie Bonacio (reeds); Kurt Dieterle, Mischa Russell, Matty Malneck, Harry Strubel (vns); Vincent Pirro (acc); Casper Reardon (h); Roy Bargy, Ramona Davies (ps); Mike Pingitore (gtr); Artie Miller (st-bs); Norman McPherson (tuba); Chet Martin, Herman Fink (pcs).
THE KING'S MEN: Ken Darby, Jon Dobson, Bud Linn, Rad Robinson.

CS-86457-2 **STARDUST**
(vc by Johnny Hauser and The King's Men)
12″-78 Victor 36159
(as by ''Paul Whiteman & His Concert Orchestra'')

CS-86458-1 **BLUE MOONLIGHT**
12″-78 Victor 36159
(as by ''Paul Whiteman & His Concert Orchestra'')

(Dana Suesse guest pianist on CS-86458-1 only.)

CS-86459-1 **DEEP FOREST**
12″-78 Victor 24852
12″-78 English HMV B-8318

CS-86460-1 **SERENADE FOR A WEALTHY WIDOW**
12″-78 Victor 24852
12″-78 English HMV B-8318

Trumbauer was paid $32.00 for this session.

17 DECEMBER 1934 (Mon): Victor Record Co., New York, NY.
PAUL WHITEMAN ORCHESTRA: Eddie Wade, Harry ''Goldie'' Goldfield, Charlie Teagarden (tpts); Hal Matthews, Bill Rank (tbns); **Frank Trumbauer**, John Cordaro, Charles Strickfaden, Bennie Bonacio (reeds); Kurt Dieterle, Mischa Russell, Matty Malneck, Harry Strubel (vns); Vincent Pirro (acc); Roy Bargy, Ramona Davies (ps); Mike Pingitore (gtr); Artie Miller (st-bs); Norman McPherson (tuba); Chet Martin, Herman Fink (pcs).
THE KING'S MEN: Ken Darby, Jon Dobson, Bud Linn, Rad Robinson.

CS-86468-1 **WHEN I GROW TOO OLD TO DREAM**
(vc by The King's Men)
10″-78 Victor 24844
10″-78 English HMV BD-130

CS-86469-1 **AU REVOIR L'AMOUR**
(vc by Johnny Hauser)
10″-78 Victor 24854
10″-78 English HMV BD-136

CS-86470-1 **THE NIGHT IS YOUNG AND YOU'RE SO BEAUTIFUL**
(vc by Bob Lawrence)
10″-78 Victor 24844
10″-78 English HMV BD-130

CS-86471-1 **SINGING A HAPPY SONG**
(vc by Ramona Davies)
10″-78 Victor 24854
10″-78 English HMV BD-136

20 DECEMBER 1934 (Thu): ***The Kraft Music Hall,*** NBC Radio Program, New York, NY.
PAUL WHITEMAN ORCHESTRA: Personnel same as for 6 December 1934.
THE KING'S MEN: Ken Darby, Jon Dobson, Bud Linn, Rad Robinson.

RHAPSODY IN BLUE (opening theme)

Medley:
a. **LET'S TAKE A WALK AROUND THE BLOCK**
b. **IF IT'S LOVE**
c. **THE GREAT WALTZ**
d. **LET'S TAKE ADVANTAGE OF NOW**

STARS FELL ON ALABAMA
(vc by The King's Men)

WE LOVE OUR PICCOLO
(vc by The King's Men)

THE NIGHT IS STILL
(vc by Helen Jepson)

A WAND'RING MINSTREL, I
(vc by Derek Oldham)

TONY'S WIFE
(vc by Ramona Davies)

CHRISTMAS FANTASY FOR CHILDREN
(featuring Ford Bond, storyteller)

CHRISTMAS NIGHT IN HARLEM
(vc by Jack Teagarden and Johnny Mercer)
12″-LP Aircheck 9 ''Teagarden & Trumbauer''
12″-LP Totem 1001 ''Teagarden & Trumbauer''

TAKE A NUMBER FROM ONE TO TEN
(vc by Peggy Healy and Johnny Hauser)

TAKE A PAIR OF SPARKLING EYES
(vc by Derek Oldham)

THE HUNDRED PIPERS
(vc by Derek Oldham)

SERENADE FOR A WEALTHY WIDOW

SILENT NIGHT, HOLY NIGHT
(vc by Helen Jepson and Chrous)

RHAPSODY IN BLUE (closing theme)

The complete 60-minute program is available on:
CASS Cassettes Only and TAPE Nostalgia MT-1299

23 JANUARY 1935 (Tue): Victor Record Co., New York, NY. PAUL WHITEMAN ORCHESTRA: Harry "Goldie" Goldfield, Charles Teagarden, Eddie Wade (tpts); Bill Rank (tbn); **Frank Trumbauer**, Benny Bonacio, John Cordaro, Charles Strickfaden (reeds); Kurt Dieterle, Mischa Russell, Matty Malneck, Harry Struble (vns); Roy Bargy, Ramona Davies (ps); Mike Pingitore (bjo/gtr); Artie Miller (st-bs); Chet Martin, Herman Fink (dms). Only one trombone was used on 23 January and 22 April sessions. The common belief is that Bill Rank was the lone trombonist.

BS-87445-1 **IF THE MOON TURNS GREEN**
(vc by Ramona Davies)
10″-78 Victor 24860

BS-87446-1 **I'M KEEPING THOSE KEEPSAKES FOR YOU**
(vc by Peggy Healy)
10″-78 Victor 24860

BS-87447-1 **LET'S SPILL THE BEANS**
(vc by Johnny Hauser)
10″-78 Victor 24887
10″-78 English HMV BD-184

BS-87448-1 **WOULD THERE BE LOVE?**
(vc by Ken Darby and Rad Robinson)
10″-78 Victor 24887
10″-78 English HMV BD-184

4 APRIL 1935 (Thu): ***The Kraft Music Hall,*** NBC Radio Program, New York, NY.

PAUL WHITEMAN ORCHESTRA: Personnel same as for 6 December 1934.

RHAPSODY IN BLUE (opening theme)

APRIL IN PARIS

RHAPSODY IN BLUE (closing theme)

Full details of program unknown at time of publication.

22 APRIL 1935 (Mon): Victor Record Co., New York, NY.
PAUL WHITEMAN ORCHESTRA: Personnel same as for 23 January 1935.
THE KING'S MEN: Ken Darby, Jon Dobson, Bud Linn, Rad Robinson.

BS-89573-1 **'WAY BACK HOME**
(vc by Johnny Hauser and The King's Men)
10″-78 Victor 25022

BS-89574-1 **NINON**
(vc by Bob Lawrence)
10″-78 Victor 25023
12″-LP Russian Melodija 33M60-41643-44

BS-89575-1 **SOMEONE I LOVE**
(vc by The King's Men)
10″-78 Victor 25023

BS-89576-1 **NOW I'M A LADY**
(vc by Ramona Davies)
10″-78 Victor 25022

16 MAY 1935: Film, ***Broadway Highlights***
Broadway Highlights (Paramount Varieties), presented by Adolph Zukor, 1935-36. 1 reel, sound. Copyright 16 May 1935, MP-5588, by Paramount Productions, Inc. No indication of renewal found. Credits: Fred Aller, Milton Hocky, Carl Timin, Fred Rath (editors); Ted Husing (narrator).

BROADWAY HIGHLIGHTS #1: A Paramount Film short in their variety series that depicts highlights of musicians originating from New York. Usually ten-minute shorts. Paul Whiteman and orchestra filmed on unknown date.

Details unknown. It is believed that Whiteman's orchestra may have been filmed in January 1935 for this short subject.

27 JUNE 1935 (Thu): ***The Kraft Music Hall,*** NBC Radio Program, New York, NY.

PAUL WHITEMAN ORCHESTRA: Personnel same as for 6 December 1934.

RHAPSODY IN BLUE (opening theme)

VALSE MODENNE

RHAPSODY IN BLUE (closing theme)

Full details of program unknown at time of publication.

9 JULY 1935 (Tue): Victor Record Co., New York, NY.

PAUL WHITEMAN ORCHESTRA: Harry "Goldie" Goldfield, Charles Teagarden, Eddie Wade (tpts); Hal Matthews, Bill Rank, Jack Teagarden (tbns); **Frank Trumbauer**, Benny Bonacio, John Cordaro, Charles Strickfaden (reeds); Roy Bargy, Ramona Davies (ps); Mike Pingitore (bjo/gtr); Artie Miller (st-bs); Larry Gomar (dms/vb).

BS-92576-1 **DODGING A DIVORCEE**
10″-78 Victor 25086
10″-78 English HMV B-8641

BS-92577-1 **THE DUKE INSISTS**
10″-78 Victor 25113

BS-92578-1 **AND THEN SOME**
(vc by Durelle Alexander)
10″-78 Victor 25088

BS-92579-1 **NOBODY'S SWEETHEART NOW**
(vc by Jack Teagarden)

10″-78 Bluebird B-10957
10″-78 Victor 23519

BS-92580-1 **AIN'T MISBEHAVIN'**
(vc by Jack Teagarden)
10″-78 Bluebird B-10957
10″-78 Victor 25086

BS-92581-1 **SUGAR PLUM**
(vc by Durelle Alexander)
10″-78 Victor 25150
10″-78 English HMV BD-5001

BS-92582-1 **BELLE OF NEW O'LEANS**
(vc by Ramona Davies)
10″-78 Victor 25150

10 JULY 1935 (Wed): Victor Record Co., New York, NY.
PAUL WHITEMAN ORCHESTRA: Harry ''Goldie'' Goldfield, Charles Teagarden, Eddie Wade (tpts); Hal Matthews, Bill Rank, Jack Teagarden (tbns); **Frank Trumbauer**, Benny Bonacio, John Cordaro, Charles Strickfaden (reeds); Kurt Dieterle, Mischa Russell, Matty Malneck, Harry Struble (vns); Roy Bargy, Ramona Davies (ps); Mike Pingitore (bjo/gtr); Artie Miller (st-bs); Larry Gomar (dms/vb).
THE KING'S MEN: Ken Darby, Jon Dobson, Bud Linn, Rad Robinson.

BS-92588-1 **I'M SITTIN' HIGH ON A HILLTOP**
(vc by Johnny Hausser)
10″-78 Victor 25151

BS-92589-1 **THANKS A MILLION**
(vc by Johnny Hauser)
10″-78 Victor 25151
10″-78 English HMV BD-5001

BS-92590-1 **I FEEL A SONG COMIN' ON**
(vc by Ramona Davies and The King's Men)
10″-78 Victor 25091
10″-78 English HMV BD-219

BS-92591-1 I'M IN THE MOOD FOR LOVE
(vc by Ramona Davies)
10″-78 Victor 25091
10″-78 English HMV BD-219

BS-92592-1 GARDEN OF WEED
10″-78 Victor 25113
10″-78 English HMV B-8641

BS-92593-1 DARKTOWN STRUTTERS' BALL
(vc by Jack Teagarden)
10″-78 Victor 25192
10″-78 English HMV B-8494

BS-92594-1 CHINA SEAS
(vc by Bob Lawrence)
10″-78 Victor 25088

7 SEPTEMBER 1935 (Sat): Victor Record Co., New York, NY.
PAUL WHITEMAN ORCHESTRA: Harry ''Goldie'' Goldfield, Charles Teagarden, Eddie Wade (tpts); Hal Matthews, Bill Rank, Jack Teagarden (tbns); **Frank Trumbauer**, Benny Bonacio, John Cordaro, Charles Strickfaden (reeds); Kurt Dieterle, Mischa Russell, Matty Malneck, Harry Struble (vns); Roy Bargy, Ramona Davies (ps); Mike Pingitore (bjo/gtr); Artie Miller (st-bs); Norman McPherson (tuba); Larry Gomar (dms/vb).
THE KING'S MEN: Ken Darby, Jon Dobson, Bud Linn, Rad Robinson.

BS-94192-1 FAREWELL BLUES
10″-78 Victor 25192
10″-78 English HMV B-8548

BS-94193-1 STOP, LOOK, AND LISTEN
10″-78 Victor 25319

BS-94194-1 WHY SHOULDN'T I?
(vc by Ramona Davies)
10″-78 Victor 25134

BS-94195-1 ME AND MARIE
(vc by The King's Men)
10″-78 Victor 25135

BS-94196-1 **WHEN LOVE COMES YOUR WAY**
(vc by Bud Linn)
10″-78 Victor 25134

BS-94197-1 **ANNOUNCER'S BLUES**
10″-78 Victor 25404

BS-94198-1 **A PICTURE OF ME WITHOUT YOU**
(vc by Ramona Davies and Ken Darby)
10″-78 Victor 25135

28 SEPTEMBER 1935 (Sat): Victor Record Co., New York, NY.
PAUL WHITEMAN ORCHESTRA: Harry ''Goldie'' Goldfield, Charles Teagarden, Eddie Wade (tpts); Hal Matthews, Bill Rank, Jack Teagarden (tbns); **Frank Trumbauer**, Benny Bonacio, John Cordaro, Charles Strickfaden (reeds); George Bamford (clt/ten-sx); Kurt Dieterle, Mischa Russell, Matty Malneck, Harry Struble (vns); Vincent Pirro (acc); Roy Bargy, Ramona Davies (ps); Mike Pingitore (bjo/gtr); Artie Miller (st-bs); Larry Gomar (dms/vb).
THE KING'S MEN: Ken Darby, Jon Dobson, Bud Linn, Rad Robinson.

CS-95095-1 ***Jubilee*** Medley (part 1):
a. **JUST ONE OF THOSE THINGS**
b. **WHY SHOULDN'T I?**
(vc by Ramona Davies)
c. **ME AND MARIE**
(vc by The King's Men)
12″-78 Victor 36775
(as by ''Paul Whiteman & His Concert Orchestra'')

CS-95096-1 ***Jubilee*** Medley (part 2):
a. **A PICTURE OF ME WITHOUT YOU**
(vc by Ramona Davies and Ken Darby)
b. **BEGIN THE BEGUINE**
c. **WHEN LOVE COMES YOUR WAY**
(vc by Bud Linn)
12″-78 Victor 36174
(as by ''Paul Whiteman & His Concert Orchestra'')
12″-78 English HMV C-2803

CS-95097-1 *Top Hat* Medley (part 1):
a. **NO STRINGS**
(vc by Durelle Alexander)
b. **ISN'T THIS A LOVELY DAY?**
(vc by Johnny Hauser)
c. **TOP HAT, WHITE TIE, AND TAILS**
(vc by The King's Men)

12″-78 Victor 36174
(as by ''Paul Whiteman & His Concert Orchestra'')
12″-78 English HMV C-2803

CS-95098-2 *Top Hat* Medley (part 2):
a. **CHEEK TO CHEEK**
(vc by Ramona Davies)
b. **PICCOLINO**
(vc by The King's Men)

12″-78 Victor 36174
(as by ''Paul Whiteman & His Concert Orchestra'')
12″-78 English HMV C-2803

29 SEPTEMBER 1935 (Sun): ***The Magic Key Of Radio,*** (première broadcast), NBC Radio program, New York, NY.

PAUL WHITEMAN ORCHESTRA: Personnel same as for 28 September 1935.

THE KING'S MEN: Ken Darby, Jon Dobson, Bud Linn, Rad Robinson.

First half of program: **RHAPSODY IN BLUE** (theme)

BELLE OF NEW O'LEANS
(vc by The King's Men, Bob Lawrence, and Ramona Davies)

Second half of program: **RHAPSODY IN BLUE** (theme)

I'M SITTING HIGH ON A HILLTOP
(vc by Johnny Hauser)

The complete 60-minute program is available on:
CASS Cassettes Only and TAPE Nostalgia MT

3 OCTOBER 1935 (Thu): ***The Kraft Music Hall,*** NBC Radio Program, New York, NY.

PAUL WHITEMAN ORCHESTRA: Personnel same as for 28 September 1935.

THE KING'S MEN: Ken Darby, Jon Dobson, Bud Linn, Rad Robinson.

RHAPSODY IN BLUE (opening theme)

THANKS A MILLION
(vc by Ramona Davies, The King's Men, Morton Downey, Ruth Brent, and Bob Lawrence)

Medley:
a. **WHISPERING**
(vc by Morton Downey)
b. **WONDERFUL ONE**
(vc by Morton Downey)
c. **WHEN DAY IS DONE**
(vc by Morton Downey)

TALES FROM THE VIENNA WOODS
(vc by Helen Jepson)

RHYTHM IS OUR BUSINESS
(vc by Ruth Brent and The King's Men)

THAT'S WHAT YOU THINK
(vc by Ruth Brent and The King's Men)

RHAPSODY IN BLUE (closing theme)

The complete 60-minute program is available on:
CASS Cassettes Only and TAPE Nostalgia MT

16 NOVEMBER 1935 (Fri): Film, ***Broadway Highlights #5,*** New York, NY.

PAUL WHITEMAN ORCHESTRA: Personnel same as for 28 September 1935.

BROADWAY HIGHLIGHTS #5: Paramount film short contains opening night footage of ***Jumbo,*** and (undated) rehearsals with the Whiteman Orchestra in the background.

Details of film unknown.

No copyright has been found for ***Broadway Highlights #5.*** Entries for 1 thru 4 and 6 thru 8 are listed but not #5.

16 NOVEMBER 1935: Film, ***Thanks A Million,*** Filmed, August 19–October 4, 1935, Hollywood, CA.

Copyright 16 November 1935, LP-7960; renewed 16 October 1963, R-324212. Roy Del Ruth (dir); Nunnally Johnson(screenplay); Arthur Lange (musical dir).

PAUL WHITEMAN ORCHESTRA: Personnel same as for 28 September 1935.

THE KING'S MEN: Ken Darby, Jon Dobson, Bud Linn, Rad Robinson.

BELLE OF NEW O'LEANS
(vc by Ramona Davies and The King's Men)

Picture completed and ready for release on 4 October 1935. Released 25 October 1935.

The Whiteman segment was filmed in New York. The exact date is unknown.

2 DECEMBER 1935 (Mon): Victor Record Co., New York, NY.

PAUL WHITEMAN ORCHESTRA: Personnel same as for 5 January 1936.

THE KING'S MEN: Ken Darby, Jon Dobson, Bud Linn, Rad Robinson.

BS-98181-1 **I DREAM TOO MUCH**
(vc by Bob Lawrence)

10″-78 Victor 25197
10″-78 English HMV BD-5027

BS-98182-1 **THE JOCKEY ON A CAROUSEL**
10″-78 Victor 25197
10″-78 English HMV BD-5027

BS-98183-1 **I'M THE ECHO**
(vc by The King's Men)
10″-78 Victor 25198

BS-98184-1 **I GOT LOVE**
10″-78 Victor 25198

26 DECEMBER 1935 (Thu): ***The Kraft Music Hall,*** NBC Radio Program, New York, NY.
PAUL WHITEMAN ORCHESTRA: Personnel same as for 5 January 1936.
THE KING'S MEN: Ken Darby, Jon Dobson, Bud Linn, Rad Robinson.

RHAPSODY IN BLUE (opening theme)

I FEEL A SONG COMIN' ON
(vc by The King's Men and Ramona Davies)

CAPRICE VIENNOIS
(arrangement by Roy Bargy)

YOU TOOK ADVANTAGE OF ME
(vc by Ramona Davies)

WHEN DAY IS DONE
(featuring Harry ''Goldie'' Goldfield, tpt)

RHAPSODY IN BLUE (closing theme)

26 December 1935 was the last ***Kraft Music Hall*** program for Paul Whiteman.

TAPE Nostalgia MT-3303.

5 JANUARY 1936 (Sun): ***Musical Varieties,*** Sponsored by Woodbury; NBC Radio program, New York, NY.

PAUL WHITEMAN ORCHESTRA: Harry ''Goldie'' Goldfield, Charlie Teagarden, Eddie Wade (tpts); Hal Matthews, Bill Rank, Jack Teagarden (tbns); **Frank Trumbauer**, George Bamford, Benny Bonacio, John Cordaro, Charles Strickfaden (reeds); Bob Lawrence, Matty Malneck, Mischa Russell, Harry Struble (vns); Roy Bargy, Ramona Davies (ps); Mike Pingitore (bjo/gtr); Artie Miller (st-bs); Bob White (dms).

THE KING'S MEN: Ken Darby, Jon Dobson, Bud Linn, Rad Robinson.

BOLERO

TONY'S WIFE
(vc by Ramona Davies)

THERE'LL BE NO SOUTH
(vc by Harry Richman)

MARDI GRAS

A LITTLE BIT INDEPENDENT
(vc by Durelle Alexander and Johnny Hauser)

I FOUND A DREAM
(vc by Harry Richman)

TAKE ME BACK TO MY BOOTS AND SADDLE
(vc by Bob Lawrence and The King's Men)

Medley:
a. **RED SAILS IN THE SUNSET**
b. **ON TREASURE ISLAND**
(vc by The King's Men)
c. **CHEEK TO CHEEK**
(vc by The King's Men)

CHINA BOY

12″-LP Aircheck 9 ''Teagarden & Trumbauer''
12″-LP Totem 1001 ''Teagarden & Trumbauer''

January 5 was the first program in the Woodbury series.

The complete 45-minute program is available on tape:
TAPE Nostalgia MT-2965

12 JANUARY 1936 (Sun): ***Musical Varieties,*** Sponsored by Woodbury; NBC Radio program, New York, NY.
PAUL WHITEMAN ORCHESTRA: Personnel same as for 5 January 1936.
THE KING'S MEN: Ken Darby, Jon Dobson, Bud Linn, Rad Robinson.

COSI COSA

THE MUSIC GOES 'ROUND AND AROUND
(vc by Jack Teagarden)
12″-LP Aircheck 24 "Jack Teagarden 'On The Air' "

MORE THAN YOU KNOW
(vc by Morton Downey)

DEEP PURPLE

GOODY, GOODY
(vc by Durelle Alexander and Johnny Hauser)

ALONE
(vc by Morton Downey)

CHLOE
(vc by Bob Lawrence)

Medley:
a. **MOON OVER MIAMI**
b. **CAN'T WE DREAM**
c. **HERE'S TO ROMANCE**
(vc by The King's Men)

THE BROKEN RECORD
(vc by Ramona Davies)

The complete program is available: TAPE Nostalgia MT-2965

19 JANUARY 1936 (Sun): ***Musical Varieties,*** Sponsored by Woodbury; NBC Radio program, New York, NY.

PAUL WHITEMAN ORCHESTRA: Personnel same as for 5 January 1936.

THE KING'S MEN: Ken Darby, Jon Dobson, Bud Linn, Rad Robinson.

VIRGINIA REEL

ALONE
(vc by Bob Lawrence)

RAISING THE RENT
(vc by Ramona Davies)

DARK EYES

ANNOUNCER'S BLUES
(featuring **Frank Trumbauer**)

12″-LP Aircheck 24 ''Jack Teagarden 'On The Air' ''
12″-LP Sandy Hook SH-

PARADE OF THE WOODEN SOLDIERS

YOU HIT THE SPOT
(vc by Durelle Alexander and Johnny Hauser)

GOT A BRAN' NEW SUIT
(vc by Jack Teagarden)

12″-LP Aircheck 24 ''Jack Teagarden 'On The Air' ''
12″-LP Sandy Hook SH-

Medley:
a. **SECRET HEART**
(vc by Bob Lawrence & The King's Men)
b. **HUGUETTE WALTZ**
c. **LOVELY LADY**
(vc by The King's Men)

REVOLT IN CUBA

The complete program is available: TAPE Nostalgia MT-2965

26 JANUARY 1936 (Sun): ***Musical Varieties,*** Sponsored by Woodbury; NBC Radio program, New York, NY.

PAUL WHITEMAN ORCHESTRA: Personnel same as for 5 January 1936.

THE KING'S MEN: Ken Darby, Jon Dobson, Bud Linn, Rad Robinson.

LIFE BEGINS WHEN YOU'RE IN LOVE
(featuring Mike Pingitore, bjo)

WAH-HOO!
(vc by Durelle Alexander, Johnny Hauser and The King's Men)

DOWN THE OREGON TRAIL
(vc by Bob Lawrence)

WABASH BLUES
12″-LP Aircheck 9 ''Teagarden & Trumbauer''
12″-LP Totem 1001 ''Teagarden & Trumbauer''

MOOD INDIGO

I FEEL LIKE A FEATHER IN THE BREEZE
(vc by Ramona Davies)

DANCE MY DARLINGS
(vc by Walter Wolf King)

SOMETHING NEW IS IN MY HEART
(vc by Nancy McCord)

I BUILT A DREAM ONE DAY
(vc by Walter Wolf King and Nancy McCord)

RAIN IN SPAIN

NOBODY'S SWEETHEART
12″-LP Aircheck 9 ''Teagarden & Trumbauer''
12″-LP Totem 1001 ''Teagarden & Trumbauer''

Medley:
a. **WITH ALL MY HEART**

b. **THANKS A MILLION**
(vc by The King's Men)
c. **MY ROMANCE**
(vc by The King's Men)

THE DUKE INSISTS

The complete program is available: TAPE Nostalgia MT-2965

2 FEBRUARY 1936 (Sun): ***Musical Varieties,*** Sponsored by Woodbury; NBC Radio program, New York, NY.
PAUL WHITEMAN ORCHESTRA: Personnel same as for 5 January 1936.
THE KING'S MEN: Ken Darby, Jon Dobson, Bud Linn, Rad Robinson.

GREAT DAY!

NEW YORK BOAT
(vc by Ramona Davies)

PLAY, FIDDLE, PLAY
(vc by Donald Novis)

I FOUND A DREAM
(vc by Donald Novis)

FLIGHT OF A HAYBAG
(featuring **Frank Trumbauer**)
12″-LP Aircheck 9 "Teagarden & Trumbauer"
12″-LP Totem 1001 "Teagarden & Trumbauer"

IF YOU LOVE ME
(vc by The King's Men)

CIRCUS ON PARADE

TAKE ME BACK TO MY BOOTS AND SADDLE
(vc by Bob Lawrence and male chorus)

I'LL NEVER SAY "NEVER AGAIN" AGAIN
(vc by Johnny Hauser and Durelle

Alexander) (lyrics sung to the melody of DON'T COUNT YOUR KISSES)

Medley:
a. **RED SAILS IN THE SUNSET**
b. **ON TREASURE ISLAND**
c. **CHEEK TO CHEEK**

VALSE MODERNE

The complete program is available: TAPE Nostalgia MT-1460

6 FEBRUARY 1936 (Thu): Victor Record Co., New York, NY.
PAUL WHITEMAN ORCHESTRA: Personnel same as for 5 January 1936.
THE KING'S MEN: Ken Darby, Jon Dobson, Bud Linn, Rad Robinson.

BS-99057-1 **THE WHEEL OF THE WAGON IS BROKEN**
(vc by Bob Lawrence)
10″-78 Victor 25251

BS-99058-2 **AWAKE IN A DREAM**
(vc by Ramona Davies and Ken Darby)
10″-78 Victor 25265
10″-78 English HMV BD-5057

BS-99059-1 **WHAT'S THE NAME OF THAT SONG?**
(vc by Johnny Hauser)
10″-78 Victor 25252

BS-99060-1 **SADDLE YOUR BLUES TO A WILD MUSTANG**
(vc by Bob Lawrence and The King's Men)
10″-78 Victor 25251

BS-99061-1 **LOOK FOR THE SILVER LINING**
(vc by The King's Men)
10″-78 Victor 25278

BS-99062-1 **WAH-HOO!**
(vc by Durelle Alexander and unidentified singers)
10″-78 Victor 25252

9 FEBRUARY 1936 (Sun): ***Musical Varieties,*** Sponsored by Woodbury; NBC Radio program, New York, NY.
PAUL WHITEMAN ORCHESTRA: Personnel same as for 5 January 1936.
THE KING'S MEN: Ken Darby, Jon Dobson, Bud Linn, Rad Robinson.

ARIA FROM *Martha*
(vc by Jon Keipura)

DARDANELLA

I'M BUILDING UP TO AN AWFUL LETDOWN
(vc by Ramona Davies)

THE MARCH OF THE CLOWNS

PARK AVENUE FANTASY

16 FEBRUARY 1936 (Sun): ***Musical Varieties,*** Sponsored by Woodbury; NBC Radio program, New York, NY.
PAUL WHITEMAN ORCHESTRA: Personnel same as for 5 January 1936.
THE KING'S MEN: Ken Darby, Jon Dobson, Bud Linn, Rad Robinson.

PHANTOM OF THE RHUMBA

GOODY, GOODY
(vc by Durelle Alexander and Johnny Hauser)

GIVE ME A HEART TO SING TO
(vc by Helen Morgan)

ST. LOUIS BLUES
12″-LP Aircheck 24 ''Jack Teagarden 'On The Air' ''

OH LORD, WHY DID YOU PUT US IN THE BAYOU
(vc by Bob Lawrence)

I'M SHOOTING HIGH
(vc by Ramona Davies)

THE MUSIC GOES 'ROUND AND AROUND
(as sung around the world)

THE JOCKEY ON A CAROUSEL

YOU ARE MY LUCKY STAR
(vc by Helen Morgan)

PLEASE BELIEVE ME

CLING TO ME
(vc by The King's Men)

UNIDENTIFIED INSTRUMENTAL

The complete program is available: TAPE Nostalgia MT-1460

23 FEBRUARY 1936 (Sun): ***Musical Varieties,*** Sponsored by Woodbury; NBC Radio program, New York, NY.
PAUL WHITEMAN ORCHESTRA: Personnel same as for 5 January 1936.
THE KING'S MEN: Ken Darby, Jon Dobson, Bud Linn, Rad Robinson.

WE SAW THE SEA
(vc by Bob Lawrence)

WHAT'S THE NAME OF THAT SONG?
(vc by Johnny Hauser)

I'M A DING DONG DADDY FROM DUMAS
(featuring the Stuff Smith Sextet)

UNIDENTIFIED TITLE
(vc by Marina Mura)

MARDI GRAS

WAH-HOO!
(vc by Durelle Alexander and The King's Men)

Medley:
a. **CORAL SEA**
b. **CARESSES**
c. **LOVE TALES**

I'M GONNA SIT RIGHT DOWN AND WRITE MYSELF A LETTER
(vc by Ramona Davies)

I'SE A MUGGIN'
(featuring the Stuff Smith Sextet)

OLD MAN OF THE MOUNTAIN
12″-LP Aircheck 9 ''Teagarden & Trumbauer''
12″-LP Totem 1001 ''Teagarden & Trumbauer''

The complete program is available: TAPE Nostalgia MT-2965

1 MARCH 1936 (Sun): ***Musical Varieties,*** Sponsored by Woodbury; NBC Radio program, New York, NY.
PAUL WHITEMAN ORCHESTRA: Personnel same as for 5 January 1936.
THE KING'S MEN: Ken Darby, Jon Dobson, Bud Linn, Rad Robinson.

A RENDEZVOUS IN HONOLULU

LIGHTS OUT
(vc by The King's Men)

Full details of the program unknown at time of publication.

8 MARCH 1936 (Sun): ***Musical Varieties,*** Sponsored by Woodbury; NBC Radio program, New York, NY.

PAUL WHITEMAN ORCHESTRA: Personnel same as for 5 January 1936.
THE KING'S MEN: Ken Darby, Jon Dobson, Bud Linn, Rad Robinson.

HINDUSTAN

IT'S BEEN SO LONG
(vc by Ramona Davies)
(featuring Red Norvo, xylophone)

IF I SHOULD LOSE YOU
(vc by Arthur Tracy)

BOUNCING BALL
(featuring **Frank Trumbauer**)

TWILIGHT ON THE TRAIL
(vc by Bob Lawrence and The King's Men)

I CAN PULL A RABBIT OUT OF MY HAT
(vc by Durelle Alexander and Johnny Hauser)

SOLILOQUY

I NEVER KNEW
(featuring Red Norvo Group, sans Whiteman)

AUF WIEDERSEHEN, MY DEAR
(vc by Arthur Tracy)

LET'S FACE THE MUSIC AND DANCE

The complete program is available: TAPE Nostalgia MT

10 MARCH 1936 (Tue): Victor Record Co., New York, NY.
PAUL WHITEMAN ORCHESTRA: Harry "Goldie" Goldfield, Eddie Wade, Charles Teagarden (tpts); Hal Matthews, Bill Rank, Jack Teagarden (tbns); **Frank Trumbauer**, Benny Bonacio, John Cordaro, George Bamford, Charles Strickfaden

(reeds); Mischa Russell, Matty Malneck, Bob Lawrence, Harry Struble (vns); Roy Bargy (p); Mike Pingitore (bjo/gtr); Artie Miller (st-bs); Bob White (dms).
THE KING'S MEN: Ken Darby, Jon Dobson, Bud Linn, Rad Robinson.

BS-99444-1 **MY ROMANCE**
(vc by Gloria Grafton and Donald Novis)
10″-78 Victor 25269

BS-99445-1 **LITTLE GIRL BLUE**
(vc by Gloria Grafton and Donald Novis)
10″-78 Victor 25269

BS-99446-1 **A WALTZ WAS BORN IN VIENNA**
(vc by The King's Men)
10″-78 Victor 25274

13 MARCH 1936 (Fri): Victor Record Co., New York, NY.
PAUL WHITEMAN ORCHESTRA: Personnel same as for 10 March 1936.

BS-99877-1 **IT'S GOT TO BE LOVE**
(vc by Johnny Hauser)
10″-78 Victor 25270

BS-99878-1 **THERE'S A SMALL HOTEL**
(vc by Durelle Alexander)
10″-78 Victor 25270

BS-99879-1 **GLOOMY SUNDAY**
(vc by Johnny Hauser)
10″-78 Victor 25274

15 MARCH 1936 (Sun): ***Musical Varieties,*** Sponsored by Woodbury; NBC Radio program, New York, NY.
PAUL WHITEMAN ORCHESTRA: Harry ''Goldie'' Goldfield, Charlie Teagarden, Eddie Wade (tpts); Hal Matthews, Bill Rank, Jack Teagarden (tbns); **Frank Trumbauer**, George Bamford, Benny Bonacio, John Cordaro, Charles Strickfaden (reeds); Bob Lawrence, Matty Malneck, Mischa Russell, Harry Struble (vns); Roy Bargy, Ramona Davies (ps); Mike Pingitore (bjo/gtr); Artie Miller (st-bs); Bob White (dms).

THE KING'S MEN: Ken Darby, Jon Dobson, Bud Linn, Rad Robinson.

St. Patrick's Day Medley:
a. **WEARING OF THE GREEN**
b. UNIDENTIFIED
c. UNIDENTIFIED

I'SE A MUGGIN'
(vc by Jack Teagarden)

UNIDENTIFIED
(vc by Phil Regan)

GLORY ROAD
(vc by Bob Lawrence and Choir)

JUBA DANCE

(IF I HAD) **RHYTHM IN MY NURSERY RHYMES**
(vc by The Tell Sisters)

NEW YORK HEART BEAT

I'D RATHER LEAD A BAND
(vc by Ramona Davies)

ALL MY LIFE
(vc by Phil Regan)

Medley:
a. **BEAUTIFUL LADY IN BLUE**
b. **ALICE BLUE GOWN**

The complete program is available: TAPE Nostalgia MT

22 MARCH 1936 (Sun): ***Musical Varieties,*** Sponsored by Woodbury; NBC Radio program, New York, NY.
PAUL WHITEMAN ORCHESTRA: Personnel same as for 15 March 1936.
THE KING'S MEN: Ken Darby, Jon Dobson, Bud Linn, Rad Robinson.

REVOLT IN CUBA

I'M PUTTING ALL MY EGGS IN ONE BASKET
(vc by Durelle Alexander and Johnny Hauser)

DOIN' THE PROM

DINNER FOR ONE PLEASE, JAMES
(vc by Helen Ault)

SADDLE YOUR BLUES TO A WILD MUSTANG

GRAND CANYON SUITE (ON THE TRAIL)
12″-LP M. F. Distributing Co. LP-94748X

DAY AFTER DAY
(vc by Helen Ault)

I HOPE GABRIEL LIKES MY MUSIC
12″-LP Aircheck 24 "Jack Teagarden 'On The Air' "

WITH EVERY BEAT OF MY HEART
(vc by Ramona Davies)

GREEN FIELDS AND BLUEBIRDS

The complete program is available: TAPE Nostalgia MT-2965

5 APRIL 1936 (Sun): ***Musical Varieties,*** Sponsored by Woodbury; NBC Radio program, New York, NY.
PAUL WHITEMAN ORCHESTRA: Personnel same as for 15 March 1936.
THE KING'S MEN: Ken Darby, Jon Dobson, Bud Linn, Rad Robinson.

HYMN TO THE SUN
12″-LP M. F. Distributing Co. LP-94748X

RHYTHM SAVED THE WORLD
(vc by Durelle Alexander)

SUNSHINE AT MIDNIGHT
(vc by Johnny Hauser)

WATER BOY
(vc by Bob Lawrence)
12″-LP M. F. Distributing Co. LP-94748X

SHAKING HANDS WITH THE DEVIL
(vc by Durelle Alexander and Johnny Hauser)

LIEBESTRAUM

UNIDENTIFIED
(vc by Ramona Davies)

GOODY, GOODY
(vc by The Collegians)

ALONE
(vc by The King's Men)

THE MAYOR OF ALABAM'
(vc by Jack Teagarden)
12″-LP Aircheck 24 "Jack Teagarden 'On The Air' "
12″-LP Sandy Hook SH-

Medley:
a. **RED SAILS IN THE SUNSET**
b. **AT SUNDOWN**
(vc by The King's Men)

The complete program is available: TAPE Nostalgia MT-2965

24 MAY 1936 (Sun): ***Musical Varieties,*** Sponsored by Woodbury; NBC Radio program, New York, NY.
PAUL WHITEMAN ORCHESTRA: Personnel same as for 15 March 1936.
THE KING'S MEN: Ken Darby, Jon Dobson, Bud Linn, Rad Robinson.

UNIDENTIFIED INSTRUMENTAL

ZAZU
(vc by Durelle Alexander & The King's Men)

ZAZU
(vc by Judy Canova)

ALEXANDER'S RAGTIME BAND

THE MELODY LINGERS ON
(vc by Frank Parker)

UNIDENTIFIED
(vc by The King's Men)

COMEDY SKETCH:
(featuring Judy Canova with Sister Anne and Cousin Zeke)

HILLBILLY SONG
(vc by Judy Canova)

UNIDENTIFIED INSTRUMENTAL

DARK EYES

IT'S GOT TO BE LOVE
(vc by Ramona Davies)

IS IT TRUE WHAT THEY SAY ABOUT DIXIE?
(featuring an unidentified pianist)

GOODY, GOODY

MEXICAN HAT DANCE

SIBONEY
(vc by Frank Parker)

The complete program is available: TAPE Nostalgia MT-2965

7 JUNE 1936 (Sun): ***Musical Varieties,*** Sponsored by Woodbury; NBC Radio program, New York, NY.

PAUL WHITEMAN ORCHESTRA: Personnel same as for 15 March 1936.
THE KING'S MEN: Ken Darby, Jon Dobson, Bud Linn, Rad Robinson.

DRESS REHEARSAL (part 5)

Full program details unknown at time of publication.

26 JUNE 1936 (Fri): Victor Record Co., New York, NY.
PAUL WHITEMAN ORCHESTRA: Harry ''Goldie'' Goldfield, Eddie Wade, Charles Teagarden (tpts); Hal Matthews, Bill Rank, Jack Teagarden (tbns); **Frank Trumbauer**, Jack Cordaro, Al Gallodoro, George Bamford, Charles Strickfaden (reeds); Mischa Russell, Harry Struble, Howard Kay, Walt Edelstein (vns); Sam Zimberlist (va); Sol Zimberlist (co); Casper Reardon (h); Vincent Pirro (acc); Roy Bargy, Ramona Davies (ps); Norman McPherson (tuba); Artie Miller (st-bs); Larry Gomar (dms).

CS-102291-1 **SLAUGHTER ON TENTH AVENUE** (part 1)
12″-78 Victor 36183
(issued as by ''Paul Whiteman & His Concert Orchestra'')
12″-78 English HMV C-2884

CS-102292-1 **SLAUGHTER ON TENTH AVENUE** (part 2)
12″-78 Victor 36183
(issued as by ''Paul Whiteman & His Concert Orchestra'')
12″-78 English HMV C-2884

BS-102293-1 **AFTERGLOW** (vc by Jimmie Brierly)
10″-78 Victor 25356
10″-78 English HMV BD-5111

BS-102294-1 **ON YOUR TOES** (vc by Ramond Davies)
10″-78 Victor 25256

5 JULY 1936 (Sun): Unidentified radio program. Fort Worth, TX.

SUMMER BREEZE
(vc by choir)

"T" FOR TEXAS
(vc by Judy Canova with sister Annie and cousin Zeke)

CROSS PATCH

The program also included a comedy sketch featuring Judy Canova with sister Annie and cousin Zeke.

Full program details not available at time of publication.

The partial program is available: TAPE Nostalgia MT

19 JULY 1936 (Sun): Radio program, Fort Worth, TX.

IT HAPPENED IN CHICAGO IN '33
(vc by The Dixie Debs)

THE NIGHT IS YOUNG AND YOU'RE SO BEAUTIFUL

TOY BALLOON
(vc by Durelle Alexander and The King's Men)

I'M GOIN' HOME
(vc by The King's Men)

YOU CAN TALK ABOUT ME
(vc by Judy Canova with sister Annie and cousin Zeke)

The program also included a comedy sketch featuring Judy Canova with sister Annie and cousin Zeke; and, a second sketch featuring Judy Canova and Jack Teagarden.

Full program details not available at time of publication.

The partial program is available: TAPE Nostalgia MT

24 MARCH 1937 (Wed): ***Birthday Salute To Paul Whiteman,*** NBC Radio Program, New York, NY.

PAUL WHITEMAN ORCHESTRA: Harry ''Goldie'' Goldfield, Charlie Teagarden, Eddie Wade (tpts); Hal Matthews, Bill Rank, Jack Teagarden (tbns); **Frank Trumbauer**, George Bamford, Murray Cohan, Jack Cordaro, Al Gallodoro (reeds); Mischa Russell, Matty Malneck, Harry Struble, Walter Edelstein, Robert Spokaney, Howard Kay, Adam Fluschman, Sam Korman, Sylvan Kirsner (vns); Ben Pellman, Fred Glickman (vas); Abe Edison, Milton Prinz (cos); Vincent Pirro (acc); Casper Reardon (h); Roy Bargy (p); Mike Pingitore (bjo); Frank Victor (gtr); Norman McPherson (tuba); Artie Miller (st-bs); Larry Gomar (dms).

RHAPSODY IN BLUE (opening theme)

THANK YOU, MR. BACH
(arrangement by Van Phillips)

RHUMBA LA BOMBA

ST. LOUIS BLUES
(featuring Casper Reardon, harp)

STARS IN MY EYES
(arrangement by Roy Bargy)

MARDI GRAS

WINTERGREEN FOR PRESIDENT

NOLA
(featuring Al Gallodoro, saxophone)

MR. GHOST GOES TO TOWN

WALTZING THROUGH THE AGES
(arrangement by Adolph Deutsch)

CHRISTMAS NIGHT IN HARLEM
(vc by Jack Teagarden and **Frank Trumbauer**)

LINGER AWHILE
(featuring Mike Pingitore, bjo)

RHAPSODY IN BLUE (closing theme)

The selection ALL POINTS WEST was to have been performed by Bob Lawrence. However it was cancelled due to illness just before broadcast time.

26 MARCH 1937 (Fri): Victor Record Co., New York, NY.
PAUL WHITEMAN ORCHESTRA: Harry ''Goldie'' Goldfield, Eddie Wade, Charles Teagarden (tpts); Hal Matthews, Bill Rank, Jack Teagarden (tbns); **Frank Trumbauer**, Jack Cordaro, Al Gallodoro, George Bamford, Murray Cohan (reeds); Mischa Russell, Matty Malneck, Harry Struble, Walter Edelstein, Robert Spokaney, Howard Kay, Adam Fluschman, Sam Korman, Sylvan Kirsner (vns); Ben Pellman, Fred Glickman (vas); Abe Edison, Milton Prinz (cos); Vincent Pirro (acc); Roy Bargy (p); Frank Victor (gtr); Norman McPherson (tuba); Artie Miller (st-bs); Larry Gomar (dms).

BS-06546-1 **SHALL WE DANCE?**
10″-78 Victor 25552
10″-78 English HMV BD-5221

BS-06547-1 **FOR YOU**
(vc by Allan Holt)
10″-78 Victor 25552

28 MARCH 1937 (Sun): Victor Record Co., New York, NY.
PAUL WHITEMAN & HIS CONCERT ORCHESTRA: Harry ''Goldie'' Goldfield, Eddie Wade, Charles Teagarden (tpts); Hal Matthews, Bill Rank, Jack Teagarden (tbns); **Frank Trumbauer**, Jack Cordaro, Al Gallodoro, George Bamford, Murray Cohan (reeds); Mischa Russell, Matty Malneck, Harry Struble, Walter Edelstein, Robert Spokaney, Howard Kay, Adam Fluschman, Sam Korman, Sylvan Kirsner (vns); Ben

Pellman, . . . Mazzuchi (vas); Abe Edison, Joe Rosenblatt (cos); Vincent Pirro (acc); Roy Bargy (p); Frank Victor (gtr); Norman McPherson (tuba); Artie Miller (st-bs); Larry Gomar (dms).

CS-06557-2 **ALL POINTS WEST** (part 1)
(vc and narration by Bob Lawrence)
12″-78 Victor 36198
(as by ''Paul Whiteman & His Concert Orchestra'')

CS-06558-1 **ALL POINTS WEST** (Part 2)
(vc and narration by Bob Lawrence)
12″-78 Victor 36198
(as by ''Paul Whiteman & His Concert Orchestra'')

CHRONOLOGY

30 MAY 1901: Orie Frank Trumbauer born in Carbondale, IL.

SEP 1906–JUN 1914: Elementary school.
SEP 1914–JUN 1916: High school.
SEP 1916–JUN 1917: Normal School.
SEP 1917–MAY 1918: Mechanical Trade School.

29 MAY 1918: Trumbauer enlisted at the Navy Recruiting Station in St. Louis. He listed his current address as that of his mother: 2304–A Russell Avenue, St. Louis. The enlistment papers noted that he had been employed by Rice Stix Dry Goods Company for the past month at the pay of $15 per week. Under occupations, Trumbauer noted ''machinist'' (6 months) and ''musician'' (1 year, 6 months).

3 JUN 1918: Trumbauer arrived at the Great Lakes Naval Training Station, outside of Chicago, IL. Assigned serial number 104-64-34. Description: height, 5 feet 10 inches; weight, 133 pounds; eyes/hair, brown; complexion, ruddy. Enlisted as LDS. Mus., Musicians 2c rating.

14 AUG 1918: Training completed. Assigned as musician.
29 AUG 1918: All bands at Great Lakes performed en masse.

17–24 SEP 1918: Trumbauer a member of the Second Regiment. The band was assigned the Wisconsin area to tour promoting the sales of U. S. Liberty Bonds.

15 OCT 1918: *America* sank at Hoboken, NJ.

22 NOV 1918: Assigned to Receiving Ship at Great Lakes, IL. Rating: Musician.

14 JAN 1919: Trumbauer honorably discharged from the U. S. Navy. Total service time: 7 months, 16 days. Salary, $41 per month. Paid $15.44 when discharged. Discharged while serving on the Receiving Ship at Great Lakes.

30 JAN 1919: Applied for membership in Musicians Local #2 in St. Louis. Trumbauer listed his address as 2304–A Russell Avenue. Length of residence as 2-1/2 years. Place of employment: Rice Stix Dry Goods Company. He listed his birth date as May 30, 1898. It should be noted that this was a game that Trumbauer enjoyed throughout his life. He always listed May 30 correctly, but he rarely cited the correct year, which he listed anywhere between 1898 and 1905.

28 FEB 1919: Accepted as full member of the St. Louis local. Joined Max Goldman's Band.

CA APR 1919: Joined Al Sarli's Band at Cicardi's Restaurant. Personnel as provided by Nick Lucas: Frank Quartell (tpt); Frank Trumbauer (sx); Louis Salemme (vn); Ted Fiorito (p); Nick Lucas (gtr); Joe Zig (dms).

8 NOV 1919: Led a band at the Armory in Carbondale.

17 JAN 1920: The Volstead Act went into effect at 12:01 A.M. Trumbauer's employment ended at Cicardi's. He went to work with the Gene Rodemich Orchestra at the West End Lyric Theatre.

CA OCT 1920: Tram worked with Gene Rodemich at the Grand Central Theatre.

8 DEC 1920: Appeared with Joe Kayser's Band in Danville, IL.

20 DEC 1920: Became a full member of the Joe Kayser Band: Leo Lambertz (tpt); Frank Trumbauer (sx); Bob Chaudet (vn); Harry Sales (p); Joe Kayser (dms).

JAN 1921: Shortly after the first of the year, Bob Marvin (bjo) replaced Leo Lambertz. The Kayser Band worked mainly Illinois, Iowa, and Wisconsin. Reportedly appeared at the Arcadia Dance Hall in Springfield, IL.

4 MAY 1921: Kayser Band opened at the Inglaterra ("The Ball Room Beautiful") in Rockford, IL.
27 MAY 1921: Kayser Band closed at the Inglaterra.
30 MAY 1921: Kayser Band opened at Harlem Park, Rockford, IL., sharing the music with Herb Bailey's Musicians of New York. Engagement booked until September 10. Trumbauer was given a watch for his birthday, inscribed "O. F. T. From Your Boys." The Elgin Watch still runs in 1993.

AUG 1921: Left the Joe Kayser Band and returned to St. Louis, MO.
21 AUG 1921: The Jansen-Trumbauer Orchestra opened at the Forest Park Highlands. Personnel, provided by Charles McHenry: Frank Trumbauer (sx); Frank Papila (acc); Charles McHenry (xyl); Charles Michener (p); Norman Rathbert (bjo); Ted Jansen (dms).

1 SEP 1921: Tram, doing double duty, opened with his own orchestra at Westminster Hall. Personnel unidentified.
4 SEP 1921: Jansen-Trumbauer engagement at Forest Park Highlands ended.
14 SEP 1921: Frank Trumbauer married Myrtle Alice Hill ("Mitzi") of Janesville, WI., at Rockford, IL.

CA OCT 1921: Tram appeared with Gene Rodemich Orchestra on Brunswick Recordings made in New York.

NOV 1921: Trumbauer featured at the Grand Central Theatre with Gene Rodemich Orchestra as "Frank Trumbauer, The Dippy Dancing Saxophonist . . . will wag a wicked wiggle, while charming sweet swaying strains from his seductive saxophone—and, boys, this bird can set all your feet to tapping."

JAN–MAY 1922: Continued to work with Gene Rodemich and various local bands, including a brief stint at the Westminster Hall with his own band.

25 MAY 1922: The Frank Trumbauer Orchestra opened at the Central Park Gardens in Rockford, Illinois. Personnel: Ray

Lodwig (tpt); unidentified (tbn); Frank Trumbauer (sx/ldr); Bonnie Ross (vn); Charlie Heckenberg (p); Bob Marvin (bjo); unidentified (tuba); ''Doc'' Kolb (dms).

10 SEP 1922: Closed at the Central Park Gardens.
11 SEP 1922: Joined Musicians Local #10 in Chicago. Issued card #4884.

OCT–DEC 1922: Bismarck Hotel, Chicago, IL.
Maurie Sherman Orchestra: Andrew Padula (tpt); Norman Lillis, Frank Trumbauer (sxs); Maurie Sherman (vn); Wallace Bradley (p); Ralph Smith (dms).

JAN 1923: Trumbauer joined the Benson Orchestra of Chicago. See Discography for full personnel.
29 JAN 1923: Benson Orchestra—Victor Records:
DOWN IN MARYLAND and TROT ALONG (rejected).
30 JAN 1923: Benson Orchestra—Victor Records:
STARLIGHT BAY and GEORGIA CABIN DOOR and TROT ALONG and SOME DAY YOU'LL CRY OVER SOMEONE (rejected) and THINK OF ME.
31 JAN 1923: Benson Orchestra—Victor Records:
LOOSE FEET and SWEET ONE (rejected) and OLD TIME MEDLEY (rejected).

25 FEB–3 MAR 1923: LeClaire Theatre and Hotel, Moline, IL.

MAR 1923: Benson Orchestra returned to Chicago engagements.

9 APR 1923: William Francis Trumbauer born, 8-1/2 pounds.
12 APR 1923: Coliseum Ballroom, Davenport, IA.
13–20 APR 1923: New World Theatre, Omaha, NE.
24–25 APR 1923: Coliseum Ballroom, Davenport, IA. Met Bix Beiderbecke.
27–28 APR 1923: Benson's Orchestra at Armory Dance.
29 APR 1923: Benson's Orchestra Concert.

MAY 1923: Return to Chicago area.

13 JUN 1923: Benson Orchestra—Victor Records:
IN A TENT and LOVE IS JUST A FLOWER and I'M DRIFTING BACK TO DREAMLAND (rejected).

14 JUN 1923: Benson Orchestra—Victor Records:
JUST FOR TONIGHT and NOBODY KNOWS BUT MY PILLOW AND ME and I NEVER MISS THE SUNSHINE.

15 JUN 1923: Benson Orchestra—Victor Records:
I'M DRIFTING BACK TO DREAMLAND and DREAMS OF INDIA and MARCH OF THE MANIKINS and THE CAT'S WHISKERS.

15 JUN 1923: Opened at Young's Million Dollar Pier, Atlantic City, NJ.

28 JUN 1923: Mitzi and Bill (age 2 months) arrived in Atlantic City. As a baby gift, Mrs. Bestor gave Mitzi white silk shoes and silk stockings for Bill.

20 JUL 1923: Benson Orchestra—Victor Records:
NO, NO NORA and WHO COULD BE SWEETER (rejected).

25 JUL 1923: Benson Orchestra—Victor Records:
SOMEBODY'S WRONG and OTHER LIPS.

17 AUG 1923: Benson Orchestra—Victor Records:
SOBBIN' BLUES and ROYAL GARDEN BLUES (rejected).

21 AUG 1923: Benson Orchestra—Victor Records:
MEAN, MEAN MAMA and SHIM-ME-SHA-WABBLE (rejected).

27 AUG 1923: Benson Orchestra—Victor Records:
FOOLISH CHILD and THAT OLD GANG OF MINE.

10 SEP 1923: Benson Orchestra—Victor Records:
WOLVERINE BLUES and THE THRILL OF LOVE (rejected).

15 SEP 1923: Engagement at Young's Million Dollar Pier ended.

17 SEP 1923: Benson Orchestra—Victor Records:
EASY MELODY and ARE YOU LONELY and IN A COVERED WAGON WITH YOU and MIDNIGHT ROSE and OH YOU LITTLE SUN-UV-ER-GUN.

Trumbauer served notice and left the Benson Orchestra on October 1 to return to St. Louis, MO.

23 OCT 1923: Tram appeared with Joe Kayser Band at Mendelssohn Club Dance in Rockford, IL.
31 OCT 1923: Trumbauer visited and sat in with the Benson Orchestra at Radeka's Hall in Kankakee, IL.

NOV 1923: Reunited with Ted Jansen Orchestra.

28 DEC 1923: Advertisement in St. Louis newspapers: "New Year's Eve Party at the Coronado. Hotel to be formally dedicated. Ted Jansen's Orchestra to feature Frank Trumbauer on trumpet. $7 per couple."
31 DEC 1923: New Year's Eve Party included personnel: Clarence Forster (tpt); Frank Trumbauer (sx); Frank Papila (acc); Charlie Michener (p); Norman Rathbert (bjo); Ted Jansen (dms).

JAN 1924: Trumbauer became ill from overwork and doctor advised a lengthy rest period.

MAR 1924: Grand Central Theatre—Gene Rodemich Orchestra. Personnel identified by Jules Blattner and Charles McHenry from photograph on wall of Local #2: Jules Blattner (tpt); Julius Robb, Frank Trumbauer, Allister Wylie (sxs); Otto Reinert, Gus Schmitt (vns); Bill Bailey (xyl); Gene Rodemich (p); Paul Spor (dms).
14 MAR 1924: Mound City Blue Blowers—Brunswick Records: SAN and RED HOT.

Frank Trumbauer joined the Ray Miller Orchestra at the Paradise Club in Newark, New Jersey. See Discography for full personnel.

28 MAR 1924: Ray Miller Orchestra—Brunswick Records: COME ON, RED and MONAVANNA.

23 APR 1924: Ray Miller Orchestra—Brunswick Records: LOTS O' MAMA and FROM ONE TILL TWO.

20 MAY 1924: Arkansas Travelers—Okeh Records: GEORGIA BLUES and LOST MY BABY BLUES.

30 MAY 1924: Gold watch given to Tram on his birthday, inscribed
"O. F. T. From The Boys And Ray Miller."

1 JUN 1924: Ray Miller Orchestra opened at the Beaux Arts Cafe in Atlantic City, NJ. (St. James and Boardwalk. Telephone: Marine 4763 or 4764).
3 JUN 1924: Ray Miller Orchestra—Brunswick Records:
MAMA'S GONE GOOD-BYE
6 JUN 1924: Ray Miller Orchestra—Brunswick Records:
WHERE IS THAT OLD GIRL OF MINE and I DIDN'T CARE TILL I LOST YOU (rejected)

10 JUL 1924: Ray Miller Orchestra—Brunswick Records:
I CAN'T GET THE ONE I WANT and SALLY LOU and LONELY, LITTLE MELODY and SOMEBODY LOVES ME
22 JUL 1924: Ray Miller Orchestra—Brunswick Records:
PLEASE and CHARLESTON CABIN and I DIDN'T CARE TILL I LOST YOU

5 AUG 1924: Ray Miller Orchestra—Brunswick Records:
BAGDAD and RED HOT MAMA and ARABIANNA
28 AUG 1924: Cinderella Night at the Cafe Beaux Arts. A pair of golden slippers awarded to the lady with the smallest foot. Abe Lyman presented the slippers to Mitzi (size 4).

1 SEP 1924: Closed at the Beaux Arts Cafe.
7 SEP 1924: Opened at the Hippodrome Theatre, New York, NY.
27 SEP 1924: Band reviewed in Billboard, page 23.
27 SEP 1924: Ray Miller Orchestra—Brunswick Records:
DOODLE-DOO-DOO and ADORING YOU

1 OCT 1924: Preview opening for press and invited guests at Arcadia Ballroom, NY.
2 OCT 1924: Grand opening for public, 2,000 attended, of Arcadia Ballroom.
4 OCT 1924: Band reviewed in *Billboard.* (Review of September 29 show).
9 OCT 1924: Sioux City Six—Gennett Records:
FLOCK O' BLUES and I'M GLAD

12 OCT 1924: Attendance at Arcadia Ballroom reached 4,100 paid admissions.

13 OCT 1924: Ray Miller Orchestra—Brunswick Records: ME AND THE BOY FRIEND

15 OCT 1924: Al Jolson—Brunswick Records: I'M GONNA TRAMP! TRAMP! TRAMP!

17 OCT 1924: Ray Miller Orchestra played on the White House Lawn, introducing the campaign song for President Calvin Coolidge, KEEP COOL WITH COOLIDGE. Al Jolson, the Dolly Sisters, and other performers entertained.

7 NOV 1924: Ray Miller Orchestra—Brunswick Records: BY THE LAKE

4 DEC 1924: Ray Miller Orchestra—Brunswick Records: WHY COULDN'T IT BE POOR LITTLE ME? and I'LL SEE YOU IN MY DREAMS

5 DEC 1924: Ray Miller Orchestra—Brunswick Records: INDIAN LOVE CALL

6 DEC 1924: Cotton Pickers—Brunswick Records: JIMTOWN BLUES

10 DEC 1924: Ray Miller Orchestra—Brunswick Records: YOU AND I (rejected) and NOBODY KNOWS WHAT A RED-HEAD MAMA CAN DO (rejected)

16 DEC 1924: Ray Miller Orchestra—Brunswick Records: YOU AND I and NOBODY KNOWS WHAT A RED-HEAD MAMA CAN DO

7 JAN 1925: Ray Miller Orchestra—Brunswick Records: TESSIE (STOP TEASING ME) and ME NEED YAH (rejected)

27 JAN 1925: Ray Miller Orchestra—Brunswick Records: ON THE WAY TO MONTEREY (rejected) and THAT'S MY GIRL (rejected)

4 FEB 1925: Rhythmodic Orchestra—Brunswick Records: HUNGARIA and EGYPTIAN ECHOES

5 FEB 1925: Ray Miller Orchestra—Brunswick Records: ON THE ROAD TO MONTEREY and THAT'S MY GIRL

6 FEB 1925: Cotton Pickers—Brunswick Records:
MISHAWAKA BLUES and JACKSONVILLE GAL

10 FEB 1925: Ray Miller Orchestra—Brunswick Records:
WILL YOU REMEMBER ME?

27 FEB 1925: Ray Miller Orchestra—Brunswick Records:
WE'RE BACK TOGETHER AGAIN and I'LL TAKE HER BACK, IF SHE WANTS TO COME BACK

13 MAR 1925: Ray Miller Orchestra—Brunswick Records:
JUST A LITTLE DRINK and MOONLIGHT AND ROSES

16 MAR 1925: Ray Miller Orchestra—Brunswick Records:
RED HOT HENRY BROWN and LET IT RAIN—LET IT POUR

9 APR 1925: Cotton Pickers—Brunswick Records:
THOSE PANAMA MAMAS and DOWN AND OUT BLUES

11 APR 1925: Ray Miller Orchestra—Brunswick Records:
PHOEBE SNOW and HOLD ME IN YOUR ARMS

1 JUL 1925: Trumbauer left the Ray Miller Orchestra and headed to Detroit to discuss with Bix Tram's offer to join his band in St. Louis.

6 JUL 1925: Detroit Musicians' Local #5 has this as transfer date on Trumbauer's union card. He listed his address as: 201 East Alexandrine Avenue (telephone: GL 3750).

Trumbauer then joined "The Breeze Blowers" band at Island Lake, MI: Bix Beiderbecke (crt); Fred Farrar (tpt); Bill Rank (tbn); Frank Trumbauer, Don Murray, Stanley "Doc" Ryker (reeds); Fred Bergin (p); Howdy Quicksell (bjo); Steve Brown (bs); Chauncey Morehouse (dms).

Detroit Musicians' Local #5 does not have anything on file that lists when Tram left their area and withdrew his transfer card. He probably only stayed a couple of weeks at Island Lake.

Red Norvo (born: Kenneth Norville), in an interview of 10 September 1990, revealed that he met Bix and Trumbauer for the first time during this period when they were playing on a Mississippi riverboat.

Variety of 1 June 1925 reported that Trumbauer was organizing a band and planned to open at the Arcadia Ballroom in St. Louis on August 29, succeeding Jack Ford's Orchestra.

8 SEP 1925: Frank Trumbauer Orchestra opened at the Arcadia Ballroom (3515-3523 Olive Street): Bix Beiderbecke (crt); Irving Kordick (tbn); Frank Trumbauer (alto/C-mel); Charles ''Pee Wee'' Russell (clt/ten-sx); Karl Spaeth (ten-sx); Louis Feldman (p); Wayne Jacobson (bjo); Anton Casertani (bs); Edgar ''Eggie'' Krewinhaus (dms); Marty Livingston (vcs). The Arcadian Serenaders played opposite Trumbauer's band every Wednesday, Saturday, and Sunday.
12 SEP 1925: Ray Thurston replaced Irving Kordick (tbn).

NOV 1925: Personnel changes: Don Gaebe replaced Anton Casertani (bs); Damon ''Bud'' Hassler replaced Karl Spaeth (ten-sx); Dee Orr replaced Edgar Krewinhaus (dms).

29 JAN 1926: Trumbauer's Orchestra appeared at the Elks' Club dance in Carbondale, IL.

8 FEB 1926: Ray Thurston replaced Sonny Lee (tbn).
9 FEB 1926: Trumbauer's Orchestra played the St. Louis University ''Prom of '26'' at the Statler Hotel.
15 FEB 1926: Vernon Brown replaced Ray Thurston (tbn).
26 FEB 1926: Trumbauer's Orchestra played at the Elks' Club dance in Carbondale, IL.

29 MAR 1926: Sonny Lee returned and replaced Vernon Brown (tbn).

3 APR 1926: Trumbauer, Beiderbecke, and rhythm section played for the opening of Thiebes Music Company.
16 APR 1926: Trumbauer's Orchestra played for the junior prom at Indiana University.

3 MAY 1926: Trumbauer's Orchestra closed at the Arcadia Ballroom in St. Louis.

Trumbauer joined the Detroit Musicians' Local #5 and was

issued card #E408; records now lost. Joined the Jean Goldkette Band

14 MAY 1926: Goldkette Orchestra at South Bend, IN. Played University of Notre Dame Senior Ball. Broadcast over WSBT.
15 MAY 1926: The Goldkette Orchestra returned to Detroit, MI. Played at the Graystone Ballroom.
21 MAY 1926: Goldkette Orchestra broadcast over WCX.
22 MAY 1926: Goldkette unit opened at Blue Lantern Inn in Hudson Lake, Indiana: Bix Beiderbecke (crt); Fred Farrar (tpt); Sonny Lee (tbn); Frank Trumbauer (alto/C-mel); Charles ''Pee Wee'' Russell (clt/ten-sx); Stanley ''Doc'' Ryker (ten-sx); Irving Riskin (p); Frank DiPrima (bjo); Dan Gaebe (bs); Dee Orr (dms). Trumbauer listed as the leader.

21 JUN 1926: Broadcast over WSBT, South Bend, IN.

26 AUG 1926: Article on Trumbauer and the band in South Bend ***Tribute.***
29 AUG 1926: Goldkette band closed at Hudson Lake.
30 AUG 1926: Tram and Bix heard Louis Armstrong with Carroll Dickerson Orchestra at Sunset Cafe, Chicago, IL.

1 SEP 1926: Trumbauer assumed leadership of the Jean Goldkette Orchestra, based in Detroit at the Graystone Ballroom: Bix Beiderbecke (crt); Fred Farrar, Ray Lodwig (tpts); Bill Rank, Newell ''Spiegle'' Willcox (tbns); Frank Trumbauer (alto/C-mel); Don Murray (clt/alto); Stanley ''Doc'' Ryker (ten-sx); Irving Riskin (p); Howdy Quicksell (bjo); Steve Brown (bs); Chauncey Morehouse (dms).
13 SEP 1926: Band left for tour of New England.
Tommy Dorsey temporarily replaced Spiegle Willcox (tbn).
21 SEP 1926: Band made its headquarters at the Hillcrest Inn, Southboro, MA. Conducted tour by bus. Spiegle rejoined the band, replacing Dorsey.
22 SEP 1926: Broadcast from WTAG, Southboro. Bill Challis joined the band as an arranger.
25 SEP 1926: ''Battle Of Bands'' at Lyonhurst Ballroom opposite Mal Hallett.

2 OCT 1926: Final appearance at Lyonhurst Ballroom.
4 OCT 1926: Band left Hillcrest Inn.
5 OCT 1926: Band arrived in New York, NY.
6 OCT 1926: Band opened at Roseland Ballroom opposite Fletcher Henderson Orchestra.
12 OCT 1926: Jean Goldkette Orchestra—Victor Records: IDOLIZING and I'D RATHER BE THE GIRL IN YOUR ARMS (rejected) and HUSH-A-BYE
15 OCT 1926: Jean Goldkette Orchestra—Victor Records: SUNDAY and COVER ME UP WITH SUNSHINE and I'D RATHER BE THE GIRL IN YOUR ARMS and JUST ONE MORE KISS
17 OCT 1926: Engagement at Roseland Ballroom ended.

5 NOV 1926: Band returned to Detroit and appeared at the Graystone Ballroom.

JAN 1927: The January issue of ***Orchestra World*** reported: ''Goldkette Orchestra will record for Vitaphone.'' Jean Goldkette, in correspondence dated November 1959, denied that they recorded for any label other than Victor Records.
20 JAN 1927: Band closed at Graystone Ballroom.
Personnel changes: Paul Mertz replaced Irving Riskin (p); Don Murray became ill, and Jimmy Dorsey replaced him when the band reached New York.
24 JAN 1927: Band opened at Roseland Ballroom, New York, NY.
28 JAN 1927: Jean Goldkette Orchestra—Victor Records: PROUD OF A BABY LIKE YOU and I'M LOOKING OVER A FOUR LEAF CLOVER
31 JAN 1927: Jean Goldkette Orchestra—Victor Records: I'M GONNA MEET MY SWEETIE NOW and HOOSIER SWEETHEART Personnel changes: Danny Polo replaced Jimmy Dorsey (sx); Don Murray still ill.

1 FEB 1927: Jean Goldkette Orchestra—Victor Records: LOOK AT THE WORLD AND SMILE and MY PRETTY GIRL and STAMPEDE (rejected)
3 FEB 1927: Jean Goldkette Orchestra—Victor Records: A LANE IN SPAIN and SUNNY DISPOSISH

4 FEB 1927: Frank Trumbauer Orchestra—Okeh Records: TRUMBOLOGY and CLARINET MARMALADE and SINGIN' THE BLUES

6 FEB 1927: Closed at Roseland Ballroom.

7–9 FEB 1927: Band appeared at Cook's Butterfly Ballroom in Springfield, MA.

11 FEB 1927: Band played University of Michigan's annual "J-Hop," along with the bands of Fletcher Henderson and Guy Lombardo.

12 FEB 1927: Returned to Detroit and Graystone Ballroom. Personnel changes: Marlin Skiles replaced Paul Mertz (p); Don Murray returned but Danny Polo remained with the band; Chris Fletcher and Ernest "Red" Ingle (vns/reeds) added.

LATE MAR 1927: Personnel changes: Irving Riskin replaced Marlin Skiles (p); Chris Fletcher and Red Ingle left; Danny Polo left. Trumbauer returned to full time playing with the band. Eddy Sheasby took over as director as Trumbauer felt that doing double duty, leader and sax section, was draining his energy.

APR 1927: Tour of midwest.

10 APR 1927: Closed at the Graystone Ballroom.

13 APR 1927: General Motors Convention, Dayton, OH.

15 APR 1927: Greystone Dance Hall (120 West 4th Street), Dayton, OH.

16 APR 1927: Greystone Dance Hall, Dayton, OH.

17 APR 1927: Valley Dale Ballroom (1590 Sunbury Road), Columbus, OH.

18 APR 1927: Hannah Neil Charity Ball, Columbus, OH.

21 APR 1927: Rose Polytechnic Institute Junior Prom, Terre Haute, IN.

22 APR 1927: Indiana University Junior Prom.

29 APR 1927: Pennsylvania State University Prom.

MAY 1927: Tour continued throughout east coast, mainly in Pennsylvania.

2 MAY 1927: Bach's Natatorium.

4 MAY 1927: Chambersburg, PA.

6 MAY 1927: Jean Goldkette Orchestra—Victor Records: SLOW RIVER

9 MAY 1927: Frank Trumbauer Orchestra—Okeh Records: OSTRICH WALK and RIVERBOAT SHUFFLE
13 MAY 1927: Frank Trumbauer Orchestra—Okeh Records: I'M COMING, VIRGINIA and WAY DOWN YONDER IN NEW ORLEANS and FOR NO REASON AT ALL IN C (credited as: Tram-Bix and Eddie . . .)
13–14 MAY 1927: Princeton University house parties.
16 MAY 1927: Jean Goldkette Orchestra—Victor Records: LILY (rejected) and IN MY MERRY OLDSMOBILE (waltz)
20 MAY 1927: Cornell University, Ithaca, NY.
21 MAY 1927: Scranton, PA.
22 MAY 1927: Harrisburg, PA.
23 MAY 1927: Jean Goldkette Orchestra—Victor Records: PLAY IT RED (rejected) and IN MY MERRY OLDSMOBILE (fox trot) Personnel change: Spiegle Willcox left the band, replaced by Lloyd Turner (tbn).
24 MAY 1927: Harrisburg, PA.
25 MAY 1927: Chambersburg, PA.
26 MAY 1927: Allentown, PA.
27 MAY 1927: Philadelphia, PA.
29 MAY 1927: Band opened at Castle Farms in Cincinnati, OH. Band was contracted to 25 June, but on 10 June their contract was extended to 1 July. Chris Fletcher and Red Ingle added.

2–8 JUL 1927: Loew State Theatre, St. Louis, MO.
Further bookings were cancelled and the band returned to Detroit and the Graystone Ballroom.

5 AUG 1927: Closed at the Graystone Ballroom. Chris Fletcher remained with the band. Don Ingle believes that his dad, Red Ingle, also continued with the band to the end.
8 AUG 1927: Opened at Young's Million Dollar Pier in Atlantic City, NJ.
23 AUG 1927: Rehearsed for Victor Recording date, but session cancelled.
25 AUG 1927: Frank Trumbauer Orchestra—Okeh Records: THREE BLIND MICE and BLUE RIVER and THERE'S A CRADLE IN CAROLINE
26 AUG 1927: Another attempt at Victor Recording date, but session cancelled again.

5 SEP 1927: Closed at Atlantic City, NJ. Chris Fletcher left the band.

8 SEP 1927: Opened at Roseland Ballroom, New York, NY.

9 SEP 1927: Tram present at Okeh Recording Studio while Bix recorded IN A MIST.

9–14 SEP 1927: Played nights with Goldkette Orchestra at Roseland Ballroom, rehearsed days with Adrian Rollini for forthcoming engagement at the Club New Yorker.

15 SEP 1927: Jean Goldkette Orchestra—Victor Records: BLUE RIVER and CLEMENTINE (FROM NEW ORLEANS)

16 SEP 1927: Adrian Rollini Orchestra photographs taken at Apeda Studios.

17 SEP 1927: Tram-Bix and Lang—Okeh Records: WRINGIN' AN' TWISTIN'

18 SEP 1927: Final night at Roseland Ballroom, New York, NY.

19–20–21 SEP 1927: Rollini rehearsed new band for Club New Yorker.

22 SEP 1927: Rollini Orchestra opened at Club New Yorker.

28 SEP 1927: Frank Trumbauer Orchestra—Okeh Records: HUMPTY DUMPTY and KRAZY KAT and THE BALTIMORE

29 SEP 1927: Broadway Bellhops—Harmony Records: THERE AIN'T NO LAND LIKE DIXIELAND TO ME and THERE'S A CRADLE IN CAROLINE and RAINBOW OF LOVE

30 SEP 1927: Frank Trumbauer Orchestra—Okeh Records: (issued as Benny Meroff Orchestra) JUST AN HOUR OF LOVE and I'M WONDERIN' WHO

4 OCT 1927: Tram, Bix, Bobby Davis, and Sylvester Ahola attended the movie ***Wings.***

8 OCT 1927: Rollini Orchestra opened at the Strand Theatre, concurrently with Club New Yorker engagement.

14 OCT 1927: Job at the Strand Theatre folded.

15 OCT 1927: Job at the Club New Yorker folded.

15–26 OCT 1927: The New Yorkers backed Jack Benny at the Aububon on 14th Street.

20 OCT 1927: Willard Robison with Chicago Loopers—Perfect Records: I'M MORE THAN SATISFIED and CLORINDA and THREE BLIND MICE

25 OCT 1927: Frank Trumbauer Orchestra—Okeh Records: CRYIN' ALL DAY and A GOOD MAN IS HARD TO FIND

26 OCT 1927: Red Nichols Stompers—Victor Records: SUGAR and MAKE MY COTTON WHERE THE COT-COT-COTTON GROWS

26 OCT 1927: Frank Trumbauer Orchestra—Okeh Records: (issued at Russell Gray Orchestra) SUGAR and DO YOU MEAN IT?

27 OCT 1927: Tram and Bix joined Paul Whiteman Orchestra at the Indiana Theatre in Indianapolis, Indiana. Personnel: Bob Mayhew, Bix Beiderbecke (crts); Henry Busse, Charles Margulis (tpts); Boyce Cullen, Wilbur Hall, Tommy Dorsey, Jack Fulton (tbns); Chet Hazlett, Hal McLean, Frank Trumbauer, Jimmy Dorsey, Jack Mayhew, Nye Mayhew, Rube Crozier, Charles Strickfaden (reeds); Kurt Dieterle (concert master), Mischa Russell, Matty Malneck, Mario Perry, Charles Gaylord, John Bowman (librarian) (vns); Tommy Satterfield, Harry Parella (ps); Mike Pingitore (bjo); Mike Trafficante (tuba); Steve Brown (bs); Harold MacDonald (dms); Harry Barris, Bing Crosby, Al Rinker (Paul Whiteman's Rhythm Boys), Austin "Skin" Young, Jack Fulton, Charles Gaylord (Paul Whiteman Trio) (vcs); Ferde Grofé, Tommy Satterfield, Bill Challis (arrs).

28 OCT 1927: Closed at Indianapolis, IN.

29 OCT 1927: Opened at the Ambassador Theatre, St. Louis, MO.

4 NOV 1927: Closed at the Ambassador Theatre, St. Louis, MO.

7–13 NOV 1927: Chicago Theatre, Chicago, IL.
During Chicago engagements, Trumbauer started taking flying lessons from "Pops" Keller.

14–20 NOV 1927: Uptown Theatre, Chicago, IL.

21 NOV 1927: Opened at the Tivoli Theatre, Chicago, IL.

22 NOV 1927: Paul Whiteman Orchestra—Victor Records: AMONG MY SOUVENIRS

25 NOV 1927: Paul Whiteman Orchestra—Victor Records: MARY

27 NOV 1927: Closed at the Tivoli Theatre. Tommy Dorsey left the band.

29 NOV 1927: Memorial Hall, Columbus, OH.

30 NOV 1927: Land O' Dance, Canton, OH.

1 DEC 1927: Madison Gardens, Toledo, OH.
2 DEC 1927: Prudden Auditorium, Lansing, MI.
4–11 DEC 1927: Allen Theatre, Cleveland, OH.
12 DEC 1927: Loew's Penn Theatre, Pittsburgh, PA.
Bill Rank (tbn) joined the band.
16 DEC 1927: Closed at Loew's Theatre, Pittsburgh, PA.
19–24 DEC 1927: Century Theatre, Baltimore, MD.
26 DEC 1927: Coliseum Ballroom, York, PA.
27 DEC 1927: Ritz-Carlton, New York, NY.
28 DEC 1927: Town Hall, Scranton, PA.
29 DEC 1927: Armory, Wilkes-Barre, PA.
30 DEC 1927: Kalurah Temple, Binghamton, NY.
31 DEC 1927: Bellevue-Stratford Hotel (stage show), Philadelphia, PA.

1–13 JAN 1928: Whiteman did not have a steady engagement booked. He told the boys, "enjoy the vacation."
3 JAN 1928: Trumbauer met with Tommy Rockwell to decide upon tunes for next Monday's recordings.
4 JAN 1928: Paul Whiteman Orchestra—Victor Records:
RAMONA and LONELY MELODY
4 JAN 1928: NBC radio program. First nationwide hookup, sponsored by the Dodge Brothers (automobiles). 10:30–11:30 P.M. EST. Los Angeles: Will Rogers, master of ceremonies.
New York: Paul Whiteman & His Orchestra; RHAPSODY IN BLUE
Chicago: Dorothy Stone and Criss Cross Four; TRUE BLUE Fred Stone; CHINESE SONG FROM CHIN CHIN Fred & Dorothy Stone; DOWN ON THE FARM (from ***Tip Top***) with Mary Cooke at the piano.
New Orleans: Al Jolson with Dave Dreyer at the piano; (first medley) CALIFORNIA, HERE I COME and ROCK-A-BYE YOUR BABY WITH A DIXIE MELODY and TOOT, TOOT, TOOTSIE (GOO'BYE) and MY MAMMY; (second medley) GOLDEN GATE and FOUR WALLS and BACK IN YOUR OWN BACKYARD
New York: Paul Whiteman & His Orchestra; RAMONA and CHANGES
5 JAN 1928: Paul Whiteman Orchestra—Victor Records:
O YA YA

9 JAN 1928: Frank Trumbauer Orchestra—Okeh Records:
TWO LETTERS FROM DIXIE (rejected) and THERE'LL COME A TIME and JUBILEE

10 JAN 1928: Columbia Records offered a contract to Trumbauer for a series of 12-inch recordings. Tram discussed the matter with Paul Whiteman, and Whiteman refused permission.

11 JAN 1928: Paul Whiteman Orchestra—Victor Records:
PARADE OF THE WOODEN SOLDIERS and OL' MAN RIVER

12 JAN 1928: Paul Whiteman Orchestra—Victor Records:
SAN

14–20 JAN 1928: Mosque Theatre, Newark, NJ.

18 JAN 1928: Recording date for Willard Robison.
Trumbauer's notes failed to list studio or tunes.

20 JAN 1928: Frank Trumbauer Orchestra—Okeh Records:
FROM MONDAY ON (rejected) and MISSISSIPPI MUD

21 JAN 1928: Paul Whiteman Orchestra—Victor Records:
TOGETHER

22–28 JAN 1928: Stanley Theatre, Philadelphia, PA.

24 JAN 1928: Paul Whiteman Orchestra—Victor Records:
MY HEART STOOD STILL and SMILE

25 JAN 1928: Trumbauer had a recording date at Okeh Records but was unable to record. Tunes not listed. Okeh studios overbooked with recording others.

26 JAN 1928: Paul Whiteman Orchestra—Victor Records:
Orchestra rehearsed but did not record, WHISPERING, with Fats Waller.

27 JAN 1928: Paul Whiteman Orchestra—Victor Records:
MAKE BELIEVE

28 JAN 1928: Paul Whiteman Orchestra—Victor Records:
BACK IN YOUR OWN BACKYARD

29 JAN 1928: Trumbauer spent the day in the dentist's chair. That evening, a party was held at Frank's (Victor?) home. Tram had to take Bix home and put him to bed. Band's day off.

30 JAN 1928: Mealey's Auditorium, Allentown, PA.

1 FEB 1928: Coliseum Ballroom, Harrisburg, PA. Roy Bargy replaced Harry Parella (p). Trumbauer noted: "Paul likes him and I think he will do well with the band."

2 FEB 1928: Cathuaum Theatre, Penn State College. "3 shows and went over good," Tram noted.

3 FEB 1928: Auditorium Dance Hall, Johnstown, PA.

4 FEB 1928: Returned to New York.

6 FEB 1928: Trumbauer discussed Whiteman's contract offer for two years with a $50 weekly increase every six months. It appears that Tram accepted the new contract.

7 FEB 1928: Paul Whiteman Orchestra—Victor Records: POOR BUTTERFLY (Tram ill, only made the one recording)

8 FEB 1928: Paul Whiteman Orchestra—Victor Records: THERE AIN'T NO SWEET MAN and A SHADY TREE (rejected)

9 FEB 1928: Paul Whiteman Orchestra—Victor Records: ORIENTAL and MEDITATION FROM "THAIS" and BY THE WATERS OF THE MINNETONKA and DARDANELLA

10 FEB 1928: Paul Whiteman Orchestra—Victor Records: LOVE NEST

13 FEB 1928: Paul Whiteman Orchestra—Victor Records: WONDERFUL ONE and MIDNIGHT REFLECTIONS and SUNSHINE and FROM MONDAY ON (Trumbauer not present)

14 FEB 1928: Paul Whiteman Orchestra—Victor Records: GRAND FANTASIA FROM WAGNERIANA (PART ONE) and GRAND FANTASIA FROM WAGNERIANA (PART TWO)

15 FEB 1928: Paul Whiteman Orchestra—Victor Records: AVALON and A SHADY TREE (Trumbauer not present on other two selections)

16 FEB 1928: Paul Whiteman Orchestra—Victor Records: THREE SHADES OF BLUE (PART ONE) and THREE SHADES OF BLUE (PART TWO)

18 FEB 1928: Paul Whiteman Orchestra—Victor Records: CAPRICE FUTURISTIC and MISSISSIPPI MUD

19 FEB 1928: Trumbauer visited Cotton Club, and noted: "Saw the boys do their bit, just can't understand all that goes on."

20 FEB 1928: Tour. Altoona, PA. Trumbauer big winner at band's poker game.

21 FEB 1928: Youngstown, OH.

22 FEB 1928: Band's day off.

23 FEB 1928: Fairmount, WV. Trumbauer purchased a .22 rifle.

24 FEB 1928: Day off.

25 FEB 1928: Pittsburgh, PA. "Played poker and lost some of previous winnings back to the boys."

26 FEB 1928: Claridge Hotel.

27 FEB 1928: Paul Whiteman Orchestra—Victor Records: CHLOE ("Played bassoon and not so bad. I like that instrument.")

28 FEB 1928: Paul Whiteman Orchestra—Victor Records: FROM MONDAY ON and HIGH WATER and SUGAR ("HIGH WATER with bassoon also and hard to do, but I did it." Tram ill.)

29 FEB 1928: Trumbauer ill, did not record on this date. Teeth problems.

1 MAR 1928: Paul Whiteman Orchestra—Victor Records: SUITE OF SERENADES and OL' MAN RIVER and SELECTIONS FROM "SHOW BOAT"

2 MAR 1928: Paul Whiteman Orchestra—Victor Records: A STUDY IN BLUE (Tram not on other selection recorded)

3 MAR 1928: Whiteman gave the band a week's vacation. Trumbauer moved to a larger hotel room as Mitzi was arriving the next day. He spent the evening watching a Broadway Play (***Octopus*** ?) and then visited the Cotton Club ("good band and show"). Returned to hotel at 5:00 A.M.

5 Mar 1928: Trumbauer received a telegram at 5:00 P.M. that informed him of his grandfather's death at 8:00 A.M. that day. Tram took the news hard, and spent the next few days recalling his youth and memories of, what Trumbauer called "my teacher and wonderful grandfather." The night of March 13, at a Whiteman musician's poker party, the first card dealt to Trumbauer was the ace of spades, causing deep concern to him.

12 MAR 1928: Paul Whiteman Orchestra—Victor Records: WHEN and DOWN IN OLD HAVANA TOWN and I'M WINGING HOME

13 MAR 1928: Paul Whiteman Orchestra—Victor Records: METROPOLIS (PART ONE) and METROPOLIS (PART TWO)

14 MAR 1928: Paul Whiteman Orchestra —Victor Records:

METROPOLIS (PART THREE) Trumbauer did not appear on Paul Whiteman recording dates of March 15 and 16.

17 MAR 1928: Paul Whiteman Orchestra—Victor Records: METROPOLIS (PART FOUR)

19 MAR 1928: Whiteman started rehearsals for Paramount Theatre engagement, starting March 31.

21 MAR 1928: Enticed by other members of the orchestra playing golf, Trumbauer played for the first time: "very sad."

24 MAR 1928: Attended concert that presented the works of Ravel, Eastwood Lane, and others. Failed to note location of performance. Made arrangements with Tommy Rockwell for April 3 and 10 Okeh Recording dates.

28 MAR 1928: Whiteman Orchestra performed for the Women's Pay Club in New York.

29 MAR 1928: Tram noted Whiteman radio program with many top movie stars.

31 MAR 1928: Whiteman Orchestra opened at the Paramount Theatre in New York. Chet Hazlett became upset when he learned that they would do five shows a day.

3 APR 1928: Frank Trumbauer Orchestra—Okeh Records: OUR BUNGALOW OF DREAMS and LILA (Trumbauer noted, "Boys all tired.")

7 APR 1928: A new show was put in at the Paramount, causing many mistakes and changes in the arrangements and program.

8 APR 1928: More changes in Paramount program.

10 APR 1928: Frank Trumbauer Orchestra—Okeh Records: BORNEO and MY PET

12 APR 1928: "Paul did it again. Show is better with a dandy for next week."

19 APR 1928: Trumbauer noted: "Saw Adrian (Rollini) and he wants 10 arrangements, which will mean settlement of our debt and some extra. Then Lodwig must be paid also and Itzy Riskin too." Payment to Lodwig and Riskin probably for arrangements they did.

21 APR 1928: Paramount Theatre engagement ended.

21 APR 1928: Paul Whiteman Orchestra—Victor Records: IN MY BOUQUET OF MEMORIES and I'M AFRAID OF YOU and MY ANGEL

22 APR 1928: Paul Whiteman Orchestra—Victor Records:

MY PET and IT WAS THE DAWN OF LOVE and DANCING SHADOWS and FORGET-ME-NOT

23 APR 1928: Paul Whiteman Orchestra—Victor Records: DIXIE DAWN and LOUISIANA

24 APR 1928: Paul Whiteman Orchestra—Victor Records: GRIEVING and DO I HEAR YOU SAYING

25 APR 1928: Paul Whiteman Orchestra—Victor Records: YOU TOOK ADVANTAGE OF ME

26 APR 1928: Played golf in Boston and played under a hundred for the first time!

27 APR 1928: Whiteman Orchestra opened at Loew's Metropolitan Theatre in Boston, MA.

During the engagement in Boston, Trumbauer was able to play golf on a regular basis, except 28 April when it rained. Tram had his first lesson on May 8 and shot 48 for nine holes. On May 9, he recorded a 91 for 18 holes. Charles Burgess was his instructor.

10 MAY 1928: Engagement at Loew's concluded.

12 MAY 1928: Paul Whiteman Orchestra—Columbia Records: LA PALOMA (rejected) and LA GOLONDRINA and MY HERO

Trumbauer formed a partnership with Chet Hazlett, investing in a Kentucky Warehouse (no details), and then to buy stock in Bank Of America. 88 on the golf course.

Fox Movietone news filmed the Paul Whiteman Orchestra at the Columbia Recording Studios. The 680 feet of film showed a long shot of Whiteman leading the orchestra, and a closeup of Whiteman leading the band tuning up. The Library Index Card of the Fox Case Corporation of New York does not list a date of the filming, generally thought to be May 12. Footage is shown in the Movietone News #25 release of May 18. Item #6: "Jazz King Tears Up Old Contract: On Stroke Of Twelve Paul Whiteman Starts His First Recording Date For Columbia Phonograph Company." An "edited" version of the event is contained on video tape produced by Yazoo #514. The selection of "My Ohio Home" runs 1 minute 45 seconds.

13 MAY 1928: Paul Whiteman Orchestra—Columbia Records: MERRY WIDOW and LAST NIGHT I DREAMED YOU KISSED ME (rejected) and EVENING STAR (rejected)

14 MAY 1928: Whiteman Orchestra opened at Loew's Metropolitan Theatre in Brooklyn. Whiteman is ill and cites "too much work" as the reason.

15 MAY 1928: Paul Whiteman Orchestra—Columbia Records: MY MELANCHOLY BABY

16 MAY 1928: Paul Whiteman Orchestra—Columbia Records: THE MAN I LOVE ("One of my best records," according to Tram.)

17 MAY 1928: Whiteman talked to Trumbauer about his wanting to put a small band on Columbia. Trumbauer is set to talk with Tommy Rockwell about new contract.

17 MAY 1928: Paul Whiteman Orchestra—Columbia Records: C-O-N-S-T-A-N-T-I-N-O-P-L-E

18 MAY 1928: Whiteman decided that Trumbauer's name should be used for the Columbia small band recordings.

19 MAY 1928: Trumbauer saw Tommy Rockwell at Okeh Records and decided upon a contract that called for eight men for Okeh, and eleven men for Columbia. Engagement at Loew's ended.

21 MAY 1928: Paul Whiteman Orchestra—Columbia Records: LA PALOMA and LAST NIGHT I DREAMED YOU KISSED ME and EVENING STAR and 'TAIN'T SO, HONEY, 'TAIN'T SO (rejected) (the last title suggested by Trumbauer)

22 MAY 1928: Paul Whiteman Orchestra—Columbia Records: IS IT GONNA BE LONG? and JAPANESE MAMMY (rejected) and GET OUT AND GET UNDER THE MOON and I'D RATHER CRY OVER YOU (Tram noted, "Eddie King is fine to me.")

23 MAY 1928: Paul Whiteman Orchestra—Columbia Records: 'TAIN'T SO, HONEY, 'TAIN'T SO (rejected) and IN THE EVENING (rejected) and OH! YOU HAVE NO IDEA and MOTHER GOOSE PARADE

24 MAY 1928: Paul Whiteman Orchestra—Columbia Records: BLUE NIGHT

25 MAY 1928: Paul Whiteman Orchestra—Columbia Records: FELIX THE CAT and CHIQUITA (The orchestra boarded a train immediately after the recording session.)

26 MAY 1928: The Whiteman Orchestra opened at the Capitol Theatre in Detroit, MI. Ward Archer loaned Trumbauer his car, so Tram could get around town and see friends.

1 JUN 1928: Engagement at Capitol Theatre ended. Orchestra traveled by train, and poker party, to Buffalo.

2–8 JUN 1928: At Shea's Buffalo Theatre, Buffalo, NY. Opening night, Irving Friedman discussed his role with Whiteman, feeling that he had been doing all the clarinet work and it is wearing on him. Whiteman discussed the matter with Trumbauer, and as of June 4, Tram shared some of the clarinet solo work. Continuous rain prohibited Trumbauer getting in a game, but the boys in the band, hindered by the rain, decided to throw a party in Trumbauer's hotel room on June 5, and had "a lot of fun." They forgot to invite Tram.

9 JUN 1928: Back to New York. Day off. Trumbauer spent the day with his family in the park.

10 JUN 1928: Paul Whiteman Orchestra—Columbia Records: 'TAIN'T SO, HONEY, 'TAIN'T SO and JAPANESE MAMMY and I'D RATHER CRY OVER YOU and IN THE EVENING and CHIQUITA

11–15 JUN 1928: Whiteman Orchestra at Lincoln Theatre, Trenton, NJ. Mitzi joined Tram on June 12. Trumbauer able to play golf daily.

17 JUN 1928: Paul Whiteman Orchestra—Columbia Records: I'M ON THE CREST OF A WAVE and THAT'S MY WEAKNESS NOW and GEORGIE PORGIE and IF YOU DON'T LOVE ME (rejected) and JUST LIKE A MELODY OUT OF THE SKY and LONESOME IN THE MOONLIGHT

18 JUN 1928: Paul Whiteman Orchestra—Columbia Records: JUST A LITTLE BIT OF DRIFTWOOD and SORRY FOR ME (rejected) and BECAUSE MY BABY DON'T MEAN MAYBE NOW and OUT O' TOWN GAL

Paul Whiteman Orchestra appeared at Hastings-On-Hudson to play for New York Mayor Jimmy Walker's party.

19 JUN 1928: Paul Whiteman Orchestra—Columbia Records: AMERICAN TUNE

19 JUN 1928: Paul Whiteman Orchestra radio program, 10:00–11:00 P.M., WEAF, New York, NY.

20 JUN 1928: Paul Whiteman Orchestra—Columbia Records: TSCHAIKOWSKIANA (PART ONE) and TSCHAIKOWSKIANA (PART TWO)

21 JUN 1928: Orchestra boarded train. Trumbauer lost $35 playing poker.

22 JUN 1928: Trumbauer visited his aunt (304 Gramercy Street) in Minneapolis, MN.

23–29 JUN 1928: At Minneapolis Theatre, Minneapolis, MN. Tram able to play golf daily, shot an 87 on June 26.

30 JUN 1928: Band arrived in Chicago. Tram played Bunker Hill Golf Course, shot a 96.

2 JUL 1928: Whiteman Orchestra opened at the Chicago Theatre, Chicago. During this engagement, Trumbauer developed a pain in his left leg. He gave serious thought to leaving the band and seeking treatment, but decided to stay with the band, as a vacation period was near.

5 JUL 1928: Frank Trumbauer Orchestra—Okeh Records: BLESS YOU SISTER and DUSKY STEVEDORE

6 JUL 1928: Pain in leg became so severe that Trumbauer had some tests run, and the results came back as "good." Tram could hardly walk at this time.

7 JUL 1928: Tram given a pair of shoes (from doctor's prescription?) and noted that he could start learning to dance, "I sang on the 1st record, and why not? I may do some thing good yet."

8 JUL 1928: Engagement at the Chicago Theatre ended. Pain grew worse in his leg.

9–15 JUL 1928: Uptown Theatre, Chicago, IL.

10 JUL 1928: Trumbauer decided to play golf. "Now or never," he remarked. "Game only fair today."

12 JUL 1928: Golf lesson. Pain persisted but Tram kept smiling.

13 JUL 1928: Chicago newspapers reported "Pop" Keller's crash and death. Trumbauer was with "Pop" the previous day, and left him only an hour before the fatal crash.

14 JUL 1928: Trumbauer decided to stay away from flying for a few days, but noted "I want to learn."

16–22 JUL 1928: Tivoli Theatre, Chicago, IL.

Whiteman gave the band a three-week vacation. Trumbauer purchased a ring for Mitzi on July 20 and presented it to her when he arrived in St. Louis for start of vacation. Tram's left leg apparently improved with the rest, as he was able to play a good many rounds of golf, i.e., 86 (July 24), but his father-in-law was taken to the hospital on July 28. The doctor's claimed (July 30) that he wasn't expected to live, but Trumbauer refused to accept their conclusions. By August 2, his father-in-law is considered as being on the road to full recovery. Trumbauer's vacation period was devoted to resting and playing golf.

13 AUG 1928: Trumbauer went to Chicago by train, and visited the doctor concerning his leg. Doctor provided prescription. Leg apparently well on the road to recovery.
14 AUG 1928: Left by train from Chicago to New York.
15 AUG 1928: Band rehearsed all day.
16 AUG 1928: Sugarcreek Pavilion, Franklin, PA.
(''Fair crowd.'' Golf: 89)
17 AUG 1928: Sunset Park, Johnstown, PA. (''Concert not well received'').
18 AUG 1928: York, PA.
(''Good crowd and people nice. Concert was well received.'')
19 AUG 1928: Willow Grove, Philadelphia, PA.
(''4 concerts. No dance. Wonderful crowd, packed all day.'')
20 AUG 1928: Carlin's, Baltimore, MD.
(''6000 people at dance. Very big crowd.'')
21 AUG 1928: Dorney Park, Allentown, PA.
22 AUG 1928: George F. Pavilion, Johnson City, PA.
(''Bad crowd. Played some golf.'')
23 AUG 1928: Lakeside, Mahoney City, PA. (''good crowd.'')
24 AUG 1928: Pennbrook Park, Wilkes-Barre, PA.
25 AUG 1928: Steel Pier, Atlantic City, NJ.
(''23,000 people and we did well, but I miss the old days that I spent there.'')
26 AUG 1928: Band travelled all day during rain storm. Trumbauer's leg acted up.
27 AUG 1928: Nutting's-On-The-Charles, Waltham, MA.
(''Fine crowd and did well.'')
28 AUG 1928: Bornehurst, New Bedford, MA. (''OK.'')
29 AUG 1928: Riverside Park, Springfield, MA.

(''Wonderful place to stay. Beat Chet even, the first time in golf.'')

30 AUG 1928: Arcadia Roof Garden, Providence, RI.
(''Big crowd. These trips are killing can't even get the laundry done.'')

31 AUG 1928: Shelburne Inn, Berlin, NH.
(''Beautiful mountains. Played golf and got beat.'')

1 SEP 1928: Palace Ballroom, Old Orchard Beach, ME.

2 SEP 1928: Crescent Gardens, Revere, MA.

4 SEP 1928: Paul Whiteman Orchestra—Columbia Records:
IN THE GOOD OLD SUMMERTIME (rejected) and
THE SIDEWALKS OF NEW YORK (rejected) and ROSES OF YESTERDAY

5 SEP 1928: Paul Whiteman Orchestra—Columbia Records:
CONCERTO IN F (PART ONE) (rejected)

6 SEP 1928: Paul Whiteman Orchestra—Columbia Records:
CONCERTO IN F (PART TWO) (rejected) and CONCERTO IN F (PART THREE) (rejected) (Trumbauer suffering with a terrific cold, felt that it affected his playing.)

7–14 SEP 1928: Loew's Metropolitan Theatre, Boston, MA.

15 SEP 1928: Paul Whiteman Orchestra—Columbia Records:
CONCERTO IN F (PART ONE) and CONCERTO IN F (PART TWO) and CONCERTO IN F (PART THREE) and CONCERTO IN F (PART FOUR)

Band not engaged. Trumbauer saw the play ***Diamond Lil.***

17 SEP 1928: Paul Whiteman Orchestra—Columbia Records:
JEANNINE and CONCERTO IN F (PART FIVE) and
CONCERTO IN F (PART SIX) (later recalled)

18 SEP 1928: Paul Whiteman Orchestra—Columbia Records:
GYPSY and SWEET SUE Paul Whiteman Orchestra radio program from Hotel Astor 9:30–11:00 P.M., NBC.

19 SEP 1928: Paul Whiteman Orchestra—Columbia Records:
CHRISTMAS MELODIES (PART ONE) and CHRISTMAS MELODIES (PART TWO)

20 SEP 1928: Frank Trumbauer Orchestra—Okeh Records:
TAKE YOUR TOMORROW and LOVE AFFAIRS and SEN-TIMENTAL BABY (rejected)

21 SEP 1928: Paul Whiteman Orchestra—Columbia Records: I CAN'T GIVE YOU ANYTHING BUT LOVE and WHERE IS THE SONG OF SONGS FOR ME? (rejected)
22 SEP 1928: Coliseum, Harrisburg, PA. (''Bad crowd.'')
24 SEP 1928: Erie, PA. (''cold and rain.'')
25 SEP 1928: Land O' Dance, Canton, PA. (''Played 'drink and smell' with the boys.'' [Ed note: A golf game the band enjoyed. Winners of the hole had a drink, while the losers got to smell the cork].)
26 SEP 1928: Market Auditorium, Wheeling, WV. (''got off 425 yard drive.'')
28 SEP 1928: Union Town
29 SEP 1928: Pittsburgh, PA. (''crowd not so bad''). Following Whiteman engagement, Chet Hazlett and Trumbauer drove back to New York. A truck ran their automobile into a ditch, and Tram felt that they were lucky to escape with their lives. They arrived in New York at 4:30 A.M. (30 Sep).

1 OCT 1928: Knights Of Columbus Hall, band rehearsed.
2 OCT 1928: Hotel Astor, New York, NY., band rehearsal continues.
3 OCT 1928: Hotel Astor, band rehearsal continues.
4 OCT 1928: Queen Anne Theatre, Bogota, NJ.
5 OCT 1928: Paul Whiteman Orchestra—Columbia Records: CONCERTO IN F (PART SIX)
5 OCT 1928: Frank Trumbauer Orchestra—Okeh Records: THE LOVE NEST and THE JAPANESE SANDMAN and HIGH UP ON A HILLTOP and SENTIMENTAL BABY
6 OCT 1928: Paul Whiteman Orchestra—Columbia Records: WHERE IS THE SONG OF SONGS FOR ME

Paul Whiteman & His Orchestra start the fall concert tour. All afternoon performances were scheduled at 2:00 P.M., and the evening performances set for 8:00 P.M.

7 OCT 1928: Carnegie Hall, New York, NY.
8 OCT 1928: Wells Theatre, Norfolk, VA. (''Played good house and did well.'')

9 OCT 1928: Academy Of Music, Lynchburg, VA.
(''good house.'') Trumbauer developed a sore mouth.
10 OCT 1928: Carolina Theatre, Greensboro, NC.
(''nice house.'') Trumbauer's sore mouth continued, and Whiteman promised to purchase a gun for Tram's collection in appreciation of his efforts though ill.
11 OCT 1928: Campus Auditorium, Greenville, NC.
(''concert went nuts.'')
12 OCT 1928: Memorial Hall, Chapel Hill, NC.
(''did the job and left. Feel better.'')
13 OCT 1928: State Theatre, Raleigh, NC.
(''Sent $150 to Mitzi. Lost $48 playing poker.'')
14 OCT 1928: War Department Theatre (Fort Bragg), Fayetteville, NC.
(''Took pictures. Played a bad game of golf. Lost another $20 to the boys.'')
15 OCT 1928: Reynolds Memorial Auditorium, Winston-Salem, NC.
16 OCT 1928: Auditorium, Charlotte, NC.
17 OCT 1928: City Auditorium, Asheville, NC. (''shot a 94.'')
18 OCT 1928: Columbia Theatre, Columbia, SC.
19 OCT 1928: Richmond Academy, August, GA. (''Yes Sir.'')
20 OCT 1928: New City Auditorium, Macon, GA.
(''We are getting the plans now for the west coast and it looks very good so far.'')
21 OCT 1928: Birmingham, AL. Band arrived in town very late. Day off.
22 OCT 1928: Municipal Auditorium, Birmingham, AL. Dance from 9:00 P.M.–1:00 A.M.
23 OCT 1928: City Auditorium, Atlanta, GA.
(''No, we did not play with Jones.'' A joke, referring to that they did not play with golf pro Bobby Jones.)
24 OCT 1928: Memorial Auditorium, Chattanooga, TN.
(''Saw the old battle grounds and took lots of pictures.'')
25 OCT 1928: Ryman Auditorium, Nashville, TN.
26 OCT 1928: Auditorium, Memphis, TN.
27 OCT 1928: Auditorium, Jackson, MS.
28 OCT 1928: St. Charles Theatre, New Orleans, LA.

(''Saw Paul Mares, had dinner out there and got half baked. Wonderful boy and I met [''Snoozer''] Quinn, the only boy alive who has it on Eddie Lang, I believe.'')

29 OCT 1928: Strand Theatre, Shreveport, LA.
(''A good town. Took lots of pictures.'')

30 OCT 1928: Baton Rouge High School, Baton Rouge, LA.

31 OCT 1928: City Auditorium, Beaumont, TX.
(''In big letters this is my state for true. I love it!'')

1 NOV 1928: Auditorium, Houston, TX.
(''flew for half hour. Pilot Dick Hair.'')

2 NOV 1928: Municipal Auditorium, San Antonio, TX.

3 NOV 1928: Hardin-Simmons University, Abilene, TX.

4 NOV 1928: Cotton Palace, Waco, TX.

5 NOV 1928: Fair Park Auditorium, Dallas, TX.
(''I got 15 minutes air work and took off alone and made a few good landings, and a lot of bad ones. William McAlister claims I'll fly sure as hell.'')

6 NOV 1928: Memorial Auditorium, Wichita Falls, TX.
(''Maybe I should stop for Bill and Mitzi, but I want to learn [to fly].'')

7 NOV 1928: City Auditorium, Amarillo, TX.
(''Ray Turner's mother met us and took us around and told about her boy and his flying.'')

8 NOV 1928: Shrine Auditorium, Oklahoma City, OK.

9 NOV 1928: University Auditorium, Norman, OK. (''our largest crowd.'')

10 NOV 1928: Convention Hall, Tulsa, OK.
(''Had a wire to go home from Tulsa. Grandmother ill. I'll get out as soon as possible.'')

11 NOV 1928: St. Louis, MO. Trumbauer did not make it in time. His grandmother died at 2:00 P.M.

12 NOV 1928: Trumbauer drove to Carbondale to get everything ready.

13 NOV 1928: Funeral in Carbondale. Trumbauer drove back to St. Louis.

14 NOV 1928: Trumbauer missed catching train to Warrensburg, MO.

15 NOV 1928: Trumbauer missed early train, caught the afternoon one and made it in time for concert at University Auditorium, Lawrence, KS. (''All the boys nice. Paul wonderful to me.'')

16 NOV 1928: Memorial Hall, Salina, KS.

17 NOV 1928: Sheridan Coliseum, Hays, KS.

18 NOV 1928: Auditorium, Omaha, NE.

19 NOV 1928: Central High School, Sioux City, IA. (''Bix day all the folks were there and landed, long and loud.'')

20 NOV 1928: Coliseum, Sioux Falls, SD. (''Bought coat for Mitzi. $135.'')

21 NOV 1928: Auditorium, St. Paul, MN.

22 NOV 1928: Shrine Temple, Cedar Rapids, IA.

23 NOV 1928: Clinton Theatre, Clinton, IA. (''A matinee and no one came.'') Poor attendance.

24 NOV 1928: Majestic Theatre, Peoria, IL. (''Great town. Bought Bill an air gun.'')

25 NOV 1928: Auditorium Theatre, Chicago, IL. (''Mitzi and Bill here. Saw all the boys.'')

26 NOV 1928: University Gym, Lafayette, IN.

27 NOV 1928: Pease Auditorium, Ypsilanti, MI. (''afternoon to a good house.'')

27 NOV 1928: Hill Auditorium, Ann Arbor, MI. (evening)

28 NOV 1928: Day off.

29 NOV 1928: Charleston High School Auditorium, Charleston, WV. (''Thanksgiving Day. Paul gave us a dinner and it was great.'')

30 NOV 1928: New Music Hall, Cleveland, OH. (''I saw Wylie to get my money. Got $50.'')

1 DEC 1928: Memorial Hall, Columbus, OH. (''Saw lots of people I know. Heard a good band and Huston a cornet player that is OK for me.'')

2 DEC 1928: Taft Auditorium, Cincinnati, OH. (''Bix still gone. Stayed in Cleveland with DTs. I spent 4 years on him to no avail.'')

3 DEC 1928: Arcadia Auditorium, Detroit, MI. (''No Bix. When he should be here, he missed the best town on the map. Saw Jean Goldkette, also Charles [Horvath?] and they liked me [Tram's playing]. Paul offered me his Stutz for my record money and I jumped at it. Boy what a car and how I can go home now to show the folks. Boy I'm very happy over the whole thing.'')

4 DEC 1928: Memorial Auditorium, Athens, OH.
(''Mitzi will pass out when she sees that car.'')

5 DEC 1928: Coliseum, Toledo, OH.
(''Guess it shows to pay to live right and treat Paul good for he is the last gasp. The greatest man I ever knew.'')

6 DEC 1928: Coliseum, Toledo, OH.
(''Our best crowd for a reception. Met Peg Thompson of the movies and other big people. Paul took me along and we woke up more people that I ever saw before. Had a great time.'')

7 DEC 1928: Consistory Auditorium, Buffalo, NY. (''bad crowd.'')

8 DEC 1928: Holy Family School Auditorium, Auburn, NY.

9 DEC 1928: Symphony Hall, Boston, MA.

10 DEC 1928: Day off. Band returned to New York.

11 DEC 1928: Paul Whiteman Orchestra—Columbia Records: I'VE GOT A FEELING I'M FALLING (rejected) and MAKIN' WHOOPEE (rejected)

12 DEC 1928: Paul Whiteman Orchestra—Columbia Records: I'M BRINGING A RED, RED ROSE (rejected) and SWEET DREAMS (rejected)

13 DEC 1928: Paul Whiteman Orchestra—Columbia Records: LIEBESTRAUM

14 DEC 1928: Paul Whiteman Orchestra—Columbia Records: LET'S DO IT, LET'S FALL IN LOVE (rejected) and HOW ABOUT ME (rejected)

Apparently, Whiteman turned over his Stutz automobile to Tram on December 14. Trumbauer noted that Whiteman would be picking up a new Cadillac tomorrow.

15 DEC 1928: Auditorium, Washington, DC.
(''This car is nuts. Had her up to sixty. Some road car.'')

16 DEC 1928: Penn Athletic Club, Philadelphia, PA.

17 DEC 1928: New York. Whiteman gave the band time off for Christmas, except for recording dates and concert on December 23.

19 DEC 1928: Paul Whiteman Orchestra—Columbia Records:

I'M BRINGING A RED, RED ROSE and HOW ABOUT ME (rejected) and I'VE GOT A FEELING I'M FALLING (rejected)

22 DEC 1928: Paul Whiteman Orchestra—Columbia Records: LET'S DO IT, LET'S FALL IN LOVE and MAKIN' WHOOPEE ("Took car in and haven't got a dime but I'll get it some how.")

23 DEC 1928: Carnegie Hall, New York. Final concert of the 1928 Fall Tour.

24 DEC 1928: Christmas trip home.
("Sunup to sundown. Going like hell. Snow. Plenty snow. Car wonderful. Made South Bend in 25 hours.")

25 DEC 1928: Christmas at home in St. Louis, MO.

27 DEC 1928: Left for New York. Arrived on December 28.

29 DEC 1928: Paul Whiteman Orchestra opened atop the New Amsterdam Theatre in New York for Ziegfeld's ***Midnight Frolic.*** Also appeared in production of ***Whoopee*** (starring Eddie Cantor, featuring Ruth Etting) on stage downstairs.

30 DEC 1928: Opened at Palace Theatre, New York, NY. Both engagements concurrently.

31 DEC 1928: Trumbauer turned in his bs-sx case to Frank Holton & Co., for needed repairs.

3 JAN 1929: Paul Whiteman Orchestra—Columbia Records: SWEET DREAMS (rejected)

5 JAN 1929: Engagement at the Palace Theatre ended. New Amsterdam continued.

10 JAN 1929: Paul Whiteman Orchestra—Columbia Records: CRADLE OF LOVE and CHINESE LULLABY

10 JAN 1929: Paul Whiteman Presents Bee Palmer with The Frank Trumbauer Orchestra—Columbia Records:
SINGIN' THE BLUES (rejected) and DON'T LEAVE ME, DADDY (rejected)

11 JAN 1929: Paul Whiteman Orchestra—Columbia Records: HOW ABOUT ME and MY ANGELINE (rejected)

11 JAN 1929: Engagement at the New Amsterdam Theatre ended.

13–19 JAN 1929: Music Hall, Cincinnati, OH.

20–26 JAN 1929: Palace Theatre, Cleveland, OH.

27 JAN 1929: General Motors Research Building, Detroit, MI. Andy Secrest joined the band.

2 FEB 1929: Engagement in Detroit ended.

3 FEB 1929: Orchestra returned to New York. Originally the Whiteman Orchestra was to travel to Hollywood to begin work on the film, ***The King Of Jazz,*** but Universal asked for a postponement.

5 FEB 1929: Paul Whiteman signed a contract with the P. Lorillard Company (Old Gold cigarettes) for a weekly radio program. Old Gold supplied complimentary cigarettes to members of the orchestra as an ongoing gesture. This was fine with Trumbauer, as this was his regular brand of cigarettes. First program, WABC, 10:00–11:00 P.M.

6 FEB 1929: Whiteman Orchestra reopened atop the New Amsterdam Theatre for the ***Midnight Frolic.*** Austin Young left the band, replaced by Ray Heatherton.

7 FEB 1929: Paul Whiteman Orchestra—Columbia Records: LOVER, COME BACK TO ME and MARIANNA

8 FEB 1929: Paul Whiteman Orchestra—Columbia Records: BUTTON UP YOUR OVERCOAT and MY LUCKY STAR

William Grant Still added to the band as an arranger.

12 FEB 1929: Old Gold Radio Program. WABC, New York, 10:00–11:00 P.M.

16 FEB 1929: Trumbauer applied to the Department Of Commerce (Washington, DC) for a pilot's license.

18 FEB 1929: Frank Holton & Co., returned Trumbauer's bass-saxophone case. Total charges for repairs and finish on the case: $55. Maurice Chevalier's first American appearance was at Ziegfeld's ***Midnight Frolic.***

19 FEB 1929: Old Gold Radio Program. WABC, New York, 10:00–11:00 P.M.

26 FEB 1929: Old Gold Radio Program. WABC, New York, 10:00–11:00 P.M.

28 FEB 1929: Paul Whiteman Orchestra—Columbia Records: MY ANGELINE (rejected) and COQUETTE

4 MAR 1929: Bix Beiderbecke returned, replacing Eddie Pinder (tpt).

5 MAR 1929: Old Gold Radio Program. WABC, New York, 10:00–11:00 P.M.

7 MAR 1929: Paul Whiteman Orchestra—Columbia Records: MY ANGELINE and NOLA

8 MAR 1929: Frank Trumbauer Orchestra—Okeh Records: FUTURISTIC RHYTHM and RAISIN' THE ROOF

12 MAR 1929: Old Gold Radio Program. WABC, New York, 10:00–11:00 P.M.

15 MAR 1929: Paul Whiteman Orchestra—Columbia Records: BLUE HAWAII and LOUISE

19 MAR 1929: Old Gold Radio Program. WABC, New York, 10:00–11:00 P.M.

22 MAR 1929: Trumbauer issued Student's Pilot License (#12859). He enrolled for pilot's training with R. J. Grabenhofer, Curtis Field, Mineola, Long Island, NY.

26 MAR 1929: Old Gold Radio Program. WABC, New York, 10:00–11:00 P.M.

2 APR 1929: Old Gold Radio Program. WABC, New York, 10:00–11:00 P.M.

5 APR 1929: Paul Whiteman Orchestra—Columbia Records: I'M IN SEVENTH HEAVEN and LITTLE PAL (rejected)

9 APR 1929: Old Gold Radio Program. WABC, New York, 10:00–11:00 P.M.

16 APR 1929: Old Gold Radio Program. WABC, New York, 10:00–11:00 P.M.

17 APR 1929: Frank Trumbauer Orchestra—Okeh Records: LOUISE and WAIT TILL YOU SEE "MA CHERIE" and BABY WON'T YOU PLEASE COME HOME

23 APR 1929: Old Gold Radio Program. WABC, New York, 10:00–11:00 P.M.

25 APR 1929: Paul Whiteman Orchestra—Columbia Records: LITTLE PAL and SONG OF INDIA

26 APR 1929: Whiteman Orchestra appeared at the Star Casino.

27 APR 1929: Engagement at the New Amsterdam Theatre ended.

30 APR 1929: Frank Trumbauer Orchestra—Okeh Records: NO ONE CAN TAKE YOUR PLACE and I LIKE THAT

30 APR 1929: Old Gold Radio Program. WABC, New York, 10:00–11:00 P.M.

MAY 1929: Release of advertisement of Holton Instruments showed a photo of Trumbauer with caption . . . "Frank

Trumbauer with Paul Whiteman and His Orchestra, using Holton's 100%. Mr. Trumbauer is regarded as one of America's foremost masters of the saxophone and none excel him in handling 'hot passages.' '' Advertisement appeared in a number of publications devoted to music and musicians.

3 MAY 1929: Paul Whiteman Orchestra—Columbia Records: WHEN MY DREAMS COME TRUE and REACHIN' FOR SOMEONE and CHINA BOY

4 MAY 1929: Paul Whiteman Orchestra—Columbia Records: OH! MISS HANNAH and YOUR MOTHER AND MINE (rejected) and ORANGE BLOSSOM TIME

4 MAY 1929: Whiteman orchestra opened Pavilion Royale, Long Island, NY.

7 MAY 1929: Old Gold Radio Program. WABC, New York, 10:00–11:00 P.M.

14 MAY 1929: Old Gold Radio Program. WABC, New York, 10:00–11:00 P.M.

15 MAY 1929: Mason-Dixon Orchestra (Frank Trumbauer)—Columbia Records: WHAT A DAY and ALABAMY SNOW

16 MAY 1929: Paul Whiteman Orchestra—Columbia Records: YOUR MOTHER AND MINE and S'POSIN' and LAUGHING MARIONETTE

18 MAY 1929: Engagement at the Pavilion Royale ended.

19 MAY 1929: Paul Whiteman Orchestra appeared at the Friar's Frolic at the Metropolitan Opera House. Eddie Lang and Joe Venuti joined the band. Matty Malneck was ill, and returned home to recuperate, replaced by Otto Landau (vn).

21 MAY 1929: Frank Trumbauer Orchestra—Okeh Records: NOBODY BUT YOU and I'VE GOT A FEELING FOR YOU

21 MAY 1929: Old Gold Radio Program. WABC, New York, 10:00–11:00 P.M.

22 MAY 1929: Frank Trumbauer Orchestra—Okeh Records: SHIVERY STOMP and REACHING FOR SOMEONE

24 MAY 1929: Paul Whiteman Orchestra appeared at the Metropolitan Opera in Philadelphia, PA. This is the first stop on the trip to California to film ***The King Of Jazz.*** It is believed that Whiteman received approximately $440,000 for the film. This included a $50,000 advance, $50,000 on the first day reporting to the studio, $50,000 upon completing the film, plus salary.

25 MAY 1929: Syria Mosque, Pittsburgh, PA.
Old Gold Radio Program. WJAS, 10:00–11:00 P.M.
26 MAY 1929: WHK Studios, Cleveland, OH. 10:00 A.M.
Armory, Toledo, OH. 2:00 P.M.
Olympia, Detroit, MI. 8:30 P.M.
27 MAY 1929: Train Station, Ft. Wayne, IN.
28 MAY 1929: Auditorium Theatre, Chicago, IL.
Old Gold Radio Program, WBBM, Chicago, IL.
29 MAY 1929: State Arsenal, Springfield, IL.
30 MAY 1929: Indianapolis 500 Race, Indianapolis, IN.
31 MAY 1929: Washington University Field House, St. Louis, MO.
Old Gold Radio Program, KMDX, St. Louis, MO.

1 JUN 1929: Convention Hall, Kansas City, MO.
1 JUN 1929: Old Gold Radio Program, KMBC, Kansas City, MO.
2 JUN 1929: City Auditorium, Omaha, NE. 2:00 P.M, radio program, KOIL. Burlington Station, Lincoln, NE. 6:30 P.M.
3 JUN 1929: Day off in Denver, CO. Matty Malneck rejoined orchestra.
4 JUN 1929: Shirley-Savoy Hotel, Denver, CO. Rehearsal, 11:00 A.M.-2:00 P.M. Municipal Auditorium Concert, Denver, CO. 3:00–4:30 P.M.
Old Gold Radio Program, 6:00–7:00 P.M., KLZ, Denver, CO.
5 JUN 1929: Granada Theatre, Salt Lake City, UT.
6 JUN 1929: Passed through Los Angeles, CA.
7 JUN 1929: Opened at the Pantages Theatre in San Francisco, CA.
11 JUN 1929: Old Gold Radio Program, KYA, San Francisco, CA.
12 JUN 1929: Whiteman Orchestra played for the Optimist Club Luncheon at Bellevue Hotel.
13 JUN 1929: Engagement at the Pantages Theatre in San Francisco ended.
15 JUN 1929: Whiteman Orchestra arrived in Los Angeles. Paraded to the Pantages Theatre for opening engagement.
16 JUN 1929: Universal Studios named Paul Fejos as director of ***The King Of Jazz.***

17 JUN 1929: Played for the Chamber of Commerce benefit dinner at the Majestic Theatre.

18 JUN 1929: Old Gold Radio Program, KMTR, Los Angeles, CA.

22 JUN 1929: Engagement at the Pantages Theatre ended.

25 JUN 1929: Old Gold Radio Program, KMTR, Los Angeles, CA.

Announcer Ted Husing returned to New York, replaced by Harry Von Zell.

28 JUN 1929: Reported to Universal Studios. According to ***Photoplay*** magazine for September 1929, terms of the contract: Whiteman was given "good will money" last fall, $50,000. If the picture isn't completed in eight weeks, Whiteman had the right to demand any salary that he wanted. In the meantime, Whiteman was to receive a weekly check of $8,000 and the band was to receive a weekly check of $4,500 for the same eight-week period. The day the band arrived on the studio lot, in their newly purchased Ford automobiles, Bob Cook shot home movie footage that has been shown in the Bix documentary entitled, ***Bix*** (Canada, 1981).

2 JUL 1929: Old Gold Radio Program, KMTR, Los Angeles, CA.

3 JUL 1929: Paul Whiteman's Rhythm Boys opened at the Montmartre Club.

9 JUL 1929: Old Gold Radio Program, KMTR, Los Angeles, CA.

15 JUL 1929: Trumbauer joined the Los Angeles Musicians' Local #47, and was issued card #586.

16 JUL 1929: Old Gold Radio Program, KMTR, Los Angeles, CA.

23 JUL 1929: Old Gold Radio Program, KMTR, Los Angeles, CA.

29 JUL 1929: In addition to their Montmartre Club engagement, The Rhythm Boys opened at the Orpheum Theatre.

30 JUL 1929: Old Gold Radio Program, KMTR, Los Angeles, CA.

31 JUL 1929: Automobile accident involving Joe Venuti and Mario Perry. Venuti suffered a broken arm, his bowing arm, and Perry's injuries proved fatal.

3 AUG 1929: Mildred Bailey hosted a party for Paul Whiteman and members of the orchestra.

5 AUG 1929: Whiteman signed Mildred Bailey as featured singer with his orchestra.
6 AUG 1929: Old Gold Radio Program, KMTR, Los Angeles, CA.
7 AUG 1929: Paul Whiteman Orchestra, along with many attractions, appeared at the Hollywood Bowl. Radio program of event over KFWB.
7 AUG 1929: Rhythm Boys closed at the Orpheum Theatre.
13 AUG 1929: Old Gold Radio Program, KMTR, Los Angeles, CA.
16 AUG 1929: Whiteman Orchestra played at the Santa Barbara Fiesta Day.
20 AUG 1929: Old Gold Radio Program, KMTR, Los Angeles, CA.
24 AUG 1929: Whiteman announced plans for a concert tour of the Pacific Coast, which do not materialize, due to Universal Studios postponing the film until November.
27 AUG 1929: Old Gold Radio Program, KMTR, Los Angeles, CA.
28 AUG 1929: Whiteman decided to return to New York. Orchestra boarded the train for New York.
31 AUG 1929: Paul Whiteman Orchestra opened the Pavilion Royale on Long Island, NY.

Universal Studio's press release announced that they had hired John Murray Anderson to direct the musical revue of ***The King Of Jazz.***

3 SEP 1929: Old Gold Radio Program, WABC, New York. Featured the Ponce Sisters: Ethel (carried the high notes) and Dorothea (the low ones).
6 SEP 1929: Paul Whiteman Orchestra—Columbia Records: AT TWILIGHT and WAITING AT THE END OF THE ROAD (rejected)
10 SEP 1929: Old Gold Radio Program. WABC, New York. Featured the Ponce Sisters.
13 SEP 1929: Paul Whiteman Orchestra—Columbia Records: WAITING AT THE END OF THE ROAD and WHEN YOU'RE COUNTING THE STARS ALONE and LOVE ME

Bix Beiderbecke left the Paul Whiteman Orchestra. Joe Venuti replaced Charles Gaylord (vn).

17 SEP 1929: Old Gold Radio Program. WABC, New York. Featured the Ponce Sisters and marked the first appearance of the "Old Gold Trio" (see text).

18 SEP 1929: Frank Trumbauer Orchestra—Okeh Records: LOVE AIN'T NOTHIN' BUT THE BLUES and HOW AM I TO KNOW?

24 SEP 1929: Old Gold Radio Program. WABC, New York, 10:00–11:00 P.M.

1 OCT 1929: Old Gold Radio Program. WABC, New York, 10:00–11:00 P.M.

8 OCT 1929: Old Gold Radio Program. WABC, New York, 10:00–11:00 P.M. Featured "Old Gold Trio."

9 OCT 1929: Paul Whiteman Orchestra—Columbia Records: NOBODY'S SWEETHEART and GREAT DAY! and WITHOUT A SONG

10 OCT 1929: Frank Trumbauer Orchestra—Okeh Records: TURN ON THE HEAT and MANHATTAN RAG and SUNNY SIDE UP

14 OCT 1929: Trumbauer took his first flight test at Roosevelt Field, New York, and was passed for a Private Pilot's License by Mr. Harwood.

15 OCT 1929: Old Gold Radio Program. WABC, New York, 10:00–11:00 P.M. Featured "Old Gold Trio."

16 OCT 1929: Paul Whiteman Orchestra—Columbia Records: I'M A DREAMER, AREN'T WE ALL? and IF I HAD A TALKING PICTURE OF YOU

Whiteman apparently left New York on October 16. An article in a Chicago newspaper, of October 17, stated: "Paul Whiteman clad in gray tweeds, stopped off here a short time today, on his way from New York to Hollywood."

18 OCT 1929: Paul Whiteman Orchestra—Columbia Records: MOONLIGHT AND ROSES MEDLEY and SOUTHERN MEDLEY and SHOULD I? A BUNDLE OF OLD LOVE LETTERS and AFTER YOU'VE GONE

18 OCT 1929: Frank Trumbauer Orchestra—Okeh Records: GREAT DAY! (rejected)

18 OCT 1929: Joe Venuti Orchestra—Okeh Records:

RUNNIN' RAGGED (aka BAMBOOZLIN' THE BASSOON) and APPLE BLOSSOMS

19 OCT 1929: Frank Trumbauer Orchestra—Okeh Records: MY SWEETER THAN SWEET and WHAT WOULDN'T I DO FOR THAT MAN

21 OCT 1929: Universal Studios announced that Whiteman arrived in town and production to start in two weeks.

22 OCT 1929: Old Gold Radio Program. WABC, New York, 10:00–11:00 P.M.

25 OCT 1929: Orchestra arrived in Los Angeles, CA.

28 OCT 1929: Universal Studios press release: ''Mr. Whiteman is 26 pounds lighter this time.''

29 OCT 1929: Old Gold Radio Program, KMTR, Los Angeles, CA.

30 OCT 1929: Trumbauer applied for readmission to Local #47. Issued card #1443.

5 NOV 1929: Old Gold Radio Program, KMTR, Los Angeles, CA.

6 NOV 1929: Department of Commerce (Washington, DC) issued Trumbauer's private pilot's license. Tram now living at 2124 North Highland Avenue, Hollywood, CA.

8 NOV 1929: Rehearsals started for film.

12 NOV 1929: Old Gold Radio Program, KMTR, Los Angeles, CA.

14 NOV 1929: Paul Whiteman and his orchestra were guest-of-honor at the Roosevelt Hotel, hosted by film colony leaders. George Olsen's orchestra provided entertainment.

19 NOV 1929: Old Gold Radio Program, KMTR, Los Angeles, CA.

Featured Nancy Carroll and Jack Oakie, stars of film ***Sweetie.*** Oakie does a number from the film, an imitation of Al Jolson, complete with blackface, on bended knee, singing ALMA MAMMY.

26 NOV 1929: Old Gold Radio Program, KMTR, Los Angeles, CA.

Universal Studios announced that E. T. White would supervise the sound of the film, and that Paul Small would appear as Mr. Whiteman's dancing double.

3 DEC 1929: Old Gold Radio Program, KMTR, Los Angeles, CA.
Featured John Boles (of stage and screen) and Jack Egan (star of film, ***Broadway Scandals***).

8 DEC 1929: Trumbauer purchased a Holton alto saxophone, model 213, finish 1, serial number 39648, and case, from Frank Holton & Co. Total price: $282.00.

10 DEC 1929: Old Gold Radio Program, KMTR, Los Angeles, CA.
Featured the Brox Sisters.

16 DEC 1929: Trumbauer passed flight test for Limited Commercial License. Approved by J. Mall.

17 DEC 1929: Old Gold Radio Program, KMTR, Los Angeles, CA.
Featured Mary Margaret Owens, who sang ***Showboat*** medleys.

24 DEC 1929: Old Gold Radio Program, KMTR, Los Angeles, CA.
Featured Polly Walker and Jack Oakie from the RKO film, ***Hit The Deck.*** The film, based on a Broadway play which ran for 325 performances, included such songs as MORE THAN YOU KNOW and SOMETIMES I'M HAPPY.

31 DEC 1929: Old Gold Radio Program, KMTR, Los Angeles, CA.
Featured Ruth Roland and husband Ben Bard. Roland was recognized as second only to Pearl White as movie serial heroine, from the silent days of movies, and had been retired since 1927. She appeared to "plug" her forthcoming sound picture, ***Reno.*** Bard had been a vaudeville comedian, but when they married in 1929, he was a theatre owner.

7 JAN 1930: Old Gold Radio Program. KMTR, Los Angeles, CA.

8 JAN 1930: Copyright date of sound short film, ***Voice Of Hollywood #3.*** Only 26 were made in this series and collectors have located only 7 or 8 to date. This short shows Whiteman being initiated into the Hollywood Breakfast Club. Musicians are seen but no music is heard.

8–15 JAN 1930: Continual rain prevented both golf and flying.

14 JAN 1930: Old Gold Radio Program. KMTR, Los Angeles, CA.
Featured Mary Nolan of the film ***Shanghai Lady.***

16 JAN 1930: As a result of his December 1929 application, Trumbauer was issued Limited Commercial Pilot's License #1146. He retained the license number throughout the remainder of his life.

18 JAN 1930: Trumbauer was able to drive to the field in hopes of flying, but was shocked when he saw fellow pilot, Dick Grace, crack-up. "Believe me, he's the last word in a flyer. Think of 35 and crack-up."

21 JAN 1930: Old Gold Radio Program. KMTR, Los Angeles, CA.

Featured three movie stars: Charles King of ***Broadway Melody,*** and Stanley Smith and Nancy Carroll of ***Sweetie.***

24 JAN 1930: Trumbauer noted: "Fine thoughts make fine deeds. Your will lets you think fine under pressure."

28 JAN 1930: Old Gold Radio Program. KMTR, Los Angeles, CA. Guests Blanche Sweet and J. Harold Murray.

4 FEB 1930: Old Gold Radio Program. KMTR, Los Angeles, CA. First anniversary program. Gala affair. Harry Richman sang selections from his first film, ***Puttin' On The Ritz,*** including I'LL GET BY. Other stars appearing included: Lew Cody, master of ceremonies, Richard Arlen, Jack Oakie, Madge Bellamy, Lola Lane, June Clyde, Lillian Roth, Sam Coslow, Lawrence Lambert, and Mildred Harris Chaplin.

Universal announced that it was exercising their option on a second picture to be made by Paul Whiteman, probably to be started in the fall.

7 FEB 1930: "Almost thru for a week or so then back March 1st to cut and add." (Trumbauer's note regarding filming).

10 FEB 1930: Paul Whiteman Orchestra—Columbia Records: HAPPY FEET and IT HAPPENED IN MONTEREY (rejected)

11 FEB 1930: Old Gold Radio Program. KMTR, Los Angeles, CA.

13–19 FEB 1930: Loew's State Theatre, 5 shows daily.

18 FEB 1930: Old Gold Radio Program. KMTR, Los Angeles, CA.

Guest is Hedda Hopper who sang numbers from her film, ***High Society Blues.***

20–23 FEB 1930: Fox Theatre, San Diego, CA.
24 FEB 1930: Whiteman rehearsed the band.
25 FEB 1930: Old Gold Radio Program. KMTR, Los Angeles, CA.
Featured Lupe Velez, star of film ***Hell Harbor.***

Universal announced that having exercised their option for a second "talkie," the bandmaster must report back to Hollywood in September. According to present plans, his second film will be a story with a musical plot, rather than a revue. John Murray Anderson will be retained as a director on the Universal lot and will probably direct Whiteman's second film.

2 MAR 1930: "I believe they [Old Gold] are not going to renew the contract in May as expected."
4 MAR 1930: Old Gold Radio Program. KMTR, Los Angeles, CA.
Featured Lillian Roth, Joe Wagstaff, Doris Kenyon, and Milton Sills.
6 MAR 1930: Back to Universal for two more weeks of work.
7 MAR 1930: "Nothing to do much but wait around and do a few shorts."
11 MAR 1930: Old Gold Radio Program. KMTR, Los Angeles, CA.
Featured Edmund Lowe and his wife, Lilyan Tashman.
16 MAR 1930: Failed to note the host, but "That party was wonderful. Billie Dove, Doug (Fairbanks) and Mary (Pickford), Dale Owen, and too many to mention."
18 MAR 1930: "Finished cartoon and that alone is wonderful. A very clever bit of work." This entry may refer to the Paul Whiteman cartoon sequence in the film ***The King Of Jazz*** *or* the soundtrack of a Walter Lantz cartoon, ***Bowery Bimbos,*** that was completed that day.
18 MAR 1930: Old Gold Radio Program. KMTR, Los Angeles, CA.
19 MAR 1930: "Making shorts and blackouts for the picture and it should be a great hit."
20 MAR 1930: "Our last day at Universal for some time."
21 MAR 1930: Paul Whiteman Orchestra—Columbia Records: IT HAPPENED IN MONTEREY and SONG OF THE DAWN

22 MAR 1930: Paul Whiteman Orchestra—Columbia Records: RAGAMUFFIN ROMEO and LIVIN' IN THE SUNLIGHT, LOVIN' IN THE MOONLIGHT

23 MAR 1930: Paul Whiteman Orchestra—Columbia Records: A BENCH IN THE PARK and I LIKE TO DO THINGS FOR YOU and YOU BROUGHT A NEW KIND OF LOVE TO ME

"All moved and everything is fine. Address 6626 Franklin. Apt. 218. Had Hall up and he did fine and I am very happy for him." "Hall" refers to Wilbur Hall who decided to leave the Whiteman Orchestra, and gave notice.

25 MAR 1930: Old Gold Radio Program. KMTR, Los Angeles, CA.
Featured Jeanne Loff and Grace Hayes from the film, ***The King Of Jazz.***

28 MAR 1930: Mitzi left to return home.

30 MAR 1930: Trumbauer withdrew his transfer card from Local #47 (effective April 1), and drove Whiteman (in Whiteman's new Cord automobile) north. Stopped in Atascadero for eats.

1 APR 1930: Old Gold Radio Program. KFRC, San Francisco, CA.

4 APR 1930: Whiteman Orchestra arrived in Vancouver, British Columbia, Canada.

5 APR 1930: Hollywood "sneak preview" of the film ***The King Of Jazz.*** Running time cut by editing three numbers from the film: (1) Sketch [William Kent?] about a suicidal flute player, with the Whiteman Orchestra performing CAPRICE VIENNOISE as background music; (2) A specialty number featuring dancer Nell O'Day, music unknown, set in a cabaret lobby; and (3) A sketch featuring Grace Hayes singing MY LOVE.

Final print ran 95 minutes: ***King Of Jazz***—Paul Whiteman and his Orchestra. Cast: John Boles, Jeanette Loff, Jeanie Lang, Stanley Smith, Grace Hayes (vcs); Nell O'Day, Tommy Atkins Dancers, Russell Markert Dancers; Sisters G (dancers/vcs); Jack White, William Kent, Slim Summerville (comics); Walter Brennan, Laura LaPlante (supporting cast).

Charles Irwin opens the giant ''Paul Whiteman Scrapbook. Walter Lantz animated cartoon on 'How Paul Became Known As The King Of Jazz.' '' Whiteman opens his lunch bucket and introduces musicians that came forth: brief conversation with Mike Pingitore and Harry Goldfield. Harry Goldfield plays HOT LIPS; Joe Venuti and Eddie Lang offer WILDCAT; Ray Mayer on flute; violin section; close up of Chester Hazlett; Roy Bargy does NOLA with Wilbur Hall, (tbn). Mike Pingitore offers LINGER AWHILE; girls' chorus line with music, MUSIC HATH CHARM, I LIKE TO DO THINGS FOR YOU, and MUSIC HATH CHARM.

''My Bridal Veil'' sketch: Wedding dresses as seen through the ages. ''Ladies Of The Press'' sketch, featuring Laura LaPlante.

MISSISSIPPI MUD and THE BLACKBIRDS AND THE BLUEBIRDS GOT TOGETHER sung by The Rhythm Boys.

IT HAPPENED IN MONTEREY sung by John Boles and Jeanette Loff.

''In Conference'' sketch.

''The Fish Store'' sketch: Jack White and members of the Whiteman Orchestra.

A BENCH IN THE PARK sung by The Rhythm Boys and The Brox Sisters.

Sketch: Slim Summerville reports a stolen car.

''All's Quiet On The Eastern Front'' sketch: includes Whiteman.

Wilbur Hall plays POP GOES THE WEASEL (vn) and STARS AND STRIPES FOREVER (bicycle pump) with Roy Bargy (p).

RHAPSODY IN BLUE featuring Roy Bargy (p).

''Oh, Forever More'' sketch featuring William Kent and goldfish.

MY RAGAMUFFIN ROMEO featuring Jeanie Lang, George Chiles, Don Rose, and Marian Statler.

Sketch: Walter Brennan (horse's neck) and Slim Summerville (horse's rear end).

''We're Not Married'' sketch.

HAPPY FEET featuring The Rhythm Boys and Sisters ''G''. Male dancer. Chorus dancers.

Sketch: Slim Summerville asking for hand in marriage. I'D LIKE TO DO THINGS FOR YOU.

HAS ANYONE HERE SEEN NELLIE sung by unidentified tenor.

SONG OF THE DAWN sung by John Boles and chorus.

''The Melting Pot'' finale showing music from all over the world melting into the pot that produced American Jazz Music.

The print that is currently available was located in a vault in England around 1968 and underwent two years of restoring process before its première in 1970. Ned Comstock, Archives Assistant, Cinema-Television Library, University of Southern California, states that Universal reedited the film in 1933. They wanted to release the film to capture the 1932 popularity that Bing Crosby gained with the film ***The Big Broadcast.*** The film was assembled as:

Reel One: Credits. On-screen appearance of Carl Laemmle, ''Countless thousands throughout the world have requested the revival of ***The King Of Jazz.*** It is my great pleasure to present it again and I hope that you, too, will thrill to its rhythm and beauty.'' Film then follows:

Animated sequence.

Sketch: Paul Whiteman and Charles Irwin.
HAPPY FEET with The Rhythm Boys.

Reel Two: Sketch (goldfish scene): Billy Kent and Walter Brennan.
IT HAPPENED IN MONTEREY with John Boles and Jeannette Loff.
Sketch (conference scene): Kathryn and Billy.

Reel Three: A BENCH IN THE PARK with The Brox Sisters and The Rhythm Boys. MY RAGAMUFFIN ROMEO with Jeanie Lang and George Chiles.

Reel Four: MY BRIDAL VEIL with Jeanette Loff.

Reel Five: SO THE BLUEBIRDS AND THE BLACKBIRDS GOT TOGETHER with The Rhythm Boys.
Sketch (Ladies Of The Press): Laura LaPlante.
SONG OF THE DAWN with John Boles.

Reel Six: RHAPSODY IN BLUE.

Reel Seven: THE MELTING POT OF MUSIC.

6 APR 1930: Left Canada and arrived in Seattle, WA.
7 APR 1930: Rehearsal, Seattle, WA.
8 APR 1930: Old Gold Radio Program. KOL, Civic Auditorium, Seattle, WA.
9–13 APR 1930: Spanish Ballroom, Olympic Hotel, Seattle, WA. Dances. Matinee show and dance on 12 April; and, grand concert, 13 April.
14 APR 1930: Auditorium, Portland, OR.
15 APR 1930: Old Gold Radio Program. KOIN, Portland, OR. Featuring Mildred Bailey, Bing Crosby, Jack Fulton, Old Gold Trio. The Rhythm Boys sang SO THE BLUEBIRDS AND THE BLACKBIRDS GOT TOGETHER.
21 APR 1930: Trumbauer's room mate, Bing Crosby, telephoned Dixie Lee in Hollywood. Bill $130.75.
22 APR 1930: Old Gold Radio Program. WABC, New York, 10:00–11:00 P.M.

29 APR 1930: Old Gold Radio Program. WABC, New York, 10:00–11:00 P.M. Featured Catherine Dale Owen.

2 MAY 1930: Paul Whiteman Orchestra opened a two-week engagement at the Roxy Theatre, New York, to promote the film ***The King Of Jazz.*** George Gershwin appeared with the orchestra during the first week.

6 MAY 1930: Old Gold Radio Program. WABC, New York, 10:00–11:00 P.M. Final Old Gold Program. Guests, Irene Dunne and John Held, Jr.

8 MAY 1930: Frank Trumbauer Orchestra—Okeh Records: HAPPY FEET and I LIKE TO DO THINGS FOR YOU

10 MAY 1930: Frank Trumbauer Orchestra—Okeh Records: GET HAPPY and DEEP HARLEM

13 MAY 1930: Closed at the Roxy Theatre.

14 MAY 1930: ***Variety*** reported that the band was taking a two-week vacation, and Whiteman would be going to Atlantic City for a rest.

23 MAY 1930: Press release is made of hand infection suffered by Paul Whiteman.

31 MAY 1930: Orchestra reassembled to play Bournehurst, Buzzard's Bay.

2 JUN 1930: Whiteman Orchestra at Nutting's-On-The-Charles, Waltham, MA.

3 JUN 1930: Whiteman Orchestra at Charlehurst, Salem Willows.

4 JUN 1930: Whiteman Orchestra at Riverside Park, Springfield.

5 JUN 1930: Whiteman Orchestra at Lyonhurst.

6 JUN 1930: Whiteman Orchestra at Roseland-On-The-Merrimack.

7 JUN 1930: Whiteman Orchestra at Wilburs-On-The-Taunton.

9 JUN 1930: Paul Whiteman Orchestra—Columbia Records: SITTIN' ON A RAINBOW and OLD NEW ENGLAND MOON

12 JUN 1930: Whiteman Orchestra scheduled to open at Hollywood Gardens, postponed due to rain.

14 JUN 1930: Whiteman Orchestra opened at the Hollywood Gardens, Pelham Bay Park, New York. Bronx Chamber Of Commerce head "Borough Day Mardi Gras" opening night.

4 JUL 1930: Whiteman Orchestra still at Hollywood Gardens. Closing date unknown.
7 JUL 1930: Trumbauer takes physical for renewal of pilot's license. Application submitted on 15 July, and approved.
22 JUL 1930: Frank Trumbauer Orchestra—Okeh Records: WHAT'S THE USE and HITTIN' THE BOTTLE
22 JUL 1930: Whiteman Orchestra appeared at the Roger Sherman Theatre, New Haven, CT.
25 JUL 1930: Paul Whiteman Orchestra—Columbia Records: SONG OF THE CONGO and WEDDING OF THE BIRDS and NEW TIGER RAG
30 JUL 1930: Whiteman Orchestra opened at Saratoga Springs to play for the "racing season."

30 AUG 1930: Whiteman Orchestra closed at Saratoga Springs.

4 SEP 1930: Trumbauer applied for Transport License.
8 SEP 1930: Frank Trumbauer Orchestra—Okeh Records: BYE-BYE BLUES and CHOO CHOO
9 SEP 1930: Trumbauer given a test in single-engine airplane, and approved by Mr. Harwood.
10 SEP 1930: Paul Whiteman Orchestra—Columbia Records: A BIG BOUQUET FOR YOU and BODY AND SOUL and SOMETHING TO REMEMBER YOU BY and IN MY HEART IT'S YOU and CHOO CHOO
13 SEP 1930: Whiteman Orchestra opened a four-week engagement at the Hotel Sinton, Cincinnati, OH.
16 SEP 1930: Transport Pilot's License, #11456, sent to Trumbauer.
19 SEP 1930: Whiteman Orchestra provided dinner music in the Forest Glade Dining Room, "where it is ten degrees cooler in the French Ball Room."

Vocal group, The Howards, hired by Whiteman during this engagement. Their group name was changed to The King's Jesters.

3 OCT 1930: Closed Hotel Sinton. Tour of one-nighters.
6 OCT 1930: Whiteman Orchestra opened a two-week engagement at the Casa Granada Cafe, Chicago. Daily programs from

11:15–11:45 P.M., WBBM, and once weekly on Chicago Variety Hour.

13 NOV 1930: Whiteman Orchestra offered a new series of dance music and broadcast over CBS network from Casa Granada Cafe, Chicago, IL. A 30-minute program.
23 NOV 1930: Began radio program, ***The Nutty Club,*** over WBBM, Chicago, IL., a weekly program.

6 DEC 1930: Whiteman Orchestra is part of a six-hour celebration on radio to announce the opening of CBS Studios in Chicago, IL.
11 DEC 1930: Whiteman conducted ***Marathon Opera*** at the Merry Garden Ballroom to aid Chicago Milk Fund Drive. Orchestra did not appear.
28 DEC 1930: Whiteman Orchestra featured in one-hour radio program from Casa Granada Cafe.
31 DEC 1930: Federal agents raid Casa Granada Cafe.

AFM Local #802 Directory listed Trumbauer's address as: The Thorndyke Hotel, West 56th Street. New York.

JAN 1931: The Whiteman Orchestra opened the month with a two-week vacation. Trumbauer flew to Cleveland (5th) to have his teeth worked on by Dr. Leonard Samartin, and Whiteman vacationed in Santa Barbara.
1 JAN 1931: Closed at Casa Granada Cafe, Chicago, IL.
16 JAN 1931: University of Iowa dance, Iowa City, IA.
17 JAN 1931: Danceland, Davenport, IA.
18–25 JAN 1931: Schroeder Hotel, Milwaukee, WI.
Doubled at Davidson Theatre.
20 JAN 1931: Press release; Whiteman made a trip to Hollywood to visit with Carl Laemmle, Jr. The outcome was that Whiteman agreed to do a series of novelty short films that Universal would release.
27 JAN 1931: Whiteman signed a contract for 52 weeks of 30-minute radio programs sponsored by Sherwin-Williams Paint Company and broadcast on the NBC network. The band was billed as: "Paul Whiteman's Allied Quality Paint Men."
27 JAN 1931: Radio program, "Paul Whiteman's Allied Quality Paint Men"

28 JAN 1931: Concert and dance, Red Oak, IA.
29 JAN 1931: American Legion Charity Ball, Omaha, NE.
30 JAN 1931: Junior Legion Hall, Lincoln, NE.

FEB 1931: During the first part of the month, Whiteman was elected as a director of the NBC network.
1 FEB 1931: Indiana Roof Ballroom, Indianapolis, IN.
3 FEB 1931: Radio program, ''Paul Whiteman's Allied Quality Paint Men''
5 FEB 1931: Dance, Hartford, WI.
6 FEB 1931: University of Wisconsin Junior Prom, Madison, WI.
7 FEB 1931: Eagles, Galena, IL.
9 FEB 1931: Casa Granada Cafe opening (after six weeks absence), Chicago, IL.
10 FEB 1931: Radio program, ''Paul Whiteman's Allied Quality Paint Men''
16 FEB 1931: Benefit Ball for stage hands, Chicago Stadium, IL.
17 FEB 1931: Radio program, ''Paul Whiteman's Allied Quality Paint Men''
22 FEB 1931: Washington's Birthday Dance, St. Louis, MO.
24 FEB 1931: Radio program, ''Paul Whiteman's Allied Quality Paint Men''

3 MAR 1931: Radio program, ''Paul Whiteman's Allied Quality Paint Men''
3 MAR 1931: Radio program, ''Roy Bargy's Maytag Radio Show.'' The Maytag programs were aired at 8:00–8:30 P.M., weekly.
7 MAR 1931: Trumbauer had a medical examination to again seek renewal of his pilot's license.
10 MAR 1931: Radio program, ''Paul Whiteman's Allied Quality Paint Men''
10 MAR 1931: Radio program, ''Roy Bargy's Maytag Radio Show''
13 MAR 1931: Application submitted (later approved).
17 MAR 1931: Radio program, ''Paul Whiteman's Allied Quality Paint Men''
17 MAR 1931: Radio program, ''Roy Bargy's Maytag Radio Show''

24 MAR 1931: Radio program, ''Paul Whiteman's Allied Quality Paint Men''

24 MAR 1931: Radio program, ''Roy Bargy's Maytag Radio Show''

31 MAR 1931: Radio program, ''Paul Whiteman's Allied Quality Paint Men''

31 MAR 1931: Radio program, ''Roy Bargy's Maytag Radio Show''

7 APR 1931: Radio program, ''Paul Whiteman's Allied Quality Paint Men''

7 APR 1931: Radio program, ''Roy Bargy's Maytag Radio Show''

10 APR 1931: Frank Trumbauer Orchestra—Brunswick Records: GEORGIA ON MY MIND (rejected) and BASS DRUM DAN and HONEYSUCKLE ROSE (rejected)

14 APR 1931: Radio program, ''Paul Whiteman's Allied Quality Paint Men''

14 APR 1931: Radio program, ''Roy Bargy's Maytag Radio Show''

18 APR 1931: Engagement at Casa Granada Cafe ended.

21 APR 1931: Radio program, ''Paul Whiteman's Allied Quality Paint Men''

21 APR 1931: Radio program, ''Roy Bargy's Maytag Radio Show''

22 APR 1931: Band began two weeks of one-nighters.

28 APR 1931: Radio program, ''Paul Whiteman's Allied Quality Paint Men''

28 APR 1931: Radio program, ''Roy Bargy's Maytag Radio Show''

29 APR 1931: Concert and dance, Carbondale, IL.

5 MAY 1931: Radio program, ''Paul Whiteman's Allied Quality Paint Men''

5 MAY 1931: Radio program, ''Roy Bargy's Maytag Radio Show''

12 MAY 1931: Radio program, ''Paul Whiteman's Allied Quality Paint Men''

12 MAY 1931: Radio program, ''Roy Bargy's Maytag Radio Show''

18 MAY 1931: Opened at the Edgewater Beach Hotel, Chicago, IL. During the band's stay at the Edgewater Beach Hotel, station KWY broadcast two 30-minute programs nightly, and once on Sunday afternoon. The times varied.

19 MAY 1931: Radio program, "Paul Whiteman's Allied Quality Paint Men"

19 MAY 1931: Radio program, "Roy Bargy's Maytag Radio Show"

24 MAY 1931: Radio remote from Edgewater Beach Hotel, Chicago, IL.

26 MAY 1931: Radio program, "Paul Whiteman's Allied Quality Paint Men"

26 MAY 1931: Radio program, "Roy Bargy's Maytag Radio Show"

31 MAY 1931: Radio remote from Edgewater Beach Hotel, Chicago, IL.

JUN 1931: In Chicago area, at Edgewater Beach Hotel.

1 JUN 1931: Radio program, "A & P Gypsies" (western). The A & P Gypsies radio programs were 30 minutes.

2 JUN 1931: Radio program, "Paul Whiteman's Allied Quality Paint Men"

2 JUN 1931: Radio program, "Roy Bargy's Maytag Radio Show"

7 JUN 1931: Radio remote from Edgewater Beach Hotel, Chicago, IL.

8 JUN 1931: Radio program, "A & P Gypsies" (western)

9 JUN 1931: Radio program, "Paul Whiteman's Allied Quality Paint Men"

9 JUN 1931: Radio program, "Roy Bargy's Maytag Radio Show"

14 JUN 1931: Radio remote from Edgewater Beach Hotel, Chicago, IL.

15 JUN 1931: Radio program, "A & P Gypsies" (western)

16 JUN 1931: Radio program, "Paul Whiteman's Allied Quality Paint Men"

16 JUN 1931: Radio program, "Roy Bargy's Maytag Radio Show"

21 JUN 1931: Radio remote from Edgewater Beach Hotel, Chicago, IL.

22 JUN 1931: Radio program, ''A & P Gypsies'' (western)
23 JUN 1931: Radio program, ''Paul Whiteman's Allied Quality Paint Men''
23 JUN 1931: Radio program, ''Roy Bargy's Maytag Radio Show''
24 JUN 1931: Frank Trumbauer Orchestra—Brunswick Records: IN THE MERRY MONTH OF MAYBE and CRAZY QUILT and GEORGIA ON MY MIND and HONEYSUCKLE ROSE
28 JUN 1931: Radio remote from Edgewater Beach Hotel, Chicago, IL.
29 JUN 1931: Radio program, ''A & P Gypsies'' (western)
30 JUN 1931: Radio program, ''Paul Whiteman's Allied Quality Paint Men''
30 JUN 1931: Radio program, ''Roy Bargy's Maytag Radio Show''

JUL 1931: In Chicago area, at Edgewater Beach Hotel.
5 JUL 1931: Radio remote from Edgewater Beach Hotel, Chicago, IL.
6 JUL 1931: Radio program, ''A & P Gypsies'' (western)
7 JUL 1931: Radio program, ''Paul Whiteman's Allied Quality Paint Men''
7 JUL 1931: Radio program, ''Roy Bargy's Maytag Radio Show''
12 JUL 1931: Radio remote from Edgewater Beach Hotel, Chicago, IL.
13 JUL 1931: Radio program, ''A & P Gypsies'' (western)
14 JUL 1931: Radio program, ''Paul Whiteman's Allied Quality Paint Men''
14 JUL 1931: Radio program, ''Roy Bargy's Maytag Radio Show''
19 JUL 1931: Radio remote from Edgewater Beach Hotel, Chicago, IL.
20 JUL 1931: Radio program, ''A & P Gypsies'' (western)
21 JUL 1931: Radio program, ''Paul Whiteman's Allied Quality Paint Men''
21 JUL 1931: Radio program, ''Roy Bargy's Maytag Radio Show''
26 JUL 1931: Radio remote from Edgewater Beach Hotel, Chicago, IL.

27 JUL 1931: Radio program, ''A & P Gypsies'' (western)
28 JUL 1931: Radio program, ''Paul Whiteman's Allied Quality Paint Men''
28 JUL 1931: Radio program, ''Roy Bargy's Maytag Radio Show''

1 AUG 1931: Whiteman radio program featured Trumbauer on his latest Brunswick recording of CRAZY QUILT.
2 AUG 1931: Radio remote from Edgewater Beach Hotel, Chicago, IL.
3 AUG 1931: Whiteman Orchestra opened at the Edgewater Beach Hotel. Trumbauer and wife moved to 611 Elmore Avenue, Park Ridge, IL. (a Chicago suburb).
3 AUG 1931: Radio program, Station KWY, Chicago, IL.
3 AUG 1931: Radio program, ''A & P Gypsies'' (western)
4 AUG 1931: Radio program, ''Paul Whiteman's Allied Quality Paint Men''
4 AUG 1931: Radio program, ''Roy Bargy's Maytag Radio Show''
9 AUG 1931: Radio remote from Edgewater Beach Hotel, Chicago, IL.
10 AUG 1931: Radio program, ''A & P Gypsies'' (western)
11 AUG 1931: Radio program, ''Paul Whiteman's Allied Quality Paint Men''
11 AUG 1931: Radio program, ''Roy Bargy's Maytag Radio Show''
14 AUG 1931: Radio program, Station KWY, Chicago, IL.
15 AUG 1931: Trumbauer's transport pilot's license renewed.
16 AUG 1931: Radio remote from Edgewater Beach Hotel, Chicago, IL.
17 AUG 1931: Radio program, ''A & P Gypsies'' (western)
18 AUG 1931: Paul Whiteman married Margaret Livingston in Denver, CO.
18 AUG 1931: Radio program, ''Paul Whiteman's Allied Quality Paint Men''
18 AUG 1931: Radio program, ''Roy Bargy's Maytag Radio Show''
23 AUG 1931: Radio remote from Edgewater Beach Hotel, Chicago, IL.
24 AUG 1931: Radio program, ''A & P Gypsies'' (western)

25 AUG 1931: Radio program, ''Paul Whiteman's Allied Quality Paint Men''

25 AUG 1931: Radio program, ''Roy Bargy's Maytag Radio Show''

30 AUG 1931: Radio remote from Edgewater Beach Hotel, Chicago, IL.

31 AUG 1931: Radio program, ''A & P Gypsies'' (western)

1 SEP 1931: Jimmy Gillespie resigned as Whiteman's business manager.

1 SEP 1931: Radio program, ''Paul Whiteman's Allied Quality Paint Men''

6 SEP 1931: Radio remote from Edgewater Beach Hotel, Chicago, IL.

8 SEP 1931: Radio program, ''Paul Whiteman's Allied Quality Paint Men''

8 SEP 1931: Radio program, ''Roy Bargy's Maytag Radio Show''

13 SEP 1931: Radio remote from Edgewater Beach Hotel, Chicago, IL.

15 SEP 1931: Radio program, ''Paul Whiteman's Allied Quality Paint Men''

15 SEP 1931: Radio program, ''Roy Bargy's Maytag Radio Show''

20 SEP 1931: Radio remote from Edgewater Beach Hotel, Chicago, IL.

22 SEP 1931: Radio program, ''Paul Whiteman's Allied Quality Paint Men''

22 SEP 1931: Radio program, ''Roy Bargy's Maytag Radio Show''

26 SEP 1931: After a brief tour, the band reopened at the Edgewater Beach Hotel, Chicago, IL.

27 SEP 1931: Radio remote from Edgewater Beach Hotel, Chicago, IL.

29 SEP 1931: Radio program, ''Paul Whiteman's Allied Quality Paint Men''

29 SEP 1931: Radio program, ''Roy Bargy's Maytag Radio Show''

30 SEP 1931: Paul Whiteman Orchestra—Victor Records: TANGO AMERICANO and VILIA and SYLVIA

1 OCT 1931: Paul Whiteman Orchestra—Victor Records: OLD PLAYMATE and WHEN THE WORLD WAS NEW and GETTIN' SENTIMENTAL

4 OCT 1931: Paul Whiteman Orchestra—Victor Records: CAN'T YOU SEE? and WHEN IT'S SLEEPY TIME DOWN SOUTH

4 OCT 1931: Radio remote from Edgewater Beach Hotel, Chicago, IL.

6 OCT 1931: Paul Whiteman Orchestra—Victor Records: CUBAN LOVE SONG and A FADED SUMMER LOVE and DANCE OF THE LITTLE DUTCH MILL and MY GOOD-BYE TO YOU and TELL ME WITH A LOVE SONG

6 OCT 1931: Radio program, "Paul Whiteman's Allied Quality Paint Men"

6 OCT 1931: Radio program, "Roy Bargy's Maytag Radio Show"

10 OCT 1931: Closed at the Edgewater Beach Hotel, Chicago, IL.

13 OCT 1931: Radio program, "Paul Whiteman's Allied Quality Paint Men"

13 OCT 1931: Radio program, "Roy Bargy's Maytag Radio Show"

20 OCT 1931: Radio program, "Paul Whiteman's Allied Quality Paint Men"

20 OCT 1931: Radio program, "Roy Bargy's Maytag Radio Show"

27 OCT 1931: Radio program, "Paul Whiteman's Allied Quality Paint Men"

27 OCT 1931: Radio program, "Roy Bargy's Maytag Radio Show"

1 NOV 1931: Chicago radio program for President Hoover's Mobilization of Relief Resources.

3 NOV 1931: Radio program, "Paul Whiteman's Allied Quality Paint Men"

8 NOV 1931: Radio remote from Edgewater Beach Hotel, Chicago, IL.

10 NOV 1931: Radio program, "Paul Whiteman's Allied Quality Paint Men"

15 NOV 1931: Radio program for Unemployed Relief Benefit, New York.

17 NOV 1931: Radio program, ''Paul Whiteman's Allied Quality Paint Men''

22 NOV 1931: Concert, Studebaker Theatre, Chicago, IL.

24 NOV 1931: Radio program, ''Paul Whiteman's Allied Quality Paint Men''

25 NOV 1931: Benefit radio program, Philadelphia, PA.

29 NOV 1931: First serious symphonic jazz concert radio program, New York, NY.

30 NOV 1931: Paul Whiteman Orchestra—Victor Records: GEORGE WHITE'S SCANDALS MEDLEY and 'LEVEN POUNDS OF HEAVEN and THERE'S A BLUE NOTE IN MY LOVE SONG

1 DEC 1931: Paul Whiteman Orchestra—Victor Records: POPULAR SELECTIONS MEDLEY and ALL OF ME

1 DEC 1931: Radio program, ''Paul Whiteman's Allied Quality Paint Men''

3 DEC 1931: Paul Whiteman Orchestra—Victor Records: A ROSE AND A KISS and BY THE SYCAMORE TREE and I DON'T SUPPOSE

8 DEC 1931: Radio program, ''Paul Whiteman's Allied Quality Paint Men''

12 DEC 1931: Emergency Relief Fund Benefit, Chicago, IL.

15 DEC 1931: Radio program, ''Paul Whiteman's Allied Quality Paint Men''

22 DEC 1931: Radio program, ''Paul Whiteman's Allied Quality Paint Men''

29 DEC 1931: Radio program, ''Paul Whiteman's Allied Quality Paint Men''

31 DEC 1931: Chicago, IL.

1932: AFM Local #802, New York, listed Trumbauer's address for 1932 as Thorndyke Hotel, West 56th Street, New York.

Paul Whiteman signed a 14-month contract with the Pontiac Motor Company for a weekly radio program. Whiteman to be billed as: ''Paul Whiteman and His Chieftains.''

2 JAN 1932: Left Edgewater Beach Hotel for a nine-week tour of RKO Theatres.

6 JAN 1932: RKO Theatre, Detroit, MI.
8–14 JAN 1932: St. Louis Theatre, St. Louis, MO.
16–22 JAN 1932: Albee Theatre (four shows daily), Cincinnati, OH.
19 JAN 1932: "Played blackjack all night. John Fulton, Chester Hazlett, Mischa Russell."
21 JAN 1932: "Good broadcast. Saw Seger Ellis."
22 JAN 1932: Radio program over WCKY, 10:00 P.M., for VFW gala.
23–29 JAN 1932: Palace Theatre, Chicago, IL. Mitzi & Bill join Tram.
30 JAN 1932: Opened at Palace Theatre, Cleveland, OH.

2 FEB 1932: Trumbauer decided to have his teeth worked on by a Cleveland dentist.
5 FEB 1932: Closed at Palace Theatre, Cleveland, OH.
6–12 FEB 1932: "Opened Downtown Detroit."
12 FEB 1932: "Played Jay Hop at Ann Arbor, also four shows, and broadcast. What a day."
13–19 FEB 1932: Shea's Buffalo Theatre, Buffalo, NY. During this engagement, Red Norvo married Mildred Bailey. "Five shows a day."
20–23 FEB 1932: Palace Theatre, Albany, NY.
20 FEB 1932: "Five shows."
21 FEB 1932: "Three shows, the only break we got so far."
22 FEB 1932: "Four shows."
24 FEB 1932: Paterson, NJ. "Over to the Irishman's. Won $2 on the nite."
26 FEB 1932: Closed Paterson, NJ. "Had party in room and $20 went the way of all good money."
27 FEB 1932: New York. "Saw Ed Wynn and Willie Hall and went to Onyx for drinks."

1 MAR 1932: Paul Whiteman Orchestra—Victor Records:
MOTHER DIXIE and FACE THE MUSIC MEDLEY and HOT CHA MEDLEY
2 MAR 1932: Paul Whiteman Orchestra—Victor Records:
FACE THE MUSIC MEDLEY and HOT CHA MEDLEY
3 MAR 1932: "Went to Connie's Inn. Gave Redman tune. Saw Tom [Rockwell] also."

4 MAR 1932: Pontiac Radio program. Left for Boston via train, and Trumbauer lost $28 in poker game. ''Get it back later.''
5 MAR 1932: Opened at Keith Theatre, Boston, MA. Five shows a day for one week. Trumbauer sent a check to Mitzi for $600.
11 MAR 1932: Closed at Keith Theatre, Boston, MA. Boarded a bus for next date.
12–18 MAR 1932: Albee Theatre, Providence, RI.
17 MAR 1932: Tram comments, ''Schedleys is the best place to eat. Biltmore Hotel is nice.''
19–25 MAR 1932: Palace Theatre, New York, NY.
26 MAR–1 APR 1932: New York, second week at the Palace. ''New show and the same hustle hurry as before. Midnite show and finished at 3:00 A.M.''

Trumbauer's pilot license was renewed. He received his medical clearance on 4 March, ''1 A Airplane Land'' on 8 March, and approved on 12 March.

1 APR 1932: Closed at the Palace Theatre, New York, NY.
2 APR 1932: Opened at Albee Theatre, Brooklyn, NY.
''Got $200 for records. Five shows, so I'm tired. The fool learns hard, so the wise man watches the fool.''
5 APR 1932: Frank Trumbauer Orchestra—Columbia Records: SIZZLING ONE-STEP MEDLEY and MEDLEY OF ISHAM JONES HITS. ''Finished at 11:55 and I'm almost finished too. I hope they are good.''
8 APR 1932: Closed at the Albee Theatre, Brooklyn, NY.
9–12 APR 1932: New York—181st Street. ''Four shows daily.''
14 APR 1932: Paul Whiteman Orchestra—Victor Records: LAWD, YOU MADE THE NIGHT TOO LONG and THE VOICE IN THE OLD VILLAGE CHOIR and DAYBREAK (Mitzi and Bill arrived for a visit.)
16–19 APR 1932: 86th Street Theatre (Flushing), New York, NY.
20–21 APR 1932: Days off
22 APR 1932: Mastbaum Theatre, Philadelphia, PA. Five shows daily.
During this engagement, Tram had considerable dental work performed by ''Doc Starr.'' Trumbauer stayed at the Stephen Girard Hotel.

26 APR 1932: Paul Whiteman Orchestra—Victor Records: GRAND CANYON SUITE (SUNRISE—Part 1) and GRAND CANYON SUITE (SUNRISE—Part 2) and GRAND CANYON SUITE (SUNRISE Part 1/SUNRISE Part 2)

27 APR 1932: Paul Whiteman Orchestra—Victor Records: GRAND CANYON SUITE (PAINTED DESERT) and GRAND CANYON SUITE (ON THE TRAIL—Part 1) and GRAND CANYON SUITE (PAINTED DESERT/ON THE TRAIL Part 1) and GRAND CANYON SUITE (ON THE TRAIL—Part 2) and GRAND CANYON SUITE (SUNSET) and GRAND CANYON SUITE (ON THE TRAIL—Part 2/ SUNSET)

28 APR 1932: Paul Whiteman Orchestra—Victor Records: GRAND CANYON SUITE (CLOUDBURST—Part 1) and GRAND CANYON SUITE (CLOUDBURST—Part 2) and GRAND CANYON SUITE (CLOUDBURST Part 1/ CLOUDBURST Part 2) and TOSELLI'S SERENADE

28 APR 1932: Closed at Mastbaum Theatre, Philadelphia, PA.

29 APR 1932: Stanley Theatre, Pittsburgh, PA.

1 MAY 1932: Band went to Steubenville, OH., for four shows. "Long ride back."

2 MAY 1932: Charles Horvath arrived to make final offer to Trumbauer for his own band. Tram accepted.

3 MAY 1932: Trumbauer notified Whiteman of his decision to leave the band.

5 MAY 1932: Band closed at Stanley Theatre, Pittsburgh, PA. Trumbauer, wondering about Whiteman's reaction to his decision, noted "Paul wonderful."

6 MAY 1932: Trumbauer arrived in Chicago, IL.
Now residing: 611 Elmore Avenue, Park Ridge, IL.

7 MAY 1932: Trumbauer met with Charles Horvath and learned that Charles had not hired any musicians.

9 MAY 1932: Unidentified radio program, $50.

11 MAY 1932: "So far spent about $500 on little things."

12 MAY 1932: First rehearsal, "and the band was sure sad but it will be better with better men."

13 MAY 1932: Unidentified radio program, $50.

16 MAY 1932: Trumbauer had negotiated for an opening in

Kansas City, but on this date, ''Calhoun wants to welch. Cut on the deal of 1750 to 1600 down to nothing.''

17 MAY 1932: Kansas City engagement wanted Trumbauer to open on 24th ''knowing I could not do it.'' Tram signed Max Connett and two others.

18 MAY 1932: ''No job. Boys all set to go and so there is the game. Statz let me down. Boys are lovely.''

Band: Max Connett (first tpt); Vance ''Chink'' Rice (second tpt); Hal Matthews (tbn); Frank Trumbauer (C-mel/altos); Gale Stout (first alto); Malcolm Elstad (third alto); Harold Jones (ten-sx); Cedric Spring (vn/acc/gtr); Leon Kaplan (vn/gtr); Herm Crone (p/arr); Craig Leitch (gtr); Charles McConnell (bs); LeRoy Buck (dms).

Vocalists: Hal Redus (baritone); Craig Leitch (tenor), Elinor Sherry.

''The Three Spooks'': Cedric Spring, Harold Jones, LeRoy Buck.

Max Connett was the business manager, and Malcolm Elstad drove the truck containing the instruments and baggage. Initial salaries were set at $60 per musician, except Max Connett who received $100 per week. Hal Redus received $45, and Elinor Sherry $40 per week. In the ensuing months, Frances Kerr replaced Elinor Sherry and received $40 per week. Russ Case was added on 1 April 1933 as an arranger and received $25 per week. During 1933, as the depression grew worse, regular salaries were forgotten and payments were made based on amounts collected. The ''steady'' salary seems to be $10 per person per engagement, with a substitute musician receiving $7. Hal received $7 and Frances $5 per night.

25 MAY 1932: Bing Crosby—Brunswick Records:
CABIN IN THE COTTON and (I'M STILL WITHOUT A SWEETHEART) WITH SUMMER COMING ON

26 MAY 1932: Bing Crosby—Brunswick Records:
LOVE ME TONIGHT and SOME OF THESE DAYS

3 JUN 1932: Chateau La Mar, Janesville, WI.
Special WCLO radio program at 8:30 P.M..

9 JUN 1932: Opening night at Bellerive Hotel, Kansas City, MO. Newspapers announced that the band would start broadcasting regularly over the Columbia Network.

25 JUN 1932: Trumbauer had minor surgery. Max Connett led the band, and informed during intermission of the birth of his daughter.

28 JUN 1932: ***Variety*** carried a review on Trumbauer and his orchestra appearing at the Bellerive Hotel.

7 JUL 1932: Trumbauer signed with Frederick Brothers' Booking Agency.

10–16 JUL 1932: Bellerive Hotel, Kansas City, MO. ($810)
"The crowd's dancing in the Terrace Cafe with its delightfully cool, dry-iced air. Band plays for luncheon, dinner and supper, daily and Sunday, except Sunday noon. Call Valentine 7047 for reservations."

17–23 JUL 1932: Bellerive Hotel, Kansas City, MO. ($775)
Band also paid $175 for two-week engagement by radio station carrying their programs.

24 JUL 1932: (Probably Frog Hop), St. Joseph, MO. ($200)

25 JUL 1932: Casa Loma Park, Abilene, KS. ($160)

26 JUL 1932: Day off.

27 JUL 1932: Orchelan Heights, Moberly, MO. ($138.10)

28 JUL 1932: Half-A-Hill Tea House, Springfield, MO. ($105.94)

29 JUL 1932: Joplin, MO. ($86.24)

30 JUL 1932: Frog Hop, St. Joseph, MO. ($88.92)

31 JUL-2 AUG 1932: Jay Hawk Theatre, Topeka, KS. (no receipts listed)

It appears that the amounts listed above represent the money netted after paying commission to booking agency, and local union tax charged to them as a travelling band.

As a publicity stunt, an article appeared in the Topeka newspapers noting that Frank Trumbauer had been a catcher in minor league baseball. They scheduled Tram to catch the offerings of Ray Lewis, star hurler of the Nehi baseball team, for one inning, during Sunday's game. Trumbauer watched Ray "warm up" and decided that he had too much "smoke" and decided against the publicity stunt. Instead, he had the team as his guest at a theatre performance.

3 AUG 1932: Casa Loma Park, Abilene, KS.
4 or 5 AUG 1932: Ogden, KS.
6 AUG 1932: Frog Hop, St. Joseph, MO.
7 AUG 1932: Frog Hop, St. Joseph, MO.
8 AUG 1932: Hotel St. Joe (presumably St. Joseph, MO.)
9 AUG 1932: Old Mill, Topeka, KS.
10 AUG 1932: Ottumwa, IA.
11 AUG 1932: Riverview Park, Des Moines, IA. A special public address amplifier system was installed to carry the music to the unexpected large crowd of dancers and spectators.
17 AUG 1932: Frank Trumbauer Orchestra—Columbia Records: CINDERELLA'S WEDDING DAY and I THINK YOU'RE A HONEY and BUSINESS IN Q and BASS DRUM DAN and THE NEWEST ST. LOUIS BLUES and BETWEEN THE DEVIL AND THE DEEP BLUE SEA

3–10 SEP 1932: Golden Pheasant, Cleveland, OH. Publicity notice given to local newspapers: "Frank Trumbauer, appearing at the Golden Pheasant, plays polo, tennis, basketball, was baseball catcher in minor leagues, golfs, rates as a crack rifle and pistol shot, served as a locomotive fireman on the B & O Railroad, served as transport pilot, can throw a knife Mexican-style, cooks swell biscuits, and rates as one of the ace sax players in these U.S."
5 SEP 1932: Trumbauer attended the Cleveland Air Races. When asked for a reaction to the event, he replied, "Everything sure is the last word. Doolittle was the guy who really went on though."
11 SEP 1932: Lincoln Tavern, Chicago, IL. "A roadhouse, three miles west of Evanston, on Dempsey Street. For reservations phone Morton Grove 1919." Newspapers reported that the band would "stay the season," and "for four weeks." Radio broadcasts over WGN, Chicago Tribune Radio Station, were at 7:30 P.M., 9:00 P.M., and 10:00 P.M.
15 SEP 1932: Trumbauer applied for renewal of his pilot's license and listed his address as 611 Elmore Avenue in Park Ridge.

21 SEP 1932: Davenport, IA.
22 SEP 1932: Ames, IA.
26 SEP 1932: Application for pilot's license renewed.

Engagement at the Lincoln Tavern ended at the closing of the month. Elinor Sherry left the band. Not immediately replaced. Harold Jones left and was replaced by Hubert Doyle (tenor saxophone). "The Three Spooks" as a vocal group was discontinued.

OCT 1932: The band did a brief tour through Southern Illinois, Texas, and into Oklahoma.
21 OCT 1932: Bartlesville, OK.
23 OCT 1932: Omaha, NE.
25 OCT 1932: Topeka, KS.
27–29 OCT 1932: Tulsa Club, Tulsa, OK. Added attraction, dance duo, Diane and DeMar. A telegram sent by the management of the Lincoln Tavern to owners of the Tulsa Club read: "Opened season with Earl Burtnett. Had Duke Ellington and Ted Weems and closed with Trumbauer. You will be fortunate if you can get Trumbauer as he did more business for me than the other three bands."

9 NOV 1932: The Hangar, Marion, IL. (Actual hangar at the airport used for dances.) Publicity release: "One of the proudest possessions of Frank Trumbauer is his collection of firearms. Excellent weapons of all kinds, ranging from automatic pistols and revolvers to antique and modern rifles and shotguns are to be found in gun racks of the den of his Park Ridge, Illinois home."
12 NOV 1932: Baker Hotel, Dallas, TX. Regular University Night Dance. "Where the cutest freshman co-ed will be chosen from eight of the most beautiful college girls you have ever seen. Presented in the Crystal Ballroom. No advance in prices, only $1 per person plus tax."
15 NOV 1932: Hollywood Club, Galveston, TX.

Trumbauer now switched booking agencies, signing with Music Corporation of America (MCA), mainly for broadcast exposure, as they advertised their bands as "On The Air—

Everywhere.'' Hal Matthews leaves and is replaced by Joe Harris (tbn). Frances Kerr, an acclaimed radio star for the NBC Network, is added as female vocalist.

16 NOV–18 DEC 1932: Sui Jen, Galveston, TX. Dancing from 9:00 P.M. until 3:00 A.M.. Manager Sam Maceo added the dance team of Diane (Diane Fea) and DeMar (Salvatore DeMarco). During the engagement, Gale Stout left and is replaced by Ken Mild (alto sax).

19 DEC 1932: Hollywood Club, Galveston, TX.
Annual supper-dance for the Red Cross.

24–31 DEC 1932: Baker Hotel, Dallas, TX. ($1600.55)
Diane & DeMar accompanied the band. Initial radio program of 7:45–8:15 P.M. was greatly expanded by WFAA to include Tuesday and Thursday from 10:00–10:30 P.M. and Saturday from 10:15 P.M. to midnight.

1–7 JAN 1933: Baker Hotel, Dallas, TX. ($1600.55)

8–14 JAN 1933: Baker Hotel, Dallas, TX. ($1329.25)

17 JAN 1933: Cooper Club, Henderson, TX. ($200)
Press release: ''Frank Trumbauer, the sax king, has been timed to tongue six notes to a beat, 150 beats to a minute, or a total of 900 notes per minute, doubling the 450 shots per minute speed of a machine gun.''

19 JAN 1933: Carbondale, IL. Dance set for this date, but due to advance ticket sales swelling the crowd's attendance, it was switched to the next night at . . .

20 JAN 1933: Danceland, Murphysboro, IL. ($200)

24 JAN 1933: Trumbauer paid his Chicago Local #10 union dues.

Band inactive. Lou Svobada replaced Cedric Spring (vn).

21 FEB 1933: Madison, WI. ($200)

25 FEB 1933: Ames, IA. ($330)

26 FEB 1933: Danceland, Davenport, IA. ($250)

MAR 1933: Cedric Spring returned, replacing Lou Svobada (vn).

16 MAR 1933: Blackhawk Cafe, Chicago, IL. ($241.17)

21 MAR 1933: Blackhawk Cafe, Chicago, IL. ($126.17)

21 MAR 1933: Trianon Ballroom, Chicago, IL. ($109.36)

Max Connett suggested that the band be divided in two so that they could play both the 21 March dates.

23 MAR 1933: Blackhawk Cafe, Chicago, IL. ($241.17)
28 MAR 1933: Blackhawk Cafe, Chicago, IL. ($241.17)

1 APR 1933: Russ Case joined the band as arranger.
4 APR 1933: Blackhawk Cafe, Chicago, IL. ($241.17)
11 APR 1933: Women's Athletic Club, Chicago, IL. ($200)
15 APR 1933: Grinnell, IA. ($200)
16 APR 1933: Davenport, IA. ($250)
18 APR 1933: Blackhawk Cafe, Chicago, IL. ($125.52)
20 APR 1933: Cedar Rapids, IA. ($150)
21 APR 1933: Omaha, NE. ($250)
22 APR 1933: Sioux City, IA. ($250)
23 APR 1933: Omaha, NE. ($250)
25 APR 1933: Andy Secrest replaced Vance Rice (trumpet).
26 APR 1933: Blackhawk Cafe, Chicago, IL. ($125.52)

MAY 1933: Band personnel: Andy Secrest (crt); Max Connett (tpt); Santo Pecora (tbn); Frank Trumbauer (C-mel/alto); Lennie Conn (first alto); Mal Elstad (third alto); Hugh Doyle (ten-sx); Cedric Spring (vn/acc/gtr); Cappy Kaplan (vn/gtr); Herman Crone (p); Craig Leitch (gtr); Charles McConnell (bs); LeRoy Buck (dms); Frances Kerr, Hal Redus (vcs). Redus left the band after the 2 May engagement.
2 MAY 1933: Blackhawk Cafe, Chicago, IL. ($125.52)
4 MAY 1933: O'Henry Park, Chicago, IL. ($500)
5 MAY 1933: Muncie, IN. ($210.91)
Paid $15 to Andy Secrest for getting the Muncie job.
11 MAY 1933: O'Henry Park, Chicago, IL. ($500)
12 MAY 1933: Edgewater Beach Hotel, Chicago, IL. ($200)
Digamma Alph Upsilon Dance.
18 MAY 1933: O'Henry Park, Chicago, IL. ($500)
18 MAY 1933: Blackhawk Cafe, Chicago, IL. ($125.52)
19 MAY 1933: Knickerbocker Hotel, Chicago, IL. ($210)
Received payment for this on 25 May 1933.

Kahn Keene replaced Santo Pecora (tbn) at this time.

25 MAY 1933: O'Henry Park, Chicago, IL. ($500)
25 MAY 1933: Blackhawk Cafe, Chicago, IL. ($125.52)
25 MAY 1933: Private party, Blackhawk Cafe, Chicago, IL. ($417.83)

"Dippy" Johnson (tpt) added for 11, 18, and 25 May engagements. He was paid $65 total. Paul Lyman replaced Cedric Spring (vn); Tommy Crume replaced Leon Kaplan (vn).

1 JUN 1933: O'Henry Park, Chicago, IL. ($666.66)
1 JUN 1933: Blackhawk Cafe, Chicago, IL. ($125.52) Payment received in advance on 25 May 1933.
8 JUN 1933: O'Henry Park, Chicago, IL. ($623.01)

Jules Fastoff replaced Kahn Keene (tbn).

15 JUN 1933: O'Henry Park, Chicago, IL. ($635.27)
22 JUN 1933: O'Henry Park, Chicago, IL. ($761.07)
30 JUN 1933: O'Henry Park, Chicago, IL. ($460)

JUL 1933: Band personnel: Andy Secrest (crt); Max Connett (tpt); Ray Barrett (tbn); Frank Trumbauer (C-mel/alto); Art Ralston (first alto); Mal Elstad (third alto); Hugh Doyle (ten-sx); Paul Lyman, Pick Mansfield (vns); Harold Wright (p); Craig Leitch (gtr); Charles McConnell (bs); Russ Morrison (dms); Frances Kerr (vcs); Russ Case (arr).
2 JUL 1933: Rochester, IN. ($200)
13 JUL 1933: Mineral Point, WI. ($150)
15 JUL 1933: Green Bay, WI. ($150)
19–25 JUL 1933: The Plantation, White Bear Lake, MN. ($1100) Added attractions for this two-week stay: Lillian LaVerne (specialty dancer) and Maurine & Norva (International dance stars).
26 JUL-2 AUG 1933: The Plantation, White Bear Lake, MN. ($1100)
"7 Course Dinner—$1.25. Dinner Dancing—Dinner Show. For reservations direct St. Paul telephone TOwer 7212, or White Bear 631. Three shows nightly."

AUG 1933: Harold Sells replaced Mal Elstad (third alto).
3 AUG 1933: Mineral Point, WI. ($175)
4 AUG 1933: Truck in for repairs at White Bear Lake. Charges, $62. (Total charges: Leasing, $105; Repairs, $441.80. Total Expenses: $546.80 [11/12/33]).
27 AUG–2 SEP 1933: Castle Farms, Cincinnati, OH. ($1050)

3 SEP 1933: Castle Farms, Cincinnati, OH. ($150)
4 SEP 1933: Castle Farms, Cincinnati, OH. ($150)
15 SEP 1933: Indiana Roof Ballroom, Indianapolis, IN. ($162.50)
16 SEP 1933: Indiana Roof Ballroom, Indianapolis, IN. ($162.50)
17 SEP 1933: Indiana Roof Ballroom, Indianapolis, IN. ($162.50)
20 SEP 1933: Indiana Roof Ballroom, Indianapolis, IN. ($162.50)
22 SEP 1933: Indiana Roof Ballroom, Indianapolis, IN. ($150)
23 SEP 1933: Indiana Roof Ballroom, Indianapolis, IN. ($150)
24 SEP 1933: Indiana Roof Ballroom, Indianapolis, IN. ($150)
27 SEP 1933: Indiana Roof Ballroom, Indianapolis, IN. ($150)
30 SEP 1933: World's Fair, Chicago, IL. ($215)

OCT 1933: Trumbauer dropped MCA and switched booking agency to Fredericks Brothers. Payments made to the agency from October on.
OCT 1933: Bill Lanshaw replaced Art Ralston (first alto).
9 OCT 1933: Trumbauer sent his bass-saxophone, serial number 28829, to Frank Holton & Co., for repairs. Repair (unlisted) charges $11.20 plus express charges, $4.47.
13 OCT 1933: Sherman Hotel, Chicago, IL. (Receipts not listed)
14–15 OCT 1933: O'Henry Park, Chicago, IL. ($522 for both nights)
18 OCT 1933: O'Henry Park, Chicago, IL. ($404.54)
26 OCT 1933: O'Henry Park, Chicago, IL. ($460)
28 OCT 1933: Lowery's, St. Paul, MN. ($200)
31 OCT 1933: Woodward, IA. ($170)

2 NOV 1933: Manning, IA. ($125)
3 NOV 1933: Manhattan, KS. ($93)
4 NOV 1933: Lawrence, KS. ($275)
5 NOV 1933: St. Joseph, MO. ($150)
7 NOV 1933: McPherson, KS. ($150)
8 NOV 1933: Trumbauer purchased a Holton alto saxophone,

model 201, finish A, serial number 115324, and case, from Frank Holton & Co. Total price: $60.50.

9–10 NOV 1933: Stayed at Stats Hotel, Kansas City, KS.

10 NOV 1933: Topeka, KS. ($130)

11 NOV 1933: Sioux City, IA. ($175)

12 NOV 1933: Omaha, NE. ($175)

13 NOV 1933: Advised Fredericks Brothers (booking agency) of decision to discontinue the band.

17 NOV 1933: Called the band together, informed them of decision, and paid off each member.

18 NOV 1933: Fredericks Brothers offered Trumbauer another band as a leader, salary of $250 per week, but no guarantee of recordings. Trumbauer turned down the offer.

20 NOV 1933: Trumbauer, Russ Case, and Max Connett leave for New York.

21 NOV 1933: Erie, PA. Had to purchase set of new tires for automobile.

22 NOV 1933: Arrived in New York.

24 NOV 1933: Trumbauer had lunch with Paul Whiteman. Whiteman offered Tram his job back, but Trumbauer told of wanting to "test the waters in New York." Accepted a job for Paul Whiteman radio program (***The Kraft Music Hall***) of 30 November.

25 NOV 1933: ***The Melody Maker:*** "Bix, Frankie and Co.—Just One Big Family." Article by Warren Scholl. Discussion of Okeh Records made by Bix and Tram.

27 NOV 1933: Ritz-Carlton Hotel. Member of Joe Moss Orchestra. ($20)

30 NOV 1933: Wysling Country Club (afternoon). Unidentified six-piece band.

30 NOV 1933: Radio program, ***The Kraft Music Hall.*** ($24) Following day, Dave Wade replaced Bunny Berigan.

DEC 1933: Trumbauer now residing at the Belvedere Hotel, 48th Street, west of Broadway, New York, NY.

1 DEC 1933: Ritz-Carlton Hotel. Member of Joe Moss Orchestra. ($20)

2 DEC 1933: Ritz-Carlton Hotel. Member of Joe Moss Orchestra. ($20)

5 DEC 1933: Rehearsed with Paul Whiteman for concert and radio program.

6 DEC 1933: Trumbauer on cover of ***Orchestra World.***
7 DEC 1933: Radio program, ***The Kraft Music Hall.***
8 DEC 1933: Attended Radio City Music Hall Show.
9 DEC 1933: Biltmore Hotel. Member of Joe Moss Orchestra. Job lasted until 6:00 A.M.. ($40)
11 DEC 1933: Informed Joe Moss of decision to join Paul Whiteman.
12–13 DEC 1933: Rehearsals with Paul Whiteman Orchestra.
14 DEC 1933: Official announcement of return to Paul Whiteman Orchestra. Salary $200 per week, minus income tax of $1.65.
14 DEC 1933: Radio program, ***The Kraft Music Hall.*** ($24) Radio program featured Tram.

For Whiteman Orchestra personnel see discography for date 14 December 1933. Whiteman received $4500 for his orchestra's weekly national programs originating from WEAF studios, New York, NY.

15 DEC 1933: Whiteman presented his Sixth Experiment in Modern Music at the Metropolitan Opera House.
16 DEC 1933–1 JAN 1934: Whiteman Orchestra appearing at the Paradise Cafe.
21 DEC 1933: Radio program, ***The Kraft Music Hall.***
23 DEC 1933: Trumbauer purchased from Frank Holton & Co., and had shipped to his mother: Alto saxophone, model 201, finish A, serial number 115078, and case. Price: $60.50. Alto saxophone, model 201, finish A, serial number 115722, and case. Price: $67.65. Both saxophones were returned by Mrs. Stevenson on 8 January 1934. Holton credited $128.15 to Trumbauer's account and advised him of their return. It is suggested that Tram purchased them, as a Christmas present, for his mother, who had a music school where she was teaching saxophone. She probably felt that it was too much money for her son to spend on her.
24 DEC 1933: Trumbauer had photographs made for use with article in ***Metronome,*** written by Johnson.
26 DEC 1933: Trumbauer met with officials of Brunswick Records. Contract contingent on Whiteman's permission, which he gladly gave!
28 DEC 1933: Radio program, ***The Kraft Music Hall.***

1–3 JAN 1934: Days off.
4 JAN 1934: Radio program, ***The Kraft Music Hall.***
Fred Kull, Vice President and General Manager of Frank Holton & Co., wrote to Trumbauer advising him that Charles Bryant, their saxophone department foreman, had invented a new octave key for alto and tenor saxophones, and they wanted to send either saxophone to Tram to demonstrate for them.
4 JAN–14 APR 1934: Casino Bleau at the Biltmore Hotel, New York, NY.
7 JAN 1934: Whiteman Orchestra concert at Brooklyn Institute of Arts & Sciences.
7 JAN 1934: Daughter, Lynne, born.
11 JAN 1934: Radio program, ***The Kraft Music Hall.***
12 JAN 1934: Frank Trumbauer Orchestra—Brunswick Records: BREAK IT DOWN and JUBA and HOW AM I TO KNOW?
16 JAN 1934: Paul Whiteman Orchestra—Victor Records: ($30) G BLUES and IF I LOVE AGAIN and MY LITTLE GRASS SHACK IN KEALAKEKUA, HAWAII and WAGON WHEELS and IT'S AN OLD FASHIONED WORLD AFTER ALL
16 JAN 1934: Trumbauer arranged an audition for Russell Morrison to sing for Whiteman. Tram's words: ''No Go.''
18 JAN 1934: Radio program, ***The Kraft Music Hall.***
20 JAN 1934: Golf with Paul Whiteman, Roy Bargy, Kurt Dieterle, Jack Fulton, ''and so on.''
25 JAN 1934: Radio program, ***The Kraft Music Hall.***

1 FEB 1934: Radio program, ***The Kraft Music Hall.***
2 FEB 1934: When Trumbauer joined the Paul Whiteman Orchestra he moved in with Mr. & Mrs. Bill Rank. Tram changed his residence to a hotel in downtown New York, probably Hotel Belvedere.
8 FEB 1934: Radio program, ***The Kraft Music Hall.***
15 FEB 1934: Radio program, ***The Kraft Music Hall.***
16 FEB 1934: Paul Whiteman Orchestra—Victor Records: ($30) THE MOONLIGHT WALTZ and TRUE and FARE-THEE-WELL TO HARLEM and SUN SPOTS and THE BOUNCING BALL
22 FEB 1934: Radio program, ***The Kraft Music Hall.***
Trumbauer ill with cold, but still played radio program.

23 FEB 1934: Frank Trumbauer Orchestra—Brunswick Records: CHINA BOY and EMALINE and IN A MIST and 'LONG ABOUT MIDNIGHT

Trumbauer somewhat disgusted about recordings. "Only one played free and easy." Illness with heavy cold continued, perhaps prompting remark to Jack Kapp about "in my hair" regarding recording session. Cold finally cleared up on 25th.

MAR 1934: Paul Whiteman Orchestra continued at the Biltmore Hotel, New York, NY.

1 MAR 1934: Radio program, ***The Kraft Music Hall.***

1 MAR 1934: Discussed possible recording date with "Jack and so on" but the guys are "tired of records."

3 MAR 1934: Talks closed for home at 8814 62nd Drive, Rego Park, Elmhurst, Long Island, NY.

4 MAR 1934: Kurt Dieterle, Roy Bargy, Bennie Bonacio, Herb Quigley, Mike Pingitore, Nat Natolie, Bill Rank, Charles Teagarden, Charles Strickfaden, Paul Whiteman, Adolph Deutsch (assistant conductor), and Trumbauer left for Cincinnati, OH. Musicians invited to perform with 125-member Cincinnati Symphony Orchestra for raising of funds to aid musicians hit hardest by the Depression. Upon arrival in town, Bargy, Rank, and Trumbauer stayed with Ray Lodwig.

5 MAR 1934: Mitzi and Bill arrived in Cincinnati around 5:30 P.M.

6 MAR 1934: Rehearsal and, that night, the concert. Whiteman group featured with Trumbauer spotlighted in third part of program playing BOUNCING BALL. Tram later remarked: "Greatest thrill I ever had, to stand up and play in that band."

7 MAR 1934: Whiteman musicians arrived back in New York.

8 MAR 1934: Radio program, ***The Kraft Music Hall.***

15 MAR 1934: Radio program, ***The Kraft Music Hall.***

16 MAR 1934: Closed deal for home in Rego Park.
Trumbauer's home telephone: HAvermeyer 96123.

17 MAR 1934: ***Melody Maker*** issue contained article on Trumbauer by Warren Scholl. Tram had problems with his teeth and arranged for dental appointment.

18 MAR 1934: Dental work performed by "Doc" Stone. Tram ill.

19 MAR 1934: Ill with teeth problems. Attended Will Rogers movie, hoping to take mind off troubles.

20 MAR 1934: Too ill to work. Trumbauer sent a substitute (name not listed).

21 MAR 1934: Returned to work, and Whiteman was upset about not being informed before job of substitute being sent the night before.

22 MAR 1934: Radio program, ***The Kraft Music Hall.***

23 MAR 1934: Recording date. Hired by Bunny Berigan. Bunny failed to show and date was cancelled. No details listed.

27 MAR 1934: Ramona (Davies)—Victor Records: ($28) THE BEAT O' MY HEART and THE HOUSE IS HAUNTED and BROADWAY'S GONE HILL-BILLY and WE'RE OUT OF THE RED

30 MAR 1934: In addition to Biltmore Hotel engagement, Whiteman signed a two-week contract to appear at the Capital Theatre (concurrently) with four shows a day! Trumbauer paid additional $90 per week for Capital job. Whiteman promised lengthy vacation after dual engagements end.

1–7 APR 1934: First week at Capital set record attendance: 78,000.

3 APR 1934: Whiteman musicians openly questioned the need for so much work. In addition to two engagements (Biltmore Hotel and Capital Theatre), he called for rehearsals sometimes two and one days prior to Kraft radio program. Add recordings, plus charity events (when Whiteman asked some of the boys to accompany him and perform for the crowd) and the musicians were finding all too few hours in the day for sleep!

4 APR 1934: Brunswick contacted Trumbauer about another recording date. Tram was unable to spare the time for such a session.

5 APR 1934: Radio program, ***The Kraft Music Hall.***

12 APR 1934: Radio program, ***The Kraft Music Hall.***

16 APR 1934: Trumbauer notes: "Much work. [Charles] Horvath arrangements and so on. All will clear Brunswick recording also."

17 APR 1934: Paul Whiteman Orchestra—Victor Records: (Tram paid $28) G BLUES and TAIL SPIN and CHRISTMAS

NIGHT IN HARLEM and CARRY ME BACK TO GREEN PASTURES and ANNINA

19 APR 1934: Radio program, ***The Kraft Music Hall.***

22 APR 1934: Trumbauer's "open house party." The following, and their wives, attended: Roy Bargy, Nat Natolie, Kurt Dieterle, Chet Hazlett, Mischa Russell, Owen Harwood, Bill Rank, Russ Case, Mike (last name unidentified). Party featured beer and eats.

26 APR 1934: Radio program, ***The Kraft Music Hall.***

26 APR 1934: Whiteman went to Denver on the 24th and called to say that he heard ***The Kraft Music Hall*** program. Band knew the program was not too good, and Paul told them exactly that!

27–29 APR 1934: Tram and Mitzi took a vacation and drove to Atlantic City. Rain all three days!

MAY 1934: Whiteman Orchestra continued vacation for first half of the month, doing only weekly radio programs for which Trumbauer is paid $50 each. During vacation period, Tram was able to return to the golf course. The brief tour found him on the links daily at each city.

3 MAY 1934: Radio program, ***The Kraft Music Hall.***

7 MAY 1934: Selmer Instruments Company releases national advertisement with photo of Trumbauer and using quote: "I have found nothing to compare with them."

10 MAY 1934: Radio program, ***The Kraft Music Hall.***

17 MAY 1934: Radio program, ***The Kraft Music Hall.***

18–22 MAY 1934: Whiteman Orchestra returned to work. Appeared at Montreal Mount Royal Hotel, Montreal, Canada. Trumbauer drove Whiteman, in Whiteman's new car (not identified), to and from engagement. Tram's salary of $200 per week now continued.

24 MAY 1934: Radio program, ***The Kraft Music Hall.***

25 MAY 1934: Ithaca, NY.

26 MAY 1934: Binghamton, NY.

27 MAY 1934: Batavia, NY.

28 MAY 1934: Toronto, Canada.

29 MAY 1934: Wilkes-Barre, PA.

30 MAY 1934: Atlantic City, NJ.

31 MAY 1934: Opened at the Biltmore Hotel, New York, NY. Closed 21 November.

31 MAY 1934: Radio program, ***The Kraft Music Hall.***

JUN 1934: Orchestra continued at the Biltmore Hotel for the month.
3 JUN 1934: Glen Oaks Golf Club. Regular group: Jack Fulton, Roy Bargy, Bill Rank, Trumbauer. Tram shot 83, other scores unknown.
7 JUN 1934: Radio program, ***The Kraft Music Hall.***
14 JUN 1934: Radio program, ***The Kraft Music Hall.***
21 JUN 1934: Radio program, ***The Kraft Music Hall.***
28 JUN 1934: Radio program, ***The Kraft Music Hall.***
29 JUN 1934: Paul Whiteman Orchestra—Victor Records: ($28) THERE'S NOTHING ELSE TO DO IN MA-LA-KA-MO-KA-LU (BUT LOVE) and BEACH BOY and BORN TO BE KISSED and LOVE IN BLOOM and I SAW YOU IN MY DREAMS

JUL 1934: Whiteman Orchestra continued at the Biltmore Hotel.
2–4 JUL 1934: Trumbauer took three days off and took family to Canada.
5 JUL 1934: Radio program, ***The Kraft Music Hall.***
12 JUL 1934: Radio program, ***The Kraft Music Hall.***
19 JUL 1934: Radio program, ***The Kraft Music Hall.***
26 JUL 1934: Radio program, ***The Kraft Music Hall.***
28 JUL 1934: The King's Men (Ken Darby, Jon Dobson, Bud Linn, and Rad Robinson) auditioned for Whiteman and were hired.
29 JUL 1934: Last week of the month, band doubled at the Manhattan Beach. Trumbauer paid $42 extra.

AUG 1934: Whiteman Orchestra continued at the Biltmore Hotel.
2 AUG 1934: Radio program, ***The Kraft Music Hall.***
9 AUG 1934: Radio program, ***The Kraft Music Hall.***
16 AUG 1934: Radio program, ***The Kraft Music Hall.***
Program discontinued until 22 November.
18 AUG 1934: Paul Whiteman Orchestra—Victor Records: ($28) PARDON MY SOUTHERN ACCENT and HERE COME THE BRITISH and ITCHOLA and I'M COUNTING ON YOU and I SAW STARS

SEP 1934: Whiteman Orchestra continued at the Biltmore Hotel.
SEP 1934: ***Metronome*** magazine, page 21, shows Trumbauer and

the Whiteman reed section endorsing: Otto Link & Company (264 West 47th Street, New York) mouthpieces. Prices: Alto $16 and C-Melody $17, but complete with Ligature, Cap, and Reed. Burnished Gold finish.

11 SEP 1934: Paul Whiteman Orchestra—Victor Records: ($20) PARK AVENUE FANTASY and DEEP PURPLE and PETER, PETER, PUMPKIN EATER (PARTS 1 & 2)

18 SEP 1934: Jack Teagarden Orchestra—Brunswick Records: JUNK MAN and STARS FELL ON ALABAMA and YOUR GUESS IS AS GOOD AS MINE

OCT 1934: Whiteman Orchestra continued at the Biltmore Hotel.

26 OCT 1934: Paul Whiteman Orchestra—Victor Records: ($36) ANYTHING GOES MEDLEY and I GET A KICK OUT OF YOU and YOU'RE THE TOP and ALL THROUGH THE NIGHT and ANYTHING GOES

NOV 1934: Whiteman Orchestra continued at the Biltmore Hotel.

20 NOV 1934: Frank Trumbauer Orchestra—Victor Records: BLUE MOON and PLANTATION MOODS and DOWN 'T UNCLE BILL'S and TROUBLES

21 NOV 1934: Whiteman Orchestra closed at the Biltmore Hotel.

22 NOV 1934: Radio program, ***The Kraft Music Hall.***

23–28 NOV 1934: Stanley Theatre, Pittsburgh, PA.

29 NOV 1934: Radio program, ***The Kraft Music Hall.***

29 NOV–6 DEC: Week's vacation.

3 DEC 1934: Trumbauer accepted as a member of "The Quiet Birdmen." This is a social organization of pilots with considerable flying experience in military, commercial, and private plane operation. Organization founded in 1921.

6 DEC 1934: Radio program, ***The Kraft Music Hall.***

7–13 DEC 1934: Whiteman Orchestra at Paradise Theatre, New York, NY.

13 DEC 1934: Radio program, ***The Kraft Music Hall.***

14 DEC 1934: Paul Whiteman Orchestra—Victor Records: ($32) STAR DUST and BLUE MOONLIGHT and DEEP FOREST and SERENADE TO A WEALTHY WIDOW

15 DEC 1934: Whiteman Orchestra at the Westchester Biltmore.

17 DEC 1934: Paul Whiteman Orchestra—Victor Records:

WHEN I GROW TOO OLD TO DREAM and AU REVOIR L'AMOUR and THE NIGHT IS YOUNG and SINGING A HAPPY SONG

28 DEC–1 JAN 1935: Whiteman Orchestra at the Mount Royal, Montreal, Canada.

JAN 1935: Paramount Pictures film short, ***Broadway Highlights #1,*** brief showing of Whiteman Orchestra.
3 JAN 1935: Radio program, ***The Kraft Music Hall.***
4 JAN 1935: Boston, MA.
10 JAN 1935: Radio program, ***The Kraft Music Hall.***
11–16 JAN 1935: Hippodrome Theatre, Baltimore, MD.
17 JAN 1935: Radio program, ***The Kraft Music Hall.***
20 JAN 1935: Savoy Ballroom, (Harlem), New York, NY.
21–22 JAN 1935: Auto Show, Baltimore, MD.
23 JAN 1935: Paul Whiteman Orchestra—Victor Records:
IF THE MOON TURNS GREEN and I'M KEEPING THOSE KEEPSAKES YOU GAVE ME and LET'S SPILL THE BEANS and WOULD THERE BE LOVE?
24 JAN 1935: Radio program, ***The Kraft Music Hall.***
26–31 JAN 1935: Shea's Buffalo Theatre, Buffalo, NY.
31 JAN 1935: Radio program, ***The Kraft Music Hall.***

1 FEB 1935: Junior League Dance, Richmond, VA.
2 FEB 1935: Dance, Jacksonville, FL.
3 FEB 1935: Midnight Sunday Dance, Orlando, FL.
4 FEB 1935: Dance, St. Petersburg, FL.
5 FEB 1935: Gasparilla Ball, Tampa, FL.
6 FEB 1935: Miami, FL.
7 FEB 1935: Radio program, ***The Kraft Music Hall.***
8 FEB 1935: Cleveland, OH.
14 FEB 1935: Radio program, ***The Kraft Music Hall.***
16 FEB 1935: Waldorf Hotel, New York, NY.
19 FEB 1935: Scranton, PA.
21 FEB 1935: Radio program, ***The Kraft Music Hall.***
22 FEB 1935: Rochester, NY.
28 FEB 1935: Radio program, ***The Kraft Music Hall.***

2 MAR 1935: Erlanger Theatre (afternoon), Atlanta, GA.
Shrine Mosque (evening), Atlanta, GA.

3 MAR 1935: Municipal Auditorium, New Orleans, LA.
7 MAR 1935: Radio program, ***The Kraft Music Hall.***
9 MAR 1935: Erlanger Theatre (afternoon), Atlanta, GA.
Shrine Mosque (evening), Atlanta, GA.
14 MAR 1935: Radio program, ***The Kraft Music Hall.***
14 MAR 1935: Midnight banquet party for Whiteman at Jack Dempsey's Restaurant, New York, NY.
21 MAR 1935: Radio program, ***The Kraft Music Hall.***
28 MAR 1935: Radio program, ***The Kraft Music Hall.***

3 APR 1935: Opened at the Paradise Restaurant, New York, NY.
4 APR 1935: Radio program, ***The Kraft Music Hall.***
11 APR 1935: Radio program, ***The Kraft Music Hall.***
18 APR 1935: Radio program, ***The Kraft Music Hall.***
22 APR 1935: Paul Whiteman Orchestra—Victor Records:
'WAY BACK HOME and NINON and SOMEONE I LOVE and NOW I'M A LADY
24 APR 1935: Roseland Ballroom, New York, NY.
Benefit for unemployed musicians.
25 APR 1935: Radio program, ***The Kraft Music Hall.***

2 MAY 1935: Radio program, ***The Kraft Music Hall.***
9 MAY 1935: Trumbauer purchased an airplane from Roger Wolfe Kahn, kept at Hangar #55 at Roosevelt Field, NY. DH Puss Moth 80-A, type designation. DH Gipsy 105 HP, engine type. DeHavilland Aircraft Co., manufacturer. 2140, serial number.
9 MAY 1935: Radio program, ***The Kraft Music Hall.***
12 MAY 1935: Tram and Mitzi flew to St. Louis to surprise his mother on Mother's Day.
14 MAY 1935: Purchase of aircraft completed.
16 MAY 1935: Sale recorded.
16 MAY 1935: Radio program, ***The Kraft Music Hall.***
17 MAY 1935: Assigned Department of Commerce number 770N.
23 MAY 1935: Radio program, ***The Kraft Music Hall.***
30 MAY 1935: Radio program, ***The Kraft Music Hall.***

6 JUN 1935: Radio program, ***The Kraft Music Hall.***
13 JUN 1935: Radio program, ***The Kraft Music Hall.***

20 JUN 1935: Radio program, ***The Kraft Music Hall.***
24 JUN 1935: Concert for Krager Grocery Chain, Grand Rapids, MI.
27 JUN 1935: Radio program, ***The Kraft Music Hall.***
30 JUN 1935: Danceland, Ocean Beach, New London, CT.

1 JUL 1935: Trumbauer replaced set of piston rings on newly acquired airplane.
4 JUL 1935: Radio program, ***The Kraft Music Hall***
5–7 JUL 1935: Convention Hall, Ashbury Park.
9 JUL 1935: Paul Whiteman Orchestra—Victor Records: DODGING A DIVORCEE and THE DUKE INSISTS and AND THEN SOME and NOBODY'S SWEETHEART NOW and AIN'T MISBEHAVIN' and SUGAR PLUM and NEW O'LEANS
10 JUL 1935: Paul Whiteman Orchestra—Victor Records: I'M SITTIN' HIGH ON A HILLTOP and THANKS A MILLION and I FEEL A SONG COMIN' ON and I'M IN THE MOOD FOR LOVE and GARDEN OF WEED and DARKTOWN STRUTTERS' BALL and CHINA SEAS
11 JUL 1935: Radio program, ***The Kraft Music Hall.***
12 JUL 1935: Carlin's, Baltimore, MD.
14–27 JUL 1935: Manhattan Beach, NY.
18 JUL 1935: Radio program, ***The Kraft Music Hall.***
25 JUL 1935: Radio program, ***The Kraft Music Hall.***
29–30 JUL 1935: Robin Hood Dell, Philadelphia, PA., Concert. Whiteman Orchestra augmented by members of the Philadelphia Symphony Orchestra.

1 AUG 1935: Radio program, ***The Kraft Music Hall.***
8 AUG 1935: Radio program, ***The Kraft Music Hall.***
15 AUG 1935: Ben Marden's Restaurant, Fort Lee, NJ.
15 AUG 1935: Radio program, ***The Kraft Music Hall***
19 AUG 1935: Astoria, Long Island, NY. Start of production on the 20th Century-Fox film, ***Thanks A Million.*** Starring Dick Powell, Ann Dvorak, Fred Allen, and Patsy Kelly. Music by Arthur Johnston, and lyrics by Gus Kahn. While the film was made on the studio lot in Hollywood, Whiteman's sequence was filmed at the Astoria Studios. The band had a brief appearance. Trumbauer was paid $115 for the film.

The Academy of Motion Pictures Arts and Sciences located an unpublished copy of the final screenplay for ***Thanks A Million,*** noting that the Whiteman Orchestra was to make two appearances: in the opening setup of the film, and then very near the end.

The establishing shot of the movie takes place in New York City in the control room of a national radio network. The script reads: ''These scenes to be shot in a real metropolitan radio station.'' The Whiteman Orchestra goes into the theme song THANKS A MILLION.

The second appearance takes place in an auditorium during a political rally. The script continues: ''. . . The People's Party takes great pleasure in presenting Mr. Paul Whiteman and his world-famous orchestra, featuring that lovely singer, Ramona.'' Two numbers were to be played, without interruption: SONG OF INDIA and NEW O'LEANS.

The songs THANKS A MILLION and SONG OF INDIA were generously cut by the film editors.

22 AUG 1935: Radio program, ***The Kraft Music Hall.***
29 AUG 1935: Radio program, ***The Kraft Music Hall.***

5 SEP 1935: Radio program, ***The Kraft Music Hall.***
7 SEP 1935: Paul Whiteman Orchestra—Victor Records: FAREWELL BLUES and STOP, LOOK AND LISTEN and WHY SHOULDN'T I? and ME AND MARIE and WHEN LOVE COMES YOUR WAY and ANNOUNCER'S BLUES and A PICTURE OF ME WITHOUT YOU
12 SEP 1935: Radio program, ***The Kraft Music Hall.***
15 SEP 1935: Trumbauer had pictures made to comply with requests from fan mail. Cost, $225.
19 SEP 1935: Radio program, ***The Kraft Music Hall.***
26 SEP 1935: Radio program, ***The Kraft Music Hall.***
28 SEP 1935: Paul Whiteman Orchestra—Victor Records: JUBILEE MEDLEY (PARTS ONE AND TWO) and TOP HAT MEDLEY (PARTS ONE AND TWO)

29 SEP 1935: Radio program, ***The Magic Key Of Radio*** (premiere program in series).

3 OCT 1935: Radio program, ***The Kraft Music Hall.***
4 OCT 1935: Film, ***Thanks A Million,*** completed.
5 OCT 1935: Trumbauer ''sold'' DH Puss Moth 80-A to William Edward Wade.
9 OCT 1935: Sale recorded.
10 OCT 1935: Radio program, ***The Kraft Music Hall.***
10 OCT 1935: Conde Nast hosted a party at his home, 1040 Park Avenue, for the Broadway opening of ***Porgy & Bess.*** Whiteman Orchestra performed at the party, and George Gershwin, at the piano, played his RHAPSODY IN BLUE with them.
10 OCT 1935: Sale voided citing ''Per New Application'' for Mr. Wade.
17 OCT 1935: Radio program, ***The Kraft Music Hall.***
24 OCT 1935: Radio program, ***The Kraft Music Hall.***
25 OCT 1935: Film, ***Thanks A Million,*** set for release.
26 OCT 1935: DH Puss Moth 80-A reregistered to Mitzi Hill Trumbauer. Sale completed to Mitzi!
31 OCT 1935: Radio program, ***The Kraft Music Hall.***

NOV 1935: ***Down Beat*** magazine contained an article by Warren Scholl entitled ''Trumbauer Still Greatest White Alto Sax Man In The Business!'' Article contained a discussion of Tram, his friendship with Bix, his work for Whiteman, and his experience with the famous hot stars.
7 NOV 1935: Radio program, ***The Kraft Music Hall.***
14 NOV 1935: Film, ***Thanks A Million,*** opened at Loew's State Theatre, New York, and Grauman's Chinese Theatre, Hollywood.
14 NOV 1935: Radio program, ***The Kraft Music Hall.***
15 NOV 1935: Trumbauer purchased additional photographs for fan mail requests. Cost, $100.
16 NOV 1935: Paul Whiteman Orchestra opened at the Hippodrome Theatre for Billy Rose's ***Jumbo.*** Production ran for 233 performances, closing on 18 April 1936. Paramount Pictures film short, ***Broadway Highlights #5*** carried opening night interviews and portions of production in rehearsal.

21 NOV 1935: Radio program, ***The Kraft Music Hall.***
28 NOV 1935: Radio program, ***The Kraft Music Hall.***

2 DEC 1935: Paul Whiteman Orchestra—Victor Records:
I DREAM TOO MUCH and THE JOCKEY ON THE CAROUSEL and I'M THE ECHO and I GOT LOVE
5 DEC 1935: Radio program, ***The Kraft Music Hall.***
Kraft announced that for the next four weeks, the program would be co-hosted by Paul Whiteman from New York, and Bing Crosby from Hollywood.
12 DEC 1935: Radio program, ***The Kraft Music Hall.***
19 DEC 1935: Radio program, ***The Kraft Music Hall.***
26 DEC 1935: Radio program, ***The Kraft Music Hall.*** Whiteman's last program for Kraft.

JAN 1936: Whiteman Orchestra at Le Casino Blue, Biltmore Hotel, New York, NY.
5 JAN 1936: Radio program 9:45–10:30 P.M., ***Musical Varieties.*** Sponsored by Woodbury Soap and Cosmetics, 45 minutes
12 JAN 1936: Radio program 9:45–10:30 P.M., ***Musical Varieties.***
19 JAN 1936: Radio program 9:45–10:30 P.M., ***Musical Varieties.***
26 JAN 1936: Radio program 9:45–10:30 P.M., ***Musical Varieties.***
29 JAN 1936: Frank Trumbauer Orchestra—Brunswick Records:
FLIGHT OF A HAYBAG and BREAKIN' IN A NEW PAIR OF SHOES and ANNOUNCER'S BLUES
30 JAN 1936: Birthday Ball at George Cromwell Centre, Pier 6, Rompkinsville, Staten Island, NY.

2 FEB 1936: Radio program 9:45–10:30 P.M., ***Musical Varieties.***
5 FEB 1936: Frank Trumbauer Orchestra—Brunswick Records:
I HOPE GABRIEL LIKES MY MUSIC
6 FEB 1936: Paul Whiteman Orchestra—Victor Records:
THE WHEEL OF THE WAGON IS BROKEN and AWAKE IN A DREAM and WHAT'S THE NAME OF THAT SONG? and SADDLE YOUR BLUES TO A WILD MUSTANG and LOOK FOR THE SILVER LINING and WAH-HOO
9 FEB 1936: Radio program 9:45–10:30 P.M., ***Musical Varieties.***

16 FEB 1936: Radio program 9:45–10:30 P.M., ***Musical Varieties.***

23 FEB 1936: Radio program 9:45–10:30 P.M., ***Musical Varieties.***

1 MAR 1936: Radio program 9:45–10:30 P.M., ***Musical Varieties.***

8 MAR 1936: Radio program 9:45–10:30 P.M., ***Musical Varieties.***

10 MAR 1936: Paul Whiteman Orchestra—Victor Records:
MY ROMANCE and LITTLE GIRL BLUE and A WALTZ WAS BORN IN VIENNA

10 MAR 1936: The Three T's—Victor Records:
I'SE A MUGGIN'

13 MAR 1936: Paul Whiteman Orchestra—Victor Records:
IT'S GOT TO BE LOVE and THERE'S A SMALL HOTEL and GLOOMY SUNDAY

15 MAR 1936: Radio program 9:45–10:30 P.M., ***Musical Varieties.***

22 MAR 1936: Radio program 9:45–10:30 P.M., ***Musical Varieties.***

29 MAR 1936: Radio program 9:45–10:30 P.M., ***Musical Varieties.***

APR 1936: ***Down Beat*** magazine requested readers to choose "A Real Musician's Band," and offered their choice of: Bix Beiderbecke (crt); Louis Armstrong, Henry "Red" Allen (tpts); Tommy Dorsey, Jack Teagarden, Miff Mole (tbns); Frank Trumbauer (alto); Coleman Hawkins (ten-sx); Adrian Rollini (bs-sx); Benny Goodman (sx/clt); Earl Hines (p); Eddie Lang (gtr); George "Pops" Foster (bs); Gene Krupa (dms).

5 APR 1936: Radio program 9:45–10:30 P.M., ***Musical Varieties.***

12 APR 1936: Radio program 9:45–10:30 P.M., ***Musical Varieties.***

18 APR 1936: Engagement for ***Jumbo*** ended.

19 APR 1936: Radio program 9:45–10:30 P.M., ***Musical Varieties.***

26 APR 1936: Radio program 9:45–10:30 P.M., ***Musical Varieties.***

27 APR 1936: Frank Trumbauer Orchestra—Brunswick Records:
SOMEBODY LOVES ME and THE MAYOR OF ALABAM' and AIN'T MISBEHAVIN' and 'S WONDERFUL

3 MAY 1936: Radio program 9:45–10:30 P.M., ***Musical Varieties.***
10 MAY 1936: Radio program 9:45–10:30 P.M., ***Musical Varieties.***
17 MAY 1936: Radio program 9:45–10:30 P.M., ***Musical Varieties.***
24 MAY 1936: Imperial Theatre, New York, NY. Paul Whiteman Orchestra is one of 17 bands taking part in a three-hour concert. Whiteman featured "The Three T's" on 'S WONDERFUL and BASIN STREET BLUES.
24 MAY 1936: Radio program 9:45–10:30 P.M., ***Musical Varieties.***
31 MAY 1936: Radio program 9:45–10:30 P.M., ***Musical Varieties.***

7 JUN 1936: Radio program 9:45–10:30 P.M., ***Musical Varieties.***
13 JUN 1936: Frank Trumbauer Orchestra—Brunswick Records: I'M AN OLD COWHAND and DIGA DIGA DOO
13 JUN 1936: Frank said to have appeared on Radio Program, ***Saturday Night Swing Club***. No details.
14 JUN 1936: Radio program 9:45–10:30 P.M., ***Musical Varieties.***
21 JUN 1936: Radio program 9:45–10:30 P.M., ***Musical Varieties.***
23–24 JUN 1936: Philadelphia, PA. **Seventh Experiment In Modern American Music**
26 JUN 1936: Paul Whiteman Orchestra—Victor Records: SLAUGHTER ON TENTH AVENUE (PART ONE) and SLAUGHTER ON TENTH AVENUE (PART TWO) and AFTERGLOW and ON YOUR TOES
28 JUN 1936: Radio program 9:45–10:30 P.M., ***Musical Varieties.***

4 JUL 1936: ***Today*** magazine article by Gretta Palmer entitled "Swing It." A story and photographs on Paul Whiteman's Three T's.
5 JUL 1936: Radio program 9:45–10:30 P.M., ***Musical Varieties.***
10 JUL 1936: Orchestra began rehearsals from Casa Mañana, Fort Worth, TX.
12 JUL 1936: Radio program 9:15–10:00 P.M., ***Musical Varieties.*** From Ringside Club, Fort Worth, TX.

16 JUL 1936: Whiteman Orchestra opened at the Casa Mañana in Fort Worth, TX. Band appeared in Billy Rose's ***Frontier Follies*** in celebration of the centennial of Texas' Independence.
19 JUL 1936: Radio program 9:15–10:00 P.M., ***Musical Varieties.***
26 JUL 1936: Radio program 9:15–10:00 P.M., ***Musical Varieties.***

AUG 1936: Casa Mañana, Fort Worth, TX.
2 AUG 1936: Radio program 9:15–10:00 P.M., ***Musical Varieties.***
9 AUG 1936: Radio program 9:15–10:00 P.M., ***Musical Varieties.***
16 AUG 1936: Radio program 9:15–10:00 P.M., ***Musical Varieties.***
23 AUG 1936: Radio program 9:15–10:00 P.M., ***Musical Varieties.***
30 AUG 1936: Radio program 9:15–10:00 P.M., ***Musical Varieties.***

1 SEP 1936: Paul Whiteman Day at the Frontier Centennial.
1 SEP 1936: Casa Mañana, Fort Worth, TX. Contract extended to 15 October.
6 SEP 1936: Radio program 9:15–10:00 P.M., ***Musical Varieties.***
13 SEP 1936: Radio program 9:15–10:00 P.M., ***Musical Varieties.***
20 SEP 1936: Radio program 9:15–10:00 P.M., ***Musical Varieties.***
27 SEP 1936: Radio program 9:15–10:00 P.M., ***Musical Varieties.***
29 SEP 1936: Band left for Austin, TX.
30 SEP 1936: Whiteman Orchestra Concert, University of Texas.

4 OCT 1936: Radio program 9:15–10:00 P.M., ***Musical Varieties.***
9 OCT 1936: Casa Mañana, Fort Worth, TX.
Contract extended to 3 November.
11 OCT 1936: Radio program 9:15–10:00 P.M., ***Musical Varieties.***
18 OCT 1936: Radio program 9:15–10:00 P.M., ***Musical Varieties.***

25 OCT 1936: Radio program 9:15–10:00 P.M., ***Musical Varieties.***

1 NOV 1936: Radio program 9:15–10:00 P.M., ***Musical Varieties.***

2 NOV 1936: Supper Dance (11:00 P.M.), Hotel Texas, Fort Worth, TX.

3 NOV 1936: First Baptist Auditorium (3:30 P.M.), Fort Worth, TX.

3 NOV 1936: Closed at Casa Mañana, Fort Worth, TX.

8 NOV 1936: Radio program 9:15–10:00 P.M., ***Musical Varieties.***

15 NOV 1936: Radio program 9:15–10:00 P.M., ***Musical Varieties.***

15 NOV 1936: The Mosque, Pittsburgh, PA.

22 NOV 1936: Radio program 9:15–10:00 P.M., ***Musical Varieties.***

27–28 NOV 1936: Concert, Philadelphia, PA. Whiteman Orchestra augmented with the Philadelphia Orchestra.

29 NOV 1936: Radio program 9:15–10:00 P.M., ***Musical Varieties.***

DEC 1936: The Three T's personnel: Charlie Teagarden (tpt); Jack Teagarden (tbn); Frank Trumbauer (C-mel/altos); Min Leibrook (bs-sx); Casper Reardon (h); Herm Crone (p); Stan King (dms). Jack Teagarden was ''Big T,'' and Trumbauer was ''Middle T,'' and Charlie Teagarden was ''Little T.''

2 DEC 1936: Opening night at the Hickory House, 144 West 52nd Street, New York, NY. Telephone Circle 7924.

4 DEC 1936: The Three T's premier radio program (remote), WEAF.

6 DEC 1936: Radio program 9:15–10:00 P.M., ***Musical Varieties.***

9 DEC 1936: Casper Reardon asked the Executive Board of the AFM Local #802 to allow him out of his contract with the band. He cited ''already overcrowded schedule'' and suggested Billy Chico as a replacement. Adele Girard was hired.

12 DEC 1936: Radio Program 6:45–7:15 P.M., ***Saturday Night Swing Club.*** The Three T's played BASIN STREET BLUES and JUNK MAN

13 DEC 1936: Radio program 9:15–10:00 P.M., ***Musical Varieties.***
20 DEC 1936: Radio program 9:15–10:00 P.M., ***Musical Varieties.***
27 DEC 1936: Radio program 9:15–10:00 P.M., ***Musical Varieties.*** Last program in series sponsored by Woodbury.

JAN 1937: Trumbauer address: 6336 Bourton Street, Rego Park, Elmhurst, Long Island, NY.
15 JAN 1937: The Three T's radio program (remote), WEAF. Announced as last program on WEAF.
27 JAN 1937: Trumbauer signed a contract with the Hickory House. Hours, 10:30 P.M.-3:30 A.M. daily, except Saturday, 10:30 P.M.-3:00 A.M.. In addition, Sunday afternoon from 3:30–5:45 P.M.. Payment of $2100 for the next three weeks, or $700 weekly for Trumbauer and five additional musicians.
30 JAN 1937: The ***New York Sun*** reported that Trumbauer broadcast every Wednesday and Thursday, over WEAF, after midnight.
12 FEB 1937: WEAF announced the radio program as the last one for Frank Trumbauer's Band.
16 FEB 1937: Hickory House engagement closed.
19 FEB 1937: Trumbauer rejoined the Paul Whiteman Orchestra at the Biscayne Kennel, Miami, FL.

5 MAR 1937: Whiteman engagement closed at the Biscayne Kennel, Miami, FL.
24 MAR 1937: WJZ Radio program, ***A Birthday Salute To Paul Whiteman,*** Combined Whiteman Orchestra with members of the N.B.C. Orchestra. 50 musicians in all.
26 MAR 1937: Paul Whiteman Orchestra—Victor Records: SHALL WE DANCE and FOR YOU
28 MAR 1937: Paul Whiteman Orchestra—Victor Records: ALL POINTS WEST (PART 1) and ALL POINTS WEST (PART 2)

1 APR 1937: Palorama , Schenectady, NY.
9 APR 1937: Opened at the Drake Hotel, Chicago, IL.

6 MAY 1937: Engagement closed at the Drake Hotel, Chicago, IL.
13–19 MAY 1937: Loew's State Theatre, New York, NY.

21–27 MAY 1937: Capitol Theatre, Washington, DC.
29 MAY 1937: ''Lumina'' W. L. I. dance, Wilmington, DE.
30 MAY 1937: Academy Of Music, Roanoke, VA.
Cavalier Beach , Virginia Beach, VA.

3 JUN 1937: Melody Hill, Dubuque, IA.
4–10 JUN 1937: RKO Palace Theatre, Chicago, IL.
12 JUN 1937: Columbus, OH.
15 JUN 1937: Lake Brady Park.
26 JUN 1937: Whiteman Orchestra opened at the Casa Mañana, Fort Worth, TX.
30 JUN 1937: NBC Summer Radio Series was presented from the auditorium at the Fort Worth Frontier Fiesta. Last mention of Trumbauer's name in Fort Worth newspapers.

1 JUL 1937: Trumbauer left Paul Whiteman's Orchestra.
13 JUL 1937: Trumbauer transferred to Los Angeles, CA., AFM Local #47. Union restrictions required a three-month waiting period before he could begin employment. Trumbauer listed his address as: 1873 Midvale Avenue, West Los Angeles, CA.

AUG 1937: Trumbauer still observing waiting period.

9 SEP 1937: Trumbauer applied for renewal of his pilot's license, listing total flying hours as 1080, but only 15 in the past six months. Approved on 21 September by George Gay.
28 SEP 1937: Trumbauer was a member of the George Stoll Orchestra that appeared on the Jack Oakie program as part of the hour long ***Camel Caravan,*** 9:30–10:30 P.M. Benny Goodman's Orchestra did the final half hour from New York. CBS radio.

OCT 1937: Trumbauer continued as a member of George Stoll's Orchestra on ***Camel Caravan.***

NOV 1937: ***Down Beat***, November 1937, page 7, carried an article on Trumbauer.

DEC 1937: ***Tempo Magazine,*** published by AFM Local #47, carried an article on Frank Trumbauer by Hal Holly. Article states that Trumbauer is continuing to play radio programs, and while he does not list any specific programs, it is known that he continued on ***Camel Caravan.*** This program, with Jack Oakie as master of ceremonies, was also known as ***Jack Oakie's College*** and ***The Jack Oakie College Of Musical Knowledge.***

It is often suggested that Trumbauer worked in various movie studio orchestras during his 1937–1938 stay in Los Angeles. Stephen LaVere did an extensive search of all movie studio payrolls for this period and was unable to locate Trumbauer's name.

15 DEC 1937: Frank Trumbauer Orchestra—Standard Transcriptions:
ITCHOLA and IN A MIST and TEMPO TAKES A HOLIDAY and BODY AND SOUL and WILDCAT and TIGER RAG FANTASY and PUT ON YOUR OLD GRAY BONNET and BIG BUTTER AND EGG MAN and BOUNCING BALL and NO RETARD and SPAGENZE/HEAT WAVE and CHANSONETTE and YOU'RE A SWEETHEART and I HIT A NEW HIGH and JUST A SWEET OLD GENT AND A QUAINT OLD LADY and I DOUBLE DARE YOU and CAN'T TEACH MY OLD HEART NEW TRICKS and WHEN LIGHTS ARE LOW and MY DAY and NAUGHTY NAUGHTY and MY FINE FEATHERED FRIEND and YOU TOOK THE WORDS RIGHT OUT OF MY MOUTH and ROCKIN' THE TOWN and A STRANGE LONELINESS

JAN 1938: Trumbauer listed his address as: 1873 Midvale Avenue, West Los Angeles, CA.

In addition to doing the weekly Jack Oakie ***Camel Caravan*** radio program, Trumbauer appeared with Leonid Leonardi's Orchestra over KFWB radio during the next few months.

28 JAN 1938: Frank Trumbauer Orchestra—Standard Transcriptions:
ODE TO A CHIMNEY SWEEPER and HOME LIFE OF THE SNORF and HERJE KATI and BLUE MONDAY/SINGIN' THE BLUES and THE JUBA and BRING BACK MY BON-

NIE TO ME and SHAG ON DOWN and HOT SPELL and LOVE IS HERE TO STAY and I WAS DOING ALL RIGHT and ROMANCE IN THE RAIN and ON THE SENTIMENTAL SIDE and TEA FOR TWO and RAISIN' THE ROOF and OL' MAN RIVER (as OLD MAN RIVER) and NIGHT WILL FALL

11 FEB 1938: Frank Trumbauer Orchestra—Standard Transcriptions:
IT'S WONDERFUL and ALWAYS AND ALWAYS and OUTSIDE OF PARADISE and YOU APPEAL TO ME and TABOO and HOMETOWN and CHUCK A BOOM and THE ONE I LOVE and TONIGHT WE LOVE and GOODNIGHT ANGEL and THE GYPSY IN MY SOUL and DID AN ANGEL KISS YOU and MY HEART IS TAKING LESSONS and BY MYSELF and HILLBILLY FROM TENTH AVENUE and DON'T CRY, SWEETHEART, DON'T CRY

8 MAR 1938: Rockwell-O'Keefe, Inc., Artists' Representative, 9028 Sunset Boulevard, Hollywood, CA., placed the following advertisement in various newspapers and publications, together with a picture of Trumbauer: "Frankie Trumbauer, who gave up his sax for a business career, will soon return to the fold leading his own band under Rockwell-O'Keefe."

17 MAR 1938: Frank Trumbauer and his Orchestra opened at the Biltmore Hotel, Los Angeles, CA. Baron Long, veteran hotel man, decided to launch a new band, after auditioning several orchestras. Trumbauer and Mannie Klein were listed as coleaders. Personnel: Mannie Klein, Joe Meyer, Bill Shaw (tpts); Joe Yukl, Lank Menge (tbns); Frank Trumbauer, Len Conn, Len Kavach, Lyall Bowen, Jimmy Oliver (reeds); Al Goering (p); Bob Hemphill (gtr); Russ Morhoff (bs); Ward Archer (dms); Deane Janis, Dave Saxon (vcs).

22 MAR 1938: The Jack Oakie ***Camel Caravan*** program ended, but Trumbauer probably ended his stay the previous week.

30 MAR 1938: Frank Trumbauer Orchestra—Standard Transcriptions:
STARS AND STRIPES FOREVER and IRISH WASHER WOMAN and FLIGHT OF A HAY BAG and MIDNIGHT OIL and THIS TIME IT'S REAL and MOMENTS LIKE THIS

and ROMANCE IN THE DARK and LOST AND FOUND and SHADOWS ON THE MOON and DON'T BE THAT WAY and CRY BABY CRY and WHERE HAVE WE MET BEFORE and HOW'DJA LIKE TO LOVE ME and IN A HAPPY FRAME OF MINE and TWO SHADOWS and WHO ARE WE TO SAY?

APR 1938: Radio remote broadcasts from the Biltmore Hotel, Los Angeles, CA., now set as:
NBC Blue Network: Thursday 7:30 P.M.
NBC Red Network (West Coast to Chicago) Monday and Tuesday 9:30 P.M.
NBC Blue Network (West Coast only) Friday 9:30 P.M. and Saturday 10:00 P.M.

APR 1938: ***Orchestra World*** spelled Trumbauer's last name as "Trombar." Various other publications and newspaper advertisements also used the same spelling. Tram changed the spelling. The spelling was used on his music stands, in the advertisements, and the Keystone issues of the Standard transcriptions.

12 APR 1938: In requesting a renewal of his pilot's license, Trumbauer listed the following: Ryan M.N.C. 17300, 12 hours 20 minutes; Cub. Con. N.C. 17583, 14 hours 20 minutes; Standard J. 15 N.C. 8756, 18 hours 30 minutes; Kinner Kinner 165 N.C. 14964, 47 hours 30 minutes; Waco J. 5 N. C. 8538, 17 hours 15 minutes.

14 APR 1938: Request submitted.

19 APR 1938: Request approved.

20 APR 1938: Frank Trumbauer Orchestra—Standard Transcriptions:
THERE'S A BOY IN HARLEM and HOW CAN YOU FORGET and I CAN'T FACE THE MUSIC and SOMETHING TELLS ME and BLUE HOLIDAY/SINGIN' THE BLUES and DO YOU KEN JOHN PEEL? and COLORADO SUNSET and A HEAVENLY PARTY and YOU'D BETTER CHANGE YOUR TUNE and IF DREAMS COME TRUE and AT YOUR BECK AND CALL and AN OLD STRAW HAT and YES, THERE AIN'T NO MOONLIGHT and WHEN THE STARS GO TO SLEEP and JUST AN ERROR IN THE NEWS and THE NIGHT YOU SAID GOOD-BYE and SO LITTLE

TIME and TELEVISION/I SAW YOU LAST NIGHT and NEVER NEVER LAND FANTASY and DIPPER MOUTH BLUES and PORTRAIT OF A PRETZEL

25 APR 1938: Frank Trumbauer Orchestra—Electro Vox Recording Studios Los Angeles, CA. THE NIGHT YOU SAID GOOD-BYE

30 APR 1938: Radio program, ***Saturday Night Swing Session***, KNX, Los Angeles, CA. Bill Goodwin, announcer. All music provided by Frank Trumbauer's Orchestra: MINNIE HA HA and NICE WORK IF YOU CAN GET IT (vc by Maxine Sullivan) and A BOY, A GIRL, AND A LAMPLIGHT (vc by Skinnay Ennis) and PORTRAIT OF A PRETZEL and NOBODY'S SWEETHEART (radio interference, uncertain of name of vocalist) and YOU TOOK ADVANTAGE OF ME (Johnny Mercer) and HAPPY BIRTHDAY TO CBS and LOCH LOMOND (vc by Maxine Sullivan) and STARS AND STRIPES FOREVER and TEMPO TAKES A HOLIDAY.

13 MAY 1938: Trumbauer wrote to Fred D. Fagg, Jr., Director of Air Commerce, Department of Commerce, Washington, DC, to inform him that on his last renewal of his Transport Pilot's License, which was renewed by Inspector Dake at Burbank Airport, a mixup occurred in Washington, and they sent him a Student Pilot Certificate. Tram requested the mistake be corrected "at the earliest possible moment." The matter was corrected and new license issued 28 June.

25 MAY 1938: Frank Trumbauer Orchestra—Standard Transcriptions:
THERE'S RAIN IN MY EYES and SWINGING ANNIE LAURIE THROUGH THE RYE and SAYS MY HEART and IT'S THE LITTLE THINGS THAT COUNT and COWBOY FROM BROOKLYN and YOU LEAVE ME BREATHLESS and CATHEDRAL IN THE PINES and SKRONTCH and SO YOU LEFT ME FOR THE LEADER OF A SWING BAND and NEGLECTED and IN THE NEIGHBORHOOD OF HEAVEN and OH MA MA! THE BUTCHER BOY and TONIGHT WILL LIVE and IT'S THE DREAMER IN ME and LITTLE LADY MAKE BELIEVE and MOONSHINE OVER KENTUCKY

JUN 1938: Radio remote broadcasts from the Biltmore Hotel, Los Angeles, CA., now changed to:
NBC Blue Network, Friday, 8:00 P.M.
NBC Red Network (West Coast to Chicago), Monday, 9:00 P.M.
NBC Blue Network (West Coast only), Monday-Thursday, 11:00 P.M.
NBC Blue Network (West Coast only), Saturday, 10:30 P.M.

8 JUL 1938: Frank Trumbauer Orchestra—Standard Transcriptions:
ONE KISS OF LOVE and LOST IN MEDITATION and ISN'T IT WONDERFUL, ISN'T IT SWELL and FLAT FOOT FLOOGIE and NATIONAL EMBLEM MARCH and BEETLE AT LARGE and ALEXANDER'S RAGTIME BAND and RUSTLE OF SWING and LATIN QUARTER and SMALL FRY and SPRING IS HERE and I LIKE MUSIC and MY WALKING STICK and THERE'S A FAR AWAY LOOK IN YOUR EYES and NOW IT CAN BE TOLD and LET'S BREAK THE GOOD NEWS and I'LL DREAM TONIGHT and YOU AND MUSIC and YOU AND ME and I'LL STILL BE LOVING YOU

9 JUL 1938: NBC Radio program. Victor Records planned to use these airchecks in an LP album, but at the time of publication they remain unissued. NATIONAL EMBLEM MARCH and TEMPO TAKES A HOLIDAY and PORTRAIT OF A PRETZEL and TIGER RAG FANTASY

31 JUL 1938: Third Hollywood Swing Concert, sponsored by AFM Local #47 and the American Legion (Musicians' Post 424), at the Palomar Ballroom, Vermont at Second. Twenty-one entertainers listed, and Trumbauer's Orchestra appeared as number 14.

AUG 1938: Band still at the Biltmore Hotel, Los Angeles, CA.

SEP 1938: Trumbauer and his family living at 166 Barlock, West Los Angeles, CA. Telephone 38419.

SEP 1938: Radio remote broadcasts from the Biltmore Hotel, Los Angeles, CA., now changed to:
NBC Blue Network, Friday 8:00 P.M.

NBC Red Network (West Coast to Chicago), Monday and Thursday, 9:00 P.M.

NBC Blue Network (West Coast only), Monday-Thursday, 11:00 P.M.

NBC Blue Network (West Coast only), Saturday, 10:30 P.M.

10 SEP 1938: Paul Whiteman's article in ***Collier's*** magazine, entitled "All American Swing Band," listed his choices for the top musicians of the day: Mannie Klein, Charlie Teagarden, Roy Eldridge, Louis Armstrong (tpts); Tommy Dorsey, Jack Teagarden, Jack Jenny (tbns); Benny Goodman, Artie Shaw (clts); Jimmy Dorsey, Benny Carter (altos); Chu Berry, Eddie Miller (ten-sxs); Frank Trumbauer (C-mel); Joe Venuti, Al Duffy, Matt Malneck, Eddie South (vns); Tito (acc); Art Tatum, Bob Zurke (ps); Carl Kress (gtr); Adrian Rollini (vb); Bobby Haggart (bs); Gene Krupa, Ray Bauduc (dms).

14 SEP 1938: Closed at the Biltmore Hotel, Los Angeles, CA.

15 SEP 1938: Trumbauer applied for renewal of his Commercial Pilot's License, which offered a rating for Flight Instructor of L-Land and 2S-Land aircraft. Tram listed students that he instructed as Ward Archer, Paul Mertz, and Charles LaVere, using aircraft N.C. 612M.

Stephen LaVere has family photographs taken on 10 June 1938 at the Santa Monica Airport showing his father (Charles) and Trumbauer flying a Fleet Warner Biplane.

SEP 1938: Weekly orchestra payroll, $1021.

Eddie Wade (first tpt, $92); Matt Hendrickson (second tpt, $60); Harold Trumbia, replaced by Max Tiff after one night (third tpt, $55); John Smith (first tbn, $68); Santo Pecora (second tbn, $75); John Ross (first alto, $70); Jimmy Oliver (clt/bar-sx, $83); Don Bonnee (clt/third alto, $85); Johnny Hamilton (tenor, $110); Buddy Cole (p, $85); Russ Soule (gtr, $55); Bill Jones (bs, $63); John Zenor (dms, $70); Vonnie King (vc, $50); Jo (Mrs. Johnny Hamilton) Hopkins (vc, salary included in husband's total); Fred Seymour (band manager, salary not listed).

Amount of money shown in parenthesis on each date denotes

amount paid to Trumbauer for that engagement. All bookings handled by Rockwell-O'Keefe Agency.

16 SEP 1938: Rainbow, Fresno, CA. ($300)
17 SEP 1938: Sweets, Sacramento, CA. ($350)
18 SEP 1938: Sweets, Sacramento, CA. ($350)
19 SEP 1938: Ambassador Ballroom, San Francisco, CA. ($250)
20 SEP 1938: Day off
21 SEP 1938: El Patio, Reno, NV. ($300)
22 SEP 1938: Day off
23 SEP 1938: Auditorium, Grass Valley, CA. ($275)
24 SEP 1938: Auditorium, San Jose, CA. ($350)
25 SEP 1938: Day off
26 SEP 1938: Coconut Grove, Salt Lake City, UT. ($225)
27–28 SEP 1938: Day off
29 SEP 1938: Lib's Park, Hastings, NE. ($350)
30 SEP 1938: Abilene, KS. ($300)

OCT 1938: On 5 October, George Simon of ***Metronome*** magazine, sent a wire to Trumbauer, which was received on 8 October. Simon requested that Tram write an article on Bix for their forthcoming November issue. Trumbauer consented and sent along the article on October 15 with the understanding that ***Metronome*** may publish the article but that Trumbauer retained the property rights to the material. The article on Bix was in the 1 November 1938 issue.
1 OCT 1938: Student Union, Lincoln, NE. ($350)
7 OCT 1938: University of Iowa Homecoming, Iowa City, IA. ($325)
8 OCT 1938: Pla Mor Ballroom, Kansas City, MO. ($300)
13 OCT 1938: Calyx Club Dance, Dallas, TX. ($108.50)
14–20 OCT 1938: Century Room of Adolphus Hotel, Dallas, TX. ($1750)
Personnel changes during Adolphus Hotel engagement: Carl Maus replaced John ''Doc'' Zenor (dms). John later became a chiropractor.
21–27 OCT 1938: Century Room of Adolphus, Dallas, TX. ($1750)
28 OCT–3 NOV 1938: Century Room of Adolphus, Dallas, TX. ($1750)

4–8 NOV 1938: Century Room of Adolphus Hotel, Dallas, TX. ($1350)
10 NOV 1938: Palm Isle, Longview, TX. ($200)
11 NOV 1938: ''Bat'' Gormley's Night Club, Lake Charles, LA. ($350)
12 NOV 1938: Texas Christian University, Ft. Worth, TX. ($350)
18 NOV 1938: ZTA Sorority (5:00–8:00 P.M.), Texas Christian University, Ft. Worth, TX. ($350)
18 NOV 1938: Union Building (9:00 P.M.-1:00 A.M.), Austin, TX. ($400)
19 NOV 1938: Goodhue Hotel, Port Arthur, TX. ($400)
20 NOV 1938: Palacios, TX. ($250)
23 NOV 1938: Shreveport Country Club, Shreveport, LA. ($350)
24 NOV 1938: Shreveport Country Club, Shreveport, LA. ($350)
25 NOV–8 DEC 1938: Rainbow Terrace of St. Anthony Hotel, San Antonio, TX. ($1500)
26 NOV 1938: Article, by Joe Kayser, in ***Billboard*** mentions Trumbauer as having been a member of his band.

1 DEC 1938: Vonnie King (vc) and Buddy Cole (p) left the band. Arnold Bliesner (p) added.
9 DEC 1938: University of Texas, Austin, TX. ($450)
10 DEC 1938: Corpus Christie Country Club, Corpus Christie, TX. ($350)
15–17 DEC 1938: Grand Theatre, Evansville, IN. ($945)
18 DEC 1938: Casa Loma Ballroom, St. Louis, MO. ($250)
23 DEC 1938: Evansville Country Club, Evansville, IN. ($250)
24 DEC 1938: Roberts Hotel, Muncie, IN. ($350)
25 DEC 1938: Savoy Ballroom, Chicago, IL. ($385)
26 DEC 1938: Casino (195 East Delaware), Chicago, IL. ($675)
27 DEC 1938: Auditorium, Saginaw, MI. ($500)
29 DEC 1938: Riverside, Green Bay, WI. ($300)
30–31 DEC 1938: Congress Hotel, Chicago, IL. ($1171)
''Spend New Year's Eve at the Congress Hotel on Michigan Boulevard. Supper—Show—Favors. $7.50 per person. Telephone: Harrison 3800.''

3 JAN 1939: Trumbauer paid his Chicago AFM Local #10 union dues.
6–9 JAN 1939: Paramount Theatre, Ft. Wayne, IN. ($1400)

13 JAN 1939: Michigan State University Sophomore Prom, Lansing, MI. ($400)
14 JAN 1939: Civic Auditorium, Grand Rapids, MI. ($350)
15 JAN 1939: Wisconsin Roof, Milwaukee, WI. ($300)
19–21 JAN 1939: Michigan Theatre, Jackson, MI. ($700)
22 JAN 1939: Pantheon Theatre, Vincennes, IN. ($300)
22 JAN 1939: Jo Hopkins (vocalist) and John Hamilton (sx) left, after playing the Pantheon Theatre. Bob McCracken (sx) added. Jean Webb (vc) joins the band just prior to 28 January.
28 JAN 1939: University of Indiana, Bloomington, IN. ($400)
29 JAN 1939: Lincoln Theatre, Decatur, IL. ($275)
30 JAN 1939: S.I.N.U. Gym, Carbondale, IL. ($300)

4 FEB 1939: University of Nebraska Interfraternity Ball, Lincoln, NE. ($400). Trumbauer's band engages in a ''Battle Of The Bands'' with Anson Weeks's Orchestra, also hired for the event. Student newspaper clearly proclaims the winner—Frank Trumbauer!
10 FEB 1939: University of Minnesota Junior Ball at Nicollet Hotel, Minneapolis, MN. ($??)
11 FEB–10 MAR 1939: The Terrace Room of Nicollet Hotel, Minneapolis, MN.($1500 per week)
16 FEB 1939: Hobart Bosworth, dean of motion picture actors, visited Nichollet Hotel and has several photographs taken with Trumbauer for local newspapers.

11 MAR 1939: Civic Auditorium, Rochester, MN. ($400)
15 MAR 1939: Mahomet, IL. ($250)
17 MAR 1939: University of Missouri, Columbia, MO. ($350)
18 MAR 1939: University of Missouri Engineers Ball, Columbia, MO. ($350)
22 MAR 1939: New York. Trumbauer appeared as a ''guest artist'' and was paid $230. Details unknown at time of publication.
23 MAR 1939: St. Louis, MO. Trumbauer applied for renewal of his commercial pilot's license, listing his address as 166 Barlock, Los Angeles, CA. Tram supplied medical records showing him to be in good health, and noted that in the last six months he only devoted 32 hours to flying. Certificate renewed on March 31.

25 MAR 1939: DePauw University Junior Ball, Greencastle, IN. ($450) Personnel changes: Guy Anderson replaced Don Bonnee. John Reynolds replaced ''Pec'' Pecora.

8 APR 1939: University Club, Tulsa, OK. ($450)
11 APR 1939: Galvez Hotel, Galveston, TX. ($350)
13 APR 1939: Auditorium, Goliad, TX. ($300)
14 APR 1939: Women's Federation Club, Austin, TX. ($400)
15 APR 1939: Bluebonnet Festival, Navasota, TX. ($200)
20 APR 1939: Oklahoma A & M Dance, Stillwater, OK. ($450)
21 APR 1939: Country Club, Austin, TX. ($450)
26 APR 1939: Liberty Hall, El Paso, TX. ($550)
27 APR 1939: Hobbs, NM. ($250)
28–30 APR 1939: Lake Worth Casino, Ft. Worth, TX. ($650)

5 MAY 1939: Mississippi State College, Starksville, MS. ($500)
6 MAY 1939: Mississippi State College, Starksville, MS. ($500)
9 MAY 1939: Tune Town Ballroom, St. Louis, MO. ($200)
11 MAY 1939: Tune Town Ballroom, St. Louis, MO. ($200)
12 MAY 1939: Phi Gamma Delta House, Columbia, MO. ($375)
13 MAY 1939: Tune Town Ballroom, St. Louis, MO. ($200)
14 MAY 1939: Tune Town Ballroom, St. Louis, MO. ($200)
16 MAY 1939: Tune Town Ballroom, St. Louis, MO. ($200)
17 MAY 1939: Coliseum, Benld, IL. ($200)
18 MAY 1939: Tune Town Ballroom, St. Louis, MO. ($200)
20 MAY 1939: Tune Town Ballroom, St. Louis, MO. ($200)
21 MAY 1939: Tune Town Ballroom, St. Louis, MO. ($200)

Trumbauer signed a contract with the management of Carsonia Park in Reading, PA. for the next four weeks. Tram would provide 14 men and a girl singer for evening dancing for the first two days, and afternoon and evening dancing the third day. Carsonia Park would arrange for radio programs during each evening dance performance, plus a weekly check of $750.

27 MAY 1939: Carsonia Park, Reading, PA. ($250)
28 MAY 1939: Carsonia Park, Reading, PA. ($250)
29 MAY 1939: New Yorker Hotel, New York, NY. ($300)
30 MAY 1939: Carsonia Park, Reading, PA. ($250)

JUN 1939: By mutual agreement with the management of Carsonia Park, the afternoon dance was discontinued. Adjustment in contract resulted in $100 less, but the radio programs continued as before.
3 JUN 1939: Carsonia Park, Reading, PA. ($250)
4 JUN 1939: Carsonia Park, Reading, PA. ($250)
5 JUN 1939: New Yorker Hotel, New York, NY. ($300)
6 JUN 1939: Copley Plaza Hotel, Boston, MA. ($400)
7 JUN 1939: Carsonia Park, Reading, PA. ($150)
8 JUN 1939: Lakewood, Mahoney City, PA. ($250)
10 JUN 1939: Carsonia Park, Reading, PA. ($250)
11 JUN 1939: Carsonia Park, Reading, PA. ($250)
12 JUN 1939: New Yorker Hotel, New York, NY. ($300)
13 JUN 1939: Irem Country Club, Dallas, PA. ($250)
14 JUN 1939: Carsonia Park, Reading, PA. ($150)
16 JUN 1939: Cornell University Ball at Willard Straight Hall, Ithaca, NY. ($550)
17 JUN 1939: Carsonia Park, Reading, PA. ($250)
18 JUN 1939: Carsonia Park, Reading, PA. ($250)
19 JUN 1939: New Yorker Hotel, New York, NY. ($300)
21 JUN 1939: Carsonia Park, Reading, PA. ($150)
24 JUN 1939: Filmont Country Club, Philadelphia, PA. ($300)

1 JUL 1939: Hershey Park, Hershey, PA. ($300)
3 JUL 1939: Century Park, White Plains, NY. ($500)
5–10 JUL 1939: Hamids Park, Atlantic City, NJ. ($857)
Eddie Wade (tpt) left, replaced by Garner Clark.

16 AUG–5 SEP 1939: Lake Worth Casino, Fort Worth, TX. ($1150 per week)

SEP 1939: 166 Barlock, West Los Angeles, CA.

OCT 1939: Lived at mother's home: 6842 Arthur, St. Louis, MO.

NOV 1939: Band personnel: Howard Lamont, Dick Dunne, Wayne Williams (tpts); Del Melton, Bernie Bahr (tbns); Frank Trumbauer (C-mel/altos); Johnny Ross (first alto); Connie Blessing (third alto); Rudy Boyer (ten-sx); Joe Schles (bar-sx);

Joe Levin (p); Jess Bourgoise (bs); Joe Becker (dms). The band did not have a girl singer. Rudy Boyer felt that he joined the band "on the road" but could not recall whom he replaced.

1 NOV 1939: Letter sent to van lines about eight-day delay in delivering instruments.

22 NOV 1939: Lansing, MI. ($350)

25 NOV 1939: Green Bay, WI. ($300)

26 NOV 1939: Green Bay, WI. ($250)

1 DEC 1939: Kirksville, MO. ($200)

2 DEC 1939: Auditorium Dance, Kansas City, MO. ($360)

6 DEC 1939: Kirksville, MO. ($250)

8 DEC 1939: Brookings, SD. ($450)

9 DEC 1939: Rapid City, SD. ($250)

11 DEC 1939: Ed Patterson Hotel, Bismarck, ND. ($400)

12 DEC 1939: Enderlin, ND. ($250)
About this time, Rene Favre replaced Joe Levin (p).

13 DEC 1939: Pencil drawing of Tram at 610 4th Street, Sioux City, SD.

15 DEC 1939: Corn Husker Hotel, Lincoln, NE.
Band checked in for three-day stay.

16 DEC 1939: Coliseum Theatre, Lincoln, NE. ($400)

18 DEC 1939: Springfield, IL. ($400)

22–26 DEC 1939: Moana Ballroom, Tulsa, OK.
Contracted for $1550, but not paid for job. See text.

29 DEC 1939: Mayfield, KY. ($400)

30 DEC 1939: Hoosier Athletic Club, Indianapolis, IN. ($350)

31 DEC 1939: Castle Farms, Cincinnati, OH. ($500)

1 JAN 1940: Trianon Ballroom, Cleveland, OH. ($250)

6 JAN 1940: Ames, IA. ($400)

20 JAN 1940: Cincinnati, OH. ($350)

24–28 JAN 1940: Graystone Ballroom, Detroit, MI. (25 JAN was off day).($780 total receipts for all four dates)

FEB 1940: February issue of ***Cosmopolitan*** magazine carried an article by Dorothy Kilgallen entitled "Swing Set" in which she selected her "Dream Band Of All Time." Louis Armstrong, Bix Beiderbecke, "King" Oliver (tpts); Miff Mole, Jimmy Harrison, Tommy Dorsey (tbns); Benny Goodman (clt); Frank

Trumbauer, Coleman Hawkins, Benny Carter, Jimmy Dorsey (sxs); Earl Hines (p); Eddie Lang (gtr); "Pops" Foster (bs); "Baby" Dodds (dms).

3 FEB 1940: Cincinnati, OH. ($265)

3 FEB 1940: Muncie, IN. While the band was in Cincinnati, Tram made a "guest appearance" in Muncie and was paid $90. Details unknown.

Trumbauer visited the home of Herman "Trigger" Alpert (4013 Boulevard Place) and hired him to replace Jesse Bourgoise (bs).

4 FEB 1940: Indianapolis, IN. ($350)
6 FEB 1940: Ottumwa, IA. ($300)
10 FEB 1940: Tromar Ballroom, Des Moines, IA. ($275)
11 FEB 1940: Trianon Ballroom, Terre Haute, IN. ($200)
14 FEB 1940: Marion, IL. ($200)
16 FEB 1940: Lansing, MI. ($450)
17 FEB 1940: Castle Farms, Cincinnati, OH. ($300)
18 FEB 1940: Castle Farms, Cincinnati, OH. ($300)
22–23 FEB 1940: Varsity Records, New York, NY. ($900)

15 MAR 1940: Address listed as 6842 Arthur, St. Louis, MO. Telephone: Sterling 1468.

18 APR 1940: International Oil Show, Tulsa, OK. Booked for one week. Trumbauer fronted the Bobby Pope Orchestra from Kansas City. Engagement lasted five days.

A national magazine reported in their April issue that Saul Gilbert (dms) would be joining Trumbauer's Orchestra for a May tour of the southwest. Gilbert's letter of October 1, 1990, reported that the tour never materialized. Instead, Mr. Gilbert returned to the Boston area and worked with various society bands.

5 JUN 1940: Applied to United States Civil Service Commission. Seeking employment at Kansas City, MO. (Fifth Region) with Civil Aeronautics Authority as a "Private Flying Specialist" with an annual salary of $3,200. Approved June 6, and Oath of Office was taken on June 10.

26 JUN 1940: Newspaper article found in Tram's scrapbook with this date, origin unknown, mentioned that Trumbauer had gone from ''Saxophone'' Ace To Air Career.

24 JUL 1940: Trumbauer was living at Boulevard Manor Hotel in Kansas City.

10 SEP 1940: Trumbauer applied from Private Flying Specialist to Private Flying Development Division and Ground School Supervisor. Home address: 5538 Park Avenue, Kansas City. Telephone: JA 2379.

11 SEP 1940: Ratings in the examination taken at Kansas City: General Test, 62.25%; Experience and Fitness, 73%; Average Percentage, 68.30%; Veteran (5 points), 73.30%. Trumbauer average needed to pass was 70.

1 NOV 1940: Article in ***Down Beat***, ''Immortals Of Jazz.''

22 NOV 1940: Report of ratings given to Trumbauer.

20 DEC 1940: Certificate 683-40 issued to Frank Trumbauer at his office of employment, 9th floor, City Hall, Kansas City, MO. Listed Trumbauer as ''Mechanic for both aircraft and aircraft engine.'' Test score, 85.

31 DEC 1940: Resignation, for purpose of promotion, on January 1, 1941.

Nature of Action: Discharge, without prejudice.

Position of: Private Flying Specialist ($3,200 per annum).

Department: Civil Pilot Training Service.

Station: Kansas City, MO. (Fifth Region).

Notation: ''Mr. Trumbauer is being discharged from the above position on the date previous to the effect date of his probational appointment as Assistant Aeronautical Inspector, CAF-9, $3,200 per annum, Kansas City, MO.''

1 JAN 1941: Probation appointment to Assistant Aeronautics Inspector, Des Moines, IA. Oath of office taken on January 2. Address listed as: 207 A Old Federal Building, Des Moines, IA. Telephone 4-4770. Living at 677 32nd Street.

17 FEB 1941: Medical examination given by Everett M. George, MD, U.S. Naval Recruiting Station, Des Moines, IA. General: 5′ 11-1/2″ (height); 171 pounds (clothed); 154 pounds (without clothes). Notation regarding Trumbauer's heart stated: ''Systolic murmur at apex, transmitted; compensated.'' Trumbauer's blood pressure was noted as 116 (systolic) over 74 (diastolic). Pulse rate of 86, and after ''X'' minutes of exercise rose to 112, but fell to 84 after a two-minute rest.

31 MAR 1941: Trumbauer applied for employment in Kansas City, noting his current position as ''on duty Des Moines, Iowa, Assistant Aeronautical Inspector.''

9 APR 1941: Davenport, IA. Trumbauer in town to inform the flight instructors of CAA programs and policies.

10 APR 1941: Davenport, IA. Trumbauer visited with Mr. and Mrs. C. B.(Bix's brother) Beiderbecke.

1 MAY 1941: Promoted to Associate Aeronautics Inspector, Kansas City, MO. Rating: CAF-10 ($3,500 per annum).

16 JUN 1941: Promoted to Aeronautics Inspectors. CAF-11 ($3,800 per annum).

4 OCT 1941: Personnel affidavit (Standard Form #47—Approved by the Bureau of the Budget, May 15, 1941. The standard government allegiance oath form). Personnel affidavit signed by Trumbauer read, in part, ''. . . during such time as I am an employee of the Federal Government, I will not advocate nor become a member of any political party or organization that advocates the overthrow of the Government of the United States by force or violence.''

5 APR 1942: Article in ***Down Beat*** on Trumbauer entitled: ''Keep 'Em Flying.''

2 MAY 1942: Test pressing found in Trumbauer's effects.
SHAME ON ME and MY LOST LOVE

5 MAY 1942: Promotion and transfer: Position from Aeronautical Inspector to Principal Flight Supervisor. Grade: CAF-11 ($3,800 per annum) to CAF-12 ($4,600 per annum). Headquarters: District No. 1, Kansas City, MO. (Fifth Region). Effective date: June 3, 1942.

Memo notation: ''It is necessary to establish a position additional identical to that held by Mr. Metzger due to the increase in the volume of work involving equivalent duties and responsibilities. It is therefore recommended that a new position of Principal Flight Supervisor be established, and as Mr. Trumbauer is considered the best qualified person available, his appointment thereto is recommended. At the completion of this assignment, Mr. Trumbauer will be reassigned to his former position.'' Approval recommended by Leonard W. Jurden, Regional Manager.

1 SEP–3 NOV 1942: Served in Washington, DC, as assistant to Fred Lanter, chief of the division of the CAA.

19 DEC 1942: Trumbauer wrote to Carl J. Christenson, Senior Aeronautical Inspector, Des Moines, Iowa, requesting assistance in arranging a transfer from his present duties to a position in which he could help with the war effort.

12 JAN 1943: Earl Southee, Chief, Standards Division, CAA War Training Service, replied to Trumbauer's letter of 19 December 1942 to Carl Christenson. ''The Adjutant General has informed us officially that under no circumstances will enlisted personnel be released, which makes it extremely difficult for us to do much but acquiesce and conform with procedure established by the War Department.''

8 MAR 1943: George C. Price, Lt. Col. Air Corps, Director of Flight Control, War Department. In reply to Trumbauer's letter of February 22: ''A man of your qualifications and experience would definitely be an asset to the Director of Flight Control. In the event you are able to secure a release from the Civil Aeronautics Administration and pass the physical examination which is required, you will have no difficulty securing a commission.''

19 MAR 1943: George C. Price's letter to Trumbauer stated that if he could obtain his release from the CAA, he would recommend a commission as Captain for him.

25 MAR 1943: Date of photograph showing the class and instructors of the CAA War Training Service of Kansas City, MO. Trumbauer is pictured.

1 JUN 1943: Trumbauer submitted his letter of resignation to Fred Lanter:

Position: Chief, General Inspection Branch. CAF-13 ($5,600 per annum) Bureau Division: Safety Regulation. General Inspection Branch. 53511-300-5001

Headquarters: Kansas City, MO. (Fifth Region)

Reason For Resigning: ''To accept a more productive position in the 100% furtherance of the war effort at a lower starting salary than is being received at present.''

Notation on Trumbauer's letter: ''Exit interview held with Regional Manager. Mr. Trumbauer stated that he felt his services could be more useful in the war effort in his proposed employment with North American Aviation, Inc. He did state it was his desire to return to the CAA at some future time. He feels that the experience which he will acquire with North American will be very beneficial to him in his future employment with the CAA.''

North American Aviation (now Rockwell International) advised on March 4, 1991, that their complete records only go as far back as 1971. Before then, things are a bit sketchy and incomplete, but they offered what they could: Trumbauer was based in Kansas City.

Trumbauer's Social Security number was: 087-10-4271.

17 JUN 1943: Worked in Department 67-18, Salary ''SM.'' Hours: 8:00 A.M.-4:42 P.M., at the position of Test Pilot 610.

1 AUG 1943: Worked in Department 67-18, Salary ''SM.''

Hours: 8:00 A.M.-unidentified, at the position of Functional Test Pilot 73.

21 OCT 1943: Article in ***Tribune*** newspaper: ''Saxophonist Trumbauer A Test Pilot Now.''

15 NOV 1943: Article in ***Down Beat:*** ''Trumbauer Swaps Sax For Speedy Bombers.''

APR 1944: Trumbauer and family residing at 429 West 59th Street, Kansas City, MO.

16 APR 1944: Trumbauer still in Department 67-18, Salary ''SM.'' Unlisted hours, at position of Test Pilot 0334. North American Aviation.

8 MAY 1944: Orders from Lt. Col. Henry Dickerson to Trumbauer to proceed to Boundary Bay, Canada.

11 MAY 1944: Trumbauer transferred to Inglewood, California Division, and received orders.

12 MAY 1944: Trumbauer assigned to Department 73-270, salary ''SM.''

Hours: 7:30 A.M.-unlisted, as a 600 Production Test Pilot.

14 MAY 1944: Trumbauer flew to Vancouver.

23 MAY 1944: Report to R. H. Rice of activities at Boundary Bay. (see text)

1 JUN 1944: R. H. Rice replied to Trumbauer's letter, noting that in actual combat the Mitchell B-25 was able to be kept afloat, after ditching, for five minutes. The construction of the aircraft has convinced the R.A.F. that it is ''a good airplane for ditching.'' Trumbauer's request for Flight Manuals were being honored.

4 JUN 1944: Trumbauer flew from Vancouver to Inglewood. Stayed, advising the Engineering Department of suggested changes in the B-25 Mitchell, and requested a return to Kansas City Division on June 11.

12 JUN 1944: D. M. Smith, Acting Commander of the R.C.A.F. ''Western Command,'' letter to North American Aviation in praise of Trumbauer's work at Boundary Bay (see text).

Trumbauer's transfer approved and he reported to work at the Kansas City Division of North American Aviation, as Production Test Pilot (contract #AC19341).

15 MAR 1945: Trumbauer's letter to Leo Cluesman, Secretary AFM, seeking reinstatement with locals 802, 10, 47, 2, and 4.

18 APR 1945: Reinstated in AFM Local #2, St. Louis, MO.
19 APR 1945: Withdrew his membership in AFM Local #10, Chicago, IL.

6 SEP 1945: Inter-Office memo from Paul C. Thornbury, Superintendent, Flight Operation, North American Aviation, Inc., of Kansas: ''During the time of employment with North American Aviation, Inc., of Kansas, Mr. Frank Trumbauer, test pilot, flew our B-25s 934 hours and the P-51 Mustang 21 hours and 35 minutes, making a total flight time of 955 hours and 35 minutes. His link time totaled 79 hours and 10 minutes.''

31 OCT 1945: Group photograph of employees at North American Aviation included Trumbauer.

2 DEC 1945: Radio program, ***The RCA Victor Show.*** Orchestra directed by Raymond Paige. Program billed as a ''musical battle'' between swing and the classics, with Deems Taylor leading the classics side and Leonard Feather on the lighter side.
9 DEC 1945: Radio program, ***The RCA Victor Show.*** Guests: Classics side Leo Smit, concert pianist, and Leonard Stokes, baritone. On the ''pop'' side: Errol Garner, pianist, and Mynell Alley, swing vocalist.
16 DEC 1945: Radio program, ***The RCA Victor Show.***
Guest: Nancy Norman, ''jive singing.''
18 DEC 1945: Perry Como—Victor Records:
ALL THROUGH THE NIGHT and PRISONER OF LOVE
20 DEC 1945: Johnny Desmond—Victor Records:
IN THE MOON MIST and DO YOU LOVE ME and DON'T YOU REMEMBER ME? and IN THE EYES OF MY IRISH COLLEEN

23 DEC 1945: Radio program, ***The RCA Victor Show.***
Guests: ''Slam'' Stewart (bs) and ''Hot Lips'' Page (tpt), for the light side, and Susan Reid, singer of ballads, for the ''longhairs.''

30 DEC 1945: Radio program, ***The RCA Victor Show.***
Guest: Maxine Sullivan.

AFM Local 802, New York, NY., was able to locate information confirming that Trumbauer was a member of their local at this time. He joined the latter part of 1945 and had his address listed in their 1946 Directory as: Forrest Hotel on West 49th Street.

The Trumbauer family moved to Santa Monica, CA., during the school break between Christmas and New Year's. They resided at 833 17th Street.

15 JAN 1946: Trumbauer was reinstated as a member of AFM Local 47, Los Angeles, CA. He listed his current address as 14 East Navajo Lane, Kansas City, MO.

14 FEB 1946: Bill Trumbauer transferred to Santa Monica.

18 FEB 1946: Apparently the home recording date with Mary Howard and Charles Bourne: BODY AND SOUL and BETWEEN THE DEVIL AND THE DEEP BLUE SEA and HEJRE KATI

Trumbauer returned to New York by March 1, and apparently rejoined Raymond Paige on the NBC radio program, ***The RCA Victor Show***. WEAF and network stations, Sunday, 4:30–5:00 P.M..

3 MAR 1946: Radio program, ***The RCA Victor Show.***
Guests: Kenneth Schon (baritone) of the Metropolitan Opera; Josh White, ballad singer; and, Peggy Mann, blues singer. Mann became a regular member of the program, starting with this date.

12 MAR 1946: Perry Como—Victor Records:
LITTLE MAN YOU'VE HAD A BUSY DAY and MORE THAN YOU KNOW

14 MAR 1946: Perry Como—Victor Records:
KENTUCKY BABE and A GARDEN IN THE RAIN

17 MAR 1946: Radio program, ***The RCA Victor Show.***
Guests: Leo Smit, concert pianist, and regular Peggy Mann.

19 MAR 1946: Perry Como—Victor Records:
BLUE SKIES and MY BLUE HEAVEN

21 MAR 1946: Perry Como—Victor Records:
YOU MUST HAVE BEEN A BEAUTIFUL BABY and IF YOU WERE THE ONLY GIRL IN THE WORLD and GIRL OF MY DREAMS

24 MAR 1946: Radio program, ***The RCA Victor Show.*** Changes in format. Peggy Mann and Robert Merrill are the soloists each week, with Mann singing popular numbers and Merrill the classics. Kenny Delmar champions the popular music in an exchange of views with Deems Taylor, offering the classics.

25 MAR 1946: Frank Trumbauer Orchestra—Capitol Records:
YOU TOOK ADVANTAGE OF ME and BETWEEN THE DEVIL AND THE DEEP BLUE SEA and CHINA BOY

Trumbauer served notice to Raymond Paige in April, probably April 1, and returned to Santa Monica, CA.

While it is pure speculation, there remains the possibility that Trumbauer did work with his son, Bill, for a couple of dance dates. Bill Trumbauer's date book lists April 26 and 27, and May 11.

26 APR 1946: Hoagy Carmichael—Teen Agers, March Field. ($16)

27 APR 1946: Hoagy Carmichael—Long Beach High School. ($16)

11 MAY 1946: Lank Menge—Club date. ($16)

14 MAY 1946: Letter from Bob Laurie, Insurance Research Service, Kansas City. Discusses offer of employment to Trumbauer, then living in Santa Monica, CA.

1 JUN 1946: Trumbauer employed by Robert Laurie, Insurance Research Service.
Title: Manager, Aviation Division.

Address: Dierks Building, Kansas City, MO.

10 JUN 1946: Bill Trumbauer's notebook lists "Back to Kansas City."

JUL 1946: Publication ***The Jazz Report,*** has an article containing information on Trumbauer entitled "White Jazz In St. Louis."

LATE 1946: Trumbauer family moved to 14 East Navajo Lane, Kansas City, MO. In 1955 he referred to his unlisted telephone number as Delmar 34921.

2 APR 1947: Trumbauer issued Commercial Pilot's License, signed by Harry Troxell, covering: Airplane Single And Multi-Engine Land—Flight Instructor—Instruments.

18 MAY 1947: Trumbauer applied for reinstatement to the CAA in Kansas City.

15 JUL 1947: Civil Aeronautics Administration, Washington, DC., approved Trumbauer's reinstatement.

18 AUG 1947: Trumbauer took oath of office and was employed by the CAA in Kansas City.

Position: Assistant to Regional Administrator (Personal Flying) P-6, $7,102.20 per annum.

Bureau Division: Office of Regional Administration. 51113-300-0001

Department or Field: Kansas City, MO. (Fifth Region) Office: City Hall, Ninth Floor.

Appointment accompanied a letter from Leonard Jurden, Regional Administrator, welcoming Tram back.

2 SEP 1947: A program was found in Tram's effects from the National Air Race Events in Cleveland, leading to speculation that he attended. The program circled the winner of the Kendall Trophy Race of 105 miles—Kendall Everson at 397.926 mph.

1 OCT 1947: CAA routinely sent a request to the F.B.I. headquarters in Washington, DC., for a Loyalty Data Report on Trumbauer.

15 NOV 1947: F.B.I. reported back to CAA "No derogatory data in F.B.I. files."

11 FEB 1948: Trumbauer's letter to Chic Cowpland regarding movie ***Young Man With A Horn.***

3 MAR 1948: University of Wyoming campus, Laramie, WY. Formation of the Flying Farmers of Wyoming. Sixty-one persons registered and took part, of which 38 charter members were signed. Trumbauer attended as part of his duties with the CAA. The Flying Farmers were founded in 1944 and has had as many as 11,000 members. While originally founded by farmers and ranchers who owned aircraft, the membership grew to individuals from all walks of life. The purpose of the organization is to create and maintain a compact, representative and centralized organization with a spirit of cooperation and mutual helpfulness among its members to explore and emphasize the importance of flying and the use of the airplane in agricultural production, including the breeding, raising and feeding of livestock and to engage in research and extension service, including publishing magazines or other periodicals to disseminate among its members information pertaining to the purposes of the organization.

Specific objectives are: to promote the practical use of the airplane in the Agriculture Industry; to sponsor education and research in agriculture and aviation; to encourage the conservation of our soil and water; to promote safe flying through continued education and upgrading; to develop public acceptance of light aircraft; to afford youth the opportunity to participate in worthwhile projects and to stimulate positive social activities under adult guidance; to encourage close-in landing strips for towns and cities; to express the ideas and opinions of farm families at a national level; to insist that aviation gasoline taxes, where collected, be used for the development of aviation; to help reduce unnecessary regulations for general aviation; to cooperate with other aviation organizations for the furtherance of general aviation through responsible aviation legislation.

12 APR 1948: Song IT TOOK A DREAM written and copyrighted by Tram.

28 APR 1948: Song SOMEONE TO LOVE ME written and copyrighted by Tram.

2 JUN 1948: Songs WATCH WHERE YOU ARE GOING and I THOUGHT I'D NEVER MEET YOU written and copyrighted by Tram.

27–29 AUG 1948: Trumbauer was the keynote speaker at the annual Ninety-Nines, Inc., held at the Muehelbach Hotel, Kansas City, MO. The Ninety-Nines is an organization of licensed women pilots founded by Amelia Earhart in 1929. There were 99 charter members, thus the name of the organization. In 1950 the membership had grown to over 1,500 members and was now an international organization.

28 OCT 1948: Song MY LOVE FOR YOU written and copyrighted by Tram.
Home recording made this date.

17 NOV 1948: Hoover Pavilion.

2 DEC 1948: Song COULDN'T WE PRETEND written and copyright by Tram. Two home recording takes made this date.

16 JAN 1949: J. A. Purdome, Sheriff, Jackson County, Missouri, made Trumbauer a Special Deputy. ". . . he has long been identified with law enforcement and bears an excellent reputation . . . he has in his possession a .38 Police Special, Smith and Wesson, number 916486."

10–11 FEB 1949: National Association of State Aviation Officials meeting, Wichita, KS. Trumbauer discussed the advantages of flight training by use of a four-place plane carrying one instructor and three students who alternate at the controls.

23–24 FEB 1949: Kansas State College, Manhattan, KS. Conference on Aerial Spraying. Trumbauer discussed CAA permits and regulations.

20 APR 1949: Article in Kansas City newspapers regarding upcoming ''Funzajumpin'.''
21–22 APR 1949: Flying Farmers Agriculture Spraying Conference, Kansas City.
22 APR 1949: ''Funzajumpin' '' at Boone School.
29 APR 1949: Song HOW WILL MY LOVE written and copyrighted by Tram.
29 APR 1949: Song SUDDENLY written and copyrighted by Tram.
Two home recording takes made this date.
29–30 APR 1949: National Flying Farmers Convention, Hastings, NE.
Trumbauer spoke on Personal Flying Development.

14 MAY 1949: Guest speaker at Flying Farmers meeting in Mexico, MO.

13 JUN 1949: Ernest Gentle, President, AERO Publishers, Inc., expressed appreciation to Trumbauer for his appearance at the California Aeronautics Commission Conference in Fresno, CA., ''a couple weeks ago.''
13–14 JUN 1949: North Dakota Safety Conference, Bismarck, ND.
Guest speaker.

23 NOV 1949: Advised of salary increase.
25 NOV 1949: Approved.
27 NOV 1949: Became effective. Position: Assistant to Regional Administrator. GS-301-13 to GS-301-14 ($8,800.00 per annum).
30 NOV–2 DEC 1949: Program for Aerial Spraying, Manhattan, KS.
Conference sponsored by KIDC Division of Aeronautics. Tram chaired opening day program discussion devoted to airport problems.

12 DEC 1949: Edward Rupp's letter to Trumbauer included his application for forthcoming Flying Farmers trip to Mexico in January 1950. Trumbauer and John Zentner were invited guests of the Flying Farmers trip to Mexico. January 17–29 1950. They flew a Beech Aircraft N8604C.

16 JAN 1950: Trumbauer was a member of the Flying Farmers gathering at Laredo, TX.
17 JAN 1950: Arrived in Monterrey. Jose Maguerza hosted a party at Casino Club.
18 JAN 1950: Airport dedication ceremonies in Saltillo. That evening, Jose Maguerza, again hosted a party at Casino Club in Monterrey.
19 JAN 1950: Mexican Airline to Mexico City. Stayed at Hotel Reforma.
20 JAN 1950: Mexico City.
21–26 JAN 1950: Acapulco.
27–28 JAN 1950: Returned to Monterrey.
29 JAN 1950: Many left for Laredo, Texas and customs clearing. Some remained a few extra days.

7–8 MAR 1950: National Flying Farmers Association, Second Annual National Agriculture Aviation Conference, Fort Worth, TX. Trumbauer presided over afternoon session.
17 MAR 1950: All Scout Dads' ''Funzajumpin' '' at Boone School Auditorium, Kansas City.
27 MAR 1950: Ken-Mar Airport, Wichita, KS. Airman meeting. Trumbauer was the guest speaker at the luncheon and attended a dinner party for the local Quiet Birdmen at Allis Hotel.
28 MAR 1950: A tour was conducted by the manufacturers of Beech, Cessna, and Boeing factories.

21 APR 1950: Song IF THAT WAS LOVE written and copyrighted by Tram.

7 JUN 1950: Trumbauer flew to El Paso, TX, and then on to California to make certain that all arrangements had been completed for the forthcoming October tour.

4–7 SEP 1950: National Flying Farmers Convention, Bemidji, MN. Guest speaker.
19 SEP 1950: Flying Farmers Day, Hutchinson, KS. Trumbauer

was principal speaker for the luncheon that was attended by over 200 people.

1 OCT 1950: Aircraft gathered at International Air Port, El Paso, TX. Approximately 50 planes partook in the "On to California" flight by Flying Farmers.

2 OCT 1950: Roll, AZ. Planes had a gasoline stop at Tucson, and then that evening were hosted by the Wayne Wright family in a barbecue.

3 OCT 1950: Santa Monica Airport, CA. Banquet at hotel. Bus tour of city, including Hollywood Bowl, several movie studios, movie stars' homes, and Farmers Market.

4 OCT 1950: Breakfast in Long Beach. Banquet at Miramar Hotel in Santa Monica, CA.

5 OCT 1950: "Free Day." Group members left on their own to tour or rest.

6 OCT 1950: Boat trip to Santa Catalina Island.

7 OCT 1950: Majority returned home, but others spent the day on a trip to the University of California Agriculture College at Davis, with a stop at the Fiorini Farm.

19–20 FEB 1951: National Agricultural Aviation Conference, Memphis, TN. Trumbauer conducted a special program opening night in the ballroom.

MAR 1951: Magazine ***Record Changer*** mentions Trumbauer.

25 APR 1951: Application for Airman Identification Card submitted by Trumbauer. Listed his passport number as 116730.

27–28 APR 1951: Annual state convention of Nebraska Flying Farmers. Beatrice, NE. Trumbauer was the guest speaker.

16 JUN 1951: Lake McConaughy Airstrip Dedication. Ogallala, NE. Speech by Trumbauer demonstrating a typical private pilot cross-country flight, utilizing all the various facilities of the CAA at the disposal of the pilot.

1 JUL 1951: Cedar Rapids, IA. Trumbauer, representing the CAA partook in the Eastern Iowa Flying Farmers (in cooperation with other private plane owners) practice airlift to ''bombed'' Cedar Rapids. The demonstration was in the event of an atomic bomb hitting the city, and the airlift that could be provided to land supplies. Aviation and military observers were well pleased with the showing.

4 FEB 1952: Airplanes met in Laredo, TX.

4–18 FEB 1952: Flying Farmers Goodwill Flight To Mexico. Upon arrival in Monterrey, every member was awarded a Mexican peso, which was a silver coin embedded in the attractive badge which was to be worn for getting acquainted purposes. The hosts, Maguerza family, said the badge was offered so that no one would go broke while in Mexico. Money rate of exchange, placed the peso at 11-1/2 cents. Group divided into two groups, after two days in Monterrey. One group made an intensive tour of the historic scenes of Saltillo, Guadalajara, etc., and then to Mexico City. The other group flew to Tamuin, then to the Taninul Hotel, for fishing and boating, and three days at Acapulco before rejoining the others in Mexico City, on the 13th. Trumbauer in second group.

29 FEB 1952: National Flying Farmers Convention, Norfolk, NE. Trumbauer is guest speaker.

5 JUN 1952: Trumbauer was given a performance rating, from 1 April 1951 through 31 March 1952, on 16 May 1952 and presented with the results on 5 June. In nine categories of his job performance, he was found satisfactory in two and outstanding in seven others.

6 JUN 1952: James Graham, Registrar, Veteran Air Pilots' Association wrote to Trumbauer and asked that he approve A. J. Hartman of Burlington, IA., for membership. Mr. Hartman had applied for membership and listed Trumbauer as a sponsor of his membership. Tram had been a member of the organization from approximately 1949.

6–7 JUN 1952: Seventh Annual Convention of the Kansas Flying Farmers. Hutchinson, KS. Trumbauer was the guest speaker at the banquet.

23 JUN 1952: Song MY BABY SMILES written and copyrighted by Tram. Home recording made this date.

22–24 JUN 1952: Flying Farmers Convention, Douglas, WY.

19 SEP 1952: Letter written to Leonard Feather.
29 SEP 1952: Song THOMPSON'S BAND written and copyrighted by Tram.
Home recording made this date.

5–9 OCT 1952: Mike Lyman's, Los Angeles, CA.
Sitting in with Red Nichols & His Five Pennies.
10 OCT 1952: Bix Tribute At The Shrine Auditorium, Los Angeles, CA.
OCT 1952: Hal Barton radio interview.

24 NOV 1952: Aviation Day, Great Bend, KS. Guest speaker.
25 NOV 1952: Article on Trumbauer in Great Bend ***Tribune.***

15 DEC 1952: Song GRANDMOTHER'S WALTZ written and copyrighted by Tram.

3 FEB 1953: Republican National Chairman, Wes Roberts, acknowledged the receipt of a letter from Glenn Tabor (Kansas Industrial Development Commission) requesting that Trumbauer be appointed as a member of the Civil Aeronautics Board.
9 FEB 1953: Kansas Republican State Committee Chairman, C. I. Money, acknowledged same letter from Glenn Tabor.

10 MAR 1953: Station WOC Tribute to Bix in Davenport, IA.
30 MAR 1953: Glenn Tabor advised by the White House that the selection (see 3 FEB 1953) was awarded to a Mr. Denny of Pittsburgh, PA.

24 APR 1953: Power Farm Equipment Show and Flying Farmers Day, Norton, KS. Trumbauer guest speaker at the noon luncheon.

1 JUL 1953: President Eisenhower ordered a national reduction in government forces, and this led to the ''domino effect'' in the CAA. As a result, Trumbauer was assigned to Supervisor, Flight Operations (GS-1681-13), under Paul Flanary, his supervisor.

18 SEP 1953: Trumbauer's application for Pilot Certification Rating was approved on 13 October, adding to his Commercial

Pilot's License #11456, the rating of: Aviation Safety Agent—Civil Aeronautics Administration—All Ratings Authorized.

24–26 SEP 1953: National Flying Farmers Convention, Wichita, KS. The surprise of the first business session was the special award given to Trumbauer as recognition for the interest and aid given to the Flying Farmers movement.

NOV 1953: Maggie's birthday party (see text).

16 NOV 1953: Letter from Lock Norton, Secretary, National Flying Farmers Association, sent Trumbauer a certificate of appreciation for his contributions on their behalf in resulting in the building of a permanent ''home'' for the association at the Wichita, KS. airport.

17 DEC 1953: Wright Brothers Banquet, Washington, DC. Trumbauer noted as attending.

20 JAN 1954: Song MY BABY SMILES written and copyrighted by Tram.

2 FEB 1954: Reply to Don Molmberg regarding request on early information about ''Doc'' Rando, soon to be a subject on Ralph Edwards' ***This Is Your Life*** television program.

26 MAR 1954: ''Funzajumpin' '' affair at Boone School.

12 APR 1954: Harry Troxell and Trumbauer met in Des Moines, IA. and went to Cedar Rapids, IA.

13 APR 1954: Troxell and Trumbauer returned to Des Moines, and then to their home destinations.

APR–SEP 1954: Trumbauer served as president of the CAA ''Toastmaster's Club.'' He originally joined in 1952.

1–5 JUN 1954: Flying Farmers Annual Convention, Yosemite National Park.

1 JUN 1954: Arrived in Fresno, CA. Executive meeting held at Hotel Fresno.

2 JUN 1954: Bus transportation from Fresno to Yosemite National Park, with a tour of Mariposa Grove of Big Trees that included a box lunch.

3 JUN 1954: Various committee meetings and crowning of national queen.

4 JUN 1954: General business sessions all day, with various reports of committees. Trumbauer was the guest speaker that evening. Tram put across his stimulating points with the aid of some startling props that had the delegates laughing and thinking at the same time. Trumbauer made three points for the flyers: Keep up physical standards, keep up mechanical standards, and don't push weather.

5 JUN 1954: Bus trip from Yosemite to Fresno.

28 JUN 1954: Civil Air Patrol, Lucas V. Beau, Maj. Gen., USAF, National Commander, appointed Trumbauer to the grade of Lieutenant Colonel, to serve as advisor to Southwest Regional Director. Serial number: 8-1-11113. Wing: Texas.

12 JUL 1954: Arrived in New York. Reservation at the Biltmore Hotel.

15 JUL 1954: Conference with the Under Secretary for Defense, Bob Anderson, in Washington, DC.

19 JUL 1954: Col. Emmett Rushing, C.A.P., Director, SW Region, wrote to Trumbauer requesting that he accept the fourth position on a committee consisting of: General Robert Harper, USAF (Ret.); Gill Robb Wilson, editor of Flying Magazine; and himself. The primary purpose of the program was to supply cadet pilot material for the armed services. The instruction would be done by CAA approved schools and operators.

31 JUL-1 AUG 1954: National Flying Farmers Tri-State Convention, Valley City, ND. Trumbauer was guest speaker.

20 AUG 1954: Leonard Jurden wrote to the Regional Administrator of the CAA endorsing the proposal. Trumbauer's appointment is unconfirmed. In 1991, the C.A.P. reported that their files of this period had been destroyed, and none of the government files searched revealed the decision.

12 SEP 1954: Letter from Charles Howes thanking Trumbauer for his "recent" speech to the Topeka (KS) Flying Association.

25 OCT 1954: Trumbauer filled out four pages of requested information based on "Security Investigation Data For Sensitive Position.'' Report filed in Washington, DC, on 29 October by E. J. Thomas, Chief Security Control Officer. Only notation is that it is to be processed under Table 4, 1–2–7, FPM, for N.A.C. No further information located in connection with this document.

12–14 NOV 1954: Texas State Aviation Convention, Galveston, TX. Trumbauer was the keynote speaker on 13 November.
NOV 1954: Trip with Judge and Mrs. Duvall Strother to Mexico.

JAN 1955: Kansas Aviation Trade Association meeting, Kansas City, KS. Trumbauer attended.

MAR 1955: Refresher course in the CAA, Oklahoma City, OK.

5 APR 1955: Trumbauer wrote to Bing Crosby regarding the proposing of Dodge City (KS) as the cowboy capital, and they were forming a committee for a National Cowboy Memorial, and Bing was asked to serve on that committee.
13 APR 1955: Crosby replied to Trumbauer and felt that it was a good suggestion for the National Cowboy Memorial but requested additional information on the plans.
14–15 APR 1955: Denver (CO) meeting to discuss the Dodge City proposal.

15–20 AUG 1955: National Flying Farmers Convention. East Lansing, MI. Trumbauer served on the Resolutions Committee.

10–16 OCT 1955: Vacation at the Broadmoor Hotel, Colorado Springs, CO. Mitzi, Bill, and a friend of Bill's accompanied Tram.
27 OCT 1955: Butler, MO. Guest speaker for the Butler Junior Chamber Of Commerce.

14 FEB 1956: Trumbauer wrote to H. W. Boggess, President of the Board of Directors, National Business Aircraft Association, Inc., Tulsa Branch, and requested the possible meeting regarding employment that he was seeking with them.

20 MAR 1956: Trumbauer's last application for renewal of his Pilot's Certificate.

Trumbauer wanted to be approved on the flight of a Douglas DC-3; he noted having spent 24 hours in this aircraft as pilot-in-command and 3,000 hours as pilot-in-command of this class of airplane. Under his record of flying time, he offered the following hours of flight: Dual: 250 plus 20 night; Co-Pilot: 300 plus 100 night; Pilot-In-Command: 7500 plus 1500 night. T. K. Archer, examiner, recommended acceptance after Trumbauer's flight test.

21 MAR 1956: Mr. Boggess replied that while they were not currently seeking to enlarge their organization, they felt Trumbauer highly qualified to be a member of their association and should expansion be considered, he would be notified.

20–22 APR 1956: Wichita, KS. Guest speaker at the annual convention of Ninety-Nines, Inc.

4 MAY 1956: Eleventh annual Kansas Flying Farmers Convention, Great Bend, KS. Trumbauer gave an address at the Smorgasbord banquet, held at the Eagles Lodge.

8 JUN 1956: Dinner guest of Harry Troxell's, Des Moines, IA.

11 JUN 1956: Frank Trumbauer died of coronary occlusion.

13 JUN 1956: Cremation at the funeral home of D. W. Newcomer's Sons, 1331 Brush Creek, Kansas City. Honorary pallbearers: Leonard Jurden, Fred Regen, Charles German, Joe Shumate, Judge DuVall Strother, Jack Ross, and H. A. Paulsen.

At the time of his passing, Trumbauer was listed as:
Supervision Flight Operations, Inspector GS-1681-13, $10,065.00 per annum.

SONG TITLE INDEX

ABE MCINTOSH (3 Part Suite)
(Meredith Willson's Composition Honoring The New York Columnist)
AUG 30 1934: Radio, Kraft Music Hall: Paul Whiteman & His Orch.

ADESTE FIDELIS
(Francis Wade-Canon Frederick Oakley)
SEP 19 1928: Col Records: Paul Whiteman & His Orch.

ADORING YOU
(Harry Tierney-Joseph McCarthy)
SEP 27 1924: Brun Records: Ray Miller & His Orch.

AFTER THE BALL MEDLEY
(Charles K. Harris)
JAN 31 1923: Vic Records: Benson Orch. (rejected)

AFTER YOU'VE GONE
(Henry Creamer-J. Turner Layton)
OCT 18 1929: Col Records: Paul Whiteman & His Orch.

AFTERGLOW
(Joe Young-Boyd Bunch-Robert M. Bilder)
JUN 26 1936: Vic Records: Paul Whiteman & His Orch.

AIN'T MISBEHAVIN'
(Andy Razaf-Harry Brooks-Thomas ''Fats'' Waller)
JUL 9 1935: Vic Records: Paul Whiteman & His Orch.
APR 27 1936: Brun Records: Frank Trumbauer & His Orch.
JAN 15 1937: Radio, Musical Varieties: The Three T's

ALABAMY SNOW
(David Lee-Billy Rose)
MAY 15 1929: Col Records: Mason Dixon Orch.

ALEXANDER'S RAGTIME BAND
(Irving Berlin)
DEC 13 1934: Radio, Kraft Music Hall: Paul Whiteman & His Orch.
MAY 24 1936: Radio, Musical Varieties: Paul Whiteman & His Orch.
JUL 8 1938: Standard Trans.: Frank Trumbauer & His Orch.

ALICE BLUE GOWN
(Joseph McCarthy-Harry Tierney)
MAR 15 1936: Radio, Musical Varieties: Paul Whiteman & His Orch.

ALICE IN WONDERLAND sketch
(composers unidentified)
JAN 25 1934: Radio, Kraft Music Hall: Paul Whiteman & His Orch.

ALL MY LIFE
(Sidney Mitchell-Sammy Stept)
MAR 15 1936: Radio, Musical Varieties: Paul Whiteman & His Orch.

ALL OF ME
(Seymour Simons-Gerald Marks)
DEC 1 1931: Vic Records: Paul Whiteman & His Orch.

ALL POINTS WEST (Part 1)
(Lorenz Hart-Richard Rodgers)
MAR 28 1937: Vic Records: Paul Whiteman & His Orch.

ALL POINTS WEST (Part 2)
(Lorenz Hart-Richard Rodgers)
MAR 28 1937: Vic Records: Paul Whiteman & His Orch.

ANNIE DOESN'T LIVE HERE ANYMORE
(Joe Young-Johnny Burke-Harold Spina)
NOV 30 1933: Radio, Kraft Music Hall: Paul Whiteman & His Orch.
JAN 4 1934: Radio, Kraft Music Hall: Paul Whiteman & His Orch.

ANNINA
(Leigh-Shubert-Friml)
APR 17 1934: Vic Records: Paul Whiteman & His Orch.

ANNOUNCER'S BLUES
(Frank Trumbauer)
SEP 7 1935: Vic Records: Paul Whiteman & His Orch.
JAN 19 1936: Radio, Musical Varieties: Paul Whiteman & His Orch.
JAN 29 1936: Brun Records: Frank Trumbauer & His Orch.

ANYTHING GOES
(Cole Porter)
OCT 26 1934: Vic Records: Paul Whiteman & His Orch.
OCT 26 1934: Vic Records: Paul Whiteman & His Orch.
NOV 22 1934: Radio, Kraft Music Hall: Paul Whiteman & His Orch.

ANYTHING GOES MEDLEY
(Cole Porter)
OCT 26 1934: Vic Records: Paul Whiteman & His Orch.

APPLE BLOSSOMS
(Fritz Kreisler)
OCT 18 1929: OK Records: Joe Venuti & His Orch.

APRIL IN PARIS
(E.Y. ''Yip'' Harburg-Vernon Duke)
APR 4 1935: Radio, Kraft Music Hall: Paul Whiteman & His Orch.

APRIL SHOWERS
(B. G. ''Buddy'' DeSylva-Louis Silvers)
OCT 1921: Brun Records: Gene Rodemich & His Orch.

ARABIANNA
(Val Howland-Fisher Thompson)
AUG 5 1924: Brun Records: Ray Miller & His Orch.

ARE YOU LONELY?
(Joseph A. Burke-Louis Herscher)
SEP 17 1923: Vic Records: Benson Orch.

ARIA FROM MARTHA
(Friedrich von Flotow)
FEB 9 1936: Radio, Musical Varieties: Paul Whiteman & His Orch.

AT SUNDOWN
(Walter Donaldson)
APR 5 1936: Radio, Musical Varieties: Paul Whiteman & His Orch.

AT TWILIGHT
(Maceo Pinkard-William G. Tracey)
SEP 6 1929: Col Records: Paul Whiteman & His Orch.

AT YOUR BECK AND CALL
(Eddie DeLange-Buck Ram)
APR 20 1938: Standard Trans.: Frank Trumbauer & His Orch.

AU REVOIR L'AMOUR
(composers unidentified)
DEC 17 1934: Vic Records: Paul Whiteman & His Orch.

AUF WIEDERSEHEN, MY DEAR
(Al Hoffman-Ed Nelson-Al Goodhart-Milton Ager)
MAR 8 1936: Radio, Musical Varieties: Paul Whiteman & His Orch.

AVALON
(Al Jolson-B. G. "Buddy" DeSylva-Vincent Rose)
FEB 15 1928: Vic Records: Paul Whiteman & His Orch.

AWAKE IN A DREAM
(composers unidentified)
FEB 6 1936: Vic Records: Paul Whiteman & His Orch.

BABY, WON'T YOU PLEASE COME HOME
(Charles Warfield-Clarence Williams)
APR 17 1929: OK Records: Frank Trumbauer & His Orch.

BACK IN YOUR OWN BACKYARD
(Al Jolson-Billy Rose-Dave Dreyer)
JAN 28 1928: Vic Records: Paul Whiteman & His Orch.

BAGDAD
(Jack Yellen-Milton Ager)
AUG 5 1924: Brun Records: Ray Miller & His Orch.

BALLATELLA-LAGLIACI
(composers unidentified)
OCT 11 1934: Radio, Kraft Music Hall: Paul Whiteman & His Orch.

BALTIMORE
(Jimmy McHugh)
SEP 28 1927: OK Records: Frank Trumbauer & His Orch.

BAMBALINA
(Otto Harbach-Oscar Hammerstein II-Vincent Youmans-Herbert Stothart)
DEC 14 1933: Radio, Kraft Music Hall: Paul Whiteman & His Orch.

BASIN STREET BLUES
(Spencer Williams)
DEC 13 1934: Radio, Kraft Music Hall: Paul Whiteman & His Orch.

BECAUSE MY BABY DON'T MEAN "MAYBE" NOW
(Walter Donaldson)
JUN 18 1928: Col Records: Paul Whiteman & His Orch.

BEE SONG, THE
(Barbara Belle-Anita Leonard Nye)
NOV 29 1934: Radio, Kraft Music Hall: Paul Whiteman & His Orch.

BEETLE AT LARGE
(composers unidentified)
JUL 8 1938: Standard Trans.: Frank Trumbauer & His Orch.

BEGIN THE BEGUINE
(Cole Porter)
SEP 28 1935: Vic Records: Paul Whiteman & His Orch.

BELLE OF NEW O'LEANS (See also: New O'Leans)
(Gus Kahn-Arthur Johnston)
AUG-SEP 1935: Film: Thanks A Million
SEP 29 1935: Radio, Magic Key Of Radio: Paul Whiteman & His Orch.

BELLS OF ST. MARY'S, THE
(Douglas Furber-Emmett Adams)
DEC 28 1933: Radio, Kraft Music Hall: Paul Whiteman & His Orch.

BENCH IN THE PARK, A
(Milton Ager-Jack Yellen)
NOV-DEC 1929: Film: King Of Jazz
MAR 22 1930: Col Records: Paul Whiteman & His Orch.

BETTER THINK TWICE
(J. Fred Coots-Tot Seymour)
DEC 7 1933: Radio, Kraft Music Hall: Paul Whiteman & His Orch.

BETWEEN THE DEVIL AND THE DEEP BLUE SEA
(Ted Koehler-Harold Arlen)
AUG 17 1932: Col Records: Frank Trumbauer & His Orch.

DEC 11 1936: Radio, Musical Varieties: The Three T's
DEC 1936: Radio, Musical Varieties: The Three T's
JAN 8 1937: Radio, Musical Varieties: The Three T's
FEB 18 1946: Record: Mary Howard
MAR 25 1946: Capitol Records: Frank Trumbauer & His Orch.

BIG BAD WOLF, THE (WHO'S AFRAID OF)
(Frank Churchill-Ann Ronell)
JAN 7 1934: Radio, Kraft Music Hall: Paul Whiteman & His Orch.

BIG BOUQUET FOR YOU, A
(Seymour Simons-Gus Kahn)
SEP 10 1930: Col Records: Paul Whiteman & His Orch.

BIG BUTTER AND EGG MAN
(Sidney Clare-Cliff Friend-Joseph H. Santly)
DEC 15 1937: Standard Trans.: Frank Trumbauer & His Orch.

BIRTH OF THE BLUES, THE
(B. G. "Buddy" DeSylva-Lew Brown-Ray Henderson)
AUG 23 1934: Radio, Kraft Music Hall: Paul Whiteman & His Orch.

BLACKBIRDS OF 1934 MEDLEY
(Ned Washington-Victor Young)
DEC 14 1933: Radio, Kraft Music Hall: Paul Whiteman & His Orch.

BLESS YOU SISTER
(Al Dubin-J. Russel Robinson)
JUL 5 1928: OK Records: Frank Trumbauer & His Orch.

BLUE HAWAII
(Abel Baer-Irving Caesar-Ira Schuster)
MAR 15 1929: Col Records: Paul Whiteman & His Orch.

BLUE HOLIDAY (aka "SINGIN' THE BLUES")
(J. Russel Robinson)
JAN 28 1938: Standard Trans.: Frank Trumbauer & His Orch.

APR 20 1938: Standard Trans.: Frank Trumbauer & His Orch.
JUL 9 1938: Radio, Frank Trumbauer & His Orch.
FEB 25 1939: Radio, Frank Trumbauer & His Orch.

BLUE MOON
(Lorenz Hart-Richard Rodgers)
NOV 20 1934: Vic Records: Frank Trumbauer & His Orch.

BLUE MOONLIGHT
(Dana Suesse)
OCT 11 1934: Radio, Kraft Music Hall: Paul Whiteman & His Orch.
DEC 14 1934: Vic Records: Paul Whiteman & His Orch.

BLUE NIGHT
(. . . Rollins- . . . Mahoney)
MAY 24 1928: Col Records: Paul Whiteman & His Orch.

BLUE RIVER
(Alfred Bryan-Joseph E. Meyer)
AUG 25 1927: OK Records: Frank Trumbauer & His Orch.
SEP 15 1927: Vic Records: Jean Goldkette & His Orch.

BLUE ROOM, THE
(Lorenz Hart-Richard Rodgers)
NOV 30 1933: Radio, Kraft Music Hall: Paul Whiteman & His Orch.
FEB 12 1937: Radio, Frank Trumbauer & His Orch.

BLUE SKIES
(Irving Berlin)
OCT 11 1934: Radio, Kraft Music Hall: Paul Whiteman & His Orch.
JAN 8 1937: Radio, Musical Varieties: The Three T's
JAN 1937: Radio, Frank Trumbauer & His Orch.
MAR 19 1946: Vic Records: Perry Como

BODY AND SOUL
(Edward Heyman-Robert Sour-Frank Eyton-Johnny Green)
SEP 10 1930: Col Records: Paul Whiteman & His Orch.

DEC 15 1937: Standard Trans.: Frank Trumbauer & His Orch.
FEB 18 1946: Record: Mary Howard

BOLERO
(Maurice Ravel)
JAN 5 1936: Radio, Musical Varieties: Paul Whiteman & His Orch.

BOOTS AND SADDLE (See: TAKE ME BACK TO MY BOOTS AND SADDLE)

BORN TO BE KISSED
(Howard Dietz-Arthur Schwartz)
JUN 29 1934: Vic Records: Paul Whiteman & His Orch.

BORNEO
(Walter Donaldson)
APR 10 1928: OK Records: Frank Trumbauer & His Orch.

BOUNCING BALL
(Frank Trumbauer)
DEC 7 1933: Radio, Kraft Music Hall: Paul Whiteman & His Orch.
DEC 14 1933: Radio, Kraft Music Hall: Paul Whiteman & His Orch.
FEB 16 1934: Vic Records: Paul Whiteman & His Orch.
NOV 29 1934: Radio, Kraft Music Hall: Paul Whiteman & His Orch.
MAR 8 1836: Radio, Musical Varieties: Paul Whiteman & His Orch.
DEC 15 1937: Standard Trans.: Frank Trumbauer & His Orch.

BOY AND GIRL ON THE SCOOTER
(composers unidentified)
DEC 14 1933: Radio, Kraft Music Hall: Paul Whiteman & His Orch.

BOY, A GIRL, AND A LAMPLIGHT, A
(composers unidentified)
APR 30 1938: Radio, Frank Trumbauer & His Orch.

BREAK IT DOWN
(David D. Rose-Frank Trumbauer)
JAN 12 1934: Brun Records: Frank Trumbauer & His Orch.

BREAKIN' IN A PAIR OF SHOES
(Ned Washington-Dave Franklin-Sammy Stept)
JAN 29 1936: Brun Records: Frank Trumbauer & His Orch.

BRING BACK MY BONNIE TO ME
(traditional)
JAN 28 1938: Standard Trans.: Frank Trumbauer & His Orch.

BROADWAY HIGHLIGHTS #1
MAY 16 1935: Paramount Studios: Paul Whiteman & His Orch.

BROADWAY HIGHLIGHTS #5
NOV 16 1935: Paramount Studios: Paul Whiteman & His Orch.

BROADWAY'S GONE HILL-BILLY
(Lew Brown-Jay Gorney)
MAR 28 1934: Vic Records: Ramona (Davies)

BROKEN RECORD, THE
(Cliff Friend-Charles Tobias-Sherman Edwards)
JAN 12 1936: Radio, Musical Varieties: Paul Whiteman & His Orch.

BUILD A LITTLE HOME
(Al Dubin-Harry Warren)
JAN 11 1934: Radio, Kraft Music Hall: Paul Whiteman & His Orch.

BUNDLE OF OLD LOVE LETTERS, A
(Arthur Freed-Nacio Herb Brown)
OCT 18 1929: Col Records: Paul Whiteman & His Orch.

BUSINESS IN Q
(Archie Bleyer)
AUG 17 1932: Col Records: Frank Trumbauer & His Orch.

BUTTON UP YOUR OVERCOAT
(B. G. "Buddy" DeSylva-Lew Brown-Ray Henderson)
FEB 8 1929: Col Records: Paul Whiteman & His Orch.

BY MYSELF
(Howard Dietz-Arthur Schwartz)
FEB 11 1938: Standard Trans.: Frank Trumbauer & His Orch.

BY THE LAKE
(Raymond W. Klages-Arthur Lange)
NOV 7 1924: Brun Records: Ray Miller & His Orch.

BY THE PYRAMIDS
(Bartley Costello-Ted Fio Rito)
OCT 1921: Brun Records: Gene Rodemich & His Orch.

BY THE SYCAMORE TREE
(Haven Gillespie-Pete Wendling)
DEC 3 1931: Vic Records: Paul Whiteman & His Orch.

BY THE WATERS OF MINNETONKA
(J. M. Cavanass-Thurlow Lieurance)
FEB 9 1928: Vic Records: Paul Whiteman & His Orch.
NOV 30 1933: Radio, Kraft Music Hall: Paul Whiteman & His Orch.

BYE BYE BLUES
(Bert Lown-Chauncey Gray-David Bennett-Fred Hamm)
SEP 8 1930: OK Records: Frank Trumbauer & His Orch.

CABIN IN THE COTTON
(Mitchell Parish-Frank Perkins)
MAY 25 1932: Brun Records: Bing Crosby

CALL OF THE SOUTH, THE
(Harold Raymond-Eugene West)
JUL 26 1934: Radio, Kraft Music Hall (Al Jolson with Paul Whiteman Orch.)

CAN'T HELP LOVIN' DAT MAN
(Oscar Hammerstein II-Jerome Kern)
MAR 1 1928: Vic Records: Paul Whiteman & His Orch.

CAN'T TEACH MY OLD HEART NEW TRICKS
(Johnny Mercer-Richard A. Whiting)
DEC 15 1937: Standard Trans.: Frank Trumbauer & His Orch.

CAN'T WE DREAM?
(Fred E. Ahlert-Joseph Young)
JAN 12 1936:Radio, Musical Varieties: Paul Whiteman & His Orch.

CAN'T YOU SEE (HOW I LOVE YOU?)
(Roy Turk-Fred E. Ahlert)
OCT 4 1931: Vic Records: Paul Whiteman & His Orch.

CAPRICE FUTURISTIC
(Matty Malneck)
FEB 18 1928: Vic Records: Paul Whiteman & His Orch.

CAPRICE VIENNOIS
(Fritz Kreisler)
DEC 26 1935: Radio, Kraft Music Hall: Paul Whiteman & His Orch.

CARESSES
(James V. Monaco)
FEB 23 1936: Radio, Musical Varieties: Paul Whiteman & His Orch.

CARRY ME BACK TO GREEN PASTURES
(Harry S. Pepper)
APR 17 1934: Vic Records: Paul Whiteman & His Orch.

CARRY ME BACK TO OLD VIRGINNY
(James A. Bland)
OCT 18 1929: Col Records: Paul Whiteman & His Orch.

CATHEDRAL IN THE PINES
(Charles Kenny-Nick Kenny)
MAY 25 1938: Standard Trans.: Frank Trumbauer & His Orch.

CATS WHISKERS
(Hugo Frey)
JUN 15 1923: Vic Records: Benson Orch.

CHANSONETTE (See: DONKEY SERENADE)

CHAPEL IN THE MOONLIGHT, (IN THE)
(Billy Hill)
DEC 1936: Radio, The Three T's
DEC 1936: Radio, The Three T's

CHARLESTON CABIN
(Sidney Holder-Roy Reber)
JUL 22 1924: Brun Records: Ray Miller & His Orch.

CHEEK TO CHEEK
(Irving Berlin)
SEP 28 1935: Vic Records: Paul Whiteman & His Orch.
JAN 5 1936: Radio, Musical Varieties: Paul Whiteman & His Orch.
FEB 2 1936: Radio, Musical Varieties: Paul Whiteman & His Orch.

CHINA BOY
(Dick Winfree-Phil Boutelje)
MAY 3 1929: Col Records: Paul Whiteman & His Orch.
FEB 23 1934: Brun Records: Frank Trumbauer & His Orch.
JAN 5 1936: Radio, Musical Varieties: Paul Whiteman & His Orch.
JAN 8 1937: Radio, Musical Varieties: The Three T's
JAN 1937: Radio, Frank Trumbauer & His Orch.
MAR 25 1946: Capitol Records: Frank Trumbauer & His Orch.

CHINA SEAS
(Arthur Freed-Nacio Herb Brown)
JUL 10 1935: Vic Records: Paul Whiteman & His Orch.

CHINESE LULLABY
(Robert Hood Bowers)
JAN 10 1929: Col Records: Paul Whiteman & His Orch.

CHIQUITA
(L. Wolfe Gilbert-Mabel Wayne)
MAY 25 1928: Col Records: Paul Whiteman & His Orch.
JUN 10 1928: Col Records: Paul Whiteman & His Orch.

CHLOE
(Gus Kahn-Neil Moret)
FEB 27 1928: Vic Records: Paul Whiteman & His Orch.
JAN 12 1936: Radio, Musical Varieties: Paul Whiteman & His Orch.

CHOO CHOO
(Matty Malneck-Frank Trumbauer)
SEP 8 1930: OK Records: Frank Trumbauer & His Orch.
SEP 10 1930: Col Records: Paul Whiteman & His Orch.

CHRISTMAS MELODIES
(John Sullivan Dwight-Adolphe Charles Adam)
SEP 19 1928: Col Records: Paul Whiteman & His Orch.

CHRISTMAS NIGHT IN HARLEM
(Mitchell Parish-Raymond Scott)
APR 17 1934: Vic Records: Paul Whiteman & His Orch.
DEC 20 1934: Radio, Kraft Music Hall: Paul Whiteman & His Orch.
DEC 25 1936: Radio, The Three T's
DEC 1936: Radio, The Three T's
MAR 24 1937: Radio, Paul Whiteman & His Orch.

CHUCK A BOOM
(George Forrest-Chris M. Schonberg)
FEB 11 1938: Standard Trans.: Frank Trumbauer & His Orch.

CINDERELLA'S WEDDING DAY
(Lew Corbey-Tom Ford)
AUG 17 1932: Col Records: Frank Trumbauer & His Orch.

CIRCUS ON PARADE, THE
(Lorenz Hart-Richard Rodgers)
FEB 2 1936: Radio, Musical Varieties: Paul Whiteman & His Orch.

CLAMBAKE — PROHIBITION
(John H. Mercer-Matt Malneck)
DEC 7 1933: Radio, Kraft Music Hall: Paul Whiteman & His Orch.

CLAMBAKE — THE FUNNIES
(John H. Mercer-Matt Malneck)
JAN 11 1934: Radio, Kraft Music Hall: Paul Whiteman & His Orch.
JAN 25 1934: Radio, Kraft Music Hall: Paul Whiteman & His Orch.

CLAMBAKE — PASSION'S PLAYTHING
(John H. Mercer-Matt Malneck)
FEB 2 1934: Radio, Kraft Music Hall: Paul Whiteman & His Orch.

CLAP YO' HANDS
(Ira Gershwin-George Gershwin)
JUN 28 1934: Radio, Kraft Music Hall: Paul Whiteman & His Orch.

CLARABELLE
(Dan Busath)
JAN 11 1934: Radio, Kraft Music Hall: Paul Whiteman & His Orch.
MAY 24 1934: Radio, Kraft Music Hall: Paul Whiteman & His Orch.

CLARINET MARMALADE
(Eddy Edwards-D.J. LaRocca-Tony Sparbaro-Larry Shields)
FEB 4 1927: OK Records: Frank Trumbauer & His Orch.

CLEMENTINE (FROM NEW ORLEANS)
(Henry Creamer-J. Turner Layton)
SEP 15 1927: Vic Records: Jean Goldkette & His Orch.

CLING TO ME
(Mack David-Al Hoffman-Jerry Livingston)
FEB 16 1936: Radio, Musical Varieties: Paul Whiteman & His Orch.

CLORINDA
(R. Orlando Morgan-Donald Heywood)
OCT 20 1927: Perfect Records: Chicago Loopers

COLORADO SUNSET
(L. Wolfe Gilbert-Con Conrad)
APR 20 1938: Standard Trans.: Frank Trumbauer & His Orch.

COME ON, RED
(Sidney Holden-Roy Reber)
MAR 28 1924: Brun Records: Ray Miller & His Orch.

COMRADES
(Robert A. King-Ballard Macdonald)
SEP 4 1928: Col Records: Paul Whiteman & His Orch.
SEP 14 1928: Col Records: Paul Whiteman & His Orch.

CONCERTO IN F (Part 1)
(George Gershwin)
SEP 5 1928: Col Records: Paul Whiteman & His Orch.
SEP 15 1928: Col Records: Paul Whiteman & His Orch.

CONCERTO IN F (Part 2)
(George Gershwin)
SEP 6 1928: Col Records: Paul Whiteman & His Orch.
SEP 15 1928: Col Records: Paul Whiteman & His Orch.

CONCERTO IN F (Part 3)
(George Gershwin)
SEP 6 1928: Col Records: Paul Whiteman & His Orch.
SEP 15 1928: Col Records: Paul Whiteman & His Orch.

CONCERTO IN F (Part 4)
(George Gershwin)
SEP 15 1928: Col Records: Paul Whiteman & His Orch.

CONCERTO IN F (Part 5)
(George Gershwin)
SEP 17 1928: Col Records: Paul Whiteman & His Orch.

CONCERTO IN F (Part 6)
(George Gershwin)
SEP 17 1928: Col Records: Paul Whiteman & His Orch.
OCT 5 1928: Col Records: Paul Whiteman & His Orch.

CONNECTICUT YANKEE sketch
(Lorenz Hart-Richard Rodgers)
OCT 11 1934: Radio, Kraft Music Hall: Paul Whiteman & His Orch.

C-0-N-S-T-A-N-T-I-N-O-P-L-E
(B. G. ''Buddy'' DeSylva-Lew Brown-Ray Henderson)
MAY 17 1928: Col Records: Paul Whiteman & His Orch.

CONTINENTAL, THE
(Herb Magidson-Con Conrad)
DEC 13 1934: Radio, Kraft Music Hall: Paul Whiteman & His Orch.

COQUETTE
(Irving Berlin)
FEB 28 1929: Col Records: Paul Whiteman & His Orch.

COQUETTE
(Gus Kahn-Carmen Lombardo-John Green)
MAR 2 1928: Vic Records: Paul Whiteman & His Orch.
JAN 15 1937: Radio, Musical Varieties: Paul Whiteman & His Orch.

CORAL SEA
(King Zany-Nacio Herb Brown)

FEB 23 1936: Radio, Musical Varieties: Paul Whiteman & His Orch.

COSI COSA
(Ned Washington-Bronislaw Kaper-Walter Jurmann)
JAN 12 1936: Radio, Musical Varieties: Paul Whiteman & His Orch.

COULDN'T WE PRETEND?
(Bill Trumbauer-Frank Trumbauer)
DEC 2 1948: Private: Frank Trumbauer

COVER ME UP WITH SUNSHINE
(Mort Dixon-Ray Henderson)
OCT 15 1926: Vic Records: Jean Goldkette & His Records

COWBOY FROM BROOKLYN
(Johnny Mercer-Harry Warren)
MAY 25 1938: Standard Trans.: Frank Trumbauer & His Orch.

COWBOY, WHERE ARE YOU RIDING?
(Howard Dietz-Arthur Schwartz)
DEC 6 1934: Radio, Kraft Music Hall: Paul Whiteman & His Orch.

CRADLE OF LOVE
(L. Wolfe Gilbert-Mabel Wayne)
JAN 10 1929: Col Records: Paul Whiteman & His Orch.

CRAZY QUILT
(Andrew B. Sterling-Paul Van Loan)
APR 10 1931: Brun Records: Frank Trumbauer & His Orch.
AUG 1 1931: Radio, Paul Whiteman & His Allied Quality Paintmen

CROSS PATCH
(Tot Seymour-Vee Lawnhurst)
JUL 5 1936: Radio, Paul Whiteman & His Orch.

CRY BABY BLUES
(George Meyer-Joe Young-Sam Lewis)
OCT 1921: Brun Records: Gene Rodemich Orch.

CRY, BABY, CRY
(Jimmy Eaton-Terry Shand-Remus Harris-Irving Melsher)
MAR 30 1938: Standard Trans.: Frank Trumbauer & His Orch.

CRYIN' ALL DAY
(Frank Trumbauer-Chauncey Morehouse)
OCT 25 1927: OK Records: Frank Trumbauer & His Orch.

CUBAN LOVE SONG
(Dorothy Fields-Jimmy McHugh-Herbert Stothart)
OCT 6 1931: Vic Records: Paul Whiteman & His Orch.

DAMES
(Al Dubin-Harry Warren)
JUL 26 1934: Radio, Kraft Music Hall: Al Jolson-vocal and Paul Whiteman & His Orch.

DANCE MY DARLINGS
(Oscar Hammerstein II-Sigmund Romberg)
JAN 26 1936: Radio, Musical Varieties: Paul Whiteman & His Orch.

DANCE OF THE HOURS
(A. Ponchielli)
JAN 11 1934: Radio, Kraft Music Hall: Paul Whiteman & His Orch.

DANCE OF THE LITTLE DUTCH DOLLS
(Bon Walker-Sydney Green)
OCT 6 1931: Vic Records: Paul Whiteman & His Orch.

DANCING SHADOWS
(Ernie Golden)
APR 22 1928: Vic Records: Paul Whiteman & His Orch.

DARDANELLA
(Fred Fisher-Felix Bernard-Johnny S. Black)
FEB 9 1928: Vic Records: Paul Whiteman & His Orch.
FEB 9 1936: Radio, Musical Varieties: Paul Whiteman & His Orch.

DARK EYES (based on the Russian folk song OTCHI TCHORNIJA)
(Anonymous)
NOV 22 1934: Radio, Kraft Music Hall: Paul Whiteman & His Orch.
JAN 19 1936: Radio, Musical Varieties: Paul Whiteman & His Orch.
MAY 24 1936: Radio, Musical Varieties: Paul Whiteman & His Orch.

DARKTOWN STRUTTERS' BALL
(Shelton Brooks)
JUL 10 1935: Vic Records: Paul Whiteman & His Orch.

DAY AFTER DAY
(B. G. ''Buddy'' DeSylva-Ralph Carmichael)
MAR 22 1936: Radio, Musical Varieties: Paul Whiteman & His Orch.

DAY OF THE LORD, THE
(composers unidentified)
NOV 29 1934: Radio, Kraft Music Hall: Paul Whiteman & His Orch.

DAYBREAK
(Harold Adamson-Ferde Grofé)
APR 14 1932: Vic Records: Paul Whiteman & His Orch.

DEAR OLD MOTHER DIXIE
(Gus Kahn-Matt Malneck)
MAR 1 1932: Vic Records: Paul Whiteman & His Orch.

DINAH
(Sam M. Lewis-Joe Young-Harry Akst)
APR 5 1932: Col Records: Frank Trumbauer & His Orch.

DINNER FOR ONE PLEASE, JAMES
(Michael Carr)
MAR 22 1936: Radio, Musical Varieties: Paul Whiteman & His Orch.

DIPPER MOUTH BLUES (See: SUGAR FOOT STOMP)

DISTRICT ATTORNEY
(composers unidentified)
DEC 7 1933: Radio, Kraft Music Hall: Paul Whiteman & His Orch.

DIXIE DAWN
(Peter DeRose-Jo Trent)
APR 23 1928: Vic Records: Paul Whiteman & His Orch.

DIXIE LEE
(Alexander Hill)
JAN 11 1934: Radio, Kraft Music Hall: Paul Whiteman & His Orch.

DO I HEAR YOU SAYING?
(Lorenz Hart-Richard Rodgers)
APR 24 1928: Vic Records: Paul Whiteman & His Orch.

DO YOU LOVE ME?
(Harry Ruby)
DEC 20 1945: Vic Records: Johnny Desmond

DO YOU MEAN IT? (aka DID YOU MEAN IT?)
(Phil Baker-Sid Silvers-Abe Lyman)
OCT 26 1927: OK Records: Russell Gray & His Orch.
DEC 4 1936: Radio, The Three T's
DEC 11 1936: Radio, The Three T's

DON'T YOU REMEMBER ME?
(Sunny Skylar-Frankie Carle)
DEC 20 1945: Vic Records: Johnny Desmond

DOODLE-DOO-DOO
(Art Kassel-Mel Stitzel)
SEP 27 1924: Brun Records: Ray Miller & His Orch.

DOWN AND OUT BLUES
(Arthur L. Sizemore)
APR 9 1924: Brun Records: Cotton Pickers

DOWN IN MARYLAND
(Bert Kalmar-Harry Ruby)
JAN 29 1923: Vic Records: Benson Orch.

DOWN IN OLD HAVANA TOWN
(Irving Caesar-Cliff Friend)
MAR 12 1928: Vic Records: Paul Whiteman & His Orch.

DOWN THE OREGON TRAIL
(composers unidentified)
JAN 26 1936: Radio, Musical Varieties: Paul Whiteman & His Orch.

DOWN TO THEIR LAST YACHT sketch
(Ann Ronell-Max Steiner)
JUN 28 1934: Radio, Kraft Music Hall: Paul Whiteman & His Orch.

DOWN T'UNCLE BILLS
(Johnny Mercer-Hoagy Carmichael)
NOV 20 1934: Vic Records: Frank Trumbauer & His Orch.

DREAMS OF INDIA
(Percy Wenrich)
JUN 15 1923: Vic Records: Benson Orch.

DRESS REHEARSALS
(composers unidentified)

ELEGIE
(Jules Massanet)
DEC 6 1934: Radio, Kraft Music Hall: Paul Whiteman & His Orch.

EMALINE
(Mitchell Parish-Frank Perkins)
FEB 23 1934: Brun Records: Frank Trumbauer & His Orch.

END OF A PERFECT DAY, THE
(Lew Brown-Rubey Cowan)
DEC 13 1934: Radio, Kraft Music Hall: Paul Whiteman & His Orch.

ESPAÑA RHAPSODY
(Emmanuel Chabrier)
DEC 6 1934: Radio, Kraft Music Hall: Paul Whiteman & His Orch.

EVENING STAR
(Roy Turk-Fred E. Ahlert)
MAY 13 1928: Col Records: Paul Whiteman & His Orch.
MAY 21 1928: Col Records: Paul Whiteman & His Orch.

"F" BLUES
(Frank Trumbauer)
DEC 28 1933: Radio, Kraft Music Hall: Paul Whiteman & His Orch.

FACE THE MUSIC MEDLEY
(Irving Berlin)
MAR 1 1932: Vic Records: Paul Whiteman & His Orch.

FADED SUMMER LOVE, A
(Phil Baxter)
OCT 6 1931: Vic Records: Paul Whiteman & His Orch.

FANCIES
(Norman Spencer)
OCT 7 1921: Brun Records: Gene Rodemich & His Orch.

FAR AWAY LOOK IN YOUR EYES
(composers unidentified)
JUL 8 1938: Standard Trans.: Frank Trumbauer & His Orch.

FARE-THEE-WELL TO HARLEM
(Johnny Mercer-Bernie Hanighen)
JAN 25 1934: Radio, Kraft Music Hall: Paul Whiteman & His Orch.
FEB 16 1934: Vic Records: Paul Whiteman & His Orch.
DEC 4 1936: Radio, The Three T's
DEC 11 1936: Radio, The Three T's

FAREWELL BLUES
(Elmer Schoebel-Paul Mares-Leon Rappolo)
SEP 7 1935: Vic Records: Paul Whiteman & His Orch.

FELIX THE CAT
(Alfred Bryan-Max Kortlander-Pete Wendling)
MAY 25 1928: Col Records: Paul Whiteman & His Orch.

FLAT FOOT FLOOGIE
(Slim Gaillard-Slam Stewart-Bud Green)
JUL 8 1938: Standard Trans.: Frank Trumbauer & His Orch.

FLIGHT OF A HAYBAG
(Frank Trumbauer)
JAN 29 1936: Brun Records: Frank Trumbauer & His Orch.
FEB 2 1936: Radio, Musical Varieties: Paul Whiteman & His Orch.

FLOCK O' BLUES
(Rube Bloom)
OCT 9 1924: Gennett Records: Sioux City Six

FOLLIES
(composers unidentified)
JAN 25 1934: Radio, Kraft Music Hall: Paul Whiteman & His Orch.

FOOLISH CHILD
(Lindsay McPhail-Roy Bargy-Jack Nelson)
AUG 27 1923: Vic Records: Benson Orch.

FOOLS
(composers unidentified)
JAN 8 1937: Radio, The Three T's

FOR NO REASON AT ALL IN C
(Joseph Meyer-Sam Lewis-Joseph Young)
MAY 13 1927: OK Records: Tram-Bix-Lang

FOR YOU
(Al Dubin-Joe Burke)
MAR 26 1937: Vic Records: Paul Whiteman & His Orch.

FORGET-ME-NOT
(. . . MacBeth)
APR 22 1928: Vic Records: Paul Whiteman & His Orch.

FORTY-SECOND STREET
(Al Dubin-Harry Warren)
FEB 10 1937: Radio, Frank Trumbauer & His Orch.
FEB 12 1937: Radio, Frank Trumbauer & His Orch.

FOUR DETECTIVES
(composers unidentified)
DEC 7 1933: Radio, Kraft Music Hall: Paul Whiteman & His Orch.

FRENCH CAFE MEDLEY
(composers unidentified)
NOV 22 1934: Radio, Kraft Music Hall: Paul Whiteman & His Orch.

FROM MONDAY ON
(Bing Crosby-Harry Barris)
JAN 20 1927: OK Records: Frank Trumbauer & His Orch.
FEB 28 1928: Vic Records: Paul Whiteman & His Orch.

FROM ONE TILL TWO
(J. Russel Robinson-Roy Turk)
APR 23 1924: Brun Records: Ray Miller Orch.

FROST ON THE MOON (See: THERE'S FROST ON THE MOON)

FUNNY LITTLE WORLD
(Ann Ronell)
JUN 28 1934: Radio, Kraft Music Hall: Paul Whiteman & His Orch.

FUTURISTIC RHYTHM
(Dorothy Fields-Jimmy McHugh)
MAR 8 1929: OK Records: Frank Trumbauer & His Orch.

"G" BLUES
(Frank Trumbauer)
JAN 16 1934: Vic Records: Paul Whiteman & His Orch.
APR 17 1934: Vic Records: Paul Whiteman & His Orch.

GARDEN IN THE RAIN, A
(James Dyrenforth-Carroll Gibbons)
MAR 14 1946: Vic Records: Perry Como

GARDEN OF WEED
(Reginald G. Foresythe)
JUL 10 1935: Vic Records: Paul Whiteman & His Orch.

GEORGE WHITE'S SCANDALS MEDLEY
(Lew Brown-Ray Henderson)
NOV 30 1931: Vic Records: Paul Whiteman & His Orch.

GEORGIA BLUES
(Billy Higgins-W. Benton Overstreet)
MAY 20 1924: OK Records: Arkansas Travelers

GEORGIA CABIN DOOR
(Eleanor Young-Harry Squires)
JAN 30 1923: Vic Records: Benson Orch.

GEORGIA ON MY MIND
(Stuart Gorrell-Hoagy Carmichael)
APR 10 1931: Brun Records: Frank Trumbauer & His Orch.
JUN 24 1931: Brun Records: Frank Trumbauer & His Orch.

GEORGIE PORGIE
(Billy Mayerl-Gerald Paul)
JUN 17 1928: Col Records: Paul Whiteman & His Orch.

GET HAPPY
(Ted Koehler-Harold Arlen)
MAY 10 1930: OK Records: Frank Trumbauer & His Orch.

GET OUT AND GET UNDER THE MOON
(Charlie Tobias-William Jerome-Larry Shay)
MAY 22 1928: Col Records: Paul Whiteman & His Orch.

GETTIN' SENTIMENTAL
(Gus Kahn-Matty Malneck)
OCT 1 1931: Vic Records: Paul Whiteman & His Orch.

GHOST OF A CHANCE, A (aka I DON'T STAND A GHOST OF A CHANCE)
(Ned Washington-Bing Crosby-Victor Young)
FEB 22 1940: Var Records: Frank Trumbauer & His Orch.

GIRL OF MY DREAMS
(Sunny Clapp)
MAR 21 1946: Vic Records: Perry Como

GIVE ME A HEART TO SING TO
(Ned Washington-Maxson E. Judell-Victor Young)
FEB 16 1936: Radio, Musical Varieties: Paul Whiteman & His Orch.

GLOOMY SUNDAY
(Sam M. Lewis-Rezso Seress)
MAR 13 1936: Vic Records: Paul Whiteman & His Orch.

GLORY ROAD
(Jacques Wolfe-Clement Wood)
MAR 15 1936: Radio, Musical Varieties: Paul Whiteman & His Orch.

GOING HOLLYWOOD MEDLEY
(Arthur Freed-Nacio Herb Brown)
NOV 30 1933: Radio, Kraft Music Hall: Paul Whiteman & His Orch.

GOOD MAN IS HARD TO FIND, A
(Eddie Green)
OCT 25 1927: OK Records: Frank Trumbauer & His Orch.

GOOD MORNING GLORY
(Mack Gordon-Harry Revel)
JAN 4 1934: Radio, Kraft Music Hall: Paul Whiteman & His Orch.

GOOD NIGHT, ANGEL
(Herb Magidson-Allie Wrubel)
FEB 11 1938: Standard Trans.: Frank Trumbauer & His Orch.

GOODNIGHT SWEETHEART
(Ray Noble-James Campbell-Reg Connelly-Rudy Vallee)
DEC 1 1931: Vic Records: Paul Whiteman & His Orch.

GOODY, GOODY
(Johnny Mercer-Matt Malneck)
JAN 12 1936: Radio, Musical Varieties: Paul Whiteman & His Orch.
FEB 16 1936: Radio, Musical Varieties: Paul Whiteman & His Orch.

GOOPY GEER
(Frank Marsales)
DEC 14 1933: Radio, Kraft Music Hall: Paul Whiteman & His Orch.

APR 5 1936: Radio, Musical Varieties: Paul Whiteman & His Orch.
MAY 24 1936: Radio, Musical Varieties: Paul Whiteman & His Orch.

GOT A BRAN' NEW SUIT
(Howard Dietz-Arthur Schwartz)
JAN 19 1936: Radio, Musical Varieties: Paul Whiteman & His Orch.

GOT A FEELING FOR YOU
(Jo Trent-Fred E. Ahlert)
MAY 21 1929: OK Records: Frank Trumbauer & His Orch.

GRAND CANYON SUITE (CLOUDBURST)
(Ferde Grofé)
APR 28 1932: Vic Records: Paul Whiteman & His Orch.

GRAND CANYON SUITE (CLOUDBURST) (Part 1)
(Ferde Grofé)
APR 28 1932: Vic Records: Paul Whiteman & His Orch.

GRAND CANYON SUITE (CLOUDBURST) (Part 2)
(Ferde Grofé)
APR 28 1932: Vic Records: Paul Whiteman & His Orch.

GRAND CANYON SUITE (ON THE TRAIL)
(Ferde Grofé)
MAR 22 1936: Radio, Musical Varieties: Paul Whiteman & His Orch.

GRAND CANYON SUITE (ON THE TRAIL) (Part 1)
(Ferde Grofé)
APR 27 1932: Vic Records: Paul Whiteman & His Orch.

GRAND CANYON SUITE (ON THE TRAIL) (Part 2)
(Ferde Grofé)
APR 27 1932: Vic Records: Paul Whiteman & His Orch.

GREAT WALTZ
(Desmond Carter-Johann Strauss Sr-Johann Strauss Jr)
DEC 20 1934: Radio, Kraft Music Hall: Paul Whiteman & His Orch.

GREEN FIELDS AND BLUEBIRDS
(Alfred Bryan-Larry Stock)
MAR 22 1936: Radio, Musical Varieties: Paul Whiteman & His Orch.

GRIEVING
(Wayland Axtell)
APR 24 1928: Vic Records: Paul Whiteman & His Orch.

GYPSY
(L. Wolfe Gilbert-Matt Malneck-Frank Signorelli)
SEP 18 1928: Col Records: Paul Whiteman & His Orch.

GYPSY BLUES
(Noble Sissle-Eubie Blake)
OCT 1921: Brun Records: Gene Rodemich Orch.

GYPSY IN MY SOUL, THE
(Moe Jaffe-Clay Boland)
FEB 11 1938: Standard Trans.: Frank Trumbauer & His Orch.

HAPPY BIRTHDAY TO C.B.S.
(Patty Smith Hill-Mildred J. Hill)
MAY 30 1938: Radio, Frank Trumbauer & His Orch.

HAPPY FEET
(Jack Yellen-Milton Ager)
NOV-DEC 1929: Film: King Of Jazz (Paul Whiteman Orch.)
FEB 10 1930: Col Records: Paul Whiteman & His Orch.
MAY 8 1930: OK Records: Frank Trumbauer & His Orch.

HAY, STRAW
(Oscar Hammerstein II-Vincent Youmans)
MAY 5 1931: Radio, Paul Whiteman & His Allied Quality Paintmen

HIGH WATER
(J. Keirn Brennan-Marsh McCurdy)
FEB 28 1928: Vic Records: Paul Whiteman & His Orch.

HILLBILLY FROM TENTH AVENUE
(M. K. Jerome-Jack Scholl)
FEB 11 1938: Standard Trans.: Frank Trumbauer & His Orch.

HILLBILLY SONG
(composers unidentified)
MAY 24 1936: Radio, Musical Varieties: Paul Whiteman & His Orch.

HINDUSTAN
(Oliver Wallace)
MAR 8 1936: Radio, Musical Varieties: Paul Whiteman & His Orch.

HITTIN' THE BOTTLE
(Ted Koehler-Harold Arlen)
JUN 22 1930: OK Records: Frank Trumbauer & His Orch.

HOLD ME IN YOUR ARMS
(S. J. Stocco)
APR 11 1925: Brun Records: Ray Miller Orch.

HOME LIFE OF THE SNORF
(composers unidentified)
JAN 28 1938: Standard Trans.: Frank Trumbauer & His Orch.

HOME ON THE RANGE
(Dan Kelley-Dr. Brewster Higley)
DEC 7 1933: Radio, Kraft Music Hall: Paul Whiteman & His Orch.

HOME TOWN
(Jim Kennedy-Michael Carr)
JAN 28 1938: Standard Trans.: Frank Trumbauer & His Orch.

HONEYSUCKLE ROSE
(Andy Razaf-Thomas ''Fats'' Waller)
APR 10 1931: Brun Records: Frank Trumbauer & His Orch.
JUN 24 1931: Brun Records: Frank Trumbauer & His Orch.
JAN 8 1937: Radio, The Three T's

HONKY TONK TRAIN BLUES
(Hal Miller)
FEB 23 1940: Var Records: Frank Trumbauer & His Orch.

HOOSIER SWEETHEART
(Paul Ash-Billy Baskett-Joe Goodwin)
JAN 31 1927: Vic Records: Jean Goldkette & His Orch.

HOSANNA
(Richard Maxwell-William F. Wirges)
MAY 5 1931: Radio, Paul Whiteman & His Allied Quality Paintmen

HOT CHA MEDLEY
(Lew Brown-Ray Henderson)
MAR 2 1932: Vic Records: Paul Whiteman & His Orch.

HOT SPELL
(composers unidentified)
JAN 28 1938: Standard Trans.: Frank Trumbauer & His Orch.

HOUSE IS HAUNTED, THE
(Billy Rose-Basil Adlam)
MAR 28 1934: Vic Records: Ramona (Davies)

HOW ABOUT ME?
(Irving Berlin)
DEC 14 1928: Col Records: Paul Whiteman & His Orch.
DEC 19 1928: Col Records: Paul Whiteman & His Orch.
JAN 11 1929: Col Records: Paul Whiteman & His Orch.

HOW AM I TO KNOW?
(Dorothy Parker-Jack King)

SEP 18 1929: OK Records: Frank Trumbauer & His Orch.
JAN 12 1934: Brun Records: Frank Trumbauer & His Orch.

HOW CAN YOU FORGET?
(Lorenz Hart-Richard Rodgers)
APR 20 1938: Standard Trans.: Frank Trumbauer & His Orch.

HOWDJA LIKE TO LOVE ME?
(Frank Loesser-Burton Lane)
MAR 30 1938: Standard Trans.: Frank Trumbauer & His Orch.

HUGUETTE WALTZ
(Brian Hooker-Rudolf Friml)
JAN 19 1936: Radio, Musical Varieties: Paul Whiteman & His Orch.

HUMPTY DUMPTY
(Fud Livingston)
SEP 28 1927: OK Records: Frank Trumbauer & His Orch.

HUNDRED PIPERS, A
(composers unidentified)
DEC 20 1934: Radio, Kraft Music Hall: Paul Whiteman & His Orch.

HUNDRED YEARS FROM TODAY, A
(Ned Washington-Joseph Young-Victor Young)
DEC 14 1933: Radio, Kraft Music Hall: Paul Whiteman & His Orch.

HUNGARIA
(composers unidentified)
FEB 4 1925: Brun Records: Rhythmodic Orch.

HUSH-A-BYE
(. . . Galvin-Robert E. Spencer)
OCT 12 1926: Vic Records: Jean Goldkette & His Orch.

HYMN TO THE SUN
(Rimsky-Korsakov)

APR 5 1936: Radio, Musical Varieties: Paul Whiteman & His Orch.

I BUILT A DREAM ONE DAY
(Oscar Hammerstein II-Sigmund Romberg)
JAN 26 1936: Radio, Musical Varieties: Paul Whiteman & His Orch.

I CAN PULL A RABBIT OUT OF MY HAT
(Mack David-Matt Malneck)
MAR 8 1936: Radio, Musical Varieties: Paul Whiteman & His Orch.

I CAN'T FACE THE MUSIC
(Rube Bloom-Ted Koehler)
APR 20 1938: Standard Trans.: Frank Trumbauer & His Orch.

I CAN'T GET THE ONE I WANT
(Lou Handman-Billy Rose-Herman Ruby)
JUL 10 1924: Brun Records: Ray Miller Orch.

I CAN'T GIVE YOU ANYTHING BUT LOVE
(Dorothy Fields-Jimmy McHugh)
SEP 21 1928: Col Records: Paul Whiteman & His Orch.

I DIDN'T CARE TILL I LOST YOU
(composers unidentified)
JUN 6 1924: Brun Records: Ray Miller Orch.
JUL 22 1924: Brun Records: Ray Miller Orch.

I DON'T SUPPOSE
(Gus Kahn-Matt Malneck)
DEC 3 1931: Vic Records: Paul Whiteman & His Orch.

I DOUBLE DARE YOU
(Terry Shand-Jimmy Eaton)
DEC 15 1937: Standard Trans.: Frank Trumbauer & His Orch.

I DREAM TOO MUCH
(Dorothy Fields-Jerome Kern)
DEC 2 1935: Vic Records: Paul Whiteman & His Orch.

I FEEL A SONG COMIN' ON
(Dorothy Fields-Jimmy McHugh-George Oppenheimer)
JUL 10 1935: Vic Records: Paul Whiteman & His Orch.
DEC 26 1935: Radio, Kraft Music Hall: Paul Whiteman & His Orch.

I FEEL LIKE A FEATHER IN THE BREEZE
(Mack Gordon-Harry Revel)
JAN 26 1936: Radio, Musical Varieties: Paul Whiteman & His Orch.

I FOUND A DREAM
(Jay Gorney-Don Hartman)
JAN 5 1936: Radio, Musical Varieties: Paul Whiteman & His Orch.
FEB 2 1936: Radio, Musical Varieties: Paul Whiteman & His Orch.

I GET A KICK OUT OF YOU
(Cole Porter)
OCT 26 1934: Vic Records: Paul Whiteman & His Orch.
OCT 26 1934: Vic Records: Paul Whiteman & His Orch.

I GOT LOVE
(composers unidentified)
DEC 2 1935: Vic Records: Paul Whiteman & His Orch.

I GOT RHYTHM (aka I'VE GOT RHYTHM)
(Ira Gershwin-George Gershwin)
DEC 25 1936: Radio, The Three T's
DEC 1936: Radio, The Three T's
DEC 1936: Radio, The Three T's
DEC 1936: Radio, The Three T's
JAN 8 1937: Radio, The Three T's

I HIT A NEW HIGH
(Harold Adamson-Jimmy McHugh)
DEC 15 1938: Standard Trans.: Frank Trumbauer & His Orch.

I HOPE GABRIEL LIKES MY MUSIC
(David Franklin)
FEB 5 1936: Brun Records: Frank Trumbauer & His Orch.
MAR 22 1936: Radio, Musical Varieties: Paul Whiteman & His Orch.

I JUST COULDN'T TAKE IT BABY
(Mann Holiner-Alberta Nichols)
DEC 14 1933: Radio, Kraft Music Hall: Paul Whiteman & His Orch.

I LIKE A BALALAIKA
(F. D. Ballard-Charles E. Henderson)
NOV 22 1934: Radio, Kraft Music Hall: Paul Whiteman & His Orch.

I LIKE MUSIC
(composers unidentified)
JUL 8 1938: Standard Trans.: Frank Trumbauer & His Orch.

I LIKE THAT
(Lennie Hayton-Frank Trumbauer)
APR 30 1929: OK Records: Frank Trumbauer & His Orch.

I LIKE THE LIKES OF YOU
(E. Y. "Yip" Harburg-Vernon Duke)
JAN 25 1934: Radio, Kraft Music Hall: Paul Whiteman & His Orch.

I LIKE TO DO THINGS FOR YOU
(Jack Yellen-Milton Ager)
NOV-DEC 1929: Film: King Of Jazz
MAR 23 1930: Col Records: Paul Whiteman & His Orch.
MAY 8 1930: OK Records: Frank Trumbauer & His Orch.

I NEVER KNEW
(Gus Kahn-Ted Fiorito)
JAN 8 1937: Radio, The Three T's
JAN 1937: Radio, Frank Trumbauer & His Orch.

I NEVER MISS THE SUNSHINE
(Norman Harvey-Neil Pardette)
JUN 14 1923: Vic Records: Benson Orch.

I SAW STARS
(Maurice Sigler-Al Goodhart-Al Hoffman)
AUG 18 1934: Vic Records: Paul Whiteman & His Orch.

I SAW YOU DANCING IN MY DREAMS
(composers unidentified)
JUN 29 1934: Vic Records: Paul Whiteman & His Orch.

I SAW YOU LAST NIGHT
(Mort Greene)
APR 20 1938: Standard Trans.: Frank Trumbauer & His Orch.

I SURRENDER, DEAR
(Gordon Clifford-Harry Barris)
FEB 22 1940: Var Records: Frank Trumbauer & His Orch.

I THINK YOU'RE A HONEY
(composers unidentified)
AUG 7 1932: Col Records: Paul Whiteman & His Orch.

I WAS DOING ALL RIGHT
(Ira Gershwin-George Gershwin)
JAN 28 1938: Standard Trans.: Frank Trumbauer & His Orch.

I'D CLIMB THE HIGHEST MOUNTAIN
(Lew Brown-Sidney Clare)
FEB 12 1937: Radio, Frank Trumbauer & His Orch.

I'D RATHER BE THE GIRL IN YOUR ARMS
(. . . Thompson-Harry Archer)

OCT 12 1926: Vic Records: Jean Goldkette & His Orch.
OCT 15 1926: Vic Records: Jean Goldkette & His Orch.

I'D RATHER CRY OVER YOU
(Jack Yellen-Dan Dougherty-Phil Ponce)
MAY 22 1928: Col Records: Paul Whiteman & His Orch.
JUN 10 1928: Col Records: Paul Whiteman & His Orch.

I'D RATHER LEAD A BAND
(Irving Berlin)
MAR 15 1936: Radio, Musical Varieties: Paul Whiteman & His Orch.

IDOLIZING
(Sam Messenheimer- . . . Abrahamson- . . . West)
OCT 12 1926: Vic Records: Jean Goldkette & His Orch.

IF DREAMS COME TRUE
(Irving Mills-Edgar Sampson-Benny Goodman)
APR 20 1938: Standard Trans.: Frank Trumbauer & His Orch.

IF I HAD A TALKING PICTURE OF YOU
(Lew Brown-Stephen W. Ballantine-B. G. ''Buddy'' DeSylva-Ray Henderson)
OCT 16 1929: Col Records: Paul Whiteman & His Orch.

IF I LOVE AGAIN
(Jack Murray-Ben Oakland)
JAN 16 1934: Vic Records: Paul Whiteman & His Orch.
MAY 24 1934: Radio, Kraft Music Hall: Paul Whiteman & His Orch.

IF I SHOULD LOSE YOU
(Leo Robin-Ralph Rainger)
MAR 8 1936: Radio, Musical Varieties: Paul Whiteman & His Orch.

IF IT'S LOVE
(Don Redman)

DEC 20 1934: Radio, Kraft Music Hall: Paul Whiteman & His Orch.

IF THE MOON TURNS GREEN
(Paul Coates-Bernie Hanighen)
JAN 23 1935: Vic Records: Paul Whiteman & His Orch.

IF YOU DON'T LOVE ME
(Jack Yellen-Milton Ager)
JUN 17 1928: Col Records: Paul Whiteman & His Orch.

IF YOU LOVE ME
(Ray Noble)
FEB 2 1936: Radio, Musical Varieties: Paul Whiteman & His Orch.

IF YOU WERE THE ONLY GIRL IN THE WORLD
(Clifford Grey-Nat D. Ayer)
MAR 21 1946: Vic Records: Perry Como

I'LL BE FAITHFUL
(Ned Washington-Allie Wrubel)
DEC 7 1933: Radio, Kraft Music Hall: Paul Whiteman & His Orch.

I'LL DREAM TONIGHT
(Johnny Mercer-Richard A. Whiting)
JUL 8 1938: Standard Trans.: Frank Trumbauer & His Orch.

I'LL NEVER SAY "NEVER AGAIN" AGAIN
(Harry Woods)
FEB 2 1936: Radio, Musical Varieties: Paul Whiteman & His Orch.

I'LL SEE YOU IN MY DREAMS
(Gus Kahn-Isham Jones)
DEC 4 1924: Brun Records: Ray Miller Orch.
APR 5 1932: Col Records: Frank Trumbauer & His Orch.

I'LL STILL BE LOVING YOU
(Al Stillman)
JUL 8 1938: Standard Trans.: Frank Trumbauer & His Orch.

I'LL TAKE HER BACK
(Ed G. Nelson-Steve Nelson-Albert J. Trace)
Feb 22 1925: Brun Records: Ray Miller Orch.

ILL WIND (YOU'RE BLOWIN' ME NO GOOD)
(Ted Koehler-Harold Arlen)
Apr 19 1934: Radio, Kraft Music Hall: Paul Whiteman & His Orch.

I'M A DING DONG DADDY FROM DUMAS
(Phil Baxter)
FEB 23 1936: Radio, Musical Varieties: Paul Whiteman & His Orch.

I'M A DREAMER, AREN'T WE ALL?
(B. G. ''Buddy'' DeSylva-Ray Henderson)
OCT 16 1929: Col Records: Paul Whiteman & His Orch.

I'M AFRAID OF YOU
(Archie Gottler-Lew Daly-Eddie Davis)
APR 21 1928: Vic Records: Paul Whiteman & His Orch.

I'M AN OLD COWHAND
(Johnny Mercer)
JUN 15 1936: Brun Records: Frank Trumbauer & His Orch.
DEC 4 1936: Radio, The Three T's
DEC 11 1936: Radio, The Three T's
DEC 18 1936: Radio, The Three T's
FEB 12 1937: Radio, Frank Trumbauer & His Orch.

I'M BRINGING A RED, RED ROSE
(Gus Kahn-Walter Donaldson)
DEC 12 1928: Col Records: Paul Whiteman & His Orch.
DEC 19 1928: Col Records: Paul Whiteman & His Orch.

I'M BUILDING UP AN AWFUL LETDOWN
(Johnny Mercer-Fred Astaire)
FEB 9 1936: Radio, Musical Varieties: Paul Whiteman & His Orch.

I'M COMING VIRGINIA
(Will Cook-Donald Heywood)
MAY 13 1927: OK Records: Frank Trumbauer & His Orch.
APR 19 1934: Radio, Kraft Music Hall: Paul Whiteman & His Orch.
FEB 3 1937: Radio, Frank Trumbauer & His Orch.

I'M COUNTING ON YOU
(Milton Drake-Ben Oakland)
AUG 18 1934: Vic Records: Paul Whiteman & His Orch.

I'M DRIFTING BACK TO DREAMLAND
(Charles F. Harrison-Jack Sadler-Florence Charlesworth)
JUN 13 1923: Vic Records: Benson Orch.
JUN 15 1923: Vic Records: Benson Orch.

I'M GLAD
(Frank Trumbauer)
OCT 9 1924: Gennett Records: Sious City Six

I'M GOING HOME
(Jules Buffano-Jimmy Durante)
JUL 19 1936: Radio, Paul Whiteman & His Orch.

I'M GONNA MEET MY SWEETIE NOW
(Jesse Greer-Benny Davis)
JAN 31 1927: Vic Records: Jean Goldkette & His Orch.

I'M GONNA SIT RIGHT DOWN AND WRITE MYSELF A LETTER
(Joe Young-Fred E. Ahlert)
FEB 23 1936: Radio, Musical Varieties: Paul Whiteman & His Orch.

I'M GONNA TRAMP! TRAMP! TRAMP!
(Stephen W. Ballantine-B. G. ''Buddy'' DeSylva-Harry M. Woods)
OCT 15 1924: Brun Records: Al Jolson

I'M IN A HAPPY FRAME OF MIND
(Rube Bloom-Mitchell Parish)
MAR 30 1938: Standard Trans.: Frank Trumbauer & His Orch.

I'M IN SEVENTH HEAVEN
(Al Jolson-B. G. ''Buddy'' DeSylva-Lew Brown-Ray Henderson)
APR 5 1928: Col Records: Paul Whiteman & His Orch.

I'M IN THE MOOD FOR LOVE
(Dorothy Fields-Jimmy McHugh)
JUL 10 1935: Vic Records: Paul Whiteman & His Orch.

I'M JUST WILD ABOUT HARRY
(Noble Sissle-Eubie Blake)
DEC 14 1933: Radio, Kraft Music Hall: Paul Whiteman & His Orch.
DEC 6 1934: Radio, Kraft Music Hall: Paul Whiteman & His Orch.

I'M KEEPING THOSE KEEPSAKES FOR YOU
(Fred E. Ahlert-Richard B. Smith)
JAN 23 1935: Vic Records: Paul Whiteman & His Orch.

I'M LOOKING OVER A FOUR LEAF CLOVER
(Mort Dixon-Harry Woods)
JAN 28 1927: Vic Records: Jean Goldkette & His Orch.

I'M MORE THAN SATISFIED
(Ted Klages-Thomas ''Fats'' Waller)
OCT 20 1927: Per Records: Willard Robison

I'M ON THE CREST OF A WAVE
(B. G. ''Buddy'' DeSylva-Lew Brown-Ray Henderson)
JUN 17 1928: Col Records: Paul Whiteman & His Orch.

I'M PUTTING ALL MY EGGS IN ONE BASKET
(Irving Berlin)
MAR 22 1936: Radio, Musical Varieties: Paul Whiteman & His Orch.

I'M SHOOTING HIGH
(Ted Koehler-Jimmy McHugh)
FEB 16 1936: Radio, Musical Varieties: Paul Whiteman & His Orch.

I'M SITTIN' HIGH ON A HILLTOP
(Gus Kahn-Arthur Johnston)
JUL 10 1935: Vic Records: Paul Whiteman & His Orch.
SEP 29 1935: Radio, Magic Key Of Radio: Paul Whiteman & His Orch.

I'M SO IN LOVE WITH YOU
(Kim Gannon-Walter Kent)
FEB 1 1934: Radio, Kraft Music Hall: Paul Whiteman & His Orch.

I'M SORRY DEAR
(Anson Weeks-Harry Tobias-Johnnie Scott)
DEC 1 1931: Vic Records: Paul Whiteman & His Orch.

I'M THE ECHO (YOU'RE THE SONG THAT I SING)
(Dorothy Fields-Jerome Kern)
DEC 2 1935: Vic Records: Paul Whiteman & His Orch.

I'M THE MAYOR OF ALABAM (See: MAYOR OF ALABAM)

I'M WALKING THE CHALK LINE
(Mann Holiner-Alberta Nichols)
DEC 14 1933: Radio, Kraft Music Hall: Paul Whiteman & His Orch.

I'M WINGING HOME
(Benee Russell-Henry Tobias)
MAR 12 1928: Vic Records: Paul Whiteman & His Orch.

IN THE EVENING
(James F. Hanley-Eddie Dowling)
MAY 23 1928: Col Records: Paul Whiteman & His Orch.
JUN 10 1928: Col Records: Paul Whiteman & His Orch.

IN THE EYES OF MY IRISH COLLEEN
(Charles Tobias-Nat Simon)
DEC 20 1945: Vic Records: Johnny Desmond

IN THE GOOD OLD SUMMERTIME
(Ren Shields-George Evans)
SEP 4 1928: Col Records: Paul Whiteman & His Orch.
SEP 14 1928: Col Records: Paul Whiteman & His Orch.

IN THE GOOD OLD SUMMERTIME MEDLEY
(Ren Shields-George Evans)
SEP 4 1928: Col Records: Paul Whiteman & His Orch.
SEP 14 1928: Col Records: Paul Whiteman & His Orch.

IN THE MERRY MONTH OF MAYBE
(Ira Gershwin-Billy Rose-Harry Warren)
JUN 24 1931: Brun Records: Frank Trumbauer & His Orch.

IN THE MOON MIST
(Jack Lawrence)
DEC 20 1945: Vic Records: Johnny Desmond

IN THE NEIGHBORHOOD OF HEAVEN
(John Jacob Loeb-Carmen Lombardo)
MAY 25 1938: Standard Trans.: Frank Trumbauer & His Orch.

INDIAN LOVE CALL
(Otto Harbach-Oscar Hammerstein II-Rudolf Friml)
DEC 5 1924: Brun Records: Ray Miller Orch.

INKA DINKA DOO
(Ben Ryan-Jimmy Durante)
JAN 25 1934: Radio, Kraft Music Hall: Paul Whiteman & His Orch.

INVICTUS
(William Ernest Hanley-Bruno Hahn)
NOV 29 1934: Radio, Kraft Music Hall: Paul Whiteman & His Orch.

IRISH WASHERWOMAN
(Traditional Irish folk dance)
MAR 30 1938: Standard Trans.: Frank Trumbauer & His Orch.
FEB 25 1939: Radio, Frank Trumbauer & His Orch.
FEB 22 1940: Var Records: Frank Trumbauer & His Orch.

IRVING BERLIN MEDLEY
(Irving Berlin)
OCT 11 1934: Radio, Kraft Music Hall: Paul Whiteman & His Orch.

IS IT GONNA BE LONG?
(Rubey Cowan-George Whiting)
MAY 22 1928: Col Records: Paul Whiteman & His Orch.

IS IT TRUE WHAT THEY SAY ABOUT DIXIE?
(Irving Caesar-Sammy Lerner-Gerald Marks)
MAY 24 1936: Radio, Musical Varieties: Paul Whiteman & His Orch.

I'SE A MUGGIN'
(Stuff Smith)
FEB 23 1936: Radio, Musical Varieties: Paul Whiteman & His Orch.
MAR 15 1936: Radio, Musical Varieties: Paul Whiteman & His Orch.

I'SE A MUGGIN (Part 1)
(Stuff Smith)
MAR 10 1937: Vic Records: The Three T's

I'SE A MUGGIN (Part 2)
(Stuff Smith)
MAR 10 1937: Vic Records: The Three T's

ISN'T THIS A LOVELY DAY?
(Irving Berlin)
SEP 28 1935: Vic Records: Paul Whiteman & His Orch.

ISN'T IT WONDERFUL, ISN'T IT SWELL
(Lew Pollack-Sidney Mitchell)
JUL 8 1938: Standard Trans.: Frank Trumbauer & His Orch.

IT HAPPENED IN CHICAGO IN '33 sketch
(Billy Rose-Irving Kahal-Dana Suesse)
JUL 19 1936: Radio, Paul Whiteman & His Orch.

IT HAPPENED IN MONTEREY
(Billy Rose-Mabel Wayne)
NOV-DEC 1929: Film: King Of Jazz
FEB 10 1930: Col Records: Paul Whiteman & His Orch.
MAR 21 1930: Col Records: Paul Whiteman & His Orch.

IT WAS THE DAWN OF LOVE
(J. Fred Coots-Lou Davis)
APR 22 1928: Vic Records: Paul Whiteman & His Orch.

ITALIAN STREET SONG
(Rida Johnson Young-Victor Herbert)
MAY 24 1934: Radio, Kraft Music Hall: Paul Whiteman & His Orch.

ITCHOLA
(David D. Rose-Frank Trumbauer)
AUG 18 1934: Vic Records: Paul Whiteman & His Orch.
DEC 15 1938: Standard Trans.: Frank Trumbauer & His Orch.

IT'S AN OLD FASHIONED WORLD AFTER ALL
(Alfred Bryan-George W. Meyer-Pete Wendling)
JAN 16 1934: Vic Records: Paul Whiteman & His Orch.

IT'S BEEN SO LONG
(Harold Adamson-Walter Donaldson)
MAR 8 1936: Radio, Musical Varieties: Paul Whiteman & His Orch.

IT'S GOT TO BE LOVE
(Lorenz Hart-Richard Rodgers)
MAR 13 1936: Vic Records: Paul Whiteman & His Orch.
MAY 24 1936: Radio, Musical Varieties: Paul Whiteman & His Orch.

IT'S THE DREAMER IN ME
(Jimmy Dorsey-Jimmy Van Heusen)
MAY 25 1938: Standard Trans.: Frank Trumbauer & His Orch.

IT'S THE LITTLE THINGS THAT COUNT
(Haven Gillespie-Seymour B. Simons)
MAY 25 1938: Standard Trans.: Frank Trumbauer & His Orch.

IT'S WONDERFUL
(B. G. ''Buddy'' DeSylva-Harold Atteridge)
FEB 11 1938: Standard Trans.: Frank Trumbauer & His Orch.

I'VE GOT A FEELIN' FOR YOU
(Jo Trent-Fred E. Ahlert)
MAY 21 1929: OK Records: Frank Trumbauer & His Orch.

I'VE GOT A FEELING I'M FALLING
(Billy Rose-Harry Link-Thomas ''Fats'' Waller)
DEC 11 1928: Col Records: Paul Whiteman & His Orch.
DEC 19 1928: Col Records: Paul Whiteman & His Orch.

I'VE GOT RHYTHM (See: I GOT RHYTHM)

JACKSONVILLE GAL
(. . . Rose)
FEB 6 1925: Brun Records: Cotton Pickers

JAPANESE MAMMY
(Gus Kahn-Walter Donaldson)
MAY 22 1928: Col Records: Paul Whiteman & His Orch.
JUN 10 1928: Col Records: Paul Whiteman & His Orch.

JAPANESE SANDMAN, THE
(Raymond B. Egan-Richard A. Whiting)
OCT 5 1928: OK Records: Frank Trumbauer & His Orch.

JAZZ ME BLUES, THE
(Tom Delaney-Lucille Hegamin)
FEB 3 1937: Radio, Frank Trumbauer & His Orch.

JEANNINE, I DREAM OF LILAC TIME
(L. Wolfe Gilbert-Nathaniel Shilkret)
SEP 17 1928: Col Records: Paul Whiteman & His Orch.

JEWEL SONG, THE
(Charles Francois Gounod)
JUN 28 1934: Radio, Kraft Music Hall: Paul Whiteman & His Orch.
DEC 6 1934: Radio, Kraft Music Hall: Paul Whiteman & His Orch.

JIMTOWN BLUES
(Fred Rose)
DEC 6 1924: Brun Records: Cotton Pickers
FEB 22 1940: Var Records: Frank Trumbauer & His Orch.

JOCKEY ON THE CAROUSEL, THE
(Dorothy Fields-Jerome Kern)
DEC 2 1935: Vic Records: Paul Whiteman & His Orch.
FEB 16 1936: Radio, Musical Varieties: Paul Whiteman & His Orch.

JOE PALOOKA MEDLEY
(authors unidentified).
DEC 28 1933: Radio, Kraft Music Hall: Paul Whiteman & His Orch.

JOHN Q. PUBLIC
(composers unidentified)
DEC 7 1933: Radio, Kraft Music Hall: Paul Whiteman & His Orch.

JUBA DANCE (aka THE JUBA)
(Nathanicl R. Dett)
JAN 12 1934: Brun Records: Frank Trumbauer & His Orch.
MAR 15 1936: Radio, Musical Varieties: Paul Whiteman & His Orch.
JAN 28 1938: Standard Trans.: Frank Trumbauer & His Orch.

JUBILEE
(Willard Robison)
JAN 9 1928: OK Records: Frank Trumbauer & His Orch.

JUBILEE MEDLEY
(Cole Porter)
SEP 28 1935: Radio, Kraft Music Hall: Paul Whiteman & His Orch.

JUNK MAN
(Frank Loesser-Joseph Meyer)
SEP 18 1934: Brun Records: Jack Teagarden & His Orch.
DEC 12 1936: Radio, Saturday Night Swing Club: The Three T's

JUST A LITTLE BIT OF DRIFTWOOD
(Benny Davis-Abe Lyman)
JUN 18 1928: Col Records: Paul Whiteman & His Orch.

JUST A LITTLE DRINK
(Byron Gay)
MAR 13 1925: Brun Records: Ray Miller & His Orch.

JUST A SWEET OLD GENT AND A QUAINT OLD LADY
(Brown-DeSylva-Henderson)
DEC 15 1937: Standard Trans.: Frank Trumbauer & His Orch.

JUST AN ERROR IN THE NEWS
(Irving Mills-Will Hudson-Henry Nemo)
APR 20 1938: Standard Trans.: Frank Trumbauer & His Orch.

JUST AN HOUR OF LOVE
(Alfred Bryan-Edward Ward)
SEP 30 1927: OK Records: Frank Trumbauer & His Orch.

JUST FOR TONIGHT
(Oscar Geiger)
JUN 14 1923: Vic Records: Benson Orch.

JUST LIKE A MELODY OUT OF THE SKY
(Walter Donaldson)
JUN 17 1928: Col Records: Paul Whiteman & His Orch.

JUST LIKE A RAINBOW
(Robert A. King-Ted Fiorito)
OCT 1921: Brun Records: Gene Rodemich & His Orch.

JUST ONE GIRL
(composers unidentified)
JAN 31 1923: Vic Records: Benson Orch.

JUST ONE MORE KISS
(. . . Owens- . . . Montgomery)
OCT 15 1926: Vic Records: Jean Goldkette & His Orch.

JUST ONE OF THOSE THINGS
(Cole Porter)
SEP 28 1935: Vic Records: Paul Whiteman & His Orch.

KEEP YOUNG AND BEAUTIFUL
(Al Dubin-Harry Warren)
JAN 11 1934: Radio, Kraft Music Hall: Paul Whiteman & His Orch.

KENTUCKY BABE
(Richard Henry Buck-Adam Geibel)
MAR 14 1946: Vic Records: Perry Como

KID IN THE THREE CORNER PANTS, THE
(Al Lewis-John Jacob Loeb)
JAN 8 1937: Radio, The Three T's

KRAZY KAT
(Frank Trumbaucr-Chauncey Morehouse)
SEP 28 1927: OK Records: Frank Trumbauer & His Orch.

L' AVE BLANC
(composers unidentified)
NOV 22 1934: Radio, Kraft Music Hall: Paul Whiteman & His Orch.

L' HENRE EXQUISE
(Reynaldo Hahn-Paul Marie Verlaine)
NOV 29 1934: Radio, Kraft Music Hall: Paul Whiteman & His Orch.

LA CUCARACHA
(Traditional Mexican folk song)
AUG 9 1934: Radio, Kraft Music Hall: Paul Whiteman & His Orch.
NOV 29 1934: Radio, Kraft Music Hall: Paul Whiteman & His Orch.

LA GOLONDRINA
(Narisisco Serradell)
MAY 12 1928: Col Records: Paul Whiteman & His Orch.

LA PALOMA
(Sebastian Yradier)
MAY 12 1928: Col Records: Paul Whiteman & His Orch.
MAY 21 1928: Col Records: Paul Whiteman & His Orch.

LADY BE GOOD (See: OH LADY, BE GOOD)

LANE IN SPAIN, A
(Al Lewis-Carmen Lombardo)
FEB 3 1927: Vic Records: Jean Goldkette & His Orch.

LAST NIGHT I DREAMED YOU KISSED ME
(Gus Kahn-Carmen Lombardo)
MAY 13 1928: Col Records: Paul Whiteman & His Orch.
MAY 21 1928: Col Records: Paul Whiteman & His Orch.

LAST ROUND-UP, THE
(Billy Hill)
JAN 4 1934: Radio, Kraft Music Hall: Paul Whiteman & His Orch.

LATIN QUARTER
(Al Dubin-Harry Warren)
JUL 8 1938: Standard Trans.: Frank Trumbauer & His Orch.

LAUGHING MARIONETTE
(Walter Collins)
MAY 16 1929: Col Records: Paul Whiteman & His Orch.

LAWD, YOU MADE THE NIGHT TOO LONG
(Sam M. Lewis-Victor Young)
APR 14 1932: Vic Records: Paul Whiteman & His Orch.

LAZIEST GAL IN TOWN, THE
(Cole Porter)
FEB 22 1940: Var Records: Frank Trumbauer & His Orch.

LAZY RIVER
(Sid Arodin-Hoagy Carmichael)
DEC 1936: Radio, The Three T's

LE CHALANO
(composers unidentified)
NOV 22 1934: Radio, Kraft Music Hall: Paul Whiteman & His Orch.

LET IT RAIN, LET IT POUR
(Cliff Friend-Walter Donaldson)
MAR 16 1925: Brun Records: Ray Miller & His Orch.

LET'S BEGIN
(Otto Harbach-Jerome Kern)
DEC 13 1934: Radio, Kraft Music Hall: Paul Whiteman & His Orch.

LET'S BREAK THE GOOD NEWS
(Joseph M. Davis-Paul Denniker-Joe Davis)
JUL 8 1938: Standard Trans.: Frank Trumbauer & His Orch.

LET'S DO IT, LET'S FALL IN LOVE
(Cole Porter)
DEC 14 1928: Col Records: Paul Whiteman & His Orch.
DEC 22 1928: Col Records: Paul Whiteman & His Orch.

LET'S FACE THE MUSIC AND DANCE
(Irving Berlin)
MAR 8 1936: Radio, Musical Varieties: Paul Whiteman & His Orch.

LET'S FALL IN LOVE
(Ted Koehler-Harold Arlen)
FEB 1 1934: Radio, Kraft Music Hall: Paul Whiteman & His Orch.

LET'S FALL IN LOVE MEDLEY
(Ted Koehler-Harold Arlen)
DEC 7 1933: Radio, Kraft Music Hall: Paul Whiteman & His Orch.

LET'S FALL IN LOVE OVER AGAIN
(James A. Noble-Wallace C. Williams)
FEB 1 1934: Radio, Musical Varieties: Paul Whiteman & His Orch.

LET'S HAVE ANOTHER CUP OF COFFEE
(Irving Berlin)
MAR 1 1932: Vic Records: Paul Whiteman & His Orch.

LET'S SPILL THE BEANS
(Mack Gordon-Harry Revel)
JAN 23 1935: Vic Records: Paul Whiteman & His Orch.

LET'S TAKE A WALK AROUND THE BLOCK
(Ira Gershwin-E. Y. ''Yip'' Harburg-Harold Arlen)

DEC 20 1934: Radio, Kraft Music Hall: Paul Whiteman & His Orch.

LET'S TAKE ADVANTAGE OF NOW
(composers unidentified)
DEC 20 1934: Radio, Kraft Music Hall: Paul Whiteman & His Orch.

'LEVEN POUNDS OF HEAVEN
(Joe McCarthy-Matt Malneck)
NOV 30 1931: Vic Records: Paul Whiteman & His Orch.

LIEBESTRAUM
(Franz Liszt)
DEC 13 1928: Col Records: Paul Whiteman & His Orch.
APR 5 1936: Radio, Musical Varieties: Paul Whiteman & His Orch.

LIFE BEGINS WHEN YOU'RE IN LOVE
(Lew Brown-Victor Schertzinger)
JAN 26 1936: Radio, Musical Varieties: Paul Whiteman & His Orch.

LIFE IS JUST A BOWL OF CHERRIES
(Lew Brown-Ray Henderson)
NOV 30 1931: Vic Records: Paul Whiteman & His Orch.

LIGHTS OUT
(Billy Hill)
MAR 1 1936: Radio, Musical Varieties: Paul Whiteman & His Orch.

LILA
(Archie Gottler-Maceo Pinkard-Charles Tobias)
APR 3 1928: OK Records: Frank Trumbauer & His Orch.

LILY
(Ballard MacDonald-Harry Warren- . . . Broones)
MAY 16 1927: Vic Records: Jean Goldkette & His Orch.

LINGER AWHILE
(Harry Owens-Vincent Rose)
MAR 24 1937: Radio, Paul Whiteman & His Orch.

LISA LOU
(composers unidentified)
DEC 6 1934: Radio, Kraft Music Hall: Paul Whiteman & His Orch.

LITTLE ANNIE ROONEY
(Michael Nolan)
JAN 31 1923: Vic Records: Benson Orch.
SEP 4 1928: Col Records: Paul Whiteman & His Orch.
SEP 14 1928: Col Records: Paul Whiteman & His Orch.

LITTLE BIT INDEPENDENT, A
(Edgar Leslie-Joe Burke)
JAN 5 1936: Radio, Musical Varieties: Paul Whiteman & His Orch.

LITTLE GIRL
(Madelina Hyde-Francis Henry)
AUG 14 1931: Radio, Paul Whiteman & His Allied Quality Paintmen

LITTLE GIRL BLUE
(Lorenz Hart-Richard Rodgers)
MAR 10 1936: Vic Records: Paul Whiteman & His Orch.

LITTLE LADY MAKE BELIEVE
(Charles Tobias-Nat Simon)
MAY 25 1938: Standard Trans.: Frank Trumbauer & His Orch.

LITTLE MAN, YOU'VE HAD A BUSY DAY
(Maurice Sigler-Al Hoffman-Mable Wayne)
MAR 12 1946: Vic Records: Perry Como

LITTLE MUCHACHA
(composers unidentified)

DEC 13 1934: Radio, Kraft Music Hall: Paul Whiteman & His Orch.

LITTLE OLD LADY
(Stanley Adams-Hoagy Carmichael)
DEC 11 1936: Radio, The Three T's
DEC 18 1936: Radio, The Three T's

LITTLE PAL
(Al Jolson-B. G. ''Buddy'' DeSylva-Lew Brown-Ray Henderson)
APR 5 1929: Col Records: Paul Whiteman & His Orch.
APR 25 1929: Col Records: Paul Whiteman & His Orch.

LITTLE ROCK GETAWAY
(Joe Sullivan)
FEB 23 1940: Frank Trumbauer & His Orch.

LITTLE WOMEN LIKE YOU
(Fred E. Ahlert-Edgar Leslie)
NOV 30 1933: Radio, Kraft Music Hall: Paul Whiteman & His Orch.

LIVIN' IN THE SUNLIGHT, LOVIN' IN THE MOONLIGHT
(Al Lewis-Al Sherman)
MAR 22 1930: Col Records: Paul Whiteman & His Orch.

LIZA (ALL THE CLOUDS'LL ROLL AWAY)
(Gus Kahn-Ira Gershwin-George Gershwin)
DEC 11 1936: Radio, The Three T's
DEC 18 1936: Radio, The Three T's

LOCH LOMOND
(Traditional Scottish folk song)
APR 30 1938: Radio, Frank Trumbauer & His Orch.

LONELY LITTLE MELODY
(Dave Stamper-Gene Buck)
JUL 10 1924: Brun Records: Ray Miller & His Orch.

LONELY MELODY
(Sam Coslow-Hal Dyson-Alfred Grunfeld-Benny Meroff)
JAN 4 1928: Vic Records: Paul Whiteman & His Orch.

LONESOME IN THE MOONLIGHT
(Abel Baer-Benee Russell)
JUN 17 1928: Col Records: Paul Whiteman & His Orch.

'LONG ABOUT MIDNIGHT
(Irving Mills-Alexander Hill)
FEB 23 1934: Brun Records: Frank Trumbauer & His Orch.

LOOK AT THE WORLD AND SMILE
(. . . Caldwell-Raymond Hubbell)
FEB 1 1927: Vic Records: Jean Goldkette & His Orch.

LOOK FOR THE SILVER LINING
(B. G. "Buddy" DeSylva-Jerome Kern)
FEB 6 1936: Vic Records: Paul Whiteman & His Orch.

LOOK IN THE LOOKING GLASS
(. . . Rosoff- . . . Heyman)
AUG 14 1931: Radio, Paul Whiteman & His Allied Quality Paintmen
AUG 1931: Radio, Paul Whiteman & His Allied Quality Paintmen

LOOSE FEET
(Spencer Williams)
JAN 31 1923: Vic Records: Benson Orch.

LOST AND FOUND
(Harold Levy-Pinky Tomlin)
MAR 30 1938: Standard Trans.: Frank Trumbauer & His Orch.

LOST IN A FOG
(Dorothy Fields-Jimmy McHugh)
OCT 11 1934: Radio, Kraft Music Hall: Paul Whiteman & His Orch.

LOST IN MEDITATION
(Irving Mills-Duke Ellington-Juan Tizol-Lou Singer)
JUL 8 1938: Standard Trans.: Frank Trumbauer & His Orch.

LOST MY BABY BLUES
(Ray Hibbeler)
MAY 20 1924: OK Records: Arkansas Travelers

LOTS O' MAMA
(Billy Meyers-Elmer Schoebel)
APR 23 1924: Brun Records: Ray Miller & His Orch.

LOUISE
(Leo Robin-Richard A. Whiting)
APR 17 1928: OK Records: Frank Trumbauer & His Orch.
MAR 15 1929: Col Records: Paul Whiteman & His Orch.

LOUISIANA
(Andy Razaf-Bob Schafer-J. C. Johnson)
APR 23 1928: Vic Records: Paul Whiteman & His Orch.

LOVE AFFAIRS
(Al Dubin-J. Russel Robinson)
SEP 20 1928: OK Records: Frank Trumbauer & His Orch.

LOVE AIN'T NOTHIN' BUT THE BLUES
(Louis Alter-Joe Goodwin-Jo Trent)
SEP 18 1929: OK Records: Frank Trumbauer & His Orch.

LOVE AND LEARN
(Edward Heyman-Arthur Schwartz)
JAN 15 1937: Radio, The Three T's

LOVE IN BLOOM
(Leo Robin-Ralph Rainger)
JUN 29 1934: Vic Records: Paul Whiteman & His Orch.

LOVE IS HERE TO STAY
(Ira Gershwin-George Gershwin)
JAN 28 1938: Standard Trans.: Frank Trumbauer & His Orch.

LOVE IS JUST A FLOWER
(A. Layman-H. Billings-A. Lyman-C. Schonberg)
JUN 13 1923: Vic Records: Benson Orch.

LOVE IS SWEEPING THE COUNTRY
(Ira Gershwin-George Gershwin)
DEC 7 1933: Radio, Kraft Music Hall: Paul Whiteman & His Orch.

LOVE ME
(. . . Aivaz- . . . Morse)
SEP 13 1929: Col Records: Paul Whiteman & His Orch.

LOVE ME TONIGHT
(Bing Crosby-Ned Washington-Victor Young)
MAY 26 1932: Brun Records: Bing Crosby

LOVE NEST, THE
(Otto Harbach-Louis A. Hirsch)
FEB 10 1928: Vic Records: Paul Whiteman & His Orch.
OCT 5 1928: OK Records: Frank Trumbauer & His Orch.

LOVE TALES
(Milton Ager-Benny Davis-Sam H. Stept)
FEB 23 1936: Radio, Musical Varieties: Paul Whiteman & His Orch.

LOVE'S OLD SWEET SONG
(James Luman Molloy-G. Clifton Bingham)
DEC 13 1934: Radio, Kraft Music Hall: Paul Whiteman & His Orch.

LOVELY LADY
(Ted Koehler-Jimmy McHugh)
JAN 19 1936: Radio, Musical Varieties: Paul Whiteman & His Orch.

LOVER, COME BACK TO ME
(Oscar Hammerstein II-Sigmund Romberg)
FEB 7 1929: Col Records: Paul Whiteman & His Orch.

LULLABY OF THE LEAVES
(Joe Young-Bernice Petkere)
SEP 20 1934: Radio, Kraft Music Hall: Paul Whiteman & His Orch.

MADAME BUTTERFLY
(Giacomo Antonio Domenico Michele Puccini)
APR 19 1934: Radio, Kraft Music Hall: Paul Whiteman & His Orch.

MAKE BELIEVE
(Oscar Hammerstein II-Jerome Kern)
JAN 27 1928: Vic Records: Paul Whiteman & His Orch.
MAR 1 1928: Vic Records: Paul Whiteman & His Orch.

MAKE MY COTTON WHERE THE COT-COT-COTTON GROWS
(Anthony Raymond H. Doll-Saul Klein)
OCT 26 1927: Vic Records: Red Nichols' Stompers

MAKIN' WHOOPEE
(Gus Kahn-Walter Donaldson)
DEC 11 1928: Col Records: Paul Whiteman & His Orch.
DEC 22 1928: Col Records: Paul Whiteman & His Orch.

MAMA'S GONE GOODBYE
(A. J. Piron)
JUN 3 1924: Brunwick Records: Ray Miller & His Orch.

MAMMY SINGER
(composers unidentified)
AUG 9 1934: Radio, Kraft Music Hall: Paul Whiteman & His Orch.

MAN I LOVE, THE
(Ira Gershwin-George Gershwin)
MAY 16 1928: Col Records: Paul Whiteman & His Orch.

MANDY
(Irving Berlin)

OCT 11 1934: Radio, Kraft Music Hall: Paul Whiteman & His Orch.

MANHATTAN RAG
(Hoagy Carmichael)
OCT 10 1929: OK Records: Frank Trumbauer & His Orch.

MARCH OF THE CLOWNS, THE
(Lorenz Hart-Richard Rodgers)
FEB 9 1936: Radio, Musical Varieties: Paul Whiteman & His Orch.

MARCH OF THE MANNIKINS
(Walter Hirsch-Domenico Savino)
JUN 15 1923: Vic Records: Benson Orch.

MARDI GRAS
(Ferde Grofé)
JAN 5 1936: Radio, Musical Varieties: Paul Whiteman & His Orch.
FEB 23 1936: Radio, Musical Varieties: Paul Whiteman & His Orch.
MAR 24 1937: Radio, Paul Whiteman & His Orch.

MARIANNA
(Oscar Hammerstein II-Victor Herbert)
FEB 7 1929: Col Records: Paul Whiteman & His Orch.

MARY
(Walter Donaldson)
NOV 25 1927: Vic Records: Paul Whiteman & His Orch.

MAURICE, LE GENDARME
(composers unidentified)
Feb 1 1934: Radio, Kraft Music Hall: Paul Whiteman & His Orch.

MAYOR OF ALABAM
(Frank Trumbauer)

APR 5 1936: Radio, Musical Varieties: Paul Whiteman & His Orch.
APR 17 1936: Brun Records: Frank Trumbauer & His Orch.

ME AND MARIE
(Cole Porter)
SEP 7 1935: Vic Records: Paul Whiteman & His Orch.
SEP 28 1935: Vic Records: Paul Whiteman & His Orch.

ME AND THE BOY FRIEND
(Sidney Clare-James V. Monaco)
OCT 13 1924: Brun Records: Ray Miller & His Orch.

ME NEED YAH
(Fleta Jan Brown-Herbert Spencer)
JAN 7 1925: Brun Records: Ray Miller & His Orch.

MEAN, MEAN, MAMA
(Mitchell Parish-Harry D. Squires)
AUG 21 1923: Vic Records: Benson Orch.

MEDITATION FROM "THAÏS"
(Jules Emile F. Massenet)
FEB 9 1928: Vic Records: Paul Whiteman & His Orch.

MEDLEY OF ISHAM JONES HITS
(Isham Jones)
APR 5 1932: Col Records: Frank Trumbauer & His Orch.

MEDLEY OF POPULAR SELECTIONS
(various composers)
DEC 1 1931: Vic Records: Paul Whiteman & His Orch.

MELODY LINGERS ON, THE
(composers unidentified)
MAY 24 1936: Radio, Musical Varieties: Paul Whiteman & His Orch.

MELTING POT OF MUSIC, THE
(composers unidentified)
NOV-DEC 1929: Film: King Of Jazz

MEMORIAL DAY OVERTURE
(composers unidentified)
MAY 24 1934: Radio, Kraft Music Hall: Paul Whiteman & His Orch.

MERRY WIDOW WALTZ
(Adrian Ross-Franz Lehar)
MAY 13 1928: Col Records: Paul Whiteman & His Orch.

METROPOLIS (Part 1)
(Ferde Grofé)
MAR 13 1928: Vic Records: Paul Whiteman & His Orch.

METROPOLIS (Part 2)
(Ferde Grofé)
MAR 13 1928: Vic Records: Paul Whiteman & His Orch.

METROPOLIS (Part 3)
(Ferde Grofé)
MAR 14 1928: Vic Records: Paul Whiteman & His Orch.

METROPOLIS (Part 4)
(Ferde Grofé)
MAR 17 1928: Vic Records: Paul Whiteman & His Orch.

MEXICAN HAT DANCE
(Traditional Mexican folk song)
MAY 24 1936: Radio, Musical Varieties: Paul Whiteman & His Orch.

MIDNIGHT OIL
(Russ Case)
MAR 30 1938: Standard Trans.: Frank Trumbauer & His Orch.

MIDNIGHT REFLECTIONS
(Matt Malneck-Frank Signorelli)
FEB 13 1928: Vic Records: Paul Whiteman & His Orch.

MIDNIGHT ROSE
(Sidney D. Mitchell-Lew Pollack)
SEP 17 1923: Vic Records: Benson Orch.

MINNIE HA HA
(John Avery Noble)
APR 30 1938: Radio, Frank Trumbauer & His Orch.

MIRRORS
(composers unidentified)
AUG 16 1934: Radio, Kraft Music Hall: Paul Whiteman & His Orch.

MISHAWAKA BLUES
(Fred Rose-Al Short-Charley Straight)
FEB 6 1925: Brun Records: Cotton Pickers

MISSISSIPPI MUD
(James Cavanaugh-Harry Barris)
JAN 20 1928: OK Records: Frank Trumbauer
FEB 18 1928: Vic Records: Paul Whiteman & His Orch.

MOMENTS LIKE THIS
(Frank Loesser-Burton Lane)
MAR 30 1938: Standard Trans.: Frank Trumbauer & His Orch.

MONAVANNA
(Fred Fisher)
MAR 28 1924: Brun Records: Ray Miller & His Orch.

MOOD INDIGO
(Irving Mills-Barney Bigard-Duke Ellington)
JAN 29 1936: Radio, Musical Varieties: Paul Whiteman & His Orch.

MR. GHOST GOES TO TOWN
(Will Hudson-Mitchell Parish-Irving Mills)
JAN 15 1937: Radio, The Three T's
FEB 10 1937: Radio, Frank Trumbauer & His Orch.
MAR 24 1937: Radio, Paul Whiteman & His Orch.

MR. "T" FROM TENNESSEE
(composers unidentified)
DEC 11 1936: Radio, The Three T's
DEC 18 1936: Radio, The Three T's
DEC 1936: Radio, The Three T's

MURDER AT THE POLES sketch
(composers unidentified)
DEC 7 1933: Radio, Kraft Music Hall: Paul Whiteman & His Orch.

MUSIC GOES 'ROUND AND AROUND, THE
(Red Hodgson-Ed Farley-Mike Riley)
JAN 12 1936: Radio, Musical Varieties: Paul Whiteman & His Orch.
FEB 16 1936: Radio, Musical Varieties: Paul Whiteman & His Orch.

MUSIC HATH CHARMS
(Jack Yellen-Milton Ager)
NOV-DEC 1929: Film: King Of Jazz

MUSIC IN MY FINGERS
(Richard Myers-Edward Heyman)
DEC 6 1934: Radio, Kraft Music Hall: Paul Whiteman & His Orch.

MY ANGEL
(Lew Pollack-Erno Rapee)
APR 21 1928: Vic Records: Paul Whiteman & His Orch.

MY ANGELINE
(L. Wolfe Gilbert-Mabel Wayne)
JAN 11 1929: Col Records: Paul Whiteman & His Orch.

FEB 28 1929: Col Records: Paul Whiteman & His Orch.
MAR 7 1929: Col Records: Paul Whiteman & His Orch.

MY BABY SMILES
(Bill Trumbauer-Frank Trumbauer)
JUN 23 1952: Private Recording: Frank Trumbauer

MY BLUE HEAVEN
(George Whiting-Walter Donaldson)
FEB 12 1937: Radio, Frank Trumbauer & His Orch.
MAR 19 1946: Vic Records: Perry Como

MY BRIDAL VEIL
(Jack Yellen-Milton Ager)
NOV-DEC 1929: Film: King Of Jazz

MY DAY
(Ed Heyman-Carmen Lombardo-John Loeb)
DEC 15 1937: Standard Trans.: Frank Trumbauer & His Orch.

MY FINE FEATHERED FRIEND
(Harold Adamson-Jimmy McHugh)
FEB 11 1938: Standard Trans.: Frank Trumbauer & His Orch.

MY GOOD-BYE TO YOU
(Gus Kahn-Matt Malneck)
OCT 6 1931: Vic Records: Paul Whiteman & His Orch.

MY HEART IS TAKING LESSONS
(Johnny Burke-James V. Monaco)
FEB 11 1938: Standard Trans.: Frank Trumbauer & His Orch.

MY HEART STOOD STILL
(Lorenz Hart-Richard Rodgers)
JAN 24 1928: Vic Records: Paul Whiteman & His Orch.

MY HERO
(Stanislaus Stange-Oscar Straus)
MAY 12 1928: Col Records: Paul Whiteman & His Orch.

MY HONEY'S LOVIN' ARMS
(Herman Ruby-Joseph Meyer)
APR 5 1932: Col Records: Frank Trumbauer & His Orch.

MY LITTLE GRASS SHACK
(Thomas J. Harrison-John Avery Noble)
JAN 16 1934: Vic Records: Paul Whiteman & His Orch.

MY LOVE FOR YOU
(Bill Trumbauer-Frank Trumbauer)
OCT 28 1948: Private Recording: Frank Trumbauer

MY LUCKY STAR
(B. G. ''Buddy'' DeSylva-Lew Brown-Ray Henderson)
FEB 8 1929: Col Records: Paul Whiteman & His Orch.

MY MELANCHOLY BABY
(George A. Norton-Ernie Burnett)
MAY 15 1928: Col Records: Paul Whiteman & His Orch.

MY MOTHER'S SON-IN-LAW
(composers unidentified).
DEC 14 1933: Radio, Kraft Music Hall: Paul Whiteman & His Orch.

MY, OH, MY
(Mack Gordon-Harry Revel)
APR 19 1934: Radio, Kraft Music Hall: Paul Whiteman & His Orch.

MY OHIO HOME
(Gus Kahn-Walter Donaldson)
MAY 12 1928: Yazoo Video 514: Paul Whiteman & His Orch.

MY OLD KENTUCKY HOME
(Stephen Collins Foster)
OCT 18 1929: Col Records: Paul Whiteman & His Orch.

MY PET
(Jack Yellen-Milton Ager)

JUL 9 1938: Radio, Frank Trumbauer & His Orch.
FEB 23 1940: Var Records: Frank Trumbauer & His Orch.

NAUGHTY NAUGHTY
(Ben Oakland-Milton Drake)
DEC 15 1937: Standard Trans.: Frank Trumbauer & His Orch.

NEGLECTED
(Joseph M. Davis-John D. Marks-Joe Davis)
MAY 25 1938: Standard Trans.: Frank Trumbauer & His Orch.

NEIGHBORHOOD OF HEAVEN (See: IN THE NEIGHBORHOOD OF HEAVEN)

NEVER NEVER LAND FANTASY
(Betty Comden-Adolph Green-Jule Styne)
APR 20 1938: Standard Trans.: Frank Trumbauer & His Orch.
FEB 23 1940: Var Records: Frank Trumbauer & His Orch.

NEVERTHELESS
(Bert Kalmar-Harry Ruby)
JUN 1931: Radio, Paul Whiteman & His Allied Quality Paintmen

NEW O'LEANS (See also: BELLE OF NEW O'LEANS)
(Gus Kahn-Arthur Johnston)
JUL 9 1935: Vic Records: Paul Whiteman & His Orch.

NEW TIGER RAG, THE
(Original Dixieland Jazz Band)
JUN 25 1930: Col Records: Paul Whiteman & His Orch.

NEW YORK BOAT
(composers unidentified)
FEB 2 1936: Radio, Musical Varieties: Paul Whiteman & His Orch.

NEW YORK HEART BEAT
(composers unidentified)

MAR 15 1936: Radio, Musical Varieties: Paul Whiteman & His Orch.

NEWEST ST. LOUIS BLUES, THE (aka ST. LOUIS BLUES)
(W. C. Handy)
AUG 17 1932: Col Records: Frank Trumbauer & His Orch.

NICE WORK IF YOU CAN GET IT
(Ira Gershwin-George Gershwin)
APR 30 1938: Radio, Frank Trumbauer & His Orch.

NIGHT IS STILL
(composers unidentified)
DEC 20 1934: Radio, Kraft Music Hall: Paul Whiteman & His Orch.

NIGHT IS YOUNG AND YOU'RE SO BEAUTIFUL, THE
(Billy Rose-Irving Kahal-Dana Suesse)
DEC 17 1934: Vic Records: Paul Whiteman & His Orch.
JUL 19 1936: Radio, Paul Whiteman & His Orch.
JAN 8 1937: Radio, The Three T's

NIGHT WILL FALL
(composers unidentified)
JAN 28 1938: Standard Trans.: Frank Trumbauer & His Orch.

NIGHT YOU SAID GOODBYE, THE
(Sam Stept)
APR 20 1938: Standard Trans.: Frank Trumbauer & His Orch.
APR 25 1938: Electro Vox: Frank Trumbauer & His Orch.

NILE AND FISHES, THE
(composers unidentified)
NOV 29 1934: Radio, Kraft Music Hall: Paul Whiteman & His Orch.

NINON
(Harold Adamson-Walter Jurmann-Bronislaw Kaper)
APR 22 1935: Vic Records: Paul Whiteman & His Orch.

NO MORE LOVE
(Al Dubin-Harry Warren)
JAN 11 1934: Radio, Kraft Music Hall: Paul Whiteman & His Orch.

NO! NO! A THOUSAND TIMES NO
(Al Sherman-Al Lewis-Abner Silver)
DEC 13 1934: Radio, Kraft Music Hall: Paul Whiteman & His Orch.

NO, NO, NORA
(Ernie Erdman-Gus Kahn-Ted Fiorito)
JUL 20 1923: Vic Records: Benson Orch.

NO ONE CAN TAKE YOUR PLACE
(L. Wolfe Gilbert-Matty Malneck-Frank Signorelli)
APR 30 1929: OK Records: Frank Trumbauer & His Orch.

NO RETARD
(composers unidentified)
DEC 15 1937: Standard Trans.: Frank Trumbauer & His Orch.
FEB 22 1940: Var Records: Frank Trumbauer & His Orch.

NO STRINGS (I'M FANCY FREE)
(Irving Berlin)
SEP 28 1935: Vic Records: Paul Whiteman & His Orch.

NOBODY BUT YOU
(Joe Goodwin-Gus Edwards)
MAY 21 1929: OK Records: Frank Trumbauer & His Orch.

NOBODY KNOWS BUT MY PILLOW AND ME
(Billy Frisch-Billy Hueston-Paul L. Specht-Nathaniel H. Vincent)
JUN 14 1923: Vic Records: Benson Orch.

NOBODY KNOWS WHAT A RED-HEAD MAMA CAN DO
(Irving Mills-Sammy Fain-Al Dubin)
DEC 10 1924: Brun Records: Ray Miller & His Orch.
DEC 16 1924: Brun Records: Ray Miller & His Orch.

NOBODY'S SWEETHEART
(Gus Kahn-Ernie Erdman-Billy Meyers-Elmer Schoebel)
OCT 9 1929: Col Records: Paul Whiteman & His Orch.
APR 5 1932: Col Records: Frank Trumbauer & His Orch.
JUL 9 1935: Vic Records: Paul Whiteman & His Orch.
JAN 26 1936: Radio, Musical Varieties: Paul Whiteman & His Orch.
APR 30 1938: Radio, Frank Trumbauer & His Orch.

NOLA
(Felix Arndt)
MAR 7 1929: Col Records: Paul Whiteman & His Orch.
MAR 24 1937: Radio, Paul Whiteman & His Orch.

NOT ON THE FIRST NIGHT, BABY
(composers unidentified)
FEB 22 1940: Var Records: Frank Trumbauer & His Orch.

NOW I'M A LADY
(Sam Coslow-Irving Kahal-Sammy Fein)
APR 22 1935: Vic Records: Paul Whiteman & His Orch.

NOW IT CAN BE TOLD
(Irving Berlin)
JUL 8 1938: Standard Trans.: Frank Trumbauer & His Orch.

O HOLY NIGHT
(Traditional)
SEP 19 1928: Col Records: Paul Whiteman & His Orch.

O YA YA
(Raymond W. Klages)
JAN 5 1928: Vic Records: Paul Whiteman & His Orch.

OBJECT OF MY AFFECTION, THE
(Pinky Tomlin-Coy Poe-Jimmie Grier)
DEC 13 1934: Radio, Kraft Music Hall: Paul Whiteman & His Orch.

ODE TO A CHIMNEY SWEEPER
(composers unidentified)
DEC 25 1936: Radio, The Three T's
JAN 28 1938: Standard Trans.: Frank Trumbauer & His Orch.

OH, LADY, BE GOOD (aka LADY BE GOOD)
(Ira Gershwin-George Gershwin)
DEC 1936: Radio, The Three T's
FEB 23 1940: Var Records: Frank Trumbauer & His Orch.

OH LORD, WHY DID YOU PUT US IN THE BAYOU
(composers unidentified)
FEB 16 1936: Radio, Musical Varieties: Paul Whiteman & His Orch.

OH! MA-MA (THE BUTCHER BOY)
(Lew Brown-Rudy Vallee-Paolo Citorello)
MAY 25 1938: Standard Trans.: Frank Trumbauer & His Orch.

OH ME! OH MY! OH YOU!
(Arthur Francis/Ira Gershwin-Vincent Youmans)
JAN 4 1934: Radio, Kraft Music Hall: Paul Whiteman & His Orch.

OH MISS HANNAH
(Thekla Hollingsworth-Jessie L. Dappen)
MAY 4 1928: Col Records: Paul Whiteman & His Orch.

OH, SAY, CAN YOU SWING?
(Basil G. Adlam-Alex Hyde-Al Stillman)
FEB 10 1937: Radio, Frank Trumbauer & His Orch.

OH! THAT KISS
(composers unidentified)
DEC 28 1933: Radio, Kraft Music Hall: Paul Whiteman & His Orch.

OH! YOU HAVE NO IDEA
(Dan Dougherty-Phil Ponce)
MAY 23 1928: Col Records: Paul Whiteman & His Orch.

OH YOU LITTLE SUN-UV-ER-GUN
(Joseph Solman-Richard Howard)
SEP 17 1923: Vic Records: Benson Orch.

OL' MAN RIVER
(Oscar Hammerstein II-Jerome Kern)
JAN 11 1928: Vic Records: Paul Whiteman & His Orch.
MAR 1 1928: Vic Records: Paul Whiteman & His Orch.
JAN 28 1938: Standard Trans.: Frank Trumbauer & His Orch.

OLD BLACK JOE (SOUTHERN MEDLEY)
(Stephen Collins Foster)
OCT 18 1929: Col Records: Paul Whiteman & His Orch.

OLD MAN OF THE MOUNTAIN, THE
(Billy Hill-Victor Young)
FEB 23 1936: Radio, Musical Varieties: Paul Whiteman & His Orch.

OLD NEW ENGLAND MOON
(John Jacob Loeb-Carmen Lombardo-Charles Tobias)
JUN 9 1930: Col Records: Paul Whiteman & His Orch.

OLD PLAYMATE
(Gus Kahn-Matt Malneck)
OCT 1 1931: Vic Records: Paul Whiteman & His Orch.
DEC 1 1931: Vic Records: Paul Whiteman & His Orch.

OLD SPINNING WHEEL, THE
(Billy Hill)
DEC 14 1933: Radio, Kraft Music Hall: Paul Whiteman & His Orch.

OLD STRAW HAT, AN
(Mack Gordon-Harry Revel)
APR 20 1938: Standard Trans.: Frank Trumbauer & His Orch.

OLD TIME MEDLEY
(various composers)
JAN 31 1923: Vic Records: Benson Orch.

OLD YAZOO
(Thomas Waller)
FEB 12 1937: Radio, Frank Trumbauer & His Orch.

ON A ROOF IN MANHATTAN
(Irving Berlin)
MAR 1 1932: Vic Records: Paul Whiteman & His Orch.

ON MOONLIGHT BAY (See: MOONLIGHT BAY)

ON THE ALAMO
(Gus Kahn-Isham Jones)
APR 5 1932: Col Records: Frank Trumbauer & His Orch.

ON THE BANKS OF THE WABASH
(Paul Dresser)
JAN 31 1923: Vic Records: Benson Orch.

ON THE SENTIMENTAL SIDE
(Johnny Burke-James V. Monaco)
JAN 28 1938: Standard Trans.: Frank Trumbauer & His Orch.

ON THE WAY TO MONTEREY
(Ben Black-Neil Moret)
JAN 27 1925: Brun Records: Ray Miller & His Orch.
FEB 5 1925: Brun Records: Ray Miller & His Orch.

ON TREASURE ISLAND
(Edgar Leslie-Joe Burke)
JAN 5 1936: Radio, Musical Varieties: Paul Whiteman & His Orch.
FEB 2 1936: Radio, Musical Varieties: Paul Whiteman & His Orch.

ON YOUR TOES
(Lorenz Hart-Richard Rodgers)
JUN 26 1936: Vic Records: Paul Whiteman & His Orch.

ONCE UPON A TIME
(Alan Tudor Blaikley-Kenneth Mackintosh-Ian Matthews)

DEC 13 1934: Radio, Kraft Music Hall: Paul Whiteman & His Orch.

ONE FINE DAY (UN BEL DI)
(Luigi Illica-Giuseppe Giacosa-Giacomo Puccini)
JAN 19 1936: Radio, Musical Varieties: Paul Whiteman & His Orch.

ONE HUNDRED YEARS FROM TODAY (See: HUNDRED YEARS FROM TODAY, A)

ONE I LOVE BELONGS TO SOMEBODY ELSE, THE
(Gus Kahn-Isham Jones)
FEB 11 1938: Standard Trans.: Frank Trumbauer & His Orch.

ONE KISS OF LOVE
(composers unidentified)
JUL 8 1938: Standard Trans.: Frank Trumbauer & His Orch.

ONE MINUTE TO ONE
(J. Fred Coots-Sam M. Lewis)
DEC 14 1933: Radio, Kraft Music Hall: Paul Whiteman & His Orch.

ONE NIGHT OF LOVE
(Gus Kahn-Victor Schertzinger)
AUG 23 1934: Radio, Kraft Music Hall: Paul Whiteman & His Orch.

OOH THAT KISS
(Mort Dixon-Joe Young-Harry Warren)
DEC 28 1933: Radio, Kraft Music Hall: Paul Whiteman & His Orch.

ORANGE BLOSSOM TIME
(Gus Edwards-Joe Goodwin)
MAY 4 1929: Col Records: Paul Whiteman & His Orch.

ORIENTAL
(Enrique Granados)
FEB 9 1928: Vic Records: Paul Whiteman & His Orch.

OSTRICH WALK
(Edwin B. Edwards-James D. LaRocca-Anthony Sbarbaro-Larry Shields)
MAY 9 1927: OK Records: Frank Trumbauer & His Orch.

OTHER LIPS
(Oliver Wallace-Mort Harris)
JUL 25 1923: Vic Records: Benson Orch.

OUR BIG LOVE SCENE
(Arthur Freed-Nacio Herb Brown)
NOV 30 1933: Radio, Kraft Music Hall: Paul Whiteman & His Orch.

OUR BUNGALOW OF DREAMS
(. . . Malie- . . . Newan-Joe Verges)
APR 3 1928: OK Records: Frank Trumbauer & His Orch.

OUR LOVE IS HERE TO STAY (See: LOVE IS HERE TO STAY)

OUT O' TOWN GAL
(Walter Donaldson)
JUN 18 1928: Col Records: Paul Whiteman & His Orch.

OUTSIDE OF PARADISE
(Jack Lawrence-Peter Tinturin)
FEB 11 1938: Standard Trans.: Frank Trumbauer & His Orch.

PARADE OF MARCHES
(various composers)
APR 19 1934: Radio, Kraft Music Hall: Paul Whiteman & His Orch.
AUG 16 1934: Radio, Kraft Music Hall: Paul Whiteman & His Orch.

PARADE OF THE WOODEN SOLDIERS, THE
(Ballard MacDonald-Leon Jessel)
JAN 11 1928: Vic Records: Paul Whiteman & His Orch.
DEC 14 1933: Radio, Kraft Music Hall: Paul Whiteman & His Orch.
JAN 19 1936: Radio, Musical Varieties: Paul Whiteman & His Orch.

PARDON MY SOUTHERN ACCENT
(Johnny Mercer-Matty Malneck)
AUG 18 1934: Vic Records: Paul Whiteman & His Orch.

PARK AVENUE FANTASY
(Matt Malneck-Frank Signorelli)
SEP 11 1934: Vic Records: Paul Whiteman & His Orch..
FEB 9 1936: Radio, Musical Varieties: Paul Whiteman & His Orch.

PARK IN PAREE
(composers unidentified)
DEC 14 1933: Radio, Kraft Music Hall: Paul Whiteman & His Orch.

PEANUT VENDOR, THE
(Marion Sunshine-L. Wolfe Gilbert-Moises Simons)
JAN 15 1937: Radio, The Three T's
JAN 1937: Radio, Frank Trumbauer & His Orch.

PERFECT PARADISE
(Paul Denniker-Jack Fulton)
FEB 1 1934: Radio, Kraft Music Hall: Paul Whiteman & His Orch.

PETER IBBETSON
(Bernard Hermann)
JAN 4 1934: Radio, Kraft Music Hall: Paul Whiteman & His Orch.

PETER, PETER, PUMPKIN EATER
(Alton Rinker)
NOV 30 1933: Radio, Kraft Music Hall: Paul Whiteman & His Orch.
DEC 7 1933: Radio, Kraft Music Hall: Paul Whiteman & His Orch.
JAN 25 1934: Radio, Kraft Music Hall: Paul Whiteman & His Orch.
SEP 11 1934: Vic Records: Paul Whiteman & His Orch.

PHANTOM OF THE RUMBA
(Al Lewis-Enric Madriguera)
NOV 29 1934: Radio, Kraft Music Hall: Paul Whiteman & His Orch.
FEB 16 1936: Radio, Musical Varieties: Paul Whiteman & His Orch.

PHOEBE SNOW
(Ray Miller-Fred Fisher-Al Kay)
APR 11 1925: Brun Records: Ray Miller & His Orch.

PICCOLINO, THE
(Irving Berlin)
SEP 28 1935: Vic Records: Paul Whiteman & His Orch.

PICTURE OF ME WITHOUT YOU, A
(Cole Porter)
SEP 7 1935: Vic Records: Paul Whiteman & His Orch.
SEP 28 1935: Vic Records: Paul Whiteman & His Orch.

PILGRIM'S PROGRESS 1933 sketch
(Edgar Stillman Kelley)
NOV 30 1933: Radio, Kraft Music Hall: Paul Whiteman & His Orch.

PLANTATION MOODS
(David Rose-Frank Trumbauer)
NOV 20 1934: Vic Records: Frank Trumbauer & His Orch.

PLAY, FIDDLE, PLAY
(Jack Lawrence-Emerey Deutsch-Arthur Altman)
FEB 2 1936: Radio, Musical Varieties: Paul Whiteman & His Orch.

PLAY IT RED
(. . . Harris)
MAY 23 1927: Vic Records: Jean Goldkette & His Orch.

PLEASE
(composers unidentified)
JUL 22 1924: Brun Records: Ray Miller & His Orch.

PLEASE BELIEVE ME
(Al Stillman-Luigi Tenco)
FEB 16 1936: Radio, Musical Varieties: Paul Whiteman & His Orch.

PLEASE DON'T TALK ABOUT ME WHEN I'M GONE
(Sidney Clare-Sam H. Stept)
AUG 1931: Radio, Paul Whiteman & His Allied Quality Paintmen

POOR BUTTERFLY
(John Golden—Raymond Hubbell)
FEB 7 1928: Vic Records: Paul Whiteman & His Orch.

POP GOES YOUR HEART
(Mort Dixon-Allie Wrubel)
DEC 6 1934: Radio, Kraft Music Hall: Paul Whiteman & His Orch.

POPULAR SELECTIONS MEDLEY
(various composers)
DEC 1 1931: Vic Records: Paul Whiteman & His Orch.

PORTRAIT OF A PRETZEL
(composers unidentified)

APR 20 1938: Standard Trans.: Frank Trumbauer & His Orch.
APR 30 1938: Radio, Frank Trumbauer & His Orch.
JUL 9 1938: Radio, Frank Trumbauer & His Orch.

PRESIDENT FRANKLIN ROOSEVELT MEDLEY
(composers unidentified)
NOV 29 1934: Radio, Kraft Music Hall: Paul Whiteman & His Orch.

PRINCE OF WAILS
(Elmer Schoebel)
DEC 4 1924: Brun Records: Cotton Pickers

PRINTEMPS
(Claude Achille Debussy)
DEC 6 1934: Radio, Kraft Music Hall: Paul Whiteman & His Orch.

PRISONER OF LOVE
(Russ Columbo-Leo Robin)
DEC 20 1945: Vic Records: Perry Como

PROUD OF A BABY LIKE YOU
(Arnold Schoenberg- . . . Stevens- . . . Helmick)
JAN 28 1927: Vic Records: Jean Goldkette & His Orch.

PUDDIN' HEAD JONES
(Alfred Bryan-Lou Handman)
NOV 30 1933: Radio, Kraft Music Hall: Paul Whiteman & His Orch.

PUT ON YOUR OLD GREY BONNET
(Stanley Murphy-Percy Wenrich)
DEC 15 1938: Standard Trans.: Frank Trumbauer & His Orch.

RACHMANINOFF'S PRELUDES
(Sergey Vassilievich Rakhmaninov/Rachmaninoff)
JAN 4 1934: Radio, Kraft Music Hall: Paul Whiteman & His Orch.

RAGAMUFFIN ROMEO
(Harry DeCosta Mabel Wayne)
NOV-DEC 1929: Film: King Of Jazz
MAR 22 1930: Col Records: Paul Whiteman & His Orch.

RAGGING THE SCALE
(Dave Ringle-Edward B. Claypool)
FEB 1 1934: Radio, Kraft Music Hall: Paul Whiteman & His Orch.

RAIN IN SPAIN
(Stanley Adams-Xavier Cugat)
JAN 26 1936: Radio, Musical Varieties: Paul Whiteman & His Orch.

RAINBOW OF LOVE
(Harry D. Squires- . . . Perry)
SEP 29 1927: Har Records: Broadway Bell Hops

RAISING THE RENT
(Ted Koehler-Harold Arlen)
JAN 19 1936: Radio, Musical Varieties: Paul Whiteman & His Orch.

RAISIN' THE ROOF
(Dorothy Fields-Jimmy McHugh)
MAR 8 1929: OK Records: Frank Trumbauer & His Orch.
JAN 28 1938: Standard Trans.: Frank Trumbauer & His Orch.

RAMONA
(L. Wolfe Gilbert-Mabel Wayne)
JAN 4 1928: Vic Records: Paul Whiteman & His Orch.

REACHING FOR SOMEONE (aka REACHIN' FOR SOMEONE)
(Edgar Leslie-Walter Donaldson)
MAY 3 1929: Col Records: Paul Whiteman & His Orch.
MAY 22 1929: OK Records: Frank Trumbauer & His Orch.

REBOUND
(composers unidentified)
JAN 15 1937: Radio, The Three T's

RED HOT
(Ted Koehler-Frank Trumbauer-Wallace Bradley-Maurie Sherman)
MAR 14 1924: Brun Records: Mound City Blue Blowers

RED HOT HENRY BROWN
(Fred Rose)
MAR 16 1925: Brun Records: Ray Miller & His Orch.

RED HOT MAMMA
(Gilbert Wells-Bud Cooper-Fred Rose)
AUG 5 1924: Brun Records: Ray Miller & His Orch.

RENDEZVOUS IN HONOLULU, A
(composers unidentified)
MAR 1 1936: Radio, Musical Varieties: Paul Whiteman & His Orch.

RED SAILS IN THE SUNSET
(Jimmy Kennedy-Hugh Williams)
JAN 5 1936: Radio, Musical Varieties: Paul Whiteman & His Orch.
FEB 2 1936: Radio, Musical Varieties: Paul Whiteman & His Orch.
APR 5 1936: Radio, Musical Varieties: Paul Whiteman & His Orch.

REVOLT IN CUBA
(Irving Berlin)
JAN 4 1934: Radio, Kraft Music Hall: Paul Whiteman & His Orch.
JAN 19 1936: Radio, Musical Varieties: Paul Whiteman & His Orch.
MAR 22 1936: Radio, Musical Varieties: Paul Whiteman & His Orch.

RHAPSODY IN BLUE
(George Gershwin)
NOV-DEC 1929: Film: King of Jazz

RHAPSODY IN BLUE was used as Paul Whiteman's theme song.

RHUMBA LA BOMBA
(composers unidentified)
MAR 24 1937: Radio, Paul Whiteman

RHYTHM IN MY NURSERY RHYMES (IF I HAD)
(Sammy Cahn-Don Raye)
MAR 15 1936: Radio, Musical Varieties: Paul Whiteman & His Orch.

RHYTHM IS OUR BUSINESS
(Sammy Cahn-Saul Chaplin-Jimmie Lunceford)
OCT 3 1935: Radio, Kraft Music Hall: Paul Whiteman & His Orch.

RHYTHM SAVED THE WORLD
(Sammy Cahn-Saul Chaplin)
APR 5 1936: Radio, Musical Varieties: Paul Whiteman & His Orch.

RIGHT OR WRONG
(Haven Gillespie-Arthur Sizemore-Paul Biese)
OCT 1921: Brun Records: Gene Rodemich & His Orch.

RIVERBOAT SHUFFLE
(Dick Voynow-Hoagy Carmichael)
MAY 9 1927: OK Records: Frank Trumbauer & His Orch.

ROBERTA MEDLEY
(Jerome Kern)
DEC 13 1934: Radio, Kraft Music Hall: Paul Whiteman & His Orch.

ROCKIN' THE TOWN
(Ted Koehler-John Green)
DEC 15 1937: Standard Trans.: Frank Trumbauer & His Orch.

ROMAN SCANDALS MEDLEY
(Harry Warren)
JAN 11 1934: Radio, Kraft Music Hall: Paul Whiteman & His Orch.

ROMANCE IN THE DARK
(Phil Boutelje-Ned Washington-Victor Young)
JAN 28 1938: Standard Trans.: Frank Trumbauer & His Orch.

ROMANCE IN THE RAIN
(Charles Newman-Isham Jones)
JAN 28 1938: Standard Trans.: Frank Trumbauer & His Orch.

ROSE AND A KISS, A
(Mabel Wayne-Benee Russell)
DEC 3 1931: Vic Records: Paul Whiteman & His Orch.

ROSES OF YESTERDAY
(Irving Berlin)
SEP 4 1928: Col Records: Paul Whiteman & His Orch.

ROSIE O'GRADY (See: SWEET ROSIE O'GRADY)

ROYAL GARDEN BLUES
(Spencer Williams-Clarence Williams)
AUG 17 1923: Vic Records: Benson Orch.

RUNNIN' RAGGED
(Joe Venuti)
OCT 18 1929: OK Records: Joe Venuti & His Orch.

RUSSIAN SAILOR'S DANCE
(composers unidentified)
NOV 22 1934: Radio, Kraft Music Hall: Paul Whiteman & His Orch.

RUSTLE OF SPRING
(Christine Sinding)
JUL 8 1938: Standard Trans.: Frank Trumbauer & His Orch.

SADDLE YOUR BLUES TO A WILD MUSTANG
(Richard A. Whiting-Buddy Bernier-William Haid)
FEB 6 1936: Vic Records: Paul Whiteman & His Orch.
MAR 22 1936: Radio, Musical Varieties: Paul Whiteman & His Orch.

SALLY LOU
(Hugo Frey)
JUL 10 1924: Brun Records: Ray Miller & His Orch.

SAM, THE OLD ACCORDION MAN
(Walter Donaldson)
DEC 7 1933: Radio, Kraft Music Hall: Paul Whiteman & His Orch.

SAN
(Lindsay McPhail-Walter Michels)
MAR 14 1923: Brun Records: Mound City Blue Blowers
JAN 10 1928: Vic Records: Paul Whiteman & His Orch.

SAY
(Lew Brown-Ray Henderson)
MAR 2 1932: Vic Records: Paul Whiteman & His Orch.

SAY IT WITH MUSIC MEDLEY
(Irving Berlin)
OCT 11 1934: Radio, Kraft Music Hall: Paul Whiteman & His Orch.

SAY URS SPINACH
(Irving Berlin)
MAR 1 1932: Vic Records: Paul Whiteman & His Orch.

SAYS MY HEART
(Frank Loesser-Burton Lane)
MAY 25 1938: Standard Trans.: Frank Trumbauer & His Orch.

SECRET HEART
(Bronislaw Kaper)
JAN 19 1936: Radio, Musical Varieties: Paul Whiteman & His Orch.

SELECTION FROM ''MANON''
(Jules Emile Frederic Massenet)
NOV 22 1934: Radio, Kraft Music Hall: Paul Whiteman & His Orch.

SELECTIONS FROM ''SHOW BOAT''
(Jerome Kern)
MAR 1 1928: Vic Records: Paul Whiteman & His Orch.

SEMPER FIDELIS
(John Philip Sousa)
FEB 22 1940: Var Records: Frank Trumbauer & His Orch.

SENTIMENTAL BABY
(Jack Palmer)
SEP 20 1928: OK Records: Frank Trumbauer & His Orch.
OCT 5 1928: OK Records: Frank Trumbauer & His Orch.

SENTIMENTAL OVER YOU
(composers unidentified)
FEB 12 1937: Radio, Frank Trumbauer & His Orch.

SERENADE FOR A WEALTHY WIDOW
(Dorothy Fields-Jimmy McHugh)
OCT 4 1934: Radio, Kraft Music Hall: Paul Whiteman & His Orch.
DEC 14 1934: Vic Records: Paul Whiteman & His Orch.
DEC 20 1934: Radio, Kraft Music Hall: Paul Whiteman & His Orch.

SHADOW WALTZ, THE
(Al Dubin-Harry Warren)
JAN 4 1934: Radio, Kraft Music Hall: Paul Whiteman & His Orch.

SHADOWS ON THE MOON
(Gus Kahn-Sigmund Romberg)
MAR 30 1938: Standard Trans.: Frank Trumbauer & His Orch.

SHADY TREE, A
(Walter Donaldson)
FEB 8 1928: Vic Records: Paul Whiteman & His Orch.
FEB 15 1928: Vic Records: Paul Whiteman & His Orch.

SHAG ON DOWN
(composers unidentified)
JAN 28 1938: Standard Trans.: Frank Trumbauer & His Orch.

SHAKING HANDS WITH THE DEVIL
(composers unidentified)
APR 5 1936: Radio, Musical Varieties: Paul Whiteman & His Orch.

SHALL WE DANCE?
(Ira Gershwin-George Gershwin)
MAR 26 1937: Vic Records: Paul Whiteman & His Orch.

SHEIK OF ARABY, THE
(Harry B. Smith-Francis Wheeler-Ted Snyder)
JAN 8 1937: Radio, The Three T's
JAN 1937: Radio, Frank Trumbauer & His Orch.
FEB 3 1937: Radio, Frank Trumbauer & His Orch.

SHIM-ME-SHA-WABBLE
(Spencer Williams)
AUG 21 1923: Vic Records: Benson Orch.

SHIVERY STOMP
(Segar Ellis)
MAY 22 1929: OK Records: Frank Trumbauer & His Orch.

SHOULD I?
(Arthur Freed-Nacio Herb Brown)
OCT 18 1929: Col Records: Paul Whiteman & His Orch.

SHOULD I BE SWEET OR HOT?
(Stephen W. Ballantine-B. G. ''Buddy'' DeSylva-Vincent Youmans)
NOV 22 1934: Radio, Kraft Music Hall: Paul Whiteman & His Orch.

SI TU LE VEUX
(Luc Hoffman)
NOV 22 1934: Radio, Kraft Music Hall: Paul Whiteman & His Orch.

SIBONEY
(Dolly Morse-Ernesto Lecuona)
MAY 24 1936: Radio, Musical Varieties: Paul Whiteman & His Orch.

SIDEWALKS OF NEW YORK, THE
(James W. Blake-Charles B. Lawlor)
SEP 4 1928: Col Records: Paul Whiteman & His Orch.
SEP 14 1928: Col Records: Paul Whiteman & His Orch.

SILENT NIGHT, HOLY NIGHT
(Joseph Mohr-Franz Gruber)
SEP 19 1928: Col Records: Paul Whiteman & His Orch.
DEC 20 1934: Radio, Kraft Music Hall: Paul Whiteman & His Orch.

SING A HAPPY SONG
(composers unidentified)
DEC 17 1934: Vic Records: Paul Whiteman & His Orch.

SING A LOW-DOWN TUNE
(composers unidentified)
JAN 11 1934: Radio, Kraft Music Hall: Paul Whiteman & His Orch.

SINGIN' THE BLUES (TILL MY DADDY COMES HOME)
(Sam M. Lewis-Joe Young-Con Conrad-J. Russel Robinson)
FEB 4 1927: OK Records: Frank Trumbauer & His Orch.
JAN 10 1929: Col Records: Bee Palmer

JAN 28 1938: Standard Trans.: Frank Trumbauer & His Orch.
APR 20 1938: Standard Trans.: Frank Trumbauer & His Orch.

SINGIN' THE BLUES was used by Frank Trumbauer as his theme song whenever he had his own band, usually opening and closing the program. Also used by The Three T's.

SITTING ON A RAINBOW
(Dan Dougherty-Jack Yellen)
JUN 9 1930: Col Records: Paul Whiteman & His Orch.

SIX SECRETARIES
(composers unidentified)
DEC 7 1933: Radio, Kraft Music Hall: Paul Whiteman & His Orch.

SIZZLING ONE-STEP MEDLEY
(various composers)
APR 5 1932: Col Records: Frank Trumbauer & His Orch.

SKITTER
(composers unidentified)
JAN 15 1937: Radio, The Three T's

SKRONTCH
(Irving Mills-Henry Nemo-Edward Kennedy "Duke" Ellington)
MAY 25 1938: Standard Trans.: Frank Trumbauer & His Orch.

SLAUGHTER ON TENTH AVENUE (Part 1)
(Richard Rodgers)
JUN 26 1936: Vic Records: Paul Whiteman & His Orch.

SLAUGHTER ON TENTH AVENUE (Part 2)
(Richard Rodgers)
JUN 26 1936: Vic Records: Paul Whiteman & His Orch.

SLEIGH RIDE
(Mitchell Parish-Leroy Anderson)
DEC 6 1934: Radio, Kraft Music Hall: Paul Whiteman & His Orch.

SLOW RIVER
(. . . Meyers- . . . Schwab)
MAY 6 1927: Vic Records: Jean Goldkette & His Orch.

SLUMMIN' ON PARK AVENUE
(Irving Berlin)
FEB 12 1937: Radio, Frank Trumbauer & His Orch.

SMALL FRY
(Frank Loesser-Hoagy Carmichael)
JUL 8 1938: Standard Trans.: Frank Trumbauer & His Orch.

SMILE
(Donald Heywood)
JAN 24 1928: Vic Records: Paul Whiteman & His Orch.

SMOKE GETS IN YOUR EYES
(Otto Harbach-Jerome Kern)
NOV 20 1933: Radio, Kraft Music Hall: Paul Whiteman & His Orch.
DEC 13 1934: Radio, Kraft Music Hall: Paul Whiteman & His Orch.

SMOKE RINGS
(Ned Washington-Gene Gifford)
NOV 30 1933: Radio, Kraft Music Hall: Paul Whiteman & His Orch.

SNOWFLAKE
(Anderson-Swanstrom-Morgan)
NOV 7 1921: Brun Records: Gene Rodemich & His Orch.

SO LITTLE TIME
(Peter DeRose-William J. Hill)
APR 20 1938: Standard Trans.: Frank Trumbauer & His Orch.

SO YOU LEFT ME FOR THE LEADER OF A SWING BAND
(Archie Gottler-Harry Kogen)
MAY 25 1938: Standard Trans.: Frank Trumbauer & His Orch.

SOMETHING TELLS ME
(John H. Mercer-Harry Warren)
APR 20 1938: Standard Trans.: Frank Trumbauer & His Orch.

SOMETHING TO REMEMBER YOU BY
(Howard Dietz-Arthur Schwartz)
SEP 10 1930: Col Records: Paul Whiteman & His Orch.

SONG HITS OF 1933 MEDLEY
JAN 4 1934: Radio, Kraft Music Hall: Paul Whiteman & His Orch.

SONG IS ENDED, BUT THE MELODY LINGERS ON, THE
(Irving Berlin)
MAY 24 1936: Radio, Musical Varieties: Paul Whiteman & His Orch.

SONG OF INDIA
(Nikolai Rimsky Korsakov)
APR 25 1929: Col Records: Paul Whiteman & His Orch.

SONG OF THE BAYOU
(Rube Bloom)
DEC 28 1933: Radio, Kraft Music Hall: Paul Whiteman & His Orch.

SONG OF THE CONGO
(Herbert Magidson-Ned Washington-Ray Perkins)
JUL 25 1930: Col Records: Paul Whiteman & His Orch.

SONG OF THE DAWN
(Jack Yellen-Milton Ager)
NOV-DEC 1929: Film: King Of Jazz
MAR 21 1930: Col Records: Paul Whiteman & His Orch.

SONG OF THE ISLANDS
(Charles E. King)
JAN 8 1937: Radio, The Three T's

SORRY FOR ME
(B. G. ''Buddy'' DeSylva-Lew Brown-Ray Henderson)
JUN 8 1928: Col Records: Paul Whiteman & His Orch.

SOUTHERN MEDLEY
(Stephen Foster)
OCT 18 1929: Col Records: Paul Whiteman & His Orch.

SPAGENZE
(composers unidentified)
DEC 15 1937: Standard Trans.: Frank Trumbauer & His Orch.

SPIRIT OF PROHIBITION
(composers unidentified)
DEC 7 1933: Radio, Kraft Music Hall: Paul Whiteman & His Orch.

S'POSIN'
(Andy Razaf-Paul Denniker)
MAY 16 1929: Col Records: Paul Whiteman & His Orch.

SPRING, BEAUTIFUL SPRING
(Paul Lincke)
JAN 11 1934: Radio, Kraft Music Hall: Paul Whiteman & His Orch.

SPRING IS HERE
(Lorenz Hart-Richard Rodgers)
JUL 8 1938: Standard Trans.: Frank Trumbauer & His Orch.

ST. LOUIS BLUES (also see: NEWEST ST. LOUIS BLUES)
(W. C. Handy)
FEB 16 1936: Radio, Musical Varieties: Paul Whiteman & His Orch.
MAR 24 1937: Radio, Paul Whiteman & His Orch.

ST. PATRICK'S DAY MEDLEY
(various composers)

MAR 15 1936: Radio, Musical Varieties: Paul Whiteman & His Orch.

STAMPEDE
(Fletcher Henderson)
FEB 1 1927: Vic Records: Jean Goldkette & His Orch.

STARDUST
(Mitchell Parish-Hoagy Carmichael)
NOV 29 1934: Radio, Kraft Music Hall: Paul Whiteman & His Orch.
DEC 14 1934: Vic Records: Paul Whiteman & His Orch.

STARLIGHT BAY
(Walter Donaldson)
JAN 30 1923: Vic Records: Benson Orch.

STARS AND STRIPES FOREVER
(John Philip Sousa)
MAR 30 1938: Standard Trans.: Frank Trumbauer & His Orch.
APR 30 1938: Radio, Frank Trumbauer & His Orch.
FEB 23 1940: Var Records: Frank Trumbauer & His Orch.

STARS FELL ON ALABAMA
(Mitchell Parish-Frank Perkins)
SEP 18 1934: Brun Records: Jack Teagarden & His Orch.
DEC 20 1934: Radio, Kraft Music Hall: Paul Whiteman & His Orch.

STARS IN MY EYES
(Dorothy Fields-Fritz Kreisler)
MAR 24 1937: Radio, Paul Whiteman & His Orch.

STAY AS SWEET AS YOU ARE
(Mack Gordon-Harry Revel)
DEC 13 1934: Radio, Kraft Music Hall: Paul Whiteman & His Orch.

SUGAR FOOT STOMP (aka DIPPER MOUTH BLUES)
(Walter Melrose-Joe "King" Oliver)
APR 20 1938: Standard Trans.: Frank Trumbauer & His Orch.
FEB 23 1940: Var Records: Frank Trumbauer & His Orch.

SUGAR PLUM
(Gus Kahn-Arthur Johnston)
JUL 9 1935: Vic Records: Paul Whiteman & His Orch.

SUITE OF SERENADES
(Victor Herbert)
MAR 1 1928: Vic Records: Paul Whiteman & His Orch.

SUMMER BREEZE
(Louis Rey)
JUL 5 1936: Radio, Paul Whiteman & His Orch.

SUMMER ROMANCE sketch
(Raymond Andrew Sterling-George Sumner)
MAY 24 1934: Radio, Kraft Music Hall: Paul Whiteman & His Orch.

SUN SPOTS
(Frank Trumbauer)
FEB 16 1934: Vic Records: Paul Whiteman & His Orch.
FEB 16 1934: Vic Records: Paul Whiteman & His Orch.

SUNDAY
(Ned Miller-Chester Conn-Jule Styne-Bennie Kreuger)
OCT 15 1926: Vic Records: Jean Goldkette & His Orch.

SUNNY DISPOSISH
(Ira Gershwin-Philip Charig)
FEB 3 1927: Vic Records: Jean Goldkette & His Orch.

SUNNY SIDE UP
(B. G. "Buddy" DeSylva-Lew Brown-Ray Henderson)
OCT 10 1929: OK Records: Frank Trumbauer & His Orch.

SWINGING ANNIE LAURIE THROUGH THE RYE
(Jack Meskill-Ted Fiorito-J. Russel Robinson)
MAY 25 1938: Standard Trans.: Frank Trumbauer & His Orch.

SWINGIN' DOWN THE LANE
(Gus Kahn-Isham Jones)
APR 5 1932: Col Records: Frank Trumbauer & His Orch.

'S WONDERFUL
(Ira Gershwin-George Gershwin)
APR 27 1936: Brun Records: Frank Trumbauer & His Orch.
DEC 4 1936: Radio, The Three T's
DEC 11 1936: Radio, The Three T's
DEC 1936: Radio, The Three T's
DEC 25 1936: Radio, The Three T's

SYLVIA
(Clinton Scollard-Oley Speaks)
SEP 30 1931: Vic Records: Paul Whiteman & His Orch.

"T" FOR TEXAS
(composers unidentified)
JUL 5 1936: Radio, Paul Whiteman & His Orch.

TABOO
(S. K. Russell-Margarita Lecuona)
FEB 11 1938: Standard Trans.: Frank Trumbauer & His Orch.

TAIL SPIN
(Jimmy Dorsey-Frank Trumbauer)
APR 17 1934: Vic Records: Paul Whiteman & His Orch.

'TAIN'T GOOD
(Billy Haid)
DEC 11 1936: Radio, The Three T's
DEC 18 1936: Radio, The Three T's

'TAIN'T SO, HONEY, 'TAIN'T SO
(Willard Robison)
MAY 21 1928: Col Records: Paul Whiteman & His Orch.

MAY 23 1928: Col Records: Paul Whiteman & His Orch.
JUN 10 1928: Col Records: Paul Whiteman & His Orch.

TAKE A NUMBER FROM ONE TO TEN
(Mack Gordon-Harry Revel)
DEC 20 1934: Radio, Kraft Music Hall: Paul Whiteman & His Orch.

TAKE A PAIR OF SPARKLING EYES
(Thomas F. Dunhill-W. S. Gilbert-Sir Arthur Sullivan)
DEC 20 1934: Radio, Kraft Music Hall: Paul Whiteman & His Orch.

TAKE ME BACK TO MY BOOTS AND SADDLE
(Walter G. Samuels-Leonard Whitcup-Teddy Powell)
JAN 5 1936: Radio, Musical Varieties: Paul Whiteman & His Orch.
FEB 2 1936: Radio, Musical Varieties: Paul Whiteman & His Orch.

TAKE YOUR TOMORROW
(Andy Razaf-J. C. Johnson)
SEP 20 1928: OK Records: Frank Trumbauer & His Orch.

TALES FROM THE VIENNA WOODS
(Johann Strauss)
AUG 23 1934: Radio, Kraft Music Hall: Paul Whiteman & His Orch.
OCT 3 1935: Radio, Kraft Music Hall: Paul Whiteman & His Orch.

TAMBALINA
(composers unidentified)
AUG 9 1934: Radio, Kraft Music Hall: Paul Whiteman & His Orch.

TAMMARY
(composers unidentified)
JAN 31 1923: Vic Records: Benson Orch.

TANGO AMERICANO
(Matty Malneck-Frank Signorelli)
SEP 30 1930: Vic Records: Paul Whiteman & His Orch.

TAPPING THE BARREL
(Ned Washington-Joseph Young-Victor Young)
DEC 14 1933: Radio, Kraft Music Hall: Paul Whiteman & His Orch.

TCHAIKOWSKIANA
(Piotr Ilyich Chaikovsky/Tschaikowsky)
JUN 20 1928: Col Records: Paul Whiteman & His Orch.

TEA FOR TWO
(Irving Caesar-Vincent Youmans)
DEC 13 1934: Radio, Kraft Music Hall: Paul Whiteman & His Orch.
DEC 4 1936: Radio, The Three T's
DEC 1936: Radio, The Three T's
DEC 18 1936: Radio, The Three T's
DEC 25 1936: Radio, The Three T's
DEC 1936: Radio, The Three T's
JAN 28 1938: Standard Trans.: Frank Trumbauer & His Orch.

TELEVISION
(Mort Greene)
APR 20 1938: Standard Trans.: Frank Trumbauer & His Orch.

TELL ME WITH A LOVE SONG
(Ted Koehler-Harold Arlen)
OCT 6 1931: Vic Records: Paul Whiteman & His Orch.

TEMPO TAKES A HOLIDAY
(composers unidentified)
DEC 15 1937: Standard Trans.: Frank Trumbauer & His Orch.
APR 30 1938: Radio, Frank Trumbauer & His Orch.
JUL 9 1938: Radio, Frank Trumbauer & His Orch.

TEMPTATION
(Arthur Freed-Nacio Herb Brown)

NOV 30 1933: Radio, Kraft Music Hall: Paul Whiteman & His Orch.

TESSIE
(Brook Johns-Ray Perkins)
JAN 7 1925: Brun Records: Ray Miller & His Orch.

THANK YOU, MR. BACH
(A Van C Phillips)
MAR 24 1937: Radio, Paul Whiteman & His Orch.

THANKS A MILLION
(Gus Kahn-Arthur Johnston)
JUL 10 1935: Vic Records: Paul Whiteman & His Orch.
OCT 3 1935: Radio, Kraft Music Hall: Paul Whiteman & His Orch.
JAN 26 1936: Radio, Musical Varieties: Paul Whiteman & His Orch.

THAT DALLAS MAN
(Harvey Brooks-Ben Ellison)
DEC 7 1933: Radio, Kraft Music Hall: Paul Whiteman & His Orch.

THAT OLD GANG OF MINE
(Billy Rose-Mort Dixon-Ray Henderson)
AUG 27 1923: Vic Records: Benson Orch.

THAT'S A PLENTY
(Henry Creamer-Bert A. Williams)
MAY 5 1931: Radio, Paul Whiteman & His Allied Quality Paintmen

THAT'S LOVE
(Lorenz Hart-Richard Rodgers)
FEB 1 1934: Radio, Kraft Music Hall: Paul Whiteman & His Orch.

THAT'S MY GIRL
(Kierman-Kerr)

JAN 27 1925: Brun Records: Ray Miller & His Orch.
FEB 5 1925: Brun Records: Ray Miller & His Orch.

THAT'S MY WEAKNESS NOW
(Bud Green)
JUN 17 1928: Col Records: Paul Whiteman & His Orch.

THAT'S WHAT YOU THINK
(Coy Poe-Pinky Tomlin)
OCT 3 1935: Radio, Kraft Music Hall: Paul Whiteman & His Orch.

THAT'S WHY DARKIES WERE BORN
(Lew Brown-Ray Henderson)
NOV 30 1931: Vic Records: Paul Whiteman & His Orch.

THERE AIN'T NO LAND LIKE DIXIELAND TO ME
(Walter Donaldson)
SEP 29 1927: Har Records: Broadway Bell Hops

THERE AIN'T NO SWEET MAN THAT'S WORTH THE SALT OF MY TEARS
(Fred Fisher)
FEB 8 1928: Vic Records: Paul Whiteman & His Orch.

THERE I GO DREAMING AGAIN
(Lew Brown-Buddy DeSylva-Ray Henderson)
MAR 2 1932: Vic Records: Paul Whiteman & His Orch.

THERE'LL BE NO SOUTH
(Harry Richman-Lew Brown-Harry Akst)
JAN 5 1936: Radio, Musical Varieties: Paul Whiteman & His Orch.

THERE'LL COME A TIME
(Wingy Manone-Miff Mole)
JAN 9 1928: OK Records: Frank Trumbauer & His Orch.

THERE'S A BLUE NOTE IN MY LOVE SONG
(Michael Carr-Ted Shapiro)
OCT 6 1931: Vic Records: Paul Whiteman & His Orch.

THERE'S A BOY IN HARLEM
(Lorenz Hart-Richard Rodgers)
APR 20 1938: Standard Trans.: Frank Trumbauer & His Orch.

THERE'S A CRADLE IN CAROLINE
(Fred E. Ahlert-Samuel M. Lewis-Joseph Young)
AUG 25 1927: OK Records: Frank Trumbauer & His Orch.
SEP 29 1927: Har Records: Broadway Bell Hops

THERE'S A FAR AWAY LOOK IN YOUR EYE
(Irving Taylor-Vic Mizzy)
JUL 8 1938: Standard Trans.: Frank Trumbauer & His Orch.

THERE'S A SMALL HOTEL
(Lorenz Hart-Richard Rodgers)
MAR 13 1936: Vic Records: Paul Whiteman & His Orch.

THERE'S FROST ON THE MOON
(Fred E. Ahlert-Joseph Young)
DEC 1936: Radio, The Three T's

THERE'S NOTHING ELSE TO DO
(Sidney D. Mitchell-Cliff Friend)
JUN 29 1934: Vic Records: Paul Whiteman & His Orch.

THERE'S RAIN IN MY EYES
(Joseph McCarthy Sr-Jean Schwartz-Milton Ager)
MAY 25 1938: Standard Trans.: Frank Trumbauer & His Orch.

THESE SACRED HALLS
(composers unidentified)
DEC 13 1934: Radio, Kraft Music Hall: Paul Whiteman & His Orch.

THEY SAY
(Edward Heymann-Paul Mann-Stephan Weiss)
FEB 25 1939: Radio, Frank Trumbauer & His Orch.

THINK OF ME
(Al Eldridge)
JAN 30 1923: Vic Records: Benson Orch.

THIS IS THE MISSUS
(Lew Brown-Ray Henderson)
NOV 30 1931: Vic Records: Paul Whiteman & His Orch.

THIS TIME IT'S REAL
(David Bartlett-Emilio Castillo-Stephen M. Kupka)
MAR 30 1938: Standard Trans.: Frank Trumbauer & His Orch.

THIS YEAR'S KISSES
(Irving Berlin)
FEB 10 1937: Radio, Frank Trumbauer & His Orch.

THOMPSON'S BAND
(Bill Trumbauer-Frank Trumbauer)
SEP 29 1952: Private Recording: Frank Trumbauer

THOSE PANAMA MAMAS
(. . . Johnson- . . . Bebo)
APR 9 1925: Brun Records: Cotton Pickers

THOUSAND GOOD NIGHTS, A
(Walter Donaldson)
APR 19 1934: Radio, Kraft Music Hall: Paul Whiteman & His Orch.

THOUSAND TIMES, NO!, A
(composers unidentified)
DEC 13 1934: Radio, Kraft Music Hall: Paul Whiteman & His Orch.

THREE BLIND MICE
(Frank Trumbauer-Chauncey Morehouse)

AUG 25 1927: OK Records: Frank Trumbauer & His Orch.
OCT 20 1927: Perfect Records: Chicago Loopers

THREE SHADES OF BLUE (Part 1)
(Ferde Grofé)
FEB 16 1928: Vic Records: Paul Whiteman & His Orch.

THREE SHADES OF BLUE (Part 2)
(Ferde Grofé)
FEB 16 1928: Vic Records: Paul Whiteman & His Orch.

THRILL OF LOVE, THE
(Tom Johnstone)
SEP 10 1923: Vic Records: Benson Orch.

TIGER RAG
(Original Dixieland Jazz Band)
JUN 1931: Radio, Paul Whiteman & His Allied Quality Paintmen
JUN 1931: Radio, Paul Whiteman & His Allied Quality Paintmen
JUN 1931: Radio, Paul Whiteman & His Allied Quality Paintmen
AUG 3 1931: Radio, Paul Whiteman & His Allied Quality Paintmen

TIGER RAG FANTASY
(composers unidentified)
DEC 11 1937: Standard Trans.: Frank Trumbauer & His Orch.
JUL 9 1938: Radio, Frank Trumbauer & His Orch.

TIJUANA
(composers unidentified)
JUL 26 1934: Radio, Kraft Music Hall: Paul Whiteman & His Orch.
AUG 2 1934: Radio, Kraft Music Hall: Paul Whiteman & His Orch.

TIL THE POPPIES BLOOM
(composers unidentified)
FEB 10 1937: Radio, Frank Trumbauer & His Orch.

TOGETHER
(B. G. ''Buddy'' DeSylva-Lew Brown-Ray Henderson)
JAN 21 1928: Vic Records: Paul Whiteman & His Orch.

TONIGHT WE LOVE
(Bobby Worth-Ray Austin-Freddy Martin-Ilyich Tschaikowsky)
FEB 11 1938: Standard Trans.: Frank Trumbauer & His Orch.

TONIGHT WILL LIVE
(Ned Washington-Augustin Lara)
MAY 25 1938: Standard Trans.: Frank Trumbauer & His Orch.

TONY'S WIFE
(Harold Adamson-Burton Lane)
DEC 20 1934: Radio, Kraft Music Hall: Paul Whiteman & His Orch.
JAN 5 1936: Radio, Musical Varieties: Paul Whiteman & His Orch.

TOP HAT, WHITE TIE AND TAILS
(Irving Berlin)
SEP 28 1935: Vic Records: Paul Whiteman & His Orch.

TOREADOR SONG, THE
(Georges Bizet)
JAN 25 1934: Radio, Kraft Music Hall: Paul Whiteman & His Orch.

TOSELLI'S SERENADE
(composers unidentified)
APR 28 1932: Vic Records: Paul Whiteman & His Orch.

TOY BALLOON
(Sidney Clare-Charles Tobias-Henry H. Tobias)
JUL 19 1936: Radio, Paul Whiteman & His Orch.

TWO SHADOWS
(Charles James Burns-Guy B. Wood)
MAR 30 1938: Standard Trans.: Frank Trumbauer & His Orch.

VALLEY OF THE MOON
(composers unidentified)
JAN 4 1934: Radio, Kraft Music Hall: Paul Whiteman & His Orch.

VALSE MODERNE
(Ben Oakland)
JUN 27 1935: Radio, Kraft Music Hall: Paul Whiteman & His Orch.
FEB 2 1936: Radio, Musical Varieties: Paul Whiteman & His Orch.

VILIA
(Adrian Ross-Franz Lehar)
SEP 30 1931: Vic Records: Paul Whiteman & His Orch.
NOV 22 1934: Radio, Kraft Music Hall: Paul Whiteman & His Orch.

VIRGINIA REEL
(composers unidentified)
FEB 1 1934: Radio, Kraft Music Hall: Paul Whiteman & His Orch.
OCT 11 1934: Radio, Kraft Music Hall: Paul Whiteman & His Orch.
JAN 19 1936: Radio, Musical Varieties: Paul Whiteman & His Orch.

VISSI D'ARTE
(Guiseppe Giacosa-John Gutman-Luigi Illica-Giacomo Puccini)
NOV 29 1934: Radio, Kraft Music Hall: Paul Whiteman & His Orch.

VOICE IN THE OLD VILLAGE CHOIR, THE
(Gus Kahn-Harry M. Woods)
APR 14 1932: Vic Records: Paul Whiteman & His Orch.

WALTZING DOWN THE AISLE
(Al Hoffman-Sammy Gallop)
OCT 26 1934: Vic Records: Paul Whiteman & His Orch.

WALTZING THROUGH THE AGES
(Adolph Deutsch)
DEC 14 1933: Radio, Kraft Music Hall: Paul Whiteman & His Orch.
NOV 22 1934: Radio, Kraft Music Hall: Paul Whiteman & His Orch.
MAR 24 1937: Radio, Paul Whiteman & His Orch.

WAND'RING MINSTREL, I, A
(W. S. Gilbert-Sir Arthur Sullivan)
DEC 20 1934: Radio, Kraft Music Hall: Paul Whiteman & His Orch.

WATER BOY
(Avery Robinson: adaptation of folk song Jack O'Diamonds
APR 5 1936: Radio, Musical Varieties: Paul Whiteman & His Orch.

WAY BACK HOME
(Al Lewis-Tom Waring)
APR 22 1935: Vic Records: Paul Whiteman & His Orch.

WAY DOWN YONDER IN NEW ORLEANS
(Henry Creamer-J. Turner Layton)
MAY 13 1927: OK Records: Frank Trumbauer & His Orch.
DEC 25 1936: Radio, The Three T's
DEC 1936: Radio, The Three T's
FEB 10 1937: Radio, Frank Trumbauer & His Orch.

WE BROUGHT OUR HARP
(composers unidentified)
AUG 23 1934: Radio, Kraft Music Hall: Paul Whiteman & His Orch.

WE LOVE OUR PICCOLO
(composers unidentified)

DEC 20 1934: Radio, Kraft Music Hall: Paul Whiteman & His Orch.

WE SAW THE SEA
(Irving Berlin)
FEB 23 1936: Radio, Musical Varieties: Paul Whiteman & His Orch.

WE'LL MAKE HAY WHILE THE SUN SHINES
(Arthur Freed-Nacio Herb Brown)
NOV 30 1933: Radio, Kraft Music Hall: Paul Whiteman & His Orch.

WE'RE BACK TOGETHER AGAIN
(Clare Monaco)
FEB 27 1925: Brun Records: Ray Miller & His Orch.

WE'RE NOT DRESSING MEDLEY
(Mack Gordon-Harry Revel)
APR 19 1934: Radio, Kraft Music Hall: Paul Whiteman & His Orch.

WE'RE OUT OF THE RED
(Lew Brown-Jay Gorney)
MAR 28 1934: Vic Records: Ramona (Davies)

WEARING OF THE GREEN
(Traditional)
MAR 15 1936: Radio, Musical Varieties: Paul Whiteman & His Orch.
FEB 25 1939: Radio, Frank Trumbauer & His Orch.
FEB 22 1940: Var Records: Frank Trumbauer & His Orch.

WEARY BLUES
(Artie Matthews)
MAY 5 1931: Radio, Paul Whiteman & His Allied Quality Paintmen

WEDDING OF THE BIRDS, THE
(Henry Tobias-Charley Kisco)
JUL 25 1930: Col Records: Paul Whiteman & His Orch.

WHAT A DAY
(Harry M. Woods)
MAY 15 1929: OK Records: Mason Dixon Orch.

WHAT IS THERE TO SAY?
(E. Y. "Yip" Harburg-Vernon Duke)
JAN 25 1934: Radio, Kraft Music Hall: Paul Whiteman & His Orch.

WHAT WOULDN'T I DO FOR THAT MAN!
(E. Y. "Yip" Harburg-Jay Gorney)
OCT 19 1929: OK Records: Frank Trumbauer & His Orch.

WHAT'S THE NAME OF THAT SONG?
(Vee Lawnhurst-Tot Seymour)
FEB 6 1936: Vic Records: Paul Whiteman & His Orch.
FEB 23 1936: Radio, Musical Varieties: Paul Whiteman & His Orch.

WHAT'S THE USE?
(Isham Jones-Charles Newman)
JUL 22 1930: OK Records: Frank Trumbauer & His Orch.

WHEEL OF THE WAGON IS BROKEN, THE
(Box-Cox-Carr)
FEB 6 1936: Vic Records: Paul Whiteman & His Orch.

WHEN
(Andy Razaf-Bob Schafer-J. C. Johnson)
MAR 12 1928: Vic Records: Paul Whiteman & His Orch.

WHEN DAY IS DONE
(B. G. "Buddy" DeSylva-Robert Katscher)
OCT 3 1935: Radio, Kraft Music Hall: Paul Whiteman & His Orch.

WHEN THE STARS GO TO SLEEP
(Harold Adamson-Jimmy McHugh)
APR 20 1938: Standard Trans.: Frank Trumbauer & His Orch.

WHEN THE WORLD WAS NEW
(Matty Malneck-Roy Bargy)
OCT 1 1931: Vic Records: Paul Whiteman & His Orch.

WHEN YOU AND I WERE YOUNG MAGGIE
(George W. Johnson-James Austin Butterfield)
JAN 31 1923: Vic Records: Benson Orch.

WHEN YOU'RE COUNTING THE STARS ALONE
(. . . Russel- . . . Rose-John Murray)
SEP 13 1929: Col Records: Paul Whiteman & His Orch.

WHEN YOU'RE WITH SOMEBODY ELSE
(. . . Etting- . . . Gilbert)
FEB 29 1928: Col Records: Paul Whiteman & His Orch.

WHERE HAVE WE MET BEFORE?
(E. Y. ''Yip'' Harburg-Vernon Duke)
MAR 30 1938: Standard Trans.: Frank Trumbauer & His Orch.

WHERE IS THAT OLD GIRL OF MINE?
(Isham Jones-Gus Kahn)
JUN 6 1924: Brun Records: Ray Miller & His Orch.

WHERE IS THE SONG OF SONGS FOR ME?
(Irving Berlin)
SEP 21 1928: Col Records: Paul Whiteman & His Orch.
OCT 6 1928: Col Records: Paul Whiteman & His Orch.

WHERE THE LAZY RIVER FLOWS
(Harold Adamson-Jimmy McHugh)
DEC 4 1936: Radio, The Three T's
DEC 18 1936: Radio, The Three T's
DEC 25 1936: Radio, The Three T's

SEP 7 1935: Vic Records: Paul Whiteman & His Orch.
SEP 28 1935: Vic Records: Paul Whiteman & His Orch.

WILDCAT
(Eddie Lang-Joe Venuti)
DEC 14 1933: Radio, Kraft Music Hall: Paul Whiteman & His Orch.
DEC 15 1937: Standard Trans.: Frank Trumbauer & His Orch.

WILL YOU REMEMBER ME?
(Davis-Santly-Richman)
FEB 10 1925: Brun Records: Ray Miller & His Orch.

WILLIAM TELL OVERTURE
(Gioacchino Antonio Rossini)
FEB 10 1937: Radio, Frank Trumbauer & His Orch.

WINTER WONDERLAND
(Richard B. Smith-Felix Bernard)
DEC 6 1934: Radio, Kraft Music Hall: Paul Whiteman & His Orch.

WINTERGREEN FOR PRESIDENT
(Ira Gershwin-George Gershwin)
SEP 13 1934: Radio, Kraft Music Hall: Paul Whiteman & His Orch.
MAR 24 1937: Radio, Paul Whiteman & His Orch.

WITH ALL MY HEART
(Gus Kahn-Jimmy McHugh)
JAN 26 1936: Radio, Musical Varieties: Paul Whiteman & His Orch.

WITH EVERY BEAT OF MY HEART
(composers unidentified)
MAR 22 1936: Radio, Musical Varieties: Paul Whiteman & His Orch.

WITH PLENTY OF MONEY AND YOU
(Al Dubin-Harry Warren)
DEC 1936: Radio, The Three T's

WITH SUMMER COMING ON (I'M STILL WITHOUT A SWEETHEART)
(Roy Turk-Fred E. Ahlert)
MAY 25 1932: Brun Records: Bing Crosby
JAN 11 1934: Radio, Kraft Music Hall: Paul Whiteman & His Orch.

WITHOUT A SONG
(Billy Rose-Edward Eliscu-Vincent Youmans)
OCT 9 1929: Col Records: Paul Whiteman & His Orch.

WOLVERINE BLUES
(John Spikes-Benjamin Spikes-Ferdinand ''Jelly Roll'' Morton)
SEP 10 1923: Vic Records: Benson Orch.

WONDERFUL ONE
(Dorothy Terriss-Paul Whiteman-Ferde Grofé)
FEB 13 1928: Vic Records: Paul Whiteman & His Orch.
OCT 3 1935: Radio, Kraft Music Hall: Paul Whiteman & His Orch.

WOULD THERE BE LOVE?
(Mack Gordon-Harry Revel)
JAN 23 1935: Vic Records: Paul Whiteman & His Orch.

WRAP YOUR TROUBLES IN DREAMS (AND DREAM YOUR TROUBLES AWAY)
(Ted Koehler-Billy Moll-Harry Barris)
FEB 23 1940: Var Records: Frank Trumbauer & His Orch.

WRINGIN' AND TWISTIN'
(Frank Trumbauer-Thomas ''Fats'' Waller)
SEP 17 1927: OK Records: Tram-Bix-Lang

YES, THERE AIN'T NO MOONLIGHT
(Archie Gottler-Jerome Gottler-Louis Prima)
APR 20 1938: Standard Trans.: Frank Trumbauer & His Orch.

YIP-I-ADDY-AY
(Will D. Cobb-John H. Flynn)
SEP 4 1928: Col Records: Paul Whiteman & His Orch.
SEP 14 1928: Col Records: Paul Whiteman & His Orch.

YOU AND I
(George Michael Cohan)
DEC 10 1924: Brun Records: Ray Miller & His Orch.
DEC 16 1924: Brun Records: Ray Miller & His Orch.

YOU AND ME
(Kurt Weill-Sam Coslow)
JUL 8 1938: Standard Trans.: Frank Trumbauer & His Orch.

YOU APPEAL TO ME
(Walter Bullock-Harold Spina)
FEB 11 1938: Standard Trans.: Frank Trumbauer & His Orch.

YOU ARE LOVE
(Oscar Hammerstein II-Jerome Kern)
MAR 1 1928: Vic Records: Paul Whiteman & His Orch.

YOU ARE MUSIC
(Frank Black)
JUL 8 1938: Standard Trans.: Frank Trumbauer & His Orch.

YOU ARE MY LUCKY STAR
(Arthur Freed-Nacio Herb Brown)
FEB 16 1936: Radio, Musical Varieties: Paul Whiteman & His Orch.

YOU BROUGHT A NEW KIND OF LOVE TO ME
(Sammy Fain-Irving Kahal-Pierre Norman)
MAR 23 1930: Col Records: Paul Whiteman & His Orch.

YOU TURNED THE TABLES ON ME
(Sidney D. Mitchell-Louis Alter)
DEC 4 1936: Radio, The Three T's

YOU'D BETTER CHANGE YOUR TUNE
(composers unidentified)
APR 20 1938: Standard Trans.: Frank Trumbauer & His Orch.

YOU'RE A SWEETHEART
(Harold Adamson-Jimmy McHugh)
DEC 15 1937: Standard Trans.: Frank Trumbauer & His Orch.

YOU'RE AN OLD SMOOTHIE
(B. G. "Buddy" DeSylva-Richard A. Whiting-Nacio Herb Brown)
JAN 11 1934: Radio, Kraft Music Hall: Paul Whiteman & His Orch.

YOU'RE NOT THE ONLY OYSTER IN THE SEA
(Harry M. Woods-Joe Marsala)
SEP 20 1934: Radio, Kraft Music Hall: Paul Whiteman & His Orch.

YOU'RE THE TOP
(Cole Porter)
OCT 26 1934: Vic Records: Paul Whiteman & His Orch.
OCT 26 1934: Vic Records: Paul Whiteman & His Orch.
NOV 29 1934: Radio, Kraft Music Hall: Paul Whiteman & His Orch.

YOUR GUESS IS AS GOOD AS MINE
(Sigler-Goodhart-Hoffman)
SEP 18 1934: Brun Records: Jack Teagarden & His Orch.

YOUR HEAD ON MY SHOULDER
(Harold Adamson-Burton Lane)
NOV 29 1934: Radio, Kraft Music Hall: Paul Whiteman & His Orch.

YOUR MOTHER AND MINE
(Joc Goodwin-Gus Edwards)
MAY 4 1929: Col Records: Paul Whiteman & His Orch.
MAY 16 1929: Col Records: Paul Whiteman & His Orch.

ZAZU
(composers unidentified)
MAY 24 1936: Radio, Musical Varieties: Paul Whiteman & His Orch.
MAY 24 1936: Radio, Musical Varieties: Paul Whiteman & His Orch.

INDEX

ABOUT THE AUTHORS

Philip R. Evans, while feature editor of his college newspaper, wrote his first serious jazz article on George Lewis in 1954. George used the article for the advance publicity during his band's tour of that year. Phil has been profiled in *The Second Line,* and has written for various publications ranging from *Record Research* to *The Mississippi Rag,* and provided liner notes for numerous albums. He has been consulted by writers and researchers from around the world, resulting in acknowledgments in over fifty books dealing with music and musicians. Phil has been a requested guest on various programs devoted to American Music, and has attended countless music festivals across the land. *Tram* is the third in his series of books devoted to biographies of American Musicians. Phil retired from 36 years of government service and currently lives with his wife, Linda, in Bakersfield, California.

Larry F. Kiner has been doing research and compiling discographies since the early 1940s with special emphasis on the personalities of the pre-1950 era. He has authored/co-authored *Nelson Eddy: A Bio-Discography* (Scarecrow Press, 1992), *Al Jolson: A Bio-Discography* (Scarecrow Press, 1992), *The Sir Harry Lauder Discography* (Scarecrow Press, 1990), *The AFRS Basic Musical Library "P" Series* (Greenwood Press, 1990), *The Cliff Edwards Discography* (Greenwood Press, 1987), *The Rudy Vallee Discography* (Greenwood Press, 1985) and *The Al Jolson Discography* (Greenwood Press, 1983). In addition, he has written numerous journal articles in similar vein including "The Ruth Etting Discography" (*American Discophile,* 1955), "The Eddie Cantor Discography" (*American Discophile,* 1955), and "The Cavalcade of America 1935–1953" (1990). He has also written technical articles for *VHF Horizons, 73 Magazine* and *Radio & TV Experimenter.* Kiner has also been involved with transferring to tape the entire Paul Whiteman and Rudy Vallee collections, as well as some of the Jessica Dragonette, Hildegarde and Bing Crosby collections.